85/-

D1357207

Economics
and
American
Industry

ECONOMICS AND AMERICAN INDUSTRY

LEONARD W. WEISS

San Jose State College

(Visiting Associate Professor,
University of Minnesota, 1960–1961)

John Wiley & Sons, Inc.

New York · London · Sydney

to Lee

SIXTH PRINTING, JANUARY, 1967

Copyright © 1961 by John Wiley & Sons, Inc.

Library of Congress Catalog Card Number: 61–11181
Printed in the United States of America

PREFACE

It has been my experience that the two main segments of modern economics differ greatly in their teachability. Macroeconomic analysis and the public finance and monetary economics that usually accompany it generate ample interest among undergraduates. The importance of these subjects to major problems of current national concern is obvious to most, and their conclusions and shortcomings can be easily illustrated in terms of well-known recent events. On the other hand, microeconomic analysis often seems far removed from reality to the typical undergraduate. Cost and distribution theory strike him as complex analytical structures developed in an ivory tower with little or no useful application. The situation is not much better for those students who are so impressed by theory that they swallow it whole. Their picture of the economic world is surely imperfect.

This book is an attempt to make the microeconomic analysis at once more palatable and more useful to the typical undergraduate by combining a systematic presentation of price and distribution theory with case studies of appropriate industries. I hope that the book can be used in three types of courses: 1. It might serve as the main text or as a supplement in a second term of economics after a one-term survey of economic institutions and macroeconomics. The term preceding this book might consist of the material in Chapters 1 through 20 of Samuelson, Chapters 1 through 19 of Bach, Chapters 1 through 16 of Harriss, Chapters 1 through 13 of Koivisto, or similar subject matter in other principles texts. 2. It might serve as a text for or supplement to many intermediate theory courses. 3. It might be the basic text in industrial organization courses if the case study approach is used and if continuity and analytical emphasis are desired. Pre-, liminary materials for this book proved successful in some or all of these uses at three quite diverse academic institutions.

The criteria for the selection of industries in this book were that they should be of major importance, that they should be reasonably amenable to analysis, and that adequate empirical material should be available. I believe that agriculture, textiles, aluminum, electric power, steel, automobiles, retailing, and the steelworkers' unions meet these requirements. Of course, no selection of seven or eight cases can possibly represent completely the great diversity that exists in the real economic world. These industry studies are presented as illustrations of important aspects of economic theory and policy, and make no claim to provide an exhaustive survey of American industry.

Each case has three main jobs to perform: 1. to present some major aspect of economic theory; 2. to evaluate it or at least to illustrate it in terms of performance within the industry being discussed; and 3. to review some important aspect of public policy. Altogether the book covers virtually all the major questions of theory and policy commonly raised in the microeconomic sections of principles courses and a large proportion of those raised in intermediate theory courses.

The theoretical concepts presented in this book appear in a fairly conventional order. Chapters 2 and 3 (agriculture) cover basic concepts of cost and demand as well as purely competitive equilibrium. Chapter 4 (textiles) introduces comparative advantage. Chapters 5 and 6 (aluminum and electric power) discuss various aspects of monopoly pricing. Chapters 7 and 8 (steel and automobiles) cover oligopoly pricing and nonprice competition. Monopolistic competition, cartels with free entry, and cartels with restricted entry are all analyzed in Chapter 9 (retailing). Chapter 10 (steelworkers) includes the customary analysis of factor pricing and income distribution as well as the impact of the union. In each case the analysis starts at an elementary level, but a sufficient degree of sophistication is developed to explain and partially evaluate realistically observed market behavior. The various theory sections of the book tend to build on one another, so at least Chapters 2, 3, 5, and 7 should be taken in the indicated order.

Much of the material on industry history, structure, and performance is necessarily verbal description, but whenever possible statistics on price, output, profits, and productivity are introduced. An effort is made to use similar concepts from chapter to chapter in presenting these statistics. For comparability, the price, output, profit, and productivity figures are presented along with those for "all manufacturing," even in nonmanufacturing industries. In particular cases, where the analytical questions under discussion seem to call for it, information on capacity adjustments, international productivity differences, price differentials, wage rates, advertising expenses, and the like are introduced as well. Most of this statistical material is presented in diagrams rather than tables because of my feeling that diagrams are much more likely to be read and understood. Chapter 11 compares the most commonly used measures of performance for all of the broad manufacturing industry groups and attempts some generalizations based on the results.

An obvious danger of a book such as this one is that it will be used to force the facts into analytical molds which they may not actually fit very well. To some extent this may be unavoidable, but I do make an effort throughout to raise questions wherever empirical data have led to doubts about analytical conclusions. In fact, I consider this one of the primary purposes of the book—to introduce more realistic qualifications to economic theory as it is taught in undergraduate courses.

Each chapter, in addition to presenting some aspect of theory and evaluating it in terms of industry performance, also covers an important facet of public policy toward business. Chapters 2, 3, and 4 cover a broad range of public policy toward depressed industries, from agricultural policies to tariffs. Chapters 5, 7, 8, and 9 taken together provide a brief survey of antitrust policy. The changing meaning of "monopolize" under the Sherman Act comes up in connection with aluminum. The development of public policy toward mergers is summarized in the steel chapter. The Robinson-Patman Act and resale price maintenance are discussed with retailing. The automobile chapter ends with a brief discussion of the possible meanings of "workable competition." Public regulation and operation of utilities is discussed in Chapter 6. Chapter 10 includes public policy toward unions. Whenever possible, the results of the analytical and performance material are integrated with the public policy discussions.

This book is meant as a text, not a treatise. Little originality can be claimed for its content. The goals of the book will have been accomplished if it can provide the general student in economics with a more meaningful picture of some of our most important markets, with a set of analytical tools that he can apply to other markets in which he may have experience, and with an incentive to apply those tools.

The author of a book of this nature must inevitably depend on the assistance of a great number of others. Most of the chapters in this book are avowedly based on other studies too numerous to be mentioned here. They are listed in footnotes and at the ends of appropriate chapters. In addition, I am especially obligated to the generous persons who have read extensive sections of the book and have made many very valuable suggestions. Of course the errors are all mine. Richard Caves of the University of California read the first half of the book and made many useful comments. A. G. Papandreau of the University of California and Lloyd G. Reynolds of Yale University also made helpful suggestions on some of that section. R. Buford Brandis of the American Cotton Manufacturers Institute went over Chapter 4, and J. Gordon Ainsworth of Kaiser Aluminum and Chemical Corporation did the same for Chapter 5. A number of persons at the Aluminum Company of America, especially Stanley V. Malcuit, gave me a great deal of help with Chapter 5. I am indebted to John F. Roberts of Pacific Gas and Electric Company, Roy Sampson of the University of Oregon, and especially C. Emery Troxel of Wayne State University for their comments on Chapter 6. Frank Norton of Bethlehem Pacific Coast Steel Corporation and Brent Upson of General Motors Corporation read Chapters 7 and 8 respectively. I owe much to the comments of Lee Preston and Richard Holton on Chapter 9, of Lloyd Ulman on Chapter 10, and of J. S. Bain on Chapter 11. All four are at the University of California. I received a great deal of help from my colleagues at San Jose State College, particularly Suzan Wiggins on Chapters 1, 5, and 10, Turley Mings on Chapters 1 and 10, Lawrence Lee on Chapter 5, William Stanton on Chapters 7, 8, and 11, Lawrence Appleton on Chapter 9, and Bud Hutcheson on Chapter 10. David Alhadeff of the University of California, Robert Einzig of the Federal Reserve Bank of San Francisco, and Walter Crafford of San Jose State all helped on some of my material. I owe a special debt to Edward Coen of the University of Minnesota and to Charles H. Berry of Yale University, who went over the entire manuscript carefully and helpfully. Finally, I owe most of all to my long-suffering wife who has read and reread and read again, and has waited patiently for her husband to become a full member of the family again.

LEONARD W. WEISS

Minneapolis, Minnesota
January, 1961

CONTENTS

1

INTRODUCTION

America has a huge and complex economy. It is made up of a great number of diverse markets: the market for beef, where hundreds of thousands of anonymous producers supply millions of anonymous consumers; the market for steel, where a handful of billion-dollar corporations sell to even fewer and huger automobile companies; the market for steel labor, where a single union bargains with the same billion-dollar corporations about the wages of a half million steelworkers; and thousands of other markets, each with unique features of its own. These markets warrant a great deal of attention. Most of our economic decisions are made within them.

The goal of this book is to provide some understanding of the important types of markets to be found in our economy. It combines the body of theory that economists have developed to analyze various market situations with descriptions of some leading cases to which it might apply. Before the book is finished it will cover agriculture, textiles, aluminum, electric power, steel, automobiles, and retailing, as well as steelworkers. The government has intervened in one way or another in practically all of these markets, so a wide range of public policies is discussed, including price supports, tariffs, antitrust laws, price regulation, and the control of union-management regulations. Some of the markets covered are old and familiar. The man in the street has earned his income from them or supplied his wants through them all his life. But there is much more to them than meets the eye. Getting beneath the surface is apt to be a fascinating

1

undertaking for those who have not yet discovered the implications of the markets with which they come in contact.

Since students and sometimes instructers seem to have a propensity for looking at trees rather than forests, it seems important that this book include a brief over-all look at the economy before starting on a study of its parts. This is the function of the present chapter, in which the concepts of supply and demand are used to describe how a perfectly operating private enterprise capitalism might work and where a realistic one falls down. This is followed by a rough statement of the extent of different types of markets in the United States today and a brief sketch of the trends in government controls over these markets. All of this is necessarily simplified at this stage. Later chapters go into most of the questions raised in this chapter much more thoroughly.

BASIC ECONOMIC DECISIONS AND THE PRIVATE ENTERPRISE ECONOMY

Scarcity

The basic problem of private enterprise capitalism, or of any other economic system for that matter, is scarcity. Americans are by far the richest people who have ever lived. We have higher per capita incomes than any previous civilization or any other nation in the world today. Yet very few of us would have any difficulty finding use for another dollar. Even our huge productive machine is unable to supply all our wants. It is true that we have been embarrassed from time to time by large surpluses of specific commodities and even by general "overcapacity" during depressions, but these have not meant that the problem of scarcity was solved. We still had a great backlog of unsatisfied wants.

The root cause of this scarcity is our limited supply of productive resources — what economists know as the *factors of production*. America will have perhaps 70 million man-years of labor and $1.5 trillion worth of plant, equipment, and natural resources available for use this year. That is an impressive accumulation but it is not nearly enough to provide everyone with all the goods and services he can use. In this environment of limited means and unlimited ends we, like everyone else in the world, must face the ancient problem of making the most of what we have. We must see to it that our most urgent wants are satisfied and that the waste of those limited means is minimized. In doing so we must solve several major sub-problems:

1. Which of the many goods and services possible shall we produce, or, more realistically, how much of each shall we produce? If we put more of our labor and equipment into making ballistic missiles, we will have less to use in producing automobiles or shoes or chewing gum. Somehow our society must determine the combination of goods it wants.

2. What methods of production shall we use? There are almost always alternatives. While many of them can be discarded as hopelessly inefficient (hand-dug oil wells), or immoral (slavery), others can only be chosen on the basis of economic considerations. For instance, what is the best way to dig a ditch? Should we use 100 men with shovels or 3 men with a trenching machine? It all depends on how scarce labor is compared with capital. The "more efficient" method is apt to be different in India and in Indiana.

3. How shall we distribute the goods that are produced? Some wants will have to go unsatisfied. Who should be pinched and how badly? There are two aspects of this question: One is income determination—how large is each person's slice of the total economic pie? The other is rationing—how is the current output of any given commodity to be distributed? There are too few shoes produced to let everyone have all he wants, so some method of rationing them must be devised.

Every society that has ever existed has had to provide some answer to these basic questions. They have often been left to slowly changing tradition. They have sometimes been handled by centralized decisions on the part of ancient priests, medieval magnates, or modern commissars. In the predominately private enterprise economy that we know, these decisions are left to millions of individual consumers and producers coordinated primarily by the market place.

Supply and Demand

Economists have erected an impressive theoretical structure to explain and evaluate the operation of such markets, but many of the key ideas can be expressed in terms of simple supply and demand. Although the reader may be familiar with this type of analysis, a brief review is probably in order.

A great many things influence the level of demand for any given commodity. The fact that sales of automobiles in 1959 came to 6,025,-

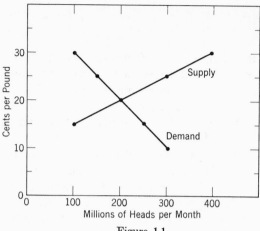

Figure 1.1

500 vehicles rather than some larger or smaller figure is only partially accounted for by their average level of price during that year. Different quantities would probably have been sold at the same price if incomes had been higher or lower, if consumers had been led by advertising or by pure caprice to view bus riding as a sign of weakness, if cars had been designed differently, or if consumers had anticipated higher prices or radical changes in style. Yet most of us can do little with so many variables at one time. We can guess how a rise in price will affect sales, but we flounder over the question of how a rise in price *and* incomes *and* quality will affect sales, especially if it rains all spring. For this reason economists usually limit themselves to one or two variables at a time in discussing demand* and assume the others constant. Price is usually selected as the key variable. Other factors such as incomes, quality, tastes, and prices of other good are assumed to be the same whatever the price.

Under such assumptions the quantity sold would normally be greater, the lower the price. This is just about inevitable because a lower price for cabbages, say, would make them appear more attractive as substitutes for other goods. The first two columns in Table 1.1 show a plausible *demand schedule* for cabbages, which is reproduced as a *demand curve* in Figure 1.1. The table and figure show the quantities of cabbage that people would buy per month, assuming that their incomes, their attitudes toward cabbage, and the prices of related commodities remain unchanged.

* Empirical studies of demand often do take a number of variables into consideration simultaneously. This is accomplished by statistical techniques. They are briefly discussed in Chapter 2, p. 71.

The supply of cabbage tends to reflect the cost of producing it. Of course, the number of cabbages coming to market in the next few weeks is almost completely determined by the numbers planted several months ago. About the same quantity will be offered whether the price is 25¢ or 5¢. However, farmers will have to anticipate a price that at least covers their costs if they are to plant another crop of cabbage next season. Ordinarily, it would take a higher price to induce greater cabbage production. This is because there is a limited amount of good cabbage land in the country. To get more cabbages

TABLE 1.1

HYPOTHETICAL DEMAND AND SUPPLY FOR CABBAGE

Price of Cabbage (cents per head)	Quantity of Cabbage Sought by Buyers per Month (millions of heads)	Quantity of Cabbage Offered by Sellers per Month (millions of heads)
30	100	400
25	150	300
20	200	200
15	250	100

more fertilizer would have to be applied to land that is now producing cabbages, or land that is less well adapted to them would have to be diverted from potatoes or strawberries. Either way costs go up with output. The result is a *supply schedule* like that in the third column of Table 1.1 or a *supply curve* like that in Figure 1.1. More cabbages are offered only at higher prices. To have an output of 200 million heads per month the price must be as high as the additional cost of the last cabbages grown—apparently 20¢ apiece. The price would have to be as high as 25¢ to bring 300 million cabbages per month to market. Supply curves do not always slope upward and to the right the way the one for the supply of cabbage did. In some industries almost any conceivable output could be achieved at the same cost per unit, given enough time for new facilities to be installed or old ones to wear out. This might be true of certain manufacturing industries, say the electric blanket industry. To get another 10,000 electric blankets per month just build another plant identical to the last one. There do not seem to be any good reasons why costs in the fiftieth plant should be any higher or lower than in the fifteenth. If this is the case, and if production cost per electric blanket is $20, then the long-run supply* would look like that in Figure 1.2. The price might be more than $20 for the time being, but if it is there will be more electric blanket factories next year, and they will keep coming so long as prices exceed cost. The price could also be less than $20 for a while

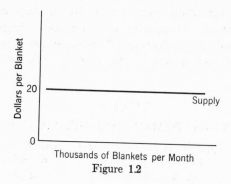

Figure 1.2

because the manufacturers might be willing to operate at a loss rather than have their plants stand idle. At such low prices, however, no new plants would be built, and if one burned down the owner would heave a sigh of relief and invest the insurance money in a more profitable business. Producers will keep leaving the industry until the price gets up to $20 again.

Some readers may be concerned about why anyone would ever be interested in producing electric blankets or anything else at prices that barely cover costs. The explanation is that the word "cost" as used by economists includes all payments necessary to bring the required resources into the industry. This often embraces considerably more than the man in the street means by cost. For instance, it includes a wage for labor, whether supplied by employees or by the owner of the business himself. Similarly, cost includes a return on capital whether put up by outsiders or by the owner again. The cost of the capital contributed by the owner of an electric blanket plant is the return he could earn on the same money invested in supermarkets or urban real estate or whatever other opportunity is open to him. If he does not earn as good a return making blankets as he could in his best alternative, he will ultimately be in another line of business. In

* Technically the *long run* is a period long enough for any factors of production to enter or leave the industry. In the *short run* some factors are committed to it. In this case the number of plants is given in the short run but can be increased or decreased in the long run. The relationship between the short and long run is taken up more thoroughly in Chapter 3.

other words, the $20 per blanket includes a return to the owner of the business as high as he can expect anywhere else.*

Equilibrium Price

Supply and demand curves, or really the thousands of individual decisions to buy or sell that they represent, interact to determine the market price. Going back to cabbages again, suppose that only 150 million heads had been planted in time to reach the market this month. For the moment, the supply of cabbages will be the vertical line in

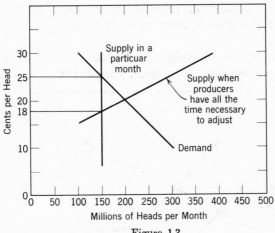

Figure 1.3

Figure 1.3. The price of cabbage will settle at 25¢. At any lower price there would be a cabbage shortage. Consumers would be trying to buy more than the 150 million heads available, and the unsatisfied buyers would bid the price up. If the price exceeded 25¢ there would be the opposite problem of too few customers, and sellers would tend to shade price rather than have large acreages of uncanned sauerkraut to clean up. At 25¢ the market is just cleared with all the cabbage being taken.

* This definition of cost by economists is not as highhanded as it may seem at first glance. It is true that many businessmen do not count their own effort or capital in calculating costs, but they should. If a druggist earned less running his own store than if he sold out and worked for a salary, he would really be taking a loss. He might be taking home enough to live on, but he could be doing better. There are thousands of farmers and little businessmen who make just this mistake. Another way of looking at it, unless all the economic costs are included, the operating expenses of running the drugstore will seem suddenly to rise when it is sold to a chain which thereafter pays its owner-turned-manager a salary.

Cabbage growers would be willing to produce 150 million cabbages for only about 18¢, however, so they must earn a pretty good profit at 25¢. If the demand situation seems permanent, other farmers will probably plant cabbages and the existing growers will try to expand. This process will continue until output rises to 200 million. By then the price will have fallen and the cost of growing more cabbage will have risen until it is no longer worthwhile for farmers to increase cabbage production. The price will just cover the extra cost of the last cabbage grown. More formally, 25¢ is the long-run *equilibrium price*. It qualifies as an equilibrium price because it shows no tendency to change, while any higher or lower price would sooner or later move toward this level.*

The equilibrium price of cabbage is not likely to stay in one place for long, however, because the demand and supply of cabbage keep

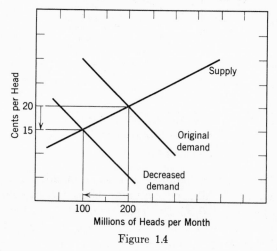

Figure 1.4

shifting about. For instance, Figure 1.4 shows a decrease in the demand for cabbage. Less cabbage can be sold at each price than before; alternatively, the same amount can be sold only at lower prices. As a result the equilibrium price falls to 15¢ and the equilibrium output to 100 million. Such a change in demand might be traceable to a drop in consumer incomes, or a fall in the price of cauliflower, or a growing conviction on the part of consumers that eating cabbage is degrading.

The one event that *cannot* cause a decline in the demand for

* The cabbage growers may take a more complicated route toward equilibrium than that described here. This discussion, like almost every other in the chapter, is considerably simplified. Some of the nuances appear in Chapter 2, p. 65.

cabbage is a rise in its price. Higher prices for cabbage could certainly make people buy less, but this would show up as a movement upward along the old demand curve rather than a shift to an entirely new one. To keep confusion on this point to a minimum, this book will reserve the phrase *decrease in demand* to describe a shift in the whole demand curve. A fall in consumer incomes could cause a decrease in demand in this sense, hence a fall in price. A rise in price could cause a decrease in the quantity of cabbage sold, but this would simply be a movement along the demand curve. A *rise* in price could hardly cause a *decline* in price.

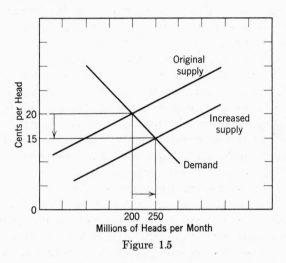

Figure 1.5

Of course, supply can change as well as demand. An increase in supply would arise because it rained or because someone found a more efficient way to grow cabbage. The increase would show up as a movement of the whole supply curve toward the southeast, as in Figure 1.5. More cabbages would be available at the same price, or the same number at lower prices. The result would be lower prices and a larger number of cabbages sold.

The reader who is not too sure of this analysis may want to stop for a minute and try shifting the demand and supply curves about for himself. What would be the effect of a stiff wage demand by the United Cabbage Workers of America? Or a tariff on cabbage imports? Or general inflation? What kinds of changes would have to occur to bring about an increase in output with no change in price? Or a fall in price with no change in output? There are all sorts of combinations possible.

Economic Decisions in Private Enterprise: What to Produce

We can now get back to the universal questions of what, how, and for whom to produce. Supply and demand on unregulated markets would provide the answers to all these questions in a perfectly working private enterprise system. For instance, the problem of what, really how much, to produce is automatically settled for cabbages when the market reaches equilibrium. When there were only 150 million cabbages, consumers were willing to spend 25¢ for another cabbage even though it cost the growers only 18¢ to produce. The growers who planted more of the crop in this case were serving the consumers' best interest as well as their own.

Consumers who paid a quarter for a cabbage were giving up the opportunity to buy 25¢ worth of other goods, which probably meant they thought the last cabbage was equivalent in satisfaction rendered to 2½ more phone calls or a pint of strawberries. If they thought otherwise, they could gain by buying more or less cabbages.

Similarly, the cost of growing another cabbage reflected the value of the services of the land, labor, and other resources used in producing it. The value of these factor services, in turn, depended on what they could produce in alternative employments. For instance, an acre of land cost the cabbage grower $100 a year, because if he had not used it for cabbage it would have produced a crop of cauliflower worth $100 net. Similarly, a man-hour of labor cost him $1.50 because if he did not pay that much the man-hour would have been out picking strawberries where it could produce and therefore earn $1.50. In other words, the cost of growing a cabbage measures the value to consumers of the other goods that could have been produced instead.

If the price of cabbage shows what consumers think it is worth in terms of other goods, and if its production costs show the value of other goods actually given up to grow it, then we can clearly gain by growing more cabbage so long as its price is more than its cost. The labor and land taken out of cauliflower and strawberry production and put into cabbages will gain the consumer more than he loses. We get goods of more dollar value from the same resources. We can go on gaining by transferring resources into cabbage production until it reaches 200 million heads per month, where the last cabbage cost just as much to produce as consumers would pay for it. Of course, this is where the growers would have stopped of their own accord.

If the initial output had been 300 million heads, so that the price had been less than the cost, the public as well as the producers would have benefited when cabbage growers switched to other products. The last few million heads produced were costing the country more in cauliflower or strawberries than they were worth in the eyes of the consumers. Again the growers, seeking their own best interest, would tend to move toward the output where the sacrifice just balanced the gain.

Economic Decisions: How to Produce

In determining the method of production, the market for productive services becomes important. The demand for any such service depends on what it can produce. This applies equally to the services of cabbage fields, Manhattan real estate, electrical engineers, pretty secretaries, locomotives, calculators, or any other factor of production. After a point, the more of any one of these resources used, the less another unit will add to production. For instance, the first electrical engineer hired by an electric blanket factory might increase output by much more than he cost. The second and third engineers in the same plant would add less and less to output because they would be doing the less essential jobs and because they would have less equipment with which to work. Still, it would be profitable to hire more engineers so long as they added at least as much to the value of output as they did to cost.

Other employers of electrical engineers would act the same way. The lower the salary they had to pay, the more engineers they would find worthwhile. The result is a demand for engineers based on the value of what they can add to output somewhere in the economy.

Figure 1.6 shows hypothetical supply and demand curves for engineers. In a perfectly working labor market an average salary of about $8000 a year would result. This is the salary that electric blanket factories or anyone else in need of an engineer would have to pay. It also is the value of additional output attributable to the 14,000th engineer. If he had added more than $8000, someone would have been willing to pay more than $8000 for his services and demand would have been higher.

This going salary regulates the use of engineers in several ways. It allocates them among employers. Engineers will only be employed in jobs where they increase the value of output by at least $8000. The last engineer employed in each firm will add just as much to the value of the product as he would in any other company that might employ him. It would be impossible to increase output by shifting engineers to different jobs. In addition, as engineers become

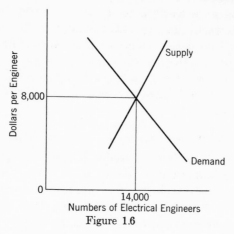

Figure 1.6

relatively scarce and capital becomes plentiful, employers will economize on the expensive engineers by providing them with automatic calculators instead of just pencils and paper. Finally, high salaries for engineers compared with other professions will probably encourage more young people to choose engineering over the law, say, once again directing labor into uses where its productivity in money terms is greatest.

Much the same can be said of calculators or cabbage land or any other productive resource. Their prices will tend to allocate them to their most productive uses and to encourage employers to substitute plentiful for scarce resources wherever possible.

Economic Decisions: Distribution

Each person's income depends on the resources he owns (including himself) and how much they can add to production. This means that each person has strong reasons for using his resources efficiently. There is the well-advertised fact that engineers have an incentive to show up for work because the more they produce, the more they earn. Just as important, though less often noticed, is the fact that output will not be carried beyond the point where it is not worth the sacrifice to resource owners. If the engineer decides not to work Saturdays because it is not worth the extra $2000 a year that he would get if he did, he is deciding that long week ends are worth more to him than mere goods. He would rather have the free time than a fancier car or a swimming pool. More *goods* could quite possibly be produced if people worked a 6-day week and a 12-hour day, but it is doubtful if more *satisfaction* would be produced.

The rationing of individual commodities is also accomplished by demand and supply in the competitive market place. Let us return to the market for cabbages: so long as the output was limited to 150 million heads per month, consumption had to be restricted to that level by some means or other. This was accomplished by a price of 25¢ which forced enough buyers out of the market to prevent a shortage. The consumers who were squeezed out were those who felt that cabbage was just not worth 25¢. Cabbage consumption was limited to those who put the highest dollar valuation on cabbages; the part of the public that was not that fond of cabbage spent their 25¢ on something which offered them more satisfaction.

If cabbage output had been 300 million, so that the problem was surplus rather than shortage, the price would have fallen far enough to induce consumers to take everything produced. Cabbages may not have been worth what they cost the producer, but once grown they would be better eaten than left to rot in the field.

To summarize: a private enterprise system *under ideal conditions* would lead to production concentrated on the goods most sought by consumers, produced by methods that get the maximum dollar output from our scarce resources, and distributed to those consumers who put the highest dollar value on them.

IMPERFECTIONS IN PRACTICE

It would be a mistake, however, to conclude that a purely private enterprise capitalism would perform as well in practice as the idealized model just described. Real-life capitalism, like every other economic system that has ever existed, falls far short of the ideal in actual experience. It contains a significant number of serious imperfections that were asumed away or disregarded just now.

1. Left to itself, our largely private enterprise economy has from time to time experienced major depressions involving large-scale unemployment of productive resources in practically every industry. The economy of the United States was certainly not providing maximum output in 1933 when national product was some 40% below capacity! Many feel instability is the greatest problem of modern capitalism. A loss of two-fifths of the nation's potential product, most of which can never be recovered, involves an economic waste that is hard to equal short of all-out war. The political future of capitalism and even democracy may well depend on our ability to

avoid the type of instability we have experienced in the past. However, this book is only incidentally concerned with the problem of economic fluctuations, and throughout most of it the assumption is made that the problem can be adequately solved. Since World War II this has seemed to be a reasonably correct assumption.

2. Economic inequality is another major problem. Goods rationed among consumers on the basis of price would satisfy the most pressing wants first only if a dollar meant about as much to each person bidding for the scarce commodities. The way incomes are distributed in reality, a beefsteak or a pair of shoes taken from a millionaire and given to a Southern sharecropper seems very likely to yield a net increase in satisfaction. Presumably the millionaire would lose less than the poor man would gain. Actually this can never be proved since we cannot compare different people's feelings. You and I can never settle an argument about which of us has the worse headache. The feeling that great inequality is undesirable is a value judgment that logic can do little to criticize or support, but it is a feeling that is widely held in our society.

3. A purely private enterprise capitalism performs imperfectly if there are costs that do not fall on producers. Economists refer to such costs as *external costs* or sometimes *external diseconomies*. For instance, American industry and commerce often result in cities that are much uglier, dirtier, and more congested than they need to be. The smog, the traffic jams, and the dreary miles of shop fronts and factories should certainly be counted as part of the cost of the goods and services produced, but they are costs to the general public, not to the producers directly. Left to their own devices, manufacturers and shopkeepers may well select the uglier or dirtier method of production or locate in a way that intensifies conjestion because such methods mean lower costs *to them*. Unless a city planning commission or other regulatory agency intervenes, they may use *high cost methods* if social costs are taken into account. These external diseconomies of modern industry must be very great to go by the billions that Americans have been willing to spend in their attempted escape to the suburbs!

4. In addition, there are important wants that cannot be expressed in the market place and will therefore not be met by private enterprise. Defense, education, roads, and public parks are familiar examples. Parks or schools or roads can seldom be operated profitably. Ballistic missiles never can. Yet few would doubt that expenditures on such items are worthwhile. An economy that puts too much reliance on private decisions expressed in the market place

is apt to have cars without adequate roads, housing developments without adequate schools, miles of city without a park, and great industrial wealth without adequate defense.

Sometimes business firms may serve social purposes for which they receive no direct payment. Apple orchards or dairy farms near the big cities may do wonders for the landscape but the farmers are not paid for the scenery. They will not continue in business if apples and milk are less profitable uses for their property than gas stations and outdoor movies. Again, the first producers in an industry often turn out a valuable supply of trained workmen worth millions to later producers and to the general public but they are seldom compensated directly for the educational services they provide. Such firms cannot be expected to take the public gain into account if it does not accrue to them. These are often referred to by economists as instances of *external economies*. A case can be made for subsidies or some other government intervention to encourage industries where significant external economies exist.

5. If for no other reason, a private enterprise system, like any other, does not perform in practice as on paper because of a whole array of imperfections comparable to the physicists' "friction." Firms may not use the lowest cost methods, workers may not take the most attractive jobs, and consumers may not find the best buys. They have trouble financing the best choice, or they do not know what alternatives are available, or they simply continue in the old ways out of inertia. The loss from such "frictional" imperfections is not small. Men will cling to dying trades for decades, and the waste that results from uninformed consumer purchases each year must run into the billions.

These imperfections should not be minimized. Some observers find them so serious that they conclude another economic system would secure the same goals more successfully. It is hard to find anyone, economist or noneconomist, who does not favor government intervention to patch up our economic system on at least some of these counts.

MONOPOLISTIC IMPERFECTONS

The main concern of this book is with imperfections in competition. In practice all modern capitalistic nations include many industries with only one or a few sellers. Yet the entire system described above was built on the assumption of competition.

Monopoly Price

To see the effect of monopoly, let us go back to the electric blanket industry. If there were a great many firms, none of them very large, and if new producers were free to enter the industry, price and quantity would be determined by supply and demand. In Figure 1.7 output would tend to settle at 10 million blankets per year, where the price just covers the $20 cost.

On the other hand, if all the electric blanket plants were part of a single U.S. Electric Blanket Corporation, and if costs were still $20 per blanket, the price would probably be higher. The price would not be set by supply and demand; it would be set by U.S. Electric Blankets. The corporation would have the choice of a wide range of prices and could make a very good profit at some of them.

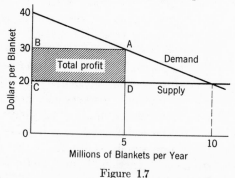

Figure 1.7

Just which price would be most profitable depends on the character of demand. In Figure 1.7 the price is represented by the distance B0 and the cost per blanket by the distance C0. The difference between the two, BC, represents the profit per blanket. Since the quantity sold is AB and the total profit is the quantity sold times the profit per unit, the total profit per year can be represented by the area of the rectangle ABCD. The lower the price, the shorter and fatter this rectangle. Its greatest area, hence, U.S. Electric Blanket's greatest profit, is to be found at a price of $30 in this case. If the demand curve had been shaped differently, the most profitable price might have been higher or lower, but at all events it would not have been as low as $20 where price just equals cost, nor as high as $40 where the quantity sold is zero.*

* This discussion involves a considerable simplification again. There is a more precise way of stating the most profitable output and price for a monopolist; it is discussed in Chapter 5.

If U.S. Electric Blankets does set a price of $30 so that output is limited to 5 million blankets per year, we will not be getting the most out of our resources. Consumers will be ready to pay $30 for an electric blanket that cost only $20 to produce. If $20 worth of resources are transferred from cabbages to electric blankets, the cabbages lost will be worth less to consumers than the electric blankets gained. But the officers of U.S. Electric Blankets will not make the move. If they set out to maximize their profits, which is only what businessman are expected to do if a private enterprise system is to work properly, they will as a matter of course raise price above cost and restrict output as a result.

Of course, a monopolist does not have to announce "Here is the output, what am I bid?" to be restricting production. He does it automatically if he sets a high price. He need not be reluctant to sell more *at that price* either. It is quite consistent for him to set a high price and then put on a big advertising campaign. Nor do monopolistic restrictions necessarily involve large-scale overcapacity or unemployment. In the long run the electric blanket combine would build plants to accommodate the expected demand at $30, not $20, and while the number of electric blanket workers might be restricted, there could still be full employment if those kept out found work in competitive industries. In other words, if electric blanket production is monopolized and cabbage growing is not, there will be too few electric blankets produced and their price will be too high at the same time that there are too many cabbages and their prices too low. High profits and wages in the electrical equipment field are likely to be associated with there being too many farmers.

A qualification is in order. If the combine had lower costs, its price might be no higher than a competitive price would be in the same industry. A hundred electric blanket makers might be inefficiently small, so that even if their price barely covered costs it would be as high or higher than U.S. Electric Blankets', which included a healthy profit. This is not to say that small firms are inefficient in all industries, but they may be in some. Incidentally, even if the monopoly price is no higher than a competitive price would be in the same industry, the consumer would still be paying more for another electric blanket than it cost to produce and would benefit if the monopolist could be induced to cut prices and sell more. The value of goods produced by another electric blanket worker would still be more than the value of cabbages that would have to be given up in transferring him.

Oligopoly

The term *oligopoly* is used to describe an industry where price and production decisions are dominated by a few firms instead of just one. It is a very common type of industrial organization, but difficult to analyze. We can make a few tentative generalizations at this point, but a great number of qualifications will be necessary before the book is finished.

Let us use the electric blanket example again. Suppose that the industry consists of two firms, A and B, and that each has costs of $20 per blanket. Suppose also that the public makes no distinction between A's and B's electric blankets. In Figure 1.8 firms

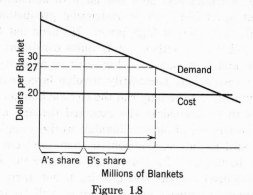

Figure 1.8

A and B each control half the market. How one seller will price his blankets depends on the reaction he expects from the other. He might expect the other to maintain the old price. Then he would gain by a small price reduction that just takes the entire market from his rival. A price of $27 would apparently do this in Figure 1.8. Such a policy would be certainly doomed to failure, however, because it assumes substandard intelligence on the part of the other seller.

A much more likely assumption is that B will meet A's price, at least when A makes a cut. Then the division of the market would be about the same after the price cut as before. This is shown in Figure 1.9. Oligopolist A might still gain by price cutting, but only if the total profits of the whole industry are increased when electric blankets sell for less. This happens to be the case with the price cut shown in Figure 1.9. A single monopolist would have cut the price under the same circumstances.

It is true that an oligopolist might be a little more reticent than a single monopolist in raising prices. However, if the price were below $30 in Figure 1.9 so that a higher price would increase both sellers' profits, there is a pretty good chance that B would go along if A led the way up. At any rate, A can always back down if he raises prices and B does not follow.

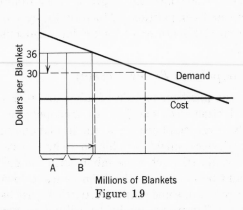

Figure 1.9

The conclusion is an old one, that two firms can generally gain by collusion, and a less obvious point, that they do not have to enter into formal agreements to price collusively. If there had been 100 electric blanket makers with the same costs the most profitable price would also have been $30, but they would not have been able to reach that price as easily as when the industry consisted only of A and B. Any one of the sellers would then be only a tiny part of the industry and would be in little danger of retaliation. He would be far more likely to shade his price in hopes of winning more of the market than either of the two giants in the oligopolistic industry had been. It would take a formal agreement with some sort of enforcement, probably by the government, to keep all 100 blanket makers in line. Otherwise their price would tend to settle at the competitive level.

The conclusion that an oligopolistic industry would tend to price the way a monopolist would, while a competitive one would not, should be taken as very tentative at this point. There might be room for some competition in quality or selling effort in the oligopoly. Firm A might cut prices even when firm B does not want to if A has lower costs or is more optimistic about potential sales at lower prices or is just by nature uncooperative.

Oligopolies in practice are a very diverse lot, and any generalization is bound to be incomplete. It makes a great deal of difference whether an oligopolistic industry is young and rapidly growing, mature and slowly growing, or actually declining; whether it sells to ill-informed consumers or to well-informed businessmen; whether there are just two big sellers or a dozen moderate-sized ones; and whether the industry is easy or hard for new firms to get into. The variations in performance between different industries all of which can be classified as oligopolies are as great as the differences between them as a group and competition. Much of the rest of this book is devoted to the special features of particular oligopolistic and competitive markets.

Monopoly on Factor Markets

Monopoly in the purchase or sale of labor or other factor services can distort production decisions just as monopoly in product sales does. The only large employer in a small manufacturing town, if left to his own devices, might be able to reduce costs by paying a low wage. He would still get some labor since the only alternatives for workers would be to stay on the farm or leave town. His policy would normally result in some output restriction, just as the monopolistic seller's did. Consumers might be willing to pay $20 for the electric blanket that one more worker would produce in a day, and the firm might be able to get the man for only $15. Yet the employer might not be willing to expand because he would have to raise everybody's pay from $14.50 to $15 if he did. The worker who is not hired is left to produce $15 worth of cabbages, say, though he might produce a $20 blanket. From a social point of view he is working on the wrong product. Consumers would be better off, and so would the worker, if the electric blanket plant employed him, but the company would not be, and it makes the decision.

Monopoly on the supply side of labor markets may be associated with a strong union. In some cases it may simply offset the power of large employers such as this isolated electric blanket plant just now. In such a situation a union-imposed wage increase might even be associated with *more* output and employment rather than less. The company would have had less incentive to limit output if it could not keep wages down by doing so.

On the other hand, a powerful union in an industry of many small producers may be able to accomplish what the firms themselves could not. If the cost of producing electric blankets can be pushed up to $30 by a union-imposed wage increase, as is shown in Figure 1.10, output will be just as much restricted as if the electric blanket manufacturers had themselves combined to push prices up and raise their profit margins.

Unions, like oligopolists, are hard to generalize about. They may

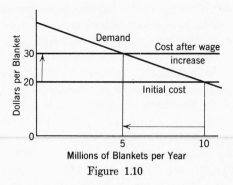

Figure 1.10

have quite different effects depending on whether they deal with big or little employers, whether the employers are competitive or monopolistic on product markets, whether the industry is fully or only partly organized, and whether the members are highly or slightly skilled. Some of the possibilities are discussed in Chapter 10.

Some Qualifications

The analysis just outlined seems to show that widespread monopoly distorts the operation of a private enterprise economy. Too little is produced in industries with one or a few large sellers and too much is produced in the more competitive fields as a result. Theory would seem to indicate that the American economy, where big business and equally big unions are familiar features, must be very far from the ideal.

Many economists have been dissatisfied with this result. They argue that while the specific conclusions may not be wrong they are often incomplete. At least three common, though controversial, explanations of why monopoly and oligopoly are not necessarily as bad as they seem in theory deserve some mention.

1. A monopolist may not be able to set prices as high as he would like because of the bargaining power of his customers. Oligopoly in the tire industry may not be a very severe problem because the big four tire makers have Sears and General Motors to deal with. Such customers can probably look after themselves. Similarly, big retailers such as Sears, Macy's, and the A&P stand between many manufacturers and the consumer. In labor markets the union may serve the same function when it organizes the workers of a powerful employer. Only a third of the American labor force is organized, but unions represent the bulk of labor employed in manufacturing, mining, and transportation where most of the large employers are to be found.

There are difficulties with this approach to monopoly, however. Some of the big sellers, such as the auto makers and the cigarette manufacturers, have no big buyers to deal with. If they are able to gain anything from their suppliers there is no one to force them to pass it on to the consumer. Moreover, the big buyers are often in a better position to exact price concessions from their relatively competitive suppliers than from the more powerful oligopolists. If the government intervenes in an attempt to build up the strength of weaker groups and distribute bargaining power more equally, the field of conflict will shift to the legislature. Then those who can exert the greatest political pressure are apt to win. At any rate, many find a world of giants glaring at each other a very unattractive prospect.

2. Some economists have argued that a certain degree of monopoly may be desirable because it can encourage firms to innovate, i.e., to try something new.* Innovation is risky. The firm cannot tell in advance whether a new location or method of merchandising will work or when the new machine will be obsolete. In view of the risks involved, the profit prospects must ordinarily be good to make such new investments worthwhile. It is a basic feature of competition, however, that profits are only temporary. Anyone in a competitive industry who finds a way to make high profits by building super-markets or moving his business to California will soon find his exceptional returns disappearing because of a host of imitators. He is in a situation of heads he loses and tails he does not win very much. Firms in concentrated industries, on the other hand, can often retain their winnings for years. As a result they may require less risk premium to find any given innovation worthwhile.

Monopolists and oligopolists have other advantages as well. They can finance new projects easily because their assured positions make them good credit risks and provide profits that can be used in self-financing. In addition, large firms (which in our enormous economy is not necessarily the same thing as monopolistic firms) can often minimize their risks by undertaking a great number of projects at once instead of putting all their eggs in one or two innovational baskets.

Monopolists and oligopolists are not inevitably good innovators, however. They have sometimes been known to drag their feet in

---

* The word *innovation* means the application of new ideas. It is not the same thing as invention. The first firm to install a machine is innovating even if the machine was invented ten years ago. So is one that tries a new line of products or a new location regardless of where the idea originated.

order to protect their plants from obsolescence. They may choose to relax and leave well enough alone. Competitors have no such options. If just a few of their number are ready to try something new, the rest will have to follow the successful innovators or lose out.

It is certainly true that if profits disappeared instantaneously in competition there would be no incentive to try anything that involved risk, but in practice there is a certain amount of friction in the economic system. Even competitive innovators can expect to retain their advantage for some time. Economists differ about how substantial the barriers to imitators must be to induce adequate rates of progress.

3. A third possible reason why monopoly may not be as bad as it seems in theory is that business leaders may not take full advantage of their monopolistic positions. They are obviously concerned about public relations. Some of them, such as the managements of U.S. Steel and du Pont, are prepared to spend millions on advertising designed primarily to improve their images in the public mind. It is quite reasonable for them to pass up occasional spectacular profits that may alienate public opinion. Many large firms did just this in the shortage years following World War II. For instance, in 1946 and 1947 newly manufactured automobiles were selling at the factories at $500 to $1000 *less* than the same cars brought on the competitive second-hand market!

Businessmen may go further. To judge by their public utterances, some of them seem to see themselves as "statesmen of industry" concerned not only with "adequate" profits for their shareholders, but also with "reasonable" prices for consumers, "fair" wages for employees, and "keen but fair" competition in dealings with other firms. Much of this is undoubtedly window dressing or self-deception, but the managers of large modern corporations are in a position to pursue goals other than maximum profits if they choose. In most cases their control of the corporation would not be in jeopardy regardless of which of a wide range of corporate policies they selected. Stockholders can seldom do much if management chooses a policy that yields 10% profits where 15% is possible. Most stockholders are too poorly informed to judge the results, and even if there is dissatisfaction stockholders almost never vote the existing management out. Thousands of stockholder elections confirm the old corporate leadership in office for every one in which it is even challenged.

The hired management of large modern corporations *can* take less than maximum profits if they want to. They undoubtedly do in some short-run situations. They take less than they might today to avoid public reaction and government intervention tomorrow. It may be that they surrender more profit than they have to because of a feeling of public spiritedness, but such an allegation would be hard to prove. We have no reliable way of reading their minds. While it is true that the robber barons of the turn of the century are practically extinct by now, it does not necessarily follow that the latter-day leaders of big business have weaker profit motives. The different behavior of big business today may be more a matter of a change in public policy than a change in heart.

Three possible qualifications to the traditional picture of monopoly have been mentioned. Some observers give considerable weight to one or another of these; others discard all of them as minor quibbles of little or no practical significance. The reader is just about free to pay his money and take his choice. These qualifications are likely to be of greater importance in some industries than in others. Probably the most fruitful method of evaluating them is by empirical studies of many specific cases.

THE OVER-ALL STRUCTURE OF AMERICAN INDUSTRY

Concentration Ratios

Although it is difficult to measure degrees of monopoly power accurately, it is certain that oligopolistic and monopolistic industries make up a substantial part of the American economy today. A commonly used, though imperfect, indicator of the monopolistic character of industries is the *concentration ratio*, the percentage of total shipments of a product made by the four largest firms.* Table 1.2 gives some indication of the degree of concentration in manufacturing according to the 1954 Census of Manufactures. Four firms made more than half the shipments in about a third of the manufacturing industries listed by the Bureau of the Census in that year.† These highly concentrated industries accounted for a little more than a quarter of all shipments made by manufacturing firms.

* Concentration ratios are discussed in more detail in Chapter 12, p. 496.

† The Census uses a "Standard Industrial Classification" in tabulating information for various types of manufacturing. Its broadest subdivisions are the two-digit "major industry groups" such as number 22, textile mill products. These are subdivided into three-digit "industry groups" such as 223, broad woven fabrics. The three-digit groups are subdivided in turn into four-digit "industries" such as 2233, cotton broad woven fabrics.

TABLE 1.2

THE NUMBER AND IMPORTANCE OF MANUFACTURING INDUSTRIES WITH VARIOUS DEGREES OF CONCENTRATION

Concentration Ratio (per cent)	Number of Industries Listed by the Census	Total Value of Shipments, 1954 (billions of dollars)	Percentage of Total Shipments of all Manufacturing Industries
75–100	40	16.4	7.8
50–75	101	35.2	16.7
25–50	157	74.5	35.3
0–25	136	84.7	40.2
	434	210.8	100.0

Source: *Concentration in American Industry*, Report of the Sub-committee on Anti-Trust and Monopoly, Committee on the Judiciary, U.S. Senate, 85th Congress, 1st Session, 1957, Table 17, p. 23.

Concentration ratios of 30 major* industries appear in Table 1.3. They shade from extremely concentrated industries such as aluminum and automobiles to'very competitive ones such as apparel and saw-mills. Concentration in some of these industries is easily sufficient to confer significant monopoly power on the firms included. Others are plainly very competitive, but any dividing line is bound to be arbitrary. Most of the industries where the four largest firms account for half or more of total shipments fall fairly clearly into the first group. If the four leaders account for no more than a quarter of total shipments, monopoly power can seldom be very great. Probably

---

The four-digit industries are the narrowest classifications for which statistics on plants, employment, and equipment are available, but the Census gathers information on shipments of more finely classified products. The group of products associated with a particular industry such as cotton broad woven fabrics is identified by the same four-digit number. These are subdivided into five-digit "product classes" such as 22334, colored yarn fabrics. These product classes are made up of seven-digit "products" such as 2233412, denims, 2.20 yard.

All the figures in Tables 1.2 and 1.3 refer to the products of four-digit industries except in the cases of steel and motor vehicles in Table 1.3. In those two instances the most important five-digit product group is used for lack of comparable information at the four-digit level.

* All of the industries shown in Table 1.3 had 1954 shipments in excess of $1 billion with the exception of aluminum. Altogether the 30 industries made about 40% of the shipments of manufacturing industries in 1954.

TABLE 1.3

CONCENTRATION RATIOS IN 30 MAJOR MANUFACTURING
INDUSTRIES, 1954

Primary aluminum	99
Passenger cars, knocked down or assembled	98
Cigarettes	82
Tin cans and other tinware	80
Synthetic fibers	79
Tires and inner tubes	78
Tractors	67
Aircraft	55
Hot rolled sheet and strip (the leading steel mill product)	53
Copper rolling and drawing	52
Electric motors and generators	48
Plastic materials	45
Meat packing products	39
Flour and meal	38
Farm machinery except tractors	36
Petroleum refining	32
Footwear except rubber	30
Pulp	29
Canned fruits and vegetables	28
Beer and ale	27
Fluid milk	21
Paper and paper board	19
Bread and related products	19
Newspapers	19
Machine tools	18
Cotton broad woven fabrics	17
Commerical printing	9
Sawmills and planing mills	6
Dresses, unit price	5
Women's suits, coats, and skirts	3

Note: The concentration ratios given here show the share of the four leading firms in total shipments of the products of the industry in question. Total shipments include quantities shipped by firms that produce that product only incidentally as well as by those that make it their main business.

· All of the industries are Census four-digit industries except for passenger cars, knocked down or assembled, and hot rolled sheet and strip. These are the most important five-digit product classes of the automobile and steel industries respectively. No concentration ratios on the basis used here are available for the four-digit industries involved because of extensive duplication owing to the intraindustry shipments.

Source: "Concentration in American Industry," *op. cit.*, Table 37.

some of the industries in the 25–50% group belong in the sector with significant monopoly power and some do not.

These concentration ratios give only a rough indication of monopoly power. Some industries, such as newspapers, are far more concentrated than Table 1.3 seems to indicate because their products are sold on local markets while Table 1.3 shows the largest firms' shares of shipments throughout the whole country.* In other cases, such as fluid milk, price competition is usually prevented by government controls. Trade union activities make some industries, such as printing, less competitive in some respects than their concentration ratios might indicate. Taking all these quibbles into account, perhaps a third to a half of American manufacturing should be classified as significantly monopolistic.

Manufacturing accounts for only about a third of present-day economic activity in the United States. Table 1.4 shows the relative importance of other types of business. Some of these are typified by large numbers of small firms. This is true of most agriculture, forestry and fishing, wholesale and retail trade, contract construction, and service industries.† Mining and finance are mixed cases. Bituminous coal, crude petroleum, and real estate are fields with large numbers of sellers, but banking, insurance, and the mining of most metals are all highly concentrated. Transportation, communication, and public utilities are also concentrated as a rule, but they are all regulated industries. With varying degrees of success, federal, state, and local governments limit competition within these fields and try to keep the firms from using their monopoly power against the public interest.

In many of the nonconcentrated fields there is some government or trade union limitation on competition. Crop restrictions and price supports in agriculture are famous. Most of the oil-producing states regulate the rate of crude oil production. Resale price maintenance laws ("Fair Trade" codes) restrict price competition among retailers to some extent, and government intervention suppresses price competition almost completely in liquor and milk distribution over much of the country. Trade unions are important monopolistic elements

---

* There are a number of other ways in which census concentration ratios may understate or overstate actual concentration. The most common overall effect is to understate concentration. See Chapter 12, p. 497.

† There are a few exceptions in most of these cases. Certain types of wholesaling are highly concentrated in most communities, although retailing seldom is. Heavy construction is sometimes quite concentrated, and, within the service field, the same can be said of motion pictures.

in coal mining and contract construction. Different economists give varying amounts of weight to these imperfections.

TABLE 1.4

NATIONAL INCOME ORIGINATING IN MAJOR INDUSTRIES, 1954

Industry	National Income Originating in the Industry in Question (billions of dollars)	Percentage of Total
Agriculture, forestry, and fisheries	16.6	5.6
Mining	5.2	1.7
Contract construction	15.7	5.3
Manufacturing	89.9	30.0
Wholesale and retail trade	52.0	17.4
Finance, insurance, and real estate	27.9	9.3
Transportation	14.6	4.8
Communication and public utilities	10.8	3.6
Services	29.8	9.9
Government	35.3	11.8
Rest of world	1.8	0.6
Total	299.6	100.0

Note: These are total factor incomes earned rather than the total shipments that were used in Tables 1.2 and 1.3. Total incomes are equivalent to net value added in production, i.e., the total value of output less purchases from other firms, depreciation, and excise taxes. The value added in manufacturing is less than the total shipments mainly because the products of manufacturing include large amounts of goods produced by farms, mines, other manufacturers, etc.

Source: *Survey of Current Business*, Feb., 1956.

Altogether America has a mixed economy. A little under a quarter of our economic activity is either carried on by federal, state, and local governments or is regulated by them. This includes the whole government sector: the armed services and schools as well as the post-office and power projects. It also includes transportation, communication, and public utilities. Another quarter, more or less, is accounted for by oligopolies of high concentration or industries where government or union activities seem definitely to result in monopolistic pricing. This quarter includes a third to a half of manufacturing, most mining, banking, insurance, and contract construction. About half of the output of our economy comes from industries with substantial amounts of competition, but in most of these there are some government or private restrictions.

MONOPOLY AND PUBLIC POLICY

Antitrust

The United States has used two main approaches to deal with the monopolistic sectors of our economy. For the largest group of industries the government has attempted to enforce competition, but in the transportation, communication, and utility fields the government has permitted and even enforced monopoly and then attempted to control it.

The basic antimonopoly legislation in the United States is the Sherman Antitrust Act passed in 1890. It provides for criminal and civil remedies against contracts or combinations "in restraint of trade" and against persons who "monopolize or attempt to monopolize" any part of interstate commerce.

The law was written in very broad terms so its meaning was really left for the courts to decide. They soon established that formal agreements to fix prices, limit output, or allocate markets among competing firms were definitely illegal. However, they were much more equivocal in their treatment of large firms. The government was successful in dissolving some of the best known combinations in the years before World War I, notably the American Tobacco Company and Standard Oil. It was the behavior of these firms that the courts condemned, not their mere size in relation to the market. In later cases it appeared that very large firms were within the law if their actions seemed "reasonable." Under this "rule of reason" the United States Steel Corporation, the nation's largest corporation at the time with about half of total steel sales, was given the court's approval (see Chapter 7).

In 1914 the Sherman Act was supplemented by the Clayton Antitrust Act and the Federal Trade Commission Act. The first spelled out and prohibited certain specific actions likely to enhance monopoly. These included interlocking directorates (where individuals served on the boards of directors of competing firms), intercorporate stock acquisitions, tying sales (where customers were required to buy a whole line of products if they wanted one of them), exclusive dealerships, and price discrimination. The second act established the Federal Trade Commission (FTC), which was to investigate competitive practices and issue orders against those deemed unfair.

Neither act produced any great changes in the 1920's and early 1930's. The prohibitions of the Clayton Act applied only "where the effect may be to substantially lessen competition or tend to create monopoly," so it left the main decisions to the judges again. In the case of the FTC, the courts limited the commission's investigating powers and retained the right to review its decisions before enforcing its orders. For many years the main job of the FTC seemed to be little more than the control of misleading advertising.

In the late 1930's the enforcement of the antitrust laws became much more vigorous, and the courts revised some of their earlier interpretations. In the Alcoa case (see Chapter 5) a corporation was convicted of "monopolizing" aluminum production mainly because it was the only domestic producer of the metal. The decision did not depend primarily on the firm's behavior. In addition, various closely parallel output or price policies in oil, tobacco, cement, and steel were prohibited although formal agreement was not definitely established. The significance of the FTC was greatly enhanced and the prohibitions of the Clayton Act began to carry more weight.

There were no great dissolutions, however. The government was prepared to tighten up on trade practices and perhaps to limit the creation of new combinations, but it was apparently not prepared to dissolve existing firms even when they were in an unquestioned position to control their markets.

The major issues of antitrust policy will be discussed in Chapters 5, 7, 8, and 9.

Regulated Industries

In the public utility fields the government regulated monopoly rather than attempted to prevent it. Regulatory commissions were established by state and federal governments to deal with the railroads in the 1880's, and state commissions to regulate utilities of all sorts became common in the early 1900's.

The regulatory approach to monopoly has a record which is about as spotty as that of the antitrust laws. The Supreme Court retained the power to review the decisions of the state and federal commissions, and its standards were especially vague in this field. Commission decisions were often overruled, and the commissions' authority was closely limited. The powers granted to the regulators by the legislatures and not weakened by the courts proved inadequate to deal with obvious problems that arose in the 1920's.

In the 1930's the powers of the state commissions were generally increased, and federal commissions were established to supplement them. At the start of the 1940's the courts seemed to withdraw from a wide range of regulatory questions, by and large accepting the findings of the commissions and reviewing only questions of procedure.

Although the powers of the regulators have been increased and judicial interference is largely gone, regulation is still imperfect. It is an extremely complex business, and regulators are only human. The problems of present-day regulation are reviewed in Chapter 6.

Instead of preventing or regulating monopolies, the government may operate them directly. In the United States, government enterprise has been pretty much limited to the public utility field and has been extremely controversial even there. Government operation of utilities is also discussed in Chapter 6.

Other Government Policies Toward Business

In some areas the government has acted to limit rather than enforce competition. The most extreme case was the National Industrial Recovery Act of 1933 which established a National Recovery Administration (NRA) with the power to approve and enforce industry "codes" controlling competition in any industry whose members chose to formulate them. The NRA lasted only two years (1933–35) before it was declared unconstitutional by the courts, but government policies to eliminate competition or at least to restrict its effects continue in such fields as agriculture, retailing, and the labor market. Moreover, tariffs, patents, and government procurement programs have often done much to enhance monopoly.

The government's actions to limit or enforce competition are only a small part of its dealings with business today. Public policy and private enterprise come in contact at a thousand different points. The government collects taxes from business; procures supplies from business; provides such services as the roads, waterways, post offices, research, and education for business; regulates the amounts of credit available to business; controls the level of business activity; regulates the wages, hours, and employment practices of business; regulates security issues and corporate organization; maintains minimum standards for business in such lines as food and drugs; and the list could go on.

These government policies are far too numerous to be discussed in a single book. This book attempts to examine fairly carefully the public policies that limit or extend monopoly in the industries studied. Other public policies toward business are mentioned only incidentally if at all.

THE REST OF THE BOOK

So far we have completed only a series of very brief and impressionistic sketches. We have outlined the ideal form of a private enterprise economy and the problem of monopoly as economists see it. We have taken a quick look at the extent of monopoly and competition in the American economy in practice; and we have reviewed briefly the general pattern of American policy toward monopoly.

In the rest of this book individual industries are studied from the same points of view but in much more detail. In each case we consider theory, practice, and policy, with the main emphasis on the degree of competition, its effect, and its control.

The fields to be studied have been selected to represent broad groups of industries both in organization and type of product. Chapters 2 and 3 develop the economist's picture of competition more completely and compare it with practice in the best known and most regulated of competitive industries—agriculture. Chapter 4 applies the same analysis to one of the most important competitive lines of manufacturing–textiles. International trade as well as domestic market performance are important here. Chapters 5 and 6 present the economists' analysis of monopoly and study the behavior of an unregulated monopoly (aluminum before World War II) and a regulated one (electric power). Chapters 7 and 8 discuss two oligopolies—steel and automobiles. The first sells a standardized product to well-informed industrial users; the second sells a highly differentiated product to the less informed general public. As a result, their performance has often been quite different. Chapter 9 is devoted to retailing, an important industry with some of the characteristics of monopoly and some of competition. The chapter covers several different cases ranging all the way from the highly competitive food stores to liquor stores where government regulates both entry and price. Chapter 10 discusses the markets for factor services. It emphasizes the labor market, comparing the economists' analysis with actual experience in the market for steel labor. A substantial part of the chapter is devoted to unions in the steel industry.

The reader must not expect to find solutions to all the great problems of competition and monopoly in this book. At the end there will be a large number of untidy strings dangling from the package which he will have to tie up for himself as best he can. The hope is that he will finish the book with a better basis for making his own judgments not only about the particular industries studied but about industries of every sort.

FURTHER READINGS

Supply, demand, and the general rationale of a private enterprise system are subjects discussed in all principles textbooks and in most books on economic theory. A fine place to brush up on these is Paul Samuelson, *Economics*, McGraw-Hill, 1958, Chapter 3, 19, and 20. Some of the qualifications of the traditional pictures of capitalism are presented in J. K. Galbraith, *American Capitalism, the Concept of Countervailing Power*, rev. ed., Houghton Mifflin, 1957, and Joseph Schumpeter, *Capitalism, Socialism, and Democracy*, Harper, 1950, Chapters VII and VIII. Both books were written for the general reader rather than for the trained economist, though the Schumpeter book is hardly light reading. Galbraith emphasizes the idea of big buyers to offset the monopoly power of sellers in a concentrated position. Schumpeter presents the innovation argument. Both books are highly controversial. For some comments on them see Edward S. Mason, *Economic Concentration and the Monopoly Problem*, Harvard University Press, 1957, Chapter 17, "The New Competition," G. Warren Nutter, "Monopoly, Bigness, and Progress," *Journal of Political Economy*, Dec. 1956, pp. 520–527, and Walter Adams, "Competition, Monopoly, and Countervailing Power," *Quarterly Journal of Economics*, Nov. 1953, pp. 469–492. The idea of the socially minded corporation appears in A. A. Berle, *The Twentieth Century Capitalist Revolution*, Harcourt & Brace, 1954, and is criticized by Carl Kaysen, "The Social Significance of the Modern Corporation," *American Economic Review*, Proceedings, May 1957, p. 311.

On the measurement of monopoly in the United States see G. Warren Nutter, *The Extent of Enterprise Monopoly in the United States, 1899–1939*, University of Chicago Press, 1951, Morris Adelman, "Measurement of Economic Concentration," *Review of Economic Statistics*, Aug. 1951, pp. 260–296, and Carl Kaysen and O. F. Turner, *Anti-Trust Policy*, Harvard University Press, 1959, Chapter II.

Most texts in economic principles contain summaries of the history of antitrust and public utility control. A good one appears in William A. Koivisto, *Principles and Problems of Modern Economics*, Wiley, 1957, Chapter 16. There are a large number of texts on government policies toward business. An outstanding one which covers a wide range of aspects of the subject quite thoroughly is Clair Wilcox, *Public Policies Toward Business*, rev. ed., Irwin, 1959.

2

PURE COMPETITION AND AGRICULTURE—SHORT RUN

Agriculture was our first industry and is still our largest. Most Americans were farmers when the country began. Today 1 worker in 11 is a farmer and as many more are employed to provide services, supplies, and equipment for farmers. Moreover, no industry has been more the subject of government policy than agriculture. Farming is the only business that has a cabinet officer and House and Senate standing committees all its own. Agricultural policy is an issue in almost every national election.

PURE COMPETITION

More important for the purposes of this book, agriculture provides some excellent material for the development fo basic ideas about cost and demand. The methods of analyzing farm cost in Chapters 2 and 3 are used with only slight variations to study costs in industries of every sort. Similarly, the demand for automobiles, aluminum, or steel is described in the same terms as those developed in Chapter 2 to describe the demand for pork. The ideas in these two chapters are absolutely essential for the understanding of the rest of this book.

In structure, agriculture comes closer to the conditions known by economists as *pure competition* than any other major industry. To be *purely competitive* a market must have all of the following characteristics: (1) a completely standardized product; (2) a large number of independent buyers and sellers so that no one of them can affect the price; (3) freedom of entry and exit for buyers and sellers; (4) complete absence of collusive agreements among buyers or sellers; and (5) free access for each buyer or seller to large numbers of alternatives on the other side of the market.* Most American industries fail to meet one or another of these requirements. Even in those fields that the trade magazines identify as "highly competitive," such as retailing or automobiles, a seller usually has some choice about the price he will charge. Either there are customers who will pay a premium for the corner grocer's smile or location, or there are only a handful of sellers and substantial barriers to new firms.

Conditions in farming are pretty close to the requirements of pure competition, however. There are about 1 million producers of hogs, 900,000 of cotton, and even 10,000 of avocados, and in each case there are more ready to start production if the situation becomes sufficiently favorable. In such a setting, no one farmer can hope to do anything about the price at which he sells. The biggest ranch in Texas might market as many as 15,000 head of cattle in a peak year, roughly 0.1% of the nation's beef supply. If it held off the market completely, it would not force the price of beef up by even 1%. It is true that actions of all the farmers, taken together, can make the price of beef or wheat or avocados rise or fall, but

---

* Pure competition is often distinguished from *perfect competition*. In addition to the requirements of pure competition, perfect competition calls for perfect market knowledge and perfect resource mobility. That is, buyers and sellers are presumed to know all the opportunities available and even to foresee the future; moreover, all resources are presumed capable of moving instantaneously to their most profitable employment, so that even temporary surpluses and shortages are avoided.

It can be shown that a perfectly competitive private enterprise economy with no external economies or diseconomies would result in the most efficient possible allocation of existing resources, given the distribution of income. Perfect competition therefore provides some sort of a standard for evaluating the various types of markets that are to be found in practice.

Of course, perfect competition has never existed anywhere and never will. Our closest approximations to it are certain almost purely competitive markets, all of which contain some imperfections of knowledge and some obstacles to mobility. Agriculture without government intervention is a good example. Pure competition as described in Chapters 2 and 3 would yield the same results as perfect competition *if none of the participants in the markets described ever made any mistakes!*

for any individual the price at which he sells is like the weather. He may grumble about it, but he must adjust to it.*

Most farm products are reasonably well graded. Buyers make no distinction between the products of two farmers as long as they come up to uniform standards. Number 2 red winter wheat is number 2 red winter wheat regardless of the grower. The leading crops are sold on great, impersonal, national exchanges like the Chicago Board of Trade or New Orleans Cotton Exchange. Quotations based on the latest transactions of these exchanges are announced throughout the country, and anyone with the means and the inclination can buy or sell almost any conceivable amount at the going price.

Individual farmers cannot take their corn or hogs all the way to Chicago, of course. There may be only a few practicable outlets available to them. The local grain or livestock dealers have a mild sort of monopoly. However, this is not a very serious imperfection in most cases. Farmers can usually go to the next town if they have to, and there is always the possibility of a new dealer or a cooperative if the old dealers take too great a cut below the Chicago price. On any one day a local dealer might be able to pay a price far out of line with Chicago and get away with it, but if he follows such a policy for long he will lose most of his business.

SHORT- AND LONG-RUN PROBLEMS OF AGRICULTURE

Farm Problems

Chapter 1 contained a rudimentary picture of pure competition. There it seemed to lead to the most efficient use of resources. In equilibrium, just the right things were produced in just the right amounts, and all resources were used where they were most productive. When we now conclude that agriculture is our best approximation to pure competition, the reader may be excused some doubts. Agriculture seems to be one of the eternal problems of our economy, and it certainly does not receive much acclamation for efficient organization. This chapter and the next will try to reconcile our seemingly rosy theory with the less rosy facts of farming.

* It is true that farmers have been able to do quite a lot about their prices by complaining to their congressmen. Later in the chapter there is an extensive discussion of farm policy, but to get a clearer picture of the issues the effect of government action on agricultural markets will be disregarded at this point.

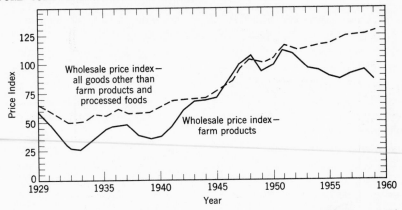

Figure 2.1. Indexes of farm and nonfarm wholesale prices (1947–49 = 100.)

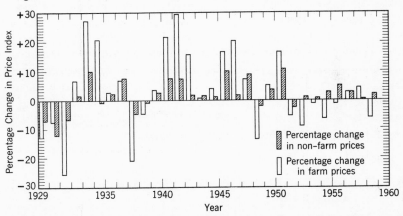

Figure 2.2. Changes in farm and nonfarm prices as percentages of previous years. Source: Bureau of Labor Statistics' Wholesale Price Index.

Modern American agriculture has two main economic problems, instability and poverty. Figure 2.1 compares farm and nonfarm prices over the last 30 years.* Both show an upward tendency, but agricultural prices have fluctuated far more from year to year than

* Actually, it compares the wholesale price index for farm and nonfarm products. Each series shows the values of representative market baskets of farm and nonfarm goods in various years. These values have been expressed as percentages of the average value of each "market basket" in 1947–49. As a result, during the 1947–49 period, both series are around 100. The reader should not conclude that there is anything sacred about 1947–49 prices, however. It is certainly correct to say that nonfarm prices have risen farther than farm prices since then, but it would be meaningless to say that farm prices are lower than nonfarm prices. That would be similar to a statement that the price of wheat is lower than the price of gasoline or automobiles.

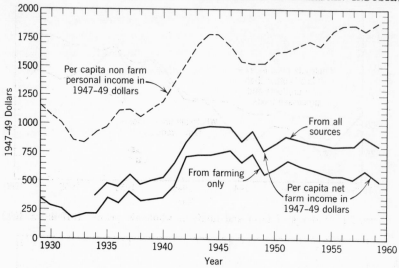

Figure 2.3. Per capita farm and nonfarm incomes in 1947–49 dollars.

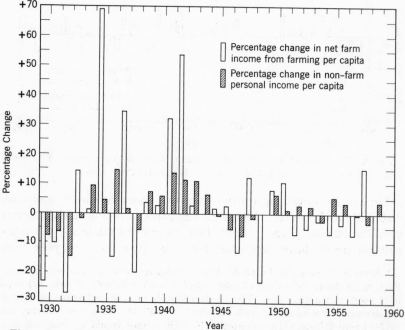

Figure 2.4. Changes in per capita real incomes as percentages of the preceding years. Note: Nonfarm income is nonfarm personal income per capita of the nonfarm population deflated by the consumer price index—Commerce Department. Farm income is per capita net farm income deflated by index of prices paid by farmers, family living items—Department of Agriculture, *The Farm Income Situation*.

nonagricultural prices. This appears more clearly in Figure 2.2, which shows each year's change in price as a percentage of the previous year's price. A 15 or 20% increase or decrease in farm prices was not uncommon, but even a 10% change in nonfarm prices occurred in only very unusual years.

Farm incomes show the same instability as farm prices. Figures 2.3 and 2.4 compare farm and nonfarm *per capita* incomes measured in 1947–49 dollars. In the depression years, farm incomes fell proportionately more than nonfarm incomes, in spite of large-scale urban unemployment. In the booms of the 1940's and the Korean War and in the subsequent slumps farm incomes moved up and down considerably more violently than city incomes even though the government was making strenuous efforts to stablize them. Farming is one of the feast and famine businesses of our economy.

Low incomes, the other major farm problem, also shows up in Figure 2.3. Per capita incomes of the farm population only reached half of the nonfarm levels in the war and early postwar years, and after the Korean War they generally declined while nonfarm incomes were rising.

This does not give a complete picture of the low incomes of much of American farming because of inequality within agriculture itself. Twelve per cent of the farms sell 58% of the farm products.* The other 88% receive very low incomes indeed. While less than a fifth of all employed men, urban and rural, reported incomes of $1500 or less in 1952, half of the country's farmers did.† From time to time in recent years there have been raised eyebrows at the farmer who flew his own airplane or drove a Cadillac. Certainly these were the exceptions. A quarter of the farmers did not even drive cars.‡

* *Census of Agriculture,* 1954. The 622,948 Class I and II farms marketed $14.5 billion, while the other 4,160,073 sold $9.9 billion worth of farm products.

† Herman P. Miller, *Income of the American People,* Wiley, 1955, pp. 22–24. 49.7% of the farmers earned $1500 or less compared with 16.9% of all employed males, including farmers.

This exaggerates farm poverty to some extent. There is undoubtedly some under-reporting. Moreover, farm products consumed on the farm are included in farm incomes at farm prices, much lower than urban retail prices.

Farm poverty was concentrated in the south, where half of the white farmers reported incomes of $1033 or less. Half the nonwhite southern farmers reported incomes of no more than $554! In the rest of the country, farm incomes ran about two-thirds of nonfarm incomes in 1952.

‡ U.S. Department of Agriculture, *Special Cooperative Survey of Farm Expenditures,* 1957. In 1956, 73% of farm families reported having automobiles.

Short Run–Long Run

The problem of instability is largely one of year to year adjustments to changes in demand or supply. The questions involved are "How much more or less will farmers produce next year if demand shifts?" and "How much more or less will consumers buy if the price changes?" In the economists' language, these are *short-run* questions. The *short run* is a period in which the number of farms or factories does not change. Any additional production must come from establishments already in the field, and the producers in the wheat or watch industry will not be able to leave if business is bad. Few, if any, factories will be built or scrapped in response to annual changes in demand, and very few farmers will move to the city or back to the farm as demand or crop conditions change from year to year.

Perennial farm poverty is a *long-run* problem. The difficulty here is the wrong types or numbers of farms. Its solution requires that resources leave agriculture or that the size and organization of farm enterprises change. It is only in the *long run*, as economists use the term, that this sort of change can occur. Then any factor of production can move into or out of a line of business, old factories or farms can be abandoned or new ones added, and firms can choose their types of organization.*

The rest of Chapter 2 covers cost and demand in the short run along with the problem of instability. Chapter 3 is concerned with cost and demand in the long run and the problem of low farm incomes.

COSTS AND OUTPUT

The General Pattern of Costs

In the short run, prices are determined by demand and supply, and supply in turn depends upon cost. At any given price a farmer or a

---

* The short run and long run are not definite periods. The time necessary to enter or leave production differs greatly from industry to industry. It takes a couple of years to build a railroad, but once built it will last a century. It takes ten years for coffee trees to start bearing fruit, and another decade or two for the trees to pass their usefulness. It may take me an afternoon to enter the local trucking business (if I can finance the truck and get a license), while it takes six or eight years for the truck to wear out. Of course, if the truck hits a telephone pole and my asset is changed into an insurance claim, the short run may be very short indeed, and I will be free to choose a new line of business immediately. Of course, I can sell the truck and leave the business immediately, even if it does not hit a pole. The truck will still be in operation, however, so a complete long-run adjustment will not have been made.

businessman will supply much or little or none at all, depending on how much it costs him to turn out the product in question.

Costs follow broadly similar patterns for most firms, whether they produce hogs, apples, shoes, steel, or automobiles. They are commonly divided into *fixed* and *variable* costs. *Fixed costs* (sometimes "overhead") are items such as interest on long-term debt, depreciation, or property taxes that are the same regardless of the level of output. Even if the firm shuts down, the equipment goes on wearing out and the interest and taxes continue to accrue. Fixed costs appear in

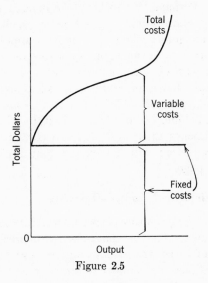

Figure 2.5

Figure 2.5 as a horizontal straight line. No matter what the level of output from zero to the greatest possible, total fixed cost is the same.

Variable costs (sometimes "prime" or "direct" or "operating" costs) are those expenses that increase or decrease with output and that *can* be avoided by closing down. They often include such items as fuel, materials, and labor when it can be laid off. They follow the pattern of the upper curve in Figure 2.5. At first variable costs are likely to rise less rapidly than output. It does not take 10 times as much labor and material to produce 10 cars or 10 bushels of wheat as it takes to produce just one. For any producer committed to a particular farm or factory, however, variable costs must sooner or later rise at an increasing rate.

The inevitable increase in the rate that variable costs rise beyond some level of production is just another way of stating the well-known principle of "diminishing returns." A cow will give more milk if her feed ration is increased, and a shoe machine will produce more insoles if more labor and leather are applied to it; but neither process can go on forever. If it did, we could slaughter all but the best cow in every region and let her supply all the milk within shipping distance of her barn. What happens in practice is that after a point additional feed will add less and less milk and presently the poor cow will just not eat any more. Again, another employee in a plant where all the machines are already being operated full blast may be able to add something. Perhaps he can keep the machinery in better repair so that breakdowns are minimized; or he can spell the other workers so that they make fewer mistakes; but it is almost a certainty that he will not contribute as much as some of his brethren who were employed when part of the machinery was idle.* Since one more laborer or one more pound of feed produces less and less after a point, the labor or feed cost of additional output must increase. Every field, factory, machine, or cow has a limit to what it can produce. As output approaches that limit variable costs rise more and more rapidly, and production will not exceed that limit even if variable costs go off the page.

Agricultural Costs—Dairying

In some types of agriculture, experimental studies have been made that show the particular cost patterns more precisely. One of the most extensive of these was in dairying. Several hundred cows at 10 experimental stations in a number of states were fed at various levels for three years and their milk production compared.

The feed "inputs" that went with the various milk outputs are shown in Table 2.1 and Figure 2.6. A cow requires a certain amount of feed simply to maintain herself. Beyond that, more feed leads to more milk, but at a decreasing rate. The cows fed at high levels produced more than less generously treated cows, but, as we would expect, milk output did not increase as fast as feed consumption.

These production figures can be used to estimate the costs of a hypothetical dairy farm. Imagine a 25-cow farm near one of the

* Diminishing returns will occur in any process where one of the factors of production is fixed. It makes no difference what the fixed factor is. If the feed were kept fixed (as with a pasture) and the number of cows increased, sooner or later extra cows would add less and less to milk production. If one worker were required to supervise more and more machines, presently additional machines would cease to contribute much to output.

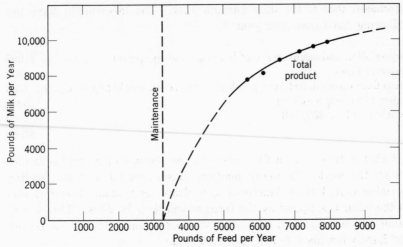

Figure 2.6. Source: Jensen et al., *op. cit.*, p. 39.

TABLE 2.1

FEED INPUT AND MILK OUTPUT PER COW PER YEAR
FOR 392 COWS FED AT SIX LEVELS

Number of Cows in Each Group	Average Total Digestible Nutrients Consumed (lb per yr)	Average 4% Fat Corrected Milk Produced (lb per yr)
65	5654	7626
60	6117	8184
66	6575	8824
55	7132	9400
52	7531	9780
94	7899	9965

Note: "Total digestible nutrients" includes all types of feed (grain, hay, etc.) expressed as pounds of carbohydrate feed (dry weight) according to feed value. A correction was applied to express all milk production as of a uniform butterfat content.

Source: Einar Jensen, John W. Klein, Emil Rauchenstein, T. E. Woodward, and Ray Smith, *Input-Output Relationships in Milk Production*, U.S. Department of Agriculture Technical Bulletin No. 815, May 1942.

large cities on the eastern seaboard. Let it produce enough hay, silage, pasture, etc., to provide 3000 pounds of feed per cow per year. It must buy any feed above that level. For simplicity, assume that purchased feed is the only variable cost. The farm might have the following fixed costs per year:*

Depreciation and maintenance of buildings and equipment	$1000
Property taxes	200
Miscellaneous (seed, fertilizer, gasoline, veterinarian, marketing costs, etc.)	1300
Labor (4000 hours at 75¢)	3000
Interest (5% on $30,000)	1500
	$7000

Labor is treated as a fixed cost because the operator and his family do all the work. In many nonfarm businesses labor is the leading variable cost, but in American agriculture more than three-quarters of the labor is supplied by the farmers and their families. This sort of labor will be employed no matter what the farm produces. A farmer can hardly fire his wife if he has a bad year.

The only way to put a value on this family labor is by looking at its *alternative cost,* i.e., what it can earn in its best alternative employment. In 1956, hired farm labor was paid about 75¢ an hour on the average. If the farmer were not earning enough from his farm to pay himself at least this wage, he would be taking a loss, all things considered. The farmer could undoubtedly earn more than this in the city, but for most American farmers a dollar on the farm is worth more than one in the city. The 75¢ is probably a reasonable implicit wage to allow the farm family in this illustration.

Interest has been treated in the same way as labor costs in this example. If the farmer had borrowed the $30,000, the interest charge would obviously be part of his fixed costs; but even if he put it up himself, the farmer's capital costs something. If he were to sell his farm and put the proceeds into securities, he could earn $1500 or so per year on his money. Farming would be profitable only if it paid enough to give him a normal return on his investment as well as the going wage for his labor. At any lower level, the farmer would be taking losses and would do well to quit if he has the opportunity.

* These costs roughly fit those of "Central Northeast Dairy Farms" in 1956 as reported in *The Dairy Situation,* Oct. 1957, and *The Farm Cost Situation,* May, 1957. Such farms were reported to have a $30,000 investment and to employ 4440 man-hours of labor per year on the average. The farm in question supplies considerably less of its feed than typical of the whole area. This farm is like those close to New York or Boston where land is too valuable for extensive farming.

Livestock costs and receipts are left out for simplicity. They would partially offset each other. Obviously some of the miscellaneous items are really variable costs, though such items as seed, fertilizer, and veterinary costs cannot be avoided very well as long as the farmer keeps his herd.

TABLE 2.2

TOTAL COSTS AT VARIOUS LEVELS OF OUTPUT

A Total Output (thousands of lb of milk per yr)	B Total Fixed Costs (dollars per yr)	C Total Variable Costs (dollars per yr)	D Total Costs (dollars per yr) B + C
0	7000	—	7,000
200	7000	3000	10,000
210	7000	3250	10,250
220	7000	3550	10,550
230	7000	3900	10,900
240	7000	4350	11,350
250	7000	5000	12,000
260	7000	6000	13,000

The total costs of this farm at various levels of output are shown in Table 2.2. Column B of Table 2.2 shows the $7000 fixed costs which apply whether the farmer sells a little or a lot or nothing at all. Column C shows the total variable costs—purchased feed in this case—assuming that he pays 4¢ a pound for concentrates. The figures in column C are approximately in line with the experimental data given in Table 2.1, but they have been rounded to make arithmetic easier.* Total costs are just the total variable and total fixed costs added together. Total costs at various outputs appear as the upward sloping total cost curve in Figure 2.7.

Cost and Revenue

Just which of the outputs in Table 2.2 is most profitable depends on the receipts that the farmer can expect. Table 2.3 compares his total costs with the prospective receipts at a price of 5¢ a pound for milk, and again at 4¢ a pound. The total receipts are simply the output times the price.

Since this is a case of pure competition, milk sells for 5¢ a pound whether Farmer Brown produces 260,000 pounds per year or 200,000

* The exact derivation of the figures in Table 2.2 is of decidedly secondary importance, but is given here for those who wish to know how it was worked out. The quantities correspond roughly to those in Table 2.1 multiplied by 25 (we are assuming a 25-cow herd). The feed per cow at each output was estimated on the basis of Table 2.1. The total variable cost is just the number of pounds of feed per cow times $1 (4¢ a pound for 25 cows). The dots in Figure 2.7 show the costs that result if the exact inputs and outputs in Table 2.1 are used without any rounding.

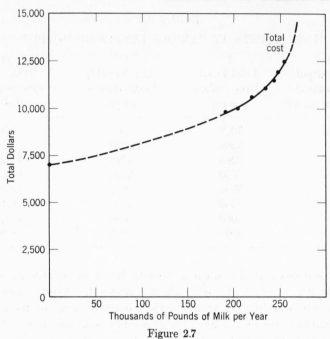

Figure 2.7

TABLE 2.3

TOTAL COSTS, TOTAL RECEIPTS, AND TOTAL PROFITS AT VARIOUS
LEVELS OF OUTPUT

A Output (thousands of lb of milk per yr)	B Total Costs (dollars per yr)	C Total Receipts at 5¢ per lb (dol- lars per yr) A × 5¢	D Total Profits at 5¢ per lb (dollars per yr) C − B	E Total Re- ceipts at 4¢ per lb (dol- lars per yr) A × 4¢	F Total Profits at 4¢ per lb (dollars per yr) E − B
0	7,000	0	−7000	0	−7000
200	10,000	10,000	0	8,000	−2000
210	10,250	10,500	250	8,400	−1850
220	10,550	11,000	450	8,800	−1750
230	10,900	11,500	600	9,200	−1700
240	11,350	12,000	650	9,600	−1750
250	12,000	12,500	500	10,000	−2000
260	13,000	13,000	0	10,400	−2600

per year or quits dairying completely. The difference between the total costs and the total receipts of the farm is its total profits. In this case the farmer would just break even at 200,000 pounds and at 260,000 pounds, but could make considerable profits at intermediate outputs. His most profitable level of operation according to column D is at 240,000 pounds per year.

Total costs, total receipts, and total profits at a price of 5¢ a pound are all reproduced as curves in Figure 2.8. Since total receipts rise

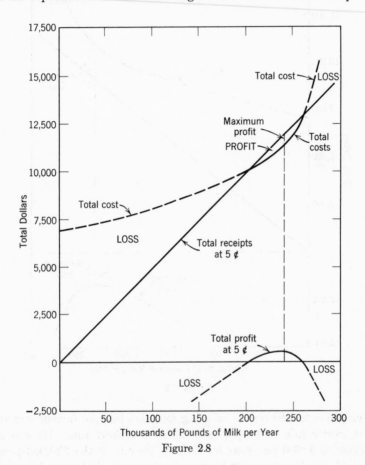

Figure 2.8

in proportion to output, the total receipts curve is a straight line. At outputs of less than 200,000 pounds or more than 260,000 pounds of milk per year, the total receipts curve of this farm is below the total cost curve and profits are negative—in other words, the farmer is taking a loss. The distance between the cost and revenue curves is greatest at 240,000 pounds of milk, the level of production that a profit-maximizing farmer would select.

Columns E and F of Table 2.3 show what would happen at a price of 4¢ a pound. They are plotted in Figure 2.9. This time there is *no* output where the farmer can make a profit or even avoid a loss.

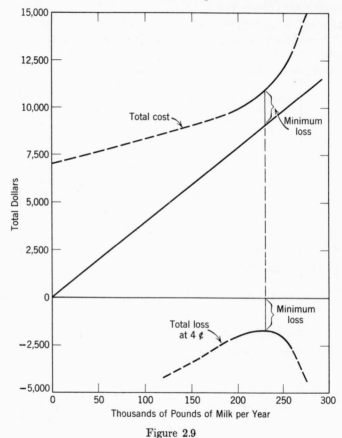

Figure 2.9

Dairying has turned out to be a big mistake, but the farmer will still find it worthwhile to keep producing in the short run. He can cut his losses to $1700 per year by keeping output at the 230,000-pound level. At any lower output he would lose more. If he tried to avoid all of his variable costs by just maintaining his herd he could lose as much as $7000 a year. So long as he sticks to dairying a loss of $1700 is the best that he can manage.

How can a businessman or a farmer operate at a loss this way?

Part of the explanation lies in the economists' definition of "cost." Remember that it includes $4500 a year for the farmer's own wages and a return on his investment in this case. A loss of $1700 means that he might have been making $1700 more in some other line of work, but so long as his money is tied up in the dairy herd he does not really have the alternative. At 4¢ a pound, dairying is not a very good business to go into, and if prices stay at that level our farmer would do well to get out when he can. So long as he remains committed to dairying, however, the best that he can do is operate his farm so that his losses will be at a minimum.*

Average Costs

It is often convenient to discuss costs on an "average" or "per unit" basis. After all, prices are quoted in cents per pound, per bushel, or per kilowatt-hour, and such prices cannot be compared directly with costs expressed in *total* dollars. This farm's average costs are worked out in Table 2.4 and plotted in Figure 2.10. *Average fixed cost* (fixed costs *per pound of milk*) and *average variable cost* (variable costs *per pound of milk*) behave quite differently, so they have been derived separately.

In this case *average fixed cost* is just the $7000 of fixed cost divided by the number of pounds of milk produced. When the output is 200,000 pounds, average fixed cost is $\dfrac{\$7,000}{200,000 \text{ pounds}} = 3.5¢$ per pound. As the output expands the $7000 is divided by larger and larger outputs so average fixed cost declines continually. If the farmer could get out 1 million pounds of milk a year he could reduce his average fixed cost to 0.7¢ per pound, but of course the cows could never do it. The larger the output, the lower the average fixed cost indefinitely. This is the famous phenomenon of "spreading the overhead."

Average variable cost is, by analogy, just total variable cost divided

---

* He does have the choice of selling the herd or even the whole farm. In fact, if he does badly enough to go bankrupt, his creditors may sell them for him. This will not change the situation significantly, however. A buyer would only be interested in the herd and the pasture if the price were low enough to offer him a reasonable return on *his* investment. Once he gets such a price he will find it profitable to keep up milk production so long as the present herd lasts, though he will not want to replace the cows as they grow old. The original farmer or his creditors will not avoid the loss either. The price that they get will have to be low enough that the new buyer can break even at 230,000 pounds of milk per year. That means that the old farmer must take a loss on the sale of the farm equivalent to $1700 per year.

TABLE 2.4

AVERAGE COSTS OF A HYPOTHETICAL NORTHEASTERN
DAIRY FARM

A	B	C	D	E	F
Quantity Produced per Yr (thousands of lb of milk)	Average Fixed Cost (cents per lb) $7000 ÷ A	Total Variable Cost (dollars per yr)	Average Variable Cost (cents per lb) C ÷ A	Total Cost (dollars per yr)	Average Cost (cents per lb) E ÷ A or B + D
200	3.50	3000	1.50	10,000	5.00
210	3.33	3250	1.55	10,250	4.88
220	3.18	3550	1.61	10,550	4.80
230	3.04	3900	1.69	10,900	4.73
240	2.91	4350	1.81	11,350	4.72
250	2.80	5000	2.00	12,000	4.80
260	2.69	6000	2.30	13,000	5.00

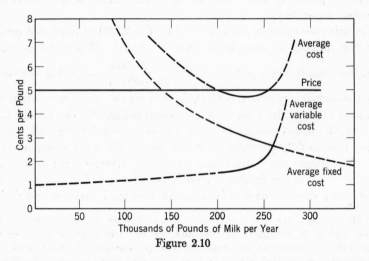

Figure 2.10

by total output. For instance, at an output of 200,000 pounds of milk per year, average variable cost comes to $\dfrac{\$3,000}{200,000 \text{ pounds}} = 1.5¢$ per pound. Total variable cost rises when the output does, so average variable cost can either increase, decrease, or remain constant over a wide range of outputs. In Table 2.4 the variable cost *per pound of milk* increases continuously, but this would not have to be the case in another enterprise. In many firms the variable labor and materials cost *per unit of output* declines for a while as production expands. Again, in some industries average variable cost seems to be almost constant over wide ranges of output. The labor and materials cost of a pair of shoes or a kilowatt-hour of electricity may be about the same whether the plant is running at 20% of capacity or 80%.

In every case where the plant is fixed, however, average variable cost *must* rise ultimately. As operations approach the capacity of the farm or factory, the feed used per pound of milk or the labor used per pair of shoes or the fuel per kilowatt-hour is bound to increase because of diminishing returns. There is a limit to the output of a farm or factory no matter how much variable feed or labor or fuel is used.

By now it should come as no surprise that *average cost* is the total cost divided by the quantity produced.* Alternatively, it is the sum of the average fixed and average variable costs. In Table 2.4 average cost declines at first and then increases, so it is roughly "U-shaped" when plotted in Figure 2.10. This is almost inevitable. So long as the enterprise being described has any appreciable fixed costs, the cost per unit will decrease at first because of the "spreading" overhead. Later, when the overhead is "spread" thin, the decrease in costs slows down, and as the output approaches capacity the rise in average variable cost results in an increase in average cost.

Price and Profit

The price of milk is expressed in cents per pound so it can be plotted directly on Figure 2.10. It appears as a horizontal straight line at 5¢. That will be the price of milk no matter how much this particular farm produces. The horizontal line might be thought of as the demand curve for this farmer's milk. He cannot sell milk at all at more than the market price, and he can sell any likely amount at that level.

The most profitable output is still not obvious. At first glance it would always seem to be at about 240,000 pounds a year where the average cost is at a minimum. This is where the margin between the price and cost per unit is greatest. The same would also be true if the price were 6¢, or 8¢, or 10¢! For that matter, 240,000 pounds would also be the output where the farmer can come closest to covering cost *per pound* when the price is no more than 4¢ and he operates at a loss.

---

* Average cost is sometimes called average total cost or total unit cost.

Something is obviously wrong here. The farmer is certainly *not* going to produce the same amount of milk regardless of the price. In fact, the earlier analysis of total costs and total receipts showed that the most profitable (least loss) levels of output were different at 5¢ and at 4¢.

The explanation is that the difference between average cost and price is profit *per pound* of milk, *not* total profit; and it is the total profit per year that the farmer will try to maximize. He wants the highest possible return on his *investment,* and he would be willing to sacrifice some profit *per pound of milk* if he could thereby enhance his profit per dollar invested in his farm.

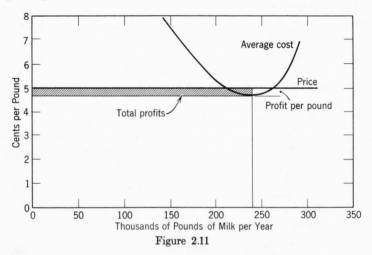

Figure 2.11

Total profit is, of course, profit per pound times the number of pounds of milk. Total profits at a price of 5¢ are represented by the shaded rectangle in Figure 2.11. The sides of the rectangle are the profit per pound and the total numbers of pounds produced, so the area of the rectangle represents the product of the two sides or total profits. Although profit per pound (the vertical distance between average cost and price) may always be at a maximum at 240,000 pounds, total profits (the rectangle) may be greater at some other output.

Marginal Cost

To determine the most profitable level of operations more precisely we need one more cost concept, that of *marginal cost.* The word *marginal* refers to the effect of a small change, so *marginal cost* is the change in cost which will accompany a small change in output. The marginal costs of this farm are worked out in Table 2.5. When milk production expands from 200,000 to 210,000 pounds per year, total costs rise by $250 from $10,000 to $10,250. If milk came in 5-ton (10,000-pound) tanks, this $250 would be the *marginal* of a tank of milk. If the unit of milk production is thought of as the pound, then the $250 is the extra cost of 10,000 more pounds of milk. Within the range from 200,000 to 210,000 the farm can produce one more pound for about $\dfrac{\$250}{10,000 \text{ pounds}}$ or 2.5¢ per pound. In general the marginal cost of any product can be thought of as the $\dfrac{\text{extra cost}}{\text{extra output}}$.

TABLE 2.5

MARGINAL COST

A Quantity of Milk per Yr (Thousands of lb)	B Total Cost (dollars)	C Change in Total Cost with Each 10,000-lb Change in Output (dollars)	D Marginal Cost (cents per lb) C ÷ 10,000	E Average Cost (cents per lb)
200	10,000			5.00
		250	2.5	
210	10,250			4.88
		300	3.0	
220	10,550			4.80
		350	3.5	
230	10,900			4.73
		450	4.5	
240	11,350			4.72
		650	6.5	
250	12,000			4.80
		1000	10.0	
260	13,000			5.01

The marginal cost derived in Table 2.5 is plotted in Figure 2.12. In the short run, marginal cost *must* sooner or late increase the way it does in Figure 2.12. This is true of any farm, factory, or power plant again, and for the same reasons that total cost and average cost

must rise. As the output approaches capacity it takes more and
more additional feed, labor, or materials to add anything more to
output.

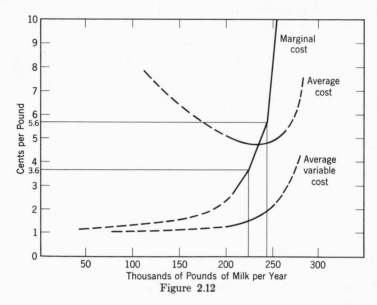

Figure 2.12

One feature to note in Figure 2.12 is that the marginal cost curve
cuts right through the lowest point on the average cost curve. This
is no accident. It is inevitable because of the character of an average. For instance, the average of the following numbers is obviously 4:

$$6 + 5 + 4 + 3 + 2 = 20 \qquad 20 \div 5 = \text{the average}$$

When a sixth number is added to the series, the average stays at 4
only if the added (or *marginal*) number is 4. If the marginal number
is more than 4, say 5, the average rises to $4\frac{1}{6}$. If the *marginal* number is less than 4, say 3, the average falls to $3\frac{5}{6}$. Note that even
though the series of numbers stops falling and even rises a bit when
the 3 is added, the *average* continues to fall so long as the new number is below it.

The same thing happens with average and marginal costs. If the
cost of one more pound of milk is less than the average cost of milk,
the average cost will have to decline. If the marginal cost is more
than the average cost, the average cost will have to rise. And if
the marginal cost is the same as the average cost, the average cost

will neither rise nor fall. When average cost stops declining, it is at its minimum.*

Maximizing Profit

We are now in a position to make a more definite statement about the most profitable level of output. The general rule is that profits will be at a maximum, or losses at a minimum, where *marginal cost equals price*. So long as marginal cost is less than price, it pays to expand since one more unit of output adds less to costs than to receipts. Once marginal cost rises above price, it is better to reduce production. The last pound of milk then increases cost by more than it does receipts. The place for the profit-maximizing producer to stop expanding is where marginal cost just reaches price.

This is an important and sometimes confusing idea which can bear some repetition. Figure 2.13 may help to clarify the point. It shows the effect of a series of 10,000-pound increases in output. Let us imagine the farmer selling 5-ton tank trucks of milk again, so that the effects of his actions will be large enough to be visible on the diagram. At a price of 5¢ a pound, each 10,000-pound increase will bring in $500 more. These additions to receipts are represented in the upper diagram by the row of uniform bars at the $500 level. The marginal cost of each new tank of milk appears as the flight of stairs rising irregularly toward the right. At low outputs these marginal costs are less than $500 so each expansion adds something to profits. The additions to profits show up as the lightly shaded segments of each receipts bar. When output gets out to a point where marginal cost is more than price, the *reductions* in profit are shown as the darkly shaded segments above the receipts bar.

The lower diagram in Figure 2.13 shows what has been happening to *total* profit while this was going on. As each of the lightly shaded additions to profits is piled on top of the previous ones, the total profit bars grow taller and taller. When output reaches 240,000 pounds where the last $50 addition has been made, total profits are at a maximum. Thereafter marginal cost exceeds price and progressive subtractions from profits reduce the height of the profits bars.

The most profitable output would be different at other prices. For

---

* The marginal cost curve will also pass through the lowest point on the average variable cost curve, if it has one, and for the same reason. Marginal costs are necessarily variable costs. Marginal *fixed* costs are always zero! In this case, where average variable costs are rising as far back as experimental data go, marginal cost is always greater than variable cost per unit.

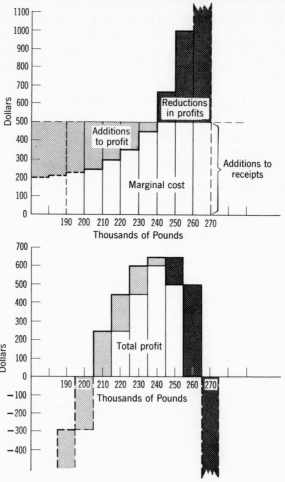

Figure 2.13

instance, if milk sold for anything from 6.5¢ to 10¢ per pound, it would have paid to expand to the 250,000-pound level, and above 10¢ the price would exceed marginal cost all the way out to the 260,000-pound level. Going in the other direction, if the price were only 4¢, an output of 230,000 pounds would yield the greatest possible profit. Of course, this time the "greatest possible profit" would be a *loss* of $1700 per year, but at any other level of production the loss would be greater. So long as the price is more than marginal cost, an increase in output will reduce losses even at 4¢, but further expansion after that point will just make them worse.

There is a limit to how low the price can go and still have the farmer find it worthwhile to produce. If the price of milk were as low as 1¢ a pound, the farmer would not earn enough even to cover his purchased feed. He would be better off then to produce no more milk than he would get just maintaining his herd, and if he feels certain that the price will stay that low he should consider selling the cows for hamburger. The reason why he was willing to keep feeding above the bare maintenance level in spite of some losses at 4¢ was that he could not avoid his fixed costs even if he did cut output. He had already "sunk" his time and money into the herd and was committed to $7000 a year in fixed costs. There was no point in crying over spilled milk. On the other hand, he *can* escape his variable costs, even in the short run, so if the price does not even cover those he would be better off not producing or at least not feeding above the maintenance level.

Marginal Cost and Supply

The marginal cost curve has turned out to be the supply of milk for the particular farm in question. At any price above the lowest average variable cost, the marginal cost curve shows the amounts that the farmer is willing to sell.

Of course, this supply is only a tiny part of the total supply of milk. If this farm was in the New York milk shed it would be only one of 48,555 producers in the area, some of them larger and some smaller, some well and some poorly managed, some near New York and some 200 miles away. The others may have higher or lower costs, but they can all be counted on to have the same general pattern of costs as this farm.

The supply of milk for New York City is derived in Figure 2.14. To simplify things, imagine that the only difference between farms is distance from New York. There are 20,000 like our farm near the

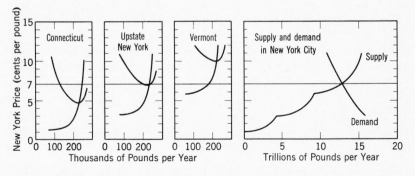

Figure 2.14

city in Connecticut or New Jersey, 20,000 more in upstate New York, and another group in Vermont and the Adirondacks. Including transportation costs in their total costs, these farms farther out have higher costs and therefore supply less at each New York price. The total amount supplied at each price by all of the farms together is shown in the right-hand diagram. At a New York price of 7¢ a pound, each of the Connecticut farms produces 250,000 pounds of milk per year, and the upstate New York farms produce 230,000. The Vermont farms produce 200,000 pounds right now, but if things do not improve they will switch to another business in the long run. At a price of 5¢, the Vermont farmers would drop out and the nearer farms would all sell less.*

If there were hundreds of small, independent buyers of bulk milk in New York City and if there were no government intervention (neither assumption is correct), the price of milk there would be determined by this total supply and the New Yorkers' demand. The price that would result is the one that our farmer, as well as all the others, would equate with his marginal cost. This farmer and all the other milk producers in the New York area help to determine the price through their supply curves, but any one of them individually can only do as the price tells him. He can do nothing about the price himself.

FARM OUTPUT IN PRACTICE

Marginal Cost

It is a little difficult to picture a typical dairy farmer carefully calculating his marginal cost and deciding to feed his cows another hundred pounds of grain as a result. Noneconomists often decide that the six or seven kinds of cost curves just developed are pure academic theorizing with little or no meaning in practice. Actually, the analysis in the last few pages was not intended to show the way that farmers or other businessmen decide at what level to produce. Usually the most profitable level of feeding on dairy farms is worked out by trial and error, not by curve and schedule. Marginal costs give us a means of describing where a profit-maximizing producer would settle. It does not matter how he gets there. If we can assume that farmers do maximize profits, our analysis will have described them properly.

* This example is hypothetical, of course. There are other markets for milk besides New York. Vermont farmers may find it worthwhile to produce for the Boston market or for cheese makers.

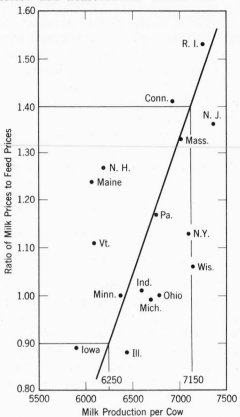

Figure 2.15. Source: Milk prices are prices received by farmers in 1955. Feed prices are average prices paid by farmers during the 12 months of 1955 for "all mixed dairy feed under 29% protein." Both are from Agricultural Marketing Service, *Agricultural Prices*. Milk per cow in 1955 is from *Agricultural Statistics 1956*, p. 371.

There is some evidence that dairy farmers really *do* tend to produce where marginal cost equals price. Figure 2.15 compares the milk-grain price ratio with the output of milk per cow in 16 northeastern dairy states in 1955.* The milk-grain price ratio is the price

* While dairying occurs in all states, these states embrace the major dairy regions of the country. There are secondary dairy centers in sections of the West and the South as well. However, differences of climate, quality of stock, and availability of year-round pasture make these areas difficult to compare with the Northeast.
There is a closer correlation between the milk-grain price ratios and the number of pounds of grain fed per cow. The output of milk was used here instead of the input of grain because it corresponded to the usual terms of marginal cost analysis more closely.

of milk per pound divided by the price of grain per pound. There is a clear trend toward heavier milk production with high milk prices. In states like Massachusetts, New Jersey, Connecticut, and Rhode Island where nearness to the great cities makes milk prices at the farm favorable, cows are fed intensively and the output per cow is high; in Iowa and Illinois, where the ratio of milk prices to feed prices is much lower, it is worthwhile to feed cows only at a lower rate and to produce less milk per cow as a result.

These statistics fit our earlier example surprisingly well. There it was assumed that feed costs 4¢ a pound. At that rate, a milk-grain price ratio of 0.90 (as in Iowa and Illinois) would mean a price of milk of 3.6¢ a pound $\left(\dfrac{3.6}{4.0} = 0.90\right)$. A ratio of 1.40 (as in Connecticut and New Jersey) would mean a milk price of 5.6¢ a pound $\left(\dfrac{5.6}{4.0} = 1.40\right)$. According to the marginal cost curve for our hypothetical farm (Figure 2.12), about 20,000 pounds more of milk (or 800 pounds per cow) would be produced at 5.6¢ than at 3.6. This is very close to the difference between the low and high price states in Figure 2.15 on the average. Variations among states in responsiveness of output to price could easily result from differences in the price of hay, the climate, and the types of stock. Northeastern dairy farmers seem to have operated at about the level where marginal cost equals price with surprising accuracy.*

Fixed Costs in Farming

Each type of business has its own cost patterns, of course. Though they generally resemble the dairy farmer in having some fixed and some variable costs and in showing short-run diminishing returns, they differ in significant ways. A very important consideration is the proportion of total costs that is fixed. For most farms this proportion is fairly high. Table 2.6 shows the main expenses of the average American farm in 1956. In addition to such obvious items as depreciation, property taxes, long-term interest, and rents, the incomes of farm operators have been included in fixed costs. The average American farm represented an investment of about $25,000 of the owner's capital in 1956 and employed 1.2 man-years of family labor.†

* The fact that all of the states produced less per cow than the cows in the experiment should not be surprising. The cows on the average farm are not of such uniform high quality nor do they receive such uniformly good attention as cows in an experimental station.

† U.S. Department of Agriculture, *The Balance Sheet of Agriculture—1957*, Agri-

TABLE 2.6

PRODUCTION EXPENSES AND RECEIPTS PER FARM, ALL UNITED STATES FARMS, 1956

Operating Expenses	Dollars	Fixed Expenses	Dollars
Feed purchased	789	Depreciation of buildings	
Livestock purchased	325	and equipment	770
Seed purchased	109	Property taxes	243
Fertilizer purchased	251	Interest on farm mortgages	86
Hired labor	562	Rents paid to nonfarm	
Repairs and operation of buildings		landlords	224
and equipment (includes gas and		Net farm income of opera-	
oil)	707	tors	2337
Miscellaneous	412		3660
	3155		

Total fixed plus operating expense (equals gross farm income per farm)   6815

Note: The costs listed are derived from *The Farm Income Situation*, July 1957, pp. 18–34. The totals have been divided by 4,964,000 (the number of farms in 1956) to find the cost per farm for each item.

The average operator's net income of $2337 per year seems a very low return on such a substantial amount of labor and capital. Some farmers were undoubtedly making more than their alternative costs, but they were probably offset by others who were taking a "loss" in view of what they could earn in the city.

Counting only the clearly fixed cost items in Table 2.6, fixed costs came to 54% of the total value of output of American farms in 1956. In addition, some of the operating costs are really overhead for many farms. Livestock purchases may be variable costs for an Iowa farmer fattening beef cattle, but for a dairy farmer they are a matter of maintaining the herd. Similarly, feed used for maintenance and building and machinery repairs would fall into the fixed cost category. Altogether, maybe 60% of the average farm's costs are fixed. In some types of agriculture the proportion of total costs that are fixed is considerably higher. The main variable costs (hired labor, feed, seed, and livestock) are only 11% of the total on spring wheat-small grain farms on the northern plains, 20% on the winter wheat farms

culture Information Bulletin No. 177, Oct. 1957, p. 20. All productive assets on farms in 1956 were valued at $124.6 billion or $25,429 per farm. Total farm debt in 1956 was $18.9 billion, but against this farmers had financial assets (securities, cash, etc.) of $18.4 billion and household furnishings of $11.6 billion.

of the southern plains, 20% on cash grain farms in the corn belt, and 26% on Wisconsin dairy farms.*

With fixed costs accounting for more than half of total costs on the average farm and about 80% on some, farmers can be expected to keep producing even if farm prices fall by half or more.†

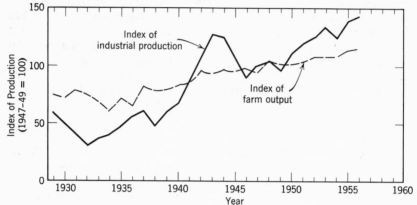

Figure 2.16. Source: *Statistical Abstract of the United States.*

This has certainly been American experience. Figure 2.16 compares the index of industrial production with an index of farm output. Industrial and farm production in each year appear as percentages of the 1947–49 levels. These indexes measure volume of output only. Price changes are left out. Industrial output grew faster than farm production, but farm output changed much less from year to year. The main ripples in farm output that did occur were due to the weather. During the depression years, when farm prices were falling disastrously, farmers continued to produce. In some deep depression years, 1931 and 1932, they actually produced more than in 1929. In other years, 1933 and 1935, they produced only slightly below the 1929 level, and even in the drought years of 1934 and 1936 farm production never fell more than 20% below the 1929 level. By contrast, industrial production was 47% below 1929 in 1932. Farmers did not stop producing when prices fell because they still had the mortgage to pay and the family to feed. By and large, they continued to pro-

* *The Farm Cost Situation,* May 1957, p. 26.

† Output can still fluctuate with price changes, depending on how flat the marginal cost curves are, but few farmers will move in and out of production because of changing prices in the short run. If, in addition, the marginal cost curves on most farms rise steeply, as they did in the dairy farm discussed a few pages back, the output would show little response to price changes.

duce and sell at whatever price they could get, even if that price barely covered their operating expenses.

Diversified Farming and Alternative Products

Even if he is committed to agriculture, the farmer often may choose between several possible crops. While some farmers are specialists in dairying or cotton or wheat, a substantial proportion of American farmers has more than one product. If the price of farm products in general declines, a diversified corn belt farm will go right on producing, but if just the price of milk falls off, the operator can feed more of his grain to hogs or beef cattle or sell it to a breakfast-food manufacturer.

In shifting between products such a farmer has to make the same sort of decision that the one-crop dairy farmer did. How much less milk should he produce at a lower price? How much feed should he divert from the milk cows to other uses? Each successive hundred pounds of corn diverted to other uses involves a larger and larger loss of milk.* The wise farmer will keep diverting grain from milk to beef or pork until the last hundred pounds adds no more in dollars-worth of pork or beef than the farmer loses in dollars-worth of milk. Any time a pound of feed (or hour of labor or acre of land) will earn more in one use than in another, the farmer will gain by making the shift. When the last pound of feed (or other resource) earns just as much in all uses, the farmer cannot improve himself; he is making his maximum profit.

Production Adjustments from Year to Year

As a result of the farmer's ability to shift between products in the short run, there can be substantial fluctuations in the output of individual farm products from year to year in response to price changes. While total farm output almost never changes as much as 20% from one year to the next, wheat or cotton marketings often do. This is partly due to regional weather conditions, which can change much more in one year than the weather of the whole country, but it is also farmers' adjustments to price changes. Figures 2.17 and 2.18 show some cases of this.

Figure 2.17 shows the total cattle population of the country since the end of the Civil War. There is a surprisingly regular cycle.

* The increase or decrease in output (milk) with one more or one less unit of imput (feed) is called the "marginal product." The marginal product is an important concept later in the book (Chapter 10). At this point, the *term* is not really very necessary.

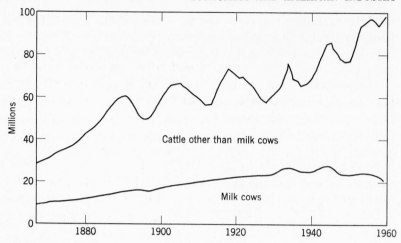

Figure 2.17. Cattle on farms as of Jan. 1, 1959. Source: Agricultural Marketing Service, Neg. 430A–57(2).

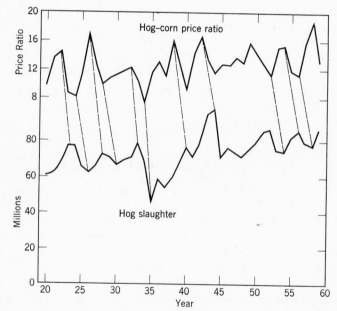

Figure 2.18. Source: *Agriculture Outlook Charts*, 1955 and 1960.

Every decade or so, cattlemen respond to good prices by increasing their herds 30 or 40%. The large numbers of marketings that result inevitably make the price unfavorable for the last part of the cycle and ranchers cut their herds back once more.

Hog producers have a similar cycle. Figure 2.18 compares hog marketings and the hog-corn price ratio since 1920. Here the fluctuations are shorter than the cattle cycle. Hogs mature in a year and have litters of a half dozen pigs, while cattle take two years or more to mature and have one calf at a time. It takes longer to build up or reduce a herd in the latter case. In Figure 2.18, a high price for hogs compared with corn is typically followed a year or two later by large marketings. All these hogs mean low prices, and these in turn are followed a year or two later by low production. It looks very much as if farmers are growing feed and hogs with an eye to prices at planting and farrowing time. Of course, it is their estimates of price at harvest that determine their output, but these estimates are often very uncertain and are strongly influenced by prices in previous years.

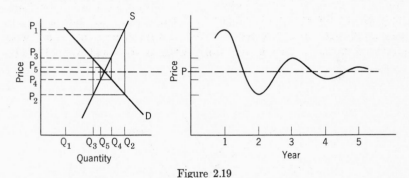

Figure 2.19

It has been suggested that unstable hog production can be explained by supply and demand curves like Figure 2.19. Suppose that in year 1 the output of hogs is low (at Q_1) so that the price is temporarily very high (P_1). Expecting this price to continue, farmers grow a large number of hogs next year (Q_2) and when they come to sell them find a price of only P_2. This leads to low output and high prices in year 3, heavy feeding and low prices in year 4, etc. This idea has come to be known as the cobweb theorem because of the way the supply and demand diagram looks after several go-arounds.*

Various writers have thought they have seen cobwebs of this sort in cattle, chickens, strawberries, coffee, and tree-grown fruits. The duration of the cycle would vary with the time it takes to increase production. In this illustration output was assumed to shift annually for simplicity, but it could just as well have taken a decade to get

* The price fluctuations do not necessarily become less severe as time passes. By flattening the supply curve or steepening the demand, you can make the price go off the page.

from year 1 to year 2. Of course, weather, crop restrictions, the prices of other goods, and changes in demand all affect the level of price so that actual price fluctuations cannot be expected to be as regular as those in Figure 2.19. If they ever were that regular, farmers could probably figure out what was happening to them. Then the cycle would be stopped, or at least changed.

ELASTICITY

Demand and Instability

Not all fluctuations in farm prices and incomes are attributable to the weather or output decisions by farmers. Shifts in demand can do drastic things to farm prices and incomes. Figures 2.1 and 2.3 showed that the really extreme changes in farm prices and incomes were associated with the reduced demand during depressions and with increased demand during the world-wide post-World War II food shortage.

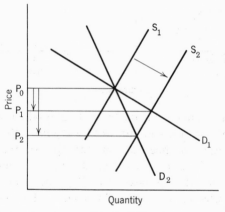

Figure 2.20

The effect of shifts in supply or demand on price and income depends on the character of demand in part. If consumption is very responsive to changes in price (D_1 in Figure 2.20), a given shift in supply will produce little change in price. Consumers will take up additional strawberries so readily that the price need not fall very much to clear the market. On the other hand, if the demand is unresponsive to price changes (D_2 in Figure 2.20), it will take a large drop in price to sell any additional output when there is a bumper crop. D_2 might represent a product like wheat. If strawberry and wheat production show similar fluctuations from year to year, strawberry prices should be more stable that wheat prices. Figure 2.21 shows this. In both the strawberry and wheat cases, output is 40% higher in odd-numbered years than in even. Prices fluctuate within a 20% range for strawberries, but by 50% for wheat.

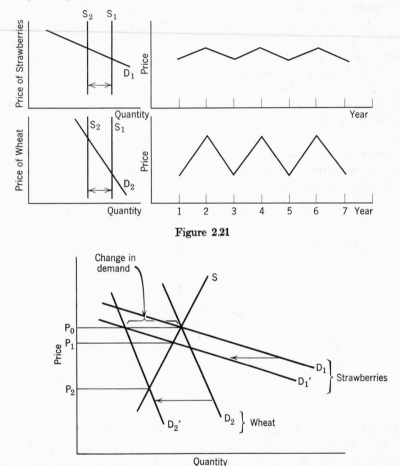

Figure 2.21

Figure 2.22

We would have had similar results if instability had been caused by shifts in demand instead of supply. In Figure 2.22, both the demand for strawberries and the demand for wheat are reduced by the same quantity at each price. It takes only a small reduction in price to bring consumers back to strawberries but it takes a large price reduction to get them to take all the extra wheat.

Elasticity

Economists have developed the concept of *elasticity* to measure the responsiveness of the quantity purchased to price changes. In the foregoing illustrations, the demand for strawberries was much more "elastic" than the demand for wheat, because changes in quantity were relatively large when the price changed. However, terms like "large" and "small" are imprecise. A 10,000-ton increase in the quantity purchased would be a large change for strawberries but an insignificant one for coal. A 25¢ fall in the price of gasoline would be earth-shaking, but a 25¢ reduction in auto prices would not even be noticed. Economists use the percentage rather than absolute changes in price and quantity to avoid this problem. A 10% increase in strawberry consumption can be compared with a 1% increase in coal, even if tons of the two commodities cannot.

The precise definition of elasticity is the

$$\frac{\text{percentage change in quantity purchased}}{\text{percentage change in price}} \quad \text{or} \quad \frac{\Delta Q}{Q} \bigg/ \frac{\Delta P^*}{P}$$

For instance, Table 2.7 shows small portions of several demand

TABLE 2.7

Quantities Purchased per Day

Price	Q_1	Q_2	Q_3	Q_4
$10	100	100	100	100
$9	120	110	105	100

schedules. In each case, the public will buy 100 units per day at a price of $10 per unit, but when the price of each commodity is reduced to $9 per unit, the public responds to the change in price more in some cases than in others. For the first commodity (Q_1), the $1 cut in price leads to 20 more sales, so that the elasticity is

* The symbol Δ (the Greek letter delta) simply means "change." ΔQ means the change in quantity. If quantity rises from 100 to 110 or declines from 100 to 90, ΔQ is 10. The percentage change in quantity would be $\Delta Q/Q$ or $\dfrac{10}{100}$ or 10% in either case.

$$\frac{\Delta Q}{Q} \Big/ \frac{\Delta P}{P} = \frac{20}{100} \Big/ \frac{1}{10} = \frac{20\%}{10\%} = 2$$

The second demand schedule has an elasticity of $\frac{10\%}{10\%}$ or 1, the third has an elasticity of $\frac{5\%}{10\%}$ or $\frac{1}{2}$, and the last has an elasticity of $\frac{0}{10\%}$ or 0.* Demand curves with these elasticities are plotted in Figure 2.23. Demands with elasticities of more than 1 (like D_1) are called "elastic." Products with elasticities of less than 1 (like D_3 or D_4) are said to have "inelastic" demands. The dividing line is where elasticity is 1—the case of "unit elasticity" (D_2). It is often convenient to draw straight-line demand curves like the one in Figure 2.24. Such a curve does not fit any of those in Figure 2.23. It has different elasticities at different prices. At a high price (P_1) a 10% drop in price doubles the quantity sold, but at a low price (P_2) a 50% cut in price increases sales by only a tenth. Exactly at the mid-point of the curve in Figure 2.24 a 10% change in price leads to a 10% change in quantity. Of course, there is no logical reason why demand curves should have the same elasticity throughout, or why they should fall in a straight line. They often appear that way in textbooks because they make calculations easy and are simple to draw.

* The equation used for elasticity here is still a little fuzzy if applied to anything but a very tiny price change. For instance, in the demand schedule at the right, a 50% cut in price leads to a 100% increase in quantity, so that elasticity is $\frac{100\%}{50\%} = 2$. However, reversing the price change, a 100% increase in price (from \$5 to \$10) leads to a 50% decrease in quantity, so that elasticity seems to be $\frac{50\%}{100\%} = \frac{1}{2}$. Both cannot be right. Actually neither is.

Price	Quantity
\$10	50
\$ 5	100

A better statement of the percentage change in price would be to compare the change with the average of the two prices, $\frac{5}{7.5}$ or $66\frac{2}{3}\%$. The percentage change in quantity would be derived the same way: $\frac{50}{75}$ or $66\frac{2}{3}\%$. Elasticity turns out to be $\frac{66\frac{2}{3}\%}{66\frac{2}{3}\%} = 1$. This method of measuring elasticity is known as "arc elasticity."

The elasticities in Table 2.7 are not quite correct because we did not go to all this trouble. The errors are not very great, however, because the change in price was fairly small. The error would disappear completely if we compared the percentage *rate* of change in quantity with the percentage *rate* of change in price at a point.

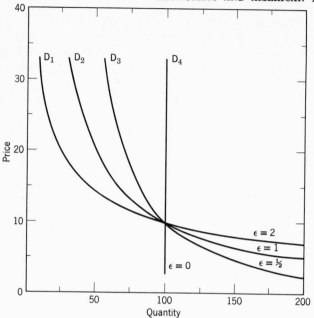

Figure 2.23

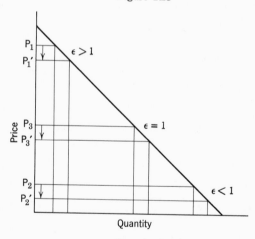

Figure 2.24

Elasticity in Practice—Pork

The elasticity of demand for some product is not always easy to discover in practice. Some of the problems involved are illustrated by Figure 2.25; it compares the average New York retail price of pork products with total national pork consumption in the years since 1930 (the years 1942–46 were left out because wartime price control and rationing limited consumer choices in those years). If we can presume that consumers were able to buy all the pork they wanted at the prevailing price each year, every dot in Figure 2.25 must be on the demand curve for pork. Yet the dots do not fall very neatly into the usual pattern of demand. They are scattered all over the map and seem to show that Americans buy *more* pork when its price is high, if anything!

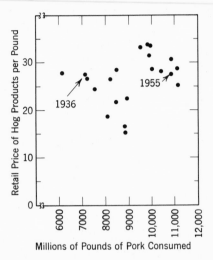

Figure 2.25. Source: Department of Agriculture, Agricultural Marketing Service, *Livestock Market News: Statistics and Related Data*–1956.

The problem is that the demand curve for pork keeps shifting about from year to year. For instance, the dots in Figure 2.25 fall easily into two groups. Those in the lower left-hand part of the chart show prices and quantities in the years 1930–41; the dots for 1947–56 are all located in the upper right-hand section. The whole demand curve for pork obviously shifted upward and to the right between the prewar and postwar years. In 1955, American consumers were willing to buy half again as much pork as they had bought in 1936 at about the same price. There are good reasons for this shift, of course. The population, the level of incomes, and the prices of goods other than pork were all much higher in the 1940's and 1950's than in the 1930's. Unfortunately, population, incomes, and other prices were also changing from year to year in the thirties, forties, and fifties, although less drastically. We cannot really tell therefore how much of any increase in consumption was attributable to a price reduction and how much to these other changes. There can be no doubt that we should draw different demand curves through the dots for 1936 and 1955, but we must be very uncertain about how steep the demand curves drawn through the dots for these two years should be.

Some of the changes in these other variables have been eliminated in Figure 2.26. For one thing, prices here are all expressed in 1956 dollars to adjust for the effect of inflation. Actually, 27¢ per pound was a much higher price in 1936 than in 1955 because of the other

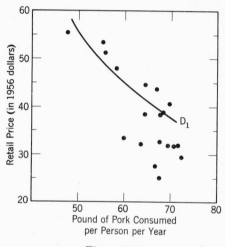

Figure 2.26

things 27¢ would buy in the two years. To express all prices in 1956 dollars, each price was divided by the consumer price index based on 1956. A price of 27 1936 cents would be about 54 1956 cents, because the general level of prices had just about doubled from 1936 to 1956.

The effect of population growth has also been eliminated in Figure 2.26. Instead of total consumption, Figure 2.26 shows consumption per person. The dots in Figure 2.26 can be thought of as points on the demand curve of Mr. Average American.

The dots in Figure 2.26 at least look something like a demand curve, but they may not show the actual demand for pork even yet. We still have such items as changing incomes to reckon with. The statisticians have a method known as multiple correlation by which they can estimate the effects of several simultaneous influences on some variable such as the quantity of pork consumed. The method is too complex to explain here, but the statistician can work out simultaneously how much the quantity changes in response to changes in the price of pork *and* to changes in consumer incomes. With his results, he can estimate how much the consumption of pork would change if only the price of pork changed, incomes remaining the same. When he does this, he has finally reached the elasticity of demand for pork, or something close to it. Various economists studying different groups of years and using somewhat different statistical techniques have estimated the elasticity of demand for pork at retail as 0.70, 0.99, and 0.86.* Taking 0.8 as a rough average of these, curves like D_1 in Figure 2.26 would seem to be a reasonable guess about the demand for pork. A 10% cut in pork prices would seem to lead to an 8% increase in consumption if nothing else changed.

Elasticity in Practice—Other Goods

Elasticity estimates have been made for a large group of commodities, many of them agricultural. Table 2.8 lists a few of these. They are not all equally reliable. Different scholars often find quite different elasticities, depending on the period they study, the exact statistical method they use, and the other variables besides price that they consider. Many of the methods used have been subject to considerable criticism. Nevertheless, these figures do show the rough patterns of demand elasticities. For one thing, the demand for beef, or pork, or mutton, each taken separately, all seem to be more elastic than the demand for all meat, and this in turn is more elastic than the demand for all food. This is to be expected. Buyers with good alternatives will drop out of a market rapidly as the price rises, but where there is no good substitute higher prices will do little to discourage consumption. In many cases, individual farm products are quite adequate substitutes for each other. It does not take an exorbitant drop in price to eliminate a surplus of beef *or* pork *or* lamb individually. But the substitutes for broad categories of goods like

* The first is from Henry Schultz, *The Theory and Measurement of Demand*, University of Chicago, 1938, p. 641. It took into account the price of beef, of lamb, and consumer incomes and was based on consumption during the years 1922–33. Schultz is the classic on this sort of study.

The second is from Elmer Working, *The Demand for Meat*, University of Chicago, 1951, p. 70. It took into account consumer incomes and the quantity of other meats consumed, based on 1922–41.

The third is from Karl A. Fox, *The Analysis of Demand for Farm Products*, U.S. Department of Agriculture Technical Bulletin No. 1081, Sept. 1953, p. 42. It was based on consumption during the years 1922–41 and took into account consumer incomes and the quantity of other meats consumed.

TABLE 2.8

Commodity	Elasticity	Source	Commodity	Elasticity	Source
Automobiles (retail)	0.8–1.5	(A)	Beef (retail)	0.8–1.1	(D, E, F)
Steel (at factory)	0.3–0.4	(B)	Pork (retail)	0.7–1.0	(D, E, F)
Aluminum (at			Lamb (retail)	1.8–2.0	(D, E)
factory)	0.2	(C)	All meat products		
Cotton (at farm)	0.1	(D)	(retail)	0.5–0.6	(E, F)
Wheat (at farm)	0.2	(D)	Milk (retail)	0.2–0.5	(G)
Corn (at farm)	0.5	(D)	Butter (retail, prewar)	0.3–0.4	(G)
Apples (retail)	1.3	(E)	Butter (retail, postwar)	1.3–1.4	(G)
Peaches (retail)	1.5	(E)	Margarine (retail,		
Citrus fruits (retail)	0.8	(E)	postwar)	0.3	(G)
All fruit	1.1	(E)	All food (retail)	0.2–0.5	(E, H, I)

Sources:

(A) See footnote, p. 334.

(B) U.S. Steel, *TNEC Papers*, Volume I, *Economic and Related Studies*. U.S. Steel, 1940, pp. 169–170.

(C) J. A. Rosenzweig, *The Demand for Aluminum*, University of Illinois Press, 1956, pp. 26–27.

(D) Henry Schultz, *loc. cit.*

(E) Karl A. Fox, *loc. cit.*

(F) Elmer Working, *op. cit.*, pp. 70 and 81.

(G) A. S. Rojko, *The Demand and Price Structure for Dairy Products*, U.S. Department of Agriculture, Technical Bulletin No. 1168, 1957, and various sources quoted in Rojko, pp. 109–110.

(H) James Tobin, "A Statistical Demand Function for Food in the U. S. A.," *Journal of the Royal Statistical Society*, Series A, Pt. II, 1950, p. 134.

(I) M. A. Girshick and Trygve Haavelmo, "Statistical Analysis of the Demand for Food," *Econometrica*, Apr. 1947.

"meat" and especially "food" are much poorer in the eyes of consumers, so that a larger drop in price is necessary to sell a surplus of all meats or all foods.

Most of the farm products in Table 2.8 have elasticities of less than 1.0. Since the substitutes for food in general, in the eyes of most consumers, are very few and very inadequate, the elasticity of demand for farm products as a whole must be very low indeed.

This is especially likely on the farm because of the processors' markups between the consumer and the farmer. The canning of peaches, the butchering of pork, or the milling of flour involves substantial costs which do not necessarily go up and down with farm prices. For many foods processing and distribution account for half or more of the consumer's dollar. Suppose that this has been true of beefsteaks, and that they have been selling for $1 a pound in the stores. If the price of beef now falls by 25¢ *at the farm*, and if the meat packers and distributors still require 50¢ a pound for their services, the retail price will fall to 75¢. The response to a 50% drop in price at the farm is likely to be disappointing because it involves only a 25% drop in price from the consumer's point of view.

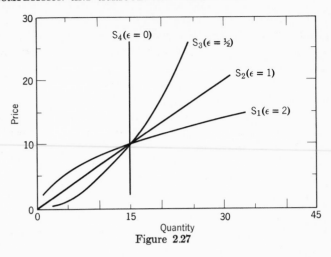

Figure 2.27

This low elasticity for farm products means unstable farm prices with changes in output or demand from year to year. Since prices fluctuate less with a more elastic demand, the problem of instability should be less severe for a single commodity with good substitutes than for farm products in general. For instance, the decline in the demand for butter that occurred as margarine became more popular in the early 1950's need not have caused surpluses of butter for long. Obviously, many consumers considered margarine a good substitute for butter. A cut in price would have won many consumers back to the dairy product. The loss of foreign demand for American food products in general as the world food shortage ended at about the same time was a much more serious problem. A substantial drop in all food prices seemed unlikely to make Americans eat much more.

Elasticity of Supply

The supplies of various commodities differ in responsiveness to price just as the demands do. The elasticity of supply is derived in the same way as the elasticity of demand, except that a fall in price normally leads to a decrease, not an increase, in the amounts offered.* If a 10% increase in price leads to a 20% increase in quantity offered, the elasticity of supply is 2; if it leads to a 5% increase in quantity, the elasticity is ½; etc. Figure 2.27 shows supply curves with several such elasticities.

* Technically, the elasticity of demand should have a minus sign. The change in price is *plus* 10% and the change in quantity, *minus* 10%, so the elasticity is a plus divided by a minus or a minus. The elasticity of supply is normally positive. Usually in economic writings elasticities are expressed without signs.

In discussing the costs of farm enterprises, we concluded that total farm output would change very little from year to year with price changes. In effect, we were concluding that supply of farm products, like demand, is inelastic. The supply of individual products may be more elastic because farmers, like consumers, can shift from one product to another when the price changes, even though they cannot stop producing much more easily than consumers can stop eating.

An inelastic supply will intensify the instability of farm prices. It will not take an impossible fall in price to remove a surplus of butter, because Iowa farmers who previously found it worthwhile to feed corn to dairy cows will now feed it to pigs, and some consumers who switched to margarine when it cost half as much as butter will switch back again when they are closer in price. It may take an intolerable fall in farm prices in general to adjust for the loss of the European market, however. Not only will consumers eat very little more; but farmers, who have to eat too, will keep right on producing in spite of the low prices.

Elasticity and Farm Incomes

The instability of farm incomes as well as farm prices can be traced in part to the inelastic demand for farm products. A fall in price does not necessarily mean a fall in the total sellers' receipts. That depends on the elasticity of demand.

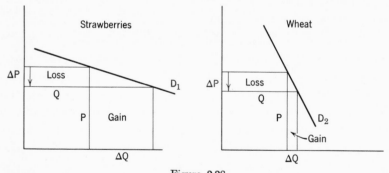

Figure 2.28

This shows up well in Figure 2.28, which compares the demand for strawberries and wheat again. Suppose there is a 10% reduction in the price of both commodities. In both cases there is an element of gain in the receipts of sellers as well as a loss. The loss results because the goods that were already selling at the higher price are now sold at a reduction. It is equal to the old quantity (Q) times the change in price (ΔP) and can be measured in Figure 2.28 by the areas of the two rectangles which have Q and ΔP for sides. The gain arises from the additional sales. It is equal to the additional quantity sold (ΔQ) times the price at which the new sales are made (P) and can be measured in Figure 2.28 by the areas of the two rectangles with P and ΔQ for sides. In the case of strawberries, so many more are sold at the lower price that they more than make up for the relatively small loss. A good crop means high incomes for strawberry growers, even though the price falls. In the case of wheat with an inelastic demand, consumers buy very little more at the lower price, so the main result is that wheat that would have been sold anyway goes for less. Thus the incomes of wheat farmers are actually reduced when there is a bumper crop.

The dividing line is an elasticity of demand of 1. Then the change in price just offsets the change in quantity so that the gain is just equal to the loss.* If the elasticity of demand for a farm product is 1, the gross receipts of producers will be the same regardless of the price.

Most of the agricultural elasticities in Table 2.8 are less than 1. This implies that fluctuations in output will make gross farm incomes rise and fall with farm prices.

An inelastic demand also implies unstable farm incomes in booms and depressions. If the demand for a product falls, total receipts of sellers are almost bound to decline regardless of the elasticity, since both the price and the quantity of sales are likely to be reduced. However, the amount of the decline will be more, or less, depending on the elasticity.

Figure 2.29 shows the effect of a decline in an inelastic demand. To isolate and dramatize the effect, assume that farmers have an elasticity of supply of 0; in other words, their supply curve is S_a. Contrast with this a situation which sometimes occurs in manu-

---

* To prove this, take the formula for elasticity $\dfrac{\Delta Q}{Q} \Big/ \dfrac{\Delta P}{P}$ and rearrange it.

Since we are dividing by a fraction, we can simply invert and multiply: $\dfrac{\Delta Q}{Q} \times \dfrac{P}{\Delta P}$

or $\dfrac{P\Delta Q}{Q\Delta P}$. But $P\Delta Q$ is the gain in revenue with a small change in price and $Q\Delta P$ is the loss in revenue with a small change in price. The elasticity of demand is therefore $\dfrac{\text{the gain in revenue}}{\text{the loss in revenue}}$. If elasticity is greater than 1, the gain must be greater than the loss. If elasticity is less than 1, the gain must be less than the loss. If elasticity is just equal to 1, the gain must just equal the loss.

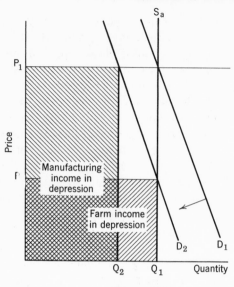

Figure 2.29

facturing, where the price of goods sold is not allowed to fall in a
recession. The manufacturers would supply any amount at P_1 out
to the capacity of the plants. A decline in demand will hurt both
industries. In manufacturing it will show up as a decline in output
and employment from Q_1 to Q_2, in agriculture as a decline in price
from P_1 to P_2. However, with an inelastic demand, the fall in price
must be very great, but the reduction in output is relatively small.
The loss in farm incomes will be much greater than the loss in manufacturing incomes. If the demand had been elastic, then a policy of
maintaining the old price would have caused an enormous drop in
employment and incomes in the city, but a policy of maintaining the
old output would have caused only a slight drop in price and income
on the farm. At least the more monopolistic manufacturers could
pick prices that minimize their losses in view of their demands, but
the farmers, acting individually, cannot keep the price from falling
when demand is inelastic. Farmers, who produce almost the same
amount, regardless of the price, and who face a very inelastic demand,
do very badly in depressions.

GOVERNMENT POLICY AND FARM INSTABILITY

The general public gains very little from only temporarily low
farm prices followed by temporarily high ones. A fairly plausible

case can be made for some government controls to level out farm prices and incomes from year to year.

The short-term fluctuations in farm prices are due to shifts in supply or demand. The main reasons for these shifts have been: (1) changes in supply as farmers overestimated or underestimated future prices, (2) changes in supply because of weather, insects, disease, etc.; and (3) changes in demand because of depressions or booms in the country as a whole. A somewhat different government policy is indicated for each of these problems.

Forward Prices for Agriculture and the Hog Cycle

When swings in output result because farmers consistently miscalculate future markets, as in the case of the hog cycle, the argument for government intervention is particularly strong. In Figure 2.30,

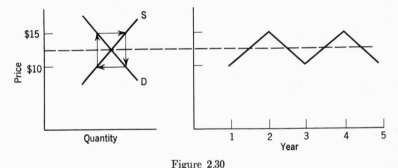

Figure 2.30

the price on an unregulated market would swing up to $15 and back to $10 indefinitely, but if government would guarantee a price of $12.50, it could avoid awkward surpluses or shortages and still stabilize the price. Farmers would be able to estimate the market correctly and would no longer overproduce and underproduce.

Of course, the trick is to determine what price will clear the market. In practice, supply and demand do not stay put year after year. The government would have to announce new guaranteed prices before each planting on the basis of its best estimate of demand and supply at harvest time. These prices would not necessarily guarantee farmers profitable prices at all times, nor even perfectly stable ones, but they would avoid price instability of the farmers' own making.

Some economists who have rejected most other proposals for agricultural price supports have continued to urge "forward prices" of the sort described here. Prices in a free market are expected to act as guides to production, but they perform that function very imperfectly if producers consistently judge future markets inaccurately.

Others have disapproved of even guaranteed forward prices, however. They feel that the Department of Agriculture statisticians would not be allowed to make objective estimates of the future demand and supply of pork or chickens because of the farm senators looking over their shoulders.

Nature, Speculators, and the Ever-Normal Granary

Government intervention to offset the effect of the weather is only a short step beyond the "forward price" proposal. The idea that government should maintain an "ever-normal granary," buying up part of bumper crops and storing them until poor years, has been suggested again and again.* By following such a policy, the government would automatically reduce price fluctuations, and for commodities with inelastic demands this would even out farm incomes as

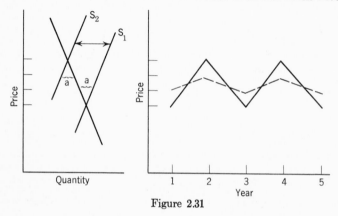

Figure 2.31

well. Figure 2.31 shows the supply of wheat in year 1, when it rained in Kansas, and in year 2, when it did not. The government might buy up quantity "a" in the good year and sell it during the drought. As a result, the price fluctuation would be reduced as in the right-hand diagram.

Private speculators might do the same sort of thing. By buying during periods of surplus when prices are low and selling during shortages, when prices are high, not only do the speculators make profits, but prices and supplies tend to be evened out, as in Figure 2.31. Speculators sometimes upset rather than stabilize the market, however. When they make up a large part of the supply and demand of a product, speculators are as likely to buy with an eye to other speculators as to the weather. When Smith buys because he

* It goes back considerably farther than the New Deal: see Genesis 41:47-57.

is sure Jones will buy, and Jones is buying because he is sure Adams will buy, and Adams is betting on Smith, etc., prices may sometimes rise farther and at other times fall farther than if there were no speculators at all. For speculation to have a stabilizing effect, speculators must be a small enough part of the market that they can generally be disregarded by the average trader and even by each other.

The government can operate an ever-normal granary even when its intervention represents a very large part of total output. In fact, if buyers and sellers become convinced that the government's action will prevent large fluctuations in price, there can be no great speculative spirals of the Smith-Jones-Adams sort. With guaranteed forward prices and a storage program offsetting changes in the weather, the speculators will have a stabilizing effect in spite of themselves.

The big problem of the government in an "ever-normal granary" program is to know when to buy and when to sell. What constitutes an unusual crop? If the large crop is due to good weather in Kansas, government purchases may be desirable, but if the bumper crop is because more farmers planted wheat this year, the government will just perpetuate the large supply by buying up part of it. By keeping the price high, the government encourages the same farmers to keep planting wheat in future years. Similarly, if the large crop is because of improved seed, the government will find itself buying wheat every year from now on. The ever-normal granary is in danger of becoming a permanent price support program unless the government limits itself to clearly temporary surpluses and shortages. It is often difficult for the Agriculture Department to determine in advance what sort of changes are temporary, especially if it is under constant pressure from a powerful group of legislators and lobbyists.

Depression and "Disaster Insurance"

The problem during a depression is a little different. If the government were to buy up some of the surplus in such years, it would be keeping farm prices and incomes high by withholding goods from the urban public which is suffering from the same depression. A better solution would be to attack the depression itself. The farmer has a strong interest in full employment in the city.

If we are unable to prevent depressions, however, there are good arguments for guaranteeing farmers some minimum income. Urban workers are guaranteed against impossible losses by unemployment insurance or, as a last resort, by direct relief. Many feel that if we hold up a net for everyone else a guarantee against complete disaster for farmers is only equitable. Since farmers are not unemployed during a depression as city workers are, their protection must take the form of some sort of price or income program rather than the insurance and welfare programs of nonfarmers.

Storage Programs Versus Direct Income Payments

A minimum price support which would apply in any period of general depression sufficient to assure the farmer, say, 75% of his predepression income is one possibility. An alternative would be to allow farm prices to fall and to make direct payments to farmers sufficient to guarantee them the same minimum income. The payments could be made in proportion to the farmers' output so that their incomes would be distributed in the same way as with the price supports. With a direct subsidy program there would be no large surpluses carried over to burden markets in subsequent years. The lower prices would benefit city people who suffer from the same depression, while the direct payments would give farmers the same incomes they would have with price supports.

The two approaches to maintaining farm incomes can be seen in Figure 2.32. In both cases, the total income of wheat farmers is to be kept at $1 billion dollars (500 million bushels at $2 a bushel). If

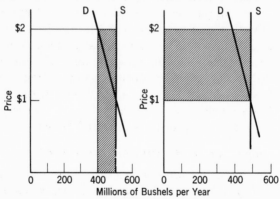

Figure 2.32

the price is to be maintained, the government must buy up 100 million bushels, the entire output in excess of consumption at $2. If the government makes direct payments to farmers instead, consumers will take all 500 billion bushels of wheat at a price of $1. Farmers will receive $1 per bushel from the grain dealer and $1 from the government. The public will have all of the wheat and at a lower price, and the farmers will be receiving the same billion dollars that they had with the price support program.

If the demand is inelastic, as is shown here, the government will have to pay more in the case of the subsidy program than in the storage program, but the total payment by *consumers plus government* will be the same in both cases. The storage program is cheaper for the government because a small purchase will force the price up a long way, while the subsidy program is relatively expensive because it takes a large price reduction to make consumers buy a little more wheat.

Direct payments to farmers instead of price supports have been proposed from time to time but have not won wide political support. Direct subsidies seem to threaten many farmers' feelings of self-sufficiency, and their relatively high cost to government in the case of commodities with inelastic demands is understandably unpopular with legislators. Direct subsidy payments to farmers are common in Europe, however, and are in use in this country in wool and sugar production.

Parity

The Department of Agriculture's price programs over the last quarter century have gone far beyond forward prices, storage against crop failure, and disaster insurance in time of depression. The government has maintained prices for many commodities so high that substantial parts of the output have gone begging even in prosperous years. It was clearly not just evening off the peaks and the valleys, but trying to bring all prices up to the peaks. The congressman or Secretary of Agriculture was more apt to seek "fair" prices than prices that would clear the market over a period of years.

The popular standard of "fair" prices for farmers is *parity*. This had its origin in the farm discontent of the 1920's. The first two decades of the century had been prosperous for farmers. During World War I and its immediate aftermath, farm prices had risen particularly rapidly. From 1920 on, however, farm prices were much less favorable, and farmers struggled under the heavy debts incurred during the earlier boom. Farm leaders tended to look back to the pre-World War I years as a time when farmers had received prices "in line" with nonfarm prices. In the 1920's, they felt, the farmer had fallen behind, and in the 1930's his position was worse yet. As the interwar years progressed, the prices of the years just before the war became established as the "fair" or "parity" prices. Their restoration became a main concern of farm pressure groups. In the Agricultural Adjustment Act of 1933, passed during the early days of the New Deal, Congress expressed its goal of restoring the relative prices of farm products to their levels of 1910–14.

Of course, the actual dollar price of wheat or cotton in 1910–14 was irrelevant because of changes in the general price level. The parity price of a bushel of wheat was to be one that gave its seller the same purchasing power as he would have had in the base period. The Department of Agriculture developed a parity index to measure the purchasing power of farm dollars.* The parity price of a bushel of wheat would be the 1910–1914 price of wheat multiplied by this index.

As 1910–14 became more and more remote this method of calculating parity became less and less appropriate. In the 50 years since then changes in diet, in export markets, and in production costs have made relatively higher prices appropriate for some commodities, such as meats, and relatively lower prices for others, such as grains. To adjust for this, parity was redefined in 1948. The parity level of farm prices generally was still to be one that would give a unit of farm output the same purchasing power as in 1910–14, but the parity price for any one commodity could now drift up or down depending on its price during the previous ten years.† The new definition was an improvement in the eyes of most economists. Parity prices of individual products could now gradually adjust to current demand and cost conditions. The new definition was less enthusiastically received by

---

* The index includes not only the items in farmers' costs of living but also production costs such as feeds, seeds, taxes, interest, and wages. It is therefore not strictly comparable to such familiar series as the consumer price index.

† The precise calculation of parity is now quite a complicated undertaking. (1) The Department of Agriculture finds the average price of the commodity in question for the previous ten years. (2) It divides this by the average level of prices received by farmers during the same period compared with 1910–14. (3) It multiplies the result by the price paid by farmers in the current year.

For instance, to find the January 1960 parity price of wheat, the department went through the following steps: (1) The average price of wheat from January 1950 to December 1959 including price support payments was $2.02 per bushel. (2) The average price received by farmers for farm products in general during the decade was 255% of the 1910–1914 level, so the department divided $2.02 by 255% to get a new base price of 79.2¢ a bushel. (3) In January 1960 the parity index stood at 299, so to give the same purchasing power per bushel as 79.2¢ had provided in 1910–14, the parity price of wheat had to be 299% of 79.2¢ or $2.37. Wheat prices have been relatively low in most years since 1950, so the new parity price is below that calculated by the old formula. If the old method still applied, the parity price of wheat would be $2.63 per bushel.

those farmers slated to suffer a price decline, however, and their opposition was enough to postpone the transition until 1956. During the intervening years the Secretary of Agriculture was instructed to determine parity prices by the old or the new formula, *whichever was higher!* Meat prices could drift upward but wheat prices could not fall. Starting in 1956, parity prices were gradually changed to the new basis and by 1960 the transition was virtually complete.*

There is still room for criticism of parity, however. While individual prices can now adjust to current conditions, the over-all level is still pegged to 1910–14 prices. These were some of the best peacetime years that the farmers had from the end of the Civil War until the present. Even in the 1920's and 1930's a nonfarmer might reasonably wonder whether a less advantageous period would not be closer to "normal" for farmers. By now, a "normal" period half a century back seems almost preposterous to many.

Price Policies—Crop Restrictions

The prices of farm products would not obediently slide up to parity levels just because Congress said that is where they were to be. Congress had to take some action to bring about the relative prices that it set as its goal in 1933. In the main these actions have consisted of (1) output restrictions and (2) price supports. Both programs began in 1933,† but the main reliance was on crop restriction in the early years.

Crop restriction, if effective, would certainly raise prices. Whether it would raise incomes or not would depend on the elasticity of demand. If the demand were inelastic (case A in Figure 2.33) the price would increase enough to more than offset the reduction in quantity sold, but if the demand were elastic (case B in Figure 2.33) the price

---

* The transition provided by law was a gradual one, and a few of the newer farm products, such as citrus fruits, had experienced such sharp price declines since 1914 that their parity prices had still depended on the old definitions in 1960.

† There had been attempts to improve farm prices before 1933. In the last part of the nineteenth century, farmers had sought inflationary policies and government regulation of monopolies to improve their price positions. Farmers who competed in an important way with imports received tariff protection. In the 1920's a program to restrict domestic supplies and export the surpluses at low foreign prices passed Congress twice but was vetoed both times. From 1929 on there was a Federal Farm Board with authority to buy and sell farm products. Its funds were insufficient to deal with the disastrous price decline of the depression, however. The Agricultural Adjustment Act of 1933 was certainly a far more drastic step than any that preceded it. Most of the present federal farm price programs are direct descendants of the 1933 legislation.

increase would reduce farm receipts, not raise them. Crop restriction makes sense because most farm products have inelastic demands. The restriction programs have been most consistently applied to a group of commodities described as "basic" in the law: cotton, wheat,

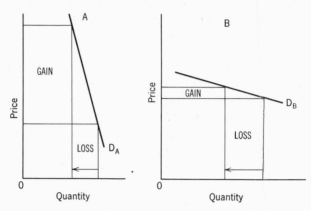

Figure 2.33

corn, rice, tobacco, and peanuts. The estimates available show extremely low elasticities for these commodities.

Crop restriction has been subject to much criticism. The waste involved has seemed obvious to many. In the depression years when living standards were already low a further reduction in the nation's output was highly vulnerable. There were many tears shed in Congress and the press for the cotton ploughed under and the little pigs slaughtered during the early New Deal programs.

Individual farmers have often resented the "regimentation" involved in crop restrictions. Some were simply objecting to the paper work or outside interference with their personal affairs, but for many the difficulty was economic. Suppose that the government sets the price of wheat at $2, as in Figure 2.34. Then Farmer Brown, whose cost curves appear at the left, will make the greatest profit at an output of 2000 bushels this year. To keep the price at $2, however, the government will have to impose production quotas. Brown cannot be allowed to produce more than 1400 bushels. From his point of view there is a fine opportunity for profit right under his nose if only he can reach out and take it, but then the bureaucrats step in. Of course, if every farmer did take advantage of these opportunities, the price would fall and they would all be in worse condition, not better.

Crop restriction programs have not always accomplished their ob-

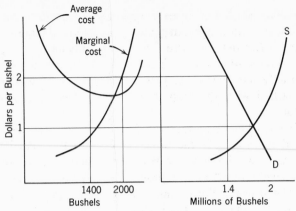

Figure 2.34

jectives. When they take the form of acreage allotments, the farmers
generally retire their least promising land and then apply their efforts
and equipment more intensively to what is left. As a result, output is
not reduced in proportion to acreage. In the first years of the New
Deal programs, the droughts on the great plains restricted output
very impressively, but after 1936 acreage allotments seemed to have
little effect on output. Most acreage restriction programs today include marketing quotas. Not only is Farmer Brown limited in the
number of acres he may plant, but he is subject to a penalty if he
sells more than a certain amount from those acres.

Crop restrictions sometimes simply move the surplus over to some
other product or region. Land retired from corn production is likely
to be planted in oats or soybeans. Then last year's corn problem
becomes this year's oats problem. Again, if the government succeeds
in raising prices by restricting output in the usual producing area,
farmers in other parts of the country are apt to start growing the
crop in question. The result is not a reduction in output but a shift
from the most suitable regions to less well-adapted ones. Of course,
Congress can restrict the crops that farmers can turn to and limit
interregional competition, but with every step in this direction the
restrictions become more complex and harder to administer. A rule
that prevents cotton production from moving to new areas under the
impetus of high prices would also prevent it from moving to new
regions which might be more efficient.

Direct Price Supports

In addition to restricting output in many years, the government has
provided a floor for at least some farm prices in every year since

1933.* At harvest time, farmers who have complied with their acreage allotments and marketing quotes and have adequate storage facilities are permitted to borrow a certain amount per bushel of their crops while storing them. The loans are "nonrecourse," meaning that if the farmers choose to just keep the money the government must be satisfied with the crop in full settlement regardless of its market value.

During the marketing period, the farmer can always pay off the loan and sell the crop. If the price rises above the loan level any time during the year, he almost certainly will do so. If it stays near the support level, the CCC will probably wind up with the crop at the end of the season. Since many farmers are guaranteed at least the loan rate, the open market price cannot fall much below that level. It sometimes gets a bit lower because of farmers who cannot arrange a commodity loan because of inadequate storage facilities or failure to cooperate in acreage allotments, or who simply think it is too much trouble.

The price levels at which loans have been made and the particular commodities supported have varied from year to year. Corn and cotton have had loan programs since 1933, though they were not used very much in some prosperous years. In the first years of the programs, whether or not to support prices and at what level to do so was entirely up to the Department of Agriculture, but after 1938 supports on corn, cotton, and wheat became "mandatory." The law required the Secretary of Agriculture to support them at no less than 52% of parity and at not more than 75%. At the start of World War II, the list of commodities with mandatory supports was increased, and the support level was raised to 90% of the parity prices. Market prices were generally above this level until 1948.

Since 1948, when surpluses became a serious problem once more, the level and rigidity of price supports have been the subject of annual debate. However, it was only in 1955 that support prices were permitted to fall below 90%. By 1960 the Secretary of Agriculture could set support prices for basics within a range from 75% to 90% of parity depending on expected surpluses.† The small degree of

---

* The main support programs are financed by the Commodity Credit Corporation (CCC), a government agency controlled by the Agriculture Department. Since 1953, acreage allotments, support prices, etc., have been administered by the Commodity Stabilization Service (CSS). The CCC and CSS use the same field staff.

† These support prices are mandatory so long as farmers accept the required crop restrictions. If farmers reject acreage allotments, support levels may be lower. For instance, in 1958 corn farmers voted for an end to acreage allotments and for price supports at 90% of the previous three years' average down to 65% of

flexibility in price supports today is far from fully accepted. Every year a group of farm state senators renews the battle for high, rigid price supports.

Figure 2.35 shows the average support prices, the average market prices, and the inventories owned by the CCC for corn, cotton, and wheat in various years. Except for the World War II and the Korean War periods, inventories were built up regularly after supports became mandatory in 1938. Even in years of flexible supports when lower prices were combined with production quotas, inventories were not reduced very much. They would not have been reduced at all if we had not developed an export subsidy program in those years. It should be no surprise that lower support prices did not reduce government inventories. All the evidence is that the elasticities of demand and supply for these commodities are very low. The 10% or 15% price reduction permitted by law was apparently insufficient to eliminate surpluses that are sometimes a third of total output for these products.

For "nonbasic" commodities, the Department of Agriculture has a wide range of price programs. The Secretary of Agriculture may support almost any farm price if he chooses. He has done so for most nonperishable goods. There have been loan programs for feed grains and oil seeds since the start of World War II, though not always at levels as high as those prescribed for "basics." Dairy prices are subject to mandatory supports at 75% to 90% of parity with the Department of Agriculture buying "surplus" butter, cheese, and dried milk from processors. In addition, regional marketing agreements for fluid milk have been worked out under which milk handlers of an area are required to pay prescribed prices. Sugar and wool producers are protected by tariffs (and import quotas in the case of sugar). Beyond that, producers of both commodities receive direct payments from the government in proportion to their marketings that bring their total receipts per pound up to a prescribed level regardless of world prices.

There are no direct price supports on perishables such as fruits, vegetables, poultry products, and meats, but the Department of Agriculture has funds for the diversion of these products from the usual consumers. They have been exported as part of aid programs, donated to states for use in welfare cases or as part of a low-cost

---

parity. In 1959 cotton farmers were allowed to choose on an individual basis between supports at 80% and at 65% of parity, the lower support level carrying with it much larger allotments.

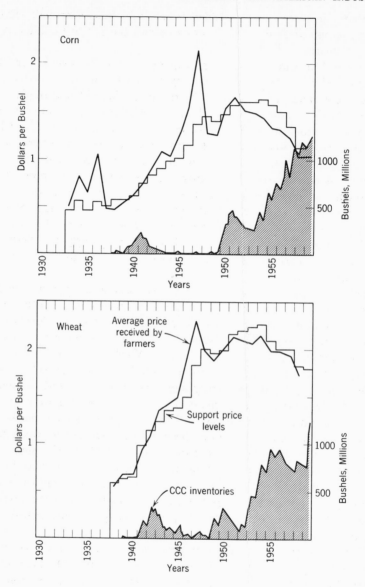

school lunch program, and diverted to new uses such as the manufacture of feed or starch from Irish potatoes. The essential point of such programs is to keep the goods away from anyone willing to pay for them. It will not increase prices to reduce supply and demand by equal amounts. The program for perishable foods has been far less substantial than that for nonperishables. Over the whole 20

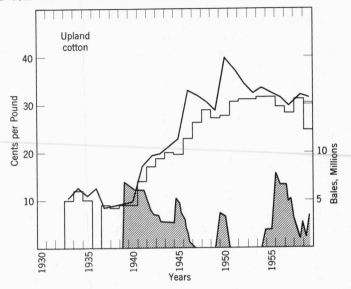

Figure 2.35. Notes: Inventories are commodities *owned* by CCC and do not include commodities pledged but still owned by farmers. Until 1938 CCC owned no inventories. In August 1939 the cotton pledged in 1934 and 1937 and still in storage was transferred to CCC.

Two support prices are shown for cotton for 1959 because individual growers were given a choice in that year between a high support price with old acreage allotments and a lower one with increased allotments.

Source: U.S. Department of Agriculture, *Commodity Credit Corporation Charts*, Feb. 1955 and March 1959, and *The Farm Price Situation, passim*.

years from 1937 to 1957, the program for all meats cost the government less than its losses on cotton alone in just one year (1956).

Price Programs and Instability

A case was made earlier for control of prices to deal with instability. Forward price guarantees to improve farmers' planning, an ever-normal granary to offset crop fluctuations, and disaster insurance against a major depression all make sense to many people. How has American farm policy performed in regard to these proposals?

The support prices have amounted to forward prices. The Secretary of Agriculture must announce support prices in advance of each crop year and keep that price throughout the season. However, the price support program has not eliminated the hog and cattle cycles (as can be seen from Figures 2.17 and 2.18) simply because price supports do not apply to livestock. Producers of nonperishables can plan accurately as long as prices are at support levels, but when they are far above those levels, as during the early postwar and the Korean War periods, the Agriculture Department programs give little guidance. At any rate, the present price program is far from the forward price proposal. Forward prices were to be set at levels that would clear the market. Support levels have been far above this in most years.

The CCC stocks do provide a buffer against bad years, of course, and twice the accumulated stocks have been largely used up. The CCC was able to dispose of most of its inventories with very little loss during World War II and the Korean War and the public generally benefited from having the stocks on hand during those shortage years. Of course, the crop restriction programs for surplus years were no help at all. By the late 1950's the commodity stocks had reached levels well above those of 1942 and 1950, and were greatly in excess of foreseeable needs. The wheat inventory has exceeded an entire year's crop for several years.

The acreage control and price support programs began as depression relief policies, but they have continued into good times. In fact, support levels in the prosperous 1940's and 1950's were far above those in the 1930's because parity had been redefined to the farmer's advantage, because price supports were at higher percentages of parity, and because price supports applied to a broader range of products. The present program would undoubtedly protect farmers against disastrously low prices in time of depression, but it goes far beyond that.

To turn from an objective of permanently supporting farm prices to simply stabilizing them, several changes in policy would be necessary:

1. Support levels would have to be far more "flexible" than they are now. The Secretary of Agriculture must be free to guarantee prices outside the 75–90% parity range if the market is to clear in normal years.

2. If minimum incomes are to be guaranteed in depression years without regulating output or developing surpluses, farmers would have to be paid direct subsidies.

3. To eliminate cyclical production errors, price guarantees would have to be extended to some perishables (such as meats and tree crops) where many of the most obvious cycles occur and prices would have to be set to avoid surpluses in normal years.

Many feel that these proposals are impossible because price guarantees cannot be separated from politics; the guaranteed prices would consistently be above the market price as they are today. To people of this opinion, a return to an unrestricted market would be a more promising policy.

Whether price programs are to be continued, made more flexible, or completely eliminated, many economists feel that the ultimate solution to low farm incomes will not be found in the direct control of farm prices at all. It is a long-run problem and requires a long-run cure.

(The Further Readings section for this chapter is combined with that of Chapter 3.)

3

PURE COMPETITION AND AGRICULTURE—LONG RUN

OVERCAPACITY

Productivity and Demand

The main reason for the continuing low incomes of farmers is the rapid increase in the supply of farm products in the face of only slowly growing demand. Figure 3.1 compares output per man-hour, total farm output, and number of man-hours used in agriculture, all as percentages of the 1947–49 levels. Tractors, hybrid seed, mechanical cotton pickers, milking machines, and other equally revolutionary changes have doubled the output per man-hour in agriculture in about 12 years. Productivity has grown faster in farming than in manufacturing in the years since World War II. The total supply of farm products has grown more slowly than this only because so many farmers have left the land in the same years.

The output, productivity, and employment series in Figure 3.1 are plotted against a ratio (or logarithmic) scale. Such diagrams will appear throughout the book and deserve some explaining. They are so constructed that equal percentage increases appear as equal distances. In Figure 3.1 the distance from 10 to 20 is the same as that from 20 to 40, that from 40 to 80, and that from 100 to 200. As a result, a constant percentage rate of growth appears as a straight line instead of a rapidly rising one. For instance, output per man-hour in farming rose at almost the same percentage rate from 1939

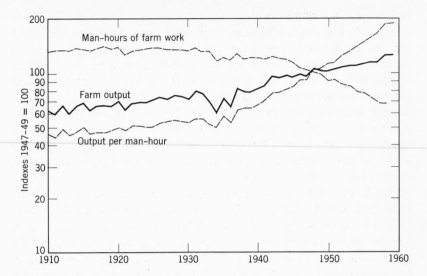

Figure 3.1.   Source: *Agricultural Outlook Charts*, 1959, and *Economic Report of the President*, 1960.

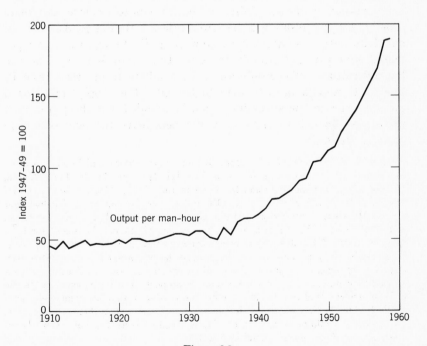

Figure 3.2

to 1959, so in Figure 3.1 that series appears as a straight line. On a conventional arithmetic scale such as Figure 3.2, the same series appears as a curve that grows steeper and steeper each year. A *constant* percentage growth means *increasing* absolute additions to output per man-hour. Ratio scales of this sort are very convenient for studying growth series because (1) it is easy to compare rates of growth at different periods; (2) fluctuations appear in their true significance—a 20-point increase in 1957 was of about the same significance as a 5-point increase in 1912; and (3) in rapidly growing series, at least, ratio scales are necessary if the whole series is to appear in a single legible chart.

The demand for farm products has not grown as fast as the supply, even with the declining number of farmers. Our demand for food increases only slowly as we get richer. On the average, a 10% increase in consumers' incomes leads to an increase in demand for farm products of only 2.5 to 4.5%.* There is only so much room in the average American stomach, and although we can switch to more expensive foods as we get richer, we are apt to spend more of our growing incomes on nonfoods.

If the demand for farm products rises less rapidly than total national output, while the ability of the farmers to produce rises more rapidly, the net result will be lower prices. In Figure 3.3, the demand for farm products might grow from D_1 to D_2, while the potential supply would grow in the same time from S_1 to S_2 if no one left agriculture. The result would be a fall in farm prices from P_1 to P_2. If enough farmers went to the city, the supply might wind up at S_3 and the price decline would be avoided, but the prospect of profits low enough to make large numbers leave the land is a farm problem in itself.

* Karl Fox, "Factors Affecting Farm Income, Farm Prices, and Food Consumption," *Agricultural Economic Research,* Vol. III, 1951, pp. 71–79; James Tobin, "A Statistical Demand Function for Food in the U.S.A.," *Journal of the Royal Statistical Society,* Series A, Pt. II, 1950, p. 134; Ser. A, and M. A. Girshick and Trygve Haavelmo, "Statistical Analysis of the Demand for Food," *Econometrica,* Apr. 1947, p. 109. In technical terms, the income elasticity of demand for farm products is 0.25–0.45. Just as the responsiveness of quantity to changes in price is measured by the price elasticity of demand, so the responsiveness of quantity purchased to changes in income is measured by income elasticity. If consumers increased their purchases of some commodity in proportion to their income, a 1% rise in income would lead to a 1% increase in consumption so that the income elasticity would be 1.0. If they increased their consumption faster than their incomes grew, the elasticity would be more than 1. If they bought less as they got richer, the income elasticity of demand would be negative.

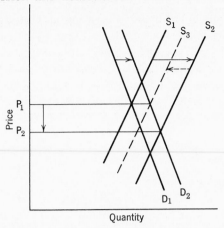

Figure 3.3

Foreign Trade and Agriculture

In one important respect, the demand for farm products has actually declined during the twentieth century. Before World War I (in the base period used in parity calculations), the United States was the world's leading exporter of agricultural products, but our position as world supplier of food and fiber has declined drastically since then. In 1910–14 we exported an average of 9 million bales of cotton per year (roughly 60% of the rest of the world's supply), but by 1950–55 this was reduced to 4 million bales per year (about 15% of the rest of the world's supply). For other commodities there has been less of a decline, but since World War I our farm export market has tended to dry up generally. Figure 3.4 shows farm exports as a percentage of farm sales since 1910. The percentage reached a peak during World War I and then fell off until after World War II. After 1945 the percentage of farm products exported returned to the level of the early 1930's, but no higher. A large part of these have been government grants of one sort or another, and many of the nongovernment farm exports have only been possible because of substantial subsidies. At times in the late 1950's private exporters of wheat were receiving subsidies of more than a third of the domestic price.

United States government policy has played a part in this loss of foreign markets. The American tariff that restricts foreign sales in the United States reduces the supply of dollars abroad and, as a result, the foreign demand for American exports. The tariff may help some farmers such as those in sugar and wool production, but since

American agriculture is traditionally a net export industry, trade restrictions hurt it generally.

The agricultural price programs described in Chapter 2 have hurt farm exports also. Price supports and crop restrictions in the 1930's raised American agricultural prices above those on world markets.

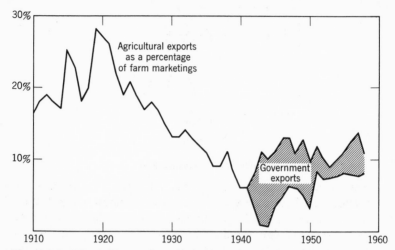

Figure 3.4. Note: Figures for 1956–58 are approximate.
Source: U.S. Department of Agriculture, Statistical Bulletin No. 179, Aug. 1956, Table 16; Murray Benedict, *Can We Solve the Farm Problem?* Appendix Table 8–3; and *Economic Reports of the President,* 1958 and 1959.

As a result, American exports declined and world prices were kept higher than would otherwise have been the case. The relatively high prices encouraged the development of new sources of supply. Much of the gain from the American cotton program went to producers in Egypt and Brazil who could take advantage of the good prices without any limitations on output. Once lost, these foreign markets have proved hard to regain.

ADJUSTMENTS IN CAPACITY

Long-Run Adjustment in Theory

In theory, unprofitably low prices should be only temporary. One of the key characteristics of pure competition is the free entry and exit of firms. If the price of some product is above its average cost, new firms can be expected to enter production; if the price is below that level, not only will no one be tempted to take up the trade, but those already in it can be counted on to leave when they have a chance. For instance, if the short-run equilibrium price is as high as P_1 in Figure 3.5, the profit prospects will attract new producers, who will keep coming as long as there are any unusual profits to be

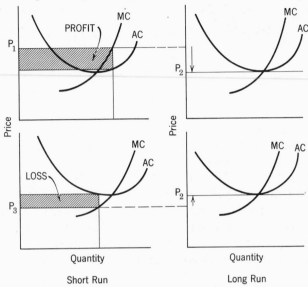

Figure 3.5

had, and will no longer be attracted when the price falls to P_2 where it barely covers their costs.* Similarly, if the price set by supply and demand in the short run is as low as P_3 so that there are losses, the reduction in the number of firms will tend to raise the price. Firms will keep leaving the industry until they have no more reason to do so; in other words, until their losses have disappeared. Then the price will be at P_2 again.

The result is a long-run supply curve like that in Figure 3.6. In the short run, the supply and demand might look like D and S_1 but the price can be at P_1 only temporarily. With enough time, new producers will appear, the supply will shift to S_2, and the price will fall to P_2. In fact, no matter what the level of demand, the price will be at P_2 in the long run. The horizontal straight line S_L is the long-run supply curve. It shows how much will be supplied when all producers who want to, have an opportunity to enter or leave the industry.

* Remember that "cost" includes a normal return to the owner of the business on his own investment.

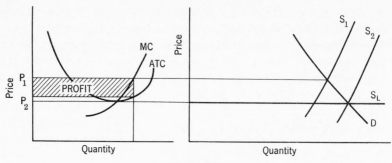

Figure 3.6

In agriculture, not all farms are equally efficient. Some have lower costs than others because of more regular rain, more fertile soil, or better access to the market. The dairy farms in the hypothetical New York milk shed discussed in Chapter 2 differed only in their distance from the city and had costs like those in Figure 3.7. In the short run, the supply of milk in this market was derived from the marginal costs of the various farms above the lowest average variable cost. The high-cost Vermont farms might be caught with a price less than their lowest average cost and still keep producing temporarily because some of their costs are fixed. Fixed costs are only fixed in the short run, however. In the long run, they can be avoided. The herd and equipment need not be replaced as they grow old, and the farmer himself can take up a new trade. In the long run, Vermonters will shift to some other product and only those farms whose costs are fully covered will remain in the industry. The long-run supply curve of the industry is the sum of the marginal cost curves of all potential producers, *starting at their lowest average cost curve* in each case. The long-run equilibrium price is just barely profitable for the highest cost producer left in the industry. With demand curve D_1 this turns out to be the New York State farms. They might be identified as

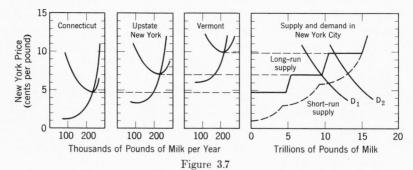

Figure 3.7

the *marginal* producers. If demand increased to D_2, the long-run equilibrium price would rise to 10¢ and more than cover the upstate New York costs.* There would then be room in the industry for some Vermont farms as well. The Vermont farms in dairying would become *marginal*, and the upstate farms, *intramarginal*. Of course, in practice, farms do not fall in big blocks like those in Figure 3.7, so the long-run supply is unlikely to be this lumpy. Whatever the price, there are some farmers whose costs are just barely covered.

Rents

The Connecticut farms in Figure 3.7 have costs considerably below those of the marginal farms and will have more than adequate receipts whether demand is at D_1 or at D_2. These farms are almost bound to be more valuable than the others. Two hundred acres only 50 miles from New York are worth much more than 200 equally fertile acres in Vermont because a competent farmer can bring in more receipts on the former than on the latter. Farmers will tend to bid up the prices of advantageous land until the good farms yield no more *per dollar invested* than the poor ones. Until this happens, farmers with enough money can be expected to sell off their Vermont farms and move to Connecticut, or vice versa. When land values are in line with returns throughout the New York milk shed, the costs in that market *including a return on the owners' investments* will look like the broken lines in Figure 3.8.

If the price were now to fall below 10¢, the Vermont farms would ultimately drop out of the market, just as they did in Figure 3.7, but upstate New York farms would continue to produce milk down to 7¢ a pound and Connecticut farms, down to 5¢. It is true that the new prices would not cover all expenses as they had previously been calculated, but this would not force Connecticut and upstate dairymen out of business. Rather it would force the value of Connecticut and upstate New York land down. When land values in those areas fell far enough, locally produced milk would just yield the landowners a normal return on their revalued property. In other words, the new low price would just cover average cost in the two areas again.

The return on land turns out to be a very peculiar sort of expense. The farmer must certainly pay for the land if he is renting it or if he has borrowed money to buy it. In fact, he should take this expense into account even if he owns the land clear, since he has the alternative of selling out and investing the proceeds elsewhere. Yet

---

* In the short run, it would rise above 10¢, until enough Vermonters were attracted into dairying.

except for the marginal farm, the cost of land does not affect output. The cost of agricultural land does not determine the prices of agricultural products—it is determin*ed by* the prices of agricultural products!

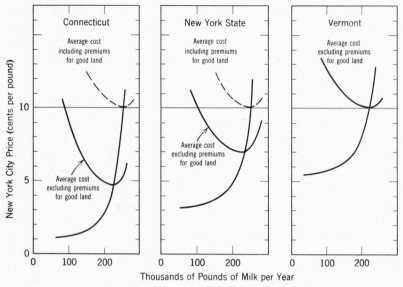

Figure 3.8

Economists use the term *rent* to refer to price-determin*ed* expenses of this sort. More precisely, *rents* are payments for factors of production over and above what is necessary to bring them into use. If a piece of land is to be used for dairying, its owner must receive as much for it as he could get in some other crop. It was such alternative costs that were represented by the solid cost curves in Figures 3.7 and 3.8. If land actually produces dairy products worth more than its alternative costs, however, it will be earning some rents. Connecticut land would produce milk at any price down to 5¢ a pound. Extra receipts above this bare minimum are very nice for Connecticut landowners, but are unnecessary to bring them into dairying. On the other hand, if the value of Connecticut land rises because of suburban development, the alternative cost of the land will have risen and the supply of milk will be reduced.

The term *rent* as the economist uses it may apply to other factors of production besides land. A farm hand who would work for $2000 but who is paid $2500 because he has a way with cows is earning a rent of $500 for his special talents. If the price of milk goes up, farmers will be willing to pay more for his services. If it goes down, he will keep producing at any salary over $2000 per year. On the other hand, if alternative jobs in the city improve, this farm hand might not stay in dairying for less than $3000. In this case, it is *alternative costs* rather than *rents* that rise, so the price of milk may be affected again. The output of milk at any given price will be less when farm hands have to be paid $3000 before they will work than when they will work for $2000.

The distinction between rents and alternative costs is important. For instance, what is a reasonable level of farm prices? A rise in costs might logically call for higher prices to keep net farm incomes the same, but what about rents? If the farmers come in asking for a higher price because farmland is so expensive these days, and if they get it, farmland values will rise even farther and the farmers will be back for more next year. The reverse is also true. If the price support programs are curtailed, farmland values will decline, too. Then farmers who acquire land at the new low prices may not be squeezed very badly in spite of low product prices.

Long-Run Adjustment in Practice

Theoretically, profits and losses are expected to disappear in pure competition. The price should just cover the cost (and rents) of all firms still in business in the long run. Since the farmers' costs include their own salaries at the rates they could earn elsewhere, this would mean that farmers should be earning as much in farming as in any other line of business.

Profits certainly disappear in farming, with a vengeance, but the losses, i.e., the low incomes, seem to be eternal. Why have farm incomes not adjusted upward as expected? How can farm incomes continue for a generation at half of city incomes?

Part of the answer is that farm incomes are not as low as they seem to be. The cost of living is lower on the farm, because food and housing supplied by the farm are included in farm incomes at much lower values than urban retail prices.* Moreover, there are many who prefer rural life. A man who likes to be his own boss and dislikes traffic and crowded apartments may get more out of life at $3000 a year on the farm than at $6000 a year in the city. In money he could better himself, but, taking nonmonetary considerations into account, he is making his maximum income on the farm.

---

* J. D. Black, in "Agriculture in the Nation's Economy," *American Economic Review*, Mar. 1956, p. 27, estimates that per capita farm incomes are understated by about $150 on this count.

There is no more reason to raise this man's low income than the rest of ours.

The exodus of people from the farm in the last 30 years shows that farm incomes are not adequate for many, however. Farmers have been adjusting, as competitive theory suggests they would. There are fewer farmers every year, but low farm incomes persist. What seems to be happening is that the problem is continuously recreated. If every year supply increases by 5% and demand by 2%, every year the equilibrium price will decline. In the face of this, people will have to leave the farms in droves just to keep the situation from getting worse.

It is not easy to leave the farm. A worker who leaves a job in the dying buggy-whip industry in the city and moves to the more sprightly spark-plug industry, must punch a new time clock and perhaps learn a new trade if skills are involved, but he goes on living in a similar environment, often even in the same house. Leaving the farm means changing your home and your whole way of life. The

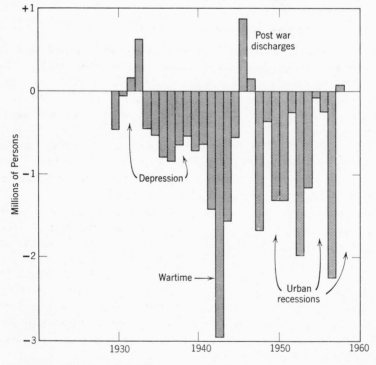

Figure 3.9. Net migration to (+) or from (−) farms. Source: *Economic Report of the President,* 1960.

upheavals that go with a move from rural or small-town life to the city are a wonderful source of all kinds of social problems according to the sociologists, psychologists, and soap operas.

Moving to the city does not make much sense if there are no jobs there. Figure 3.9 shows that the great exodus occurred in prosperous years, which were often good years for farmers too. In the depression years very few left the farm, and in the really bad years some of the unemployed left the city. Back home on the farm they could at least eat.

It is not just urban depressions that keep too many people in agriculture. If monopolistic production practices or trade union activities actually limit the level of output and hence the number of jobs in some urban industries, people will stay on the farm even though their incomes are lower than city incomes. They cannot hope for the high returns that others earn because they are not free to move into the highly paid fields.

ADJUSTMENTS IN SCALE

Farm Size and Efficiency

Not all farmers are poor by any means. In spite of relatively low prices in recent years, some have prospered. The great differences in income between farmers are largely due to divergences in size and technique. Agricultural enterprises, like most others, have a variety of possible sizes and shapes, and some are more efficient than others.

The 1954 Census of Agriculture collected information about productivity on farms of various scales. The Census divided all commercial farms into six size categories:

Class   I: Large scale—more than $25,000 sales annually
Class   II: Large family scale—$10,000 to $24,999 sales
Class III: Upper medium family scale—$5000 to $9999 sales
Class IV: Lower medium family scale—$2500 to $4999 sales
Class   V: Small family scale—$1200 to $2499 sales
Class VI: Small scale—$250 to $1199, provided that the operator
           did less than 100 days of work off the farm

In all but the first category, the operator and his family generally provide the bulk of the labor. These six classes include only the commercial farms where farming is clearly a business. Part-time and residential farms are segregated in the statistics.

The Census findings for northeastern dairy farms are shown in Table 3.1. The large-scale, 75-cow farms sold more milk per cow,

TABLE 3.1

PRODUCTIVITY AND COSTS ON NORTHEASTERN DAIRY FARMS OF VARIOUS SIZES

A	B	C	D	E	F	G	H	I
Census Class of Farm	Average Number of Milk Cows per Farm	Number of Farms	Milk Sold per Cow (pounds per year)	Gross Sales per Man-Year (dollars)	Man-Years per $100 Gross Sales	Investment in Land, Buildings & Equip. per $100 Gross Sales (dollars)	Materials Purchased per $100 Gross Sales (approx.) (dollars)	Estimated Costs of $100 Gross Sales (dollars)
I	75	1,215	8036	6846	0.016	221	49	92
II	39	12,525	7549	6446	0.017	266	54	101
III	24	24,658	6441	4775	0.021	325	58	116
IV	16	19,447	5361	3463	0.029	431	62	142
V	10	7,965	4361	2228	0.045	631	72	194
VI	7	1,717	2782	1003	0.100	1039	88	340
All commercial farms	24	67,521	6526	4837	0.021	320	58	116

Source: Columns A–G from *Census of Agriculture*, 1954, Vol. III, Pt. 9, Ch. V. The same source gives expenditures on feed, fertilizer, and gas and oil. Purchases in column H were estimated on the basis of those expenditures and the ratios of those items to all purchased production goods and services given in *Census of Agriculture*, 1954, Vol. III, Pt. 9, Ch. IX. Column I cost estimates were derived by multiplying the labor input in column F by $2000, multiplying the investment by 5%, and adding the two products to the estimate of purchased materials in column H.

per man, and per dollar invested than the 39-cow farms, and they in turn sold more on each count than the 24-cow farms, and so on down. More of the smaller farms' output was consumed rather than sold, and therefore does not appear in Table 3.1, but these farms also seem to have purchased more materials per $100 of sales so that their *net* output is exaggerated in columns D, E, and G.

Column I shows some rough estimates of the cost of $100 gross sales on various farms if labor is valued at $2000 a year and if the capital yields a return of 5% (this will have to include depreciation). The Class I farms at these rates could make some profit over and above their costs, the Class II farms just about broke even on the average, and the smaller farms experienced losses. Their operators paid themselves less than $2000 a year.*

* These losses are exaggerated because of output consumed on the farm and because farmers did not always report all their sales to the census takers. Taking these things into account, the Class II farms might well have made as much profit as the Class I farms, and the Class III farms may have broken even. It is hard to believe that these factors can make up for the large apparent losses of the Class IV, V, and VI farms, however.

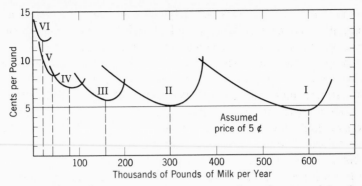

Figure 3.10. Approximate average cost curves of northeastern dairy farms in 1954.

In a sense, the costs shown in Table 3.1 represent the alternatives available to the farmer discussed in Chapter 2 *in the long run*. In the short run, the farmer was committed to a Class III farm and had no choice about its scale and organization. With enough time, however, he has a choice of leaving for a more profitable business, or of changing his farm for a more efficient one.

The choices available to a northeastern dairy farmer in 1954 are shown graphically in Figure 3.10.* Each size of farm still has a U-shaped average cost curve. Whether a farm has 75 cows or 7, it still has some fixed costs and there is still a limit to what it can produce. Of course, capacity is reached much sooner for some farms than for others.

The lowest cost of very small scale farms is inevitably higher than for larger ones because some equipment is too expensive to use in such small enterprises; or if it is installed, it will stand idle a large part of the time. The farmer himself may not have enough to keep him busy at very useful work, and at any rate he can produce much more if he has more land and animals to work with. Larger farms show lower costs as equipment and labor are used more fully and more complex mechanization becomes worthwhile, but costs cannot keep declining with increased scale forever. A 5000-cow herd would be pretty inefficient. If nothing else, some of the pasture would have to be miles away from the barns, and the task of administering that many cows would make it a very confused affair.

The pattern of costs in Figure 3.10 applies to most types of agri-

* Figure 3.10 was derived from Table 3.1, assuming that the average farm in each class was operating at its most profitable level and that the price of milk was 5¢ a pound.

culture.   The 1954 Census showed that sales per man-year and per dollar invested were higher on Class I and II farms than on smaller farms in every type of farming.   However, in most lines, there is probably a maximum size beyond which administrative problems make it difficult to gain any lower costs by expanding.

What was most efficient in 1954 may not be in 1964.   The best methods of agriculture are changing all the time.   For instance, the average dairy farm has grown consistently over the years.   In the days before milking machines, a man could not milk more than 10 or 15 cows per day so that larger scale dairies required many hired hands. With mechanization, the possibilities changed from perhaps the broken lines in Figure 3.11 to the solid curves.

In most types of agriculture, as the shift from hand labor has occurred, the average size of the farm has increased.   This has not

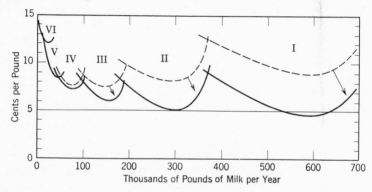

Figure 3.11.   Hypothetical average total cost curves of northeastern dairy farms before and after milking machines.

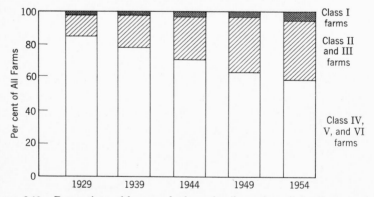

Figure 3.12.   Proportions of large scale, large family, and small family farms to all commercial farms, 1929–54. Source: *Agricultural Outlook Charts,* 1957, Table 6. In all years farms were classified by 1954 class boundaries. Values of sales in earlier years were measured in 1954 prices.

meant a disappearance of the family farm, however. As Figure 3.12 shows, while the proportions of small-scale farms has fallen rapidly, Class I farms are still a small part of the total. It is the large family farm (Classes II and III) that is growing. Most labor is supplied by the operator and his family, but they use much more equipment and better methods and can work much more land.

Adjustments in Scale in Practice

In spite of the rapid adjustment shown in Figure 3.12, more than half the farms in the country were still in the smaller classes in 1954. This included 42% of the northeastern dairy farms. These inefficiently organized farms had to compete with the larger ones. Prices tended to fall to a level that left the Class I and II farms profitable, but made the owners of Class IV, V, and VI farms miserable.

Farm property values have tended to rise in spite of relatively low farm prices partly for the same reason. Figure 3.13 shows how agricultural land values and farm prices have moved in opposite directions in the 1950's. Properly organized, a 400-acre Iowa farm can be

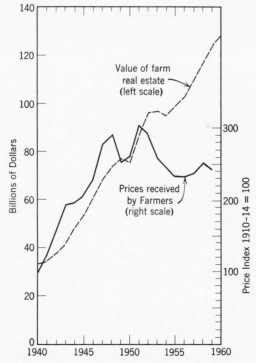

Figure 3.13. Farm prices compared with value of farm real estate. Source: *Balance Sheet of Agriculture,* 1959, and *Economic Report of the President,* 1960.

profitable even with somewhat declining prices, but three or four smaller farms on the same land will yield very low total receipts. When new methods make for lower costs and more profits, land prices rise. The smaller, less efficient farms that continue in production find their land costs rising as well as their prices falling.*

In theory, in pure competition the low-cost producers should force the high-cost firms out of production. Profit prospects would result in an increase in Class I, and perhaps Class II, farms until prices fell so far that they just covered the costs of such farms. The Class III, IV, V, and VI farms would then be forced out of business.

In practice, inefficiently small farms seem to persist for years. Partly, this is due to the old problems of constant change and immobility. Farms that were up to date a generation ago are obsolete today. The need for larger farms means fewer farmers, and, as we have seen, it is not easy to pull up roots and move to the city.

To a considerable extent, the problem of inefficient farms is traceable to inadequate sources of capital. An efficient farm may involve an investment of $50,000 or more and many farmers are simply unable to raise that kind of money. They recognize that they would be better off with more land and a combine, but they do not have the funds themselves, and lenders understandably put limits on the amount of money they will lend to a small enterprise, especially in such an uncertain business as agriculture. Capital is typically rationed to borrowers in proportion to their assets and the stability of their earnings. On both grounds, millions of farmers are limited to farms that are too small and inadequately equipped.

It is also important to notice who it is that moves to the city. Theory suggests that it would be the high-cost farmers who would be forced off the land. This may be correct, but remember that the "cost" of labor supplied by the owner is what it could earn in another employment. A modern Iowa farmer with a good education and substantial capital assets might be able to earn $8000 or $10,000 a year in the city, while a sharecropper with little education and no capital has very doubtful alternatives. Counting their alternative earnings at, say, $8000 in the first case and bare subsistence in the second, it may often be that the technically "efficient" large farmer is the one with high "costs."†

* Improving techniques are not the only reason for rising farmland values. As the cities pushed out into the countryside in the postwar years, some farmland values went up because of the high price of urban real estate.

† Some of those who stay on the farm are really half retired. A substantial proportion of the Class V and VI farms have elderly operators. This does not apply to the much more numerous Class IV farms, however.

GOVERNMENT POLICY AND LONG-RUN ADJUSTMENTS

Price Supports Once More

Unregulated private enterprise may theoretically lead to "low-cost" methods of production without any overcapacity or undercapacity in the long run, but with immobility, limited alternatives in the city, and capital rationing these "low costs" may be socially undesirable and the long run may be very long in coming. If the market place, left to its own devices, yields less than ideal results, what government policies will improve the situation?

The price support and crop control program is certainly of limited value in dealing with low farm incomes and farm poverty. At best it is a palliative, providing higher incomes by subsidy or protection without dealing with the cause of the poverty. It is like aspirin, which reduces the unpleasant symptoms of a disease but does not cure it. Aspirin may be a good idea for an occasional headache that lasts only a short time, but it is better to clear up the basic cause of a longer term disease.

The price support program is not even a very good palliative for farm poverty. It does very little about the really low income farmers. Programs that raise farm prices help farmers in proportion to the amounts they sell. The large farms reap most of the benefits. The really poor of agriculture, who have very little to sell, do not gain much from price supports.

Price supports intensify the basic farm problem to some extent. By keeping prices and incomes from falling they reduce the pressure on farmers to leave agriculture. On the demand side, high prices discourage the expansion of consumption.

Export Subsidies and Trade Restrictions

Where exports have been important, price supports are particularly likely to discourage sales. To keep up our exports, the Department of Agriculture has had to sell our crops abroad at a loss.* The government explains that it is simply selling at the world price, having maintained a price above the world level at home. To the Canadian wheat farmer or the Egyptian cotton grower, however, it looks very

---

* In some cases, the exports were grants made as part of foreign aid programs. In others, the Department of Agriculture has sold at American prices but has accepted payment in inconvertible currencies. Generally, these could only be used in the purchasing country so they were of limited value to the United States. Private exporters of wheat and cotton have received direct subsidies to make exports possible.

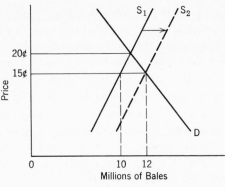

Figure 3.14

much like the "dumping" that the Americans so condemn in others. In Figure 3.14, if S_1 and D represent the supply and demand for cotton in world markets without American export subsidies, the world price is 20¢ a pound. If the United States decides to reduce its surpluses by 2 million bales by selling them at "world market prices," the supply of cotton will be increased to S_2 and the world price will be 5¢ less than otherwise. Foreign growers are apt to resent having to compete with excess United States cotton so that American farmers can have higher prices and incomes.

The policy of supporting prices above world levels has attracted imports, even in crops where we have domestic surpluses. To avoid subsidizing foreign producers, we have had to impose import quotas and prohibitions in many fields. Foreign sellers are subject to more severe restrictions in agricultural commodities than in manufactured goods today. Of course, we would not normally import many of these crops, but it is difficult to permit "normal" imports and exclude "abnormal" ones. Canadian producers of feed grains have been particularly critical of these controls.

The export subsidy and import restriction programs have been embarrassing to the State Department. We have attempted to lead the world in encouraging trade and to raise incomes in many countries of the world by direct economic assistance. Yet our agricultural policy has required trade restrictions and export subsidies of the very sort we object to abroad and it often tends to undermine foreign producers' incomes.

Farm Education and Research

If the price programs provide only a temporary solution to a long-run problem, and that imperfectly, what alternative policies are there?

How can we attack farm inefficiency and the surplus of farmers directly? A number of government policies attempt to do this.

Government-subsidized education and research to increase farm efficiency is not new. Under the Morrill Act of 1862, the federal government made substantial grants of land to the states to endow state agricultural colleges. These land grant colleges continue to be the main centers of agricultural research and education and are still government-financed, largely on the state level today. In addition, the federal government has made annual grants to the states since 1887 to help finance state experimental stations as well as conducting large-scale agricultural research of its own.

Both the federal and state governments have programs to get the new techniques to the farmers. Since 1914 there has been a regular national extension service. The key man in this is the county agent, a permanent local advisor, demonstrator, and teacher whose main job is to get the better techniques into use. He has often played an important though informal role in the local organization of federal price and output programs as well. He is financed partly by the federal extension service, partly by the state government, partly by the county in which he serves, and to a small extent by private farmers and businessmen.*

Altogether, it has been estimated that the federal, state, and local governments spend about $250 million annually on agricultural research and education.† This is less than 1% of the total farm output, certainly not an excessive amount compared with the research and educational expenses connected with much of manufacturing.

These programs have certainly done much to increase farm efficiency. Since they lead to lower prices, they are of benefit to the consumer as well as the farmer. This part of the farm program has unquestionably been in the public interest.

Does it solve the problem of low farm incomes, however? The recurring surpluses are at least partly attributable to the rapidly

* With the county agent came the county Farm Bureaus, local organizations of farmers who cooperated in furthering better methods of agriculture. These were principally educational groups at first, but they became the most powerful of American farm pressure groups with the organization of The American Farm Bureau Federation in 1919. The national organization was the source of much of the farm agitation during the 1920's and 1930's and was important in the formation of the "farm block" in Congress in the 1920's. Since it developed around the introduction of improved farming, it is not surprising that the Farm Bureau has tended to represent the more efficient farmer primarily.

† Murray Benedict, *Can We Solve the Farm Problem?* Twentieth Century Fund, 1955, p. 60.

increasing productivity that these programs promote. Moreover, in the past the services of land grant colleges, county agents, and experimental station bulletins have been used primarily by the better farmers, thus intensifying the competitive pressure on the poorer ones. It is not the sharecropper who goes to college.

Efforts have been made to reach the small-scale farmers. The federal government contributes $10 million per year to help finance high school training in agriculture, and state and local governments do more. Some southern states have systems of Negro county agents. However, the funds allocated to these programs have been small compared with those that reach the more efficient farmers. At any rate, educational services can help only if farmers use them. Many of the techniques of modern agriculture require more training and financial resources than most small farmers have.

Financing the ordinary public schools is a problem in many rural areas. Birth rates are usually higher on the farm than in the city, and it is working-age people who go to the city. School-age children are consequently a disproportionately large part of the farm population. This is particularly true in the South, where the worst farm poverty coincides with the densest school-age population. As a result, although many farm areas put an unusually large share of their total income into schools, the total expenditure per pupil is relatively small. Many states transfer funds from urban to rural areas for educational purposes, and the federal aid to education proposals are aimed at the same problem in part. Regional inequality in educational resources is much more than a farm problem, of course, but it contributes to income inequality both within agriculture and between the city and the farm.

It also makes a difference what the rural schools teach. By and large, the emphasis has been on agricultural methods, but, to help solve the problem of too many farmers, a large part of the educational program should be directed toward training rural young people for city jobs. Rural high schools should teach more shorthand and drafting as well as agricultural methods.

Farm Credit

The problem of credit for farmers has been a recurrent subject of public policy. Since the first years of our country "reformers" have been going to Washington from the agricultural districts to get easier credit for the farmer.*

---

* A good deal of the agitation of the nineteenth century was concerned with price levels as much as with direct credit for farmers, though both were considerations

In the twentieth century, special government credit facilities for farmers have developed. Twelve Federal Land Banks were established in 1916 and 12 Intermediate Credit Banks in 1923. The main purpose of these agencies was to improve the terms of regular farm loans.* With the depression, the federal credit programs were turned to emergency relief. The collapse of farm prices led to wholesale foreclosures. A Farm Credit Administration (FCA) was formed in 1933. It embraced the two older agencies and added several more. One of these, the Federal Farm Mortgage Corporation, purchased and refinanced a large proportion of the farm mortgages then outstanding and saved innumerable farms for their owners. The Production Credit Corporation, which set up local short-term credit associations for farmers, and the Bank for Cooperatives were also established at that time.

These FCA programs have provided longer repayment periods and better interest rates for farmers, and in the crisis of the early 1930's they saved many farmers from disaster, but they were all run on a regular business basis, lending to reasonable credit risks. In other words, they benefited primarily the larger, more progressive farms who also enjoyed most of the benefits of the extension service and the price support programs.

Credit for farmers who cannot borrow elsewhere has been handled by the Farmers Home Administration (FHA)† since 1946. It makes "production and subsistence" loans to small farms for specific improvements such as increased use of fertilizer, better livestock, or new crops. The loans are carefully supervised and farm methods often receive supervision in the process so that the FHA is conducting an educational as well as a credit program. The FHA also makes farm purchase and farm expansion loans to small tenants or operators

---

in the western opposition to the Banks of the United States in the early part of the century and to the gold standard during the greenback and silver eras. The midwestern farmer built up a strong distrust of "Wall Street" in large part because it was the banker who seemed to be his main obstacle to progress and efficiency. There were wonderful opportunities almost within his grasp but for the eastern bankers.

* Bank mortgages in that day had to be renewed every three to five years and short-term credit, normally every three months. In bad times, farmers were apt to find it difficult to renew these loans. The land banks amortized mortgages over many years so that the farmer's obligation in any one year was far less likely to cause a disaster than if the whole debt came due at once. The Intermediate Credit Banks discounted agricultural paper of up to two and three years' duration so that commercial banks could lend to farmers to carry livestock, machinery, etc.

† Not to be confused with the Federal Housing Administration, also FHA.

unable to make sufficient down payments to be eligible for conventional mortgages. The total amount of these loans is limited so that only the more promising applicants receive them and farmers whose assets and earnings are large enough are graduated to conventional lenders. Disaster relief loans made to farmers affected by flood, drought, grasshoppers, etc., are also supervised by the FHA.

These FHA programs have been subject to more criticism than the FCA lending. The interest charges are not sufficient to cover the high supervisory costs and the risks involved so that the program includes a subsidy. The programs seem paternalistic and unbusinesslike to many "self-reliant" farmers and congressmen.* The disaster loans, although politically popular, are criticized by some economists, at least in cases where they occur year after year. They preserve in operation farms that should probably be converted to grassland or forest.

Although the FHA program has grown, the bulk of federal agricultural credit goes to the more prosperous farmers. In 1958 the FHA made loans totaling $330 million (and $63 million of this was disaster loans available to farmers generally). This was more than it had lent in any previous year. In the same year, the various FCA agencies made loans of $3.4 billion, primarily to relatively large farmers.† The FCA loans in that one year exceeded the total loans made to small farmers by the FHA and its predecessors from the start of their programs in the mid-thirties through 1958.‡

Farm Adjustments and Economic Activity

Farm adjustment requires above all else opportunities for employment in the city. The most essential part of a workable farm program is general prosperity. The city must absorb all the net increase in rural populations plus the net outflow to adjust for the rapid increase in productivity and the slow increase in demand. In some years, more than 2 million persons have left farming. This can only occur with a rapid increase in output and jobs in the city.

Solving the problem of small and inefficient farms also requires

* Some of this criticism applies more to the resettlement programs of the 1930's that were administered by FHA's predecessors. Actually, all of the resettlement work of that era affected only a few thousand families. Only the credit programs continued after 1946.

† *U.S. Government Organization Manual*, 1959–60, pp. 272 and 378.

‡ The production and subsistence loans and the farm purchase and expansion loans came to about $2.5 billion over their whole history through 1958. Benedict, *op. cit.*, pp. 202–204, 209, and 214, and *U.S. Government Organization Manuals*, 1955–56, 1956–57, 1957–58, 1958–59, and 1959–60.

urban prosperity. The way to have larger farms in a region of small ones is for the more promising small farmers to buy the others out, and the others must have a place to go. The greatest problem has been in the South. Its rapid industrialization since World War II has provided many new employment opportunities. This is one of the most important factors in the declining number of inefficiently small farms in recent years. Perhaps the most promising government policy to deal with farm overcapacity and poverty would be a program to further accelerate the industrial development of those areas with surplus farm populations.

The growth in urban incomes and population will help solve the farm surplus problem on the demand side as well. Many feel that with the large increase in population in prospect the farm problem will solve itself. Indeed, by the end of the century, some predict an opposite problem of too little food and too high prices.

The Acreage Reserve Plan

Guarantees of farm credit, education, and research programs and the maintenance of general prosperity are all means of making a shift out of agriculture or to more efficient agriculture feasible. Some propose that the government go a step further and use its financial powers to retire resources from farming. There have been many such programs on a short-term limited scale already. The crop restriction plans of the 1930's paid farmers for acreage not planted. Later, in attempts to improve farming practice and check soil erosion as well as to eliminate surpluses, farmers were paid to plant soil-conserving crops. Under the Republican administration, a "soil bank" was tried in which farmers received payments to take land out of their regular acreage allotments.

These programs all restricted the amounts of land planted in basic crops and supplemented farm incomes, but they were of limited value in reducing farm output, and they seldom resulted in people leaving agriculture. Most farmers stayed in farming and let the payments and the output from the remaining land make up for the retired acreage.

To expedite the flow of resources out of agriculture, it has been proposed* that the government offer to purchase or lease an appropriate

* This proposal was advanced by the Committee for Economic Development (CED), an organization of prominent businessmen and economists: *Toward a Realistic Farm Program* CED, Dec. 1957. There were a few experiments with whole farm retirement under the soil bank, but for the most part it was a partial retirement plan.

number of farms on a whole farm basis. The prices offered would have to be attractive if the program were to work, so the expense might be substantial. However, the advocates of this program hold that these expenditures would help to solve the basic problem and would be of a once-for-all sort, while the price support and crop restriction costs tend to perpetuate the problem, if anything, and promise to go on forever.

This proposal for a permanent, large-scale federal acreage reserve could be adapted to deal with other farm problems in addition to the current surpluses. Purchase or lease programs could be concentrated on inefficiently small farms and farms where soil erosion is a great danger. Since the inefficient small farmer sells so little, some relatively efficient farms might have to be bought out as well. The better farms could be returned to production later if and when the long-term increase in demand occurs. The basic purpose of the proposal, of course, would be to increase total output in our country by idling surplus land, which has practically no alternative uses, and to transfer farmers, who *do* have other uses, to other jobs.

However, this program might inhibit the adjustment to more efficient farms. The government's leases or purchases would tend to bid up the price of agricultural land, making the formation of larger farms even more expensive and difficult than it is today.

There would be substantial administrative problems in the permanent acreage reserve plan. The terms offered by the government would have to be profitable to work, and it would be up to the administrator to say just how advantageous they could be and still serve the nation's best interests.

The acreage reserve proposal was made in the hope of reducing the government's role in agricultural markets. Since the program would be voluntary (farmers would not have to sell out or lease unless they liked the terms offered), it would mean less "regimentation" than acreage· reduction through present crop restrictions. Although the government would wind up as owner or lessor of a substantial proportion of the farmland in the country, the farms actually in production would be privately owned and would sell their output in a market which advocates intend should be less regulated than the present one.

SUMMARY

Unstable prices and incomes are the natural result of very inelastic demand, high fixed costs, and large year to year changes in market conditions owing to weather, shifts between crops, and general business fluctuations. Low farm incomes and inefficient farmers are consistent with competition if mobility is difficult and credit is rationed, especially in a setting of rapidly improving techniques and slowly growing demand.

A plausible case can be made for government intervention to even out the extreme fluctuations in farm incomes and prices and to improve the farmer's adjustment to long-term changes in market conditions and techniques. However, present-day policy provides only a partial solution to instability and practically none for poverty and inefficiency. Price supports are far above the level that would clear the market, taking one year with another, and they do little or nothing for some commodities such as meat products where prices and incomes are least stable. They are of only minor assistance to the inefficient small farmer who sells only a small proportion of total farm marketings. The larger part of government expenditures for farm credit and for education and research have also been on programs helpful primarily to the more substantial farmers. They have probably intensified the problems of the less efficient farmer, if anything, though the general public certainly gains from a more efficient farm economy. Farm poverty has been reduced in recent years, but more because of urban prosperity, especially in the South, than because of the government's policy.

To deal with agricultural instability economists have proposed forward prices, a true ever-normal granary, and emergency payments in time of depression. To deal with poverty and inefficiency some economists would propose a permanent acreage reserve involving the elimination of whole farms as well as credit and education programs aimed more at assisting the less efficient farmer. These programs taken together would leave the government with a substantial role to play in farming but would let market prices eliminate shortages and surpluses and direct farm output. They would attack the underlying causes of farm instability and poverty rather than simply treating the symptoms.

Many oppose some or all of these plans and advocate a more complete withdrawal of government from farm markets. Others would retain more of the present programs. Either policy may work without impossible hardship for farmers or expense for the government if something turns up. That something might well be our rapidly growing population and incomes. The most important farm policy is one of maintaining general prosperity.

FURTHER READINGS FOR CHAPTERS 2 AND 3

Agricultural economics is a whole discipline in itself. *The Journal of Farm Economics* is a regular professional journal devoted almost exclusively to the subject. New contributions to the field are likely to appear there. There are a large number of basic textbooks on the subject. Two good ones are J. D. Black, *Introduction to Economics for Agriculture*, Macmillan, 1953, and C. E. Bishop and W. D. Toussaint, *Introduction to Agricultural Economic Analysis*, Wiley, 1958. On a more advanced level, J. D. Black, M. Clawson, S. R. Sayre, and W. W. Wilcox, *Farm Management*, Macmillan, 1947, develops cost examples for various types of farms in detail, and Earl O. Heady, *Economics of Agricultural Production and Resource Use*, Prentice-Hall, 1952, is a good intermediate theory book with many applications of analysis to agriculture. W. H. Nicholls, *Imperfect Competition within Agricultural Industries*, Iowa State College Press, 1941, also contains much careful analysis of the position of the farmer relative to his suppliers and processors, though much of Nicholls' material applies more appropriately to Chapters 5–9 of this book. R. L. Mighell and J. D. Black, *Interregional Competition in Agriculture*, Harvard University Press, 1951, approaches the northeastern dairy industry from another, very interesting angle. Theodore Schultz, *The Economic Organization of Agriculture*, McGraw-Hill, 1953, is a useful collection of essays on a wide variety of agricultural subjects. R. L. Mighell, *American Agriculture: Its Structure and Place in the Economy*, Wiley, 1955, gives a good over-all picture of the farm industry based mainly on the 1950 Census. There is an almost limitless supply of material on the agricultural economy from the Department of Agriculture and the Bureau of the Census.

On agricultural policy: J. D. Black, *Parity, Parity, Parity*, Harvard Committee on the Social Sciences, 1943, gives an interesting history of the origin of American farm policy. D. G. Johnson, *Forward Prices for Agriculture*, University of Chicago, 1947, and *Trade and Agriculture: A Study of Inconsistent Policies*, Wiley, 1950, contain careful criticisms of American policies and many of the proposals for change discussed in Chapters 2 and 3. A comprehensive and exhaustive review of American farm policy is to be found in Murray Benedict, *Farm Policies of the United States, 1790–1950*, Benedict, *Can We Solve the Farm Problem?* and Benedict and O. C. Stine, *The Agricultural Commodity Programs*, all Twentieth Century Fund, 1953, 1955, and 1956.

The price theory developed in these two chapters had its initial complete statement in Alfred Marshall, *Principles of Economics*, 8th ed., Macmillan, 1920. Much of the diagrammatics originated with Jacob Viner, "Cost Curves and Supply Curves," reprinted in *Readings in Price Theory*, Irwin, 1954. The classic on elasticity is Henry Schultz, *The Theory and Measurement of Demand*, University of Chicago, 1938. The analysis of cost, demand, and competitive price is presented in almost every principles book (Lawrence Abbott, *Economics and the Modern World*, Harcourt, Brace, 1960, Chapters 20 and 21, is a good one for this), and in all economic analysis texts (Kenneth Boulding, *Economic Analysis*, 3rd ed. Harper, 1955, is a well-written one).

4

COMPETITIVE
MANUFACTURING–TEXTILES

$\mathbb{P}$ure competition is rare in modern America. Most of our industries fail to meet one or another of its major requirements. Either they contain sellers that are so large as to significantly affect supply, or they deal with similarly large buyers, or their products are not really standardized.

Among our major manufacturing industries, textile production comes as close as any to meeting the formal requirements of pure competition, though even here events of the last two decades have moved it away from the perfect textbook case.

THE TEXTILE INDUSTRY

Stagnation

Textile manufacturing is one of our oldest and most important industries. Textile making of all sorts employs just under 1 million people. According to the 1954 Census of Manufactures, the weaving of cotton cloth, the largest single subdivision of the industry, employed 296,000, more than any other industry except automobiles, steel, aircraft, and sawmills. Textile production was the first step of the industrial revolution in Britain in the eighteenth century, in the United States in the early nineteenth century, and in most other nations that have industrialized since.

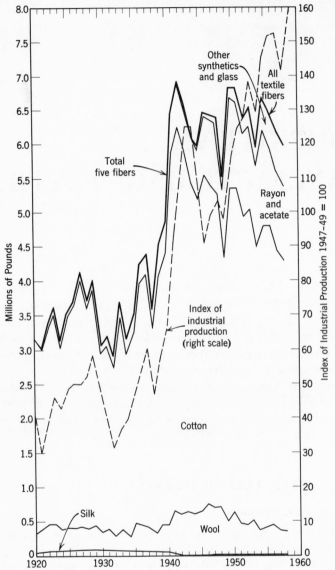

Figure 4.1. Mill consumption of certain textile fibers. Source: *Textile Organon*, March 1959.

Old industries often grow very slowly, and this is certainly true of textiles. The top curve in Figure 4.1 shows the total consumption of major textile fibers since 1920. The only important growth occurred in connection with World War II, but even with that boom textile fiber consumption only doubled between 1920 and 1958. In the same years over-all industrial production, shown as the broken line in Figure 4.1, increased four times. Since World War II textile fiber consumption has actually declined somewhat.

The new man-made fibers have made things even worse for large segments of the industry. Both cotton and rayon consumption have declined from their postwar peaks by about 20%. The use of wool has been cut in half so that it is now no more than it was in 1920. Only the new synthetics such as nylon have continued to gain.

The Textile-Making Process

Figure 4.2 gives some idea of what a complicated path the various textile fibers follow on their way to the consumer. After leaving the farm or chemical plant, they pass through four main stages.

First comes *yarn production*. The natural fibers, cotton and wool, are cleaned, carded and/or combed, and then spun into yarn. About one-third* of the synthetic fibers are shipped as staple—short fibers similar to cotton and wool—and these are spun in a similar process. The other two-thirds come from the chemical plants as filament yarn,* strands of filaments twisted together slightly, which may be used directly or after having been further twisted to the desired consistency in throwing mills.

The second step is *fabric production*, either *weaving* or *knitting*. About 10% of the yarn is knitted into fabrics such as jersey or into final products such as hosiery, gloves, underwear, or outerwear, and a small part is woven into "narrow fabrics" such as ribbons, belting, and labels. However, much the largest part of it goes into broad woven fabrics from which most of the familiar textile products are made.

Third comes *finishing*. Most broad woven goods retain the natural color of the fibers from which they are made. The cotton fabrics at this stage are known as "gray goods" and the synthetics are said to be woven in the "greige." For the majority of uses these products still require considerable processing: bleaching, printing, dyeing, pre-shrinking, and shaping. They may be given relatively permanent textures of various sorts by application of resins and sizings and the use of high temperature and pressure. Finishing is important mainly in cotton and synthetic production. For most wool products and some synthetics or cottons (e.g. ginghams), the yarn is dyed before weaving and the pattern is woven into the fabric.

Finally, the finished cloth is *fabricated* into a great variety of ap-

---

* In 1954, 958 million pounds of rayon, acetate, and other synthetic filament yarns and 483 million pounds of staple, tow, and waste were shipped. The bulk of this 483 million pounds was staple. *Census of Manufactures,* Vol. II, pp. 28B-18.

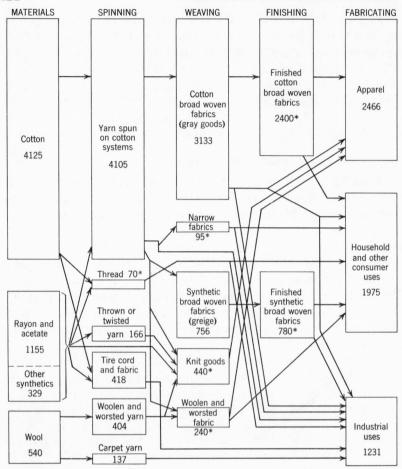

* Weights of certain products have been estimated on the basis of weights of sub-categories (thread), or yarns consumed (narrow fabrics, knit goods, and woolen and worsted fabrics), or on the proportion of gray goods yardage finished (cotton and synthetic finished broad woven fabrics).

Figure 4.2. Approximate flow of major textile fibers in 1954 (figures in millions of pounds). Source: Raw materials and fabrication from *Textile Organon*, Mar., 1959. Spun, woven, and finished products from *Census of Manufactures*, 1954, Vol. II, Section 22B.

parel, household, and industrial products. Some of the simpler of these, such as bags, sheets, towels, pillowcases, blankets, and drapery, are produced by the textile mills themselves, but goods to be made into apparel or the more complex housewares are usually sold to the cutting trades for fabrication.

Although it has lost ground to synthetics, cotton is still the most important fiber and cotton system yarns and cotton broad woven fabrics are the leading textile products. Moreover, much of the synthetic output goes through a similar process, being spun on the cotton system and broad woven. This chapter's main emphasis is on cotton spinning, broad weaving, and finishing.

Textile Mills

Most of the mills in the textile industry are highly specialized. Knitting, narrow weaving, and broad weaving are almost always carried on in separate mills, and there is little overlapping among wool, cotton, and synthetic fabric production.* Indeed, most cotton mills are themselves specialized, producing only a limited range of weaves and widths, though for about 75% of the cotton cloth produced, mills can shift from one product to another fairly easily.†

At the heart of the textile industry are somewhat more than 400 *integrated* mills—mills that combine spinning and weaving. They may buy or sell some yarn, but most of what they spin they also weave. These mills account for about four-fifths of cotton system spinning and broad weaving capacity.‡ The other fifth is to be found in mills specializing in spinning or weaving. The yarn mills supply knitters, specialist weavers, and industrial users such as the tire industry. The specialist weavers produce mainly complex fabrics such as table linens and upholstery fabrics.

Even the relatively large integrated mills do not do their own finishing, as a rule,§ so the textile industry also contains hundreds of separate finishing mills. The finishers do a large part of their work on a custom basis for "converters." These are merchants, mostly in the New York area, who buy gray cloth and have it finished to their specifications before selling it to cutters and wholesalers.

Textile Firms

A generation ago most of the vast array of mills in the textile industry were individually owned by small, local companies. Some

---

* About 7% of the synthetic mills' shipments were cotton goods and only 2% of the cotton mills' shipments were synthetics in 1954. *Census of Manufactures, 1954*, Vol. II, p. 22B-1.

† Jules Bachman and M. R. Gainsbrugh, *The Cotton Textile Industry*, National Industrial Conference Board, 1946, p. 43.

‡ In 1954 there were 458 such mills with 82% of the cotton system spindles and 84% of the cotton and synthetic broad looms. *Census of Manufactures*, Vol. II, p. 22B-32.

§ In 1954 only 16% of all cotton and synthetic integrated mills reported finishing facilities. *Census of Manufactures*, Vol. II, p. 22B-4.

still are, but more than half of total textile capacity today is controlled by large corporations with from 5 to more than 100 mills each.* Table 4.1 lists 25 of the largest of these with their vital statistics for 1958.

TABLE 4.1

MAJOR TEXTILE INTERESTS IN THE UNITED STATES: EMPLOYMENT, EQUIPMENT, AND PLANTS IN THE YARN AND FABRIC INDUSTRY, NOVEMBER 1958

| | Basic Textiles (Excludes Knitting, etc.) | | | | All Textiles | |
Rank and Interest (Ranked in Order of Magnitude of Basic Textile Employment)	Textile Employees	Spindles (thousands)	Looms	Plants (Includes Finishing Plants)	Plants	Employees
1. Burlington Industries, Inc.	45,000	1362	24,900	78	98	52,000
2. J. P. Stevens & Co., Inc.	30,500	1020	25,000	44	44	30,500
3. Cannon Mills Co., interests	23,200	452	12,325	19	21	24,300
4. Dan River Mills interests	17,200	821	18,500	17	17	17,200
5. Abney-Ervin interests	16,300	700	15,575	23	23	16,300
6. Deering, Milliken & Co.	16,100	803	20,200	27	28	16,700
7. M. Lowenstein & Sons, Inc.	15,000	584	14,500	11	11	15,000
8. Cone Mills Corp.	14,500	550	13,500	18	18	14,500
9. Springs Cotton Mills	12,000	639	14,240	8	8	12,000
10. West Point Manufacturing Co. interests	10,800	390	7,497	16	18	11,500
11. United Merchants & Manufacturers, Inc.	8,800	375	9,592	16	17	9,000
12. Pepperell Manufacturing Co.	7,600	301	6,502	6	6	7,600
13. Textron, Inc., interests	7,100	133	8,550	16	16	7,100
14. Riegel Textile Corp.	6,600	197	4,400	3	3	6,600
15. Bibb Manufacturing Co.	6,500	247	2,750	12	12	6,500
16. Comer interests	6,300	289	5,200	12	12	6,300
17. Berkshire Hathaway, Inc.	6,000	505	13,600	8	8	6,000
18. Reeves Bros., Inc.	5,700	200	4,050	9	9	5,700
19. Lineburger-Stowe interests	5,500	380	....	23	29	6,600
20. Abernethy-Shuford and associated Berdon-Levine interests	5,400	224	2,200	18	20	5,600
21. Callaway Mills	5,200	132	2,680	6	8	6,100
22. Greenwood Mills	5,000	292	6,860	5	5	5,000
23. American Thread Co., Inc.	4,500	243	....	7	7	4,500
24. Swift and Illges interests	4,500	121	2,450	5	5	4,500
25. Kendall Co.	4,400	322	6,990	10	13	5,000

Source: *Problems of the Domestic Textile Industry*, Hearings before a subcommittee of the Senate Committee on Interstate and Foreign Commerce, 85th Congress, 2nd Session, Pt. 5, 1958, p. 1898

* Burlington Industries reported 106 separate plants in 1959, *Moody's Industrial Manual*, 1959.

Integration and Merger

The growth of such multiplant firms may be accomplished by either internal or external growth. *Internal growth* is a matter of building additional facilities, something that does not happen very much in stagnant industries. Most of the large textile firms are therefore the products of *external growth*—the merging of formerly independent firms.*

Economists distinguish three main directions of corporate growth. *Vertical integration* is the combination of different steps on the way from the raw material to the consumer, such as the textile firms that do their own spinning, weaving, and converting.† *Horizontal integration* is the combination of two or more plants performing essentially the same function, such as textile firms with two or more broad woven fabric mills. *Conglomerate integration* is the combination of unrelated or only distantly related processes, such as textile firms that are also in the electronics business.

The big new firms in the textile industry have grown in all three directions at once. One study of textile mergers from 1930 to 1948 found that about a third of the mills changing hands were involved in vertical combinations and another third in clearly horizontal combinations. The largest part of the remaining mergers combined mills producing different textile products.‡

Motives for Merger

There were important mergers in the 1920's and 1930's but the largest number occurred during and since World War II. They had a variety of purposes.

* The term *merger* is used in this book to cover any combination of formerly independent firms no matter what legal form it takes. There is quite a variety of possibilities. One firm may absorb another by (1) issuing its own stock in exchange for the controlling stock of the other corporation; (2) purchasing the controlling stock for cash; (3) purchasing the assets of the other firm for stock or cash; or (4) taking a long-term lease on the other firm's assets. There may be different financial or legal problems in using one or another of these approaches, but they all have the same effect economically.

† In common speech the word *integrated* is often used by itself to mean vertically integrated. An *integrated* textile mill is one that combines spinning and weaving. A *fully integrated* firm is one that combines spinning, weaving, converting, and selling.

‡ Jesse W. Markham, "Integration in the Textile Industry," *Harvard Business Review*, Jan. 1950, p. 78. 370 acquisitions represented horizontal integration, 331 were cases of vertical integration, and 109 combined different fibers. Between 1940 and 1947, when the mergers were at their height, 331 mills were acquired, of which 109 were in horizontal mergers and 135 in vertical mergers.

The first great wave of mergers in 1940–48 was connected with wartime shortages and controls. Price controls were stricter on gray than finished goods, so many firms became their own converters for a time, retaining title to the products while they were being finished. Some mills acquired their own finishing mills or selling agencies. At the same time the larger commission houses and converters set out to acquire mills to assure themselves of supplies. For instance, J. P. Stevens and M. Lowenstein, the second and seventh firms in Table 4.1, were respectively the country's leading selling agent and converter until 1946.

Vertical mergers continued to be popular after the postwar shortages were long past. A main purpose of such combinations in recent years seems to have been to win direct access to the consumer. Gray goods lose their identity before they reach him. A firm must expand at least to the converting stage if it expects to build up brand names that people recognize. Some firms, like Burlington Industries and United Merchants and Manufacturers, have merged right into fabrication and even wholesaling and retailing. Promotion that develops dependable consumer loyalty offers such firms a certain amount of shelter in a declining market. The firms that fail to integrate and promote are apt to be even harder hit by declining demand as a result.

Another goal of textile mergers has been diversification. When demand shifts from one fiber to the next, the way for a textile company to keep alive is to shift with it. Many cotton firms acquired synthetic capacity by merger in the 1930's and 1940's. The 1950's saw the acquisition of leading woolen mills by such large firms as Burlington, Lowenstein, Textron, and United Merchants, though there were other motives besides diversification in these cases. Some firms have diversified outside of textiles. Textron makes plywood, machine tools, electronics equipment, chemicals, aluminum and steel castings, precision testing equipment, nuts and bolts. It even ran a steamship for a while.

Some mergers have been salvage operations. When textile firms face bankruptcy and have to sell out, their most likely buyers are other textile firms. The unprofitable firms are usually available at bargain prices. In some cases their stock has declined in value until it can be bought up for less than their liquidation value so that it may pay to buy a firm and close its mills.

The tax laws encourage such mergers. A firm may carry losses forward for five years and backward for two in calculating its federal corporate income tax obligation. For instance, losses in 1958 can be subtracted from profits in any year as early as 1956 or as late as 1963 with taxes payable only on the balance. This way the government participates in losses as well as profits. Without this rule taxes would fall more heavily on firms that suffer losses from time to time than on firms with stable incomes.

One effect of the tax loss provision is to encourage the merger of successful firms with unprofitable ones. Some of the firms that picked up woolen mills in the 1950's were able to keep their entire incomes tax-free. At a tax rate of 52% it was possible by mergers to more than double their profits after tax. They could afford to make generous offers to the stockholders in the unprofitable companies even if the mills were simply liquidated afterwards.* In fact, in some cases the tax losses were greater than the profits of the acquiring companies, and they found it worthwhile to buy up successful enterprises to have enough profits against which to offset all the losses. This is part of the reason why Textron is spread all over the map.

Some mergers are no more than personal empires for corporate officers with Napoleon complexes. An attitude of bigness for bigness' sake is not necessarily irrational for such men. Executives in big firms have more power and prestige and often more pay than those in small ones, and it is the executives who make most of the merger decisions.

Outside of the textile industry, many mergers have been directed toward monopoly control over markets or toward the economies of large-scale production. As we shall see, monopoly is a long way off in most textiles, and a larger scale offers little in improved production efficiency.

Concentration

The textile industry is still not very concentrated in spite of the large firms. Table 4.2 shows the numbers of firms and concentration ratios for various textile industries at the time of the 1954 census. Except for the relatively unimportant throwing and wool finishing trades, the four largest firms never control more than 30% of total shipments in any of these fields—less than the largest *single* firm in the aluminum and automobile industries to be discussed later in this book. In cotton broad woven fabrics, the most important textile industry, the figure is only 18%. There are fewer firms in the production of particular types of cloth, but the ease with which most of them can shift from one to another makes this fact of minor im-

* The mills could not be liquidated immediately. The Treasury will not recognize tax losses that result from mergers unless the acquired property is operated for at least two years after acquisition.

TABLE 4.2

CONCENTRATION IN TEXTILE INDUSTRIES—1954

Industry	Total Shipments (millions of dollars)	Number of Firms	Percentage of Sales by Four Largest Firms
Cotton system yarn mills	1030	278	26
Cotton broad woven fabrics	2790	413	18
Yarn throwing mills	99	118	39
Synthetic broad woven fabrics	1143	396	30
Yarn mills, wool except carpet	252	157	20
Woolen and worsted fabrics	890	285	27
Finished textiles except wool	998	680	24
Finished woolen textiles	33	54	44
Converters	884	587	..

Note: Shipments of finished textiles does not include custom work for converters except for the commissions earned by the finishers. Realistically, the converters' shipments and the finished goods shipments (but not commissions) should be taken together. If they were, the concentration ratio for finished textiles might well be lower.

Source: Senate Judiciary Committee, *Concentration in American Industry*, 85th Congress, 1st session, 1957, and *Census of Manufacturers* (for converters).

portance. These were 1954 figures, and the mergers have continued since then. Yet the four largest firms in Table 4.1, which shows conditions in 1958, still had only 19% of the country's spindles and 25% of its looms.

TEXTILE COSTS AND MARKETS

Textile Costs—Short Run

Textile mills use relatively little capital and great amounts of labor. Table 4.3 compares capital per worker and the relative importance of payroll in the major manufacturing industry groups. Only three industries used less capital per worker than textiles. Motor vehicles and primary metals (including steel and aluminum) used twice as much and petroleum used ten times as much. Payroll was a larger proportion of value added in textile production than in any other industry group.

In addition, materials are an important cost. Purchased materials and energy amount to 59% of shipments in cotton broad woven fabrics, 63% in synthetic broad woven fabrics, and 71% in cotton system spinning mills.* Altogether, an exceptionally high proportion of textile mill costs seem to be variable.

TABLE 4.3

CAPITAL PER WORKER AND PAYROLL AS A PERCENTAGE
OF VALUE ADDED IN 19 INDUSTRY GROUPS—1954

Industry	Capital per Worker (dollars)	Payroll as a Percentage of Value Added
Apparel	3,523	62.2
Leather and leather products	4,106	62.7
Lumber and furniture	6,205	60.8[a]
Textile mill products	8,009	63.9
Fabricated metal products	8,387[b]	57.9
Transportation equipment other than motor vehicles	8,673[b]	[c]
Electric machinery	9,779	53.4
Printing and publishing	10,194	57.9
Instruments and related products	10,639	56.4
Stone clay and glass products	10,915	50.7
Machinery, except electric	12,685	58.3
Paper and allied products	13,340	48.4
Rubber products	13,579	55.6
Food and beverages	14,992	46.3
Motor vehicles and equipment	15,713	[c]
Primary metals	15,765	54.4
Chemicals	25,479	36.1
Tobacco products	30,009	26.3
Petroleum	90,921	42.7[d]

[a] Lumber mill products 60.6 and furniture 60.9.

[b] Fabricated metal products includes ordnance. Transportation equipment other than motor vehicles is mainly aircraft. In both industries a large part of the capital is provided by the government rather than the business firm.

[c] Payroll as a percentage of value added is 59.6% for the whole transportation equipment industry including motor vehicles.

[d] 42.7% is for petroleum and coal products.

Source: The Conference Board, *Economic Almanac*, 1959.

* Cost of materials as percentages of value of shipments reported in the 1954 *Census of Manufactures.*

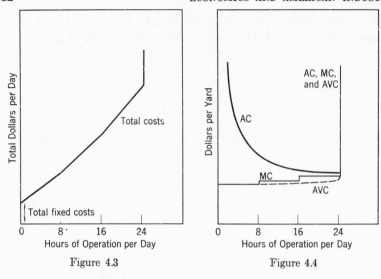

Figure 4.3   Figure 4.4

Marginal costs are probably pretty close to constant during. any given shift in a textile mill. It would take the same amount of additional labor, yarn, and power to produce the five hundredth yard of cloth as the fifth yard. Textile mills can operate on a one-, two-, or three-shift basis, however, and one more yard of cloth is apt to add more to costs on the swing and night shifts than on the day shift. If nothing else, the mills pay premium rates for night shift and often for swing shift work.

The result is a total cost curve like that in Figure 4.3. Total fixed costs are shown as a small part of total costs at any but very low outputs. Total costs, variable plus fixed, rise at a constant rate out to the 8-hour-a-day operating rate, then at a slightly faster rate out to 16 hours, and faster yet out to 24. When a mill is working its equipment around the clock, no further output is possible no matter how much labor or material is employed, so total costs are shown as rising abruptly at 24 hours. If there were some high-cost stand-by equipment available, the plant could produce something beyond its normal operating capacity and costs would rise less suddenly.

The average and marginal costs implied in Figure 4.3 are shown in Figure 4.4. Marginal cost is constant within each shift but rises between shifts. Average cost is shown as declining right out to capacity, as the mill's overhead is spread over more and more output, but it does not decline very rapidly during the second and third shifts because fixed costs are not a very large part of the total then. Average variable cost rises gradually after the first shift is over because the more expensive swing and night shifts are being averaged in. All three rise abruptly when the mill reaches capacity.

Textile Costs—Long Run

Textile production is one industry in which large-scale mills have little or no advantage over smaller ones. Mills that employ only a few hundred people are large enough to use the most advanced methods of production at each stage in the textile process.

In spinning, a study financed by the Department of Agriculture concluded that mills with from 7000 to 14,000 spindles would be large enough for efficient operations in producing the widely used coarse yarn, though somewhat larger mills were necessary for the efficient production of fine yarns. The study projected a "model" spinning mill with 10,000 spindles,* about 0.04% of the total cotton system spindles in the country!

Integrated mills need to be somewhat larger. A major manufacturer estimated that efficient production of fine cotton woven goods would require 60,000 spindles and 1300 looms, some 0.3% of total national capacity.†

Finishing mills often process the output of a number of different weavers, but they are still very small. Only 12% of them employed as many as 100 persons against 67% of the yarn mills and 70% of the cotton broad woven fabric mills.‡

Most of the large new combinations have found it worthwhile to maintain large numbers of separate mills, often producing similar products and within a few miles of each other. These large firms' main advantages seem to lie in promotion, diversification, and finance rather than in production. Their vertical integration into converting makes promotional activities feasible. Their volume is enough to support national advertising campaigns and selling organizations. Their size also makes them better credit risks, facilitating the financing of capital expansion and further merger.

Regional Competition

There are important regional cost differences in textile production. Our first textile mills were in the North, mainly in New England. At

* *Costs of Manufacturing Carded Yarns and Means of Improvement,* U.S. Department of Agriculture Technical Bulletin No. 1033, 1951, p. 10.

† Letter from Chairman of Board, Berkshire Fine Spinning Associates, May 12, 1952, quoted in *Report on the New England Textile Industry by a Committee Appointed by the Conference of New England Governors,* 1952, p. 207.

‡ *Census of Manufactures,* 1954, Vol. II, pp. 22B-8 and 9.

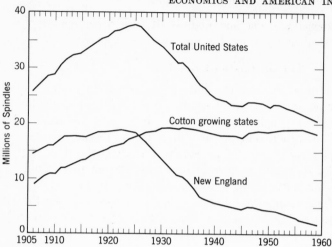

Figure 4.5. Cotton system spindles in place. Source: *Statistical Abstract of the United States* and *Facts for Industry*, Series M22P.

the turn of the century the Northeast still had the bulk of textile capacity, but since then the South has largely displaced it. Figure 4.5 shows what has happened to the numbers of northern and southern spindles since 1906. Both grew until after World War I, but the South advanced faster. Since 1923 New England has experienced an almost continuous decline. Today the South has nine-tenths of the spinning capacity. New England's textile employment has not fallen this fast because it changed to two- and three-shift operations between World Wars I and II and because it lost spinning capacity faster than weaving and finishing capacity.

The heavy labor costs in textile production account for much of the attraction that the South holds for textile mills. At the end of the last century northern wage rates were almost double those in the South. Northern labor did have more skills as a rule, but this was a minor advantage in the making of many textile products.

Mills located in small communities in the Carolinas and Georgia could get labor for 40¢ a day* in some cases because the only alternative employment was hoeing cotton on the hillside. Southern public opinion was generally hostile to unions so the mills were in little danger of being organized. In fact, very few of them are even yet. Southern state legislatures treated the new mills with great tenderness, imposing little or no social legislation.

* D. L. Cohn, *The Life and Times of King Cotton,* Oxford University Press, 1956, p. 216.

Conditions in the South are far better today. With the improvement of southern agriculture and the further industrialization of the region, the differential has narrowed. Southern wages are only about 8% less than New England textile wages today.* Northern labor costs are still considerably higher because Northern mills give fringe benefits not available in the South, such as wage differentials on the swing shift and paid holidays.† Moreover, work standards are generally higher in the South. Southern mill workers often handle half again as many looms as their northern counterparts.‡

Northern textile wages are certainly not high compared with most manufacturing. The union has been in a very weak position to demand more because any increase not matched in the South was likely to mean more runaway mills. Much of the cry for higher national minimum wage rates has come from the northern textile industry and its employees, but for the most part the minimums set have been a bit below the actual southern textile pay scales.§

The South has other advantages, though they are less significant than its labor cost differential. Many southern communities have set out to raise themselves from rural poverty by attracting industry. The early southern mills were often financed locally by solicitations from citizens that appealed as much to their local patriotism as to their profit motives. It is still fairly common for southern towns to grant tax exemptions to new mills for specified periods or to offer to build mills and lease them at low rents. Southern locations can usually offer low power rates and fuel prices as well.

Incidentally, nearness of the cotton fields does not help the southern mills much. Cotton has a high value per pound so that transportation costs are not very important. At any rate, the largest part of the cotton crop today comes from Mississippi or farther west so that Carolina and Georgia mills are little closer than other sections of the country.

These days the southward migration is less a question of where new mills will locate than one of which old mills will close. The South has a definite advantage in this respect, since more of its mills are

* Department of Labor, *Employment and Earnings, May 1959.* Average hourly earnings, straight time pay, broad woven fabric mills, cotton, silk, and synthetics, for 1958 were $1.53 in New England and $1.42 in the South.

† Bureau of Labor Statistics, Report No. 118, *Factory Workers' Earnings in Five Industry Groups,* Apr. 1956, p. 40.

‡ *Report on the New England Textile Industry by a Committee Appointed by the Conference of New England Governors,* 1952, pp. 167–169.

§ Bureau of Labor Statistics, Report No. 118, *op. cit.,* p. 7.

of fairly recent vintage. On the average, they contain more modern equipment and are more efficient as a result.

Textile Markets—Gray Goods

Regardless of mill location, textile markets are centered in New York City. In selling gray goods the mills were traditionally represented by a small group of commission houses there. Many of these had been associated with particular groups of mills for years. They were the main sources of market information as well as the main outlets for their clients. Many of the recent vertical mergers have simply cemented old ties. The large firms that have resulted from the mergers typically have their own selling offices which in some cases serve as agents for other firms as well.

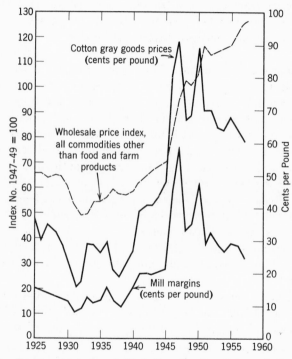

Figure 4.6. Source: Agricultural Marketing Service, *Prices of Cotton Cloth and Raw Cotton and Mill Margins for Certain Constructions of Unfinished Cloth* and *Statistical Abstract*.

The largest part of the gray goods are of standard "constructions" such as print cloths, sheetings, or drills of particular widths, thread counts, and weights. Asking prices are regularly available from the various selling offices and commission houses by telephone. Prices quoted by different sellers may differ slightly at any one moment, but no one can hope to sell gray goods at much above the going price. Prices are constantly being adjusted. Altogether, the gray goods market is a close approximation to pure competition.

Gray goods prices fluctuate considerably more violently than do wholesale prices in general. Figure 4.6 compares the two. Some of these gyrations reflect changes in the raw cotton markets, but mill margins, the difference in price per pound between gray goods and raw cotton, can also rise or fall by as much as a third in one year. These mill margins are what the mill operators receive to cover all their costs other than cotton itself.

The prices of different types of gray goods tend to move together. Figure 4.7 shows what has happened to the prices of four important

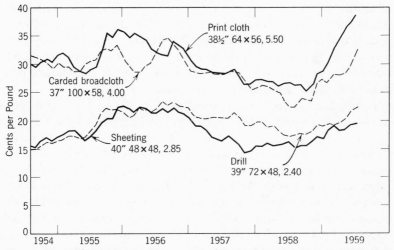

Figure 4.7. Mill margins on four constructions of gray cotton cloth. Source: Agricultural Marketing Service, *Prices of Cotton Cloth and Raw Cotton and Mill Margins for Certain Constructions of Unfinished Cloth,* Sept. 1958 and season 1958–1959.

constructions of cotton gray goods in the years 1954–59. Occasionally the market has changed and left one or another of these in oversupply or undersupply, and mill margins have risen or fallen in response. The slumps in the margins on broadcloth in 1956 and in sheeting in 1957 are examples. Such discrepancies never last very long because mills shift from the less profitable to the more profitable lines. Ordinarily price differences among the various sorts of cloth reflect differences in production costs, not differences in profit.

Textile Markets—Finished Goods

Finished goods are less standardized than gray goods. There are an infinite number of possible designs and textures. No two sellers' lines of fabrics are exactly the same. The converters and the fully integrated textile firms compete by constantly trying to bring out new finishes that are unique but within the current fashion. Since fashions change unpredictably, converting is a risky business.

Finished goods are distributed through salesmen or jobbers to the cutting trades, department stores, and mail order houses. Considerable promotional effort goes into such contacts. In recent years there has been an increasing amount of promotion aimed directly at the consumer, and textile brand names have become more familiar as a result. Compared with other industries, however, the amount of textile advertising is still very small. In 1956–57 advertising took 0.7% of textile mill total receipts as against 1.2% for manufacturing as a whole and 4.8% in tobacco products.* Outside of household linens, textile brands are still of secondary importance. A woman may recognize the mill's name when she sees it on a garment today, but in most cases it is the style and possibly the retailer or the fabricator's brand name that count when she buys the dress.

Finished goods prices are usually more stable than gray goods prices. A large part of the apparel and piece goods sold in this country are "price lined," i.e., they are sold at traditional prices such as $8.95 dresses, $49 suits, or $1.98 a yard drapery fabric. The consumers come to group goods by the price at which they sell, so the prices continue year after year. To stay within these price lines in the face of fluctuations on the gray goods market, converters often change quality to some extent. When gray goods prices rise, say, converters put a similar finish on cloth of lighter construction so that they can supply the cutters or retailers at the same price.†

While converters set the prices at which they sell, the prices they select must be in line with their competitors if they want to do any business. You and I can be misled by a skilled finisher with a handful of sizing, but most of the converters' sales are to expert cutters or retailers who can tell what they are getting. They are not likely to buy a product at prices much above those going for similar quality elsewhere. Occasionally a distinctive new finish will give a firm a

---

* Derived from Treasury Department, *Statistics of Income,* 1956–57, all corporations with balance sheets.

† The possibility of such changes in quality is one of the main reasons why price control on finished goods did not work very well during World War II.

special market for a time, but successful designs or textures are often copied and the originator who tries to make a big profit will soon be undersold.

Figure 4.8 compares fluctuations in gray goods prices with those of percale piece goods at retail. The finished goods prices did rise

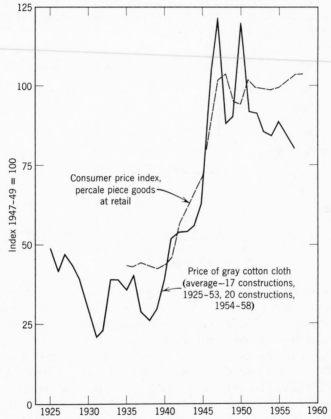

Figure 4.8. Source: Agricultural Marketing Service, *op. cit.*, and Bureau of Labor Statistics, Bulletin 1256, *Consumer Prices in the United States*, 1953–1958.

faster during the shortages of World War II. That was when the mills found it profitable to become converters. In the nonshortage years, such as 1935–40, and 1951–59, however, the finished goods prices remained stable in the face of wide changes in the gray goods markets.

The market for finished goods does not meet all of the requirements of pure competition. However, with large numbers of sellers, expert buyers, and easy imitation of successful finishes, the discrepancies are only moderate. The analysis developed so far in this book will not give a perfect picture of the market for finished textiles, but it should not be wildly off the mark.*

Prices and Output

Theoretically, changes in price should lead to changes in output. When demand is high (D_1 in Figure 4.9), both the high- and low-cost mills may find it worthwhile to operate all three shifts. If demand falls (D_2) and gray goods prices drop (P_2), both raw cotton prices and mill margins are likely to decline as well. In Figure 4.9 the drop in raw cotton prices shows up as a decline in marginal costs for

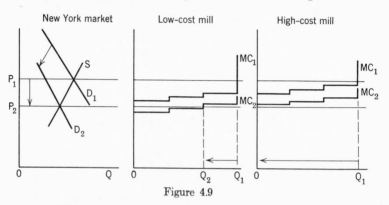

Figure 4.9

the two mills from MC_1 to MC_2. Margins have also fallen in Figure 4.9 because prices fell more than marginal costs. After the drop in price the low-cost mill would find it profitable to run only two shifts and the high-cost mill would close down.

Textile mills do act this way to some extent. Figure 4.10 shows how they have adjusted to market fluctuations since World War II. In peak years, like 1948, 1951, 1953, and 1955, the number of idle spindles has run slightly over 1 million and the active spindles have operated close to 120 hours a week on the average; 120 hours corresponds to three shifts, five days a week. There has been a slight upward trend in the average number of operating hours as the New England mills have adopted three-instead of two-shift operations. In bad years like 1949, 1952, 1954, and 1957, the number of inactive spindles has risen to about 2 million while enough of the active spindles were operated on restricted schedules to reduce the over-all average operating rate by five or ten hours a week from previous peaks.

* An alternative analysis of such a market, known as "monopolistic competition," is discussed in Chapter 9.

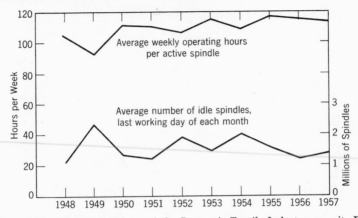

Figure 4.10. Source: *Problems of the Domestic Textile Industry, op. cit.*, Pt. 5, p. 1962. Derived from figures given there.

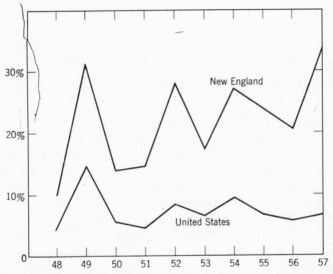

Figure 4.11. Percentage of installed spindles idle last working day of July. Source: *Problems of the Domestic Textile Industry, op. cit.*, Pt. 1, p. 256, and *Facts for Industry*, Series M22P.

Moreover, it was in the high-cost northern mills that the idle spindles appeared. Figure 4.11 compares the percentages of installed spindles that were inactive in New England and in the country as a whole. In bad years 30% or more of New England's spinning capacity stood idle against 8 to 14% for the whole of the United States. The New England mills were the marginal producers who bore the brunt of any declines.

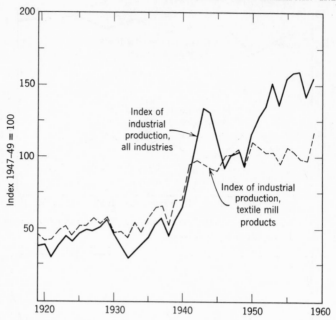

Figure 4.12. Source: *Historical Statistics of the United States* and *Federal Reserve Bulletins*.

One aspect of mill operations is puzzling at first. One would expect that if it is worthwhile to operate a shift at all it would pay to operate it all week. There is no very good reason why the night shift on Thursday should have any higher marginal costs than the night shift on Wednesday. Yet mills often operate more or less than a full work week. In January 1959, toward the end of a recession period, 15.3% of the active looms were run more than 80 hours (two full shifts) but less than 120 hours (three full shifts). In January 1960, a more prosperous period, only 2.9% of the looms were operated at such rates.*

Some economists have explained this behavior as a matter of the mills trying to keep their labor force intact.† Many mills are located in isolated communities where they are the only important employers. If they lay their help off completely it is likely to drift away. To

---

* American Cotton Manufacturers Institute, *Textile Hi Lights*, July 1959, p. 19, for the 1959 figure, and correspondence for the 1960 figure. In January 1959, 19.6% were operating below the 120-hour level, but 4.3% were not run on the third shift at all, leaving 15.3% more than two shifts but less than three. In January 1960, the corresponding figures were 6.9, 4.0, and 2.9%.

† R. Robson, *The Cotton Industry in Britain*, St. Martin's Press, 1957, p. 204.

retain all their workers, mills in such situations find it profitable to employ them for less than full weeks. In other words, these mills treat a portion of their payroll as a fixed cost.

Textile output has usually avoided the most severe fluctuations of industrial output generally, as can be seen in Figure 4.12. The mills' maintenance of output in bad years to preserve their working force is probably one of the reasons. Another is that the demand for textiles is more stable than for more durable commodities. When a pair of pants wear out, they have to be replaced pretty quickly. Finally, the readiness with which price or quality adjust to market conditions may account for some of the stability of output.

The Inventory Cycle

The mild ups and downs that do occur in textile output and the wilder ones that appear in textile prices are at least partly attributable to the irregular accumulation of inventories. Converters and cutters accumulate materials in advance when they anticipate a rising market, and this pushes prices up further. If demand for finished products seems to be flattening out, they keep their inventories stable, which means a drop in demand at the mill. If the converters and cutters foresee a decline, they try to cut their inventories and this intensifies any drop in output that does occur.

The mills themselves may produce for inventory in slack periods rather than close down or sell at a loss. Much of the time this turns out to be a wise policy. They are able to sell the cloth they have produced at profitable prices later on. If the recovery in demand is late in coming, however, they may have more inventory than they can finance. Then they have to sell what they have produced at the bottom of the market and depress things further.

All this has added up to a fairly regular textile cycle. Before World War II the textile industry was relatively prosperous in most odd-numbered years and in trouble in even-numbered ones. Since World War II the textile cycle has corresponded to the general fluctuations in business activity except that the textile mills succeeded in having one more recession than the rest of us (in 1952).

This instability could be avoided, at least in part, if the many different people in the textile business could be kept better informed about who had what inventory. One of the main arguments presented in favor of the mergers since World War II is that the vertically integrated firms can coordinate operations at various levels more plausibly and maintain inventories in a more stable fashion.

PROFITS, CAPACITY, AND LONG-RUN ADJUSTMENTS

Profits in Theory and Practice

When we turn to the long-run performance of an industry, profits become important. Figure 4.13 compares the profit rates reported by textile firms with those reported by all manufacturing corporations. Similar comparisons will be made for the rest of the industries discussed in this book. Such accounting profit figures are the best we have, so we must use them, but it would be a good idea to spell out the differences that may exist between what the economists and the accountants have in mind.

1. For one thing, Figure 4.13 shows the rate of return on stockholders' equity, i.e., it shows reported profits as a percentage of corporate assets less corporate liabilities. This figure might be quite different for two economically identical firms, depending on how they were financed. The firm with the larger debt outstanding will show higher earnings on equity so long as its interest charge per dollar borrowed is less than it earns on its total assets. Of course, the debt-financed firm also is in greater danger of turning in a loss in bad years since the interest has to be paid regardless of what the firm earns. In other words, the profits on equity will fluctuate more widely from year to year for the company with large debts, even if the economic performance of the two firms is the same.*

2. Corporations may show high or low costs and profits on their books depending on which of a number of quite plausible accounting methods they use. For instance, the more rapidly they depreciate their equipment, the higher their "costs" will be and the lower their owners' equity. Quite honest and competent accountants also differ on how they evaluate such thing as inventories, accounts receivable, or patents and trademarks. As a result, two companies may show widely different returns on owners' equities, not because they are economically any different but because their accountants have different predilections.

3. Sometimes profits or losses disappear from corporate accounts because of property transfers. A textile mill that cost $5 million to

---

* One way around this problem would be to take profits plus interest as a percentage of total assets. This would be just as workable as the profits-to-equity ratio as far as textiles go, but we find later in the book, when public utilities are discussed, that the return on total assets cannot be compared very easily with those of other industries. At any rate, it is the return on owners' equity that businessmen are presumably trying to maximize.

build might sell for only $1 million if business were really bad. A buyer would only be interested if the price were low enough to offer him at least as good a return on his money as he could get elsewhere. If he guesses right about future profit prospects for the business he is acquiring, the new owner should show a reasonable "profit" according to his books, even if the original owner of the mill would have been taking a "loss" if he had kept it.

This can work the other way, too. If some mill is exceptionally profitably, perhaps because of a familiar trademark, it can be sold for a price that reflects its high profits. Thereafter the new owner may show only a normal return on *his* investment, but the profits are not gone. The old owner, now on the beach somewhere clipping coupons, is still getting them. In other words, profits and losses may change into *rents* and be lost from view as far as the accounts go.

4. Profits can also be disguised as wages and salaries. Economically it would make very little difference whether the stockholder-officers of a small corporation paid themselves salaries or dividends, though the first would be a "cost" and the second would not. For that matter, highly profitable firms often let their employees in on their good fortune. In textiles low profits and losses are more common, and the workers seem to have participated in those as well. At least, textile wages are among the lowest in manufacturing. This is true even within the South,* and in the North the disparity between wages in textiles and most other manufacturing is more extreme. In recent years, when textiles have been particularly badly hit, textile wage rates have risen only half as fast as manufacturing wages in general.†

5. Yet another reason why one firm might show larger accounting profits than another would be that its plant was built at a time when construction costs were lower. If a mill was built for $3 million once upon a time, and if it would cost $5 million to replace it now, the owner of the $3 million mill would show a large profit even if new $5 million mills were built until *their* profits completely disappeared. In these days of regularly rising prices, profits of firms with old mills will be exaggerated compared with those that constructed their mills recently.

6. Finally, when profits "disappear" in the economic sense, there is still something left in the accounting sense. The return on the

* See Chapter 11, pp. 507–508.

† Between 1947 and 1957 average hourly earnings in manufacturing in general rose from $1.24 to $2.07 an hour, or 67%. In the same years hourly earnings of textile workers rose from $1.04 to $1.50, or 44%. Senate Report No. 42, *Problems of the Domestic Textile Industry*, 86th Congress, 1st Session, 1959, p. 6.

owner's investment necessary to get him into the industry is counted as a "cost" in economics. If a man could earn 5% on common stock or real estate, and if he is really earning only 2% on an equally risky textile mill, he is not making an economic profit. He is taking a loss! In the long run he will leave the industry.

Textile Profits

After all this qualification we can finally get back to textiles. The industry was able to make exceptional profits in the years just after the two world wars (1919–23 and 1946–48) but those are about the only times. The rest of the twenties, the thirties, and the fifties have

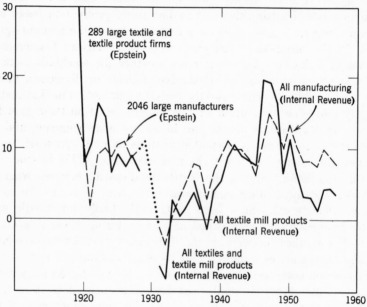

Figure 4.13. Net income after tax as percentages of owners' equity—textiles and all manufacturing. Source: Ralph Epstein, *Industrial Profits in the United States*, National Bureau of Economic Research, 1934, and Internal Revenue Service, *Statistics of Income*.

been long dreary years for textile makers. They were probably drearier than even Figure 4.13 indicates. Owners' equity is understated there because many mills changed hands at low prices and because more of textile capacity was built before the inflation of capital equipment prices than in most industries. The low wages of textile workers make things even blacker. Except for the war and postwar shortage periods a large proportion of the mill owners did not earn as much on their properties as they would have if they had put their money into government bonds!

Long-Run Adjustments

Figure 4.14 shows how the industry has adjusted in response to its varying fortunes. The top line indicates the amount by which textile profits on owners' equity exceeded or fell short of profits in manufacturing generally. The second line shows the net change in the number of cotton system spindles in place in the United States from one year to the next, i.e., it shows the installation of new spindles less the scrappage of old spindles. During the two postwar booms when profits exceeded those available elsewhere, the textile makers expanded capacity. In other years, when profits were lower than in most industries, they scrapped and failed to replace great numbers of spindles—often as many as a million a year.

The industry was more cautious about adding capacity in response to the high profits of the late forties than it had been during the early twenties. This is understandable in view of the dismal intervening experience. It is not current profits that count in decisions to enter new industries so much as long-run prospects for profit. Even at the peak of the boom, there was plently of room for doubt in the case of textiles.

As one might expect, it was the high-cost northern mills that left the industry. The third and fourth lines in Figure 4.14 show the net additions to spinning capacity in New England and in the South since 1919. Even in the booms the northern mills added very few spindles and in the slumps they did most of the contracting. The southern mills were adding to capacity until 1931 and experienced little net contraction until recently.

In the 1950's even the South was hit. From 1952 to 1958 115 mill closings involving 31,855 employees were reported in southern states.[*] In the same years New England reported 234 mills closed with 95,830 employees idled.[†]

Profits so low as to be virtual economic losses have persisted in spite of the liquidations for much the same reason that the farm problem never seems to be solved. Productivity has grown while demand has remained stagnant. The change from one to three-shift operations increased the output per mill and intensified the overcapacity in the industry. Output per man-hour has also been on the increase. Figure 4.15 compares the growth in man-hour productivity in cotton

[*] *Problems of the Domestic Textile Industry, op. cit.,* p. III, pp. 1974–1976.

[†] *Ibid.,* p. 601

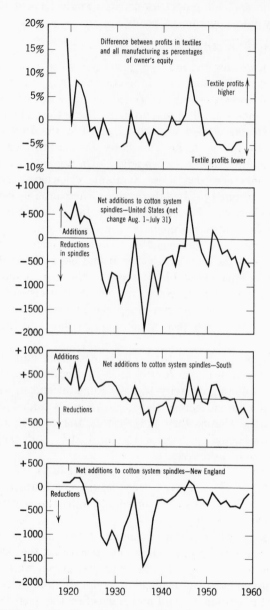

Figure 4.14. Source: Epstein, *op. cit., Statistics of Income,* and *Statistical Abstract* (derived from Figures 4.5 and 4.13).

textiles and in all manufacturing.   In the 1920's textile productivity hardly grew at all, but since then it has apparently increased as fast as in manufacturing generally.   The elimination of high-cost mills, the rise in production standards in the nonunion South, the use of more automatic equipment and improvements in the physical arrangement

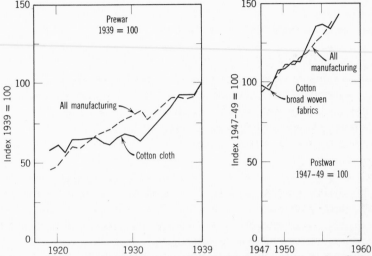

Figure 4.15.   Output per man-hour, cotton cloth and all manufacturing. Source: Prewar, Bureau of Labor Statistics, *Handbook of Labor Statistics*, 1950. Postwar, *Economic Indicators, Historical and Descriptive Supplement*, 1957; and Textile Workers Union of America, exhibition in *Problems of the Domestic Textile Industry, op. cit.*, Pt. 2, p. 949. This is just linear yards of cotton broad woven fabric per man-hour. In both cases these figures are for production workers only.

of mills have all been cited as reasons.   At any rate, the competitive nature of the industry does not seem to have made progress impossible.

While productivity grew, demand leveled off.   With better heating, less formal living habits, and longer-lasting fabrics, Americans have spent most of their extra income on products other than textiles. Industrial use of textile products in particular has fallen off.   As a result we need fewer textile mills and fewer textile workers each year.

The elimination of high-cost plants and surplus capacity does not occur in a sterilized test tube.   In real life, it is an extremely painful adjustment.   The liquidations of the last four decades have left ghost towns all over New England.   The communities' investments in shops, streets, schools, and houses are often lost along with the mill.   Even worse, the towns become pockets of unemployment that persist for years.   The dead mill leaves a great number of unskilled workers or workers with obsolete skills, often in isolated areas.   Many of them are middle-aged. Declining industries do not hire many new workers. These people are very hard to place even in boom years like the 1950's. Important New England textile centers like Lowell, Lawrence, Fall River, and New Bedford were almost continuously among the Labor Department's "surplus labor areas" in the 1950's.

GOVERNMENT POLICY—TRADE RESTRICTIONS

Easing the Adjustment

In the long run the rest of us gain more than the New Englanders lose. The South has certainly found its salvation in industrialization, though textiles no longer offer it the prospect they once did. The nation as a whole will obviously produce more if its resources are withdrawn from industries in which they are superfluous and shifted to other uses.

The adjustment of textile production to the country's needs is requiring a few unlucky textile mill operators and workers to pay for what we all gain, however, and a good case can be made for the rest of us compensating the losers, at least in part. The maximum eligibility for unemployment insurance might be extended in the special case of mill liquidations in surplus labor areas. The unemployment that results in such instances is certainly very different from the periodic and temporary unemployment common in other industries. Government-financed retraining or worker transfer programs might be developed. Mill owners are already compensated by the government in part in that the loss write-off provisions of the corporate income tax make a mill that takes heavy losses still worth something on the market place.

Much attention has been given in recent years to government measures to assist depressed areas. As far back as 1951 some mild and not very effective efforts were made to give such areas preference in defense contracts. A more ambitious program was regularly debated in the late 1950's, and, by January 1961, seemed to have a good chance of becoming law. A bill introduced then provided for Federal loans or loan guarantees for firms establishing new operations in distressed areas or to state or local government projects designed to attract industry. Federal aid in regional planning and in worker retraining were also included.

Textiles and the Tariff

Another remedy that Congress periodically discusses is the tariff. Tariffs and textiles have been connected from the beginning in the

United States. The young New England mills at the beginning of the nineteenth century were sheltered from British competition by one of our first protective tariffs. After that, tariffs on textiles and almost anything else we could conceivably produce at home were regularly revised, usually upward. By 1930 Americans were paying duties that averaged about 35% of the value of cotton textiles they imported and 85% on woolen and worsted textiles.

The United States turned a corner in 1934 when the Reciprocal Trade Agreements Act was passed. It permitted the President to reduce American duties in return for tariff concessions by countries to which we export. If the President had used all of his authority under the act and under various extensions of it since, he might have reduced tariffs by more than 80% by now.* Textile duties were not reduced anywhere nearly this much. They are down about a third from the 1930 rates.†

Figure 4.16 shows how cotton textiles have fared in world trade. America has consistently exported more cotton cloth than it has let into the country, but neither imports nor exports have actually amounted to much. In recent years imports have run about 1% of domestic production, and exports, 5%. We export the mass-produced fabrics such as denims and print cloths mainly to Canada and the Philippine Islands where location or preferential duties give us an advantage. We import ginghams, velveteens, and table damask, items that require much hand labor. The main reason imports are so small is that the American tariff was especially constructed to keep most of them out. This is even more so of wool fabrics (not shown in Figure 4.16), where we export practically nothing and, because of the tariff, imported only 7.8% of domestic consumption in 1958.

At the end of World War II, when most of the textile industries of the world were in need of reconstruction and when textiles were in short supply everywhere, the American cotton industry became the

---

* Under the 1934 act he could reduce duties by as much as 50% in negotiations with other countries In 1945 the act was extended and the President was allowed to make reductions of 50% from the 1945 level. If he had taken the full reduction allowed before 1945, he could then get the tariff down to 25% of 1930 rates. When the act was extended in 1955 and in 1958, the President received authority to make further reductions of 5% per year from the 1955 or 1958 levels. Altogether, by 1962 when the act will be up for renewal again, these would have permitted a maximum reduction of 82% from 1930 rates.

† Based on U.S. Tariff Commission, *United States Import Duties*, 1958. Duties on cotton fabrics are all down by about a third. Duties on woolens may be down by as much as 50% or more on the more expensive fabrics and by less than a third on cheaper fabrics. In addition to these formal reductions, inflation has made existing duties less significant than they were in the 1930's.

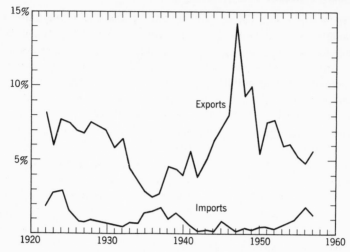

Figure 4.16.   Cotton cloth exports and imports as percentages of domestic production. Source: Backman and Gainsbrugh, *op. cit.*, pp. 176 and 181, and *Problems of the Domestic Textile Industry, op. cit.*, Pt. 4, pp. 1615 and 1617.

world's leading exporter for a while.   As the rest of the world's industries recovered, our exports fell back to their old levels and our imports rose.   The reduction in tariffs contributed to the increase in imports.

This coming on top of the industry's domestic problems has brought mill owners, unions, and just about everyone else connected with the industry to Congress seeking protection.   Southern congressmen, who have habitually opposed tariffs, did an about-face on the issue.

The industry has been demanding import quotas as well.   Imports would be limited to specified quantities regardless of foreign and domestic prices.   So far the American government has been able to avoid textile quotas directly, but in 1956 it persuaded the Japanese to establish quotas on their textile exports to us.

COMPARATIVE ADVANTAGE

The Gains from Trade

Most economists would oppose the use of trade restrictions to solve the textile industry's problems.   Their basic objection depends on a fundamental concept known as *comparative advantage*.   This is a fairly sophisticated idea.   It can best be stated in terms of a numerical example.

To keep things simple, suppose that there are only two commodities, automobiles and cotton cloth, and only two countries, America and Britain. A study made of American and British industries showed that in the 1930's American output per worker was three times that of the British in automobile production but only 1½ times that of the British in cotton spinning and weaving.* Perhaps one Englishman could produce 1 car or 1000 yards of cloth in a year. Then an American worker would produce 3 cars or 1500 yards of cloth per year. These hypothetical outputs are shown in Table 4.4.

TABLE 4.4

HYPOTHETICAL OUTPUT PER MAN-YEAR

	America	Britain
Automobiles	3	1
Cloth	1500	1000
Price ratios without trade	1A = 500C	1A = 1000C
Possible price ratio with trade	1A = 750C	

If trade between the two countries were prohibited, 1 automobile would be the equivalent of 500 yards of cloth in America. That is, if cars cost $2000, cloth should cost $4 per yard. Similarly, in Britain the two products would exchange at a rate of 1 car to 1000 yards of cloth.

Now let all restrictions on trade be removed. The two different price ratios cannot last. A single price would have to develop at 1A = 500C or 1A = 1000C or some place in between. 1A = 750C is a nice convenient number. At this rate both sides will gain from trade.

In America:

Without trade, two men might produce   3A + 1500C
With trade, America would specialize in automobiles and the same two men would be able to produce   6A
If America kept three of these automobiles and sold the others at the international rate of 1A = 750C, it would have   3A + 2250C

* G. D. A. MacDougall, "Brtish and American Exports, A Study Suggested by the Theory of Comparative Costs," *Economic Journal*, Dec. 1951, p. 700. The exact ratio of output per worker in America to output per worker in Britain was 3.1 to 1 for motor vehicles and 1.5 to 1 for cotton spinning and weaving. This illustration uses 3.0 and 1.5 because they make the arithmetic easier.

With trade America would have just as many automobiles as before and more cloth for the same effort. The cheapest way for Americans to get cloth is to make automobiles and trade them for it. Incidentally, America would have gained in this example, no matter what combination of automobiles and cloth it chose to consume, so long as it wanted any cloth at all.

The Americans were not getting rich at the expense of the British. Britain was playing the same game.

In Britain:

Without trade, two men might produce   1A + 1000C

With trade, Britain would specialize in cloth and the same two men could then produce   2000C

If Britain traded 750 yards of cloth at the international price for 1 automobile, would have   1A + 1250C

Like the Americans, the British wind up with as many automobiles as before and more cloth.

America in this example had a *comparative advantage* in automobiles, and Britain in cloth. In absolute terms, American labor was more productive in both fields, but its advantage was greatest in automobiles. The British disadvantage was least in cloth. Both countries gained by specializing where their comparative advantage was greatest. The result did not depend on the numbers chosen. There would have been some gain to be had from trade no matter what figures were used so long as the productivity ratios were different. The greater the difference, the greater the possible gain.

Comparative Advantage and Common Sense

At this point, students often suspect some sleight of hand. One reason for their doubts is the suspiciously long list of assumptions. We obviously do not live in a world with only two countries and two commodities, and other expenses besides labor count for something. None of these assumptions were really necessary, however. We would have reached the same sort of results using any number of countries and commodities, and taking all types of expense into account, but the chapter would have been a lot longer.

Actually, the principle involved here is not really new to most people. It simply says that it pays to specialize. A lawyer whose time is worth $25 an hour should hire someone to handle his letters, even if he can type twice as fast as the average $2-an-hour stenographer. Otherwise, every hour he spends typing letters he will save $4 on secretarial services and lose $25 as a lawyer. He has a comparative advantage in law just as America did in automobiles.

The proposition obviously applies to different regions within the country. If each state tried to be self-sufficient, we would all certainly be poorer. If Michigan set out to make its own textiles and North Carolina its own cars, they would both have to take resources out of their most efficient industries and put them into less productive ones. Yet illogically a great number of people are convinced that the situation is suddenly reversed when they reach the international frontier.

Comparative Advantage in Practice

In real life, of course, American importers do not ordinarily buy foreign cloth with automobiles. They usually use money. Whether they import or not depends on the money price of goods abroad compared with that at home. This complication is easy to handle, however. In the 1930's when the productivity comparisons used here were made, American wage rates averaged about twice the British levels.* America was the low-cost source of automobiles in spite of this because its 3 to 1 productivity advantage more than made up for its higher wages. On the other hand, in textiles where Americans produced only 1½ times as much per man-hour, British mills had lower money costs. With free trade, American cars and British textiles were in strong positions to undersell their rivals in the other country.

The Americans actually sent very few cars to Britain and they imported even fewer cotton textiles in those days. The main reason for this was that the keepers of the public trust in the two countries had seen fit to impose tariffs of 35% on textile imports into the United States and 33⅓% on auto imports into Britain—just about enough to erase any gains from trade.

The comparative advantages of the British and American manufacturers did show up, however, when they were shipping to third countries where neither of them had much special advantage. America exported more than four times as many automobiles as Britain in those days while British exports of cotton textiles were nine times as great as those of the Americans.† The American and British

---

* The ratios differed from industry to industry. Auto wages were just double the British but textile wages were 1.7 times the British. MacDougall, *op. cit.*, p. 707.

† *Ibid.*, p. 700.

people would both have been richer if their governments had permitted them to specialize in supplying each other as well as in dealings with the rest of the world. The fact that they did not was largely the doing of a great number of special interests in both countries seeking protection for particular industries.

TARIFF ARGUMENTS

The protectionists have an imposing line of arguments to present. Some are pure hokum and can be disposed of quickly. Others have an element of truth to them and deserve some attention.

In the hokum category is the old saw about "keeping the money at home." If I buy a suit from Britain, I have the suit but the British have the money. If I buy it in the United States, Americans get both the suit and the money. Won't we be better off? No! If I had bought the suit in Britain my money would have gotten back to some American exporter and we would have had the advantages of international specialization as well.

Again, some people think that trade restrictions raise incomes instead of lowering them because of the obvious help given to the protected industry. There can be little question but what total textile incomes are higher than they would be without the tariff, but the country as a whole is poorer because its resources are not being used efficiently. For every dollar the textile makers gain the rest of us lose more. Specifically, we pay more for our shirts and suits, and we produce, and therefore earn, less than we might because of the inefficient industries we are protecting.

"Pauper Labor"

A stock argument of the textile makers concerns the "pauper labor" of other textile-producing countries. How, they ask, can they hope to compete with British mills that pay only 60¢ an hour or, even worse, the Japanese who pay 13¢?* At first glance this complaint seems reasonable enough, but somehow many other American industries do not have the same problem. In fact, many American producers succeed in exporting considerable amounts to Britain and Japan in spite of wages far higher than in textiles. This should not be surprising. Their advantage in productivity more than makes up for their wage costs. That is why they are export industries.

Actually, the low wages abroad reflect conditions that make trade

* *Problems of the Domestic Textile Industry, op. cit.,* Pt. 1, p. 268.

worthwhile. To a considerable extent the reason different countries have comparative advantages in particular commodities is that they are endowed with different combinations of resources. Japan's low wages reflect her relatively great supply of labor and her lack of capital and natural resources. These low wages give her a big advantage in textiles, where labor is important, less help in automobiles, and practically none at all in chemicals. At the same time, her shortage of capital and of some natural resources hurts her badly in chemicals, somewhat in automobiles, and very little in textiles. The Japanese might turn the American mills' argument around and object that they cannot compete with the cheap land and capital of the United States.* If every industry in the world that has to compete with comparatively low cost foreign producers were able to get protection, there would be very little profitable trade left. In general, cheap foreign labor, or cheap foreign capital, or cheap foreign resources of any sort are a good argument for trade, not against it.†

The Scientific Tariff

Some of the bad logic of the cheap foreign labor argument has even been written into the law. In the Smoot-Hawley Tariff Act of 1930 (which is still our basic tariff law) the Tariff Commission was instructed to set import duties just equal to the difference between costs of production at home and abroad. What could be fairer? Producers at home and abroad were to start competing on the same footing. This is known as the "scientific tariff" approach.

Of course, if the commission takes its task seriously, it will eliminate trade completely. Doubtless we could raise our own bananas—in hot houses—if the commission would only put a duty. of $5 or $10 a pound and equalize the costs. The whole point to trade is that

---

* This is not as ridiculous as it may sound. Most European countries have severe restrictions on agricultural imports, primarily because their farmers cannot compete with what might be called "cheap American land."

† There is a grain of truth in the "pauper labor" argument. If America removed its restrictions on trade it would be textiles and other industries using great amounts of labor that would contract and automobiles and other industries using great amounts of capital that would expand. Labor's share of the national income would very likely fall as a result. The whole national income would be larger, however, and it would be possible to compensate the losers and have every one better off. This is really just one of a large number of instances where a public policy action hurts one group and helps another. If no action could be taken unless everyone gained, very little could ever be done. Incidentally, removing trade restrictions in countries like Japan would raise labor's share of their national income. In those countries it is capital-using industries that are protected.

foreign goods are cheaper, and the greater the differences between domestic and foreign costs, the greater the gain possible.*

Infant Industries

Not all of the tariff arguments are this absurd. Some have validity under the right circumstances, but they should all be weighed against the near certainty that trade restrictions will make the country poorer, at least at first.

The original basis for the textile tariff in this country was the "infant industry" argument. The new American mills at the start of the nineteenth century could not compete with England, but given a few years of protection, they would presumably be able to hold their own in the world. The tariff might make the country poorer at first, but in the long run it would result in a new, low-cost industry.

There are pitfalls in this approach. For one thing, it is hard to pick promising infants in advance, especially when anyone who has to compete with imported goods will gladly demonstrate his eligibility. If doubtful infants are protected, the country is apt to be saddled with high-cost rather than low-cost industries, which are very painful to eliminate once established. A good case can be made that we should never have had a woolen industry or at least not one of major proportions. It came into existence after a high tariff was installed in 1828 and it has had to have protection to survive ever since. The duty on wool fabrics may run to 50% or more today, depending on the quality of cloth involved. It is one of the highest American tariffs in effect, and still the industry is in trouble.†

Truly promising infants are likely to grow up even without protection. The southern textile industry was surely an infant industry half a century ago. It had to compete with the well-entrenched New

---

* It is possible for a country's prices to be so high that it cannot export enough to pay for its imports. However, with lower prices and wages, or with lower exchange rates, the goods in which it had the greatest advantage would be relatively cheap and would be exported, while the goods in which it had the least advantage would be expensive and it would still import. The problem of adjusting *total* imports to *total* exports is a complicated one which we simply do not have space for here.

† The comparative disadvantage of the American woolen industry showed up clearly in the productivity study cited earlier. Workers in American woolen and worsted mills produced only 1.35 times as much as their British counterparts and earned 2.0 times as much in wage rates. MacDougall, *op. cit.*, p. 707. To offset this disadvantage the average tariff at that time ran 85%! There have been some reductions in duty since.

England mills and had no shelter at all, but it developed just the same.

The American textile industries would have a very hard time arguing that they are infants today. In fact, part of the reason why cottons have lost their foreign markets in recent years is that the low income countries of the world are now taking the same path that the United States once took. They turn naturally to textile manufacturing, which requires little of the capital and skills that they find so scarce and meets demands that exist in even the poorest of populations. One of the first steps on the road to industrialization for such countries is to install a textile tariff.

Revenue

The tariff also provides a fine source of revenue for underdeveloped countries, mainly because it is easy to collect. Well-trained civil servants are usually scarce in such places and business record-keeping is rudimentary or nonexistent, so income and sales taxes do not work very well. To collect the tariff, however, all they need is a few customs officers in the ports checking the ships as they come in.

In the nineteenth century, the tariff was the leading source of federal revenue in the United States, too, but it produces only 2% of government receipts today. We just do not use it for revenue. If we did we would put the tariff on coffee, not textiles. Actually, we could increase our tariff revenues by *reducing* many of the duties now in effect to the point where something actually comes into the country and is taxed.

Military Self-Sufficiency

The textile makers, like almost everyone else seeking protection, have claimed that they are essential in time of war and should therefore be kept alive by trade restrictions in normal times. Again, there is something to this, or at least there used to be. A country can become so specialized that it is unable to survive a blockade. But protection costs something. There is plenty of room for doubt about how much the country should pay in peacetime inefficiency to have wartime textiles. It is hard to avoid the feeling that if the textile industry were subsidized directly, rather than through the tariff, the appropriation would not last very long. The military self-sufficiency argument, like the revenue argument, makes much more sense for other countries than for the United States. By and large, the industries in which we have a comparative advantage, those requiring capital and skilled labor, are just the ones required for modern war.

The military self-sufficiency argument may well be obsolete by now. It is hard to imagine that it would make any difference whether we had a textile industry or not in one of the 48-hour nuclear wars the press talks about today. In limited wars, such as the Korean War, our trade with the rest of the free world would probably not be interrupted.

Distributing the Burden

The basic valid case for a textile tariff today* is that we already have one and its removal would be a disaster for people committed to the industry. The workers and investors who went into the textile production in good faith did not put the tariff there. Eliminating it now would force great sacrifices upon them to improve the standard of living of the rest of us. It would not be so bad if the industry were a growing one. Then freer trade might just mean that fewer young people should enter the business and few new plants be built. But for the textile industries, more imports would mean even greater overcapacity and unemployment in an industry that already has some of the country's lowest wages and profits.

There are two ways of dealing with this case. The easiest answer is to keep protection intact and increase it if necessary. The industry would be helped, but the old inefficient allocation of resources would be passed on for yet another generation.

Alternatively, we can try to ease the adjustment of those who are displaced. This would call for the same sort of measures as those discussed in connection with the problem of New England: special unemployment compensation, training programs, tax adjustments, and special efforts to develop new industry in the distressed communities. This approach would eliminate the inefficient segments of the industry permanently and leave the country as a whole more productive.

The parts of the industry that survive in the face of foreign competition would have to do so by increased productivity. The government might contribute to this sort of adjustment also, by financing research and training as it has in agriculture.

---

* The cotton textile industry has some special claim to tariff protection because of the government's raw cotton program. The Department of Agriculture has been selling American cotton abroad at about 20% less than domestic prices in recent years. The American mills receive comparable subsidies on cloth that they export, but without a tariff foreign mills would have an advantage in selling the American textile market. Actually the duties on the cotton textiles more than make up for low raw cotton prices abroad.

Why We Have Tariffs

A natural question after all this is: if trade restrictions are so awful, why do we have them? The answer is that the gain from tariffs is concentrated on a small group of people but the loss is diffused throughout the whole country. If the woolen tariff were removed, the general public might have its over-all level of living increased by maybe one-half of one per cent. The export industries might find that because of the increased availability of dollars abroad they would be able to sell a few millions more in foreign markets, a tiny part of total present exports. For most consumers or exporters it would not be worthwhile to even write their congressmen. On the other hand, the congressmen from New England would be deluged with letters, telegrams, and delegations from the mill owners and workers who felt their lives were at stake. It is understandable that these congressmen should proceed to roll logs and scratch backs all over Washington until their constituents were saved. Since most congressmen have some constituents who need this kind of salvation, tariffs have a way of going up in Congress and are terribly hard to get down again.

SUMMARY

The textile industry probably comes as close to meeting the requirements of unfettered pure competition as is realistically possible. It is still an industry of large numbers and low concentration in spite of the mergers of recent years. Most gray goods are unquestionably standardized products and are sold on an almost perfect market. The same is not true of finished goods, but even here the expert buyers to which the industry sells and the ease with which successful finishes can be copied keep the industry close to pure competition.

By and large, textile markets perform as theory suggests they would. In the short run gray goods prices and mill margins fluctuate continuously in response to changes in demand and supply. Finished goods prices are more stable, but the quality of cloth sold at established price lines may change in response to market conditions, and this can amount to the same thing. Output is adjusted to these price changes by mills increasing or decreasing operations on their expensive night shifts and by the high-cost New England mills entering or leaving production.

In the long run the industry has consistently responded to relatively high or low profits by expanding or contracting capacity. High or low profits for particular constructions of cloth are usually eliminated in a matter of months by mills changing their products. Overcapacity has been eliminated by the liquidation of large numbers of high-cost mills, mainly in the North, but increasing productivity in the face of stagnant demand is constantly renewing the problem. Altogether, the industry deserves high marks for flexibility in the face of drastic changes in product, region, and method of production.

Life in this competitive market place has not been easy. Textile wages are exceptionally low and are rising more slowly than in most industries. Textile profits have been among the lowest in manufacturing except in the postwar booms. The competitive changes have left a wake of unemployment and distressed communities all over New England.

The industry has borne the brunt of an adjustment from which we all benefit. A good case can be made for regional development programs and similar policies by which the country as a whole can make adjustments in such industries less painful.

The case for trade restrictions to protect the industry is not nearly as good. Trade restrictions make the country as a whole poorer by preventing international specialization. We could produce more as a nation if we shifted our resources to those industries in which we have a comparative advantage and traded for other goods. For the most part we have a comparative *dis*advantage in textiles. They require large amounts of labor, which is relatively scarce in America, and small amounts of capital and natural resources, which are plentiful. Textiles are the sort of product we would import except for our relatively high textile tariffs.

In spite of the gains from international specialization, it may still pay a country to employ tariffs for revenue or defense or to protect promising infant industries. In the past some of these considerations were important in the United States, but they no longer make much sense here. There is a case for assisting depressed industries such as textile production, but trade restrictions, which impose inefficient industries upon us permanently, are a poor solution to the problem. A much better solution would be measures to ease the shift to more productive industries.

FURTHER READINGS

There are a limited number of studies of the textile industry available. One of the best is Jules Backman and M. R. Gainsbrugh, *Economics of the Cotton Textile Industry*, National Industrial Conference Board, 1946, but it is dated. A good current book on the British industry with many insights into the

American industry is R. Robson, *The Cotton Industry in Britain*, St. Martin's Press, 1957. Much of the recent information in the chapter came from the hearings of a subcommittee of the Senate Committee on Interstate and Foreign Commerce, *Problems of the Domestic Textile Industry*, 1958, and earlier hearings of the House Judiciary on *The Merger Movement in the Textile Industry*, 1955. The reports in 1952 and 1956 of the New England Governors' Textile Committee whose chairman, Seymour Harris, is a well-known economist, are also very useful. L. D. Howell, *Changes in the American Textile Industry*, Department of Agriculture Technical Bulletin 1210, 1959, brings together a great deal of statistical and descriptive material on the industry.

The idea of comparative advantage and the pros and cons of trade restriction are discussed in all principles textbooks. P. T. Homan, A. G. Hart, and Sametz, *The Economic Order*, Harcourt, Brace, 1958, Chapter 29, is a good one. The subject of international trade and payments is a large one and was barely touched here. Good texts on the subject is P. T. Elsworth, *The International Economy*, rev. ed., Macmillan, 1958, and Delbert Snider, *Introduction to International Economics*, Irwin, 1959. The particular example used in this book came from G. D. A. MacDougall, "British and American Exports, A Study Suggested by the Theory of Comparative Costs," *Economic Journal*, Dec. 1951.

5

PURE MONOPOLY— ALUMINUM BEFORE WORLD WAR II

THE MEANING OF MONOPOLY

Pure monopoly, when there is only one seller in some market, is at least as hard to find in practice as pure competition. Both are theoretical constructions, like the physicists' perfect vacuum or frictionless plane. They are approached but never quite reached in reality. They are worth discussing because they provide methods of analysis and evaluation that can be used to study the great bulk of American industry that falls between these two extremes. Moreover, while only a small number of industries even approximate pure monopoly, the cases that do have often been subject to unusual amounts of regulation and therefore have often been debated.

Many of the industries that approach pure monopoly in practice fall into the directly regulated public utility field. This is true of the electric power producers to be discussed in the next chapter. Outside of the public utility field, International Shoe Machinery is the only American producer of certain types of equipment, and American Metal-Climax controls about 90% of the world's molybdenum output. International Business Machines and International Nickel have both held similar positions until recently. Probably the outstanding example of an unregulated, nearly pure monopoly in recent

American history, however, is the Aluminum Company of America, which from 1893 to 1940 was the only producer of primary aluminum in the United States. The size of Alcoa, the importance of its product, and the significance of legal action connected with it make this industry particularly worthy of study.

Alcoa, like most of the other firms mentioned, was not completely free of competition. There were several large and efficient foreign producers capable of selling in the United States market. There was a substantial domestic stock of scrap aluminum at times. In addition, Alcoa had to compete with other materials such as steel, copper, and magnesium. The difference between such competition and that of Fords with Chryslers and Buicks is only a matter of degree.

Markets and Industries

Economists measure the degree of competition between two products by the *cross elasticity of demand*—the responsiveness of sales of one product to changes in the price of others. The formula for ordinary price elasticity in Chapter 2 was $\dfrac{\text{the percentage change in quantity}}{\text{the percentage change in price}}$

The cross elasticity of demand for aluminum with respect to copper is $\dfrac{\text{the percentage change in the quantity of aluminum}}{\text{the percentage change in the price of copper}}$ If this expression is high (say $+10$, so that a 1% increase in copper prices leads to a 10% increase in the quantity of aluminum sold) the products are good substitutes. If it is low, (so that a change in the price of copper has little effect on aluminum sales) the two commodities obviously do not compete very closely.

In pure competition the cross elasticity of demand between the products of two firms would be infinite. Farmer Brown could not raise his price for cotton by even a tiny amount without losing all of his customers to other producers. In *pure* monopoly the cross elasticity of demand between the monopolist's product and any other product would be zero. Regardless of the price of any other goods, the national insulin monopoly (if there were one) could sell the same amount of insulin. In realistic cases the cross elasticity of demand will fall between these two extremes. A firm will approach pure monopoly when the cross elasticity of demand between it and its nearest substitute is low.

Two firms whose products have high cross elasticities are said to be selling in the same *market*. The reader should note that it is consumer attitudes rather than technological similarities that make for such substitutability and the resulting competition. Park Avenue penthouses are hardly in the same market with lower East Side slums even though they are both technologically "New York rental housing." The penthouses could more reasonably be classified in the same market with technologically very different Cadillacs and trips to Europe.

The term *industry* may cause some confusion. In theoretical discussions it usually means all the firms selling on the same market, but in empirical studies it often refers to all the firms using a technically similar process, whether or not they compete. We are apt to hear about the rental housing industry or the American dairy industry even though penthouses and tenements, or California and Wisconsin milk producers, have few customers in common. Often there is no difficulty, of course. Firms in the aluminum, textile, wheat, automobile, and cigarette industries do compete among themselves.

The different firms of the United States can be thought of as being located on a "map" where differences between products are represented by distances between points. Whether any two of these are in the same market depends on what arbitrary standard we want to set. If we make a rule that two firms are in the same market any time that the cross elasticity of demand between their products exceeds zero, then most producers are parts of a single, enormous, national market, since most products compete with one another for the consumer's dollar. If we require an infinite cross elasticity, then only those products that are identical so that the points are superimposed in Figure 5.1 can be counted as in the same market. This is true of Farmer Brown's and Farmer Smith's cotton at point F in Figure 5.1. If we set a realistic rule like a minimum cross elasticity of 1.0 or 0.5, then some firms have no competitors and others many. The lower the cross elasticity we allow, the fewer the monopolists, and the more "competing" products for each firm.

Alcoa was in a position like point A on this "map." There were substitutes for aluminum, but they were not nearly such good substitutes as those available for the products of other firms. As a result Alcoa's nearest competitors at points B, C, and D (perhaps Bethlehem Steel, Anaconda Copper, and Dow Chemical) are shown as much farther away than are the nearest competitors of most firms on the "map."

The reader should not take this "map" too seriously. It is not suggested as a method of precise analysis. For one thing, to give a correct picture of the complex American economy we would probably need several more dimensions. There would be all sorts of difficulties in handling firms that produce many products, and comple-

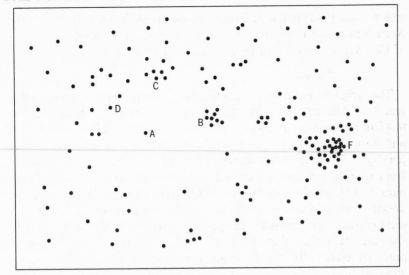

Figure 5.1. A hypothetical "map" of competing firms.

mentary goods, such as tires and gasoline, could not be mapped at all.

The reason for presenting this "map" is to suggest a useful way of thinking. Any "market" or "industry" we talk about is apt to have fuzzy edges, and the boundaries we draw will generally be more or less arbitrary. Most of the firms in America can be thought of as on a continuum, competing closely with neighbors and less so with more distant firms, and with greatly differing degrees of separation among neighbors. All but Farmer Brown are to some degree monopolists, and none is a pure monopolist in the strictest sense.

RESTRICTIONS ON ENTRY

Cases approaching pure monopoly cannot exist, or at least cannot involve significant monopoly profits, unless there is some restriction to keep new firms from producing closely competing goods. It is the entry of new producers that makes exceptional profits disappear in pure competition, and this cannot be permitted to happen if the monopolist is to have any real power. In some cases Nature or the government provides the monopolist with such restriction through the patent system, municipal utility franchises, or geographical concentration of natural resources. If Nature or Washington is not so benevolent, the monopolist can often perform the service for himself.

who formed the Pittsburgh Reduction Company in 1888 to exploit the Alcoa's long and profitable monopoly seems to be attributable to acts of God and Congress and to acts of Alcoa as well.

Patents

The original restriction working in Alcoa's favor, as with IBM and International Shoe Machinery, was a patent. Aluminum was not isolated in the laboratory until well into the nineteenth century, and until ·the 1880's it was so expensive that it was used mainly for jewelry. Then in 1886 Charles M. Hall, who had just graduated from Oberlin College, discovered that alumina (concentrated aluminum oxide) would dissolve in molten cryolite (sodium aluminum fluoride) after which it could be reduced to metallic aluminum by electrolysis. Hall patented his process in the United States at about the same time that Paul L. T. Heroult, an equally young Parisian, patented essentially the same discovery in Europe. After a false start with the Cowles Electric Smelting and Aluminum Company, Hall was able to get the backing of a group of Pittsburgh businessmen process.*

The patent provided the Pittsburgh firm with a monopoly in the United States until 1906, but not without a fight. There was an electrochemical revolution in the 1880's to which many persons besides Hall had contributed. As a result, the Pittsburgh Reduction Company had to contend with two other firms in a half-dozen patent cases over its first 15 years to establish its monopoly. First the Cowles firm with which Hall had initially worked was forced to stop using the Hall process after a price war and a series of infringement suits. Then Cowles threatened to re-enter the industry using a patent of another American, C. S. Bradley, which they claimed covered the Hall process. A third firm founded for the purpose by Grosvenor P. Lowrey, a patent lawyer, laid claim to the Bradley patent and also proposed to produce aluminum under it. The litigation over who owned the patent and what it covered lasted until 1903. It was finally determined that Cowles controlled it and that both the Bradley and Hall patents were necessary to produce aluminum. Lowrey was out and Cowles and Pittsburgh were left dependent on each other.

* The firm changed its name in 1907 to the Aluminum Company of America without changing its organization. Alfred E. Hunt was one of the original investors, Arthur V. Davis was the first regular employee (he retired as Chairman of the Board of the firm in 1957), Andrew W. and Richard B. Mellon began acquiring stock in 1890, held about 12% by 1894, and about a third of the stock from 1920 on. The Hunt, Davis, and Mellon families still hold a substantial part of the company's common stock.

Although the Cowles firm had originally set out to regain part of the market, after the 1903 decision it agreed to license its patent to the Pittsburgh firm exclusively in return for a cash settlement, royalties, and regular deliveries of aluminum at less than list price. By the early 1900's the Pittsburgh firm had undoubtedly developed a mass of unpatentable technical knowledge that newcomers would have had to learn the hard way. Even without patents, an established firm has an edge that competitors can only wear away after considerable expense and hardship.

In addition to creating a patent lawyer's paradise, all this litigation seems to have had the net result of re-enforcing monopoly. Two and possibly three aluminum firms could quite conceivably have resulted. Instead, the agreement of 1903 enhanced the aluminum monopoly by excluding Cowles and Lowrey and, since Bradley's patent expired three years later than Hall's, by extending the legal monopoly until 1909.*

Tariffs and Cartels

The government contributes to the maintenance of monopoly through the tariff as well as the patent. Using the Heroult patents, efficient producers of aluminum grew in Switzerland, France, and Britain at the same time that Alcoa was developing. Alcoa's exclusive position in the United States was assured in spite of these other firms as a result of a substantial import duty. The rates of duty are shown in Table 5.1. The 15¢ tariff was established two years after the Pittsburgh Reduction Company was founded; and, although the duty was subsequently reduced, the price fell faster. Except for the Underwood Tariff Act during World War I when the Europeans were not exporting anyway. Alcoa was continuously protected by a duty in the neighborhood of 20% of its domestic list price. In spite of this, as can be seen in Figure 5.2, the United States imported from 10 to 30% of its domestic aluminum consumption in all years after 1909 except for the deepest depression years and World War I. In effect, then, the government has required the American consumer to subsidize one of our most powerful monopolies by up to a fifth of its price over almost its entire life until World War II.

European cartels were quite possibly as important as the tariff in limiting foreign competition in the United States. Under the Hall and Heroult patents Pittsburgh Reduction and the major European

---

* For a more complete review of the Cowles-Pittsburgh-Lowrey litigation see Appendixes A and B of D. H. Wallace, *Market Control in the Aluminum Industry*, Harvard University Press, 1937.

firms had an agreement reserving their respective domestic markets. Since the expiration of the Heroult patent in 1901 Alcoa has not participated directly in such international agreements, but the Northern Aluminum Company,* then Alcoa's Canadian subsidiary, was a member of both the first (1901–08) and second (1912) cartels. It was not a party to the third cartel (1926–30), but in 1928 most of Alcoa's foreign assets were transferred to Alumininum, Limited (a

TABLE 5.1

UNITED STATES IMPORT DUTIES ON ALUMINUM INGOT
AND THEIR APPROXIMATE AD VALORUM EQUIVALENTS

Year	Import Duty (cents per pound)	Duty as a Percentage of Average New York Prices
1890–1894	15	7–15
1894–1897	10	17–25
1897–1909	8	20–33
1909–1913	7	20–34
1913–1922	2	6–10
1922–1930	5	18–24
1930–1939	4	17–20
1939–1947	3	15–21
1948–1951	2	10–13
1951–1956	1.5	6–8
1956–1957	1.4	5–6
1957–1958	1.3	5
1958–	1.25	5

Source: Office of Defense Mobilization, *Materials Survey, Aluminum*, 1956, pp. VII-23 and 24 and Tariff Commission.

Canadian corporation) which was a leading member of the fourth and most effective cartel (known as the Alliance Aluminum Company, 1931–46, effective 1931–38). Alumininum, Limited was technically separate from Alcoa but its stock was held by Alcoa's shareholders and its top officers had been drawn from Alcoa.

It is hard to believe that Northern Aluminum and Aluminium, Limited would consent to agreements that did not protect Alcoa's

* The name of the Northern Aluminum Company was changed in 1925 to the Aluminum Company of Canada (Alcan). This firm is now the leading operating company owned by Aluminium, Limited.

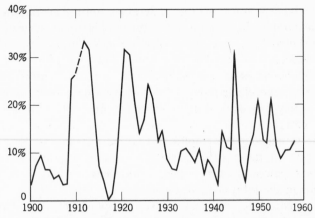

Figure 5.2.   United States aluminum imports as a percentage of apparent consumption. Source: Wallace, *op. cit.*, Appendix E for 1900–14.   Office of Defense Mobilization, *op. cit.*, p. VIII-27 for 1913–53. *Minerals Yearbooks* for 1951–58.

interests.   Alcoa could be provided for without its formal participation,* since the American tariff automatically gave Alcoa an inside track on about half the world aluminum market.   Figure 5.2 shows that the main inroads of European producers on Alcoa's preserve occurred in 1909–12, after the breakdown of the first cartel, and in 1919–26, when there was no cartel in existence.

Limitation of Resources

Alcoa seems to have been exceptionally profitable in the pre-World War I years and earned good profits throughout the 1920's (see p. 201).   Yet no successful domestic rival arose until 1940.   In some industries an initial patent monopoly like Alcoa's has been extended for many years by patents on refinements that, for practical purposes, prohibit the use of the original process long after the first patent has lapsed.   The Hall process was too simple for this.   None of the several possible new producers after 1909 seems to have been concerned about its right to use all the essential processes.

In a few industries geographical concentration of resources has accounted for monopoly.   The fact that a large part of the world's

* The Alliance Aluminum Company established output quotas and these probably did prevent exports to the United States even though no quotas on exports to this country were set.   The collapse of world aluminum prices in 1921 had occasioned a high level of exports to this country.   In the great depression of the 1930's, no comparable price collapse occurred so imports declined rather than increased.

known molybdenum ore is in a single mountain in Colorado makes it almost inevitable that the owner of that mountain, American Metal-Climax, should be a near monopolist. Something similar applies to the International Nickel Company in Sudbury, Ontario.

The key resources in the production of aluminum are bauxite (the original ore) and electric power.* Both are too widely available to be completely pre-empted by any single firm. In a sense, every bank of clay is a low-quality ore deposit, and high-grade bauxite is available throughout the tropics as well as in Arkansas, France, and the Balkans in the temperate zones. Similarly, means of developing electric power are everywhere, and Alcoa accounted for only a small part of the total demand for it.

Electric power sources and bauxite supplies both differ in cost, however. Bauxite may be expensive to process if low in aluminum content or high in silica (Arkansas) or if located far from refining facilities (India, Indonesia). Electric power may be relatively costly if it is technically expensive to develop (steam power until recently), if there are large numbers of other users to bid up its price (Niagara), or if it is far from bauxite and markets (Pacific Northwest). Until recently the only power cheap enough to compete in the aluminum industry was hydropower in isolated sites close to either bauxite deposits (the French Alps, Tennessee) or Atlantic shipping (Norway, Quebec).

During the period from 1900 to 1914 Alcoa bought up a large part of the then useful reserves of bauxite in the United States,† acquired a large part of the reserves in British and Dutch Guiana, established plants at Niagara, Massena, N. Y. (on the St. Lawrence below Lake Ontario) and Shawinigan Falls (between Quebec and Montreal), and bought up power rights along the length of the Little Tennessee River near Knoxville, Tenn. Alcoa had not taken all the low-cost hydrosites, of course, but it had started acquiring sites when the electrochemical industry was young, and any new competition in later years might find that Alcoa had an advantage they could not achieve.

There were several more or less serious attempts to enter the industry. In 1912 a group from L'Aluminium Français (the central

---

* It takes about 7 kilowatt-hours of electricity to produce 1 pound of aluminum—enough to keep a 100-watt light bulb burning all night every night for a week.

† The United States government claimed that Alcoa controlled 90% of the useful American deposits in an antitrust suit in 1912. Alcoa was not required to give up the deposits, though some restrictive provisions in the purchase agreements were stricken. It is interesting to note that a large part of present-day output by both Alcoa and Reynolds is from low-grade Arkansas bauxite, then considered unusable.

sales agency of the French aluminum industry) formed the Southern
Aluminum Company in the United States and began work on a plant
in North Carolina.* They expected to use ores from their own
reserves in France. During an inquiry in the 1920's representatives
from the firm indicated that American ore was available but that
French bauxite was cheaper.† The implication was that Alcoa controlled all the ore that could compete with foreign sources. The
French firm was never able to get into production. With the start
of World War I its foreign financing and foreign sources of bauxite
disappeared, and when it was unable to find American financial support it sold out to the only buyer, Alcoa, in 1915.

Just after World War I the Uihlein family (owners of the Schlitz
Brewery) began investigating sources of bauxite. Although they were
actually able to acquire some Guiana ore, they ultimately decided
against an attempt at aluminum production because it would be "too
much work."‡ They sold off their Guiana ore, a third interest going
to Alcoa.

In 1924, J. B. Duke (of the American Tobacco Company) appeared as another threat. Duke was developing power rights along
the Saguenay River, about 150 miles downstream from the city of
Quebec, and was looking for a use for his enormous potential power
supply in the wilderness. He and George D. Haskell, president of
Baush Machine Tool Company, made plans for aluminum production
there. Duke formed the Quebec Aluminium Company in December
1924, which had the assurance of European alumina and a good
chance at the bauxite deposits reserved for the crown in British
Guiana. But in January 1925, Duke's power company merged with
Alcoa and the rich potential of the Saguenay was added to Alcoa's
already substantial resources. Quebec Aluminium died aborning in
the process. One plant was built on the Saguenay, 1927–30, but the
bulk of its development waited until World War II. Haskell brought
an antitrust suit against Alcoa and the Duke estate, but the award
he was granted by a district court was reversed by the circuit court.§

The three attempts to enter the industry after the Hall patent
expired all depended on foreign bauxite, two of the three hoping to
get some of the Guiana bauxite, a large part of which seemed to be

* Office of Defense Mobilization, *op. cit.*

† Senate Document No. 67, 69th Congress, 1st Session, pp. 113–116 (a report by
the Justice Department in 1926 on alleged Alcoa antitrust violations).

‡ FTC Docket 1335, record p. 2204, quoted in Wallace, *op. cit.*, p. 131.

§ Haskell v. Perkins (1929), 31 Fed 2nd 54.

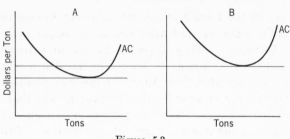

Figure 5.3

pre-empted by Alcoa.* Ultimately all three sold their ores, power rights, or plants to Alcoa, enhancing its already preponderant power.

Alcoa, at the end of the 1920's, appeared to hold a definite cost advantage. As seen by potential competitors in those days, the technical and locational character of different bauxite and power sites might be described by the average cost curves shown in Figure 5.3. Alcoa already seemed to operate or to have rights to the plants of type A. New firms would have to use distant ores and high-cost power and would have costs like plant B. There always was the possibility of low-cost sites if the methods were developed or the ores discovered, but these are easier to see by hindsight than in advance.

The experience of Reynolds Metals when it finally decided to enter the aluminum industry in 1940 bears this picture out. Reynolds planned to use bauxite from Indonesia,† and its power supply (from TVA) actually cost more than Alcoa's.‡ After the Pacific campaign of World War II began, Reynolds depended on Alcoa's Guiana ores and the low-quality Arkansas bauxite.

Since World War II the discovery of large reserves in Jamaica and the other West Indies has completely altered the bauxite picture. Cheap power for the wartime expansion was available from govern-

* Alcoa maintained at the time that its ore holdings were only prudent and that the tropics were full of bauxite deposits, a view that has been borne out by experience since.

† Bureau of Mines, *Minerals Yearbook,* 1941, p. 667.

‡ In 1949 power costs at Alcoa were 1.78¢ per pound and 2.32¢ at Reynolds, 91 F. Supp. 375. Power costs were identical on facilities in the Pacific Northwest. The differences occurred entirely in their plants in the Southeast (where Reynolds and Alcoa had their main plants in 1940). Incidentally, the difference in power cost is much less today (1.94¢ for Alcoa against 2.28¢ for Reynolds in 1957—153 F. Supp. 132). The change is due to the large-scale expansion of both firms and their increasing dependence on steam power.

ment plants in the Pacific Northwest and TVA. Since then, while there has been spectacular private hydropower development connected with aluminum production in Canada, most of the new United States plants have either made further use of government hydropower or have turned to Texas-Louisiana natural gas or lignite or Ohio Valley coal. Improvements in the efficiency of steam plants and the technical and sometimes political difficulties in developing the remaining American hydrosites have apparently been enough to divert practically all of the industry to the use of steam power.

Economies of Scale

Monopoly is inevitable in some industries because of costs. In competitive industries the plants available to a firm in the long run follow the pattern of Figure 5.4. There is presumably a least-cost plant (plant E) where all the advantages of scale are available. A bigger plant would have no advantage over plant E, and might even be less efficient because of administrative problems. A 5000-head dairy herd would probably be too badly handled to give the most milk per pound of feed.*

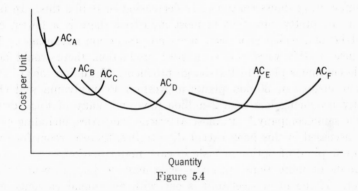

Quantity

Figure 5.4

However, there are industries where costs seem to continue to fall the larger the operation (Figure 5.5). A one-track railroad (plant A) might be the lowest cost way to serve Podunk Center (one train a day), but if there were enough traffic (one train each way) one track with sidings (plant B) would give lower costs; two tracks would be better: and three, four, five, etc., would continue to cut operating costs so long as demand warranted the growth. Even here there is probably a hypothetical lowest cost plant. A 26-track railroad might be so confusing that, even though no train ever had to

* See Chapter 3, p. 107.

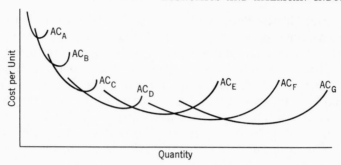

Figure 5.5

wait for another, an electronic computer would be needed at every switch to avoid accidents.

Competition cannot last in such an industry. A firm with capacity equal to the total demand can easily undersell any other producer. Even if the government could force 20 firm A's on such an industry it probably should not because of the high-cost methods that would result.

The reader should not conclude that all or even most of large-scale manufacturing shows continuously decreasing costs like this. In fact, he can be pretty sure that in most industries there is a lowest cost plant beyond which expansion offers no production advantages. For instance, if this were not so in steel production, there would be a single enormous plant in Pittsburgh producing 25 million tons of steel a year instead of 30-odd plants in western Pennsylvania and Ohio mostly producing less than 2 million tons and many of them owned by the same company.* In most American industries, including every one discussed in this book except the utilities, there is room for more than one plant of optimum scale in each major market.†

Plants of more than optimum scale may do just as well but no better. If the ideal steel mill is one with an annual capacity of 3 million tons, the way to build an efficient 6- or 9-million ton plant is to build two or three optimum plants side by side. The prospective builder of a steel mill would have the choice of average cost curves like those in Figure 5.6. The lowest cost per unit of the big plants would be no better than in the 3-million ton plant. Cost patterns like those in Figure 5.6 seem to occur in many industries. At least

* Bureau of Mines, *Minerals, Facts and Problems,* pp. 374–375. These figures were for 1954.

† See Chapter 11, pp. 512–513.

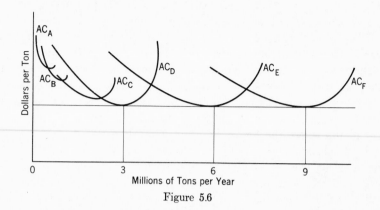

Figure 5.6

it is common to find firms of widely differing sizes surviving profitably side by side for years.

In some instances, firms might be so huge as to have cost *dis*advantages compared with those of more moderate size. They would be just too big for effective administration. It is quite possible that Figure 5.6, if extended off the page to the right, would show organizations at, say, 40 million tons capacity which could not get costs down to the level of the 3-million ton mill at any output. Such an outcome would be especially likely in the case of huge organizations combining large numbers of diverse plants.*

Economies of Scale in Aluminum

Alcoa's costs probably did help to preserve its monopoly. There are four major stages in aluminum production: (1) bauxite mining, (2) alumina refining, (3) electrolytic reduction (smelting), and (4) fabrication (into sheets, foil, bars, wire, pots and pans). On three of these levels (1, 3, and 4) reasonably small plants seem to be quite efficient. Bauxite mining is a fairly simple process and large-scale operations probably result more from concentration of holdings than from low cost.

Most of the fabrication processes are feasible on a very small scale. There were more than 24,000 firms in the field in 1955.† The bulk of these were producing final products, but there were some small firms at most of the intermediate steps. The one exception was the rolling

---

* This may have been true in steel for many years though it seems less so today. See Chapter 7, pp. 316–317.

† 84th Congress, 2nd Session, House Report 2954, Report of Subcommittee No. 3 to the Select Committee on Small Business, July 27, 1956, p. 7.

of heat-treatable sheet where Alcoa was the only producer for years*
and where only four firms have facilities even today.

Electrolytic reduction is a basically simple process. A single pot
has a capacity of about 1500 pounds per day (450 pounds in the
1930's) and a plant is expanded by just adding pots. In practice,
they are installed in series, but additional lines involve few savings.
One estimate has it that doubling the size of a reduction plant will
increase capital outlays by 90% or more by contrast to many chemical plants where the figure would be more like 50%.†

Hydroelectric sites may have affected the size of reduction works
when Alcoa was developing its own power. Some power sites might
require very large operations. If Alcoa had been permitted to develop the St. Lawrence below Lake Ontario, it would have had a single
power project large enough to provide for the entire American aluminum market until World War II. Aluminium, Limited is developing
a single site at Kitamat, British Columbia, with an ultimate capacity
of 550,000 tons, more than twice the North American market in 1940.

Actually, Alcoa operated several plants from an early date.
Through the late 1920's and the 1930's there were four smelting plants
in the United States and two in Canada. Since the 1930's electricity
for new plants has been purchased from the government or produced
in steam or gas plants so that power facilities no longer dictate
size. In 1959 there were smelting facilities at 22 different sites in
the United States.‡

In the refining of alumina from bauxite, however, there seem to be
substantial gains from size. Until 1938 there was only one alumina
plant in the United States. One study estimated that in 1940 a
100,000-ton alumina plant would have costs 20% higher than a
500,000-ton plant.§ One ton of aluminum takes 2 of alumina so the
latter plant would correspond to 250,000 tons of metal. The United
States did not reach an annual consumption of 250,000 tons of aluminum until 1942. Eight alumina plants were constructed from 1941 to

* 84th Congress, 2nd Session, House Report 2954, *op. cit.*, p. 10.

† Cecil H. Chilton, "Sixth Tenth Factor Applies to Complete Plant Costs,"
Chemical Engineering, Apr. 1950, pp. 112–114.

‡ *American Metal Market,* Mar. 17, 1959.

§ N. H. Engle, E. E. Gregory, and R. Mosse, *Aluminum, An Industrial Marketing
Appraisal,* Irwin, 1945, p. 222. Part of their cost differences depended on location
rather than size. They used the new private plants in operation in 1943. But even
eliminating locational items, there was a 10% difference in cost between the large
and small plants.

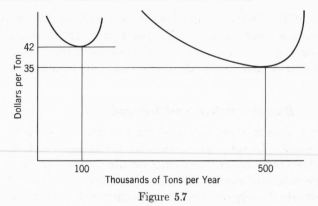

Figure 5.7

1958 with capacities ranging from 350,000 to 985,500 tons per year.*
For alumina production, costs appear to follow the pattern in Figure
5.7. Any firm that entered the industry before 1940 would have had
to depend on Alcoa or foreign supplies for alumina (and there was a
tariff of about 20% on alumina most of the time) or face higher
costs. Since alumina made up about a third of total costs, a firm
using a small plant would have a 7% disadvantage (about 1¢ a
pound).

Just the initial investment necessary to build an empire from the
mines through the reduction works so as to be independent of Alcoa
was enough to keep most contenders out. When Reynolds went into
production in 1940 it imported bauxite, bought power from TVA, and
built a small (100,000-ton) alumina plant which it no longer operates. In spite of the limited nature of its venture, Reynolds could
find no lenders but RFC (a government lending agency) even though
Reynolds was established in fabricating and had lots of family connections. In 1955 Reynolds estimated that completely new, fully
integrated facilities would cost $1500 per ton.† At that rate, an
alumina plant of optimum scale and the reduction and fabricating
facilities to go with it would cost a quarter of a billion dollars.‡
Even a high-cost 100,000-ton alumina plant and a 50,000-ton reduction mill would cost $75 million. New plant costs have risen sharply

* *Minerals Yearbook*, Pt. II, 1957, p. 242.

† Written answer to a questionnaire submitted by Reynolds Metals Company to
Subcommittee No. 3 to the Select Committee on Small Business. *Aluminum Industry*, Pt. II, p. 502.

‡ The latest firm to enter the industry spent $285 million building an integrated
set of plants around an alumina plant of 345,000-ton capacity. Ormet Corporation
press release, July 1, 1958.

since the 1930's, but even in those days aluminum was hardly an industry of low capital outlays. For many years only financial giants could even hope to break into it. Capital rationing, that kept the farms too many and too small, keeps aluminum producers few and big.

Buyers, Outlets, and Demand

In many industries demand is at least as great a problem as cost for new firms. In some cases, such as automobiles and cigarettes, existing firms build up such consumer loyalty that new producers have very little chance of success. Or again, new firms may have difficulty finding outlets if early producers have nation-wide systems of dealerships (automobiles or gasoline). Neither consideration could have been a major deterrent to competition in aluminum. Most buyers of aluminum are industrial users for whom aluminum is aluminum. Alcoa has provided plenty of technical assistance and undoubtedly has many loyal customers, but other firms could do the same.

Alcoa did expand into the fabrication of every kind of semimanufacture (sheets, bars, cable, wire, etc.) and some final products. They even established a subsidiary to produce and market aluminumware, bypassing the retailer. It is doubtful if this forward integration was especially designed to keep out competitors, however. Alcoa usually had a hard time finding fabricators ready to try their new metal. They often had to develop new uses themselves before anyone else would take the plunge.* Alcoa also seems to have used its fabrication as a means of price discrimination (see pp. 192–193). At any rate, the existence of a number of independent fabricators and the ready market for imports suggests that Alcoa's fabrication and selling activities were only a minor barrier to potential competitors in the 1920's and 1930's.†

If Alcoa did have any deliberate policy of exclusion, it lay in its expansion. Until the late 1930's Alcoa almost always had sufficient capacity to supply 70–90% of the United States market, and usually had facilities that could easily be expanded if the demand warranted this. If Figure 5.8 can represent the demand for aluminum and P_1 and Q_1 are Alcoa's price and output respectively, an added firm of anything like an efficient size would increase national capacity to Q_2, resulting in either overcapacity for both firms or a fall in

---

* E. R. Corey, *The Development of Markets for New Materials,* Harvard University Press, 1956, gives some interesting analyses of the problems of Alcoa in introducing such new uses as aluminum window frames and aluminum truck bodies.

† The situation since World War II is very different in this respect. See p. 217.

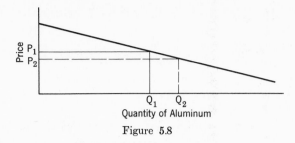

Figure 5.8

prices to P_2. Either way the new firm could not hope for the profits of the old one.

This was certainly Reynolds' experience. On August 1, 1940, the very day Reynolds signed its first RFC contract, Alcoa reduced the price of 99% ingots from 19¢ to 18¢.* The price was further reduced to 17¢ on November 18, 1940, and to 15¢ on October 1, 1941. The last reduction was the result of negotiations with the federal government,† rather than a direct attack on Reynolds, but it meant that Reynolds' profits would be lower nevertheless.

Barriers to Entry—Summary

It is not difficult to find reasons for Alcoa's long monopoly. Alcoa had all the trained staff in America, many of the lowest cost sources of supply, all the cost advantages of large scale, and a capacity capable of supplying most of the market in almost every year. Yet very few of Alcoa's actions were reprehensible by the standards of the general public. The popularly condemned sins of monopolists do not usually include too low costs, too rapid development of new products and markets, and too rapid expansion of plant. Monopoly might not have been inevitable in the aluminum industry to start with, but Alcoa, once established, was able to hang on to its exclusive position while usually staying well within the bounds of normal business ethics. Although challenged by some substantial business groups, Alcoa's monopoly was only broken when the government intervened.

MONOPOLY PRICE POLICY

Marginal Revenue

The fundamental difference between a perfectly competitive seller and a monopolist lies in the character of demand for their products.

* Written reply to questionnaire, Reynolds, Subcommittee No. 3, *op. cit.*, p. 501.

† Press release of Federal Loan Agency, Aug. 20, 1941 (FLA 359).

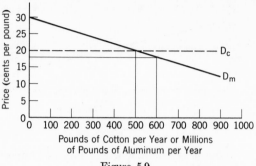

Figure 5.9

Figure 5.9 shows demand curves for a hypothetical cotton producer, Farmer Brown (D_c) and for a less hypothetical monopolist, Alcoa (D_m). Once Mr. Brown has an estimate of this year's market price, his only concern is production costs. He will get the same price no matter how many acres he harvests. On the other hand, if Alcoa has a 500 million-pound capacity and is contemplating another 100 million-pound plant, it will have to consider the 2¢ cut in price necessary to sell the extra output as well as production costs in the new mill. Alcoa would find it profitable to build the new plant if it could add more to receipts than to costs by so doing.

In the jargon of economists, it will pay a monopolist to expand so long as marginal cost is less than *marginal revenue*. As one might guess, marginal revenue is simply the extra receipts attributable to one more unit of output. So long as another pound of aluminum adds more to the total revenue of Alcoa than it does to Alcoa's total cost, the firm can improve its profits by producing more.

The extra receipts from the new plant in Figure 5.10 would certainly be less than the total value of sales at that plant. The new 100 million pounds sell for 18¢, bringing in $18 million a year, but the old 500 million must be sold at 18¢ too, instead of 20¢, so that Alcoa loses 2¢ a pound or $10 million a year on this count. It is only worth installing the new facilities if their annual total cost is $8 million

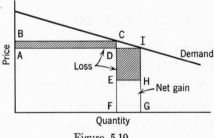

Figure 5.10

or less per year. In terms of Figure 5.10 the quantity FG produced at the new plant sells at a price of DF so that its total value can be represented by the area of the rectangle DEFGHI; but to find the marginal revenue we must subtract the area ABCD, which represents the loss on the sales that could occur at 20¢. Area ABCD = area DEHI (both shaded in Figure 5.10). This leaves only EFGH as a *net* addition to Alcoa's receipts. In any case, with a downward sloping demand curve, i.e., wherever there is a limit to what the firm can sell at any given price, the marginal revenue from expanded production is bound to be less than its market value.

Actually we have been careless with the term "marginal revenue." Generally it refers to the additional receipts *per unit of a small change* in output. Instead of speaking of $8 million from 100 million extra pounds, it would be more precise to say that the marginal revenue of the 550 millionth pound is 8¢ or that over the range 500–600 million pounds the marginal revenue averages 8¢ a pound.

Table 5.2 illustrates the calculation of marginal revenue. Columns

TABLE 5.2

A	B	C	D	E
		Total	Change in	
Price	Quantity	Revenue	Total Revenue	
(cents per	(millions	(millions	(millions of	Marginal Revenue
pound)	of pounds)	of dollars)	dollars)	(cents per pound)
30	0	0		
			28	28
28	100	28		
			24	24
26	200	52		
			20	20
24	300	72		
			16	16
22	400	88		
			12	12
20	500	100		
			8	8
18	600	108		
			4	4
16	700	112		
			0	0
14	800	112		
			−4	−4
12	900	108		

A and B are simply Alcoa's demand function. Column C is the total
revenue at each price—the products of the prices and quantities in
the first two columns. Column D shows the change in these totals
with each addition of 100 million pounds. For instance, when output
grew from 0 to 100 million there was a change in revenue of $28
million; when output grew from 100 to 200 million, revenue increased
from $28 million to $52 million or by $24 million, etc. Column E
shows an approximation of marginal revenue on a per pound basis;
the change in total revenue (column D) is divided by the change in
total output (100 million in each case).

The demand and marginal revenue schedules in Table 5.2 (columns
A and E) are plotted in the upper part of Figure 5.11, and the total
revenue schedule (column C) in the lower part. As output expands,
revenue increases but at a declining rate because of the falling price.
The additional receipts attributable to the first six 100 million-pound
additions to output are indicated by the vertical distances $\triangle R_1$, $\triangle R_2$,
etc., on the lower chart. To find marginal revenue these must be
divided by the corresponding changes in quantity which are all equal
in this case. Marginal revenue $\left(\dfrac{\triangle R}{\triangle Q}\right)$ then clearly declines as output grows.

Marginal Costs

A monopolist must consider both his costs and his receipts. His
marginal costs might follow the pattern described for farmers and
textile makers in earlier chapters and increase with output. Alternatively, they might remain constant or even decrease over the relevant range of operations.

It is commonly supposed that marginal costs in much of manufacturing are fairly close to constant. Whether Alcoa operates at
10% of capacity or 90%, it would presumably have to use another
7 kilowatt-hours of electricity, another 2 pounds of alumina, and
another 2 man-minutes of labor to produce another pound of aluminum. If this were correct, Alcoa's costs would look like those in
Figure 5.12. Every extra pound of aluminum would add perhaps
8¢ to total costs right out to capacity. As a result, the marginal cost
and average variable cost would coincide in the horizontal straight
line at 8¢ a pound, as in the upper diagram in Figure 5.12. Average
cost would still decline, however, because Alcoa would have its very
substantial fixed costs to spread over more and more aluminum as the
output increased.

Alcoa's costs have never fit this pattern exactly. The firm usually
had several plants of varying ages, and the older plants were apt to

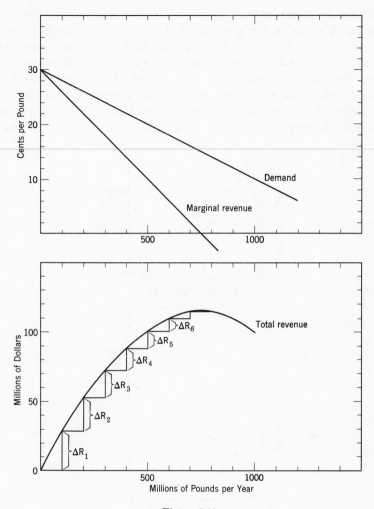

Figure 5.11

be poorly located or to contain obsolete equipment because of changes in technology, markets, or power costs. At low levels of output Alcoa could stick to its low-cost facilities, but when they reached capacity it would have to turn to more expensive plants.*

* A good example of this occurred during the Korean War. The government paid Alcoa a subsidy equal to the extra power costs of the company's high-cost facilities at Massena and in North Carolina. The government was able to get more aluminum and at the same time economize its total subsidy bill by subsidizing only the high-cost plants which would have required a higher price to come into production.

In the long run, when Alcoa could replace its obsolete plants or build more capacity, the assumption of constant costs would be more plausible. If Alcoa could always get another 100 million pounds of aluminum by building another plant like the last one, it would have costs like those in Figure 5.13. Given enough time to build more capacity, it could always produce another pound of aluminum for 10¢ more. The reason that the long-run marginal cost is higher than the short-run marginal cost in this example is that it includes costs

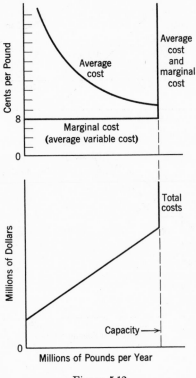

Figure 5.12

that were fixed in the short run. To get another pound of aluminum in the long run, the company would have to provide more plant as well as more electricity, alumina, and labor.

The long-run marginal cost curve does not *have* to be a horizontal straight line, of course. It might rise because Alcoa would have to turn to more expensive sources of materials or power or because of administrative problems. It might also decrease if there were continuing economies of scale, something that is possible in monopoly though not inevitable.

We will make the assumption of constant costs in the long run in this chapter because (1) it is at least plausible over a wide range of outputs, and (2) it makes the analysis considerably easier. Decreasing costs in the long run, which might also have been a plausible assumption for Alcoa before World War II, are analyzed in the next chapter.

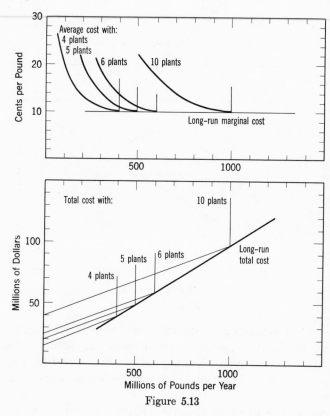

Figure 5.13

Monopoly Price in Theory

The most profitable output and price for a monopolist depends on his marginal cost and marginal revenue. If Alcoa had cost and revenue curves like those shown in Figure 5.14, its most profitable output would be at 500 million pounds per year. At any lower output the marginal revenue would be greater than the marginal cost. An-

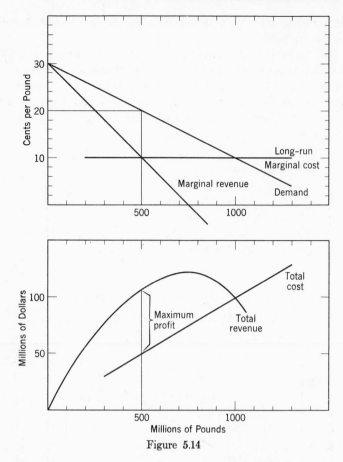

Figure 5.14

other pound of aluminum would add more to receipts than to costs so profits would increase or losses decrease as output expanded. Beyond the 500 million level, marginal revenue would be less than marginal cost, so profits would decrease or losses increase as output grew.

In terms of the lower diagram in Figure 5.14, total revenue rises faster than total cost out to 500 million pounds, meaning that the two curves are diverging and the difference between them, total profits, is growing. Beyond 500 million, total cost is rising faster than total revenue so the two curves are converging. Right at 500 million, total cost and total revenue are farthest apart, so in this example Alcoa's profits would be at a maximum.

From Alcoa's point of view 500 million pounds per year might be the best level of output, but a higher output would be preferable for the public as a whole. According to the demand curve, consumers were ready to pay 20¢ for another pound of aluminum that would have cost only 10¢ to produce. This means that another kilowatt-hour of electricity and another man-hour of labor taken out of the textile industry, for example, and employed by Alcoa would have produced aluminum worth more to the public than the textile products given up. The country would stand to gain from more aluminum production. Alcoa decided the scale of aluminum operations, however, and since Alcoa would have less profits at the higher output the extra expansion was not likely to be forthcoming. Of course, Alcoa was eager to sell more aluminum but in this example it was not willing to charge less than 20¢ to accomplish that goal.

Whether a monopolist sets his price far above marginal cost or only slightly above depends on the elasticity of demand for his product. If its elasticity is high he can increase sales greatly by making only small price cuts, so price will be only a little way above the marginal cost. On the other hand, if elasticity is low, he cannot gain very much by price cuts, so the most profitable price will exceed marginal cost by a wide margin. Since commodities with high elasticities are those with good substitutes, this amounts to saying that monopolists will be less inclined to take large markups when their customers have good alternatives. It should come as no surprise that monopoly power is not very great when there are competing products nearby.

Alcoa's Price Policy

To go by the public statements of its officers, Alcoa used a very different method to reach its prices during the 1920's and 1930's from that described just now, but the results may have been similar. One officer described the company's policy in the following terms:

In setting our prices we set them so that if, and when, and as we have a normal expected load in our plants, we will make approximately 15 to 20 per cent return on the capital used in connection with the operations for producing that particular aluminum commodity.

Now that results after taxes—over the long period of years—that results in a profit to the company of about 10 per cent on the equity capital in the business. That is the history that has been shown and litigated over in the antitrust case, and I think is not disputed at all. But, that is the basis on which we set our prices.*

* Statement of I. W. Wilson, president of Alcoa, in *House Judiciary Study of Monopoly Power,* 82nd Congress, 1st Session, Serial 1, Pt. 1, *Aluminum,* 1951, p. 634.

The "normal expected load" he refers to is reported elsewhere to be 70% of capacity.* With the prices that Alcoa set, Alcoa would earn more than its target profit whenever output exceeded 70% of capacity and would earn less whenever it fell short of 70%. The price would change if there were changes in cost but not in response to year to year changes in rate of operation.

This does not sound much like setting marginal cost equal to marginal revenue, but it *could* amount to the same thing over the years. If the target profit were the management's best guess about the most they could make, taking one year with the next, they would in effect be setting a price where marginal cost equaled marginal revenue even if they did not operate in such terms intentionally. It is true that their price policy would result in prices that remained stable regardless of output, and, since demand shifts about continuously, their prices could not have been the most profitable possible on every day of every year. Counting the cost of price changes in terms of management time, accounting adjustments, new catalogues, and possible customer antagonism, however, stable prices may well have been more profitable than constantly changing prices, especially since the leaders of Alcoa could never have had more than a rough idea of demand. At any rate, if the analysis can tell us even approximately what price will be charged it will tell us quite a bit.

The fact that the managers of Alcoa did not use marginal cost and marginal revenue explicitly in reaching their price and output does not make the formal theory of monopoly price useless. One economist has likened the analysis to a theory of passing a truck. How many feet does a car accelerating from 35 to 55 miles per hour need to pass a truck going 35? The analysis necessary to solve such a problem precisely would be very complicated—probably far beyond the capacity of the average motorist. Yet the vast majority of us obviously do succeed in passing trucks, often with little to spare. A theory that tells us how much space we need to do it and therefore how far from the crest of the hill we should paint the yellow lines would be useful, even though nobody ever applied the theory consciously when driving a car. Similarly, a theory that tells us what price a firm will select if it maximizes profits may give us a basis for evaluating that price which can be useful, even if the firm never consciously applies it in making company price policy.

* A. D. H. Kaplan, J. B. Dirlam, and R. F. Lanzillotti, *Pricing in Big Business*, The Brookings Institute, 1958, p. 26.

PRICE DISCRIMINATION

Price Discrimination in Theory

So far we have treated Alcoa's pricing policy as if all aluminum were identical and Alcoa had to charge all customers the same price. Realistically, monopolists can often enhance their profits by selling the same goods to some customers at higher prices than others are charged, i.e., by engaging in *price discrimination.*

The reason that price discrimination can increase monopoly profits is that different customers react differently to price changes. For instance, in the 1930's the aircraft industry probably would not have stopped using aluminum even if the price had been two or three times what it actually was. There was no other cheap, easily worked light metal to turn to. On the other hand, the demand for aluminum for electric transmission cable where it had to compete with copper was very elastic. Aluminum would be too expensive to be used for cable if its price was more than double that of copper. On the other hand, when its price fell below that of copper after World War II, aluminum took over the whole market.*

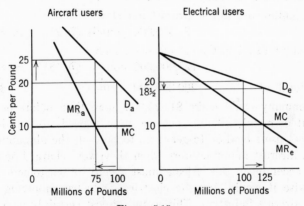

Figure 5.15

In such a situation Alcoa could enhance its profits by charging the electrical users less than the aircraft manufacturers. The aircraft and electrical demand for aluminum at that time might have looked like curves D_a and D_e in Figure 5.15. Each curve has its own marginal revenue curve reflecting the different elasticities. To make

* Aluminum weighs less than copper, so a pound of aluminum provides considerably more cable than a pound of copper.

maximum profits here, Alcoa should set a price in each market so that marginal cost is just equal to the appropriate marginal revenue. This means it should charge a high price where demand is less elastic and a low one where it is more so. Any time that Alcoa is tempted to cut price and sell more aluminum, it should do so in the market where the *marginal revenue* is highest, not necessarily where the *price* is highest.

This is a difficult piece of analysis. It may help to work out an illustration. In Figure 5.15 the marginal cost is 10¢ a pound regardless of where the aluminum is sold. If Alcoa had to sell to all comers at the same price, it would make its greatest profit at a price of 20¢.* At that price it would be receiving:

on aluminum sold to the aircraft industry:
$$100,000,000 \text{ pounds @ } 20¢ = \$20,000,000$$
on aluminum sold to the electrical industry:
$$100,000,000 \text{ pounds @ } 20¢ = \$20,000,000$$

or a total of   200,000,000 pounds $40,000,000

Now if Alcoa charged the aircraft industry 25¢ instead of 20¢ for its aluminum, Alcoa could divert 25 million pounds into electrical use. Then the company would receive:

on aluminum sold to the aircraft industry:
$$75,000,000 \text{ pounds @ } 25¢ = \$18,750,000$$
on aluminum sold to the electrical industry:
$$125,000,000 \text{ pounds @ } 18\frac{1}{2}¢ = \$23,125,000$$

or a total of   200,000,000 pounds $41,875,000

The company could make $1,875,000 more than before on the same amount of metal. This is because it only needs to cut the price to electrical users by 1.5¢ to get them to take all the aluminum released by the aircraft manufacturers when they were charged 5¢ more!

To accomplish this Alcoa must keep its customers separated. Otherwise it would find the electrical industry supplying aluminum to the aircraft industry. This would almost certainly have happened if Alcoa had tried to sell ingot aluminum at different prices to the two industries. To keep its customers apart Alcoa had to become a fabricator. Then it could set a lower price on the aluminum contained in cable than on strong alloy sheet for aircraft.

* To work this out, add up the total amounts that Alcoa could sell in the two markets taken together at each price. The result is the over-all demand for aluminum. Now derive the marginal revenue from this total demand. The most profitable single price in the combined market would be the one that yielded sales of 200 million pounds where marginal revenue equals 10¢.

Of course, different products, such as transmission cable and strong alloy sheet, usually have different fabricating costs. Alcoa would be engaging in *price discrimination* in the economic sense of the term if it were taking a larger markup over costs on some commodities than on others.* In effect, it would be charging more for the aluminum included in some of its products than in others.

Price Discrimination at Alcoa

Alcoa has a large number of cases of price discrimination in its history. The company has more than a half century of remarkable growth behind it mainly because it was continuously finding further uses for its new metal, and in most cases the new uses meant taking over markets from old established materials. Alcoa has almost always had some product or other on which it was taking less than its target profit in an attempt to win new customers.

Before World War I, when it was trying to popularize the use of aluminum in the fabrication of consumers goods, it discriminated in favor of the buyers of pots and pans. In the 1920's and 1930's it maintained low margins on transmission cable to compete with copper, but when copper was priced out of the market after World War II, Alcoa set prices on cable that were in line with those on its other products. Similarly, Alcoa was unable to attain its target return on structural aluminum shapes because they could only be sold if their prices did not exceed those of corresponding structural steel shapes by more than a small margin.† In each of these cases Alcoa was cutting price where additional sales were most likely to be forthcoming while maintaining its usual profit objectives on other goods where demand was probably less elastic.

Alcoa was able to pursue a policy of price discrimination because it was a monopolist in a field where entry was highly restricted. In the textile industry price differences between products which did not reflect cost differences disappeared rapidly as firms shifted toward the more profitable lines. This could not happen for most aluminum products. In a few types of fabrication, however, entry was relatively easy and in such instances Alcoa was sometimes unable to maintain its target profits even when the over-all demand for the product involved did not seem very elastic. For instance, in transmission cable once more, the high profits after World War II induced a large num-

* This often is not discrimination in legal terms, however. A producer may often take wildly different profits on two different products and be within the law. See Chapter 9, pp. 403–404.

† All of these examples came from Kaplan et al., *op. cit.*, pp. 33–36.

ber of firms to install stranding equipment. By 1954 Alcoa and the other primary producers were having to reduce their margins on cable even though copper was now too expensive to offer effective competition. This time they were meeting the price competition of these new fabricators.* Of course, this meant that Alcoa was discriminating again, this time in favor of the markets where it had many competitors. The over-all demand for aluminum cable might not have been very elastic, but the demand for Alcoa's cable certainly was in view of all the alternatives available to buyers.

Not all instances of price discrimination are attributable to differing elasticities of demand in different markets. Some discrimination is almost inevitable if a firm is to avoid impossible amounts of paper work. Technically speaking, a shoe store discriminates when it charges two customers the same price even though one takes two minutes to be fitted while the other keeps a salesman for an hour and a half. The post office also discriminates when it charges 4¢ for a letter whether it goes from New York to Hoboken or to Honolulu. Alcoa has been discriminating in the same way consistently since 1921, when it started selling aluminum products at identical prices throughout the country. Users near Alcoa's plants have paid just as much for their aluminum as customers at the other end of the country even though Alcoa had to pay much less freight in getting it to them.†

Another possible reason for price discrimination would be to drive competitors out of business. Alcoa has been accused of doing this in the case of sheet in the late 1920's. In a year and a half in 1926 and 1927 it reduced the margin between aluminum ingot and certain types of sheet from 16¢ a pound to 7¢ a pound and then kept it there until 1932. By their own statements, 7¢ was not even enough to cover their own fabricating costs. Two independent rollers of aluminum sheet brought antitrust suits against Alcoa, which, after much litigation, were settled out of court. Later in another case brought by the Justice Department, the courts ruled that Alcoa had employed an illegal "price squeeze" against its competitors. Actually Alcoa's policy may not have been meant to do the smaller firms in at all. Alcoa may have simply been cutting price in a market where demand seemed particularly elastic. The development of hard aluminum alloys and of stainless steel brought aluminum sheet into closer competition

---

* *Ibid.*

† Incidentally, this is one of the reasons that the aluminum industry has been shifting back to the Mississippi and Ohio Valleys in recent years. Power costs have not been rising but freight costs have. As a result the advantage that the Pacific Northwest once had in cheap hydropower has been overcome by the rising cost of hauling aluminum to the industrial centers in the East and the Midwest.

with steel than previously. There was even talk at the time of aluminum automobile bodies, though the change was never adopted. The price cuts may have been aimed at winning such big new markets —something that Alcoa could not do without hurting the other fabricators.*

Finally, some sellers have been forced to make special price concessions in negotiations with exceptionally powerful buyers and have in effect discriminated against the rest of their customers in the process. The huge firms of the automobile industry have often been able to insist on special discounts from their suppliers. In the late 1950's the primary aluminum producers, beginning with Reynolds, agreed to sell molten aluminum to the automobile producers at prices 10% below the list price of aluminum pig,† a price concession that many in the trade felt exceeded any cost savings.

By and large, Alcoa discriminated in pricing at just about the points where theory would have suggested they should to maximize profits. It has generally charged less where the elasticity of demand for its product was high because of competing products or because of actual or potential competition from other fabricators. It is important to notice that Alcoa was quite ready to break its general pricing rules when such deviations offered to enhance its profits. This lends plausibility to the notion that Alcoa's over-all pricing policy was a rough rule-of-thumb way of reaching its most profitable price and output. When its general price policy did not seem to lead to optimum results, Alcoa's management would simply discard it.

PERFORMANCE

Price and Output in Practice

Alcoa's actual price and output performance in its years as an almost pure monopoly were very impressive. Figure 5.16 compares

---

* This case is based on Wallace, *op. cit.*, pp. 382–388. Alcoa's statement about fabricating costs were quoted by Wallace from Baush Machine Tools v. Alcoa, Exhibits 133 and 313.

Alcoa could have tried to break into the new sheet markets without discriminating by cutting all aluminum prices, but this was not a very likely policy from a profit-maximizing corporation.

† Agreements between Reynolds Metals Company and General Motors reproduced in *Aluminum Industry,* Hearings of Subcommittee No. 3 of Select Committee on Small Business, House of Representatives, 1958, pp. 403–410. GM saves not only 10% of the average list price of the previous month but also Reynolds' average transportation cost on pig delivered in the previous quarter.

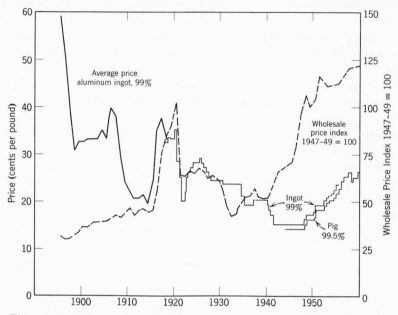

Figure 5.16.   Primary aluminum prices and wholesale prices.   Source: Aluminum prices, Office of Defense Mobilization, *op. cit.,* p. IV-6 (1895–1918), and correspondence with Alcoa (1918–59).   Wholesale price index, *Economic Almanac* and *Economic Report of the President,* 1960.

primary aluminum prices with wholesale prices since the turn of the century, and Figure 5.17 compares American aluminum production and consumption with over-all industrial production over the same period.   In both comparisons Alcoa far outperformed the economy generally.   Aluminum prices declined regularly.   The only important price increases from 1906 to 1949 were those connected with World War I, when other prices rose more, and with the tariff increase of 1922.   By 1949 aluminum prices were only slightly more than a third of their 1906 levels and just about half of those in 1926.   Wholesale prices generally were respectively three and two *times* as high in 1949 as in the two earlier years!   In the same period aluminum production grew roughly three times as fast as industry generally.

This is hardly the sort of price and output policy that ordinarily comes to mind in discussions of monopolistic exploitation, but it is what might be expected of a monopolist with a new product in a rapidly growing market.   Production costs for such commodities usually fall because of improving techniques, accumulating skills, increasing scale, and development of efficient sources of supply.   In the case of aluminum, electric power costs in particular were dropping rapidly because the generation of electricity was itself a new industry.

Even a profit-maximizing monopolist can be expected to cut price if his costs fall. In Figure 5.18 a decline in marginal cost from MC_1 to MC_2 makes it worthwhile to cut price from P_1 to P_2. The result is an increase in output until the marginal revenue gets down to the new marginal cost. Alcoa's costs were unquestionably falling in the periods of its main price cuts (see pp. 219–220).

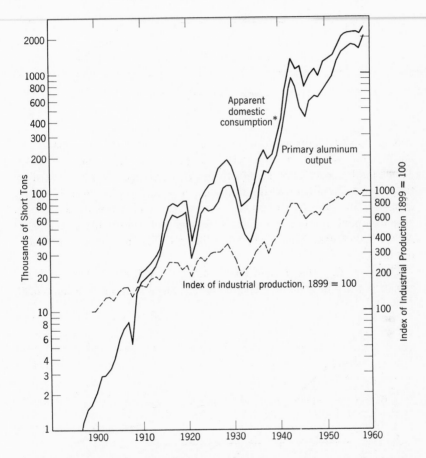

* Apparent domestic consumption is output plus scrap recovery plus imports minus exports. 1959 production and consumption estimates.

Figure 5.17. Aluminum consumption and output. Source: Office of Defense Mobilization, *op. cit.*, pp. VIII-26–28; J. E. Rosenzweig, *The Demand for Aluminum,* University of Illinois Press, p. 64; *Minerals Yearbook; Historical Statistics of the United States;* and *Federal Reserve Bulletins.*

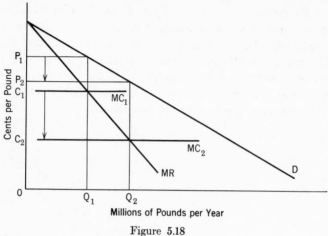

Figure 5.18

A monopoly might also find it profitable to cut price if demand for its product became more elastic. Figure 5.19 shows such a case. This might account for some of Alcoa's price reductions at various times. As new alloys made aluminum a feasible substitute for other materials in one after another market, Alcoa might very well have been tempted to win the new customers not attainable previously. As we have seen, Alcoa certainly did just this in pricing particular products.

The mere fact that a firm has a monopoly will not prevent it from expanding production in response to increased demand. Figure 5.20

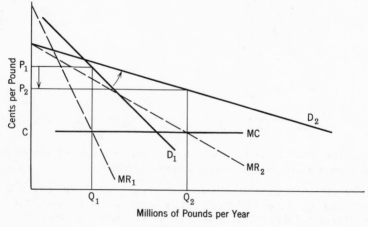

Figure 5.19

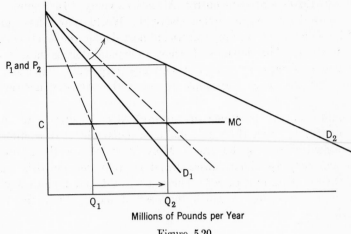

Figure 5.20

shows such an increase. With constant marginal costs, the most profitable reaction of the monopolist turns out to be to increase output from Q_1 to Q_2 and leave price the same as demand shifts from D_1 to D_2. There can be no doubt about the rapid increase in demand for aluminum over the history of Alcoa's monopoly. It was due, of course, to the new uses that were constantly appearing for the new metal. Alcoa itself did its best to develop those new uses and hence to shift the demand curve upward and to the right.

Building Capacity

In Alcoa's case there could have been little question about the profitability of expanding output so long as it could be done from existing plants. Where increased production required additional capacity, however, the company was faced with a different sort of problem. On a number of occasions it did not erect enough new facilities to meet the demand that soon developed.

Shortages due to inadequate capacity have been a recurrent problem in the aluminum industry. During the period 1940 to 1945 and 1950 to 1955, World War II and the Korean War were obviously the main reason for the difficulty, but a shortage also developed during the mid-1920's when military demand was not important. Alcoa had expanded rapidly during World War I and appeared to have excess capacity when the war ended. The depression of 1920–21 saw an unparalleled collapse of aluminum prices and a drop in output to less than half of capacity. After that the company was very cautious about expanding further. The demand for aluminum grew rapidly during the 1920's and soon outran Alcoa's capacity. In Figure 5.17 Alcoa's output did not rise much above the World War I level until 1928,* by which time consumption was almost double the level reached during the war. The slowness of Alcoa to expand during these years resulted in shortages and delays in delivery, large-scale imports (see p. 171), and the several attempts to enter the industry mentioned earlier.

It would probably be wrong to interpret Alcoa's slowness to build more capacity between 1918 and 1927 as a monopolistic restriction of supply aimed at raising the price. More likely, it was the result of a conservative guess about future demand. Why run big risks until the market is definitely there? There is an old and famous saying in economics according to which the best of monopoly profits is a quiet life.

Alcoa's Profits

Alcoa's reported profits on owner's equity are shown in Figure 5.21. Just as in the textile industry, these accounting "profits" are only rough approximations of "profits" in the economic sense. Unlike textiles, however, aluminum profits are probably understated for several reasons:

1. Some of the economic profits of Alcoa were transformed into rents. The owners of the Bradley patents and the Duke rights on the Sagueney River were in a position to exact a share of the monopoly profits that they were conveying to Alcoa. The profits were still there, but someone else besides the old owners of Alcoa was enjoying them. On Alcoa's books they appeared as "costs."

2. Some of Alcoa's profits went to the firm's employees as exceptional wages, as well. Alcoa regularly pays wages well above the average for the regions in which its plants are located. While this may be partly due to special skills, it seems reasonable that Alcoa was letting its employees in on its good fortune.†

* Alcoa had built four pot rooms in 1918 but had never equipped them because the war ended before they were complete. It only began installing equipment in 1927. (Based on information from Alcoa.) Canadian output, which was controlled by Alcoa, did not get much above the wartime peak until 1927 either. European capacity expanded considerably faster in those years, but there was still a world shortage of aluminum. See Wallace, *op. cit.*, pp. 291–292 and 307–308.

† Aluminum wages have sometimes been compared unfavorably with steel wages, a comparison that is relevant because the United Steel Workers organizes the majority of aluminum workers. However, the steelworkers are some of the best paid workers in American industry (see Chapter 10, p. 482) and the aluminum workers do not lag far behind them.

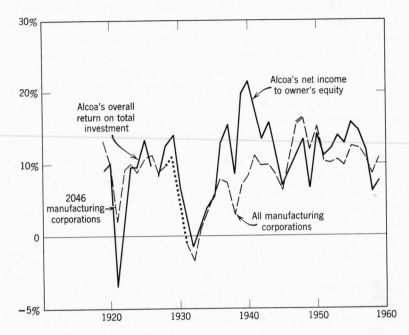

Figure 5.21. Profits after tax as a percentage of owner's equity—Alcoa and all manufacturers.

Notes: Alcoa's profits before 1926 are income plus interest as returns on total equity plus long-term debt. Since interest payments are fixed, this is probably lower in prosperous years and higher in bad years than income on owner's equity.

Alcoa revised its depreciation policy in 1955. Profit figures for 1947–55 have been revised to reflect this change. Only figures for 1951–54 actually differ appreciably from those originally reported.

Profit figures for all manufacturing after 1947 were taken from samples of corporate reports made quarterly by the Federal Trade Commission and the Securities and Exchange Commission. The Internal Revenue series used for 1931–48 (and for 1931–58 in other chapters) are not strictly comparable with Alcoa's financial reports because of various special income tax deductions. The difference between the Internal Revenue series and the FTC-SEC series is not very serious until the Korean War, but rapid amortization since then has made the Internal Revenue series consistently 1–2% lower. The FTC-SEC data will be used whenever profit figures for particular industries come from regular financial statements.

Source: Alcoa: Return on total investment, 1919–26, Wallace, op. cit., pp. 538–546. Net income to owner's equity, 1927–48 and 1956–59, Moody's Industrial Manual, 1947–55, 153 F. Supp. 132.

All manufacturing: 2046 manufacturers 1919–27, R. C. Epstein, Industrial Profits in the United States, National Bureau of Economic Research, 1934, pp. 56, 156. All manufacturing corporations with balance sheets 1931–48, Bureau of Internal Revenue, Statistics of Income. 1947–59, FTC-SEC, Quarterly Financial Reports, United States Manufacturing Corporations.

3. In addition, Alcoa seems to have been exceptionally conservative in its accounting policy, depreciating its plant and equipment considerably more rapidly than other firms in the industry. This would tend to understate its profits so long as the firm's plant is growing rapidly.*

4. Finally, it has been suggested that in the 1920's, at least, Alcoa's profits were low because the company was holding large reserves of undeveloped resources and incomplete plant that appeared in the owner's equity but yielded little or no return.

Alcoa's reported profits were about in line with those of manufacturing generally in the 1920's and again in the 1940's and 1950's. Of course, "all manufacturing" includes some very concentrated industries, and such competitive industries as textiles generally did more poorly than Alcoa. On the other hand, an industry expanding as fast as aluminum would show profits even if purely competitive.

In the 1930's, on the other hand, Alcoa did make exceptional profits. Even in the worst years of the depression it did not report as much loss as most manufacturing although its production fell below a third of capacity for a time. In the late 1930's it earned a higher return than in the booming 1920's and 1950's. The explanation is probably its price policy. Referring back to Figure 5.16, Alcoa made only one price cut of 1¢ in the whole collapse of 1929–33—a period when most prices were falling by a third or more! In the late 1930's prices were reduced somewhat, though by no more than Alcoa's cost savings (see Figure 5.23).

Limitations on Monopoly Profit

Why did Alcoa not take higher profits? It may be that the Mellons, Hunts, and Davises had weak profit motives, but their policy probably made sense for profit-maximizing monopolists. If they had set out to make maximum profits in 1926, disregarding what happened in subsequent years, they could undoubtedly have made more than they did—in 1926! Realistically, what they were trying to maximize was the whole stream of profits year after year into the next century. For several reasons they could hope to improve their total profits over the years by taking somewhat less than they might in any one year:

1. For one thing, the elasticity of demand for aluminum is certainly much higher over the long pull than in any one year. An estimate of

---

* "The Splendid Retreat of Alcoa," *Fortune*, Oct. 1955, p. 246, and "Alcoa, 1960," *Modern Metals*, June 1959, p. 30.

the demand for aluminum based on year to year fluctuations yielded an elasticity of only 0.3.* If this is right, a profit-maximizing Alcoa should certainly charge more. Any time that elasticity is less than 1 a monopolist can gain by raising prices. He will receive more total revenue for less output.

On the other hand, one officer of Alcoa explained the company's policies to the author in the following terms:

Profits were consistently held down in order to broaden markets. Aluminum has no markets that have not been wrested from some other metal or material, and even where aluminum was plainly feasible, a price concession was usually involved in order to break into an established relationship with another product.†

This man clearly thought that the elasticity of demand for their product was much more than 1. Otherwise, breaking into new markets by cutting price just would not have paid.

Probably both appraisals are correct. Not many consumers can be expected to shift back and forth between aluminum and other materials in response to short-term price changes, but a price of 20¢ instead of 25¢ for ten years may mean twice as many buyers at the end of the decade. Since the company was undoubtedly aiming for long-run profits, it was the long-run demand curve that generally concerned it.

The stable price of the depression years makes sense in view of these elasticities. A depression is a short-run problem. When thinking in decades, Alcoa leadership was willing to cut price to win new customers, but with a temporary problem of low demand, a price cut would not bring in enough more trade to be worthwhile.

2. Another reason why the goal of maximum profits over the years would probably require Alcoa to take less than it might in any one year is the possibility of attracting new competitors at high prices. The over-all demand for aluminum might look like curve ACD in Figure 5.22 but this was not Alcoa's long-run demand curve even when the company had a monopoly. Suppose that at any price above 25¢ someone like Duke or Reynolds or the Uihleins would come into the aluminum business. Then Alcoa's long-run demand curve would really be curve BCD. At any price above 25¢ it would simply lose its market in the long run. The harder it is for new firms to enter the industry, the more profit a monopolist can get away with on this count.

* Rosenzweig, *op. cit.*, pp. 26–27.

† Correspondence with an officer of Alcoa.

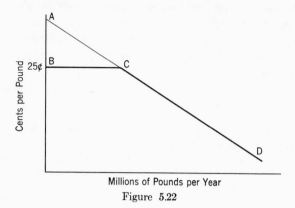

Figure 5.22

3. Finally, public opinion was certainly important in determining Alcoa's long-run profit and price policy.   Between 1912 and 1940 Alcoa was the subject of five antitrust cases, three FTC complaints, and a number of congressional investigations.   The position of one of its main stockholders, Andrew Mellon, as Secretary of the Treasury under Coolidge and Hoover made the firm especially subject to public scrutiny.   Alcoa could conceivably have lost its existence as a single firm if it had pursued an obviously exploitative policy.

ANTITRUST

"Monopolizing"

Four years after the birth of Alcoa in Pittsburgh the Sherman Antitrust Act was passed.   The two have developed simultaneously and each has played an important role in the other's history.

Among other things, the Sherman Act provides that:

(Section 2) Every person who shall monopolize, or attempt to monopolize, or combine or conspire with any other person or persons, to monopolize any part of the trade or commerce among the several states, or with foreign nations, shall be deemed guilty of a misdemeanor.

Alcoa's healthy existence in the face of a law that seemed to make it one big, continuous violation is due largely to the meaning that lawyers assigned to the word "monopolize." Over most of the history of the act this term meant getting and keeping monopoly by predatory moves against competitors or potential competitors, but the mere possession of a monopoly was not enough to convict a firm of "monopolizing." The courts have been willing to condemn offenders who, by overt actions such as localized price wars, have forced competitors out of business, but until recently the courts have been reluctant to decide against a company that did no direct harm to other firms, especially if its policy toward the general public seemed reasonable. The law did not appear to prohibit all monopolies, just nasty ones.

Alcoa's first Sherman Act case, in 1912, illustrates the meaning of the act at that time. (1) The decree voided certain clauses in Alcoa's contracts with bauxite companies preventing them from supplying any other aluminum producer. (2) It ordered Alcoa to cease its participation in the second international cartel through its Canadian subsidiary. (3) It enjoined Alcoa from limiting supplies of metal to independent fabricators or charging them excessive prices. These results were fairly representative of the main prohibitions of antitrust at the time: (1) acts of exclusion aimed at monopoly, (2) agreements in restraint of trade, and (3) unfair methods of competition. On the other hand, the decree did nothing about Alcoa's position as the sole American seller.*

Cases brought by the FTC and private parties during the 1920's and 1930's dealt with Alcoa's acquisition of an independent fabricator during World War I (which Alcoa lost), its acquisition of the Duke rights on the Sagueney (which it ultimately won), and its method of competition, particularly the price squeeze on aluminum sheet (where it finally settled out of court).

The "New" Sherman Act

The Justice Department brought a second momentous suit against Alcoa in 1937. Both Alcoa and the law were fundamentally changed as a result of the case. It was argued for more than two years and added up to more than 56,000 pages of testimony and exhibits. One of the attorneys involved became a father twice during the trial! The case was appealed and the last remnants of it were only disposed of 20 years later, in 1957.

In the District Court the case was handled along the old lines. The trial judge concluded (1) that Alcoa had not excluded competition—its purchases of ore and power reserves were only prudent foresight; (2) that Alcoa had not competed unfairly—he could find no price squeeze aimed at harming competitors; and (3) that Alcoa

---

* This was a consent decree; i.e., it was an order of the court growing out of negotiations between the Justice Department and the company rather than a court trial. There is no admission or finding of guilt in a consent decree, though the person involved must comply with its provision. The terms of this decree are found in Wallace, *op. cit.*, pp. 547–55.

had not been party to the latest cartel while Aluminium, Limited, as a separate Canadian firm, was free to participate. In general he found that Alcoa was a "good" monopolist.

The government's appeal was several years finding a court because so many members of the Supreme Court had been connected with the case that there was no quorum. A special act of Congress had to be passed making the appropriate Circuit Court the court of last resort in such a case. The decision was read by one of the country's leading jurists, Learned Hand, in 1945. The date is important. World War II had intervened, and more than half of the aluminum capacity in the country at the time was owned by the government.

Hand upheld the lower court on most counts of exclusion and unfair competition, although he did conclude that there had been a price squeeze in sheet and he convicted Limited, but not Alcoa, of participation in the international cartel.*

Far more important, however, Hand decided that Alcoa was guilty of monopolizing in a much broader sense. His first concern was Alcoa's share of the market, and once he had determined that Alcoa had made about 90% of domestic sales of primary aluminum he concluded that the long discussion of Alcoa's performance was beside the point.

> . . . the whole issue is irrelevant anyway, for it is no excuse for "monopolizing" a market that the monopoly has not been used to extract from the consumer more than a "fair" profit. The Act has wider purposes. Indeed, even though we disregarded all but economic considerations, it would by no means follow that such concentration of producing power is to be desired, when it has not been used extortionately. Many people believe that possession of unchallenged economic power deadens initiative, discourages thrift, and depresses energy; that immunity from competition is a narcotic, and rivalry is a stimulant to industrial progress; that the spur of constant stress is necessary to counteract an inevitable disposition to let well enough alone. Such people believe that competitors, versed in the craft as no consumer can be, will be quick to detect opportunities for saving and new shifts in production, and be eager to profit by them. In any event, the mere fact that a producer, having command of the domestic market, has not been able to make more than a "fair" profit is no evidence that a "fair" profit could not have been made at lower prices.†

* Alcoa was adjudged separate from Limited even though more than half of the stock in the two companies was held by the same persons and the presidents of Alcoa and Limited were brothers.

† 148 Fed 2nd 427.

In other words, he was revising the definition of "monopolize." According to this decision, a firm that intentionally acquired and maintained a monopoly was prohibited by the Act regardless of how well it had performed. The new concept of "monopolize" came much closer to the economist's meaning of the term. A monopolist who does what businessmen are expected to do in a capitalistic system and seeks maximum profits will, as a matter of course, produce too little and charge too much. This is true even if he does cut price and increase output over the years.

Judge Hand did acknowledge that a monopolist might be within the law if monopoly had been "thrust upon" him (for instance, because of superior products or lower costs), but he found it hard to accept this as an explanation for Alcoa's monopoly position. Antitrust decisions since Alcoa have put more emphasis on the behavior of the firms involved. No one has been convicted of monopolizing since then *simply* because he was a monopolist. Some overt action to exclude competition has always played a role. The 1945 decision may not have reversed the earlier meaning of the law as much as was thought at the time, therefore, but it still ushered in a period of far more vigorous antitrust enforcement when the full force of the Sherman Act could be brought to bear on many subtle but important restrictions on competition for the first time.

As to what to do about his decision, Hand made it clear that the remedy should be devised to improve the situation rather than especially to punish Alcoa. However, in view of the uncertain status of the government plants in 1945, Hand postponed the final remedy.

The New Rivals

Alcoa had built and operated most of the government's plants, and it tried to buy the best of them after the war. The Surplus Property Board rejected Alcoa's proposal, but it had difficulty finding any other takers for the plants. The market for aluminum was in doubt because of great quantities of government-owned scrap. The plants available were very large scale and required considerable expenditure on conversion. The two alumina plants owned by the government had been built around patents owned by Alcoa. And any new firm had both the powerful Alcoa and the new, low-cost plants of Aluminium, Limited to contend with.

The Surplus Property Board made heroic efforts to dispose of the plants. It persuaded Alcoa to license its alumina patents on a royalty-free basis, it provided for the orderly disposition of government-owned scrap, it arranged for a modification of the terms on which power was sold from government facilities to the aluminum plants, and it agreed to sell the plants at prices reflecting prospective earning power rather than original or replacement cost. On these terms it was able to find buyers in Reynolds and in Kaiser, a West Coast dam builder, ship builder, magnesium maker, and general handy man of multimillion-dollar dimensions. Two economists reviewing the disposal of war plants concluded that these strenuous efforts in the case of aluminum resulted in the only real success from an antitrust point of view in the whole surplus disposal program.*

The court decided on the question of remedies in the Alcoa case in 1951.† It denied the government's motion that Alcoa be broken into two firms, but it did order the main Alcoa stockholders to dispose of their stock in Limited, and the case was kept under review for five years.

Economists, who for years had pressed for more realistic antitrust thinking, had hailed Hand's conclusion in 1945, but many of them were very critical of the final decision on dissolution. They felt that three firms with Alcoa still strongest were little better than one, while the separation of Alcoa and Limited would be meaningless because of personal and traditional ties between the two. If the Canadian giant should become truly independent, they feared that the tariff would be restored.‡

An alternative proposal is difficult to name, however. Alcoa had only two alumina plants, so it could have been broken into only two fully integrated firms. Moreover, one of the two would have been saddled with the obsolete East St. Louis plant§ and would have been at a disadvantage. Starting from scratch, society might have benefited from an industry with smaller alumina plants, but the courts could hardly have the 1951 plants dismantled. Again, by 1951 there could have been quite a number of firms at the smelting and fabricat-

---

* Walter Adams and Horace Gray, *Monopoly in America*, Macmillan, 1955, pp. 126–132.

† 91 F. Supp. 333.

‡ The case occasioned a considerable discussion among economists in the early 1950's. Walter Adams, "The Aluminum Case: Legal Victory—Economic Defeat," *American Economic Review*, Dec. 1951, p. 915; comments by T. Levitt, W. H. Martin, and Adams, *American Economic Review*, Dec. 1952, pp. 893, 895, 900; J. V. Krutilla, "Aluminum, A Dilemma for Anti-Trust Aims," *Southern Economic Journal*, Oct. 1955; and J. B. Dirlam and A. E. Kahn, *Fair Competition*, Cornell University Press, 1954, pp. 58–65, 152–161.

§ It was closed in 1958.

ing levels if they were separated from the alumina plants, but there would still have been concentration at the alumina level. Anyway, the government had for practical purposes already decided against vertical dissolution when it permitted Kaiser and Reynolds to acquire fully integrated organizations.

OLIGOPOLY IN ALUMINUM

Postwar Expansion

The wartime growth, the new government policies, and the new firms have altered some, but not all, of the characteristics of the aluminum industry.

Many of the old barriers to entry seem still intact. The minimum initial investment increased because of rising costs and plant sizes. In addition to alumina and smelting plants, new firms almost had to have fabricating facilities since the production of ingot itself was relatively unprofitable in the United States after World War II. On the other hand, the shift to steam power and the development of bauxite deposits all over the Carribean area have removed some of the obstacles to new firms that seemed important earlier.

During the Korean War the government tried to stimulate another rapid expansion. Producers were permitted to depreciate new equipment rapidly for tax purposes and thus postpone their tax obligations. Sometimes the government guaranteed loans or agreed to buy any unsold output of the new plants for stockpiling during the first five years of operation.

Each of the existing firms expanded capacity by about equal amounts, but Alcoa grew less proportionately because it was larger to start with. No new firms appeared until 1955, but since then three have entered primary aluminum production—Anaconda Aluminum, Harvey Aluminum, and ORMET (Olin-Revere Metals)—while the Canadian-British Aluminium Company has become the second Canadian producer.* All the new firms had fabricating facilities already. ORMET was the only one that built a fully integrated organization, the others depended on existing firms for alumina. Several other

---

* Anaconda is owned by Anaconda Copper. Harvey is a Los Angeles fabricator. ORMET is owned half by Olin-Mathieson Chemicals and half by Revere Copper and Brass. The two companies market their fabricated aluminum products separately. The Canadian-British Aluminium Company is owned jointly by the Quebec Northshore Paper Company (in turn owned by the Chicago Tribune) and by the British Aluminium Company (in which Reynolds acquired a 49% interest in 1959).

TABLE 5.3

PRIMARY ALUMINUM CAPACITY IN NORTH AMERICA

Company	1946 Capacity		1959–60 Capacity	
	Thousands of Tons	Per-centage	Thousands of Tons[a]	Per-centage
United States				
Alcoa	325	31.1	1001	28.1
Reynolds	190	18.2	701	19.7
Kaiser	129	12.4	610	17.1
Anaconda	...	....	60	1.7
ORMET	...	....	180	5.1
Harvey	...	....	54	1.5
Canada				
Aluminium, Limited	400[b]	38.3	866	24.3
Canadian-British	...	....	90	2.5
Total North America	1044	100.0	3562	100.0

[a] 1959 capacities include 510,000 tons in plants under construction.

[b] Aluminium, Limited "capacity" in 1946 is maximum attained output to date.

Source: Office of Defense Mobilization, *op. cit.*, p. VII-9, and *American Metal Market*, Mar. 17, 1959.

firms made gestures toward entering the industry during 1951–55 but did not, giving such reasons as the lack of fabricating facilities, the lack of capital, or the inability to get tax amortization privileges before September 1955 when the program expired.*

Altogether, aluminum capacity grew by some 340% from the end of World War II to 1960 in response to the high Korean War demand, the upsurge in civilian demand, and the government's rapid amortization and loan or market guarantee programs. Over much of the decade aluminum was in very short supply. However, for a short period in 1954 and during most of 1957–59 there was excess capacity in the industry. The prospect seemed to be for somewhat slower domestic expansion in subsequent years.

Table 5.3 compares aluminum capacities at the end of World War II and in 1959–60. Alcoa was still the leader at the end of the period, but its share of primary capacity was decreasing. It had not grown as fast as the other firms: it had only tripled its plant in 15 years!

* 153 F. Supp. 142.

Table 5.3 understates Alcoa's share in both 1946 and 1959-60 because it has more fabricating facilities than the other integrated producers.*

The next wave of expansion in primary capacity seems to be occurring overseas. In 1959 the Bureau of Mines† could list ten projects for the construction of smelting plants in Africa and Latin America with total prospective capacity in excess of 1 million tons! All of the major North American firms were involved: Alcoa in Surinam, Kaiser in Ghana, Reynolds in the Congo,‡ Olin-Mathieson in Guinea, and Limited in several African and Latin American locations at once. In addition, Belgian, British, French, German, Portuguese, and Swiss firms were all involved in one or more of the African proposals. Local governments also played a role in many cases.

These locations all offered abundant undeveloped water power and, in many cases, local bauxite deposits. Postwar reductions in trade restrictions had given them increased access to the American and European markets. At any rate, it seems likely that with their drive for rapid economic development many of these tropical countries will probably be building aluminum industries whether the American and European firms participate or not.

Postwar Price Making

Alcoa has less complete control over aluminum prices in the new setting than it did in the monopoly period, but this certainly does not mean that aluminum prices are set by impersonal forces of supply and demand. The various aluminum producers announce their prices much as Alcoa did before the war, and since their products are largely standardized their prices are ordinarily identical. Aluminum is still sold at a uniform price throughout the United States regardless of where the customer is located, so there is no problem of differential delivery charges to complicate pricing practices. When a price change occurs, one firm makes a move and the others generally duplicate it within a few days. Table 5.4 shows the amounts and dates of general price changes by the five leading firms during the 1950's. Alcoa led in 9 of the 13 changes shown, Kaiser in two, and Reynolds and

* As a result Alcoa's sales exceed those of Reynolds and Kaiser more than its primary capacity does. In 1959 Alcoa's sales came to $858 million, Reynolds' to $489 million, and Kaiser's to $435 million. *Moody's Industrial Manual,* 1960. Their advantage was even greater in earlier years.

† Bureau of Mines, *Minerals Yearbook,* 1958, Vol. I, p. 168.

‡ In addition to the ten projects listed by the Bureau of Mines, Reynolds later announced a plan to build a plant in Venezuela. *Moody's Industrial Manual,* 1960.

Limited in one each. Limited pursued an openly passive price policy until 1958. Its officers made public statements that their approach was to accept the announced prices in the countries in which they trade rather than to "strangle competition."* This was an understandable policy in view of the company's dependence on exports. An aggressive low price policy might well have resulted in trade restrictions excluding it from its main markets.

TABLE 5.4

CHANGES IN PRICE OF ALUMINUM PIG
(99% MINIMUM AVERAGE), 1950-58

Price (cents)	Alcoa Date	Reynolds Date	Kaiser Date	Limited Date
16.5	May 22, 1950	May 23, 1950	May 25, 1950	May 23, 1950
18	Sept. 25, 1950	Sept. 29, 1950	Sept. 28, 1950	Sept. 25, 1950
19	Aug. 4, 1952	Aug, 4, 1952	Aug. 4, 1952	Aug. 7, 1952
19.5	Jan. 23, 1953	Jan. 23, 1953	Jan. 22, 1953	Jan. 23, 1953
20	July 15, 1953	July 20, 1953	July 20, 1953	July 21, 1953
20.5	Aug. 5, 1954	Aug. 6, 1954	Aug. 6, 1954	Aug. 6, 1954
21.5	Jan. 13, 1955	Jan. 10, 1955	Jan. 12, 1955	Jan. 14, 1955
22.5	Aug. 1, 1955	Aug. 6, 1944	Aug. 2, 1955	Aug. 8, 1955
24	Mar. 29, 1956	Mar. 27, 1956	Mar. 26, 1956	Mar. 31, 1956
25	Aug. 10, 1956	Aug. 13, 1956	Aug. 11, 1956	not available
26	Aug. 1, 1957	Aug. 1, 1957	Aug. 1, 1957	Aug. 5, 1957
24	Apr. 1, 1958	Apr. 1, 1958	Apr. 1, 1958	Apr. 1, 1958
24.7	Aug. 1, 1958	Aug. 1, 1958	Aug. 4, 1958	Aug. 2, 1958*

* Limited raised price in the United States only.
Source: 153 F. Supp. 151 and *Iron Age, passim.*

The fact that other firms besides Alcoa sometimes took the lead in price changes did not mean that price competition had broken out. It would have been fatuous for one of three or four firms or even one of six or eight to think it could win customers from its rivals with a general price cut. They were certain to meet any changes almost immediately. Actually all but one of the 15† price changes from the end of World War II to 1960 were upward. Any one of the major firms could have vetoed any of these increases by simply

* Aluminium, Limited, Unlimited Aluminum," *Fortune*, June 1954, p. 108.
† There were increases in Oct. 11, 1948 and on Dec. 17, 1959 not shown in Table 5.4. Alcoa led in both of them but dates on which other firms changed price are not available.

refusing to go along. The fact that they generally did not probably indicates that all of them thought the higher prices would be more profitable. In other words, they were raising price to enhance the profits of *every one in the industry*. Of course, this is just why Alcoa itself would have raised price when it *was* the whole industry.

This is very different from the way that prices are determined in a purely competitive industry such as textile weaving or beef production. No textile mill operator or cattle rancher can raise his price and expect the rest of the industry to follow him, even if it is perfectly plain that every producer would be better off at the higher price. If any mill operators or ranchers have unsold surpluses, they will shade their prices until the extra cloth or cattle can be sold, even if the whole industry loses in the process. No such thing can happen in aluminum because no major aluminum producer can rationally expect that the other firms in the industry will disregard its moves.

Elements of Price Competition

The new organization of the aluminum industry does leave room for a limited degree of competition that did not exist previously. For instance, the 10% price concessions made to Ford and General Motors in the hot metal contracts mentioned earlier were a new development in the late 1950's. Alcoa had resisted pressure for such concessions earlier, but after Reynolds had agreed to them Alcoa had little choice if it wanted to keep up. The existence of several firms rather than just one firm in the industry undoubtedly improve the bargaining position of the big buyers. The lower prices in the hot metal contracts may be a mixed blessing for price competition generally, however. If such agreements become common they may act to exclude competitors at both the aluminum-producing and aluminum-using levels. It takes enormous firms to use enough metal to make the contracts worthwhile. Both Ford and General Motors have built facilities near Alcoa or Reynolds plants which take substantial parts of the output of those plants. At the same time, the producers of secondary aluminum are to some extent excluded from supplying the large firms. This may not have been Reynolds' purpose in signing the contracts, but it seems to be a likely result.

Another way that prices in the new oligopoly might come out differently than if the old monopoly had continued is the possibility of differences of opinion about what price would be most profitable. Alcoa seems to have preferred lower prices than Kaiser and Reynolds in the early years. Ordinarily it called the tune. Reynolds did announce an increase in July 1950, shortly after the Korean War had begun, but Alcoa refused to follow. The next day President Truman appealed to industry generally to hold the price line, and Reynolds backed down.*

The only general price reduction from the end of the war to 1960 was initiated by Limited during the 1958 recession. Some price cutting had developed in Europe, and the Russians were causing a great uproar by openly selling aluminum at 2¢ less than Limited's price. At the bottom of the recession, Limited abandoned its previous passive policy and announced a price cut of 2¢. The rest of the aluminum producers and the Russians immediately cut price accordingly, so Limited could not have won any significant amount of business from its rivals by the move. The management of Limited has explained that the price cut was designed to "make aluminum more competitive with other metals" rather than meet the price competition.† If the explanation given reflects Limited's true motives, it indicates that the firm was cutting price for the same reason that the others had been raising price previously—to increase profits even with the whole industry meeting the move. Either Limited made a mistake or it simply differed with the other firms about which price would be most profitable.

In addition to the price cut by Aluminium, Limited, some of the cheap European metal available in 1958 was reaching America, and the primary producers were finding themselves undersold in some markets. They also met price competition in secondary aluminum and in certain fabricating fields where independent producers could use imported or secondary aluminum. By and large, price competition developed in those fields where large numbers of small firms had appeared since the war such as scrap recovery and the production of some aluminum extrusions. The effect of this sort of price competition can be exaggerated, however. So long as Alcoa and the other integrated producers held the price line, the independent fabricators, the secondary foundries, and the importers only needed to offer a small margin below Alcoa's prices to win business.‡

* Kaplan et al., *op. cit.*, p. 33.

† *Iron Age*, Apr. 3, 1958, p. 53, and June 26, 1958, p. 57.

‡ In a few cases, particularly soft extrusions, Alcoa lost so much business that it cut price "due to the competitive situation." It reported that the prices quoted earlier were "almost impossible to adhere to." *Iron Age*, Aug. 21, 1958, p. 138. In such instances the numbers of small new firms were so large that the particular segment of the aluminum industry involved began to behave very much as a competitive industry. All extrusions together, including many where price competition did not break out, came to only about 15% of Alcoa's fabricating capacity. **153 F. Supp. 149.**

Import Restrictions Once More?

The aluminum industry did not accept the newly imported price competition of 1958 with equanimity. It made an appeal for protection.* It cited the Russian "dumping," the low wages paid by its foreign competitors, domestic unemployment and overcapacity, and its militarily essential character. Then it went on to say in boldface type:

AN IMAGINATIVE GOVERNMENT PROGRAM IS NEEDED, BOTH TO END THE EXISTING SURPLUS OF ALUMINUM THROUGHOUT THE FREE WORLD, AND TO STEM THE PRESENT FLOW OF SURPLUS ALUMINUM TO THE UNITED STATES MARKET.

The "imaginative program" proposed turned out to be import quotas:

To limit the great advantage which foreign producers have because of low wage costs, the aluminum industry believes that the present tariff is entirely inadequate. It recognizes, however, that in the present international situation legislation to increase tariffs might have unfortunate international repercussions, and may seem undesirable, however sound economically. If a tariff increase is not now feasible, however, other means must be found to normalize imports.

This requires the establishment of controls which will effectively limit the imports from foreign suppliers in times of surplus. Such imports should bear some reasonable relationship to imports which have customarily been made from the same suppliers in normal times and in times of scarcity. Controls could be established in terms of absolute tonnages, or in terms of percentages of past shipments made in a base period.†

It is difficult to imagine a move that would be less "sound economically." Import quotas might have been a good thing for the primary aluminum producers, but certainly not from a public point of view. Most of the arguments were the same old points that the textile makers and every one else seeking protection had trotted out with no more validity in this case than in others. The most spectacular point raised, the Russian "dumping," was greatly exaggerated. Al-

* Memorandum submitted by representatives of the Primary Aluminum Industry of the United States to the U.S. State Department in Washington, D. C., on Monday, July 14, 1958, entitled "Causes and Effects of Imports of Aluminum and the Need for Government Action."

† *Ibid.*, pp. 12–13. The industry also proposed an American-Canadian program of stockpiling and a government program to "channel" surplus aluminum to the parts of the world where aluminum consumption was low. They cited the export program for agricultural surpluses as an example. While the proposal was quite vague on this point, apparently the industry wanted export subsidies!

together, Russian sales in the free world in 1958 ran about 5% of Limited's.* United States imports of aluminum and aluminum products increased by only 35,000 tons in that year over 1957, less than 2% of apparent domestic consumption.† It is difficult to see that this little aluminum could have made such a difference. The main fault in the Russian "dumping" was the open price competition!‡

The proposal was never put into effect in the case of aluminum, but something similar was done in other industries. The United States imposed quotas on the importation of crude oil, lead, and zinc during the 1958 recession or shortly thereafter.

The Pattern of Postwar Prices

The prices of aluminum from 1940 to 1960 were surprisingly low. Ingot prices were reduced by 25% when Reynolds entered the industry in 1940–41, and they remained at that level until 1948. Even in 1960 primary aluminum sold for only about a third more than in 1939,§ whereas wholesale prices in general had more than doubled. For much of the period primary aluminum was in short supply. Secondary ingot sold at prices well above primary in 1950–53 and 1955–56. The aluminum producers obviously could have charged more.

* During 1958 Aluminium, Limited produced 549,000 tons in Canada (*Moody's Industrial Manual,* 1960). In the same year the leading aluminum-using countries imported a little over 30,000 tons (27,688 *metric* tons) of aluminum from Russia (UN Statistical Papers, Series D, Vol. VIII, No. 4). This includes all imports by major Western European and North American users, the British Dominions, and Japan. Russia's total aluminum exports were greater (94,000 tons in 1957— *Minerals Yearbook,* 1958, p. 166. 1958 figure not available), but the largest part of Russian trade is with other communist countries. England, the largest importer of Russian aluminum, received only 5.3% of its 1958 aluminum imports from that source. (UN, *op. cit.*)

† *Minerals Yearbook,* 1958. Three-quarters of our imports came from Canada, and none of them came directly from Russia. However, some of our relatively small imports of fabricated aluminum undoubtedly contained Russian metal. *All* of our imports of fabricated aluminum in 1958 came to 40,300 tons or about 2% of domestic consumption. (Bureau of Census, FT110, calendar year, 1958).

‡ The proposed base date for the import quotas was 1955 when imports from Europe were practically nil. As a result, the quotas would have virtually eliminated all possible competition in primary aluminum except for the eight North American firms!

§ In 1939 the most commonly quoted price for primary aluminum was that of 99% ingot, but after 1956 aluminum pig was the most widely used form of primary aluminum. Pig has generally been 1¢ to 2¢ cheaper than ingot.

The prices of many fabricated products did not fall as much as ingot prices in the 1940's and the greater margins were maintained in the 1950's.* In part this was because fabricating costs rose faster than smelting costs, but fabrication does seem to have been the more profitable end of the business in those years. The great issue of the early 1950's was who would get the scarce primary aluminum for fabricating. All of the new primary producers were fabricators trying to assure themselves of a supply of metal. The nonintegrated fabricators were regularly before Congress complaining that the integrated firms were keeping too much of the metal for themselves.† The government insisted that the major firms offer two-thirds of the primary aluminum produced in their new plants to nonintegrated firms before it would guarantee to buy any surplus aluminum from those plants.

This was a complete reversal of the price situation of the early 1930's when fabricated products had been especially cheap, if anything. One reason for the change was the antitrust case. In view of its finding of a price "squeeze," the court ordered Alcoa to price its sheet at a level that covered the selling price of ingot plus the manufacturing cost of sheet. The order referred only to sheet, but Alcoa's officers extended the principle to other products where they had competitors.‡

One effect of the new policy was a great influx of fabricators. Their numbers grew from 4500 in 1945 to more than 24,000 in 1955.§ Most of these were making finished products for consumer or industrial use, but an influx occurred in the production of intermediate products as well. The number of extruders grew from 6 during World War II¶ to 109 in 1959. By then some 50 other firms were competing with primary producers in rolling or drawing various semifinished products

---

* Office of Defense Mobilization, *op. cit.*, p. IV-7. In December 1952, ingot prices were the same as in 1939 but most sheet, foil, extrusions, and wire sold for about 10% more than in 1939.

† *Aluminum Industry,* Hearings of Subcommittee No. 3 of House Select Committee on Small Business, 84th Congress, 1st Ssession, 1955, *passim;* and report of same committee, July 27, 1956. The claims of the independents were exaggerated. They received about the same percentage of the total aluminum supply in the tight years of the 1950's as they did in the easier late 1940's. A substantial part of this was the result of government insistence or imports, however. 153 F. Supp. 182–192.

‡ Kaplan et al., *op. cit.,* p. 143.

§ House Report 2954, 84th Congress, 2nd Session, *op. cit.,* p. 7.

¶ *Ibid.,* p. 10.

such as sheet, bars, wire, and tube.* On the other hand, the relatively low price of primary aluminum probably discouraged new firms at the smelting stage except for large fabricators seeking assured supplies. The most reliable source of supply for the nonintegrated fabricators, especially those making semifinished products, turned out to be Aluminium, Limited, which had few fabricating facilities and sold mainly primary products.†

In a few cases so many fabricators appeared that Alcoa found it impossible to maintain its high margins on fabricated items. This happened in the case of soft (nonheat-treated) extrusions such as those used in making window casements. These products required very little equipment and could be made on a small scale. The numbers of extruders increased so rapidly that the major integrated producers found their sales declining in spite of a rising total market. Alcoa reacted by reducing the margin between pig and extrusions by about an eighth between 1955 and 1958.‡ By the second year, the margin was almost as low as it had been in 1939.§ Alcoa explained its policy as necessary to stay in the business.¶

Especially low prices were also charged for products with particularly elastic demands. For instance, Alcoa introduced aluminum screen wire in 1948 and maintained almost the same price for the product for the following decade.‖ During the same period primary

---

* Census, "Facts for Industry," Series 33-2, *Aluminum Ingot and Mill Products,* Dec. 1959; this source showed 166 producers of mill products. 109 of these were extruders and 6 were primary producers, leaving 51 other firms. There were 29 rolling sheet and plate, 13 rolling foil, 11 drawing cable, and 13 drawing tube. The greatest concentration was in heat-treatable sheet where only the 4 large producers had facilities.

† To meet their obligation to supply primary aluminum to nonintegrated firms, Alcoa and Kaiser made long-term contracts for large amounts of Limited's metal. In spite of these, however, Limited regularly sold more than half of the aluminum that it shipped to the United States to nonintegrated firms after the start of the Korean War. 153 F. Supp. 192.

‡ Office of Defense Mobilization, *op. cit.,* p. IV-7, and Alcoa price lists.

§ *Ibid.* In 1939 the margin over pig was 19¢. By 1955 it was 23.9¢ but it was reduced to 20¢ again by 1958.

¶ 84th Congress, 2nd Session, Hearings of Subcommittee No. 3, House Judiciary, Pt. II, p. 548.

‖ Kaplan et al., *op cit.,* pp. 35–6, 326. Aluminum screen wire was introduced at 66¢ a pound. It reached 68.7¢ a pound in August 1955, but its price was reduced after that. Even at the peak, screen wire had advanced only 4%. Pig prices rose from 14¢ to 22.5¢ or 61% in the same period and went on rising later.

aluminum prices were rising regularly. Aluminum screening offered an excellent substitute for galvanized or bronze screening provided that its price was not too far out of line with those of the older products.

In spite of its five domestic rivals, Alcoa is still able to discriminate in many of the same ways that it did when it was the only primary producer. It charges low prices for those products where the easy entry of competing firms or the availability of substitutes make the demand for the company's products exceptionally elastic, just as before.

Technical Progress

In his decision in 1945 Judge Hand had emphasized progress as well as price in arguing for further competition. Progress is extremely difficult to measure in any industry, and this is especially true in aluminum where even the productivity figures used in other cases are not available. We do have Alcoa's reported mill costs over the period 1926–37 and 1947–56, however. The upper diagram in Figure 5.23 compares them with the wholesale price index for goods other than food and farm products during the same period. The lower diagram shows the cost of aluminum deflated by that index. It can be thought of as roughly representing production costs expressed in 1947–49 dollars. The cost information for 1926–37 and 1947–56 are only roughly comparable. It was presented to the courts at two different hearings two decades apart, and it refers to two different products, aluminum ingot in the 1920's and 1930's and aluminum pig in the 1940's and 1950's. Pig sold for 1¢ less than ingot during most of the period 1943–53.

Over the years covered in Figure 5.23 wages rose regularly at Alcoa as in most of American industry. Stable costs in the face of these increasing wage rates would only have been possible if output per man-hour employed had been increasing. The apparent sharp declines in aluminum mill costs measured in 1947–49 dollars in 1927–29 and 1937–47 probably meant that productivity was increasing faster in aluminum than in most of industry. These apparent declines in Alcoa's costs coincided with rapid increases in its capacity. There was only a slight drop in cost between 1929 and 1937,* when Alcoa was doing very little expanding.

* The increase in cost per pound of aluminum from 1929–34 was attributable to operations at far less than capacity so that fixed costs per pound were greatly increased. Even in 1936 and 1937 when output was higher than in 1929, however, Alcoa's costs were only slightly below the 1929 level.

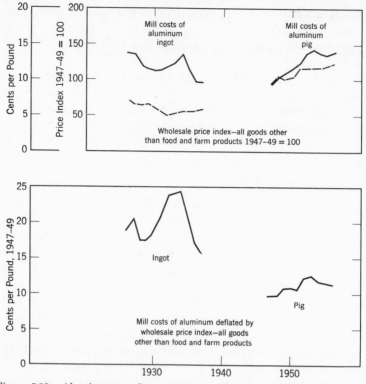

Figure 5.23.   Alcoa's costs.   Source: Justice Department Exhibit 718 in US v. Alcoa, quoted in Engle, Gregory, and Mosse, *op. cit.*, and 153 F. Supp. 185.

There is a marked contrast between the performance of Alcoa's costs in the 1920's and the 1940's on the one hand and in the third period of expansion in the 1950's on the other.   Costs expressed in 1947–49 dollars seemed to rise between 1950 and 1956 even though the plant was growing as fast as in the two earlier periods.   It is easy to find plausible explanations.   The early years of an industry might be expected to produce more cost-saving changes than later ones.   Moreover, Alcoa was very possibly still winning economies of scale as it expanded down to World War II, while in the 1950's each of the major firms was larger than Alcoa had been in 1939.   Aluminum wages were rising considerably faster than in most of industry in the 1950's under pressure from the United Steel Workers, a union that was only organized in 1937 and reached its strongest bargaining power in the 1950's.*   Finally, the higher costs of the 1950's reflected in part the rapid rise in the price of capital equipment at that time.

* See Chapter 10, pp. 482–483.

This was especially important in the aluminum industry because it tripled its capacity during the period of rising equipment costs.

All these quibbles make it difficult to evaluate the performance of aluminum costs in the 1950's compared with the 1920's and 1940's. Nevertheless, it would certainly be hard for anyone to conclude that Alcoa was progressing any faster in the 1950's, when it had several rivals, than it did previously, when it had none.

Progress takes other forms besides increasing productivity. In the aluminum industry the introduction of new products has been of particular importance. Back in the monopoly period Alcoa was continuously developing new uses for its metal, but the new rivals have been no less active along the same lines. In fact, Reynolds has taken something of a lead in popularizing aluminum products at the consumer level, as distinct from the industrial level. As a result, the general public is far more conscious of the potentialities of the metal than before.

It is practically impossible to appraise this sort of innovation statistically, but it is worth noting that the growth in demand from 1947 to 1957 was about as rapid as from 1923 to 1929. Since most industries show an early history of rapid growth which subsequently slows down, the continued increase in aluminum sales after a lapse of several decades is impressive.

Altogether, the industry probably deserves good marks for innovation in both the monopoly period up to World War II and the years of oligopoly since. The inadequate evidence available gives little basis for choosing the record of either period as particularly superior to the other. There is no way of knowing whether the same industry would have been more or less progressive if it had been more competitively organized over its history.

CONCLUSIONS

After 20 years of government intervention, what has been accomplished? Just how harmful was Alcoa's monopoly in the first place? And in what ways has the situation changed?

Alcoa's price and output policies in the monopoly period were consistent with a goal of maximum long-run profit, but they were still very impressive. The elastic long-run demand likely in the case of new products, the prospect of new competitors, and the possibility of government action all put limits on Alcoa's monopoly profits. In view of its rapidly expanding market and declining costs, Alcoa's prices and profits may have been no higher in prosperous years than might have been expected in a purely competitive industry under similar circumstances. Alcoa did engage in price discrimination that would have been impossible in pure competition, however, and it certainly exploited its monopoly position in the depression years when it was largely able to avoid price cuts and losses in spite of a collapse in demand. In addition, its strong position permitted it to hold off on installing new plant until shortages had developed and the market seemed assured.

The antitrust suit and the government's efforts to nurture new firms have eliminated Alcoa's exclusive position, but the primary aluminum industry is still one of the most concentrated in the United States. There have been changes in aluminum pricing as a result of concessions to large buyers, differences between firms in policy, and competition from domestic fabricators in those lines where large numbers of small firms have appeared. The progressively lower aluminum tariff after World War II also permitted price competition from imports during slack periods. In general, however, aluminum prices are still under the control of the great integrated firms. The prices set by the oligopoly were lower than they might have been much of the time, especially on primary metal. The integrated producers have vied with one another to expand plant and even overdid it temporarily in the late 1950's.

The actual performance of the aluminum industry before and after the antitrust action should not be the sole criterion for judging the success of the government's massive intervention. The tremendous growth of the industry will not go on forever. Alcoa might have performed more poorly if it had retained its monopoly in some later year when demand was growing slowly, costs were no longer declining, and the prospect for new markets was dimmer. At any rate, if new firms were ever to enter the industry it had to be in the period of rapid expansion. In this case there seems to have been no other way to assure some possibility of new rivals than large-scale intervention.

For the future, the best prospect for more competition at the primary aluminum stage seems to lie in the further growth in foreign sources of supply. It seems possible that the development of smelting capacity in the tropical countries will tend to transform the domestic producers into fabricators. Since fabrication is the line of the aluminum business where further competition is most possible, this change could basically alter the structure of the industry. On the other hand, the government might do much to eliminate this possibility of more competition by imposing new trade restrictions, something it has already done in several industries.

FURTHER READINGS

The classic on the aluminum industry, and one of the most highly regarded industry studies of any sort, is Donald H. Wallace's *Market Control in the Aluminum Industry*, Harvard University Press, 1937. For Alcoa's point of view, see Charles C. Carr, *Alcoa, An American Enterprise*, Rinehart (copyright by Alcoa), 1952. Much of the material in this chapter on aluminum since the monopoly period is based on the Office of Defense Mobilization's *Materials Survey, Aluminum*, Government Printing Office, 1956, a complete and authoritative survey of the industry including present-day technology, structure, uses, and regulation, with a very full bibliography. A good detailed discussion of price policy and practices in a number of industries is to be found in A. D. H. Kaplan, J. B. Dirlam, and R. F. Lanzillotti, *Pricing in Big Business*, The Brookings Institute, 1958. Its sections on aluminum are among its best studies. There are several good congressional investigations of aluminum, especially that of the Subcommittee on the Study of Monopoly Power, Committee on the Judiciary, House of Representatives, 82nd Congress, 1st Session, 1951. A book which promises to provide more information and analysis of the postwar aluminum industry is M. J. Peck, *Market Behavior in the American Aluminum Industry, 1946–1956* (forthcoming).

The great precise statement of monopoly theory appears in Joan Robinson, *The Economics of Imperfect Competition*, Macmillan, 1933, but the beginning student may find it tough going. It is discussed in all principles and economic theory texts as well. A number of the ideas discussed in connection with monopoly profits in this chapter are presented in George Stigler, *Theory of Price*, rev. ed., Macmillan, 1952, Chapter 12. An extensive discussion of barriers to entry in a large number of industries (not aluminum) appears in J. S. Bain, *Barriers to New Competition*, Harvard University Press, 1956.

Most modern books on public control of business discuss the Alcoa decisions of 1945 and 1951. A. G. Papandreau and J. T. Wheeler, *Competition and Its Regulation*, Prentice-Hall, 1954, Chapter 17, provides a good discussion. Simon N. Whitney, *Anti-Trust Policies*, Twentieth Century Fund, 1958, is a discussion of antitrust in ten industries followed by an analysis of ten famous cases. The Alcoa case is one of the latter. His discussion includes a survey of the aftermath (Vol. II, pp. 85–118).

6

REGULATED INDUSTRIES—
ELECTRIC POWER

For industries representing about a tenth of the nation's output, we do not even make a pretense of maintaining competitive conditions. Most enterprises in the transportation, communication, and public utility fields are either closely regulated or directly operated by agencies of federal, state, or local governments. In these industries, instead of relying on competition to produce private decisions in the public interest, officials try to order businessmen to pursue the desired policies. Since this is a completely different tack from that usually followed by American governmental agencies, the peculiarities of these industries and the problems involved in this approach to business warrant some special study. To keep the discussion within bounds, most of this chapter will have to do with electric power, but many of the conclusions reached apply generally to regulated industries and their regulators.

UTILITY COSTS AND MONOPOLY

The Pattern of Costs

In many public utilities, including electric power, it would be intolerably inefficient to have more than one seller. For industries with tentacles running into every part of the city such as electric, telephone, gas, and street railway utilities, two or more competing firms would involve obvious duplication of facilities and public inconvenience. At any rate there is only room for so many tracks in city streets and so many transmission lines along or under them.

In many, though not all, public utilities, the character of production costs probably makes monopoly the most efficient method of producing even without regard to the distribution system. It was suggested in Chapter 5 that this might be true of railroads, where the larger the plant, the lower the cost per ton-mile, provided that there is enough business to keep it all in use.

The same seems to be true in electric power production out to very large scales of operation. About 80% of the power generated in the United States comes from thermoelectric plants, i.e., plants converting the energy of fuels such as coal, oil, or gas into electricity, usually by means of steam turbines. The Federal Power Commission (FPC) makes an annual survey of the steam plants in the country and publishes statistics on their costs. Estimated average costs of plants in the New York area based on the 1958 report are shown in Figure 6.1. These costs per kilowatt-hour seem to be lower the larger the plant, at least out to the 300,000 to 400,000 kw level of capacity,* and some of the larger plants were able to attain almost the same low costs. The higher costs for some of the largest plants (all located in New York City itself) were apparently attributable to the dates at which they were built more than to their sizes. At any rate, it has proved worthwhile to install plants of more than 1 million kw capacity in a number of areas in the last few years and these plants have ranked among the highest in fuel consumption performance.†

Even plants in the 300,000 to 400,000 kw range are enormous. One such plant would be enough to meet the needs of cities like Omaha

---

* A kilowatt (1000 watts) is a measure of power equivalent to about 1.34 horsepower. It is used to describe the amount of power needed to operate a piece of electrical equipment (such as a 100-watt light bulb) or the amount of power a plant can produce (such as Grand Coulee Dam with a capacity of 1,960,000 kw). The amount of electricity actually produced can only be measured over time. If a 100-watt bulb were to run for 1 hour, it would use $\frac{1}{10}$ kw-hr, or if it ran for 10 hours, 1 kw-hr of electricity. If Grand Coulee is run at capacity for 1 hour, it will produce 1,960,000 kw-hr of electricity or enough to light the bulb for 2237 years.

† The federal government put six steam plants in the Tennessee Valley area into operation between 1951 and 1956. All of them reported practically the same average costs although they ranged from 540,000 to 1,440,000 kw in capacity. A single unit installed in one of these plants in 1959 had a capacity of 500,000 kw. Tennessee Valley Authority, *Annual Report,* June 1959, p. 7.

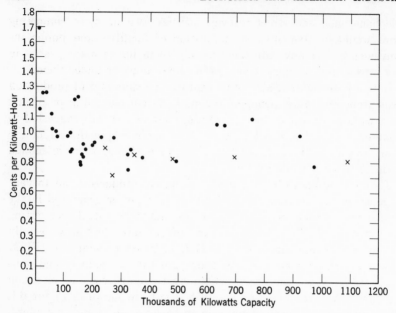

Figure 6.1. Estimated production costs of plants in the New York area—1958. Note: Construction costs were adjusted for regional differences by eliminating the cost of land. Operating costs were adjusted by recalculating fuel expenses to a price of 40¢ per million Btu for all plants. Total cost is operating cost plus an estimate of average fixed cost assuming that annual depreciation, interest, and property taxes came to 10% of total construction costs and that all plants were operated 5000 hours a year (about 57% of the time). This survey was limited to New York, New Jersey, and Connecticut to avoid national differences in types of plant and building costs. Observations marked with a ✕ are cases where new equipment was installed during 1958 so that operating expense had to be estimated on the basis of expense per kilowatt-hour.

Source: Derived from material in FPC, *Steam Electric Plant Construction Costs and Annual Operating Expenses,* Ninth Annual Supplement, 1958 (published 1959).

or Atlanta, and just before World War II it could have supplied all of Washington, D. C., or the entire state of Nebraska. Utilities cannot safely rely on a single source of power if they are to avoid major interruptions of service. As a result, only a handful of the utilities in the country are large enough to build plants beyond the 300,000 to 400,000 kw levels of capacity.

Among hydroelectric stations, which account for about 20% of the power generated in the United States, the optimum plant clearly depends on the site used. Large sites are not always superior to small ones, but on the average, again, the larger the project the lower the cost per kilowatt-hour produced.* At any rate, capacities in the hundreds of thousands or even millions of kilowatts have been necessary to make the most efficient use of some of the best sites.

Load Factors, Fixed Costs, and Scale

It is often possible to reduce costs by expanding beyond the size of a single large plant. An electric utility must meet all of its regular customers' needs whenever they arise. Yet it is selling a service that cannot be stored. The only way to meet every demand is to have capacity at least as large as the peak load. If the demand is irregular, this means excess capacity much of the time. It is quite common for a city to use four or five times as much electricity at 6:00 P.M. on December 23 as it does at 3:00 A.M. on May 10. To meet the high demand two or three nights before Christmas, the power company may have to operate at 20% of capacity at other times of the day or year.

Operating at less than capacity means high costs per unit because electric companies, like most public utilities, have high fixed costs. Much more of the cost of electricity is in interest, depreciation, and property taxes than for most industries because it requires so much plant for each dollar of sale. Table 6.1 shows the total assets of firms in various fields as proportions of their annual sales. While manufacturing usually requires investments of less than a year's revenue, many utilities have assets of three times their annual receipts or more. Many of the labor costs of electric utilities are also fixed. A large part of the maintenance, administration, and accounting expenses must be incurred regardless of the level of output.

With such high fixed costs, an electric utility might have average cost curves like those in Figure 6.2. In this illustration, a firm operating at 20% of capacity would have costs of above 2.5¢ per kw-hr, but at capacity electricity could be produced at less than 1¢. Some excess capacity is inevitable and desirable. Even on December 22, the company will want a reserve generator in case something goes wrong, and in an expanding market it will probably build plants larger than immediate needs in order to have the advantages of scale later on.

---

* FPC, *Electric Utility Cost Units, Hydro-Electric Generating Stations* (FPC S78), a study of all reporting hydroelectric stations in the country, showed clearly decreasing construction and operating costs with increasing scale in 1947. However, it has been worthwhile in recent years to develop some sites with less than 1000 kw capacity.

TABLE 6.1

TOTAL ASSETS AS PERCENTAGES OF ANNUAL SALES
IN VARIOUS INDUSTRIES

Nonutilities	Per Cent	Utilities	Per Cent
Motor vehicles and equipment	60	Class A and B electric utilities	425
Textile mill products	68	Natural gas pipelines	285
Primary iron and steel	85	Class I railroads	287
Aluminum	163	Telephone (AT&T and principal	
All manufacturing	69	telephone subsidiaries)	285

Source: Federal Trade Commission, *Quarterly Financial Report, United States
Manufacturing Corporations, Fourth Quarter, 1959,* and *Moody's Public Utilities*
and *Industrial Manuals*–1960. All figures are for 1959.

The utilities often pursue the same policy as parents who buy pants
that are too long for a growing son. However, by keeping as close
to capacity as possible, the company can keep costs per kilowatt-
hour to a minimum.

The ratio of average demand over the year to peak demand is called
the *load factor*. If a utility runs at 120,000 kw on the average but
demand gets up to 200,000 kw sometime during the year, it has a load
factor of $\dfrac{120,000}{200,000}$ or 60%. Average cost is less, the higher the load
factor, so buyers who use power continuously, i.e., those who
have load factors approaching 100%, are very desirable customers.

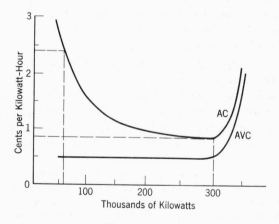

Figure 6.2

The aluminum industry is this sort of user except for occasional low levels of operation during depressions.

One way to even out production and reduce average cost would be to diversify customers. For instance, imagine three neighboring cities, one primarily residential (city R), one industrial (city I), and one comercial (city C). They might have the demand patterns shown in Table 6.2. If each city had its own plant, each would have to have a capacity of 100, making a total of 300, but since their peaks do not coincide, a single company could supply all three cities with a capacity of only 230. Electricity cannot be sent much more than 300 miles economically, so there is a limit to the area that a

TABLE 6.2

TIME OF DAY

City	2 P.M.	5 P.M.	7 P.M.	2 A.M.
R	30	60	100	20
I	100	60	60	40
C	60	100	70	10
Total	190	220	230	70

utility can serve, but there is often great diversity possible within a fairly compact region.

Public Utility Holding Companies

Because of their high fixed costs, uneven demand, and the need to supply power whenever the customer throws the switch, there has been a strong tendency for consolidation among power companies. In the first years of the industry every town had its own power company and the large cities often had many independent firms serving different parts of town, but today most metropolitan areas have single, unified companies, while smaller cities are usually served by regional power systems.

A common means of consolidating electric utilities in the 1910's and 1920's was the *holding company,* a firm holding the stock of other firms. Figure 6.3 gives a simplified picture of holding company organization. The single block at the top represents a holding company, the assets of which consist of the controlling stock in the four

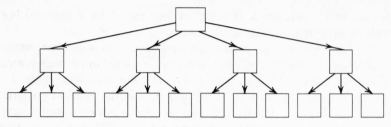

Figure 6.3

middle firms. These in turn hold stock in the 12 operating companies which are shown in the bottom tier in Figure 6.3. As a result, the persons who control the first company also control all 16 others. Operating utilities often raise as much as half of their capital in bonds and appreciable parts of the rest with preferred stock. Ordinarily, neither type of security has voting rights, so all the holding company needs for unquestioned control of its subsidiaries is a majority of their common stocks. This might amount to no more than 10 or 15% of the operating companies' total assets in some cases. If the middle tier of companies also borrow to finance their stock holdings, $1 million invested in the top level holding company in Figure 6.3 may be able to control operating companies with assets in the tens of millions.

The holding companies sometimes purchased controlling interests in their subsidiaries for cash, but in many instances they simply issued their own stock in return for the stock of the subsidiaries. Holding company stock could be very profitable partly because of the technical gains from consolidation, but also because of the large amounts of debt in public utility holding company structures. A numerical example may help to show how this came about. Imagine an operating utility with the following financial characteristics:

On total assets of	$1,000,000	it earns	$100,000 a year or 10%
But it has issued bonds of	$500,000	on which it pays interest of	$25,000 a year or 5%
This leaves stock of	$500,000	which earns	$75,000 a year or 15%

A holding company might acquire this stock, after which it could have the following financial characteristics:

On total assets of	$500,000	it would earn	$75,000 a year or 15%
It might issue bonds of	$200,000	on which it would pay interest of	$15,000 a year or 7½%
This would leave stock of	$300,000	earning	$60,000 a year or 20%

So long as the operating companies or the lower level holding companies can borrow money at interest rates below the rate of return on their assets, large amounts of debt in a holding company empire will enhance the rate of profit at the top. Of course, a heavy load of debt also makes the business more risky since the interest obligation on all these bonds does not cease when operating incomes decline. If the operating companies barely make enough to pay their interest during a depression, the first level holding companies would have no income with which to pay interest on their debts, and the higher level holding companies would be in even worse condition. Many industries are too unstable to undertake much borrowing, but electric utility incomes are traditionally very reliable. For this reason elaborate holding company structures containing heavy loads of debt blossomed particularly luxuriantly in the utility field.

The holding company structure in Figure 6.3 is conservative compared with some that were built in the 1920's. By the end of the decade there were public utility holding companies with assets of more than $1 billion each. In some of these, ultimate control was held by men with no more than million-dollar interests. There were cases where the center of power was six steps away from the operating firm. The organizers of these companies sometimes paid themselves spectacular promotors' fees, leaving the firms with large debts against questionable assets. Rival systems bid recklessly for small obsolete plants, sometimes incurring more debts in the process. Some of the holding companies sold supplies and services to their operating subsidiaries at very profitable prices. A few even borrowed from the subsidiaries, seeming to raise themselves by their own bootstraps.

Not all of the consolidations reduced costs. While some unified the utilities of a region, others had properties all over the country. One controlled utilities in 23 states!

When the depression came and the incomes of operating firms dropped off, the holding companies saw their receipts (their subsidiaries' dividends) fall drastically. Then the excessive debts of some structures brought them down in collapse, and the public suddenly became aware of holding company abuses. In 1935 Congress passed the Public Utility Holding Company Act under which holding company structures have since been drastically simplified. Holding companies more than two steps removed from operating firms have been eliminated, each company's holdings have been reduced to an "integrated" system in a contiguous area, and the accounting, service fees, dividends, security issues, and consolidations of utilities and holding companies have become subject to public control.

FORMS OF REGULATION

Franchises

Electricity production has had public utility status from its beginning, but regulation has taken several different forms at various times. When the first central station opened in New York City in 1882, local governments were attempting to control public utilities through their *franchises*, special charters which permitted the companies to operate under specified conditions and granted such privileges as the use of the streets and the power of eminent domain. The conditions set were not usually very exacting in the first years. Advantageous franchises were offered by public-spirited governments to get power companies into their cities and further their growth.

Later, the franchise became more a matter of control and less ot promotion. In franchise renewals or revisions, the city councils often attempted to include better rate and service provisions, but with limited success. The franchise was a poor method of control. City councils were inexpert in utility affairs and unable to judge the reasonableness of proposed rates. Further, once set the franchise provisions often could not be changed for long periods. In many cities, the awarding of franchises and the setting of their terms became a matter of wholesale graft. Much of the civic corruption at the turn of the century had to do with public utility franchises.

State Public Utility Commissions

One of the main reforms of the "progressive era" was the transfer of public utility regulation to expert supervisory commissions at the state level. Most of the states established public utility commissions in the decade before World War I with power to set rates and regulate service. Most public utility regulation is in the hands of such commissions today. Locally issued franchises still exist, but in most states they have little significance. The commissions have control over electric utilities in 43 of the 50 states.*

Federal Regulation

The federal government has played an important role in the control of electric utilities since 1935.† Its participation was necessary for several reasons. The constitution gave the federal government jurisdiction over navigable streams and rivers, and in the eyes of the courts this meant that Congress or its appointees could determine who might develop most of our hydroelectric sites. The FPC was formed in 1920 to issue licenses for such development.

With the long-distance transmission of electric power, interstate commerce became involved. The courts ruled that neither the commissions in consuming nor in generating states could regulate rates in such cases. To fill this gap, a reorganized FPC was given power over rates and service in interstate commerce beginning in 1935. For similar reasons, it was also given control over the interstate transmission of natural gas beginning in 1938.

Because of the financial excesses of the 1920's and the inability of the state commissions to deal with them, the FPC was also given extensive power over accounting, security issues, and consolidations within its jurisdiction. It was at the same time that the Securities and Exchange Commission (SEC) received the job of simplifying the organization and finances of public utility holding companies.

State commissions still have the main job in regulating electric utilities, but the new federal agencies have taken the lead in introducing many new methods and policies. The FPC was more aggres-

* The exceptions in 1954 (the most recent tabulation published by the FPC) were Iowa, Minnesota, Mississippi, Nebraska, South Dakota, Texas, and what was then the Territory of Alaska. FPC, *State Commission Jurisdiction and Regulation of Electric and Gas Utilities*, 1954.

† Federal regulation came earlier in some fields. The Interstate Commerce Commission (ICC) was established in 1887 to regulate the railroads, though its powers were very limited by the courts until additional legislation was passed in 1906. It also controlled pipelines from 1906 and was given some power over interstate telephone, telegraph, and cable service after 1910. In the 1920's the federal government began licensing hydroelectric developments, radio stations, and airlines but no rate regulation was involved. After 1935, federal regulation was expanded and reorganized. The ICC was given control over trucking and, later, some inland water carriers, a Federal Communications Commission (FCC) was formed with more power over telephone and telegraph companies than ICC had and with control over radio and television licenses, and a Civil Aeronautics Board (CAB) was established to regulate rates and services on the airlines.

sive than many state commissions and its rules were often stricter on such matters as accounting. Some companies actually disposed of their interstate connections to avoid federal jurisdiction. The FPC attempted to cooperate with state commissions though conflicts did arise. For the most part, its orders supplemented rather than over-rode those of state agencies.

THE GOALS OF PUBLIC UTILITY REGULATION

Monopoly Pricing and Rate Making

An unregulated electric utility would probably be a more powerful monopolist than Alcoa was. The demand for its product is not likely to be very elastic, because, unlike aluminum, electricity has very inadequate substitutes in the eyes of most users. Moreover, there is practically no threat of new competition at high prices, a considera-tion that seems to have been important to Alcoa.

The power company's policy can be analyzed in the same way that Alcoa's was. To simplify matters, we might start with the assump-tion made about marginal costs in Chapter 5: that in the long run any amount can be produced at the same cost by just installing more or less plant. To make the most profit in the situation shown in Figure 6.4, the utility would set a rate of 4¢ per kw-hr and build only enough capacity to supply the 100,000 kw-hr it could sell at that price.

This price and output would certainly not be in the public's best interest. Consumers are apparently willing to pay 4¢ for another kilowatt-hour and it would cost only 2¢ to produce one. They would be better off with more capacity and lower rates.

To eliminate the effect of the utility's monopoly position, the reg-ulator would have to set a price of 2¢ per kw-hr in this case. At that rate, there would be no monopoly profits for the firm. If it sold to all comers at 2¢, power production would be expanded until the last bit of current produced would cost just as much as someone would pay for it. Then there would be just enough electric power produced compared with other commodities.

The result of this analysis is a bit surprising. Normally one thinks of a price reduction leading to decreased output. Yet here a govern-ment-imposed price reduction resulted in new facilities and expanded production. The reason is that with a public utility commission ruling that the rate must be 2¢ no matter what, the heavy horizontal line in Figure 6.4 becomes the effective demand curve of the utility.

The company would not be allowed to force the price above 2¢ by keeping the plant at the 100,000 kw level, and if it is to satisfy its customers' demands it would have to expand.

Public utility commissions seldom have much to say about "marginal cost" in their deliberations. Their usual policy is to set rates that will cover costs of production and yield a "fair" return on the company's capital. However, in a case like Figure 6.4, where marginal costs are constant and therefore identical with average costs, the commissions' policy and the economists' recommendation would come to about the same thing. Remember that "cost," as the economist uses the word, includes a return on the owner's investment equal to what he can earn anywhere else. The utility in Figure 6.4 would be making enough to keep it in business if its rate were set at 2¢.

The usual rule of public utility regulation with regard to service is that the firm must stand ready to supply all comers within its regular market area. The company may not be required to send a line ten miles up Wildcat Gulch to the only house up there, but if new customers can be served without excessive loss the company is bound to do so. In the simple case of Figure 6.4, the commissioners would require the power company to supply everyone who is ready to pay 2¢ per kw-hr. Its output would have to expand to the 200,000 level.

Decreasing Costs

Things are more complicated if the costs of a regulated firm decline as capacity increases, and that is apparently the case with most electric utilities. Table 6.3 shows such a situation. If average hourly production is 120,000 kw, cost per unit will be less than at 100,000 kw (assuming load factors are the same in both cases) because larger plants have lower costs. As is always the case when the cost per

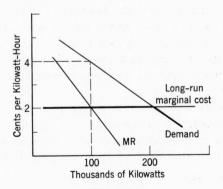

Figure 6.4

TABLE 6.3

Average Output per Hour (kw)	Total Cost per Hour (dollars)	Average Cost (cents per kilowatt-hour)	Marginal Cost (cents per kilowatt-hour)
100,000	2000	$\dfrac{\$2000}{100{,}000 \text{ kw}} = 2.0\cancel{c}$	$\dfrac{\$280}{20{,}000 \text{ kw}} = 1.4\cancel{c}$
120,000	2280	$\dfrac{\$2280}{120{,}000 \text{ kw}} = 1.9\cancel{c}$	

unit declines, the marginal cost turns out to be less than the average cost.* If the commission were to set a price equal to the marginal cost in this case, it would leave the utility operating at a loss!

Public utility commissions cannot set rates that impose losses in this way. In the eyes of the law such rates would amount to confiscation of the company's property. Under the constitutional provisions preventing the government from taking property without "due process of law," the courts have repeatedly ruled that commissions must allow public utility owners a reasonable return on their investments if market conditions permit. A public utility regulator would hardly be prudent to require operation at a loss anyway. Utility companies would be unable to raise new capital or render adequate service if such a situation continued for very long.

A decreasing average cost curve and the marginal cost curve that goes with it are shown in Figure 6.5. If the commission applied its usual standards in this case, it would have to set a rate of 2¢ per kw-hr, meaning an output of the 100,000 kw level; but at that rate consumers would be willing to pay considerably more than its marginal cost for additional current. Economic theory suggests that the public interest would be better served by a rate of 1.4¢, where the last unit produced cost just as much as it was worth to its buyer, but that would involve the company in a loss of 0.5¢ on every kilowatt-hour sold. To get such a rate, the government would have to pay a subsidy equal to the loss.

By and large, we have not been willing to subsidize public utilities in this way. Indeed, it is more usual to put especially heavy taxes on them. These taxes may have made some sense as a way to recoup monopoly profits in the days of weak controls, but now, when the

* See Chapter 2, p. 54.

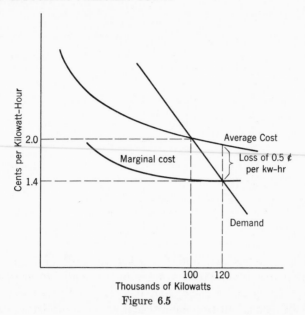

Figure 6.5

public utility commissions set prices that give the companies normal returns *after taxes*, these exactions simply raise rates and discourage service. Whether or not subsidization of public utility rates is feasible, there is a good case for the elimination of special taxes on public utilities at least in situations where regulation seems to work.*

PROBLEMS OF PUBLIC UTILITY REGULATION

It is one thing to decide that utility rates should cover costs plus a reasonable return and quite another to actually set such rates. Competitive markets automatically determine what production costs

---

* There is another criticism that applies to excise taxes in general including public utility taxes. Such taxes have the general fault that they distort consumer choice and lead people to buy the second best. A good example is a tax New England towns used to have on windows. As a result, New Englanders built houses with few windows, but of course they did not pay any less total taxes because the government had to raise just as much money as before. Similarly, a tax on public utilities leads the consumer to buy less electricity. As a result, he is not only out the tax, he also has a darker house just as his New England forebears did. To the extent that electricity is a decreasing cost industry, he also pays higher utility rates in addition to the tax. The tax raises the price, discourages consumption, and as a result keeps output at a high cost level.

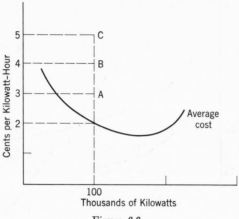

Figure 6.6

and normal profits are, and the entry and exit of firms results in prices that just cover these. In the utility field, however, a government agency must somehow find out the appropriate costs, profits, and prices. Public utility commissions face a bewildering list of difficulties that no one has to deal with in competitive markets.

Costs

For one thing, what costs should the rates cover? When economists construct average cost curves like the one in Figure 6.6 and conclude that at an output of 100,000 kw it costs 2¢ per kw-hr to produce electric power, they are discussing only the lowest possible cost. It is perfectly feasible to produce 100,000 kw at 3¢ or 4¢ or 5¢: points A, B, and C in Figure 6.6. The writer feels confident that he personally could contrive to produce electricity at costs as high as $10 or $15 per kw-hr. Cost curves are drawn as they are because we normally assume that profit-seeking businessmen will use the best methods available. In situations where the public utility commission sets rates that cover costs, however, the pressure to keep costs down may not be very great.

At any rate, some costs need scrutiny. What is there to stop the managers from giving themselves fine salaries and letting the customers foot the bill? How much can the holding company legitimately charge its subsidiaries for supplies and services? Should the utility have prices that cover obviously foolish expenditures? Some mistakes may have seemed wise in advance. If every wage increase leads automatically to a rate increase, how can the company be made to bargain effectively with the union? May advertising expenses legitimately be included in the price of power, especially when many of them are intended primarily to improve the company's political position? To be effective, a commission must carefully scrutinize the books of the utility and rule on many such issues before it sets rates.

Accounting

This is likely to be a difficult job because accounting is a complex art. When the accountant presents a picture of the firm's incomes and property, he must make a large number of more or less arbitrary estimates, and in many cases there are a variety of recognized ways of making these.

Depreciation is an important example. No one can say with certainty how long a piece of machinery will last or when it will become obsolete. If the company accountants conclude that their machinery has a short life or depreciates rapidly at first and slowly later on, their costs will seem high, at least in the first years, and the company's investment low. The opposite assumptions yield low costs and large assets. Since amortization and returns on the investment are a large part of utility costs, it makes a great deal of difference for electric rates how equipment is presumed to depreciate.

Depreciation is just one of a large number of accounting problems. Public utility commissions have found it necessary to specify accounting methods if their regulation is to be workable.

The Rate Base

In addition to production costs, the commission as a rule allows the utility a "fair" return on its investment. To do so, it must decide how much the company's investment is and what rate of return is "fair."

The firm's investment, properly evaluated for purposes of rate regulation, is known as the *rate base*. There are a variety of possible ways of determining it, and the battle over which method should be used raged violently in the courts and commissions for decades.

One possibility can be ruled out immediately. It will not do to use the market value of the utility's property or of its outstanding securities. The amount that the firm or its securities will sell for depends on what it earns, so any rate could be justified on this basis. If the commission were lax, market values would go up and high rates would seem appropriate. If it were strict, the company would have a lower value to investors, so the low rates would also seem justified.

To determine a reasonable rate base, the commission must put a value on the actual plant and equipment of the company. But what value? When the rate base was a major issue in the 1920's and 1930's, commissions tended to favor the original cost of installing the utility plant. At least it is fairly easy to calculate. The companies argued that it was unfair to evaluate their plants at prices of 20 years before and that the rate base should depend on the cost of reproducing them now.

The standard used by the courts until the 1940's was something called "fair value" which required that *both* original *and* reproduction costs "be given such weight as may be just and right in each case."* Moreover, the courts insisted on their power to review the evidence and conclusions of commission hearings in detail. Rate cases took years, and with such vague standards the commissions were always in danger of being overruled. The net result was a ritual suitable for musical comedy in which an august body of judges, commissioners, engineers, lawyers, and accountants labored to determine a hypothetical value for a utility so that it would not be deprived of its property without due process of law while the price of its common stock soared. The simple way to avoid all this was for the commission to be relatively lax in its regulation and keep disputes from arising. Then of course the stock soared even more.

The long and futile legal battles over rate base questions have largely been ended as a result of the FPC's case against the Hope Natural Gas Company, decided in 1944. The FPC had used methods in evaluating the gas company's assets that were considerably stricter than those required by the courts in previous decisions, and it ordered a substantial reduction in wholesale gas prices as a result. Hope Natural Gas was a very prosperous firm with a good dividend and earnings record. There was no question of the FPC undermining the company. The court decided that, in such circumstances, it was the results that counted and that since the property was obviously not being confiscated the court had no reason to intervene. "If the total effect of the rate order cannot be said to be unjust and unreasonable, judicial inquiry under the Act is at an end."†

Since the Hope case, the courts have generally been willing to respect the expert findings of regulatory commissions and to review only questions of procedure. The commissions have been free to

---

* Smyth v. Ames, 169 US 546 (1898).

† FPC v. Hope Natural Gas Co., 320 US 602 (1944).

settle rate base questions pretty much for themselves. Most of them now use original cost.*

Original Cost Versus Reproduction Cost

The legal and administrative questions about how to evaluate the utilities' plants may be settled for the time being, but the economic question is still open.† If the criteria used to judge the economic efficiency of other industries can be trusted, the original cost standard is subject to some criticism.

In *purely competitive* industries, the problem would be solved automatically. The long-run equilibrium price would be one that afforded a normal return to the last firms to enter the industry. The value of their plants would depend on the *current* cost of erecting them. If the original cost of an older plant in a purely competitive industry exceeded the current cost of building the same amount of capacity, the owners of the old plant would show less than normal profits on their books until their plants wore out. If the old plants cost less to build than their current replacements, the owners of the old plants in an expanding industry would show more than normal book profits as long as their plants lasted. No one could compete away their profits even with completely free entry because all firms would have higher dollar costs. In other words, purely competitive prices tend to settle at levels that cover replacement, *not* original costs.

The widespread use of original cost in public utility rate making could result in rates that are *too low* for economic efficiency after a period of rapidly rising plant construction costs. A price for electricity that covers the cost of power plants built in 1939 might be considerably below the long-run marginal cost of power in 1959. The long-run marginal cost in an expanding industry depends on the cost of new plants, not old ones. A price below the long-run marginal cost would encourage consumers to buy too much electricity. They would increase their consumption beyond the point where they are just paying the full cost of the last kilowatt-hour used.

* FPC, *State Commission Jurisdiction . . . , op cit.* Of 43 reporting commissions, 29 said that they preferred an original cost base, one (Ohio) was required to use replacement cost by law, and 13 reported that they used "fair value" or "considered all elements."

† Moreover, a somewhat related issue about how to evaluate plant for income tax purposes is the subject of much debate in such industries as steel. See Chapter 7, pp. 312–313.

There are good arguments against using replacement cost, however. As we have seen, decreasing costs, public utility taxes, or ineffective regulation may result in rates that are *more than* long-run marginal costs. To some extent, at least, the tendency for rates to be too high on these counts and the tendency for them to be too low in time of inflation because of original cost valuation will cancel each other out.

The main argument for original cost is that it makes regulation much easier and therefore more effective. Replacement costs would require continuous changes in the accounts of the firms because of changing price levels and changing technology. They would provide much more room for argument in evaluating plant than original costs do. Moreover, replacement costs would probably be an acceptable substitute for original costs only so long as construction costs rose. If rapid improvements in technique resulted in a *reduction* in the cost of a kilowatt of capacity, the commission would probably not be able to reduce its valuation of existing plants. In a competitive market the owner of an obsolete plant may incur losses as long as his plant lasts, but for a commission to set rates that impose money losses on the utility companies would be taking property without due process of law!

Even in the heyday of "fair value" the utility commissions did not use replacement costs in this sense. They used "reproduction cost," the cost of reproducing the *same* plant at current prices even if the plant was out of date and no one would think of actually reproducing it. There is some plausible economic justification for using replacement costs but reproduction costs made a mockery of any logic there might have been.

The most common argument presented by the public utilities against original cost valuations had to do with questions of "fairness" rather than economic efficiency. They claimed that their stockholders were being cheated out of some of their property because of the commissions' actions. By using original cost in evaluating the plants, the commissions were maintaining the dollar return to the investors, but in time of inflation when the dollar was decreasing in value, this meant that the stockholders received less in purchasing power than they had when the plants were first built.

There is little question but what a constant dollar income means a declining real income in time of inflation, but whether the public utility commissions have an obligation to make up for inflation with higher rates is open to question. After all, the same thing happened to anyone who bought bonds or mortgages or life insurance during the same period, but few would argue that the government (or the public utilities themselves) should scale up the interest on bonds that have already been sold.* People who bought public utility stocks knew they were buying securities that offered stable incomes, just as the buyers of bonds did.

Fair Return

Having arrived at some sort of rate base, the commission must next decide what rate of return is reasonable. In view of all the uproar over valuation, the commissions worried surprisingly little about the return. They often selected some convenient figure, such as 6%, and applied it generally year after year. However, in recent years, with the rate base question settled, the rate of return has taken its place as a major issue.

A number of commissions have attempted to determine the interest, dividends, and retained earnings necessary to raise the company's capital on current security markets and have set rates that would cover these. In other words, they have attempted to determine the rate of return on the basis of the "cost of capital," just as they cover the cost of labor and of other factors employed. Since the "cost of capital" for utilities depends on what investors can earn on their money elsewhere, it might approximate the "normal return" of pure competition.

Difficulties can arise in calculating the "cost of capital." For instance, what combination of stocks and bonds should be used? Since interest on bonds is ordinarily lower than the dividends and retained earnings assignable to common stock, the cost of capital is apt to be lower the greater the proportion of bonds to stock. On the other hand, a utility financed primarily with bonds would be too shaky to serve the public interest well. Or again, what proportion of earnings should be paid out in dividends? Other things being equal the higher the proportion paid out, the lower the total earnings necessary to make stock attractive to investors as a rule. In other words, a low level of retained earnings may mean a low "cost of capital." It will also mean a smaller cushion of owners' equity, however. If accumulation of retained earnings is too low, the company will be in a poor position

---

* It is often necessary for the government or other borrowers to pay more interest on *new* bonds to make particular issues more attractive during an inflation, but this is a different point. The analogous argument that public utilities need higher yields to attract capital is taken up in the next section.

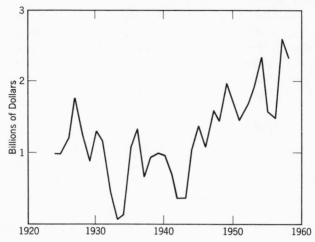

Figure 6.7.   Security issues of electric utilities.   Source: *Moody's Public Utility Manual*, 1959.

to face a decline in earnings.   To properly appraise the "cost of capital" a commission must decide upon a desirable bond ratio and a desirable dividend payout ratio.

From time to time the utilities have predicted that with their rate bases fixed at original cost and with strict regulation of returns they would have difficulty in raising capital in the future.   The "cost of capital" approach would automatically solve this problem, however. If new issues could only be sold at higher interest or dividend rates, the commissions would have to allow higher earnings.   The "cost of capital" would have risen.   In practice, the drying up of sources of capital has yet to appear.   Figure 6.7 shows the dollar amounts of electric utility stock and bonds issued from 1924 to 1958.   Altogether the electric utilities raised some $24 billion in the 14 years from the end of World War II to 1958, and the annual amounts have been increasing if anything.   Utility issues as a whole accounted for more than 40% of the security offerings of all corporations combined during the 1950's.*   The ease with which new utility issues have been sold leaves room for doubt about how seriously the owners of utility stock have felt themselves cheated by inflation.

* Between 1951 and 1959 electric, gas, water, and communication utilities offered securities with gross proceeds of $40 billion.   All corporate offerings came to $94 billion in the same nine years, so the utility share came to 42.5% on the average. Derived from Security and Exchange Commission, *Statistical Bulletins, passim.*

Utility Rates

Finally, having determined allowable expenses, a valuation of the rate base, and a rate of return, the commission must set a price that will cover these. What prices will yield a company a profit of $15 million a year? The answer obviously depends on the elasticity of demand, something we usually have to guess about. Commissions seldom study demand very carefully. They often act as if the elasticity of demand were 0 so that a 10% decrease in rates would reduce total revenue by 10%.

The effect of this assumption is shown in Figure 6.8. Suppose that the commission is faced with a situation where rates are 3¢ and output 75,000 kw. If it assumes that there will be no change in the

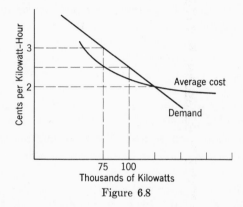

Figure 6.8

quantity purchased when rates change (i.e., that elasticity of demand is 0) it will cut rates to 2.5¢, eliminating the excess profits. At first the commission may seem to be right. It takes time for people to buy deep freezes and air conditioners in response to lower rates. But before long output will be up to the 100,000 level because elasticity really was more than 0. Then, with decreasing costs, the company will be making large profits again and another rate reduction will be in order.

Since it takes a long time for each rate decision and subsequent demand adjustment, it will be years before rates reach 2¢ in Figure 6.8. If the regulated firms could take temporary losses, rates could be reduced from 3¢ to 2¢ immediately and the public would have the advantage of lower rates and more service much sooner. Federal power projects in the Tennessee Valley and the Pacific Northwest have priced electricity on the assumption of a fairly elastic demand

and have had spectacular results.* Per capita residential consumption in the Tennessee Valley is about double the national average. Some cities in the area have even higher levels of consumption. Chattanooga is the national leader in this respect; four-fifths of the houses in the city are heated electrically.

Rate Differentials

Electric utilities seldom charge the same rates to all customers. Commonly there are different rates for residential, commercial, and various types of industrial buyers, as well as quantity discounts. Power companies are in a better position to maintain price differences of this sort than Alcoa was because it is practically impossible for users who pay low rates to resell to those who pay more.

It was rate discrimination as much as anything else that led to the demand for regulation of the railroads in the late 1800's. The public rightly associated discrimination with monopolistic exploitation. There was also strong criticism of the advantages large industrial buyers had over their smaller competitors as a result of the rebates and discounts they were able to win. Consumers who pay high rates have understandably objected, and economists have raised the further criticism that prices do not ration goods among consumers as efficiently with discrimination as when there are uniform rates.

In spite of a long-standing public distrust of price discrimination, however, public utility commissions have allowed much of it to remain. Blatant inequities have sometimes been disallowed, but an aggressive regulator is more likely to scale down all rates, leaving rate differentials intact.

There is some justification for rate differentials. For one thing, they are not always discriminatory. If electricity delivered to the only house at the head of Wildcat Gulch costs twice as much as that sold to a house in the middle of town, a uniform rate will really discriminate against the people who live close in. Of course, it often does not pay to bill customers on a different basis because of only slightly different costs, but customers can be grouped in broad categories and treated differently according to the costs of the different services.

* Part of this was an increase in the whole demand curve rather than a movement along the old demand curve. The coming of TVA brought higher incomes to the Tennessee Valley area in particular, and these led to higher demand for power. Yet Tennessee Valley residential consumption in 1959 came to 7863 kw-hr per person against 3450 kw-hr per person over the whole country. The 1¢ per kw-hr bills against 2.5¢ for most of us must account for much of this. TVA, *op. cit.*, p. 42.

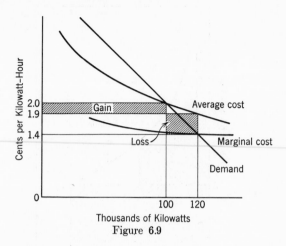

Figure 6.9

A class of customers would be less costly to serve if it had a large off-peak demand requiring no additional plant, if it had a steady demand over time so that it could be served with little excess capacity, or if it offered a large demand at one point so that the company could save on distribution and office costs. Some, though not all, of the advantageous rates paid by industrial users can be defended on this basis.*. However, the utilities have good reason to set lower rates for large industrial users than for the rest of us even when there is no cost advantage. Since the large user has the alternative of supplying his own power or locating in another part of the country, he has a much more elastic demand for electricity than other buyers. A profit-maximizing electric utility would normally discriminate in favor of such a customer.

Some price discrimination may be in the public interest in an industry with decreasing costs. Figure 6.9 shows such a case. Here a commission that must set a single rate can go no lower than 2¢ per kw-hr, so output cannot exceed 100,000 kw. If the utility is permitted to charge 2¢ for the first 100,000 kw of consumption and 1.4¢ for additional power, however, it can operate profitably at 120,000 kw, producing power out to the point where consumers are just willing to pay the cost of the last bit produced. It costs 1.9¢ per kw-hr to produce at 120,000 kw, but the company does not take a loss by selling some power at 1.4¢ because of the profits made on the

* Initially, industrial demand coming at midday was clearly off-peak and required no extra capacity. In many areas today, however, industrial demand far exceeds residential demand, and it is as likely to be the reason for new plant as household use.

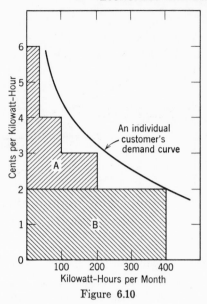

Figure 6.10

rest which sells at 2¢. In this case nobody pays more for power than with the single rate, some pay less, and output is expanded.*

Most electric utilities charge block rates, i.e., lower rates for increased consumption like the following:

First	25 kw-hr per month		6¢
Next	75 kw-hr per month		4¢
Next	100 kw-hr per month		3¢
Next	200 kw-hr per month		2¢

Instead of cutting the price on all electricity in order to sell more, they cut only the price on additional sales.† If their rate schedules

---

* Strictly speaking, the demand curve in Figure 6.9 is not quite the same as demand curves shown elsewhere in this book. Demand curves usually show the amounts that would be bought at various uniform prices. This one differs on two counts: (1) a general price cut would permit all consumers to expand consumption, but in discriminating the utilities are apt to cut rates for only some customers, especially industrial users with elastic demands. The rest of us are left at the 2¢ level and buy no more than before. (2) A general price cut would leave us with a bit more money than a partial one, and we would very likely spend some of it on extra electricity. On both counts, the quantity of electricity would be somewhat greater if all rates were cut to 1.4¢ instead of just some of them.

† To some extent these block rates reflect cost differences. The distribution line, meter, and billing expenses are likely to cost the company as much in total for the 25 kw-hr household as for the 75 kw-hr household.

fit buyers' demand curves, as in Figure 6.10, they can come close to the level of sales that they would have with a simple price of 2¢, but they would earn total revenues equal to the entire shaded area (A plus B) rather than just that below the 2¢ line (B).

Public utility rates are very complex. Railroads charge so many different rates for various types of freight and for different distances and regions that their rates fill volumes. Electric utility rates are simpler, but it is not uncommon to find 30 different rate classifications in a single town, not to mention quantity discounts. It is close to impossible for commissioners to determine whether these rate differences are all justified by cost or additional service. The regulators often accept the rate structures that the companies propose and try to regulate their over-all levels.

The Regulators

Although the details of the last few pages may seem complicated to anyone new to the subject, he should be warned that this discussion has really only skimmed over the surface of rate making. Perhaps the most important conclusion he should draw is that public utility regulators have a very complex set of questions to consider. It is no simple task to duplicate the effects of competition in a monopolistic industry.

Not all public utility commissions have been equal to the tasks imposed upon them. The funds appropriated for their use are often inadequate. In many states, technical staffs are too small. Salaries are often too low to attract good men. In 1954, the average state paid its public utility commissioners $8300 and ten paid them $6000 or less.* Utility companies often pay engineers, attorneys, and accountants higher starting salaries than this.

Commissioners are appointed in some states and elected in others. If elected, they are fairly far down a long ballot and unknown names to most voters. It is really the nominating machinery that determines who gets the job. It often goes to a loyal party worker. The best commissions are appointed, but some appointed commissions are far from the ideal. The governor may find that the public utility commission is an excellent place to reward his political supporters.

Most states have legal provisions protecting the commissioners' independence by such devices as long tenure and staggered terms. However, legislative and administrative officials sometimes do influence their decisions, and outright graft has occurred. The federal agencies like the FPC, the FCC, and the SEC are among the best

* FPC, *State Commission Jurisdiction . . . , op. cit.*, p. 34.

staffed and paid, but in the late 1950's congressional investigations turned up a number of questionable cases in several of these commissions involving the resignation of the presidential assistant and of two FCC commissioners, one of whom was later prosecuted.

Some observers have felt that even scrupulously honest and clearly competent commissions see things too much from the point of view of the regulated industry. It takes only a short step for commissioners to conclude that their job is not only to prevent excessive profits but also to assure normal ones, at least so long as the management is reasonably careful. Again, it is probably not in the public's interest to dog the companies' heels and adjust rates immediately whenever some small cost saving is achieved. If they could not look forward to even temporarily high profits, the utilities would have no incentive to increase efficiency. Yet, if this point of view is carried far enough, there is very little regulation left.

Probably most commissioners have sought what they felt was the public's best interest, but different persons have different ideas about what that might be. The ICC saw fit to consistently oppose the development of the St. Lawrence Seaway for a generation because the commissioners thought that by weakening the position of the railways it would hurt the country.

PERFORMANCE

Production

The experience of the electric power industry during this century is indicated in the output, price, profit and productivity series shown in Figures 6.11, 6.12, 6.13, and 6.14. In each case, they are compared with similar series for all manufacturing.

Figure 6.11 shows the electric industry's output record. The generation of electric power, like aluminum production, is a new industry which has grown much faster than industry generally. On the average, electricity output has doubled every 7 years since the turn of the century. By comparison aluminum production doubled every 6 years and industrial production, every 18. This is to be expected. Not only were the power companies supplying the needs of a growing country; they also provided a convenient substitute for the human, animal, and direct steam power that had been the main source of energy previously.

The growth in electric power production has been much more steady

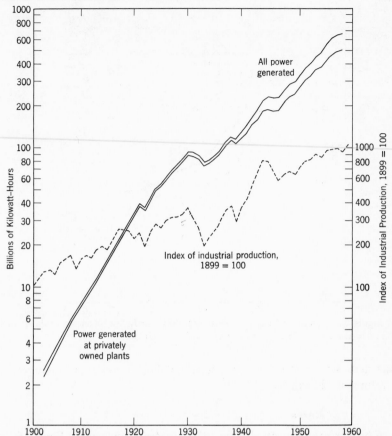

Figure **6.11**. Source: *Historical Statistics of the United States;* FPC, *Statistics of Electric Utilities in the United States,* 1958; and *Federal Reserve Bulletins.*

than the growth in most of industry. Once electricity had won new users, it never lost them again. Even in major depressions, demand barely declined. This was due in large part to the character of the product. In household use, at least, the income elasticity of demand must be very low. Once the high fixed costs of wiring the house and buying the refrigerator have been incurred, few people will pull out the plug to save the small marginal cost—the electric bill—even if their incomes fall. Moreover, electric power is the most fleeting of perishable commodities. Consumers and businessmen can use last year's refrigerator or last year's power lines when a depression hits, but they cannot use last year's power. At any rate, the stability of electric power demand was certainly not a matter of rate policy dur-

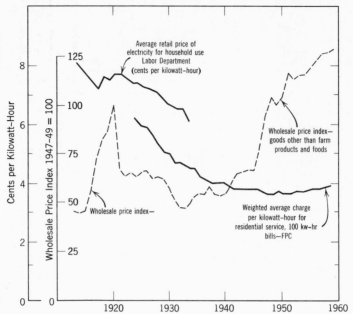

Figure 6.12.   Source: *Statistical Abstract, 1934* (for Labor Department data), and FPC, *Statistics of Electric Utilities in the United States.*

ing depression years.   Rates just do not fall in response to temporary declines in demand.

Rates

The performance of electric utility rates is shown in Figure 6.12. Of course, electric rates depend on who is paying them and how much he consumes.   The FPC series, starting in 1924, shows the average rate paid in cities of more than 50,000 population by residential consumers buying 100 kw-hr per month.   An earlier series (1913–33) collected by the Department of Labor is also shown.   It is a less reliable figure, though the best available.   The Labor Department rates are higher than those reported by the FPC because they assume that buyers are taking smaller amounts of electricity.

Electric power is almost the only industry whose prices have consistently declined since 1913.*   In part, this is simply another case of

* Residential rates for 100 kw-hr bills did increase about 8% from the low in 1948 to 1958.   In the same period, however, the wholesale price index for nonfarm, nonfood products generally was rising by 24%.   The average consumer's rate did not even increase by 8% because most people were buying more electricity in 1958 than in 1948.

a new industry with decreasing costs and an expanding market. In the 1920's, rapid technical progress and increasing scale resulted in continuously falling rates even though that was ·the period when the regulatory commissions were most weakened by judicial decisions. A number of rate reductions at that time were made voluntarily without orders from the commissions, implying that the commissions were ordering rates *higher* than the levels that seemed most profitable to the companies!

In the depression years of 1931–35 utility rates fell more slowly at a time when most prices were falling drastically. In part, this was the result of the rate-making formula. When output declined, the overhead had to be carried by a smaller number of kilowatt-hours so that average cost increased. This was offset in part by reductions in labor and fuel expenses, but commissions were in no position to require rate reductions using their old standards.* Alcoa maintained stable prices during the depression years also, and in that case it was interpreted as a monopolist exercising his monopoly power to protect himself. It is interesting that commission regulation resulted in a similar policy.

There was a sharp decline in rates in 1935. That was the year when the tougher federal legislation dealing with electric power was passed, so the industry was under close scrutiny. It also marked the return of electricity output to the predepression level so fixed costs per kilowatt-hour fell once more.

In the years since 1936, the remarkable thing about electricity prices has been their stability. In a period of general inflation, the failure of electric rates to rise amounts to a continuation of the downward trend of the 1920's.

Rate stability in time of rising prices is a common characteristic of public utilities. It is a result of regulatory practices again. The machinery of rate changes is so slow-moving that upward adjustments are apt to lag behind general price increases. As a result, regulated firms are often unprofitable during periods of rapid inflation. Moreover, the present-day basis for rate regulation permits very little upward adjustment in many cases. If plants are evaluated at their original cost, then depreciation, property taxes, and a stable return on the company's investment cannot increase except as new plant is

---

* On the basis of reduced traffic and high overhead the railroads were actually permitted to raise rates during these years. In retrospect, this was probably not a very wise move on the part of the regulators or the railroads. The demand for their service was certainly not inelastic in view of the alternative means of transportation available. A rate reduction might have increased railroad earnings more.

added and even then they will creep up slowly. Labor and fuel costs
can rise rapidly, but in the power industry these are less than half
the total. Moreover, even in these cases the slow-moving regulatory
machinery results in a lag of months or even years between cost and
rate increases.

The power industry continued to accomplish cost savings in the
1940's and 1950's. Technical changes, a great increase in scale, more
even loads owing to increased industrial use, the use of low-cost
natural gas, and cheap government power all played a part. Their net
effect was to reduce costs fast enough to make up for rising labor and
construction expenses.

Profits

Figure 6.13 shows electric utility profits compared with those of all
manufacturing corporations. The FPC required all electric utilities
falling under its jurisdiction to adopt uniform accounting practices
beginning January 1, 1937. Earnings shown for electric firms from
that date onward are reported by the FPC.

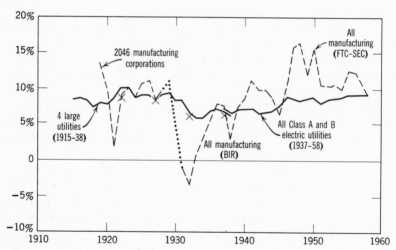

Figure 6.13. Profits after tax in electric utilities and manufacturing. Source:
Electric utilities: 1915–38, Annual reports of Boston Edison, Consolidated Gas and
Electric Light and Power of Baltimore, Detroit Edison, and Pacific Gas and Electric
as presented in *Moody's Public Utilities Manuals;* the ✕'s represent returns from
the 1922, 1927, 1932, and 1937 Censuses of Electrical Industries. 1937–58, all Class A
and B utilities, FPC, *Statistics of Electric Utilities . . . , op. cit.*

All manufacturing: 1919–28, R. C. Epstein, *Industrial Profits in the United States,*
National Bureau of Economic Research, 1934. 1931–47, Bureau of Internal Revenue,
Statistics of Income; 1947–58. FTC-SEC, *Quarterly Financial Reports, United
States Manufacturing Corporations.*

For earlier years the figures are poor. Public utility accounting yielded amazing results at times during the 1920's. The FPC has required the companies to write off or amortize about 20% of the assets they claimed in 1937, and to increase greatly the rates at which they depreciate their equipment. It is clear that company accounts for earlier years exaggerated the value of the firms so that reported rates of profit before 1937 are too low. Rates of profit in Figure 6.12 for 1915–38 are based on the annual reports of four large utilities that remained independent of outside holding companies over the whole period. There were very few such companies. These check fairly closely with the results of the Censuses of Electrical Industries in 1922, 1927, 1932, and 1937 (the x's in Figure 6.13).

Even with some understatement, the reported profits of these companies were as good as those of the average manufacturer in the 1920's. In the 1930's, when their sales fell less than most firms' and their prices stayed up, the electric companies did much better than most of industry. The electric utilities did not participate in the high profits common in inflationary years like 1941–42, 1946–48, and 1950 because they did not participate in the inflations, but they were normally prosperous even in those years.

Over the whole period shown in Figure 6.13 the most remarkable thing about electric utility earnings is their stability. The character of demand and the standards of regulation seem to assure a regular return. Since there is apparently less risk in this sort of industry, earnings need not include such large risk premiums as elsewhere. In other words, taking the record into account, the utilities are really quite prosperous when they show only average rates of profit.

Productivity

Figure 6.14 compares estimates of the increase in output per man-hour in manufacturing, in electric power (1917–43), and in all public utilities and communications industries (1889–1954). Whichever estimate is used, productivity has grown much faster in the utilities than in manufacturing. This is to be expected in the first years of an industry, especially where economies of scale are apparently very great. The continuation of the trend in productivity for two-thirds of a century without slowing up is quite impressive, nevertheless. The rapid increase in productivity in the electric utilities is an important reason, along with the commissions' emphasis on original costs, for their declining or stable rates when most prices were rising.

The electric power industry can hardly be charged with any failure to make progress in spite of the monopoly positions of its members.

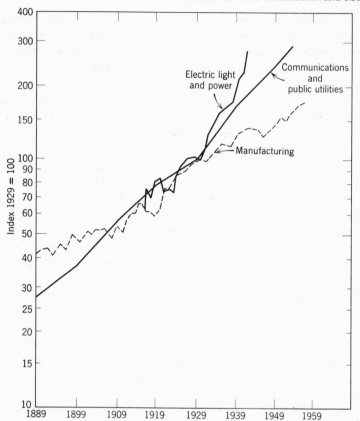

Figure 6.14. Output per man-hour, 1929 = 100. Source: Manufacturing and communications and public utilities from Solomon Fabricant, *Basic Facts of Productivity Change*, National Bureau of Economic Research, Occasional Paper 63, 1959, Chart 4. Electric light and power, Jacob Gould, *Output and Productivity in Electric and Gas Utilities 1899–1942*, National Bureau of Economic Research, 1946, p. 70.

On the other hand, the utilities have an exceptionally standardized and unchanging product. Their innovations have been primarily cost-saving rather than product-improving changes. The utilities had rapidly expanding markets with a demand that was quite stable during short-run fluctuations and with no threat of competitors who might make their plants prematurely obsolete. In such a setting, the installation of usually well-tested new equipment and techniques would be far less risky than the innovations in most of manufacturing. The development of this new equipment was an impressive achievement, but this was done primarily outside of the industry. It was firms in the electrical equipment industry such as General Electric and Westinghouse that developed the huge new equipment, and firms in the metallurgical fields that were responsible for the new metals which made the high temperatures and pressures of the new equipment possible. The equipment manufacturers have also carried on most of the private research on atomic power, though a few of the larger utilities have cooperated in building pilot plants. The electrical equipment manufacturers are in a position where they must make progress or lose out to their rivals. The electric utilities have no rivals.

UNPROFITABLE UTILITIES

The Goals of Regulation Once More

Electric power production has experienced an almost continuous boom during the last 70 years, but not all regulated industries have been as fortunate. Some, including many railroads in the last century and the airlines until recently, were built in advance of demand and had to wait many unprosperous years until the markets they were designed to serve caught up with them. Some were just poor ideas to begin with. Finally, many of the once prosperous railroads and urban transit systems have simply fallen on hard times as new means of transportation have taken their place.

Regulation in cases of this sort involves very different problems from the regulation of prosperous utilities like electric power. The main goal is no longer the elimination of monopolistic profits—there are no profits to eliminate. In fact, the problem becomes one of keeping the company afloat and the service available.

Figure 6.15 illustrates the regulatory problem in the case of a railroad where demand has fallen off. Since the plant (roadbed, track, bridges, tunnels, etc.) is already installed, the short-run cost curve for that plant is shown. Average cost inevitably declines as the large overhead of the railroad is spread over more and more service. The demand in this particular case is such that there is only one rate that would cover costs. At any higher or lower rate the firm would take losses. The regulatory commission trying to set rates that yield a normal profit *must* approve a price of 2¢, just what the most exploitative of monopolists would charge.

Of course, there may not be any rate that would be profitable. This is the case in Figure 6.16. If the commission is to keep *losses*

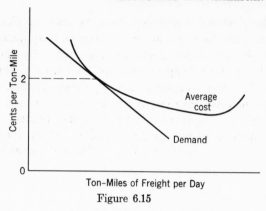

Figure 6.15

at a minimum it must again set the most exploitative possible price, 2¢ in this case.

Rate Discrimination Once More

It might be possible to completely avoid losses in a situation like that shown in Figure 6.16 by rate discrimination. Instead of charging all customers 2¢, the railroad might set a rate of 3¢ per ton-mile for those who would pay it (customers with more valuable freight, at least if they have no alternative means of transportation) and 1¢ a mile for other groups who cannot or will not pay 2¢ (perhaps shippers with very bulky products or those at ocean or lake ports). The additional revenues indicated by rectangles A and B make up all the losses that the company would suffer without discrimination.

It is difficult to object to discrimination when it keeps in operation a company that would otherwise go under. It might be better not to build the railroad from scratch starting today, but with it already in existence we might as well use it. If by discrimination we can get the facilities used closer to the point where the last carload of freight is just worth its extra costs, the public as well as the firm may be better off.

Some of our railroads would probably *never* have been profitable if no discrimination had been allowed. In these cases discrimination was a way of subsidizing an unprofitable enterprise. Ordinarily such a policy means encouraging businessmen to make the wrong investments, but if there are external economies, it may make possible publically desirable projects. Many of the nineteenth century railroads that opened up new regions obviously did offer rapid economic development that in many cases made the investment worthwhile for society even if not for the companies.

Discriminatory rates are universal on the railroads and are so complicated that only experts with years of experience can understand the entire structure. To be sure, the law does not allow railroads to discriminate between individuals within the same class, but classes are defined minutely, and the railroads have been permitted to discriminate among groups of customers according to "what the traffic will bear." There are special rates for hundreds of different commodities. Rates are sometimes more in one direction than the other, and in one part of the country than another. In Canada, where the waterways freeze up, there are even higher rates in winter than in summer. Of course, the marginal costs are not the same for all services rendered by the railroads, but freight rates and marginal costs show no consistent relationship.

Competition

In the days before the ICC, unregulated rate discrimination sometimes got the railroads into trouble. As good monopolists, they set low rates where elasticities were high (i.e., where they had lots of competition) and made up for it with high charges on noncompetitive business. Since most of their competition in those days came from other railroads, this meant occasionally spectacular rate wars. Agreements among the roads to prevent such rate rivalry were common and caused much discontent among shippers, especially in the farm belt.

One of the main effects of regulation on the railroads was the suppression of rate competition among the different lines. Wholesale discrimination continued, but the ICC coordinated rate policies between lines.

After trucking became a serious competitor of the railroads that, too, was brought under ICC control. In 1935 the ICC was empowered to license interstate truckers (with some major exceptions such as those handling farm products and those hauling their own freight) and to regulate their rates. In 1940 its authority was extended to

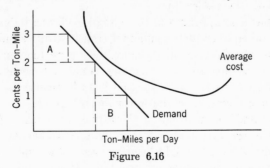

Figure 6.16

common carriers on inland waterways. In both cases, the government provides the roadbeds (highways and waterways), and the carriers pay for them only in license fees and gasoline taxes. As a result, the investments necessary to start business are relatively small so the two industries are potentially very competitive. With federal regulation, however, the number of common carriers is limited and price competition is suppressed.

When it became responsible for the rates of these other freight carriers, the ICC *in effect* had the unpleasant job of deciding on each group's share of the market. At rates that have prevailed over the last two decades truck and barge traffic has increased enormously in spite of obvious railroad overcapacity, but whenever railroads seek rate reductions on traffic in competition with the trucks and barges the other carriers object that such changes would be discriminatory. Of course, this is true, though rail rates are discriminatory anyway. With the strong opposition of these other groups the ICC has been slow to make changes. In recent years the railroads have sponsored and other carriers have opposed legislation that would limit the ICC's power to prevent rate *reductions*. They have recognized a change in the elasticity of demand for some of their services and are trying to change their rates accordingly.

Subsidies

Even the most advantageous level and structure of rates may not be enough to make some utilities profitable. If not, the firms must either be subsidized or go bankrupt ultimately. Both have happened. In the early years of the railroads the federal and state governments made large land grants to firms that built lines across the West. State and local governments often offered tax exemptions and even built some facilities for the railroads in the early days. Similarly, the federal government subsidized the airlines through advantageous postal contracts, built many airports and air navigation aids, and still subsidizes the feeder lines.

Subsidy has also appeared in the case of declining industries. Some cities have taken over their municipal transit utilities, not because of a trend toward socialism but because they were too unprofitable for private firms to operate. The service could not be abandoned because downtown business depended on it and because it was the main means of transportation of the lower income group.

The cities had to run some of these lines at a loss. A subsidy in this case was unavoidable, but there was still the question of how much subsidy. The city might keep its losses at a minimum by taking full advantage of its monopoly position. It could set rates at 25¢

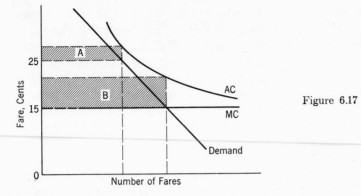

Figure 6.17

in a case like Figure 6.17, experience only a small loss (area A), and run half-empty busses. Alternatively, the city could set a rate such as 15¢ in Figure 6.17. The busses would be more fully used, and the price would meet the marginal cost standard, but the city would be involved in a more substantial loss (area B). In fact, the higher fare might actually be more expensive to the city over-all. This could happen because the city would have to build more parking lots and widen more streets for people who drove to work instead of riding the busses or subways. The point is that all our cities subsidize automobile commuters in this way. In many cases it may be cheaper to pay a bigger subsidy on busses and subways and save traffic costs.

Reorganizations

The alternative to subsidy in some of these cases is for the company to go broke. Although a pretty drastic remedy, this can sometimes solve the problem. Usually the firm will not go out of business as a result; it will simply be reorganized. Stockholders will lose their claim on the company and creditors may accept a reduced claim as better than nothing at all, or the facilities will be sold for what they will bring, and the new buyer will operate the firm. The buyer will not pay the full original cost, of course, but only a price that seems warranted in view of the prospective returns. After the reorganization, then only a part of the original fixed costs must be borne by the firm. Figure 6.18 shows the cost curves of a railroad which took $100 million to build and which went into receivership. After it was sold for $50 million, or its obligations were scaled down to that level, it could again operate without losses.*

* If the reorganized firm is to be workable, the claims must be scaled down to a suitable level. Since this means that someone must lose out, it has not always happened. In the case of railroads the ICC as well as security holders must now approve any reorganization plan.

There is not enough revenue here to cover the cost of a complete railroad. If it ever wears out it will not pay to build a new one; but until then, if receipts cover operating expenses, the trains can be kept running. This is another illustration of a point made in Chapter 2. A firm will keep in operation so long as it at least covers its variable costs. It does not have to cover fixed costs as well. Reorganizations of this sort are far from rare. Most railroads in the country have passed through receivership, some of them several times.

Abandonments

In the case of a declining industry, the abandonment of service is a difficult problem. The regulatory commission cannot make a company keep operating if it takes losses over-all, but it can require a firm that plans to stay in business to continue some unprofitable service. Commissioners often listen sympathetically to the objections of home owners on bus lines to be abandoned and of small towns on unprofitable railroad branches. A common result is the grudging continuation of poor service with nobody very happy. Yet by abandoning some lines and consolidating parallel roads, some railways could be kept in operation which might otherwise go completely under.

There is much more to the plight of the railroads than what is outlined here. They pay very heavy taxes while their rivals often do not pay all the costs of their operations. They are saddled with large amounts of obsolete plant and loss-producing commuter services with abandonment difficult or impossible. They are bedeviled with expensive make-work union rules. Their low profits have made it difficult to raise capital so that needed improvements are not made

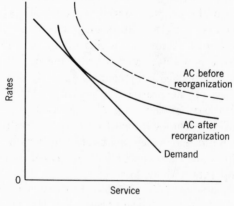

Figure 6.18

and service deteriorates. If they are to survive, at least in the long-distance hauling of freight where they still appear to be considerably more efficient than other carriers, there will have to be some major changes in policy in the future.

SUMMARY

It is not an easy job to eliminate the undesirable effects of monopoly by direct control of private business. Under the best of conditions in prosperous industries such as electric power, regulation is necessarily imperfect simply because of the mechanical complexities of rate making. Conditions have often been less than the best owing to interference from the courts and to the inadequacies of regulators. Moreover, even the most efficient commission is apt to set rates that are too high if it applies the usual standards to firms with decreasing costs. While discrimination or the undervaluation of utility property may make up for this to some extent, both are subject to criticism themselves.

In unprofitable industries regulation is even less likely to eliminate monopolistic pricing. Rates set to keep losses or subsidies to a minimum automatically exploit the monopolists' positions. The commission in such circumstances is likely to use its powers to reduce competition both within the industry and with other industries. Regulation in such fields does protect the public against abandonment of service, but we might be better served if more of the abandonments were permitted.

In regulated industries of every sort it has been found that a legal control of rates and service is not enough to accomplish the objectives of regulation. Experience has shown that the commission must control accounting methods, security issues, related companies, property acquisitions, and reorganizations as well. In fact, regulation implies supervision of almost every aspect of the business. The "private enterprise" that exists in such a setting is very different from the "private enterprise" to be found in competitive fields. It is no light decision to assign public utility status to an industry.

If regulation is imperfect, what alternative is there? Few would advocate uncontrolled private enterprise for all regulated industries, though some feel that intercity transportation might perform better with less ICC supervision. With trains, trucks, barges, airlines, and private automobiles all competing for the business, no carrier has the monopolistic position that the railroads occupied when regulation was established 75 years ago.

For utilities like electric power, where competition is practically impossible, the only plausible alternative to regulation seems to be direct government ownership.

PUBLIC VERSUS PRIVATE POWER

Government Operation

Although it is hotly debated, public operation of utilities is not new in the United States. One of the oldest public utility enterprises, the post office, has been a government concern from the beginning. In the early days of the electric power industry, some cities installed their own generating facilities, either because no private firms were forthcoming, or because of public despair at ineffective regulation. With the development of large-scale power networks many of these municipal utilities proved inefficiently small. Some sold out during the consolidation period, and all but the largest of those that survive now buy power and distribute it.*

In the 1930's the federal government became important in the power industry, mainly in the development of our large hydroelectric sites. There had been a few federal developments earlier, and one of these, Muscle Shoals on the Tennessee River, became the nucleus of TVA, a government corporation formed in 1933 to develop the resources of the whole valley.

The Tennessee is the main stream draining the southern Appalachians, an area with some of the heaviest rainfall and highest elevations in the eastern half of the country, so it had one of the largest power (and flood) potentials in the nation. Moreover, the area embraces a substantial part of the depressed southern agricultural region described in Chapter 3. There was an obvious need for improved methods of agriculture and for local industrialization to draw excess farmers into the city. The valley therefore provided an ideal setting for a large-scale experiment in economic development.

The TVA spent some $2 billion between 1933 and 1956 building or acquiring 20 major dams and 7 large steam-generating plants with a

---

* The cities of Los Angeles, Seattle, and Tacoma have large and efficient power facilities of long standing, Nebraska has a power system distributing electric energy to public agencies in practically every town in the state, and New York State produces a large amount of power at Niagara and on the St. Lawrence which it sells to industrial users and private utilities.

total capacity of more than 8 million kw. It created a distribution system made up almost entirely of municipal, cooperative, or other publicly owned utilities* covering almost all of Tennessee, important parts of Alabama, Mississippi, and Kentucky, and bits of three other states. It established the Tennessee Valley as one of the main centers of low-cost power. In addition to electricity production, the TVA put a check to heavy floods that had been common in the region, provided a 650-mile navigable channel into the southern Appalachian coal fields, and engaged in extensive programs of agricultural improvement and reforestation. The region has experienced a rapid growth under TVA. Per capita incomes have risen much faster there than in the country as a whole, though the same is true in most of the South.

The federal government has been responsible for a large number of other hydroelectric developments† during the last three decades. Between 1935 and 1955 federal generating capacity grew from 300,000 to 17 million kw—from less than 1% of total national generating capacity to about 14%. The Army Corps of Engineers and the Interior Department's Bureau of Reclamation have built most of these facilities. In the Pacific Northwest, where the largest part of the government's facilities outside of TVA are located, power is distributed by the Bonneville Power Administration, which does some regional planning as well as providing most of the area's transmission system. However, Congress has balked at single, unified, independent planning agencies for regions other than the Tennessee Valley. In most cases, the government has given preference to public agencies and cooperatives in the distribution of its power, but outside of the TVA area some private utilities continue to sell power to the public.

Public Power—Pro

Federal power projects have been the subject of great controversy. Often the discussion generated more heat than light, but valid arguments have appeared on both sides.

Defenders of public power put great emphasis on the multiple purposes of many federal projects. Private firms might never have undertaken them because the power produced was not enough to pay for the entire investments, but the public gained in many ways

* However, TVA sells more than half of its power directly to industrial users (such as Alcoa and Reynolds) and to government agencies (such as the Atomic Energy Commission).

† Many of these were built primarily as irrigation projects with electric power as a by-product.

where full remuneration was not feasible. It would be virtually impossible to collect flood protection fees downstream, though the economic gain in some instances is obvious. Similarly, irrigation projects are usually not directly self-financing and inland waterways and the recreational facilities yield no revenue at all. Even if electric power production were enough to pay for some of these other services, private firms might not build the facilities that best meet the public needs. The FPC, in licensing private projects, can require specific facilities, but in practice there is a limit to the extra expense it can ask private firms to bear without remuneration.

Many of the projects in the 1930's, at any rate, can be defended as means of accelerating economic development. Like the railroads of the nineteenth century, the power projects were enormous investments that had to be in place before their users could develop. Unless heavily subsidized, private capital was not available to finance such large undertakings when the potential market was far in the future if it existed at all.

Most of the early large-scale projects were undertaken as fiscal policy measures to help get the country out of the depression. However, in the prosperous and sometimes inflationary years of the 1940's and 1950's, reduced rather than increased government spending was called for. Unless a project were warranted for other reasons, it certainly could not then be defended because of the stimulus it gave the economy. The largest part of federal expenditures on power development has occurred in the years since World War II. The government installed or acquired 4.8 million kw of generating capacity between 1933 and 1945 compared with 11.9 million from 1946 to 1955.

It is sometimes suggested that public power projects serve as yardsticks by which private power companies and their regulation can be judged. Comparisons between private and public power are not easy to make, however. Most private power comes from steam plants, while outside of TVA federal agencies produce almost entirely hydroelectricity, often at projects far larger than any private hydrostations. At any rate, there is almost unlimited room for debate about what the appropriate costs of federal power are. There is no universally approved method of dividing the cost of the government's investment between electricity and the other purposes of most projects. Again, though federal projects often make payments in lieu of taxes to local governments, these are much less than the local taxes of private utilities, not to mention their federal corporate taxes. Interest costs are not comparable either, because the Treasury rather than the investor bears all the risks on federal projects.

It is not at all clear that public power stations should try to duplicate private conditions. As was pointed out earlier, there is a case for subsidizing or at least not taxing such a decreasing cost industry. Anyway, if considerations of flood control, irrigation, or just plain politics ordain that a dam be built, it is clearly in the public interest that the power potential be used, even if rates are too low to cover all the costs.

In practice, TVA and the Bonneville Power Administration have very low rates compared with their predecessors and other private utilities. Their rate structures are also simpler. If nothing else, TVA and the Bonneville Power Administration have shown very little inclination to exploit their monopoly positions, something that cannot be said of every producer of electricity.

Public Power—Con

Critics of public power hold that many projects are clear misallocations of the nation's resources. Not all creeks are worth developing, but if political conditions are right many of them will be anyway. Private investments are subject to the standards of the market place and, unless promising, will not be undertaken. Public funds are likely to go to states with powerful congressmen, whether or not the projects are economically worthwhile. The pork barrel is an old American institution and well worth watching.

Some critics have doubted the value of many of the multipurpose projects. It might be cheaper to have only partial protection against the sort of flood that comes once in a century than to build a dam across every creek in Kansas. Again, how much are inland waterways worth to a country well supplied with half-idle railroads, and how valuable is new irrigated cottonland when the Department of Agriculture is restricting acreage on what we already have? This does not mean that flood control, navigation, and irrigation projects are all worthless, but it is not always easy to determine their true social value.

One social value that probably gets underrated is recreation. In a nation that puts several billion a year into television, bowling, professional sports, and the like, considerable public expenditure for forests, campgrounds, and just open space is probably warranted. Power projects have inundated or threatened to inundate substantial sections of such public preserves as Glacier Park and Dinosaur National Monument. Many feel that the power and water just are not worth the permanent loss of some of our scarce, undeveloped countryside.

Much of the criticism of public power is a matter of ideology. A large part of American opinion is clearly convinced that private enterprise is superior to public and that government should stay out wherever private business can serve. Some are seriously concerned about the future of personal freedom as government grows larger and acquires increased control over a greater segment of the economy. Those who see no danger to our democracy from government-owned instead of government-regulated utilities may still fear the power of a government monopoly. In the electric industry this may be a minor consideration, but in other fields, such as transportation, a government-owned enterprise might be in a better position to suppress competition than a private firm or its regulatory commission.

Probably more widespread than either of these concerns is doubt about the efficiency of government-operated enterprises. The slow-moving bureaucracy tangled in red tape and staffed by uninspired civil servants is a familiar caricature. Private business, subject to the threat of competition, is usually supposed to be forced onto a higher level of efficiency. Private utilities are certainly on the border line between government and competitive business, however. Government regulation that sets rates on the basis of cost plus a reasonable profit is a very imperfect substitute for competition when it comes to forcing producers to innovate and increase efficiency.

The public-private power conflict is far from settled. One effect of the controversy has been to hold up the development of hydroelectric power. Public power advocates oppose the licensing of private firms for the development of choice sites, while private power groups try to stop appropriations for further public expansion. The Columbia basin, with the largest hydroelectric potential in the country, has become an area of power shortage because of the conflict in part.

Elections in states like Washington, Oregon, and Tennessee seem to point toward the continuation of federally sponsored multipurpose projects, but beyond that there seems to be little sentiment for further substitution of public for private power utilities at present.

FURTHER READINGS

The study of public utilities is a major subdivision of the field of economics. There are a number of good textbooks devoted to it exclusively, including C. E. Troxel, *The Economics of Public Utilities*, Rinehart, 1947, which emphasizes the theoretical aspects of the subject, and Eli W. Clemens, *Economics and Public Utilities*, Appleton-Century-Crofts, 1950, which emphasizes the institutional aspects. *Land Economics*, a quarterly journal published at the University of Wisconsin, prints many articles on regulated industries and regulation.

The suggestion that marginal costs be used in setting public utility rates is ordinarily attributed to Harold Hotelling, "The General Welfare in Relation to the Problems of Taxation and of Railroad and Public Utility Rates," *Econometrica*, July 1938. It was debated widely among economists in the 1940's. A good summary and evaluation of the literature appears in two articles by Nancy Ruggles on marginal cost pricing in the *Review of Economic Studies*, Nos. 42 and 43, 1949–50.

Transportation is yet another subdivision of economics. The material on the subject in this chapter hardly scratched the surface. There are a number of texts again, including Troxel, *Economics of Transport*, Rinehart, 1955, for the theoretical approach, and D. P. Locklin, *Economics of Transport*, 4th ed., Irwin, 1954, for an institutional book. For some light reading on the recent plight of the railroads see "America's Freight Cartel," *Fortune*, Jan. 1957.

7

OLIGOPOLY—STEEL

While monopoly is rare outside of regulated industries, *oligopoly*, where a few firms dominate, is a common situation in the American economy. Aluminum production falls into this category today, as do steel, automobiles, oil, chemicals, tires, farm equipment, and many other important industries. Steel has probably received more attention than any other oligopoly. It is the perennial subject of investigation by Congress, the courts, and economists. In the eyes of the American public it has long been the symbol of big business, and it is the symbol of industrial prowess and economic growth throughout the whole world.

INTEGRATION

The Steel-Making Process

Steel making is a complicated process. The steel industry consists of hundreds of firms performing any or all of the tasks shown in Table 7.1

While there are at least a few firms specializing at each step, the bulk of the steel produced in the United States today comes from great integrated companies which combine at least steps 2 through 6 and often go farther.

Table 7.2 shows the share of such firms in total steel capacities of various sorts. Semi-integrated firms buy pig iron from merchant furnaces or fully integrated firms but make their own steel. Non-integrated firms buy raw or semifinished steel and process it. Some

270

of the most important semi-integrated firms produce mainly special steels: alloys, stainless steel, etc. Theirs is almost a separate field from the high tonnage, mass production industry which supplies the materials for tin cans, automobiles, buildings, railroads, and thousands of other products. There has been a consistent trend toward full integration in the mass production field that most people think of as "steel."

Steel Plants

Integration offers definite advantages, at least from the coke ovens through the finishing mills. If blast furnaces, open hearth furnaces,

TABLE 7.1

Process	Product	Plant
1. Mining	Coal, iron ore, and and limestone	Mines, quarries, steamships, docks, railroads
2. Preparation of materials	Coke Ore concentrates	Coke ovens "Beneficiation" plants (more or less complex depending on qualities of the ore)
3. Smelting	Pig iron	Blast furnaces
4. Refining	Ingot steel	Open hearth furnaces (89% of total capacity), Bessemer converters and oxygen process (1%), and electric furnaces (10%)—mainly for alloy and stainless steel)
5. Rolling	Semifinished steel (blooms, billets, bars, slabs, tube rounds, and rods)	Rolling mills
6. Finishing	Finished steel products (sheet, strip, plates, bars, rails, tin plate, pipe, wire, structural shapes)	Rolling mills, tin plate mills, pipe mills, and a great variety of other finishing mills.
7. Fabrication[a]	Manufactured steel products (ships, woven fence, buildings, bridges, oil field equipment)	Manufacturing plants and contracting offices of all sorts
8. Distribution		Warehouses (15–20% of sales) and salesmen

[a] Note that "fabrication" does not include finishing as it did in the aluminum industry.

and rolling mills are at one location, pig iron and ingot steel can be kept at high temperatures as they move from one stage to the next, avoiding much reheating. Moreover, gases and waste heat from the coke ovens, blast furnaces, and open hearth furnaces can provide heat and power elsewhere in the plant.

The ideal steel plant is unavoidably big. The average blast furnace in 1957 had an annual capacity of 331,000 tons and new ones had twice that.* Rolling mills are often much larger. A modern continuous rolling mill may cover 40 acres and be capable of rolling

TABLE 7.2

Per Cent of National Capacity (1957)

Type of Firm	Number of Firms	Pig Iron	Ingot Steel	Finished Hot Rolled Products
Fully integrated	24	95	92	89
Semi-integrated	58	..	8	10
Nonintegrated[a]	147	..	..	1
Merchant furnaces	10	5	..	..

[a] Only 21 of the 147 nonintegrated firms listed in the directory produced hot-rolled products, so the 1% figure understates their importance. Non-integrated firms were quite significant in some fields of steel finishing. There were 36 nonintegrated firms producing 11% of the plain steel wire and 37 nonintegrated firms producing 42% of the electric-weld pipe in 1957.

Source: Derived from American Iron and Steel Institute, *Directory of Iron and Steel Works in the United States and Canada—1957*. Nonintegrated firms are all listed firms with some finishing capacity other than subsidiaries of other firms.

sheet or strip for auto bodies at a rate of 4 tons a minute—something like 30 miles an hour! The capacities of such mills often exceed 1 million tons a year and some are as large as 3 million tons.

Steel companies have a strong incentive to diversify their products. A producer of sheet for automobiles and appliances or of railroad products will experience all the instability of those industries. By producing, say, tin plate or wire products as well, he can keep his furnaces in more regular use.

If a firm is to offer anything like a complete line of steel products,

* Derived from American Iron and Steel Institute, *Annual Statistical Report*, 1958; on Jan. 1, 1958, there were 262 blast furnaces reporting a total pig iron capacity of 86.8 million tons per year.

it cannot limit itself to one finishing mill. The equipment for making other steel products does not always have such giant capacities as sheet mills have, but none can be described as small. Altogether a diversified list of products requires a tremendous flow of materials. To keep this equipment continuously busy, integrated steel plants usually have several blast furnaces. Then, to keep up with 2 or 3 blast furnaces, a plant must have 10 or 15 open hearth furnaces and coke ovens in the hundreds.

With all these facilities, a modern integrated steel plant is a very large and expensive affair. The average steel mill in 1957 had a capacity of over 1 million tons, and there were six with more than 4 million tons capacity.*

Steel producers surveyed in 1951–52 estimated that a plant of 1 to 2.5 million tons capacity was necessary to operate efficiently.† At the price levels of the late 1950's such a plant would cost $300–750 million dollars. The Fairless Works built by United States Steel (hereafter USS) in 1951–52 has a capacity of 2.2 million and was reported to have cost $600 million.‡

It does not follow that simply because the most efficient plant is in the quarter or half billion dollar class the steel industry must inevitably be dominated by a few giants. The total steel capacity of the country in 1959 was 148 million tons, large enough to include 67 Fairless Works. There actually were 87 plants with open hearth capacity. Yet three firms accounted for more than half of the industry's capacity. Control of steel production is far more concentrated than the industry's large plants require.

It is an open question whether steel producers gain in .*efficiency* by operating more than one plant. Steel men themselves differed on the question when surveyed in 1951–52.§ They can attain greater diversification and geographically wider sales with more plants. Yet some of the most successful steel producers have been one- and two-plant firms (see pp. 314–316).

Raw Materials

Most major steel companies today own raw material sources and product outlets as well as integrated mills. The savings that can

---

* Derived from *Annual Statistical Report, ibid.,* p. 54. On Jan. 1, 1958, there were 87 plants with open hearth furnaces. Their total capacity was 122 million tons or 1.4 million per plant.

† J. S. Bain, *Barriers to New Competition,* Harvard University Press, Cambridge, 1956, pp. 158, 236.

‡ "The Transformation of U.S. Steel," *Fortune,* Jan. 1956, p. 200.

§ Bain, *op. cit.,* p. 254.

be accomplished by combining mine, mill, and warehouse in this way are less obvious than the economies of mass production within the the steel mills.

One gain that is sometimes claimed is simply not there. Students often conclude that if a company acquires its suppliers or outlets it can avoid paying their profits and thus cut costs. The trouble with this is that the mill will have to put as much capital into mines, steamships, and warehouses as the independent firms did. This investment must earn a return, whoever makes it. The businessman who thinks he is saving money by making the investment himself is just not allowing a return on his own money. Of course, the suppliers and outlets might have more profitable businesses than the mill; but the mill that buys them out will normally have to pay a price in line with their prospective earnings.

There is perhaps something to be gained in coordination of operations at various levels by combining them all under one management. The qualities of ore and coal may be carefully controlled and levels of output at various stages can be kept in line. If materials and outlets are regularly available on competitive markets, however, there seems to be no need for such integration in many lines of manufacture. Flour mills, meat packers, and cigarette manufacturers never seem to find it necessary to own farms and grocery stores.

Steel firms gain little in timing by acquiring ore and coal mines. Most of them buy some coal. They depend on their own (captive) mines for regular supplies and buy varying amounts from independents. In other words, it is the independent coal mines whose output must be coordinated with steel production, not the captives. Exact coordination of iron ore production with steel operations is virtually impossible because ore shipped on the Great Lakes must move during the ice-free months and be stockpiled at the mills, regardless of when the steel is produced.

Whether or not they gain anything in efficiency, steel companies certainly gain in security by owning their own ore and outlets. It is understandable that steel men want to be assured of supplies in boom years and outlets in bad before sinking hundreds of millions into a permanent plant. An active competitive market could give such assurance again. Textile mills do not worry about being shut off from their cotton supplies, nor meat packers from shipments of cattle and hogs. They can always buy on the same basis as their competitors.

In the early days of the steel industry, the mills bought most of their supplies from independent coal mines and ore "merchants." Then in 1896 Andrew Carnegie, the largest steel producer, acquired a substantial part of the northern Minnesota ore reserves under a long-term lease. While this assured him of an ore supply, it meant that other steel producers had to make similar arrangements or expect trouble. There followed a race to buy up ore lands and companies that owned ore lands. Today practically all useful domestic ore is either owned by, or under long-term contract to, major steel producers. The nine largest companies produced 86% of the country's ore in 1948.* The few merchants that remain have close ties with major steel companies. Most of their output goes to the majors because of the steel companies' rights to jointly owned mines or because of long-term contracts.

In some cases steel firms may have to invest in raw material production simply because no one else will. This has not been true of Appalachian coal, Great Lakes shipping, or high-grade Minnesota iron ore, where large numbers of independent firms exist, or at least existed until the steel companies came along. In the 1950's, however, the industry had to turn to other sources as the high-grade Lake Superior ore approached exhaustion. Most of the new projects have been on a scale that only very large firms could handle. USS's ore deposits at Cerro Bolivar are in a largely undeveloped section of central Venezuela and required a 90-mile railroad, a 150-mile deep sea channel on the Orinoco River, and a tropical city. The mines on the Labrador-Quebec border were financed jointly by six large steel and two ore companies and involved a 360-mile railroad, a large hydroelectric development, and another city, this time in the northern wilderness. (They were also one of the main reasons for the St. Lawrence Seaway.) The low-grade taconite ores of Minnesota require complex beneficiation in very large scale plants which have again been cooperative ventures of major steel and ore companies. Each of these new ore developments has required an initial investment of more than $100 million dollars. Some have come as high as $300 million.†

Outlets

The forward integration of steel companies into such fields as ship-building, oil field supply, fencing, structural steel work, steel drums, and warehousing makes sense mainly from the point of view

* Report of the Federal Trade Commission on the Control of Iron Ore, for the Anti-Trust Subcommittee, House of Representatives, Dec. 24, 1952, p. 32.

† The cost of the various projects came from *Moody's Industrial Manual*, 1960; Federal Trade Commission, *op. cit.*; and testimony of several witnesses at the Subcommittee on Anti-Trust and Monopoly, *Administered Prices*, 1957 (hereafter *Administered Prices*), esp. p. 841.

of security again. By acquiring outlets, an individual steel company could assure itself of markets without a fight. Logically, it was in the depression years of the 1930's that the forward integration movement really got under way, though it has continued since. Of course, what one firm gained the others lost, so the forward integration movement became another race. In the 1930's and 1940's the eight leading steel companies absorbed 104 fabrication and warehouse companies, including some of the largest in their respective fields.* By 1947 integrated steel producers sold 79% of the country's wire fence and gates, 45% of its steel barrels and drums, 39% of its steel building supplies, 24% of its ships, and 15% of its oil field machinery.†

Vertical Integration and Competition

Whatever the purpose, expansion of steel companies back to the raw materials and forward toward the consumer had the effect of restricting competition.‡ The number of companies that can build such empires is certainly limited. Once the empires are built, such nonintegrated raw material producers and steel outlets as remain can hardly by very independent. They are beholden to the major steel companies for markets in bad times and for supplies in good.

The control of ore has been particularly important. Even among the major steel companies, only USS and National Steel are completely self-sufficient. The others must buy part of their ore. One of the chief sellers is USS! The others are in a poor position for vigorous, independent action.

The dominant position in ore held by USS since the turn of the century does not seem to be abating. As luck would have it, USS won the prize in the search for overseas ore when it discovered Cerro Bolivar. At home it has more reserves of both high-grade and taconite ore than the other firms, and more of its ore seems to be capable of low-cost open pit mining.§

---

* House of Representatives, Select Committee on Small Business, 81st Congress, 2nd Session, *Steel—Acquisitions, Mergers, and Expansion of Twelve Major Companies, 1900–1950,* 1950, *passim.*

† *Ibid.,* p. 77.

‡ Vertical integration need not reduce competition in all industries just because it seems to in steel. The possibility that large-scale retailers may become their own wholesalers or suppliers is a potent source of competitive pressure in many fields.

§ Federal Trade Commission, *op. cit.,* pp. 133–134. In 1948 USS reported 62% of the Great Lakes reserves, 85.5% of low-cost open pit reserves, 59% of total Great Lakes ore production, and 73.2% of open pit production. Against this, it produced only 33% of the ingot steel in the same year.

If the independence of steel firms other than USS is limited by their requirements for outside ore, the prospects for new firms are particularly restricted. As far back as 1911 a very knowledgeable steel man predicted that further development in the industry would be by companies already in existence rather than by new firms "for the reason that the possibility of a new company getting a sufficiently large supply of raw materials would make it exceedingly difficult, if not impossible."* Actually, one firm (National Steel) did appear later, acquiring its ore by merger, but there seem to be no similar opportunities today. Any large new producer must now buy into existing holdings at high prices, turn to less efficient sources of ore, be extremely lucky in finding new deposits, or depend on the others for ore. These prospects may be minor obstacles to specialty steel makers, who buy little ore, and to regional companies in the West and Southwest who depend on local deposits; but investors planning to enter the mass production markets at the main centers of American industry face substantial barriers under present circumstances.

CONCENTRATION

Steel Before 1900

Until the Civil War steel was an expensive speciality product used by tool makers. The basic material of industry was wrought iron. The development of the Bessemer and open hearth furnaces in the 1850's and 1860's offered industry cheap steel for the first time, and the new metal rapidly displaced other materials. The market that steel took over grew spectacularly in the subsequent period with the building of the railroads and the industrialization of much of America. Steel production grew as fast at that time as aluminum and electric power have in this century. Steel output multiplied 17 times from the end of the Civil War to 1900—almost exactly as much as aluminum production grew in another 35-year period from 1920 to 1955.

In the early years steel, like wrought iron before it, was produced on a very small scale. The advantages of integration led to the construction of huge steel mills in the 1870's and 1880's by such men as Andrew Carnegie, but even then the industry was not very concentrated. In 1892 the four largest firms accounted for only 18%

* Charles M. Schwab (then president of Bethlehem Steel and former president of USS) at the Stanley Committee Hearings, Vol. 2, p. 1291. Quoted in Federal Trade Commission, *op. cit.*, p. 27.

of the country's blast furnaces and 28% of its rolling mill capacity.* The industry was about as concentrated then as the textile industry is today.

The steel industry was noted for sharp competition in those days. Wide price fluctuations occurred, and large rebates were often given to big buyers. Agreements to fix price or output or to divide up the market were common, but they were notable mainly for the frequency with which they were broken. After 1898 they were also illegal. In that year Judge (later President) Taft ruled in the case of a cast iron pipe pool that any overt agreement with the sole purpose of restricting competition was forbidden by the Sherman Act, regardless of the purported "reasonableness" of the prices that resulted.† His decision set a precedent. While the courts have changed their interpretation of other sections of the antitrust laws, Taft's prohibition of overt agreements in restraint of trade remains virtually intact today.

United States Steel

At the end of the 1890's the steel industry contracted merger fever. Table 7.3 lists some of the important mergers that occurred between 1898 and 1901.

Finally in 1901, a group of citizens led by J. P. Morgan contrived to merge the mergers. They brought all of the combinations listed in Table 7.3 plus the lion's share of Minnesota iron ore reserves under a single roof entitled United States Steel.‡ The corporation was the largest of its kind ever organized in the United States up to that time. It was America's first billion-dollar corporation. It controlled 44% of the country's reported steel ingot capacity,§ and 66% of output. Its subsidiaries had even greater predominance in some finished lines such as pipe, wire, and rails. Moreover, the ingot capacity of USS was regionally concentrated. When originally organized, the corporation had no important basic plants east of the Pitts-

* Temporary National Economic Committee (hereafter TNEC) Monograph No. 27, *The Structure of Industry*, 1941, pp. 257–259; ingot capacity not given.

† US v. Addyston Pipe and Steel Co., 85 F. 271 (1898).

‡ There were a number of other mergers of the same period (1898–1901) that were not included in USS. Two that are still important are Republic Steel (1899), which combined 30 rolling mill companies, and Crucible Steel (1900), which combined practically all of the nation's crucible steel capacity. Schroeder, *op. cit.*, p. 51, 71.

§ It seems likely that USS'S share of ingot capacity at that time was understated because other firms overstated their capacity. George Stigler, "Monopoly & Oligopoly by Merger," *American Economic Review*, Proceedings, May 1950, p. 30.

burgh area, south of the Ohio, or west of the Mississippi, so that within the lake states it was even more powerful than in the country as a whole. In 1907 it acquired the Tennessee Coal, Iron and Railroad Company and thus became the dominant producer in the South. It only began producing steel in the West in 1930 and it started building its first fully integrated eastern plant in 1951.

TABLE 7.3

Year and Company		Number of Companies
Basic Steel Producers:		
1898 Federal Steel	15% of ingot capacity	a
1899 National Steel	12% of ingot capacity	8
1900 Carnegie Steel	18% of ingot capacity	a
Steel Finishers:		
1898 American Tin Plate	About 75% of tin plate output	36
1898 American Steel and Wire	About 80% of wire and wire products	19
1899 National Tube	75% of wrought tubing	13
1899 American Steel Hoop	Barrel hoops and cotton ties	9
1900 American Sheet Steel	About 70% of sheet steel capacity	17
1900 American Bridge	About half of structural steel business	26
1900 Shelby Steel Tube	About 90% of seamless tube output	13

ᵃ Federal Steel combined two major steel producers and a number of ore and transportation firms. Carnegie Steel was a reorganization of an earlier group of affiliated firms.

Source: This mighty list of combinations was derived from the Commissioner of Corporations, *Report on the Steel Industry*, 1911, Pt. I, pp. 2–5. Select Committee on Small Business, *op. cit.*, and Gertrude G. Schroeder, *The Growth of Major Steel Companies, 1900–1950*, "Johns Hopkins University Studies in Historical and Political Science," Series LXX, No. 2, Johns Hopkins University Press, 1952, pp. 36–38.

USS was a holding company somewhat like the public utility holding companies of later years. Owners of the operating firms and of the combinations of 1898–1900 exchanged their stock for securities of the new merger. They were willing to do this because they usually received securities worth more than those they surrendered. Owners of a $1 million firm would receive stock and bonds with a face value of $2 million.* Of course, a share of stock need not sell at its par value. On the stock market a share with $100 printed clearly on its face may sell for $200 or $20 or $2. However, the securities issued by USS held up in value, and the owners of the old companies prospered.

By what alchemy were J. P. Morgan and his friends able to change a $1 million asset into a $2 million asset? Buyers must have been convinced that USS combined had much better profit prospects than USS in bits and pieces. This is hardly surprising. A near monopoly is likely to do much better than its parts in competition with one another. The owners of the original firms whose participation made the combine possible were able to take most of the prospective extra profits in one lump by selling out at a large gain. Buyers of USS stock bid its price up until it yielded only normal returns *to them.* Incidentally, the organizers did not go unrewarded. Morgan and the other firms that participated in these mergers received securities worth more than $60 million as their fees.†

The chairman of the board of the new corporation was Judge Elbert H. Gary, not a steel man but a Chicago attorney who played an important role in the earlier consolidations and had the confidence of Morgan. He led the corporation for its first three decades, and more than any other man he set the tone of business in the steel industry.

He was convinced that the only policy for USS was to avoid acts of aggression and to cooperate with other steel producers for the good of the whoe industry.‡ As America's biggest company in a basic industry with a spectacular organizational history, USS was always in the public eye, and its prospects for survival in the trust-busting days of the 1900's would have been dim if it had followed the aggres-

---

* The Commissioner of Corporations attempted to estimate the value of USS's components at the time of its organization. He arrived at $676 million by a historical study of the tangible assets of the component firms, $682 million by an attempt to measure replacement costs, and $792 million by adding up the market value of the securities of the component firms. Against this, USS had securities outstanding with face values of $1402 million in 1901. Commissioner of Corporations, *op. cit.,* p. 15.

† Commissioner of Corporations, *op. cit.,* p. xix.

‡ His attitudes are well documented. See Ida M. Tarbell, *The Life of Elbert H. Gary,* Appleton and Co., 1925, especially pp. 124, 126–151, and 240, and Arundel Cotter, *The Authentic History of the United States Steel Corporation,* Moody Magazine and Book Co., 1916, pp. 171–186. Tarbell presents Gary as a sort of evangelizer preaching cooperation and public relations to the formerly buccaneering steel men.

sive policies of the tobacco and oil trusts. Instead, Gary sought stability and good public relations.

Price Policy—The Gary Dinners

Judge Gary is best known for the pricing policy he inaugurated. USS had not absorbed everyone in the industry. There were still a number of producers of a workable size, though the largest had only about 5% of the nation's steel capacity.* The cooperation of these smaller firms was essential.

In 1907 there began a famous series of "Gary dinners" which all the important steel producers attended. They were repeated often. Permanent committees were appointed to deal with specific products such as steel bars, ore and pig, and rails and billets. The participants made no formal agreements because to do so would have been illegal. They did make declarations of policy and each felt honor bound to notify his dinner associates if he chose to change. The members of the industry turned out to be very cooperative. Judge Gary reported in a speech made October 24, 1910:

> Since 1907 . . . we have in large measure at least worked together; we have secured as a rule the maintenance of fair prices; we have avoided injuring our neighbors who are in competition with us; we have helped one another almost daily and have secured and maintained conditions that are much better than they were during the times many years ago when, regardless of public sentiment, contracts were actually made though not kept, to establish and maintain prices.†

For the most part USS set the pattern and the others followed. It sold all of its products at their Pittsburgh price plus rail freight from Pittsburgh, regardless of where they were actually produced, and all the other steel producers did the same, even those whose only plants were in the Chicago or Philadelphia areas.‡ The major steel companies published identical lists of "extras," charges for goods of other then standard specifications. When USS changed the prices of its

---

* In 1908 Lackawanna Steel was second to USS in blast furnace capacity (3.7%) and Jones and Laughlin was second in rolling mill capacity (4.2%). Jones and Laughlin was apparently second in ingot capacity; it had 5.0% of the total in 1901 and 4.8% in 1920. Figures for intermediate years not available. TNEC Monograph 27, *op. cit.*, p. 258, and Select Committee on Small Business, *op. cit.*, p. 38.

† Addresses and Statements by Elbert H. Gary, 1904–1927 (pamphlets, speeches, and statements collected by J. A. Farrell and bound, in Baker Library, Harvard), quoted in Louis Marengo, *Basing Point Pricing in the Steel Industry*, Doctoral Dissertation, Harvard University, June 1950, p. 300.

‡ This system of pricing, known as the basing point system, will be discussed more fully on pp. 300–303.

products, other manufacturers of the same items made equivalent changes.

The Gary dinners ended in 1911, but cooperation among steel makers did not. Established pricing practices such as Pittsburgh-plus, uniform lists of extras, and price leadership continued. This was understandable. Small firms, one-tenth the size of "big steel," were not likely to challenge its position of leadership. Generally they had no reason to. Why should they be eager to return to price competition? In a subsequent antitrust case against the corporation, the other firms had nothing but good to say about USS.

The corporation had unquestioned control over steel prices most of the time, and presumably it set them with an eye to its own profits. However, a profitable price for USS was apt to be a profitable price for the smaller firms that had not been absorbed and for prospective new ones as well. If the corporation took full advantage of its powerful position, it would provide a strong incentive for new firms to enter the industry and for old ones to expand. Actually it had little choice. It had to take fairly substantial economic profits in view of the great amount of securities that had been issued at its birth. If it had not it would have offered very low returns to the holders of those securities.

The new conditions in steel did attract new steel producers. Many of the leading companies of the industry today either were organized or built their first major plants in the decade after the emergence of USS seemed to offer stable and profitable prices to anyone who could get under its big umbrella.* In the nineteenth century the corporation might have tried to keep the newcomers out with price wars or by excluding them from ore supplies, but such tactics were not consistent with Judge Gary's new policies. He was probably right in view of the new vigor of antitrust prosecutions at the time. However, the policy has resulted in an almost continuous decline in the corporation's share of steel production (Figure 7.1) and steel capacity (Figure 7.2). USS has grown, but the steel industry has grown considerably faster.†

* This was true of Inland Steel, Bethlehem Steel, Youngstown Sheet and Tube, Weirton Steel (predecessor of National Steel), and to a lesser extent, Armco. The other two major firms besides USS are Republic Steel, formed at the height of the merger movement in 1899, and Jones and Laughlin, the only firm in the group that was a major producer in its present form in the nineteenth century.

† There were other reasons for USS's declining share of the steel market. As part of his public relations policy, Gary seems to have decided to limit the size of his corporation to less than 50% of the industry (Tarbell, *op. cit.*, p. 257) and to avoid absorbing further competitors after 1907. Location and managerial efficiency were also important; they are discussed later.

Antitrust

In spite of Judge Gary's efforts to keep his company out of court, the federal government brought an antitrust suit against it in 1911, attacking it and its components as combinations in restraint of trade. The case was not concluded until 1920. The Supreme Court decided in favor of the corporation.*

The court emphasized the gains in efficiency presumably attained by the corporation. It concluded that even if there may have been an intent to monopolize when the corporation was formed monopoly

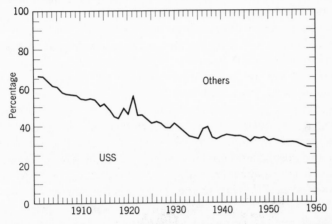

Figure 7.1. USS's share of national steel ingot production. Source: USS, *Business —Big and Small—Built America* (materials presented at Celler Committee Hearings, 1950), *Moody's Industrial Manual*, 1960, and American Iron and Steel Institute, *Annual Statistical Report*.

was not in fact achieved. The corporation's share of the market was declining and it had to have the cooperation of other firms to control prices.

The court acknowledged that the "pools, associations, trade meetings, and . . . social dinners" in which USS led the industry during the first decade of life had perhaps been illegal, but they had been discontinued nine months before the antitrust case began. Informal price leadership was apparently within the law. The court dismissed the government's attack on the "universal imitation" of the Corporation's policy. It cited the testimony of a large number of competitors, dealers, and customers that "no adventitious interference was employed to either fix or maintain prices."

Probably the most important conclusion of the court's decision

* US v. United States Steel, 251 US 417 (1920).

was that the Corporation had not misused whatever power it possessed:

> The Corporation is undoubtedly of impressive size and it takes an effort of resolution not to be affected by it or to exaggerate its influence. But we must adhere to the law and the law does not make mere size an offense or the existence of unexerted power an offense. It, we repeat, requires overt acts and trusts to its prohibition of them and its power to repress or punish them. It does not compel competition, nor require all that is possible.

In other words, so long as a firm seemed to behave well—i.e., so long as it did not abuse its rivals or appear to exploit the public—it was legal under the Sherman Act, even if it comprised half of a basic industry. Since it is difficult to establish that a price is too high, this amounts to an injunction to keep the other firms in the industry happy and maintain good public relations. Judge Gary's policy had been vindicated.

The decision in this case has been criticized by many who have studied it.* As we shall see later, there is reason to doubt the efficiency gained by the big steel merger. As far as the failure to attain monopoly goes, the Sherman Act applied explicitly to "every person who shall monopolize, *or attempt to monopolize. . . .*" At any rate, it makes little difference to the public whether there is formal agreement among the firms of an industry or informal price leadership. And, of course, a monopolist who sets out to make maximum profits will not cease to exploit his position simply because he adopts Judge Gary's idea of public relations.

The court's decision in the steel case probably reflected the sentiments of a large part of the American public at the time. Some practices of big business in the past were certainly reprehensible. Reasonable men could see something wrong with Jim Fisk stealing a railroad by stock manipulation, or American Tobacco getting out a special brand of cigarettes for the sole purpose of conducting local price wars with its rivals. Gary and his associates had done none

---

* Only four justices supported the decision. Three felt that USS was an illegal combination and should be dissolved. Two justices, Brandeis and MacRenolds, did not take part in the decision. Moreover, there has been considerable criticism of the government's presentation of the case. USS seemed particularly public-spirited in the inflation of 1919–20 anyway. It maintained a stable price when it clearly could have charged much more.

of these things. USS acted in the interests of other steel companies rather than undermining them. It kept honest records and made them public. Its leaders were responsible businessmen protecting the interests of their stockholders and stabilizing the industry. It was difficult for many people to find their actions criminal. Of course, the interests of big steel's stockholders and of the smaller steel companies are not always the same as the interests of the consuming public, but it is difficult to understand and evaluate the effects of monopoly.

The decision in the steel case set the tone of antitrust in the 1920's and early 1930's. It was clearly illegal for independent firms to enter formal price-fixing or market-sharing agreements, but it was not illegal for them to merge. Moreover, if the formation of one or a few dominant firms led naturally to parallel price policies without formal agreement, this too was within the law. The point of view expressed in the steel case was not basically changed until the Alcoa decision in 1945. In the meanwhile, a second large-scale combination movement got under way.

MERGERS

Mergers among the Independents

Steel is no longer an industry of one dominant seller. USS is still the largest producer, but it is one of eight big firms. Figure 7.2 shows the relative shares of ingot capacity of USS and of its major rivals over the years. While USS was declining to less than a third of the industry, new giants were arising. Most of these were the result of more mergers.

Bethlehem Steel was the child of Charles M. Schwab, an executive of Carnegie Steel and first president of USS. In 1904 he left USS and acquired the United States Shipbuilding Company which comprised several unprofitable shipyards and the small Bethlehem Steel works. He built up Bethlehem by exploiting the new Grey process for making wide flange structural shapes. Then, in 1916 he merged it with Pennsylvania Steel and Maryland Steel and in 1922–23 he acquired the plants of Cambria Steel and Lackawanna Steel. Bethlehem thus acquired the third, fourth, sixth, and eighth ranking steel

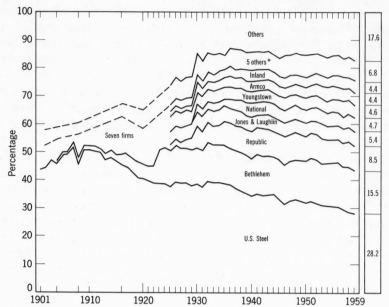

* Colorado Fuel and Iron (2% in 1959), Wheeling Steel (1.7%), Crucible Steel
(1.2%), Pittsburgh (1.0%), and Sharon (0.9). Wheeling Steel not included until
1920.

Figure 7.2. Shares of total steel ingot capacity. Source: Schroeder, *op. cit.*, and
American Iron and Steel Institute, *Annual Statistical Report*, 1960.

producers of 1904* and combined virtually all basic steel capacity
east of Pittsburgh.

Republic Steel was the result of a merger of 30 small producers in
1899. From then until the late 1920's its main concern was the
replacement of obsolete equipment and the unification of its enterprise.
In 1927 it represented 2.2 of total ingot capacity. In that year Cyrus
S. Eaton, a Cleveland financier, acquired control of the company and
proceeded, over the next ten years, to engineer mergers with nine
major steel producers. By 1937 Republic was the third ranking steel
maker with 9.0% of capacity.

The growth of many of the smaller companies has also been by
merger, though there are some exceptions. One study of 12 large
companies concluded that about 30% of their assets' growth through
1950 was attributable to merger rather than new construction. Inland

* Bethlehem itself was fifteenth in 1904. Schroeder, *op. cit.*, p. 96.

Steel acquired only 4.3% of its assets from the outside, but Republic acquired a full 50.0% that way.*

All of the important increases in market shares shown in Figure 7.2 are attributable to mergers. No firm has been able to increase its share by more than 4% of industry capacity by any other means since the turn of the century. Among the big three, only Bethlehem has been able to increase its share by as much as 2% by internal growth. Steel companies usually found it more profitable to grow by acquiring and expanding firms than by building new plants from scratch, because (1) investment costs were usually less that way; (2) there was a ready-made set of customers with every newly acquired plant; and (3) a potential competitor was eliminated. From the public point of view, the results were not always so good, because (1) there were fewer firms and less possibility of competition; and (2) there may have been less investment in new steel capacity than otherwise.

The Government and Mergers

The government made repeated efforts to check the merger movement in steel, all of them unsuccessful until very recently. The Clayton Antitrust Act was passed in 1914 to spell out particular offenses that might have gone uncontested under the Sherman Act. Among these were mergers. No corporation is to acquire the stock of another competing firm "where the effect of such acquisition may be substantially to lessen competition."† The Federal Trade Commission (FTC) filed a complaint under this provision against the Bethlehem mergers of 1922–23. However, it was unable to bring about a dissolution because of a Supreme Court ruling in 1926. The court concluded that the law had prohibited the acquisition of the stock but not of the plants, mines, and other assets of competing companies.‡ This loophole was only removed by an amendment to the Clayton Act in 1950.

In 1935 the Justice Department contested one of the Republic mergers, but this was no more successful. This time the court concluded that the combination involved did not lessen competition "substantially."§

* Schroeder, *op. cit.*, pp. 93–94.

† Clayton Act, Section 7.

‡ Thatcher Manufacturing Co. v. FTC 272 US 552 (1926).

§ US v. Republic Steel Corp., 11 F. Supp. 5152 (1935).

During World War II the federal government financed most of the expansion in steel plant. By the end of the war it owned 6% of total steel capacity.* For the most part these new facilities were sold to firms already in the industry. Some of them were so-called "scrambled" facilities, built as part of existing plants, which had only one likely buyer, but there were also four separate, fully integrated plants, all of which went to large steel producers. The most significant of these was the Geneva plant in Utah. Bids were made by several firms, but the Surplus Property Board finally accepted the offer of USS. It took a substantial loss in doing so, though the loss would probably have been greater if it had pursued a policy like that used in the aluminum industry. On the other hand, by this one move the government made USS the largest producer in the West and extended the corporation's dominant position into a new section of the country.

When USS subsequently acquired Consolidated Steel, a West Coast fabricator, the Justice Department took another tack, this time challenging the move as a case of "monopolizing" under the Sherman Act. The courts ruled against the government once more, however, arguing that the merger was too small to constitute "monopolizing." A minority of the court dissented, arguing that if a firm the size of USS was free to make small mergers, the decision might result in the gradual elimination of competition.†

The government's long history of failures in its attempts to check mergers seems to have ended with the passage of the Celler Antimerger Act amending the Clayton Act in 1950. For the first time mergers of every form were covered and the government could stop a merger if there was a reasonable presumption that it might "substantially lessen competition." It did not have to prove "monopolization" to prevent a merger, the way it did in Sherman Act cases.

One of the first cases to be tried under the new act was the proposed merger of Bethlehem Steel with Youngstown Sheet and Tube, currently the second and fifth ranking steel producers. Combined they would have produced more than a fifth of the nation's steel. The companies argued in defense of the merger that they did not compete significantly since Youngstown's plants were in the Midwest while Bethlehem's were on the two coasts. The avowed purpose of the merger was to permit Bethlehem to expand Youngstown's plants, especially those in the Chicago area. They argued that the merger

---

* *War Plant Disposal—Iron and Steel Plants,* Joint Hearings, Subcommittee on Surplus Property and Special Committee on Post War Economic Policy and Planning, 1945, p. 5.

† US v. Columbia Steel, 334 US 495 (1948).

offered the public the benefits of additional structural shape and plate capacity in the Chicago area and a firm capable of offering "challenging competition" to the USS. The court rejected these arguments. It found that the two firms did ship substantial amounts of goods to common markets, especially in Michigan and Ohio. It also doubted that the merger was necessary to create additional Chicago capacity. Both companies had proved quite capable of rapid growth by internal expansion; in fact, Bethlehem increased its own capacity during the case by more than it proposed to expand the Youngstown plants. Moreover, both USS and Inland built more structural shape capacity near Chicago while the case was being argued, and National Steel has since begun a whole new plant in the same area starting from scratch. At any rate, the supposed virtues of the merger were irrelevant since the law made no exceptions for "good mergers" if they could reasonably be supposed to "substantially lessen competition." Finally, the trial judge argued that if the merger of these two huge firms could be allowed, the door would be open to practically any other conceivable merger in the industry. The merger was therefore enjoined.* The decision was not appealed.

The result in the Bethlehem-Youngstown case seems to indicate that the new act has real teeth in it and that the legal control of mergers is at last to be fully enforced. The door that was left wide open by the USS decision in 1920 seems finally to have been closed.

OLIGOPOLY PRICING

The Oligopolist's Two Demand Curves

The steel industry with several large firms is apt to act very much as it did with one dominant one. The position of an oligopolist of this sort is illustrated in Figure 7.3. The price of steel just happens to be $100 a ton. We will decide later how it got there. The firm can be thought of as having two different demand curves depending on assumptions made about the reaction of other firms. D_1 is drawn on the assumption that no one else does anything when this firm changes its price. D_1 is very elastic because steel is a standardized product. Steel is made to specifications, and anyone with the necessary plant can meet them. A firm may be able to win some loyal customers by filling orders promptly and accurately, meeting their

* US v. Bethlehem Steel Corporation and Youngstown Sheet and Tube Company, 168 F. Supp. 576 (1958).

needs when steel is scarce, and entertaining their officers when they come to town, but that loyalty would be pretty badly strained if the firm raised its prices by a few dollars and the rest of the industry did not.

The other demand curve, D_2, shows the amounts of steel this firm could sell if all its rivals moved their prices up and down right along with it. D_2 slopes downward and to the right like all good demand curves, but it is much steeper than D_1. The only way in which this firm can sell more at $50 than at $100 is for the public to buy more steel in general at the lower prices. This company will not gain at the expense of the other steel firms, because the others cut prices as much as it does. D_2 is roughly this firm's share of the total demand for steel.

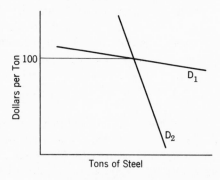

Figure 7.3

The D_2 curve has been drawn steeply because the demand for steel is probably not very elastic. For one thing, most steel reaches the ultimate consumer as an ingredient of some other commodity. A change in steel prices will not affect the prices of most of these finished goods very much. For instance, there is about $150 worth of steel in a present-day automobile. If the steel companies can shave 10% from their prices they will reduce auto prices by $15, maybe 0.5%, which certainly will not sell many more cars.

The substitutes for steel are not very good either. This is because steel is so cheap. In 1960 aluminum cost 26¢ a pound, copper 33¢, and finished steel 6.2¢.* It is true that many of the gains of aluminum in recent years have been at the expense of steel, but, so far at least, while these have been important for aluminum they have been small for steel.

Economists retained by USS in 1938 estimated the elasticity of

* *Iron Age,* Apr. 14, 1960.

demand for steel to be 0.3 to 0.4* They were concerned mainly with the short-run elasticity—what would happen if prices were reduced in a depression. Considering the possibility of developing new uses for steel, the long-run elasticity of demand may be more than this, but it is still probably pretty low.

Oligopoly Price Policy

What policy a firm would follow with a demand situation like that in Figure 7.3 depends on its assumptions about the other companies. In view of the standardized character of steel, a very plausible assumption is that any price reduction by this firm will be promptly met by the rest of the industry. Steel executives have testified repeatedly that they think along these lines. For instance, Ernest T. Weir, then chairman of National Steel, told a congressional committee in 1950:

Practically every steel consumer buys material from more than one producer. Most consumers have a number of steel suppliers. When one producer lowers a price, the other producers learn about it immediately from customers. If consumers can get a lower price from one producer, they want that same price from all producers. If one producer raises a price, that becomes known too. If other producers do not follow, the consumer naturally switches his buying to the producers with lower prices.†

On such an assumption, the firm would have to use D_2 in considering any price reduction. It might still decide that a reduction was worthwhile. Figure 7.4 shows such an instance. Even counting the D_2 curve here, marginal revenue is greater than marginal cost. However, since this firm's D_2 curve is approximately a scale model of the industry demand curve, a steel *monopolist* with the same marginal costs as this firm would find a price reduction profitable in these circumstances also. If the other firms in the industry have similar cost and D_2 curves, they will gain just as the price cutter did. If this firm finds it worthwhile to cut prices, it will be increasing the profits of the whole industry just as a monopolist would.

A price increase is more difficult to analyze. The firm is bound to lose if others do not follow. It will find itself moving up its very elastic D_1 curve. On the other hand, a price increase may well be in this firm's best interest if the others can be counted on to follow. They are most likely to follow if the price increase is plainly in their

* USS, *TNEC Papers*, Vol. I, *Economic and Related Studies*, USS, 1940, p. 170.

† Hearings before Subcommittee on Study of Monopoly Power, House of Representatives, 81st Congress, 2nd Session, Serial No. 14, Pt. 4A, *Steel* (hereafter Study of Monopoly Power), pp. 810–811.

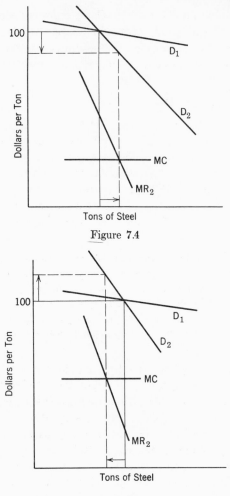

Figure 7.4

Figure 7.5

interests also. All any rate, if they do not follow, the initiator is usually free to retreat. Figure 7.5 shows a case where a price increase is worthwhile, presuming that other companies have similar costs.

It is the D_2 curve, again, that indicates that a price increase is called for. In other words, in increasing prices an oligopolist is also likely to follow in the monopolist's footsteps. It would seem that oligopolists can arrive at the most profitable price for the whole industry by just following their individual best interests. It would certainly pay to get together and work out the price among themselves, but they can have the same effect by not communicating at all.

Things may not be quite this easy. Someone may misinterpret his costs or industry demand. After all, the most profitable price can only be roughly estimated at best. Or someone may misinterpret another company's actions. Or one of the firms may not understand the rules of the game very well. Then the industry may wind up with prices lower than the optimum (from its point of view).

Steel men (and some economists) have often emphasized the dangers of price competition in steel.* Demand for their product is apt to fluctuate violently. They have fairly high fixed costs, though nothing like those of the public utilities. When demand gets down to half of capacity, which is not uncommon during recessions, individual firms are tempted to try to pick up a bit more business and spread their overhead by shading prices. With their inelastic demand, steel men feel that they are almost bound to lose from such "ruinous" competition.

Price Leadership

The steel industry has been able to accomplish necessary price changes with few lapses into price competition because of USS's leadership. The corporation is no longer a giant among many small firms, but as a rule the other companies still follow where it leads. Eugene Grace, then president of Bethlehem Steel, the second firm in the industry, told a congressional committee in 1939:

I am telling you what the general practice is from our company standpoint. Whether we have ever initiated any [price reductions] I just couldn't say, but in the main we would normally await the schedules of the Steel Corporation.†

And again:

When we put out a schedule, what we call our official prices, they usually represent and are the same as our competitor has put in the market, and in most instances, as a general practice, not looking for a little difference here and there, as a general practice that pace is set, if that is a good word, by the Steel Corporation.‡

* A number of statements to this effect are collected in George Stocking, *Basing Point Pricing and Regional Development,* University of North Carolina Press, 1954, Chapters I and II.

† TNEC Hearings, Pt. 19, Iron and Steel Industry, 1939, p. 10601.

‡ *Ibid.,* p. 10602.

His successor, A. B. Homer, told another committee 18 years later:

When we price our products in the East we generally wait to see how the nationwide competitive price pattern will develop, and then we price our products on a basis that we think will give us the best competitive position in the East.*

He went on to give a series of examples. In each case a price at one of the USS plants was given as the "competitive" level.

USS led in 11 of the 12 general steel price increases from World War II to 1960. The one exception is interesting. On July 1, 1958, a substantial automatic wage increase occurred under union contracts. Everybody's marginal cost curve had shifted upward by a uniform amount. There was general agreement that a price increase was indicated. The press was full of speculation about it. There were comments about USS's responsibility to the industry. But nothing happened. USS simply did not lead. One small producer (about 0.3% of the industry's capacity) raised his price but he had to retreat when nobody followed him. The rest of the steel producers milled about for a whole month. Finally Armco (with 4.4% of ingot capacity) announced a price increase and the others, including USS, fell into line.†

If it can assume that other companies will price as it does, USS is bound to consider its D_2 curve in either price increases or price decreases. It will be setting prices in the interests of the whole industry.

The price leadership pattern in steel does not *necessarily* imply formal conspiracy.‡ Several companies with a standardized product

* *Administered Prices, op. cit.,* Pt. 2, p. 615.

† A running account of this price change is available in *Iron Age* for the weeks June 26 to Aug. 7, 1958. The comment about USS's "responsibility" appeared in the June 26 issue. An interesting explanation for the price increase appeared in the Aug. 7 issue (p. 95): "Meanwhile steel earnings reports for the second quarter and the first half showed why steel prices had to go up. While profits were somewhat better in the second quarter than the first, six-months' earnings for most firms were still far below the same period in 1957." The argument was further re-enforced by a statement that at least five steel firms were taking losses in 1958. This is clearly the thinking of an oligopolist. The low profits of early 1958 were due mainly to decreased demand during the sharp recession of that period. In a highly competitive industry where price is set by supply and demand, this would certainly have meant a decrease in price, not an increase. In short-run situations, competitive prices do not conveniently go up just because producers are having a tough time. Of course, wages would not be very likely to rise during a recession in a competitive market either.

‡ On the other hand, there is evidence that steel executives have consulted about price at times. TNEC Monograph No. 42, *The Basing Point Problem,* 1941, has 11 pages of specific instances between 1935 (when NRA ended) and 1939 (pp. 94–105).

are bound to have the same prices if they all expect to sell. Any changes must be made by someone, and the others are automatically followers. In an industry where the largest firm has led for almost 60 years, its continued leadership is hardly surprising and certainly cannot be taken as conclusive evidence of illegal collusion.

The pricing practices of the steel industry are not any the less monopolistic even if they come naturally. Regardless of how innocent modern steel executives may be of latter-day Gary dinners, USS still must set its price with an eye to its demand curve, which is a near replica of the whole industry's.

Happenings Under the Counter

In deep depressions, when they find themselves operating at far less than capacity, individual steel companies sometimes attempt to gain customers by making secret price reductions. They try to slide down their flat D_1 curves by not letting the others know what they are doing and thus avoiding retaliation. If such price cutting becomes widespread the industry leaders may see fit to adjust official prices to reflect it.

Sub rosa price competition occurred during the depressions of 1921–22, 1931–33, and 1938. These occasional lapses into price competition are instructive.

The 1921–22 episode resulted from very unequal amounts of over-capacity. USS had maintained stable prices during the post-World War I steel shortage while many of the independents had charged much higher prices, and earned the antagonism of their customers. When the boom suddenly changed to depression, the smaller steel companies were in trouble. USS was able to keep operating at reasonable levels but the independents were running at 20% to 35% of capacity. At such low rates of operation many were taking severe losses and offered price concessions to get some customers back. The price competition that resulted came to an end when Judge Gary announced (for quotation in trade journals) that USS would there-after meet any price cut by a major independent that it became aware of, and the organization of mergers embracing the leading price cutters was begun.*

Under the counter price cutting appears when at least some firms are grasping at straws because of tremendous overcapacity. If some important firm has much more overcapacity than others, it may

---

* TNEC Monograph No. 13, *Relative Efficiency of Large, Medium-Sized, and Small Business*, 1941, pp. 232–248. The Bethlehem mergers of 1922–23 seem to have grown out of this episode.

temporarily become the price leader even though another may have that role traditionally.

Cost Differences

In the early 1930's a regular source of price cuts was National Steel, a combination of Weirton Steel, Great Lakes Steel, and some properties of the M. A. Hanna Company. It was organized just one week after the market crash in 1929. Weirton was a rapidly expanding firm which had installed one of the first continuous strip mills just before the depression. Great Lakes was not only one of the newest firms in the industry (its plant was completed in 1929) but also the only integrated steel producer in the Detroit area. M. A. Hanna was one of the major ore companies so that National Steel, like USS and unlike many of the others, was able to meet all of its own iron ore needs. With efficient new plants, its own ore, and an aggressive management, National was in a better position for independent action than most steel firms.

Most steel prices declined during the great depression, but the price cuts were much greater on some steel products than on others. On the average, finished steel prices fell about 20% from 1929 to the low in 1933, but the prices of heavy steel products such as rails, plates, and structural shapes fell less than this while prices of sheet and strip fell more. Rail prices went down only 9% while cold rolled strip prices fell by 39%.* This is remarkable because the demand for sheet and strip fell much *less* than the demand for most heavy steel products. Sheet and strip go in large part into consumer goods such as tin cans, appliances, and automobiles, but heavy steel products are used primarily in capital goods and construction, the fields where activity declined most in the depression.

Part of the explanation for the lower prices on sheet and strip is that firms like National, which had installed the new continuous strip mills, experienced great reductions in costs and could afford lower prices. The other high-cost producers had no choice but to go along with their prices. Another factor was that sheet production was considerably less concentrated than many heavy products.†

* TNEC Hearings, *op. cit.*, pp. 10719–10721. The composite price of finished steel products published in *Iron Age* fell a little less than 20%; the prices actually realized by USS subsidiaries fell slightly more than that.

† In 1937 there were only 5 firms making rails and 14 making heavy structural shapes. The 1935 concentration ratio in heavy shapes was 89% (1937 figure not available), and it must have been higher in rails. By contrast, there were 30 producers of sheet in 1937 and the concentration ratio in that line stood at 55%. TNEC Monograph 27, *op. cit.*, pp. 468, 488.

USS was a relatively small part of the sheet and strip part of the industry but it dominated the output of rails and shapes.* Finally, a large part of sheet and strip output went to big buyers, especially the automobile companies, who were in a strong position to demand price concessions.

This time government action stopped the price competition. When the National Industrial Recovery Act was passed (1933) permitting industries to work out "codes" to control competition and providing government enforcement, the steel industry was one of the first to participate. Its code went into effect seven weeks after the Act was passed. It formalized the old pricing rules of the industry and provided fines for those who did not observe them. To guarantee against secret price concessions, producers were required to file their minimum prices with the American Iron and Steel Institute and to give ten days notice prior to price changes. Since this almost guaranteed that price cuts would be met, in effect the code was forcing members of the industry to operate on their D_2 curves. Most firms filed simultaneous, identical prices, but even under the conditions set by the NRA code, National Steel refused to go along with several price increases and it initiated some important price cuts.†

National Steel was probably acting in its own best interests when it took the role of price cutter in the 1930's. The price competition that it inaugurated may have been "ruinous" for the others, but not for National. It was the only major steel company to make profits in every year during the depression. Its average rate of return over the whole decade was second only to Inland Steel's,‡ an amazing record for a company whose first years of business coincided with the nation's greatest depression.

The explanation is only partly secret price concessions. Others could and did do the same, though some companies with large and inflexible organizations were at a disadvantage in making individual price bargains. Even considering its D_2 curve, as it had to under the NRA code, National preferred lower prices than the others. With its new plants and good locations it had some of the lowest costs in the industry. Figure 7.6 illustrates such a case. The optimum price

---

* TNEC Hearings, *op. cit.*, Pt. 18, p. 10409. USS had 57% of the industry capacity in rails, 53% in structural shapes, but only 11% in cold rolled sheets. National had 15% in cold rolled sheets.

† C. R. Daugherty, M. G. De Chazeau, and S. S. Stratton, *Economics of the Iron and Steel Industry*, McGraw-Hill, 1937, pp. 667–671.

‡ Schroeder, *op. cit.*, p. 175.

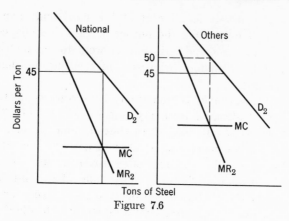

Figure 7.6

for National Steel, on the left, might be $45, but for the older firms with higher costs $50 would be preferable. The firm that sets the lower price is apt to win the argument.

The Size of Secret Price Concessions

Secret price cutting returned in the depression of 1937–39. Some information is available on the extent of secret price cuts as a result of a study made in connection with wartime price control in 1943. Over 1000 firms were asked about the prices they had actually paid for various steel products before the war. Results for eight major items representing about half of steel output were made public. For the worst period studied (second and third quarters of 1939) actual prices averaged only 2 to 4% below announced prices for merchant bars, cold finished bars, plates, and structural shapes. The average concession on hot and cold rolled sheets and strip was from 6 to 11%, however.* These concessions were in addition to formal price reductions made by USS in 1938 when its announced prices had become unrealistic. The formal cuts ran from 5 to 8% for bars, plates, and shapes, but 11 to 17% for sheet and strip.† Even on sheet and strip, however, the over-all reduction both above and below the table was only moderate for an industry operating at less than half of capacity much of the time. During the same depression cotton gray goods prices fell by a third,‡ somewhat more than the maximum decline for

* The study described here was made by the Bureau of Labor Statistics in 1943 and is quoted in Stocking, *op. cit,* pp. 119–123.

† TNEC Hearings, *op. cit.,* 19, Pt. p. 10719.

‡ U.S. Department of Agriculture, "Prices of Cotton Cloth and Raw Cotton and Mill Margins for Certain Constructions of Unfinished Cloth, 1925–1952," p. 10.

sheet and strip and several times the total price concessions on heavier steel products. Yet steel production had fallen off by more than twice as much as cotton textile output.

The price concessions in steel were not available to all buyers equally. Some of the smaller steel users paid full list price throughout the period in which the survey was made, while large buyers were able to win concessions much greater than the averages given in some cases. This seems to have been particularly true of the automobile companies.

Altogether, the price cutting that has occasionally occurred under the table in the steel industry has been an imperfect substitute for the price competition to be found in a purely competitive market. The cuts appear to be relatively small. They are limited to certain commodities and therefore imply price discrimination in the economic sense of the term. They often mean discrimination in favor of the large buyer as well. And they are sporadic occurrences. Even in the mid-1930's the industry was able to avoid price cutting for considerable periods. No important cases of it came to light in the 15 years from the end of World War II to 1960.

GEOGRAPHICAL PRICE POLICY

Transportation Costs

Transportation costs present special problems in the pricing of steel. If there are two producing centers, Pittsburgh and Chicago (Figure 7.7), the boundary between their market areas depends on their prices. If they both have f.o.b. mill prices of $100 per ton* and if freight between Pittsburgh and Chicago is $6 per ton and is proportional to distance, the boundary between Pittsburgh's and Chicago's market areas would be line I, halfway between them. A buyer at point A would pay $103 for steel shipped from either city. Buyers east of the line would find Pittsburgh steel cheaper, and those west of it would pay less for Chicago steel.

Customers and steel plants are not scattered evenly over the countryside. There is a concentration of steel capacity in the Pittsburgh-Youngstown-Wheeling area greatly in excess of the region's demand, while other places such as Chicago, Detroit, and the East Coast have insufficient plants to meet their needs and must import, at least in

---

* F.o.b. means "free on board," which means the customer pays the transportation charge in addition to the price. Most mail order merchandise is sold f.o.b.

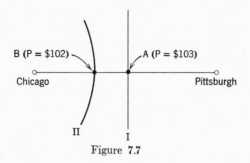

Figure 7.7

prosperous times. Pittsburgh plants have to pick up customers west of line I (in Figure 7.7) or operate at an unsatisfactory level.

In pure competition this problem would be solved by a change in price. Prices in the surplus area would be enough less than those in deficit areas that the entire surplus supply would be taken. For instance, this is the way Vermont succeeded in exporting milk to New York in the discussion in Chapters 2 and 3. If the steel industry worked this way, the Pittsburgh plants could move their market boundary to line II by cutting prices to $98. Customers at point B would pay $102 whether they bought from Pittsburgh ($98 plus $4 freight) or Chicago ($100 plus $2 freight). Customers between lines I and II who previously found Chicago cheaper would now turn to Pittsburgh.

This comes perilously close to price competition, however. Pittsburgh can pick up some of Chicago's customers by cutting price a bit; but Chicago plants are apt to meet the new Pittsburgh prices. Then the boundary will be at line I again, and Pittsburgh will be right back where it started from but with lower prices all around.

The Basing Point System

The steel industry's solution to this problem was the *basing point* system. Until the 1920's all steel producers, no matter where they were located, quoted prices as if they were shipping from Pittsburgh. A customer right next door to a steel mill in Chicago would have to pay the same freight (known as "phantom freight") that he would pay if he had ordered his steel all the way from Pittsburgh. In terms of Figure 7.7, if the Pittsburgh price were $100, steel would sell for $103 at point A, $104 at point B, and $106 at Chicago. Chicago and Pittsburgh plants would quote the same *delivered* prices at any point.*

---

* In the steel industry, to assure identical delivered prices the American Iron and Steel Institute compiled and distributed a freight book showing rail freight rates from Pittsburgh to every point in the country. Customers were charged rail

This marvelous invention meant that any producer who wanted to could solicit business in any part of the country without bringing a price war down on his head and without making price concessions to buyers in his own neighborhood. Pittsburgh mills could get into other markets if they needed to. Chicago mills could sell in the area toward Pittsburgh, too, but they had to "absorb freight" to do it (i.e., they had to accept a lower mill price, net of freight). Of course, there was no law saying that different mills had to charge the same Pittsburgh prices, but the normal behavior of oligopolists took care of that most of the time.

In 1924 the FTC ordered USS to discontinue this system of pricing. Thereafter USS and the rest of the industry established basing points at Gary, Birmingham, and occasionally at other cities as well as at Pittsburgh. The governing basing point depended on which city was nearest to the customer. The advantage of the old basing point system was preserved. Competitive price cutting was avoided, but anyone could sell in any market if he were willing to absorb enough freight.*

The basing point system had a number of unfortunate effects from a national point of view. It discouraged the development of steel-using industries away from basing points because they paid high prices for steel, even if they bought from mills right next door. The basing point system probably slowed the industrial development of the South and perhaps the West.

It probably slowed the transfer of steel-producing capacity away from obsolete locations as well. Technological and economic developments have reduced Pittsburgh's advantage in steel making. Originally, it was close to the main markets, to ore ports on Lake Erie, and especially to Appalachian coal. Since then the markets of the Midwest and, more recently, the South and the Far West have grown. At the same time scrap has become an important raw material and great savings in coal used per ton of steel have been accomplished. With coal less important than previously, new steel centers have developed next to the steel-consuming and scrap-producing centers, especially those at ore ports such as Chicago, Detroit, Baltimore, and

---

freight, even when steel was shipped by truck, or barge, and were discouraged by penalty prices from picking steel up in their own trucks.

* The old basing point prices were largely maintained because base prices at Chicago and Birmingham were higher than at Pittsburgh. This did not reflect cost differences. Birmingham, in particular, appears to have had lower costs than Pittsburgh, if anything (Stocking, *op. cit.*, p. 83). Midwestern and southern base prices were equalized in 1938. East and West Coast mill prices have remained higher to this day.

Philadelphia.*　The basing point system slowed the shift to these new locations by permitting the older mills to sell there and by preventing the local mills from undercutting them.　USS in particular had a large investment in Pittsburgh plants and dragged its feet in expanding facilities at new locations.†

Steel Without Basing Points

In 1948 the Supreme Court declared a basing point system similar to steel's illegal.‡　Since then steel prices have been set on an f.o.b. mill basis.　Sellers in the Midwest and the South generally set uniform mill prices, so that any given customer would be quoted different prices (including freight) from each mill.　Since steel shortages were common in the years that followed, poorly located mills were able to keep operating at capacity along with the rest of the industry.　A small freight difference did not deter the buyer if he found someone with steel for early delivery.

To keep exporting steel in more normal times, mills in surplus areas have had to meet prices of mills nearer to customers.　They have done so by absorbing freight again.　In terms of Figure 7.7 the announced f.o.b. prices at Pittsburgh and Chicago (and most other plants) would be 100, but Pittsburgh plants could sell anywhere in the Chicago (or other) territory by taking a low enough price net of freight on those sales.　In effect, they discriminate against nearby steel users, offering lower prices to customers near other plants.　The new arrangement is a sort of basing point system itself, with a basing point at every plant, but it is not quite so easy for a steel maker to calculate his rivals' delivered price as it used to be.§

* W. Isard and W. M. Capron, "The Future Locational Pattern of Iron and Steel Production in the United States," *Journal of Political Economy*, Apr. 1, 1949, p. 126.

† A firm of independent engineers retained by USS concluded that the Birmingham plants rather than those in the Midwest would have been the cheapest source of supply of oil country goods in the Southwest and of certain products on the East and West Coasts.　Study of Monopoly Power, *op. cit.*, Serial No. 14, Pt. 4A, pp. 640–642.

‡ FTC v. Cement Institute, 333 US 683 (1948).　There were a number of other cases at about the same time which also bore on the basing point system.　The one that applied specifically to steel was an order issued by the FTC (1951) prohibiting various practices such as the American Iron and Steel Institute's rate book, collaboration in determining charges for extras, and refusal to quote prices f.o.b.　The industry did not contest the order.

§ The new system differs from the old basing point system in a number of respects: (1) Every plant is a basing point.　(2) Customers may buy at the mill

What has been gained by eliminating the old basing point system? There has been a rapid decentralization of the steel industry in the past ten years, and the financial press has attributed this to f.o.b. pricing in part.* In 32 basing point years (1916–48) the Pittsburgh-Youngstown area's share of the nation's steel capacity declined from 46% to 41%. In the next ten years, without basing point pricing, the area's share fell to 35%.† During the decade ending 1958, steel capacity in the Pittsburgh-Youngstown area grew by only 11% against 36% for Chicago and more than 50% in the East, South, Far West, and Cleveland-Detroit districts.‡

Better steel prices in the South since World War II should probably be given some credit for its rapid industrialization. However, every chapter of this book so far has accounted for that growth in part. The elimination of price discrimination against southern steel users was only one of many factors.

One thing that f.o.b. pricing has not done is to eliminate price leadership and uniformity. These were the result of the fewness of firms, the character of the product, and the traditions of the industry. The basing point decisions did not change these conditions. The leaders of the industry proved quite capable of working out a new pricing system with little more danger of price competition than previously.

THE MONOPOLY POWER OF STEEL

Entry

Although the half-dozen leading steel producers are almost bound to set prices with an eye to the industry demand curve, it does not *necessarily* follow that their prices will be terribly exploitative. If good substitutes are plentiful or entry is easy, an industry with only a few sellers will not be able to take excessive profits. The only two

without penalty. (3) Delivered prices include freight by the cheapest means of transportation, whether truck, barge or rail. (4) Every company must work out its own freight charges and those of its rivals for itself.

* "The Transformation of U.S. Steel," *loc. cit.*

† Derived from American Iron and Steel Institute, *Directory of Iron and Steel Work in the U.S. and Canada, 1916,* and *Annual Statistical Report,* 1957, p. 56. 1916 figure is an estimate based on the assumption that Jones & Laughlin had 5% of capacity.

‡ *Annual Statistical Report, loc. cit.*

hotels in town probably will not engage in violent price competition, but if the suburbs are full of motor courts, their oligopoly cannot result in exorbitant prices or excessive profits.

The ability of steel producers to agree tacitly on price *is* significant, because the firms in the industry have more monopoly power as a group than the hotels in this illustration. The elasticity of demand for steel seems to be low, and there are substantial barriers to the entry of new firms.

New firms have not been a common occurrence in the steel industry over the last generation. In 1948 there were 62 companies with ingot capacity. All but eight of these were incorporated before 1916. Of the eight that did appear in those 32 years, only one, Kaiser Steel in California, had reached the million-ton class by 1948.*

Most of the new competition, such as it is, must come from non-integrated and semi-integrated firms already in the industry. Many of the major independents of today had such antecedents, and some new competition in the tonnage steel industry continues to appear from this group. In the 1950's Granite City Steel (near St. Louis) and McLouth Steel (Detroit) became fully integrated firms with a capacity of more than 1 million tons each. This category of firm, the "others" in Figure 7.2, offers only a moderate threat of new competition, however. Most of the small producers are specialty steel producers. Even including these, the group accounted for only 17.6% of total steel capacity in 1959. Their share has crept up by about five percentage points in the quarter-century since the last major Republic mergers, but this growth has been so slow that the established integrated firms might well decide that it was not worth sacrificing current profits to prevent.

New competition is not impossible in the mass production steel industry, but it is of limited significance. This was the conclusion of one careful scholar who investigated the restrictions on entry in 20 industries in the early 1950's. He concluded that the barriers in steel were not so high as those in automobiles, cigarettes, and a few other industries, but they were substantially higher than in such fields as cement, meat packing, metal containers, and tires.†

The Character of the Market

One important limitation on the steel industry's monopoly power has been the character of the markets on which it sells. A number

---

* Schroeder, *op. cit.*, pp. 200–202. Excluded from this 62-company figure are subsidiaries of other steel firms and companies only incidentally engaged in steel production.

† Bain, *op. cit.*, pp. 170–180.

of its customers are huge firms such as the automobile companies and the tin can manufacturers. Such buyers are good matches for the big steel companies in any negotiations. In depression times they were such important customers that steel suppliers were ready to make price concessions to win their business. Moreover, even though entry was difficult for other would-be steel producers, some of these huge steel consumers have proved quite capable of breaking into the field if they feel it necessary. Ford has had its own steel plant since 1922.

Not all of steel's customers are giants, but most of them are well-informed businessmen. They know the products they are buying very well and generally have much better ideas of the prices available to them than the typical consumer buying shoes or toothpaste. Steel companies have very few opportunities to divert customers to high-priced sources of supply with advertising or superficial frills; and it is next to impossible to keep steel users in the dark about real differences in price or quality. The well-informed character of the customers contributed to the breakdown of tacit collusion in depression years and has deprived the steel makers of profit opportunities available to some consumer goods manufacturers.

Public Opinion

Like Alcoa, USS and the other large steel companies have had to keep public relations in mind when setting policy. USS has long been famous for its concern about public opinion. In the early days the continued existence of the corporation was probably at stake. In the years since World War II the industry has had to explain its periodic price increases to congressmen in their almost annual investigations.

It is clear that this public pressure kept the steel companies' prices below their most profitable levels in some instances. This is especially true of the inflationary years after World War II. Steel was in very short supply and some distributors were able to resell such steel as they did acquire at great profits on the "grey" market. Yet announced steel prices remained stable or increased only moderately, and the companies rationed steel by administrative decision rather than price.

PERFORMANCE

Capacity and Output

Figure 7.8 shows the ingot capacity and ingot production of the American steel industry since 1901. Steel capacity has grown a little

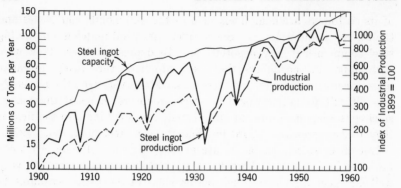

Figure 7.8.   Source: Steel capacity and production: USS, *TNEC Papers*, Vol. II, and American Iron and Steel Institute, *Annual Statistical Reports,* 1957.   Industrial production: National Bureau of Economic Research and Federal Reserve Board.

more slowly than total industrial production and much more slowly than aluminum and electricity.   This does not necessarily mean that steel was dragging its feet.   It was well established as one of our key industries at the turn of the century, while electric power and aluminum production were only beginning then.

Instability

The most notable feature of Figure 7.8 is the instability of steel production.   Output has been as low as 20% of capacity in one year, and it has often dropped below half capacity.*

This volatility is the result of the market for steel.   Steel and things made from steel are durable, so purchases can be postponed in bad years.   Moreover, a large proportion of the steel produced goes into capital goods such as machinery and buildings.   Demand for such items is particularly unstable because it depends upon *changes* in the demand for ultimate consumer goods.†   For instance, a shoe firm may normally need to replace 20 machines per year.   In a recession when sales drop by perhaps 10%, it may be able to get along with no new equipment at all, and in a boom when shoe sales increase by 10% it may have to install 40 new machines instead of just 20.   A 10%

---

* Since Figure 7.8 gives annual production figures, it does not show the extremes that occur in some months.   Relatively mild recessions like those of 1949 and 1958 included months when the steel industry was at less than 60% of capacity.   On the other hand, there were periods in a number of the postwar years when steel output exceeded 100% of *rated* capacity!

† Readers with a good economic vocabulary will recognize this as the accelerator effect.

rise or fall in demand for shoes may lead to a 100% rise or fall in machinery (and steel) orders.

Overcapacity

The steel industry had a long history of overcapacity until World War II. Even in prosperous years like 1909–13 and 1923–29, the industry as a whole ran at well below capacity, though there were individual plants with much better records. The rapid growth after the consolidations at the turn of the century and during World War I provided more than enough plant for subsequent years, and the conservative pricing policies of the industry protected obsolete plants that would probably have been eliminated in more vigorously competitive industries.*

Because of this excess capacity, there were fairly long periods with little expansion in steel facilities. Looking at the shape of the capacity curve before 1940 and the rates of utilization, it is easy to see how people could conclude that the industry was reaching "maturity."† More than half of the relatively small expansion during World War II was undertaken by the government and not all of that was retained after the war. In the period from 1945 to 1950 there were only modest additions to plant. This was a period of steel shortage, and pressure was put on the industry to expand. President Truman once proposed that the government build facilities if private firms would not. After the Korean War the industry finally began to make up for the previous 30 years' slow growth. Accelerated depreciation under the tax laws helped, but even after that had ended the expansion continued.

The slowness of the industry to grow in the 1920's, 1930's, and 1940's cannot be interpreted as monopolistic restriction in the usual sense. A monopolist seeking maximum profits would build plant if he could sell its output at prices selected by him. However, the monopolistic position of the steel industry did permit it to make decisions on the safe side. There were few impatient upstarts to force its hand. When a race for additional capacity finally did occur in the 1950's, it may have gone too far. Overcapacity in prosperous

---

* *Fortune* magazine, in "U.S. Steel," Mar. 1936, made a careful study of USS. One of their conclusions was:

"And so the chief energies of the men who guided the corporation were directed to preventing deterioration in the investment value of the enormous properties confided to their care. To achieve this they consistently tried to freeze the steel industry at present, or better yet, past levels" (p. 170).

† *Ibid.*, p. 164.

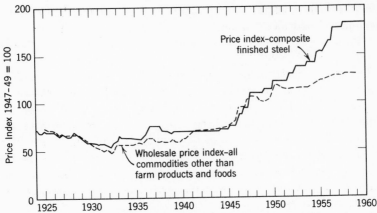

Figure 7.9. Wholesale prices—steel products and all commodities other than farm products and foods. Source: Composite finished steel index from *Steel* magazine, quoted in *Surveys of Current Business*. Wholesale price index from *Statistical Abstract*.

years, like that of the 1920's, became a serious possibility again by 1960.

Price Rigidity

Steel prices are compared with wholesale prices of all manufactured goods in Figure 7.9. Steel prices proved somewhat more stable during the twenties and thirties than industrial prices in spite of the extreme loss of sales by steel firms. As was pointed out earlier, prices of steel products where concentration was high, such as rails and heavy structural shapes, were particularly rigid.

Price rigidity is a common characteristic of oligopolies. An ingenious explanation has been developed. The effective demand curve of a conservative oligopolist is a combination of D_1 and D_2. If he cuts his price he must count on the other companies following, but if he raises his price they may not. If he is a careful man, the oligopolist will consider D_2 on the way down and D_1 on the way up. In other words, the demand curve that concerns him is the heavy portions of D_1 and D_2 in Figure 7.10.

With such a demand curve, the oligopolist is apt to leave well enough alone. If a price rise leads to a rapid loss of market and a drop means small additional sales, circumstances will have to be extreme before a change is in order.

While this analysis may account for the price rigidity of some oligopolies, it does not make too much sense in the steel industry with its traditions of price leadership. USS can almost disregard its D_1 curve in making formal price changes.

Price rigidity would make sense even disregarding this "kinked" demand curve. If nothing else, price changes mean work. New catalogues have to be prepared and thousands of new prices have to be determined. Small changes are likely to be fruitless anyway. Steel makers cannot really tell if conditions would be better or worse at a price of $100 instead of $101.

Consumer reactions to price changes also encourage rigid prices. If low demand means low prices and high demand high ones, buyers are apt to hold off ordering on a declining market and vice versa, thus making the industry's instability worse. The reader may recall that the textile industry has been plagued by just such a problem. At any rate, temporary price reductions in time of depression probably will not increase steel sales very much because the short-run demand for steel is certainly inelastic.

From a public relations point of view price flexibility has its disadvantages. If Congress investigates whenever the price goes up, increases will occur only when they are obviously worthwhile and preferably when there is a good excuse such as a wage increase or a change in the tax law. Similarly, sellers will want to be very sure before cutting prices because it is so unpleasant getting them back up again.

Finally, in an oligopoly where every seller's welfare depends on an unenforced tacit agreement, every change may be dangerous. The industry may be better off taking decent profits at a long-established price that is accepted by everybody than trying to wrest the last penny from the market by changing price often and risking a price war each time.

The rigidity of steel prices during periods of depression gives some

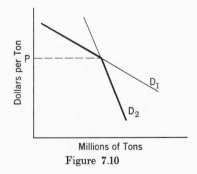

Figure 7.10

indication of the steel companies' control over price. They were not able to keep their prices up as well as Alcoa or the electric utilities in 1931–33, but prices in purely competitive fields could hardly have remained as stable as steel prices in the face of a 75% drop in demand, especially in a field with fairly high fixed costs. In milder depression years, such as 1958, the steel companies were actually able to raise prices.

"Creeping Inflation"

In the 1950's steel prices increased more than most. The annual steel price increase became something of a national institution and was widely damned as a major source of our "creeping inflation." The mere fact that a price is rising is not necessarily a basis for criticism. Some prices would always be going up and others down in a purely competitive economy depending on where shortages and surpluses appeared. In the early 1950's steel was undoubtedly in short supply, but this was not the explanation of price increases in the latter half of the decade when there was usually some unused capacity in the industry.

The price increases usually coincided with wage increases, and there was much debate about whether they were justified. The union ordinarily argued that with their profits and with rising productivity, the steel companies could afford to absorb the raises. The companies claimed that the price advances did not cover their higher costs.

Figure 7.11 shows steel wages, unit labor costs, and steel prices, all as percentages of the 1947–49 levels. Labor costs per unit of output do not rise as fast as wages because of increasing productivity. In fact, they fell in the 1920's and 1930's. Steel prices fell also, though not quite as rapidly. During the war and postwar inflations steel prices did not rise as fast as employment costs. After 1949, however, the steel companies raised their prices right along with wages and considerably faster than unit labor costs. The regular increase in unit labor costs in those years occurred because wages were rising faster than output per man-hour. In other words, both the companies and the union were contributing to the increase in steel prices during the 1950's.

A plausible explanation of this behavior on the part of the steel companies might be that they had not been able to take full advantage of their position earlier because of public pressure and were just getting their prices up to what they felt was an optimum level. Steel makers defended their profits in 1956 and 1957 along these lines:

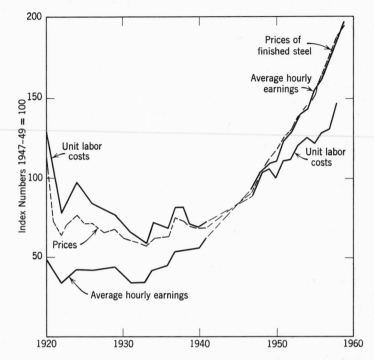

Figure 7.11. Source: Average hourly earnings from Bureau of Labor Statistics, Bulletin 567; *Wages and Hours in the Iron and Steel Industry*, 1931; *Statistical Abstract;* and *Monthly Labor Reviews.*

Unit labor cost is average hourly earnings divided by index of output per man-hour of production worker.

Index of output per man-hour from Bureau of Labor Statistics, Bulletin 1200, and *Index of Output per Man-Hour for Selected Industries, 1919–1959.* Prices from *Steel* magazine quoted in *Survey of Current Business, op. cit.*

We started out through the war with a control on prices, and unfortunately control was not exercised to the same extent on wages or other things we had to buy, and we found ourselves at the end of the war in a position where we had been squeezed down to the three percent profit on our sales dollar . . . and we have spent the next decade trying to catch up.*

The rapid rise in steel wages had a somewhat similar explanation. They had increased less than most wages from 1939 to 1949, and their more rapid rise in the 1950's brought them back to their 1939 level

* Statement of Robert C. Tyson, Chairman of the Finance Committee, USS, *Administered Prices, op. cit.,* p. 278.

relative to other wage rates.*   In both 1939 and 1959 steel wages were well above wage rates in manufacturing generally.

Foreign Competition

Wherever the responsibility for rising steel prices lay, one result was as increase in foreign competition. Steel prices had not risen as much abroad as in the United States, so by the end of the 1950's it was becoming profitable to import certain iron and steel products from Europe and Japan. The main competition arose on the two coasts, where mill prices were generally above those in the Midwest and where freight from abroad was low.

The increasing foreign competition caused considerable alarm at the time of the 1959 steel strike, but it was still quite small. The total tonnage of steel mill products imported in 1958 came to less than 2% of American steel output in that year. Our exports were still more than double our imports of steel mill products.† Even if they are small, however, these imports and the threat of more if steel prices continue to rise more rapidly here than abroad serve a useful function by providing an element of competition that can offer some check on the power of the steel companies and the steel union.

Steel Profits

Figure 7.12 shows earnings in the iron and steel industry compared with all manufacturing concerns. The steel companies have not earned particularly high profits in most years. The overcapacity of the 1920's and 1930's made steel one of the low profit fields. Government and public pressure did the same in the 1940's. The industry was finally able to get its profits into line with those of most manufacturing in the 1950's, a fact which seems to bear out the hypothesis that steel prices rose faster than steel costs in that period.

Representatives of the steel industry have urged repeatedly in recent years that their profits were overstated because of inflation. Their depreciation allowances are based on the original cost of their plants, but with inflation, replacement costs are usually greater than original costs today. As a result, they claim they are understating their actual depreciation and overstating their profits in their accounts. This argument applies to other manufacturers besides steel makers, but

---

* See Chapter 10, pp. 482–483.

† Census, *Quarterly Summary of Foreign Commerce*, Dec. 1958. Imports did exceed exports and rose above the 2% level in 1959, but this was generally presumed to be a temporary situation associated with the long steel strike of that year. *Economic Report of the President*, Jan. 1960, pp. 35, 114, 116.

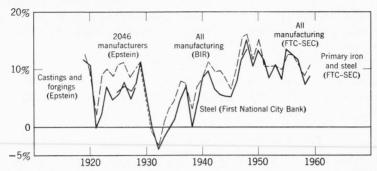

Figure 7.12. Source: 1919–28, R. C. Epstein, *Industrial Profits in the United States,* National Bureau of Economic Research, 1934.

Steel 1925–47, First National City Bank, *News Letters.*

All manufacturing: 1931–47, Internal Revenue Service, *Statistics of Income;* 1957–59, FTC-SEC, *Quarterly Financial Reports, United States Manufacturing Corporations.*

the overstatement of profits may be somewhat greater in steel than in most businesses because steel mills require somewhat more plant per dollar of sale than the average and are very long-lived.

As far as it goes, this argument is correct. If a steel company were to distribute all its accounting profits as dividends, it would find itself with less and less steel capacity over a period of rising replacement costs.

The companies have gone on to argue for some adjustment in the corporate income tax to recognize their overstated profits, but this is a much more controversial question. It would be difficult to argue that the companies should receive tax relief as a matter of fairness. Inflation has hurt many other people much more than it has the owners of steel mills, but few would argue that the owners of bonds or insurance policies should have some of their taxes excused. As a matter of fact, common stocks, including steel stocks, have become popular refuges *from* inflation in recent years, the corporate income tax notwithstanding.

It is also argued that the tax, as now collected, may discourage investment. But investors are buying *new* plant at current prices and will have realistic depreciation allowances so long as replacement costs rise no farther in the future. It is the owners of old plants built at pre-World War II construction costs who overstate their profits most. These firms with old plants may not be able to finance all the expansion they would like from their profits because some profits have to be diverted to replacement, but they have the alternative of issuing new securities. This is how smaller firms such as

Kaiser and Granite City Steel have financed their more-than-average expansions in recent years. Larger and more established firms should certainly be able to find a market for their securities.

While the companies' claims to special tax treatment are open to question, the apparent overstatement of profits from old plants probably does mean that economic profits in the steel industry were not exceptionally high even in the prosperous 1950's.

Profitability and Scale

Not all steel companies earned equally good profits. Table 7.4 shows the average rates of profit of 12 companies from their earliest

Table 7.4

RATES OF RETURN ON INVESTMENT OF 12 LARGE STEEL COMPANIES

Company	Ingot Capacity −1948 (millions of tons per year)	Average Annual Rate of Return on Total Investment (All Years with Records)		
		Years	Average Return	1946–50
USS	31.2	1901–50	9.4	9.3
Bethlehem	13.8	1905–50	9.3	13.3
Republic	8.6	1901–50	9.3	14.7
Jones and Laughlin	4.8	1920–50	5.9	11.0
National	4.2	1930–50	12.0	19.4
Youngstown Sheet and Tube	4.0	1901–50	12.6	15.4
Armco	3.4	1901–50	12.2	21.4
Inland	3.4	1905–50	15.7	20.1
Sharon	1.6	1905–50	18.3	27.4
Wheeling	1.4	1920–50	6.3	13.7
Crucible	1.3	1901–50	11.6	5.4
Pittsburgh	1.1	1910–50	7.5	8.7

Source: Schroeder, *op. cit.*, p. 175.

published records to 1950 as well as for the years 1946–50. These are returns on total investment (stockholders' equity stock *plus* long-term debt) so that variations between firms because of different types of financing are eliminated. The initial overstatement of USS's capital was also eliminated. The four largest steel companies, and USS in

TABLE 7.5

RATES OF GROWTH OF 12 LARGE STEEL COMPANIES

Company	Steel Ingot Capacity		Percentage Growth 1948–58
	1958	1948	
USS	40.2	31.2	28.8%
Bethlehem	23.0	13.8	66.7
Republic	12.2	8.6	41.9
Jones and Laughlin	7.5	4.8	56.3
National	6.8	4.2	61.9
Youngstown Sheet and Tube	6.5	4.0	62.5
Armco	6.3	3.4	85.3
Inland	5.5	3.4	61.8
Wheeling	2.4	1.4	70.9
Sharon	1.4	1.6	−10.8
Crucible	1.4	1.3	12.0
Pittsburgh	1.4	1.1	30.8

Source: American Iron and Steel Institute, *Directory of Steel Works and Rolling Mills in the United States and Canada*, 1948; *Moody's Industrial Manual*, 1958.

particular, had only mediocre records,* as did some of the smaller ones. The highest profits were earned by the middle-sized firms: National, Youngstown, Armco, and Inland.

These differences in profitability do not result from unequal monopoly power. Good steel prices for one are good steel prices for all. They could reflect differences in bargaining power in the purchase of supplies. The middle-sized firms might do better than the small ones in this respect, but the large firms should be more profitable rather than less.

In part, the profit variations reflect location. Inland, near Chicago, is particularly well located, while Republic, Jones and Laughlin, and USS have many Pittsburgh-Youngstown facilities. USS has a smaller proportion of its capacity in the Pittsburgh district than National, Youngstown, Sharon, Jones and Laughlin, or Wheeling Steel, however, and Bethlehem is certainly one of the well-located companies. Similarly, some steel products are more profitable than others. The firm that produces railroad products will not do as well as one selling tin plate these days.

Both location and product mix are matters of managerial decision. A firm that consistently produces the wrong thing in the wrong place

* Bethlehem is famous for the very high salaries of its officers. If these include some profits, Bethlehem has a better record than shown here.

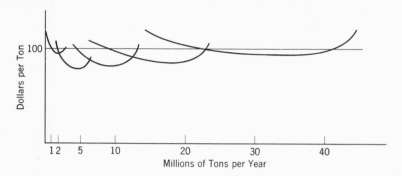

Figure 7.13. Hypothetical average total cost curves for the steel industry.

does not display much ability to adjust to change. In that sense it is less efficient than the others.

The rates of growth of these 12 firms between 1948 and 1958 (shown in Table 7.5) tell much the same story as the profit figures. Mergers were not important in adding to ingot capacity during the period in question. While Bethlehem among the very large firms and Wheeling among the smaller ones* grew rapidly, all of the middle-sized firms did.

Great empires engaged in a hundred different businesses are difficult to control. The more compact firms have done better. All this suggests that the long-run average total cost curves of the steel industry look like Figure 7.13.

The Efficiency of USS

USS in particular had a reputation for mediocre management until recently. Its weakness became especially evident when, during the great depression, it operated at a loss for four consecutive years and displayed one of the poorest profit records in the industry. After the death of Judge Gary in 1927 and especially after the start of the depression, the corporation undertook a major campaign of self-improvement. There was a drastic shake-up in command associated with Myron Taylor, the new Chairman of the Board, and Benjamin Fairless, the new president. As part of its effort to revitalize itself the corporation engaged an independent firm of engineers to review

* Table 7.5 was made up of the same firms as Table 7.4 for comparability. Actually, some of the fastest growing firms were new ones whose profit records were not comparable to those in Table 7.4 because so much of their plant was built after the postwar inflation. Three of these, Kaiser, McLauth, and Granite City, grew mainly by internal expansion. A fourth, Colorado Fuel and Iron, is an old firm which went through receivership during the 1930's and has grown rapidly by merger in recent years.

and evaluate it. Their 200-volume report completed in 1938 has never been made public, but much of its content was revealed during congressional hearings in 1950.* George Stocking, an economist testifying at the same hearings, made the following summary:

> This committee heard its counsel read extracts from the report of the industrial engineers . . . which pictured the Steel Corporation as a big sprawling inert giant whose production operations were improperly coordinated; suffering from a lack of long run planning agency; relying on an antiquated system of cost accounting; with an inadequate knowledge of the costs or of the relative profitability of the many thousands of items it sold; with production and cost standards generally below those considered every day practice in other industries; with inadequate knowledge of its domestic markets and no clear appreciation of its opportunities in foreign markets; with less efficient production facilities than its rivals had; slow in introducing new processes and new products.
>
> Specifically, according to the engineers, it was slow in introducing the continuous rolling mill; slow in getting into production of cold rolled steel products; slow in recognizing the potentials of the wire business; slow to adopt the heat treating process for the production of sheets; slow in getting into stainless steel products; slow in producing cold rolled sheets, slow in tin plate developments; slow in utilizing waste gases; slow in utilizing low cost water transportation because of its consideration for the railroads; in short, slow to grasp the remarkable business opportunities that a dynamic America offered it. The corporation was apparently a follower, not a leader in industrial efficiency.
>
> The report . . . represents perhaps the most devastating indictment by experts of big business on the charge of inefficiency that has ever been made public.†

Since the 1930's, big steel has apparently made great strides in revamping itself. One reason for its slow growth in the 1940's and 1950's was a large-scale program of renovation. Antiquated plants in the Pittsburgh area were abandoned or combined, and facilities throughout the rest of the country were rapidly built up. The corporation has developed a good-sized research program and modern cost accounting organization.‡

By the late 1950's these changes were showing up in profits. Figure 7.14 compares USS's profit with those of the industry as a whole.

---

* Study of Monopoly Power, *op. cit.*, testimony of Benjamin Fairless, pp. 626–628, 640–650.

† Study of Monopoly Power, *op. cit.*, pp. 966–967.

‡ For a review of the policy changes see "The Transformation of U. S. Steel," *op. cit.*, p. 88, and "Why Big Steel is Successful," *Iron Age*, Aug. 14, 1958, p. 48.

Figure 7.14. Net income as a percentage of owner's equity. Source: *Administered Prices, op. cit.,* p. 526, and *Steel,* Apr. 14, 1960 (for 1958 and 1959).

USS has gradually changed from one of the least profitable to one of the most profitable firms. This does not prove that USS excels the others in technical efficiency. Since it has been growing more slowly than the others, its accounts would show a smaller proportion of new, high-priced plant. Moreover, it has an advantage over the other firms in its ore supply. However, the corporation is unquestionably a more efficient organization than it once was.

The very large firm may be at less of a disadvantage today in many industries than it was previously. Revolutionary new methods of communication and record keeping have developed. A few decades ago an organization the size of USS probably had just too many parts to be understood and efficiently controlled by a few human minds. Since then, business has acquired increasingly sophisticated methods of cost accounting, highly refined methods of statistical quality control, and calculating equipment capable of storing and combining far more information than a mere human mind can use unassisted.

The improved ability of modern managements to handle huge quantities of information should tend to reduce the cost disadvantage of large-scale producers. The result would be a shift in the long-run cost curves of big firms as shown in Figure 7.15. However, while big steel may no longer be at a disadvantage, it certainly cannot be shown that the middle-sized firms are any the less workable. The nation would have no less efficient a steel industry if it were made up of a half-dozen more Inland or National Steels and one less USS.

Bigness and Progress in Steel

A common defense of bigness and monopoly is that it encourages innovation. Large firms are supposed to face less risk in trying new things because they need not put all their eggs in one basket. Monopolists presumably have a greater incentive to innovate because if they do pick a winner they are protected from the host of imitators common in competitive industries.

USS has seldom been the leader in innovation. The most important change of the century, the continuous strip mill, was patented by Armco. National led in electrolytic tin plating. Bethlehem made its name with the Gray process for making heavy structural shapes. Republic and the smaller specialty steel makers have done the most with alloys. The electric furnace, stainless steel, and the by-product coke oven all originated in Europe.

Time and again it was the smaller firms that developed new products or methods or locations. This was the way for them to break into the industry. Established firms had no such pressing incentives. Of course, the smaller companies are big business by most standards. Armco, the seventh or eighth in capacity and probably

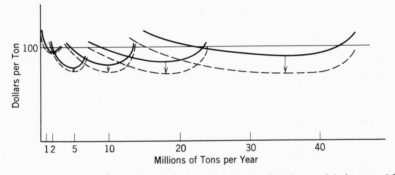

Figure 7.15. Hypothetical average total cost curves for the steel industry with and without modern management techniques and equipment.

the leader in innovation, is about the size of Alcoa. Moreover, such advantages as monopoly may offer accrue to all members of the industry, not just the big ones.

The record of the industry as a whole is hard to evaluate, but such evidence as there is seems to give steel only an average record for progress. Figures 7.16 shows that steel productivity (output per man-hour) grew faster than in most manufacturing during World War II but just kept up at other times. Similarly, new types and uses of steel have been sufficient to keep the industry growing about as fast as manufacturing generally, but no faster. Of course, an established industry like steel cannot be expected to make the progress of new industries like aluminum or electric power, but the innovational argument for bigness is certainly not given strong support by events in steel.

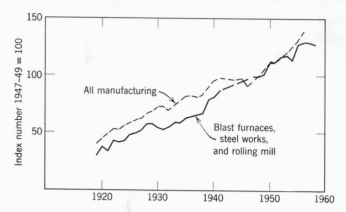

Figure 7.16. Output per man-hour. Source: Bureau of Labor Statistics, Bulletin 1200, "Man Hours Per Unit of Output in the Basic Steel Industry"; Bureau of Labor Statistics, *Handbook of Labor Statistics*, 1950, Bureau of Labor Statistics, *Index of Output per Man Hour for Selected Industries*, 1919–58.

The basic process in steel production has undergone surprisingly little change since the turn of the century. The blast furnace is centuries old, and except for the use of pure oxygen (introduced by Republic in 1944) all the techniques of the modern furnace were in use at the turn of the century. The open hearth furnace was developed in the 1860's, though its complete victory over the Bessemer converter waited until the start of this century. Most of the changes in this century have been in increased scale, in improved materials handling and control, and in rolling and finishing.

In recent years considerable attention has been given to several potentially revolutionary changes in steel technology. Direct reduction of iron would bypass the blast furnace, remove the need for coke, and make possible the production of steel with natural gas, soft coal, or almost any other fuel. The oxygen process of steel making avoids many of the defects of the Bessemer converter while retaining its advantages. The continuous casting of steel and new types of rolling mills may reduce the large scale and initial investment involved in modern steel making.

Of these, the only process now in commercial use in the United States is the oxygen process (first installed by two small firms, Kaiser and McLauth Steel). Bethlehem, USS, and Esso all have pilot plants working on the direct reduction process. Continuous casting and the new rolling processes are in use in Europe and Canada, but American steel men testify that they are not now suitable for the mass scale of American tonnage steel making. A large part of the work on all of these developments so far has been outside the American steel industry, much of it in Europe.

If these developments become practical the steel industry may be spectacularly changed in the future. All of them point toward smaller plants with less investment per ton of capacity. The direct reduction process would make it profitable to produce steel far from coking coal and thus hasten the decentralization of the industry. At present these are all in the maybe stages.*

CONCLUSIONS

The steel industry is unavoidably one of very large firms, at least with present techniques. However, it need not have been as concentrated as it has been in practice. The industry would probably have been no less efficient if the big merger of 1901 had never occurred or if the government had won the dissolution suit of 1920. It might well have been more efficient.

An oligopolistic industry like steel is apt to display a price policy similar to a monopolist's. Some price competition may occur if costs differ among firms or if some firms are in desperate condition as in time of depression. It is likely to be sporadic and undercover, however.

The steel industry has a long history of resistance to price competition through such devices as uniform lists of extras, the basing point system, and price leadership. The Federal Trade Commission has forced the abandonment or modification of these practices and has probably accomplished something in shifting the location of industry as a result. Its prohibitions have not succeeded in eliminating tacit cooperation on price, however.

The price policy of the steel industry has been oriented toward stability and good public relations. Profits have not been excessive compared with other manufacturing, but established firms have seemed to take the safe position. They have often been slow to develop new techniques or locations. As a result, profit prospects have at times been good enough to encourage the rise of relatively small firms in spite of obstacles that have seemed prohibitive to some observers. By taking advantage of opportunities not grasped by the large firms, a number of small ones have become important.

* Sources on new processes in steel: "Bypassing the Blast Furnace," *Fortune*, Oct. 1956, pp. 164–167, and *Administered Prices, op. cit.*, pp. 675–793, 1057–1060.

From time to time economists have proposed the dissolution of USS as the most likely means of accomplishing more competition and innovation in the steel industry. Such a change is unlikely in the future in view of the corporation's declining share of the industry and recent evidence of its increased efficiency. Further combinations among the leading firms of the industry can be prevented, however. These firms are all of a size clearly capable of efficient operation and progress, as their histories indicate. This does not mean that all merger within the industry is of necessity against the public's interest. Combinations of small firms, such as the merger that established National, have sometimes led to increased rather than reduced competition in the past.

The main barriers to new firms are the large initial investment and the concentrated control over ore reserves. The first can only be altered by a change in the basic techniques of the industry, something which may conceivably be in the offing. The raw material barrier can only be removed by the separation of steel mills from their ore holdings. In view of the large investment necessary for the development of overseas deposits and taconite beneficiation, this again does not seem likely. New competition must therefore be of limited significance in the mass production steel industry.

FURTHER READINGS

A good history of the leading steel companies which has been used extensively in this chapter is Gertrude G. Schroeder, *The Growth of Major Steel Companies, 1900–1950,* "Johns Hopkins University Studies in Historical and Political Science," Series LXX, No. 2, Johns Hopkins University Press, 1952. A good analysis and evaluation of the steel industry in all respects, not just the basing point system, appears in George W. Stocking, *Basing Point Pricing and Regional Development,* University of North Carolina Press, 1954. There are great quantities of official materials on the industry arising from its perennial investigations. The three most complete studies were the hearings and monographs of the Temporary National Economic Committee (1938–41), the Subcommittee on the Study of Monopoly Power (Celler Committee, 1950), and the Subcommittee on Anti-Trust and Monopoly (Kefauver Committee, 1957). The materials presented by USS for each of these are very useful. The TNEC papers of USS are especially widely quoted.

The classic on the oligopolist and his two demand curves is Edward Chamberlin, *The Theory of Monopolistic Competition,* Harvard University Press, 1933. Part of the analysis of price leadership and of location in this chapter was based on Kenneth Boulding, *Economic Analysis,* 3rd ed., Harper, 1955. The kinked demand curve was the invention of Paul Sweezy, "Demand Under Conditions of Oligopoly." It is criticized in George Stigler, "The Kinky Oligopoly Demand Curve and Rigid Prices," both reprinted in *Readings in*

Price Theory, Irwin (for American Economic Association), 1955. A good source on oligopoly theory in general is William Fellner, *Competition Among the Few,* Knopf, 1949.

On the question of mergers see J. F. Weston, *The Role of Mergers in the Growth of Large Firms,* University of California Press, 1953, R. L. Nelson, *Merger Movements in American Industry,* Princeton University Press, 1959, and George Stigler, "Monopoly and Oligopoly by Merger," reprinted in *Readings in Industrial Organization and Public Policy,* Irwin, 1958.

On the basing point system, a good textbook discussion appears in Clair Wilcox, *Public Policies Toward Business,* rev. ed., Irwin, 1960, Chapter 10. For other readings on the subject see Stocking, mentioned above, Fritz Machlup, *The Basing Point System,* Blakiston, 1949, and Carl Kaysen, "Basing Point Pricing and Public Policy," reproduced in *Readings in Industrial Organization and Public Policy,* Irwin, 1958.

Steel is another industry covered in S. N. Whitney, *Anti-Trust Policies,* Twentieth Century Fund, 1958, Chapter 5.

8

OLIGOPOLY
WITH DIFFERENTIATED
PRODUCTS—AUTOMOBILES

Oligopoly performs differently in different situations.
To most questions about oligopoly economists have
to answer "it depends." The analysis presented for the steel industry
in the last chapter has wide application, but it leaves a lot out of
the picture for many industries. Oligopolies are apt to perform differently if (1) they are selling to the general public (cigarettes) or to
a few large buyers (tires); (2) if they have complete control of
supply (steel) or have their supply set for them by someone else
(meat packing); (3) if entry of new firms is relatively easy (meat
packing again) or very difficult (cigarettes); (4) if the industry is
young and rapidly growing (aluminum) or mature and slowly growing (steel) or actually declining (flour milling).

PRODUCT DIFFERENTIATION

A very important distinction is whether the product of an industry
is *standardized* or *differentiated*. Most of the industries discussed in
this book so far have been selling largely standardized products. Of
course, not all milk or eggs or aluminum or steel are alike, but customers who want grade A large white eggs or steel rails of a particular

324

size, shape, and chemical composition do not care much which producer they buy from so long as prices are the same. In addition to raw and semiprocessed materials, a surprisingly large proportion of the tools and machinery produced in this country are practically standardized products. If there is a set of specifications to be met and if the rival firms can meet them equally well, even so unique and complex a piece of equipment as a ship might be treated as virtually the same regardless of which firm builds it.

Products like candy bars, breakfast food, and refrigerators are differentiated. Here each firm does offer something that seems distinct to the buyer. Customers develop loyalties to one brand or another and will keep buying it even at somewhat higher prices than those charged for rival products. The actual chemical and physical differences are not important for this distinction. Two laundry soaps may be exactly the same in the test tube, but if some housewives always use soap A and others swear by soap B, the soap companies can be expected to act as sellers of differentiated products.

Industries with differentiated products may show a number of special characteristics: (1) There may be room for some price differences. A firm can raise its prices slightly and not lose the whole market to its rivals, or vice versa. (2) Firms with differentiated products are apt to engage in large amounts of *nonprice competition* —advertising, salesmen, styling, and the like—in an effort to build up loyalties. (3) Nonprice competition, in turn, may have important effects on entry, likelihood of competitive behavior, and the ability of existing firms to survive.

THE STRUCTURE OF THE AUTOMOBILE INDUSTRY

The Automobile Industry

The automobile industry is an outstanding example of an oligopoly with differentiated products. It can make a good claim to being our most important manufacturing industry. Recent censuses show that the motor vehicle industry has employed more people and produced more goods than any other line of manufacturing.* In 1954 it ac-

* The census industry group 3713, motor vehicles and parts, employed 649,274 persons in 1954 and produced a value added of $6,111,554,000. Industry group 3312, steel works and rolling mills, employed 518,690 and had a value added of $4,040,-515,000. No other four-digit census industry employed as many as 500,000 persons or had a value added of as much as $4 billion. The motor vehicles and parts industry produces trucks, busses, and parts as well as passenger cars, the main concern of this chapter. The $9,471,779,000 in shipments of passenger cars far exceeded the 1954 shipments of any other commodity in the whole census.

counted for 7% of total manufactured output and 2% of the whole national income. Considering tires, petroleum refining, automobile distribution and repair, highway construction, and the industry's shares of steel, aluminum, glass, and textile production, the whole automotive complex may account for an eighth of the nation's total output!

Few industries have products as differentiated as the automobile. A large proportion of the nation's automobile owners are at least as devoted to their brands of cars as to their political parties. Winning and keeping consumer loyalty is absolutely essential for success in automobile manufacturing.

Increasing Concentration

Auto making is one of the most concentrated of American industries. By the late 1950's there were only five domestic producers though there was a small but growing import trade as well. General Motors (hereafter GM) accounted for about half of total sales by itself, and the big three, GM, Ford, and Chrysler, were selling 80 to 90% of the cars.

Automobile production is one of the few major American industries that have displayed a significant and almost continuous increase in concentration over the years. This shows up well in Figures 8.1 and 8.2. The first gives the percentage of new automobile registrations accounted for by the big three and their predecessors and by the rest of the auto makers in various years. The second shows the number of makes of cars and of automobile companies in each year. The number of makes has not fallen as fast as the number of firms because each of the big three now produces makes in several different price classes. The share of each make in 1958 is shown in Table 8.1.

Half a century ago there were 15 times as many automakers as there are now, and Ford and GM accounted for only a third of total sales. The auto makers of that day did little more than assemble parts produced by a complex of machine shops that had already developed in the Detroit area. Even the motors and bodies were often purchased. There was a large unsatisfied demand, so sales were no problem. Parts makers sold on credit while dealers paid cash, so new firms could be financed on a shoestring. Profits were enormous for those who could get workable cars on the road—more than 100% of owners' equity in some cases.* With such incentives and few

---

* Ford had profits in excess of 100% on equity from 1904 to 1914 except for 1906. It earned 377.6% in 1907, i.e., profits were nearly four times as much as owners' equity! Seltzer, *op. cit.*, p. 129.

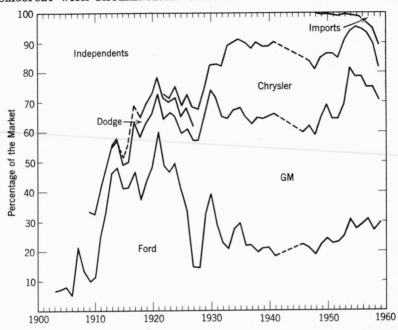

Figure 8.1. Source: Lawrence Seltzer, *A Financial History of the American Automobile Industry,* Houghton Mifflin, 1928, and *Automotive Industries, 1927–59.*

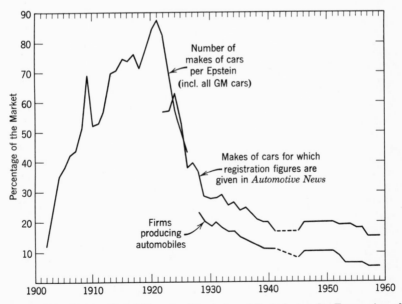

Figure 8.2. Source: Ralph Epstein, *The Automobile Industry, Its Economic and Commercial Development,* A. W. Shaw, 1928, p. 176, and *Automotive News, Almanac Issue,* 1951 and 1959.

TABLE 8.1

1958 NEW AUTOMOBILE REGISTRATIONS BY MAKE

Company and Make	Number of Units (thousands)	Percentage of Total
General Motors		
Chevrolet	1234	26.52
Pontiac	230	4.94
Buick	263	5.67
Oldsmobile	306	6.59
Cadillac	123	2.63
Total	2156	46.35
Ford		
Ford	1028	22.11
Mercury	136	2.93
Edsel	38	0.83
Lincoln and Continental	27	0.57
Total	1229	26.44
Chrysler		
Plymouth	391	8.40
Dodge	135	2.91
DeSoto	48	1.03
Chrysler	59	1.26
Imperial	15	0.32
Total	648	13.92
American Motors		
Rambler	186	4.00
Studebaker-Packard		
Studebaker Lark	48	1.03
Packard	2	0.06
Total	50	1.09
Foreign Cars		
Volkswagen	78	1.68
Renault	48	1.03
English Ford	33	0.72
Fiat	21	0.47
Others	197	4.22
Total	377	8.12

Data furnished by R. L. Polk & Co. Further re-use prohibited.

barriers to entry, firms flocked into the industry, but most of them had short lives because of production problems. By 1907 a few firms, particularly Ford, Buick, Cadillac, Olds, Maxwell, and Reo, were already established leaders, but altogether they controlled about half of total output, far less than their descendents do today.

Several key events transformed this industry into its present form. In order of occurrence they were: (1) the rise of Ford and GM to dominance, (2) the vertical integration of those and other firms, (3) the "saturation" of the market, and (4) the elimination of the independents.

The Growth of the Giants

GM was formed by merger. William C. Durant, owner of Buick, set GM up as a holding company in 1908 and used it to acquire some 25 companies including his Buick, the popular Cadillac, the once-great Olds, eight other auto makers of doubtful value, and a variety of parts makers.* Altogether it produced a quarter of the cars in 1908. Durant had attempted to acquire Reo, Maxwell, and Ford as well, but had failed for lack of financing. The acquisitions he did make so taxed GM's resources that it could only be saved from bankruptcy in 1910 by a surrender of control to a banking group. Under their supervision it fell to 9% of the industry by 1915.

Ford rose to dominance by internal growth. In 1908 automobile prices and production costs were still very high. In that year Ford brought out the Model T at a reasonable, though not a spectacularly low, price. It proved very popular and brought Ford enough customers to permit the introduction of assembly line techniques for some components. When costs fell, Ford cut his price and won yet more customers, and the process could be repeated. By 1913 he was doing enough business to warrant a complete assembly line, had halved his prices, and had become the unquestioned leader of the industry.†

* Seltzer, *op. cit.*, pp. 153–157.

† This is a simplification. Ford was already producing a popular and relatively cheap car before the Model T and had already used some mass production techniques. Moreover, those were made possible by the development of such precision in parts making that components could be made completely interchangeable. A great number of people, inside and outside of Ford, played important roles in these developments. An authoritative history of the early years at Ford is Allan Nevins, *Ford, The Times, The Man, The Company*, Scribners, 1954.

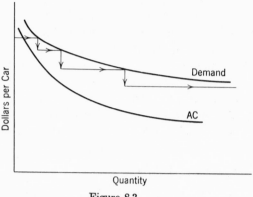

Figure 8.3

Figure 8.3 gives an idea of what was happening. In the decade before 1908 cars had become sufficiently reliable to make a substantial part of the public into potential buyers. The elasticity of demand for automobiles was probably greater in the 1910's than before, when cars had been playthings of the rich, or since, when they have been sold mainly as replacements for older cars. At the same time, mass production offered perhaps the most spectacular economies of scale in the history of modern industry. Ford could slide down his elastic demand curve, cutting costs as he went and making unprecedented profits.

Most of the important auto makers of the period were following just the opposite policy. Their cars were getting bigger and more expensive. The average wholesale price of new cars shipped more than doubled from 1904 to 1908.* Most of the firms seem to have thought their demand curve to be fairly inelastic and their marginal costs to be high (D_2 and MC in the left-hand diagram in Figure 8.4). They could see nothing to gain from price cuts below the P_1 level. Ford apparently thought that the demand for automobiles was more elastic and that marginal costs would decrease with volume (D_2 and MC in the right-hand diagram in Figure 8.4). A price of P_2 would appear more profitable to him. When oligopolists do not agree on what the elasticity of demand or the prospective level of costs is like, price agreements are apt to break down. Those like Ford who expect

---

* The average wholesale value (wholesale value of cars shipped divided by their numbers) rose from $1055 in 1904 to $2129 in 1908. Ford first sold the Model T touring car for $950, at the low end of the range though there were cheaper cars. He cut the price to $360 by 1916. After the World War I inflation ended he cut it again, getting down to $260 by 1925. Nevins, *op. cit.*, p. 641.

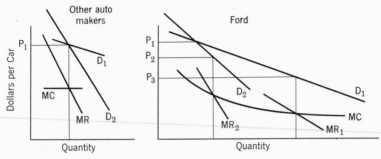

Figure 8.4

the demand to be elastic and costs to be low are likely to win the argument.

Ford had an added incentive to cut his prices at first because most of the other companies tried to keep theirs up. Their products were sufficiently differentiated and demand was growing fast enough for them to retain a respectable number of customers in spite of higher prices.* As long as he was the only important price cutter, Ford could slide down his very elastic D_1 curve all the way to P_3 level. By so doing he won himself half the market and joined the ranks of the fantastically rich.

Vertical Integration

As they accumulated capital the larger auto makers began producing some of the components for their cars. By the start of World War I practically all of the firms of lasting importance were producing at least their own motors so that they could plausibly claim distinct and superior products.† During the shortages of World War I, the drive of manufacturers to produce their own supplies was accelerated.

---

* There was an attempt at collusion among the other auto makers during the early years. George Seldon, a New York patent attorney, had been granted a broadly worded patent which appeared to cover all gasoline automobiles. In 1903 most of the major producers formed an Association of Licensed Automobile Manufacturers which, in return for a small royalty, was allowed to determine who could be licensed. Ford refused to join, and the long and noisy infringement suit that followed was only settled in Ford's interest in 1911. Any restriction of competition that occurred was in the early years. As a result of the suit, licenses were freely available by the time the Model T appeared. The main upshot of the affair was a large amount of advertising for Ford and the development of technical cooperation among the other firms on such matters as standardized parts. See Nevins, *op. cit.*, p. 419, and Seltzer, *op. cit.*, pp. 95–97.

† Epstein, *op. cit.*, p. 52.

Ford seems to have become obsessed with self-sufficiency. On the River Rouge on the edge of Detroit he built an enormous plant where, by 1922, he was producing practically all his own parts and even his own steel and glass. The Dodge Brothers, who originally had supplied Ford's motors, transmissions, and other key parts, integrated in the other direction, joining the ranks of leading auto makers in 1914.

GM integrated by merger. After losing control of GM, Durant managed to acquire control of the young Chevrolet Motor Company which he used, with the help of the du Pont family, to regain control of GM in 1915. Once back in power he resumed his merger campaign, this time concentrating on parts makers such as Hyatt Roller Bearings, Dayton Engineering Laboratories (Delco electrical systems), and Fisher Body. GM also began to move into other industries at this time by acquiring Guardian Refrigerator Company, now Frigidaire. Durant lost control for a second and last time in the depression of 1921, but GM was saved by the du Ponts and came out almost as integrated as Ford.

This vertical integration did not always turn out to be profitable. Ford's steel and glass plants had reputations as high-cost ventures, and GM later disposed of a number of Durant's acquisitions. Even the largest of auto makers today finds it worthwhile to buy many parts.

A very important effect of vertical integration was the closure of entry into the industry. Capital requirements in the beginning had been little more than an investment in parts and payroll while cars were in process, but any new automobile producer from World War I on had to invest millions in plant and equipment as well.

The "Saturated" Market

Auto production had been growing at an amazing rate while all this was happening. The number of new cars registered each year (the lowest curve in Figure 8.5) grew far faster than total industrial production (the broken curve in Figure 8.5) until about 1923. Since then, however, they have moved roughly together. The reason that the growth in output slowed down is shown by the two upper curves in Figure 8.5. They compare *total* automobile registrations (the total number of cars on the road, old and new) with the number of households in the country. Until the early 1920's there were large numbers of potential new car buyers indicated by the wide gap between the number of households and total registrations. Since then the automobile population has continued to creep up on the number

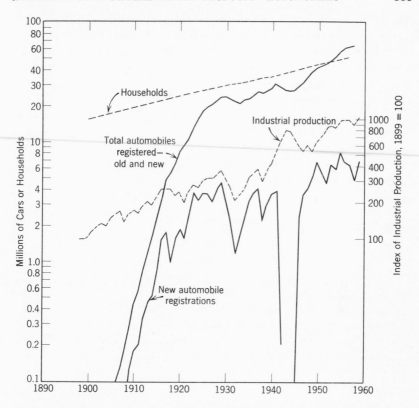

Figure 8.5. Source: Automobile Manufacturers Association, *Automobile Facts and Figures; Automotive News, Almanac Issue*, 1959; and *Historical Statistics of the United States.*

of households as the remaining recalcitrants were convinced and as higher incomes and the move to the suburbs made two-car families more common, but it is clear that from about 1923 on, most new car sales had to be to old car owners.

This "saturation" of the automobile market was a common subject of concern in the industry in the 1920's. It showed up as a "used car problem." By the mid-1920's trade-ins had become important, which meant that producers and dealers would thereafter have to compete with a large stock of old cars as well as with each other.

One effect of the "saturation" of the market was probably a reduction in the elasticity of demand. A 10% price cut offered a car owner a slightly better alternative to his repair bills, but that was about all. A number of studies of automobile demand from the 1920's on have yielded elasticity estimates that range from 0.8 to 1.5, depending on the years covered and the variables considered. By and large, the later the period covered the lower the elasticity estimate. The main estimates are given in Table 8.2. If we take the elasticity to be 1, a price cut would add nothing to industry revenues and would lower industry profits if the extra cars sold cost anything at all to produce.*

On the other hand, model changes that made the older cars seem obsolete were likely to increase sales. One of Ford's policies that had brought his costs so low was keeping the Model T virtually unchanged year after year, thus avoiding retooling. He clung to his old formula that had been so successful until 1927, even continuing to make some price cuts. His unwillingness to change his product

TABLE 8.2

Source	Years Covered	Elasticity Estimate
C. F. Roos and Victor Von Szeliski, "Factors Governing Changes in Domestic Automobile Demand," in *The Dynamics of Automobile Demand*, GM, 1939, pp. 90–91.	1920–38	1.5
L. J. Atkinson, "Demand for Consumer Durable Goods," *Survey of Current Business*, Apr. 1952, p. 20.	1925–40	1.4
G. C. Chow, *The Demand for Automobiles in the United States*, North Holland Publishing Company, 1957, p. 34.	1921–53	1.1
Daniel B. Suits, "The Demand for New Automobiles in the United States 1929–1956," *Review of Economics and Statistics*, June 1958, p. 273.	1929–56	0.8

made model improvement all the more profitable for other firms. GM's Chevrolet in particular was able to gain rapidly in spite of a premium price by offering more attractive styling, more comfort, and such improvements as starters as standard equipment in the low-price field.

Ford finally set out to produce a new car in 1927. While his plants were closed for the change-over, GM took the industry leadership.

* The industry knew this. Donaldson Brown, then financial vice president of GM, demonstrated in 1926 that a 5% price cut could not increase the industry's profits unless sales increased by 34% and that with existing patterns of automobile ownership this would not happen. Perrin Stryker, "P and C for Profit," *Fortune* Apr. 1952, p. 129.

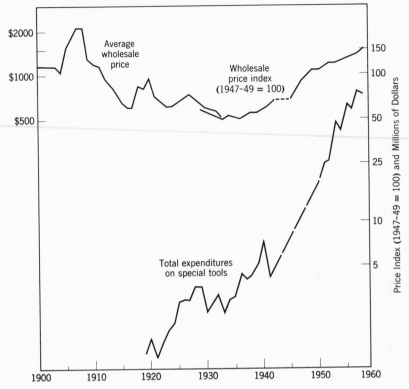

Figure 8.6.   Source: *Automotive Industries, Statistical Issue*, 1958.; *Survey of Current Business*, May 1942, p. 14; *Moody's Industrial Manuals*.

The Model A regained the lead for Ford in 1929 and 1930, but GM has been the largest firm ever since.

The new emphasis on quality,* and especially the Model A change-over, established the pattern of competition in the industry. Since the late 1920's automobile manufacturers have had to produce an "all new" car every two to four years and perform "face lifts" in intervening years if they wanted to keep up.

The shift from price to quality competition shows up in Figure 8.6, which compares the industry's prices and its expenditure on

---

* Words like "quality" and "improvement," which will have to be used through-out this chapter, are loaded. Many people would question whether more chromium or horsepower are "really" improvements. It is obviously a matter of taste. This chapter will attempt to avoid the question by saying that a product is "improved" or of greater "quality" whenever people are willing to buy more of it as a result of the change.

special tools. Automobile prices fell from 1908 until World War I and from the end of the war until 1923. After that they fluctuated around the 1923 level. They fell below it in the depression years, but most other prices fell much farther.*

There is no good measure of the extent of quality competition, but the industry's annual expenditure on special tools provides a very rough indicator of the amounts that the industry has. devoted to model changes. Tooling costs have risen almost continuously since the early 1920's. In fact, they have grown so rapidly that the series had to be presented on a logarithmic scale. Only part of the increase can be attributed to increasing output. About the same number of cars were sold in 1923 and in 1940, but special tools cost ten times as much in the second year. Or again, about twice as many cars were sold in 1957 as in 1923, but tooling costs seem to have been 100 times as great!†

One final effect of the new emphasis on selling was an increased concern about the quality of dealer services. In the early years automobiles were mostly distributed through independent wholesalers. In the 1920's and early 1930's the large manufacturers took over the wholesale function. Most *retail* dealers are still formally independent businessmen, but the factory can now supervise them much more closely.

All these changes raised the barriers to entry still higher. From the mid-1920's on automobile companies had to make large-scale investments in advertising, model changes, and a wholesaling system as well as in plant. Since then, except for the period of shortage just after World War II, the only new makes of cars have been imports or from firms already in the industry attempting to invade new price brackets.

* Prices before 1929 are average wholesale values, i.e., the wholesale value of cars shipped divided by the numbers shipped. From 1929 on, the wholesale price index for motor vehicles of the Bureau of Labor Statistics was used. The earlier figures overstate the fluctuation in price. As people shifted from the Model T to more expensive cars in 1923–27, the average wholesale value of cars shipped rose although the prices of most individual makes did not. When they shifted back to the Model A in 1928 and 1929, the average wholesale value declined again, although prices of individual cars did not. The BLS series from 1929 on avoids this problem. In considering both series, it should be remembered that the buyer was generally getting more car for his money as time passed.

† The expenditure on special tools before World War II is total expenditure on "nondepreciable tools, jigs, and dies" derived from *Survey of Current Business*, May 1942, p. 15. The series from 1950 to 1959 is based on the corporate reports of Chrysler, GM, and Ford. The two series may not be strictly comparable because of possible changes in definitions by the industry and because the postwar figures do not include the independents.

The Elimination of the Independents

After reaching a peak in 1921 the number of firms producing automobiles declined rapidly. Many of these were insignificant and their elimination had little effect on the degree of competition. They simply did not attain enough size to have workable costs, and they certainly were not capable of the large investment in plant and selling required for life in the automobile industry from the 1920's on.

There were nine or ten firms independent of Ford and GM that at one time or another during the 1920's attained enough volume to operate an assembly line efficiently.* They accounted for 30 to 40% of the market then, depending on the year. Yet by 1957 there were only two "independents" (a third had become a "major") and they had only 3% of the market.

The independents had several disadvantages. A firm needed a volume of about 250,000 cars a year to make full use of its special tools in the 1930's,† something few of the independents ever attained even fleetingly. They could therefore compete only in the medium- and high-price lines where the large companies had small volume too.

The independents also suffered from lack of diversification. If Buick did badly, GM was likely to make it up with Chevrolet or some other car, but if the Studebaker car did badly, so did the company. This defect was particularly harmful when the depression squeezed great numbers of buyers out of the high- and medium-price ranges where most of the independents were.

Finally, the independents were at a disadvantage in the risky annual model change because of their relatively few assets. The automobile business had taken on the aspect of a big poker game, where each firm made a several million dollar bet each year as it retooled for its new model. The game was one with very unevenly distributed chips. A few bad choices could ruin an independent company, but large firms like Ford could survive many years of bad luck or poor play.

The obvious solution to all of these problems was for an independent to break into the low-price field and win itself a place beside Ford and GM. Most of the leading independents tried it at one time or another, usually without success.

* Taking 50,000 cars a year as adequate (see footnote, p. 340), they were Chrysler, Dodge, Durant, Graham-Paige, Hudson, Huppmobile, Nash, Studebaker, and Willys. In addition, Packard, while never quite reaching 50,000 cars during the 1920's, dominated the luxury car market until about 1935. *Automotive News, Almanac Issue,* 1951, p. 72.

† TNEC Hearings, Vol. 21, p. 11218. Paul Hoffman, then president of Studebaker, testified that the average life of body dies was then about 250,000 units. He felt that 100,000 units was sufficient to permit his firm to compete with the big three, however.

The one exception was Chrysler. Walter Chrysler founded the Chrysler Corporation among the remains of the old Maxwell Company in 1925. His new car was very successful and the firm expanded rapidly. Then in a 1928 merger with Dodge he acquired a large integrated plant and a powerful dealer organization. He introduced the low-priced Plymouth and the medium-priced DeSoto in the same year. The Plymouth compared favorably with the Model A and the Chevrolet in size and power and offered a number of features of higher priced cars, notably four-wheel brakes. Chrysler then began an all-out campaign. His advertising budget far exceeded everyone else's except GM's.*. Over the next four years he made several model changes, increased the Plymouth's horsepower by 56%, and cut its price 23%.† From 1928 through 1931 his share of the market stayed at about 8%, but by 1933 he had made it to the top and was selling a quarter of the new cars in the country.

The failure of any of the other independents to duplicate Chrysler's achievement was because they lacked the resources to put on his kind of campaign and to wait several years for acceptance. A number of them offered light, low-powered cars in attempts to get prices down, but these proved inadequate to win a mass market. Others offered automobiles of competitive quality, but though sales climbed the companies were unable to wait out sufficiently long campaigns and graded their cars up to the medium-price field.‡

In the shortage years right after World War II everyone in the automobile industry was able to do well. Two firms, Crosley and Kaiser-Frazer, even attempted to enter, though only the latter was ever really a factor. It was another of the Kaiser ventures that seem to appear regularly in this book, but, unlike the steel and aluminum companies, it was not successful. It had experienced executives, the backing of a powerful industrial empire, and auto-

---

* His advertising expenditure *per car* did exceed all the other important auto makers. See p. 359.

† Federal Trade Commission, *Report on the Motor Vehicle Industry*, 76th Congress, 1st Session, House Doc. 468 (1939), p. 894.

‡ Some of the light car producers were Durant and Willys in the 1920's and practically everybody who was left in the 1950's. The Hudson Terraplane and the Nash LaFayette, two standard cars, were introduced in 1932 and 1934. See Harold G. Vatter, "The Closure of Entry in the American Automobile Industry," *Oxford Economic Papers*, Oct. 1952, pp. 213–234. Studebaker introduced the light Champion in 1939 with the express intention of entering the low-price field (TNEC Hearings, *op. cit.*, p. 11221) and did reach profitable volume. In this case its expansion was stopped by World War II.

mobile industry connections through the Graham-Paige organization that it inherited. It acquired a new plant on favorable terms and raised more than $200 million in stock issues and borrowing, much of it from government agencies. It entered when the market was practically insatiable and succeeded in producing a car in record time that proved to be a style leader. Yet it was unable to keep up. It had great trouble financing its 1949 model and had to curtail its advertising program. By 1954 it had withdrawn from production. Its founders concluded that they needed at least $150 million more in equity capital.* In view of such a record by one of the country's champion industry-enterers, the idea of any further entry into the industry today seems preposterous!

In the 1950's the old problems returned. Expenditures on special tools were several times prewar levels. The ante in the styling poker game had been raised and the players with few chips had a hard time staying in. Many of them tried to find some specialized demand too small to attract the big three, typically in the light economy car field. Something like the "saturated" market of the 1920's returned in about 1953—in fact, sales reached a peak in 1955 that was not regained for years. From 1953 on, selling pressure was severe and the independents' disadvantages in distribution reappeared. The remaining independents retreated into merger,† but even in combination they were not able to maintain profitable volume until the late 1950's when a good segment of public taste shifted over to smaller cars. Indeed, American Motors, the leader in the compact car campaign, reached 6% of the market by itself in 1959 and became one of the most profitable corporations in the country. By 1960 the big three were making compact cars too, however. The long-run prospects for the independents were still open to some question.

ECONOMIES OF SCALE

This history seems to imply large economies of scale. They are to be found at several stages: production, advertising, retailing, and the winning of public acceptance.

* "Kaiser-Frazer, The Roughest Thing We Ever Tackled," *Fortune,* July 1951, pp. 75–77, 154–162.

† In 1953 Kaiser acquired Willys, but both were out of production by 1956. In 1954 Nash and Hudson combined to form American Motors and Studebaker and Packard, to form Studebaker-Packard. By 1960 both companies were producing only one make of car each.

Production

The gains in automobile assembly, while spectacular, can be reached at outputs that are small by today's standards.* The president of American Motors testified that his engineers find the optimum assembly line output to be 62.5 units per hour, which would come to about 100,000 per year on a single shift or 200,000 per year on a two-shift basis.† This is only 2-5% of total national output, which has run 5–6 million units in recent years. The main advantage of large firms in automobile assembly today results from savings in transportation costs. By scattering assembly lines about the country they can ship parts instead of finished cars and save millions in freight.

Very large scale also offers rewards in the manufacture of bodies and engines. It is here that the special tools come in. To make fullest use of these tools, even GM finds it worthwhile to use some of the same parts on all five of its makes—on 2–3 million cars per year!‡ A small firm has the choice of fewer model changes, the scrapping of tools before their lives are exhausted, or the use of higher cost, more general tools.

The economies of scale at the body and engine plants have increased since World War II. The rise in tooling costs from $70 million in 1940 to the neighborhood of $1 billion a year in 1959–60 has intensified the disadvantage of small volume models. In addition, the automation of many of the engine and body operations has typically required very large scale to be worthwhile. Ford's Cleveland Engine Plant can produce 98 V-8 engines or 144 six-cylinder engines

---

* When Ford opened his first assembly line in 1913 it had a capacity close to a quarter of total industry output, but the market today is 10 or 15 times what it was then, while the optimum assembly plant has apparently grown very little.

† *Administered Prices,* Hearings of the Senate Subcommittee on Anti-Trust and Monopoly, 85th Congress, 2nd Session, 1958, Pt. 6, p. 2851. Testimony of George Romney. He indicated that before World War II a rate of 30 units per hour or something like 50,000–100,000 per year would have been optimum. Other sources give this latter figure: G. Maxcy and A. Silberston, *The Motor Industry,* Allen and Unwin, 1959, p. 75, and J. S. Bain, *Barriers to New Competition,* Harvard University Press, 1956, p. 245.

‡ For years GM used three body shells, one for the Chevrolet and Pontiac, one for Oldsmobile and some Buicks, and one for Cadillac and the rest of the Buicks. It changed one of these each year. However, beginning with the 1959 models, it has found it worthwhile to use a single basic body shell for all five makes. It will vary the body shell each year hereafter. *Business Week,* June 21, 1958, p. 29.

per hour—roughly 300,000 and 450,000 per year. New specialized press shops using mechanical handling and multiple spot welding can produce in the neighborhood of 4000 roof or door panels per day— close to 1 million a year.*

In addition to low-cost plants, their enormous size gives the big automobile producers a very strong buying position. The hot metal contracts with the aluminum producers and the concessions made by the steel companies at various times on sheet and strip are typical. In dealings with parts makers they have the added advantage of being able to produce their own supplies if they care to. Most of these special prices seem to be available to everybody in the automobile industry in normal times, but in periods of shortage the largest firms may have had an advantage.†

Only very sketchy information is available on the actual savings of large-scale producers. An English manufacturer estimated that average costs would be respectively 8%, 11%, and 13% lower in firms with 200,000-, 300,000-, and 400,000-car outputs compared with firms producing only 100,000 cars.‡ No comparable figures are available for the American companies, but one scholar concluded that a firm producing a single make must reach the 300,000 level at least if it is to attain "low costs" and that it would have "probably added advantages" out to 600,000 units.§ The president of American Motors testified that 400,000 units per year were needed to make full use of a balanced plant.‖ It would appear that a firm must reach 5 to 10% of the present American market for efficiency, and that if it falls very far short of that it will have costs so high as to make profitable operations difficult.

* Both figures from OEEC, *Some Aspects of the Motor Industry in the US,* Paris, 1952, pp. 17–18.

† George Romney of American Motors reported that he paid premium prices for more of his steel during the Korean War than GM did. *Administered Prices, op. cit.,* p. 2855.

‡ Maxcy and Silberston, *op. cit.,* p. 94.

§ Bain, *loc. cit.* Multiple line firms would not have to attain these volumes on each make of car because of equipment and parts that could be included in more than one car. Bain goes on to comment that "the firms in the automobile industry seem generally uninterested in publicizing their plant and firm cost curves."

‖ *Administered Prices, op. cit.,* p. 2851. This allows for one engine and body line and two assembly lines so it clearly does not have transportation savings made possible by scattered assembly plants.

Advertising

Automobiles are sold on a national market, so promotional programs are necessarily big. Advertising campaigns must blanket the whole country, not just a corner of it. And since public acceptance is built up only gradually, advertising campaigns must go on year after year to be worthwhile.

The automobile industry is the nation's number one advertiser. GM has a larger advertising budget than any other firm in any industry, and Ford and Chrysler rank third and fourth (Procter and Gamble is second).* Because of their high total sales, however, the auto makers advertise less per dollar of sales than a number of other industries such as cigarettes and soap.

Table 8.3 shows the average advertising budgets of the five automobile producers from 1954 to 1957. Ford and GM made approxi-

* Printers' Ink, *Advertisers Guide to Marketing for 1959.*

TABLE 8.3

NATIONAL ADVERTISING EXPENDITURES (ANNUAL AVERAGES,
1954–57) OF AUTOMOBILE COMPANIES

A	B	C	D
	Total Expenditure on National Time and Space	Approx. Expenditure Devoted to Passenger Cars	Approx. Auto. Advertising per Car Sold (dollars
Company	(millions of dollars)		per car)
GM	106.2	80.7	26.56
Ford	55.1	49.0	27.22
Chrysler	48.5	47.0	47.76
Studebaker-Packard	8.5	7.3	64.04
American Motors	7.9	6.6	57.89

Note: Total advertising expenditure includes purchases of national time and space in newspapers, magazines, farm papers, network radio and TV, business publications, and outdoor advertising. It does *not* include expenditure on advertising staff or entertainers *nor* does it cover local advertising, such as that carried on by distributors. It is based on Printers' Ink, *loc. cit.*

Some of the advertising for these firms is for trucks, parts, or nonautomotive products such as appliances. The approximate percentages of such advertising in 1957 were: GM 24%, Ford 11%, Chrysler 3%, Studebaker-Packard 14%, and

American Motors 17%. These were derived from *National Advertising Investments*, Vol. 9, 1957. This source gives advertising expenditure by product as well as by firm, but it does not cover as many media as the Printers' Ink figures. Column C was derived from column B by deducting these percentages. General promotional advertising, advertisements of automobiles and other products together, and advertisements for Fisher Body products were included in column C. Advertisements for trucks alone or for parts other than Fisher Body products were excluded.

mately equal expenditures per car sold (column D) while Chrysler spent about $20 more per car. Over-all expenditure on automobile advertising (column C) is probably a better indicator of market coverage, however. On that score GM was well ahead of the other two because of its greater volume. To accomplish the same market coverage, Ford and Chrysler would have had to spend twice as much per car as GM did. The two smaller companies did spend more than twice as much per car, and even then were only able to match the big three's advertising on a few of their less advertised medium-priced makes. In other words, large-scale national advertising offers further advantages to very large firms.

Dealers

A car buyer is most likely to go to a dealer in his own community, so the automobile producers must blanket the country with outlets. Most automobile dealerships are independent businesses operating under sales agreements with automobile companies. To be successful, auto makers must sell enough cars to keep several thousand of these dealers reasonably healthy. Table 8.4 shows the number of dealers for the various makes on January 1, 1959. It would appear that something like 2500–3000 outlets is the minimum number necessary for success in all but the high-price field. In the early 1950's it was estimated that a line of cars had to sell 100,000–150,000 units per year to keep an adequate number of dealers.* The minimum number of cars has probably increased since then as tougher competition at the retail level has reduced the amount that dealers make on each sale.

An automobile producer can increase the number of outlets by letting dealers carry more than one make of car. Chrysler established a large network of outlets for the Plymouth very quickly by "dualing" it with other Chrysler products. The automobile industry

* Bain, *op. cit.*, p. 306.

TABLE 8.4

NUMBERS OF FRANCHISED AUTOMOBILE DEALERS
BY MAKE OF CAR, JANUARY, 1959

	Exclusive[a] Franchises	Total Franchises	Total Net Franchises
General Motors			
Chevrolet	5,192	7,246	
Pontiac	1,690	3,690	
Oldsmobile	1,395	3,710	
Buick	1,640	3,215	
Cadillac	175	1,777	
Total	10,092	19,638	14,685
Ford			
Ford	5,660	6,897	
Edsel	224	1,561	
Mercury	135	2,781	
Lincoln-Continental	0	1,132	
Total	6,019	12,371	8,840
Chrysler			
Plymouth	176	6,843	
Dodge	292	3,229	
DeSoto	38	2,053	
Chrysler	60	2,579	
Imperial	0	1,358	
Total	566	16,062	8,037
American Motors			
Rambler	2,743[a]	2,743	2,743
Studebaker-Packard			
Studebaker	2,479[a]	2,479	2,479
TOTAL	21,899	53,293	36,784
Less intercorporate duals			−1,245
TOTAL			35,539

[a] Dealers with "exclusive" franchises may handle the cars of more than one manufacturer.   This is especially likely for the two independents.

Source: *Automotive News, Almanac Issue*, 1959, p. 185.

has generally felt that such arrangements result in poorer selling effort for each line of cars, however.*

* When Ford introduced its new Edsel line in 1957 it set out to get dealers who would handle that car exclusively. "How Edsel Got Those Dealers," *Fortune* Sept.

The quality of dealerships is as important as the numbers, and here again the large volume models are at an advantage. As a matter of fact, there are fewer Ford and Chevrolet dealers now than before World War II. The manufacturers intentionally reduced the number of dealerships to improve them.* Not only were they able to weed out the less effective dealers, but by making their franchises more valuable they could supervise distribution efforts of their dealers more completely. In effect, they were increasing the monopoly power of their dealers within local markets and using that power as an incentive for franchise holders to sell hard. The large automobile manufacturers today specify the showrooms and repair facilities that their dealers must maintain and set sales quotas. Because Ford and Chevrolet franchises are too valuable to lose, most dealers will go to great lengths to meet the standards set for them. Firms with smaller volume or cars that are harder to sell are in a poor position to require as much from their dealers, since their dealers have less to lose. New producers would be at an even greater disadvantage, since much of the dealers' income comes from servicing cars already on the road, something a new firm does not have.

Automobile dealers have complained loudly about factory pressure. In 1956 a great number of them descended on Washington to list their grievances before Congressional committees.† Most of their franchises could be canceled on notice without any recourse. They had been forced, they said, to adopt unprofitable and perhaps unethical practices because of factory pressure for volume.

The franchise agreements were certainly one-sided affairs. On the other hand, the Ford and Chevrolet dealers usually made very high profits compared with most retailers, largely because of company policy that restricts their numbers. And reducing pressure on the dealers is hardly likely to increase competition among them.

The big three have since altered their franchise agreement, making most of them five-year contracts cancelable only for cause. At the same time Congress amended the antitrust laws making express

---

1957, p. 145. Later when the car sold less well than had been expected the company had to give in and dual its dealers with other Ford cars to keep an adequate number of outlets.

* Paul Banner, "Competition in the Automobile Industry," unpublished Ph.D. thesis at Harvard, 1953, pp. 218–220. See also Alfred P. Sloan statement quoted in *Automobile Marketing Practices,* Hearings of a Subcommittee of the Senate Committee on Interstate and Foreign Commerce, 84th Congress, 2nd Session, 1956, Pt. I, pp. 80–87.

† *Automobile Marketing Practices, op. cit., passim.*

provision for dealer suits against the manufacturers if they fail to act in "good faith" in canceling or failing to renew franchises.*

Consumer Confidence

Large automobile companies seem to have an intangible advantage in the public mind in building and maintaining their reputations. For most makes in most years, the larger the company, the slower its cars depreciate on the secondhand market. One reason is that Chrysler and the smaller firms of the past typically priced their cars a little above Ford and GM cars of equal size and power, and their prices had farther to fall. In addition, buyers have had good reason to feel that the cars of the smaller companies might become "orphans." Finally, many buyers seem to be swayed by a general bandwagon effect. Chevrolet and Ford probably find it easier to be fashionable than other makes simply because so many new Chevrolets and Fords are soon visible on the city streets after a new model year begins.

There are exceptions to all these points. The Rambler and the Volkswagen have not depreciated as fast as the big three cars in recent years, partly because of their fairly stable design. There are a certain number of people who want to be different and tend to leap *off* bandwagons. And Ford and GM can create flops, as witness the failure of the Edsel in 1959. Over most of the history of the industry, however, the smaller producers have had to struggle for consumer loyalty.

Automobile people sometimes argue that the line of causation is the other way around. A good car leads to popularity and large scale for its producer. This is certainly true in the long run. Ford's growth in the 1910's, Chevrolet's in the 1920's, Chrysler's in the early 1930's, and American Motors' in the late 1950's were all matters of riding a popular wave up. In any one year, however, an established producer seems capable of selling a style to a large segment of the market which, if introduced by an independent, might simply have looked queer.

To the extent that the products of smaller companies really tend to depreciate more rapidly, they will be hard to sell. Owners have

---

* The Franchised Automobile Dealers' Act, 70 Stat 1125. Bills have also been introduced to permit manufacturers to guarantee their dealers' territories and fine those who sell in other territories; and to prohibit "bootlegging," the selling of new cars to secondhand dealers at low prices. The effect of these measures, if they were to become law, would certainly be to increase the local monopoly power of the franchised automobile dealer.

either to keep their cars longer or suffer more depreciation per year than those who buy products of major companies. Dealers have to offer large discounts on trade-ins, and manufacturers have to give discounts from announced prices to keep their dealers profitable.

Nonprice Competition and the Economies of Scale

Altogether, the past experience of the industry and the disadvantages of small firms in production, advertising, retailing, and possibly in winning public confidence seem to imply that concentration is inevitable and that the entry of new producers is virtually impossible in automobile production.

It is important to note the role that nonprice competition plays in this conclusion. The disadvantages of small, and especially of new, firms in advertising and distribution are clearly attributable to the intense nonprice competition of the industry. Some of the production disadvantages are matters of technology, especially those connected with automation and the distribution of assembly plants about the country. Even in production, however, the advantages of the large firm would be reduced if style competition were less severe and model changes less frequent. Tooling would be less expensive to begin with, and the smaller firms could amortize tools over many years. Technical considerations would still require firms perhaps the size of American Motors. Yet if there were less nonprice competition, the possibility of new entry would certainly be enhanced, and a gradual decline in concentration as the American market grows would be at least feasible.

This is not to say that the big three became large-scale advertisers and began making annual model changes with the conscious intention of building a wall around the industry or of doing the little producers in. Nonprice competition makes good sense for them on its own merits. Moreover, it may serve useful social functions under the right circumstances. But nonprice competition does seem to intensify concentration and restrict entry in this industry, nevertheless.

Decentralization

GM now makes sales each year of from $9–12 billion dollars! Its total sales exceed those of any other privately owned manufacturing firm anywhere in the world. It leads USS in both sales and assets by wide margins and produces at least as complex an array of products. Why doesn't such an enormous empire suffer from the *dis*-economies of scale that seemed to plague USS over so much of its history? Why have the smaller, more compact firms been unable to gain enough in administrative efficiency and maneuverability to make up for GM's production and selling advantages?

The answer seems to lie in GM's famous decentralization policy. GM pioneered in the development of this sort of organization. After a near disaster in 1921, a financial staff was brought in from du Pont to revise GM's organization. The main characteristics of the plan established at that time are still intact.

GM is subdivided into 34 operating divisions which have many of the characteristics of independent firms. Many were independent firms before GM acquired them, though they have sometimes been transformed in everything but name since. Some of the divisions such as Chevrolet and Frigidaire are familiar to everybody, producing mainly final products for sale to the public, but the corporation also contains a large number of parts divisions such as Fisher Body and Ternstedt which sell the bulk of their output to other divisions.

These divisions are in large part autonomous.* The central management sets company goals, makes long-range plans, decides the broad limits for each division's operations,† passes on top personnel and investment decisions, and reviews the various divisions' performance. Within these broad limits, division managers decide on personnel, plant and equipment, type of product, advertising, sales, and dealer organization. They may buy supplies inside or outside the corporation, whichever is most advantageous.

The division objectives, such as the target rates of return on total investment, are set by central management. Divisions are evaluated on how well they achieve these targets, though conditions in the particular markets where the divisions sell are taken into account. There are huge rewards for success. GM annually distributes a bonus among its executives which may be as much as 12% of its earnings above 5% on equity. In 1955, a peak year, $95 million were distributed to 13,284 persons.‡ Most of this went to men earning salaries of more than $10,000 per year. There were 12 GM executives

---

* The following discussion is based on Peter F. Drucker, *Concept of the Corporation,* John Day, 1946, Pt. II, Ch. 2; Stryker, *op. cit.,* p. 128; OEEC, *op. cit.,* pp. 14–15 and 55–57. and W. F. Anderson, "The Organization of General Motors," GM, 1953.

† These limits do not always preclude competition among divisions. Buick overlaps most of the other GM automobile divisions, having some models that compete with Chevrolet and others with Cadillac.

‡ *Moody's Industrial Manual,* 1956.

receiving more than $250,000 each.* On the other hand, GM is quite capable of removing executives who do not perform and even of selling off or otherwise eliminating whole divisions that do not come up to GM's profit standards. The corporation has often found it cheaper to buy supplies from outsiders than to produce for itself.†

Certain key functions must be partially centralized if the organization is to work efficiently. For obvious reasons the central management requires all the divisions to record costs and profits by standardized accounting procedures and serves as a court of last resort in disputes. It also puts great emphasis on market research for use in evaluating division performance as well as in guiding division product and sales policies. In addition, financial, legal, and labor relations problems are administered centrally. Finally, there is a large general staff organization working on styling, technical research, and broad marketing policy with considerable authority over the divisions. An important function of this staff organization is to diffuse new methods developed in one part of the company to the rest of it.

The GM decentralization policy has been widely acclaimed and copied in recent years. The reorganization of USS described in Chapter 7 involved many of these features. Ford, long a one-man firm, undertook to transform itself in GM's image after Henry Ford II became president in 1945. Top management was almost entirely replaced, in large part by executives with GM training. Modern, standardized cost accounting and market research systems were introduced. Ford was divided into divisions and a bonus plan was started.

If profit rates and market shares may be used as a standard, the change seems to have been highly successful. As Figure 8.7 shows, Ford's rate of profit has gradually risen toward GM's. At the same time, Ford's share of the total automobile market has gone back up from 20% to about 30% (see Figure 8.1).

* Perrin Stryker, "The Executive Bonus," *Fortune,* Dec. 1956, pp. 130, 164. 40% of the 1955 bonus was distributed among divisions on the basis of salaries paid, 40% on the basis of profits earned, and 20% on the basis of top management's rating of division performance.

† One GM representative indicated that GM's financial policy committee would not ordinarily authorize investment projects that did not repay themselves in three years and that it therefore found it worthwhile to buy components from outside firms (OEEC, *op. cit.,* p. 17). Either the outsiders had economies that GM did not have or they had lower profit goals. Since GM, supplying itself, would be making parts for 2–3 million cars, it would be hard to imagine that parts makers would have many advantages of scale today.

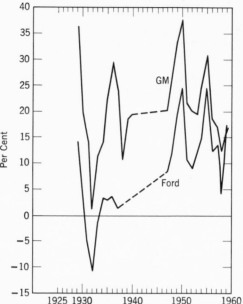

Figure 8.7. Profits on average stockholders' investment. Source: *Administered Prices, Automobiles,* Senate Report, 85th Congress, 2nd Session, p. 195, and *Moody's Industrial Manual,* 1960.

If decentralization of this sort can eliminate most of the diseconomies of scale in some of the world's largest and most complex corporations, the economic barriers to increased concentration may tend to disappear in many industries in the future.

AUTOMOBILE PRICING

Price Performance

The three firms that make up the bulk of the present automobile industry can compete by varying price, quality, promotional effort, or, more realistically, all three simultaneously. A higher price might or might not be more profitable depending on what is done to the size, shape, or power of the car. Automobile executives have a very complex problem to solve in deciding which combination to use.

The prices they have chosen for their low-priced, four-door sedans are shown in Figure 8.8. The lower diagram shows prices before World War II, the upper one after the war. One feature that appears immediately is the degree of control over price that these firms exercise. The depression brought no price wars to the automobile manu-

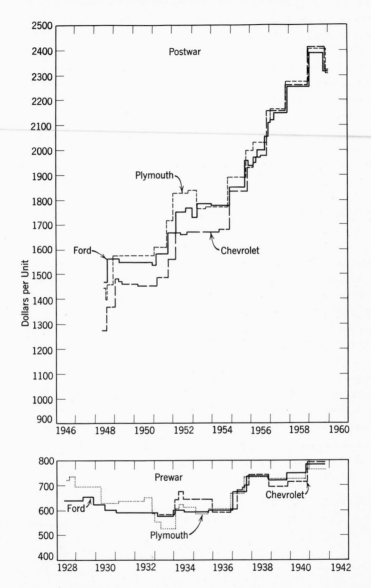

Figure 8.8. Suggested retail price of cheapest four-door sedan in high-powered line. Source: 1928–38 FTC, *op. cit.,* pp. 894, 896; 1932–42 Hans Brems, *Product Equilibrium Under Monopolistic Competition,* Harvard University Press, 1951, p. 41; 1947–59 *Automotive News, passim.*

facturers as it did to steel. Though 1932 output was less than a quarter of 1929, the prices shown in Figure 8.8 fell by only 12% (Ford) to 24% (Plymouth), and the big Plymouth price cut was more a matter of that firm breaking into the low-price field than a reaction to the depression. Price reductions in such recession years as 1937, 1949, 1954, and 1958 have been nominal or nonexistent. Price increases have been the rule in the other postwar years.

Another notable feature of Figure 8.8 is that, unlike prices of standardized products, automobile prices are not always identical. Consumer loyalties are sufficient for a firm to hold some customers in spite of premium prices. It will lose some sales,* but it may feel that it makes up for them in terms of total profits by charging the higher price.

Occasionally one or another firm has found itself too far above the others and has had to retreat. For instance, in the postwar boom years when the automobile companies were all selling for less than they might have, Plymouth and for a while Ford charged considerably more than Chevrolet and still sold everything they could produce. When selling became a problem again in 1953, Plymouth came back down toward the level of the others.

Price Leadership

In spite of their differences, the three prices have usually moved together. In the 1930's Ford set the price and the others clustered around. The other firms were not always happy about the prices he chose. A vice president of GM told other members of the Automobile Manufacturing Association:

> Mr. Ford who won't play is pretty much the price setter in this industry. I'll bet if Mr. Ford's car were $50 higher ours would be $50 higher. We care about Ford. We have been struggling with him for years.†

Since World War II it has been GM that has determined the general levels of automobile prices with the others following.

This is not price leadership as practiced in the steel industry. The automobile makers do not wait around for GM to move. Ford or Chrysler often bring out their new models first, but in setting their prices they try to anticipate what GM will do. L. L. Colbert, Presi-

---

* One economist working with Ford and Chevrolet prices estimated that a 1% increase in the ratio of Ford to Chevrolet prices would lead to a 1.79% reduction in the ratio of Fords to Chevrolets sold. Brems, *op. cit.*, pp. 45–46.

† FTC, *op. cit.*, p. 33.

dent of Chrysler Corporation, described his pricing procedure this way:

We estimate, for example, what consumers will be paying for competitive cars. In doing this we rely heavily on our knowledge of the prevailing prices and specifications of current competitive models, our knowledge of periodic design cost changes in competitive products, and the knowledge we have gained through analysis of economic changes as they relate to our new model costs. So far as our competitors' design cost changes are concerned, we rely on rough calculations, but we know that price changes in basic commodities and changes in wage rates will have an effect on unit costs of competitive products similar to the effect on our own.*

In other words, they try to guess their competitors' (GM's) prices and meet them. Ford apparently has a similar approach, going by its behavior when the new model Fords precede the Chevrolets, as in the autumns of 1955 and 1956 (1956 and 1957 models). In 1955, Chevrolet came out 1½ months after Ford with prices about $25 lower. Ford came down to within a few dollars of the Chevrolet level inside of a month. In the fall of 1956, Ford again led off, this time with a $58 increase. Two weeks later the new Chevrolets appeared with $180 price increases. Ford immediately tacked $50 more on its price, and within three months was only $1 to $10 under Chevrolet.† Ford would charge a slightly lower price for advertising purposes, but was apparently unwilling to set its prices far enough below Chevrolet to make any significant difference.

Standard Volume

GM itself has a concept known as "standard volume" which it uses in pricing. It was developed as part of the reorganization of GM in the early 1920's and remains almost unchanged today.‡ Officers of the company report that their average variable costs are practically constant,§ i.e., their total variable costs rise proportion-

* *Administered Prices, op. cit.*, p. 2777.

† These price moves refer to list prices presented in *Automotive News*, 1955–1957.

‡ It was described by Donaldson Brown, financial vice president of GM, as far back as 1924 in "Pricing Policy in Relation to Financial Control," *Management and Administration*, Feb., Mar. and Apr. 1924, pp. 195, 283, 417. 34 years later Harlow Curtice, President of GM, told a Senate Committee almost exactly the same story: *Administered Prices, op. cit.*, pp. 2518–2520, 2525. A good discussion of the procedure and the unanswered questions raised appears in A. D. H. Kaplan, J. B. Dirlam, and R. F. Lanzilotti, *Pricing in Big Business*, The Brookings Institute, 1958, pp. 48–55.

§ *Administered Prices, op. cit.*, Pt. 6, p. 2519.

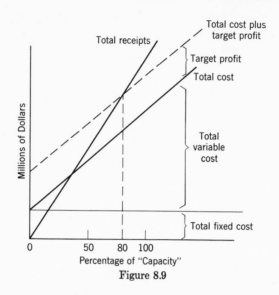

Figure 8.9

ately with output. This means that the company must have a total cost curve like that shown in Figure 8.9. The company wants to cover these costs, of course, and in addition to earn a specified target amount of profit. The profit is usually expressed as a percentage return on investment, not sales, so the dollar amount of hoped-for profit would be the same regardless of the level of output. Total cost plus target profit appears as the broken line in Figure 8.9.

Which price will cover costs and yield this profit depends on the volume of sales. When volume is low, a high price is necessary, but with large volume a lower price is adequate. However, this means raising prices during a depression and vice versa. Rather than do that, GM determines a "standard volume" which is supposed to be an estimate of the long-run operating rate of the company's plants, and then tries to set a price that yields the target profit at that output. When production exceeds the standard volume the company makes more than expected profits, and when it falls short GM's profits are less than the target figure. Traditionally standard volume has been 80% of GM's capacity. GM can sometimes get well beyond "capacity," however, by working overtime and by reducing the period that it is closed for model changes. For instance, in 1955 GM's standard volume was 3 million cars so that its "capacity" was 3.75 million.* It actually produced 4.64 million and earned a profit after

* *Ibid.*, p. 2521.

tax of 28% on owners' equity as a result!* If standard volume does turn out to be an accurate estimate of the long-run operating rate of GM's plants, the company's profits should average out to about the target rate of return.

In explaining standard volume, GM's officers usually make a point of saying that prices may differ from those indicated by the formula because of "competition" or "the market."† Presumably the qualification about "competition" means that GM would meet price cuts by other producers if it were necessary to retain markets, even if they had to surrender their target profits to do so. In the days when Ford was the industry leader this would have been an important qualification. The target profit would then have been primarily a basis for judging the efficiency of GM's operations. The situation is different today. One officer testified that prices "established in relation to competition" yielded results "close enough to what we have had in mind so it has not been a major problem."‡ The implication was that GM was able to set the prices and reach the profits that it wanted—a result that should not be surprising in view of its dominant position in the industry.

This standard volume pricing formula leaves some important questions unanswered. For one thing, how does the company decide how much plant to build, and hence how great the standard volume is to be? Presumably plant is constructed to satisfy expected demand, but in estimating demand the firm must certainly take elasticity into account, as any profit-maximizing monopolist would.

Again, where does the target return come from? It certainly is not the economists' "normal profit" nor the public utility commissions' "fair return."§ GM executives report their target profit to be 15% after tax on total investment or 15 to 20% after tax on owner's equity.‖ Such returns would mean some of the highest profits in all

* *Moody's Industrial Manual,* 1960.

† *Administered Prices, op. cit.,* Pt. 6, p. 2518.

‡ *A Study of the Anti-Trust Laws,* Hearings before the Subcommittee on Anti-Trust and Monopoly of the Senate Judiciary, 84th Congress, 1st Session, 1955, p. 3586.

§ GM's costs contain a number of items that a public utility commission would question, such as the large executive bonuses, and its capital was inflated in early years by writing up the assets of acquired companies, much as the electric utilities did in the same period. GM was criticized for some of these practices by the FTC. *op. cit.,* pp. 504–511.

‖ *Administered Prices, op. cit.,* Pt. 6, pp. 2524, 2527.

of American industry. GM actually did even better. It averaged 21.7% on owner's equity from 1927 to 1957.*

One of the originators of GM's pricing system has described the target rate of return as "the highest attainable return commensurate with capital turnover and enjoyment of wholesome expansion."† Such statements are always hard to interpret, but this one sounds very much like management's best guess about maximum long-run profit. If that is what it means, the GM pricing procedure is just a rule-of-thumb way of setting prices so that marginal revenue will equal marginal cost. The exceptions made to deal with competition or "the market" seem to reinforce this interpretation. GM will apparently drop the standard volume formula when it seems profitable to do so.

Other auto makers are not as free to set prices as GM seems to be. The financial vice president of Ford testified:

As I show later on, in our particular company we do not have a simple cost plus formula. We do not have any simple way in which you go from cost to price.

We have to look at our competitive situation. Ordinarily what we find is this: We have very little leeway. If we would reduce the price very substantially to meet competition we could not make a respectable profit.‡

Prices at Retail

The prices shown in Figure 8.8 were "suggested" retail prices and do not always show what the consumer actually pays. They are made up of the announced wholesale price including taxes plus the suggested retail margin (24% of the retail price today). What the price to the prospective auto buyer actually is has often been a deep mystery. Automobile dealers have been likened to Arabian rug peddlers in their selling techniques. In the shortage period after World War II many of them were able to find ways to sell cars for far more than the suggested prices. When automobiles became harder to sell in the mid-1950's, they developed an amazing sleight of hand in pricing their wares. The customer was often quoted a grossly inflated trade-in on his old car which was more or less made up for by a large "pack" included in the quoted price, financing charges,

* *Ibid.*, Pt. 7, p. 3862. If adjustments are made for executive bonuses and for the writing up of asset values, the average rate of profit comes to 23.9%.

† Brown, *op. cit.*, p. 197.

‡ Testimony of T. O. Yntemna at hearings on *Administered Prices, op. cit.*, Pt. 5, p. 2683. Mr. Yntemma was formerly an economist at the University of Chicago.

and "extras." Well-informed buyers could often get cars at substantial savings compared with suggested prices. Uninformed customers sometimes wound up paying much more than list price, especially if their credit was poor and they were financed by the dealers.

As a result of recent legislation, automobile buyers can now at least start bargaining from the same point. Manufacturers are required to fix stickers on the car windows showing suggested retail prices, and dealers may not remove them.* Dealers may still sell below list price or offer more for trade-ins than they are worth, so price competition is not necessarily eliminated.†

Retail prices are particularly subject to shading toward the end of the model year when both the dealer and the manufacturer have stock to clean out. Actual prices are apt to be well below the announced price then, and buyers who do not mind being a little out of date as soon as they get their cars can find bargains. Manufacturers often help the dealers by giving them discounts toward the end of the model year or by running "contests" where dealers who sell certain percentages of their summer month quotas receive bonuses of so much per car.

NONPRICE COMPETITION

Quality Competition

The manufacturers' price decisions cannot really be separated from the quality of car they choose to produce. The compact cars of 1960 were cheaper than their big brothers of the year before, but the move can hardly be counted as a price reduction. Similarly, part of the price increases in the previous years were just payments for more car.

There is no very good measure of automobile quality—something that consists of varying amounts of chromium, horsepower, and flat or sloping hoods—but tooling expenditures give a rough indication of effort devoted to such "improvement." The left-hand chart in Figure 8.10 shows the annual amortization of special tools, dies, and patterns

* The Automobile Information Disclosure Act of 1959, 72 Stat 325.

† The dealers may find it easier to resist price competition, however. The president of the National Automobile Dealers Association told a convention of dealers: "They [the manufacturers] want volume price cuts so as to undermine the labeling law. But you can stick with the stickers and stay competitive on the basis of quality and profits first and foremost." *Automotive News,* May 18, 1959, p. 3.

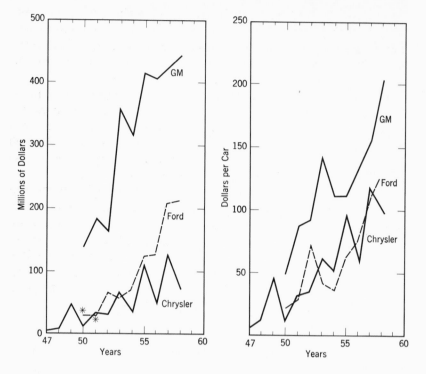

* Estimates.

Figure 8.10.   Left: Total expenditure on special tools. Right: Tooling expenditures per car.   Source: *Administered Prices, Automobiles,* Senate Report, 85th Congress, 2nd Session, p. 123, and *Moody's Industrial Manuals.*

by the big three in various postwar years; the right-hand chart shows their expenses per car. GM has apparently led the race in this respect, though its nonautomobile output may account for some of its higher tooling costs.

There certainly is no evidence of any limitation on competition here. As late as 1950 Chrysler could get by with only $10 per car in new tooling but by the late 1950's $100 per car was required even in years with only "face lifts."   Part of the increase was rising prices for tools, but capital equipment prices in general rose only 50% between 1950 and 1958,* while tooling costs per car for the big three were rising 400 to 1000%.

* In 1958 the Wholesale Price Index for "producers' finished goods" stood at 150.3 on a 1947–49 base. Tools and dies may have risen a bit more or less, but certainly not 350% more.

Advertising

Estimates of the big three's expenditures on national time and space devoted to automotive advertising since 1926 are shown in Figure 8.11. They were widely dispersed in the late 1920's and early 1930's when Chrysler was putting on an all-out campaign and Ford was just beginning to use advertising. In the late 1930's and the years 1947–52, advertising budgets per car were similar. The automobile companies had an advertising as well as a style race from 1953 on. In that race Chrysler and Ford's total advertising budgets and Ford's and GM's advertising expenditure per car moved together very closely.

Nonprice Competition in Theory

How do the automobile companies decide how much to put into advertising and into styling? To keep things simple to start with, suppose that price and quality have already been chosen but that the firm can still sell more cars by spending more on advertising. It would be faced with a series of alternatives represented by the total cost

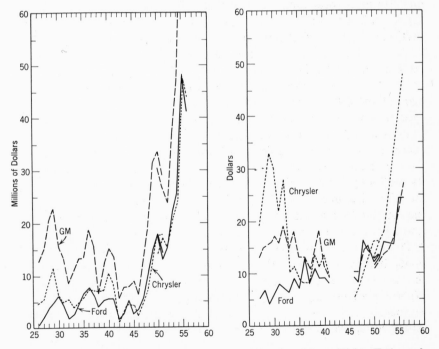

Figure 8.11. Left: Estimated total automobile advertising. Right: Estimated advertising expenditure per car. Source: Banner, *op. cit.*, p. 147, and *Automotive News, Almanac Issue*, 1958.

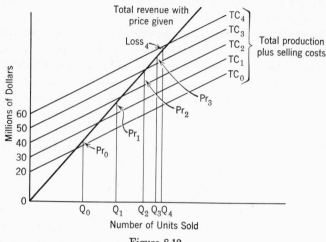

Figure 8.12

curves is Figure 8.12. It might try to get by with no advertising at all. Its total costs would be low then (TC_0) but so would its sales (Q_0). In Figure 8.12 it is shown as making a small profit without advertising (Pr_0) though it could quite plausibly have been a loss instead. Alternatively, the firm could try a $10 million advertising campaign. Its costs would be TC_1, sales Q_1, and profits Pr_1. Figure 8.12 also shows total costs, sales, and profits with advertising campaigns of $20 million, $30 million, and $40 million.

Sales increase with advertising, but sooner or later the growth in sales is bound to slow down. After a car is advertised on five TV shows a week it may be able to pick up a few more customers with a sixth, but probably not many. The firm in Figure 8.12 can increase its profits by increasing its advertising budget as far as $20 million, but after that more advertising brings in so few additional customers that profits decline. In fact, if this firm were to put $40 million a year into advertising it would take a loss.

To be profitable, another ad must increase revenue *after* any extra production costs by more than the cost of the ad itself. So long as this is true the firm can gain by increasing its advertising coverage. When the advertising budget reaches the point where the additions to revenue with further sales just cover the additional production *plus* selling costs, profits will be at a maximum.*

---

* In the jargon of economists, the most profitable selling budget is where *marginal selling cost* just equals *marginal net revenue*. As might be expected, marginal selling costs are the extra cost of a little extra selling effort—the cost of another ad or salesman. Marginal *net* revenue is the additional revenue induced by the

We might have reached the same sort of conclusions if we had varied the car instead of the advertising budget.* The $10, $20, $30, and $40 million additions to costs in Figure 8.12 might have been the expense of designing and tooling for model changes of various degrees of completeness. The most profitable level of such expenditure would be where another improvement adds just as much to revenue as to costs. Again the addition cost must include both the styling and production expense.

The story is still not complete. The automobile companies can vary price, advertising, and product all at once. Which combination should they choose? To work out an answer we would have to find the optimal level of advertising for each style and price and then pick out the most profitable of the lot.

There is a way to simplify this gargantuan-sounding problem. To find his most profitable combination, an auto maker should substitute quality for advertising, quality for price cuts, and advertising for price cuts whenever one offers a cheaper way of winning a few more sales than another. If the last styling dollar brings in $5 of trade and the last advertising dollar, $10, the company can make the same sales more profitably with a little less styling and a few more ads. Price cuts cost the company something, too. The cost of getting new business is the revenue lost on sales that would have occurred anyway. If the last styling dollar brings in $5 in new sales, and if price cuts bring in only 2 new dollars for every one given up on cars that were selling anyway, then the company can increase its profits by raising price and spending a bit more on style. For every additional dollar spent on styling it can raise prices enough to add $2.50 to receipts without losing any sales.

The gain from new sales for every dollar lost on old ones when the price is cut depends on the elasticity of demand. If elasticity of demand is high, the price cuts produce new revenue with little loss, and vice versa.† The higher the elasticity of demand, the more likely

---

extra selling effort *less* the marginal (production) cost. This book has contained quite a number of "marginals," however, and this particular concept is probably one of the less essential of them.

* Strictly speaking, this is correct only if improvements affect fixed but not variable costs. A restyled hood or fender that requires new designs and tools but no more steel or production time would be a case. If the new model requires more chrome per car, say, variable costs would rise as well. The analysis would then be more complex, though results would be similar. The reader who is interested and who can read simple calculus might look up the solution in Robert Dorfman and Peter Steiner, "Optimal Advertising and Optimal Quality," *American Economic Review,* Dec. 1954, pp. 826–836.

† See Chapter 2, pp. 76–77.

that price cuts will pay and the more productive that advertising or model changes must be to prove worthwhile.*

Realistically, it must be admitted that the automobile companies can make only rough guesses about the elasticity of demand for their products or about the marginal effectiveness of their advertising, and sometimes they do not even know whether a particular model change will raise volume or lower it! Their choice of advertising and styling effort can only approximate the elaborate analysis presented here. They certainly make great efforts to find out how their various policies will affect sales, however. Both GM and Ford have financed extensive scholarly studies of the elasticity of demand, and their high-powered market research staffs are famous.

Oligopoly and Quality Competition

A big part of being a successful auto maker is knowing the market and how it will react to a given price, style, and advertising mix. But automobile production is an oligopoly. Another big part of being a successful auto maker, or at least a successful Ford, is knowing GM well and how it will react to Ford's policies. A price cut, an extra ad, or a power ash tray may do much or little for Ford depending on what happens at Chevrolet.

The price cut can apparently be just about ruled out except for small changes for advertising purposes. If Ford made a large enough cut to really accomplish much, GM could readily meet it. Only if Ford were convinced that it would gain even with GM meeting its prices would Ford find serious reductions profitable.

Quality competition is different on several counts. For one thing, it is much more difficult to evaluate another firm's moves, or to counter them very exactly. Who can say what a power ash tray or a set of fins will do for the rival's sales or what countermoves will offset their effect? This means that the sort of stand-off where both sides tacitly agree not to compete would be harder to come by in styling than in price.

Secondly, quality changes, at least in automobiles, take a year or two of planning, design, and tooling. If plans can be kept secret, a firm can hope for at least a year of successful sales at the rival's expense without retaliation. Automobile firms lean over backward to keep their new models secret. GM is reported to have ordered tools for its 1960 Chevrolet Corvair through an Australian subsidiary and

---

* This can be presented with considerably more precision; Dorfman and Steiner, *loc. cit.*

placed conventional tool orders in the United States to disguise the fact that its engine would be in the rear.*

Finally, as pointed out earlier, model changes are a wonderful way to compete with a large stock of last year's cars.   Price cuts are not.

Oligopoly and Advertising

Competition in advertising probably falls somewhere between price and product competition as far as its likelihood in oligopoly goes. There is some of the same uncertainty that appeared with quality competition.   A million dollars spent by Ford on advertising may be more or less effective than a million spent by GM, depending on the ability and luck of their advertising executives.   On the other hand, a large and effective advertising campaign can be countered more rapidly than a model change.

A rough stand-off on advertising like that suggested with prices is at least conceivable.   If each firm knew that its rivals would approximately duplicate any advertising expenditure it made, it might be chary about starting a big campaign.

Ford and GM do a pretty good job of duplicating each other's advertising expenditure per car, and Chrysler keeps up with Ford in its total advertising bill.   Moreover, from the early 1930's to the early 1950's, a stabilization of their per-unit advertising budgets did seem to occur.   There has been very little stability in automobile advertising since 1953, however.   With cars difficult to sell, each automobile company seems to have decided on the big campaign regardless of possible retaliation.   Now with all their advertising budgets much higher, no one can afford to back down.

Quality Competition—Pro and Con

The automobile producers certainly compete, but is it a kind of competition that does the public any good?   The answer is not necessarily the same for quality and for advertising, so the two will be discussed separately.

There can be little doubt but what the public has received an improved car over the years.   The average motor vehicle, when scrapped, is roughly twice as old today as it was in 1925 and has gone more than four times as many miles.†   As the progress of the Ford shown in

* "Detroit Shoots the Work," *Fortune,* June 1959, p. 102.

† *Automobile Facts and Figures,* 1957, p. 8.   The estimated average life went from 6.5 years in 1925 to 12.3 in 1955; the mileage from 25,750 in 1925 to 110,000 in 1955.   Both had grown almost continuously until the break in production during World War II began to shorten average age at scrappage in about 1953.

Table 8.5 indicates, it has become continuously larger and more power-ful, yet gasoline mileage has remained about the same. Cars are also safe, more comfortable, and easier to drive as a result of such im-provements as safety glass, four wheel brakes, all-steel bodies, shock absorbers, sealed beam headlights, automatic transmissions, and a host of other changes that most people would count as improvements. The changes from 1925 to 1939 involved little increase in price. Those since World War II have cost more. Ford prices have tripled since 1939 while consumers prices in general have only doubled.

The main concern of people who criticize quality competition is that it may result in quality that a large part of the public does not really

TABLE 8.5

SPECIFICATIONS AND PRICES OF FORD FOUR-DOOR SEDANS, 1925, 1929, 1939, 1949, and 1959

	1925	1929	1939	1949	1959
Maximum brake horsepower	20	40	89	100	200
Number of cylinders	4	4	8	8	8
Weight (pounds)	1927	2417	2805	3030	3439
Wheelbase (inches)	100	107	112	114	118
Suggested retail price—standard four-door sedan, less tax	$660	$650	$705	$1454	$2226
Federal excise tax	26	—	18	106	165
Suggested price including tax	686	650	723	1560	2391

Source: FTC, *op. cit.*, p. 896; *Automotive Industries, Statistical Issue*, 1949; and *Automotive News, Almanac Issue*, 1959.

want to pay for. Suppose that Chevrolet offers wings on its car this year, and that Ford does not. The change may attract enough volume that Chevrolet will not have to charge any more for its fancier car. To keep up, Ford will have to offer a similar improvement next year. Then with both cars' sales back to normal but with higher costs we will probably end up paying for the improvement. It may be that many of us feel that a car with wings is superior to one without at the same price but that we would not pay $50 more for them. We are likely to pay the extra $50 anyway.

There would be little danger of consumers having quality rammed down their throats if they had a wide choice of cars, but with only a few producers a large segment of the market may not get just what it

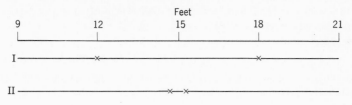

Figure 8.13

wants. Suppose that the lines in Figure 8.13 represent the spectrum of consumers' preferences in over-all automobile length. Imagine that they are about equally distributed from 9 to 21 feet. If there could be only two cars produced, we could come closest to satisfying everyone by producing one car 12 feet long and another 18 feet long, as in line I. Nobody would be more than 3 feet away from the car he really wanted.

During the 1950's, at least, the big three seemed more inclined to snuggle up to each other as the two hypothetical firms on line II have. This leaves more people dissatisfied than might be the case. Some would have cars almost 6 feet longer or shorter than they wanted.*

One reason why two producers might snuggle up to each other as in Figure 8.13 might be that either of them on line I could improve his market by moving toward his rival. For instance, the short car would not lose any customers at its end of the spectrum if it moved from 12 to 15 feet, and it would pick up some of the other car's market. The other producer could play the same sort of game—in fact, it would have to if it wanted to retain its share of the business.†

A second reason why oligopolists might turn out similar products is the uncertainty that goes with model changes. No one can tell in advance how various innovations will strike the public. One way for an automobile company to protect itself is to produce a car that offers practically all the features of its rivals. Then, whatever the big selling point turns out to be, it will not be left behind.

This bunching together of producers, leaving large segments of the market unsatisfied, can be avoided if there are a substantial number

---

* Realistically, people are not evenly distributed along the spectrum of tastes as this illustration assumes. The ideal might not be cars at 12 and 18 feet, therefore. Nevertheless, if the oligopolists get out duplicate cars they will not do as good a job of satisfying every one as they might—unless everyone in the country has identical tastes.

† A third firm, however, would do better to locate in one of the big empty segments left by the other two. The big three did not act this way in the late 1950's, however. All three of them were trying to sell a similar low-priced car.

of competitors or potential competitors in the industry. Then someone would be bound to find it profitable to fill any conspicuous gaps.

The experience of the automobile industry at the end of the 1950's provides a good example. From 1955 to 1959 the big three, which started the period with 95% of domestic registrations, were offering increasingly similar low-priced cars, each of which was moved farther toward the big car end of the spectrum with each new year. One story of the race for bigness and power tells how the GM high command heard in 1955 that Ford was going to build its car "as big as the Buick" for 1957, so it designed a big Chevrolet "to meet the threat."* At any rate, a gap was opening up at the small car end of the spectrum which none of the big three seemed ready to fill.

The segments of public taste that preferred smaller cars was able to find alternatives, however. There was an unprecedented influx of small European cars, and the only two remaining independents turned out cars designed to fill the demand not satisfied by the big three. In fact, American Motors, which in the mid-1950's seemed to be on its last legs, proved to be a tail capable of wagging the dog. By 1960 all American producers were selling compact cars and consumers had a greater variety of domestic cars to choose from than they had seen in years.

The moral of this story is that the existence of independent producers and the free access of foreign producers to the American market is perhaps the best guarantee that quality competition will be directed into useful channels. In the past the large numbers of firms in the business guaranteed that there would be a car for every taste. The two remaining independents continue to serve this important function, but with far fewer firms in the market than previously it becomes increasingly essential that American consumers remain free to buy foreign cars without trade restrictions.

Advertising—Pro

Advertising is even more controversial. It can do great things for the seller, but what does it do for you or me?

The main economic virtue claimed for it lies in the information it provides. We have an enormous and complex economy and some

* This account, including the two brief quotations, appeared in "Detroit Shoots the Works," *op. cit.*, pp. 248–250. Later, when GM started work on a compact Chevrolet for 1960, Ford and Chrysler were "obliged to follow" according to this story, even though Detroit was full of misgivings about the prospects for compact cars. There was no certainty that the public would buy large cars in 1957 or small ones in 1960, but if one of the big three made a move, the others apparently felt the only safe thing to do was to follow.

means of gathering and distributing information is essential for it to work properly. Advertising may improve the allocation of resources in the market place if it gives the buying public a better idea of what is available at what price.

The informative function of advertising can increase competition in some industries. Price cuts and product improvements will only bring in more business if people know about them. And new firms may find it easier to enter a market if they can use ads to build up volume quickly.

Perhaps most important is that advertising can encourage innovation. A firm which has to wait years for the market may be discouraged from developing a better mousetrap, but by advertising it can look forward to reasonable acceptance early. In fact, if increased production means lower operating costs, as it did in the early days of the automobile, advertising expenditure may actually lead to lower prices for the consumer during the developmental period.

In addition to its informative function, some people argue that advertising is necessary to sustain a growing economy. Without it consumers would presumably save so much that we would be faced with depression. This argument cuts both ways, however. In years when inflation is a threat, efforts to increase demand make things worse. At any rate, there are other means of maintaining full employment.

Advertising—Con

The critics of advertising have a number of other arguments on their side. To begin with, much of modern advertising offers little or no information value. It is hard to imagine that ads saying simply "Buy Fords" or even "Buy Fords, They're Beautiful" impart any new information to anyone. This sort of ad simply manipulates our tastes.

The auto makers probably deserve somewhat better marks for the information value of their advertising than do such industries as cigarettes or soaps or soft drinks. After all, automobiles do have new features to announce each year. Much of their effort is devoted to manipulation, nevertheless.

Advertising is expensive. It costs the country something like $10 billion a year—about as much as we spend on the whole navy!* Part of this goes to finance radio, TV, newspapers, and magazines that we

---

* Printers' Ink, *op. cit.*, p. 155, estimates total 1957 advertising volume at $10,311,-000,000. This was expenditure for space and time only and did not include entertainers, advertising staff, and the like. The navy's expenditures for fiscal 1958 (July 1957–June 1958) came to $10,906,000,000. *The Budget of the United States, 1960*, p. 449.

would pay for anyway, but a large part is attributable to advertising, pure and simple. Unless advertising provides information or something else of real value, it involves a waste of our resources.

Instead of increasing competition, advertising may actually create or intensify monopoly. The millions of dollars and many years necessary to develop brand loyalties stand as one of the great barriers to entry in such industries as cigarettes and automobiles. Moreover, much advertising is devoted to convincing the public that there is no substitute for particular brands. To the extent that it is successful, it gives the owners of those brands some degree of monopoly power, as witness the premium prices that well-advertised brands of soap, aspirin, or gasoline can command.

The information value of advertising obviously depends on whether the information imparted is correct or not. Outright misrepresentation does occur, although the FTC can issue orders against it today. Misplaced emphasis is a more common sin. Firms spend millions to convince consumers that essentially similar products are different. Great emphasis on unimportant differences or vague implications that some product is "better" or has a special claim to social prestige are typical. It is perhaps significant that advertising budgets of firms selling industrial supplies are seldom very large. They are selling to expert buyers who are not likely to be convinced that identical goods are different or that insignificant features count.

Aside from the economic faults of advertising, many people regret the over-all effect of Madison Avenue on our lives. Ads that say "be a conformist" or "be a snob" or "indulge yourself" are hardly designed to promote the traditional virtues. Ads that say "be a materialist" and "consume more" make it difficult for the United States to raise the taxes necessary to finance an adequate educational or defense program because so much goes into personal consumption. In addition, the propensity of many advertisers to support tabloid journalism and TV programs at the fifth grade level are old subjects of complaint, though these might plausibly be blamed on the readers and viewers, or at least on the readers and viewers who can be swayed. Finally, some object to advertising in general, regardless of its appeal, because it puts Mr. Average Man on a treadmill where he cannot be satisfied no matter how rich he gets.

Detroit spends a quarter of a billion dollars more or less on advertising today, so it is difficult for any American to avoid contact with auto ads. The reader can make his own judgments about how well they are justified for their information value and whether they mislead, emphasize the unimportant at the expense of the important, or transgress for some other reason.

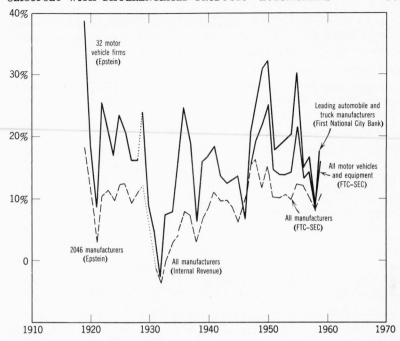

Figure 8.14.   Note: 1959 figures for three quarters only. Source: R. C. Epstein, *Industrial Profits in the United States,* National Bureau of Economic Research, 1934.
Internal Revenue Service, *Statistics of Income.*
First National City Bank, *News Letters.*
FTC-SEC, *Quarterly Financial Reports, United States Manufacturing Corporations.*

PERFORMANCE

Automobile Profits

The large-scale advertising and quality competition carried on in the automobile industry today has certainly not resulted in the elimination of profits.   Figure 8.14 compares the rate of return on owners' equity of major motor vehicle manufacturers with· profits in manufacturing generally.   The upper solid curve shows earnings of a few important automobile and truck producers (32 in the 1920's, 14 in 1957).*   The lower solid curve after 1947 shows profits of all motor vehicle and equipment manufacturers.   The inclusion of the parts makers in the lower curve consistently reduces the average rate of profit.

* Ford is not included until 1950 because it was a family-owned corporation and published no corporate report.   If it had been included the profits of the automobile and truck manufacturers would have appeared a bit lower in most years.

The automobile industry has consistently earned profits far above the average. Only in 1933 did it show a loss, and only in 1946, a period of strikes and change-over from war production, did it show less profits than all manufacturers.

Of course, large profits can exist in pure competition in the case of a rapidly growing industry, but this is no explanation of the automobile record. The industry has not been expanding rapidly since 1923. In fact, it reached a peak in 1929 and another in 1955 which remained high water marks for long periods thereafter, but profits well in excess of the average continued to persist even when demand was virtually stagnant.

Not all the automobile manufacturers did this well. Table 8.6 shows how the five remaining companies fared from 1955 to 1959. The

TABLE 8.6

AVERAGE RATES OF PROFIT OF FIVE AUTOMOBILE
MANUFACTURERS 1955–59

	Percentage Return on Owners' Equity	Profit per Automobile Produced in the United States
GM	19.1%	$299
Ford	14.0	172
Chrysler	5.9	37
American Motors	6.8	53
Studebaker-Packard	deficit	deficit

Note: Averages are total net income for five years divided by total cars produced in five years and average net income by average equity over five years.
Source: *Moody's Industrial Manuals.*

exceptional profits were going mainly to GM, though Ford also participated. The other three had very uncertain records, though both Chrysler and American Motors could show years in which they did exceptionally well. The years 1955–59 were not unusual in this respect. There have been few years in this history of the industry when some firm was not losing money or on the verge of doing so.

Most industries have marginal firms which earn much lower profits than the average for the industry, so there is nothing inappropriate about comparing automobile profits as a whole with manufacturing profits as a whole. What is different about automobiles is that there are only five producers. If some of the marginal firms in textiles or even steel went under, there would be little change in the structure of the industry, but the loss of some of the less profitable automobile manufacturers could make a major difference in the future performance of the industry. If GM were to reduce its profit per car by $100 out of a feeling of public responsibility, the result would very likely be the destruction of two or three of the five firms that remain.

Automobiles and Innovation

There are no current productivity figures for the automobile industry, but there can be little question about its technical progressiveness. Automobile manufacturing is practically synonomous with mass production.* It has probably played as important a role as any other industry in the development of precision machining, standardized interchangeable parts, the assembly line, and "automation." The industry's product has been continuously improved from an engineering standpoint, regardless of what one thinks of its styling.

It is not clear that firms as large as the big three are necessary for this degree of progress, however. Most of the major independents of the 1920's and 1930's could list significant innovations, including such items as the sedan, all-steel bodies, four-wheel brakes, overdrive, and single-unit construction, along with the big three. This should not be surprising. The independents lived by producing for the demand that the majors did not meet. For many of them it was innovate or perish.

Most of the contributions of American automobile firms have taken the form of applied engineering rather than basic scientific research. In recent years GM and Ford have established very large and impressive research organizations, but thus far they are unproved. Though GM probably spends more on nondefense research and development than any other corporation, its research staff has nothing like the professional reputation of the Bell Laboratories.†

"WORKABLE COMPETITION"

Automobiles and Antitrust

The auto industry has shown some of the highest profits in the country, far above any other covered in this book. It is as concentrated as aluminum today, and concentration has been on the increase for half a century. Its prices fell less in the depression and rose more in the postwar boom than did those of manufacturing generally. The

* This was almost literally true in Europe in the 1920's when the word for mass production in French slang was *Fordisme*.

† "How Strong is GM Research?" *Fortune,* June 1956, p. 139.

barriers to entry are among the highest in American industry. At first glance it would appear to be the most eligible of candidates for the antitrust division's corrective surgery.

Automakers have had several run-ins with the antitrust authorities, but all have dealt with peripheral problems. GM was once found in violation of the Clayton Act for requiring its dealers to finance sales through General Motors Acceptance Corporation.* It was also convicted of conspiring to monopolize the bus business by means of contracts with bus holding companies to which it had supplied capital.† In 1957 the Supreme Court found that the du Pont holdings of GM stock gave du Pont an advantage in supplying synthetic fabrics and body lacquer which might substantially lessen competition.‡

None of these actions even approaches a frontal attack on concentration in the automobile industry. The General Motors Acceptance Corporation and the National Bus Lines decisions dealt with competitive practices on the fringe of the industry. The du Pont decision may affect the possibility of stockholder control at GM and, conceivably, where GM buys its supplies, but it is unlikely to alter significantly GM's position in the industry or its methods of competition. Recent amendments to the antitrust laws covering the automobile dealers§ may actually decrease price competition if it makes it more difficult for the manufacturers to press their dealers for sales.

The failure over many years of the antitrust authorities to take major action against the automakers has not been for lack of interest. The industry has been investigated repeatedly. A common conclusion has been that industry performance is adequate and that little or no government action is required. For instance, the FTC in 1939, after an extensive study, decided that

Consumer benefits from competition in the automobile manufacturing in-

* US v. General Motors Corporation, 121 Fed 2nd 376 (1941).

† US v. National City Lines, et al., 186 Fed 2nd 562 (1951). GM along with Firestone, Phillips Petroleum, Mack Truck, Standard Oil of California, and Federal Engineering purchased preferred stock in National City Lines. The firm was then able to gain control of some 46 local bus lines. Each of the supplying companies received agreements that the bus lines would buy from them exclusively.

‡ US v. E. I. du Pont de Nemours and Co., et al., 353 US 586 (1957).

§ The Franchised Automobile Dealers Act 70 Stat 1125, and The Automobile Information Disclosure Act 72 Stat 325, see pp. 24 and 39.

dustry have probably been more substantial than in any other large industry studied by this commission.*

Workable Competition

Many economists have agreed. The automobile industry has often been cited as a case of *workable competition*. They recognize that nothing even resembling perfect competition† is possible for large segments of industry today. A law requiring that the automobile industry consist of 50 or 100 firms and have a standardized product would be in the same category with a law preventing the tide from coming in. *Workable competition* consists of what various economists consider an acceptable and realistic alternative to perfect competition.

Inevitably, workable competition has different meanings to different people. For some it means no more than a mild relaxation of the requirements of pure competition. They set attainable approximations of pure competition as their standards, such as "reasonably" large numbers of firms, no formal or tacit collusion, and no permanent disadvantages for new firms.‡

Others have gone farther. One economist has made the following list of requirements for an industry to be workably competitive in his eyes:

1. There must be an appreciable number of sources of supply and an appreciable number of potential customers for substantially the same product or service. Suppliers and customers do not need to be so numerous that each trader is entirely without individual influence, but their number must be great enough that persons on the other side of the market may readily turn away from any particular trader and may find a variety of other alternatives.

2. No trader must be so powerful as to be able to coerce his rivals, nor so large that the remaining traders lack the capacity to take over at least a substantial portion of his trade.

3. Traders must be responsive to incentives of profit and loss; that is, they must not be so large, so diversified, so devoted to political rather than commercial purposes, subsidized, or otherwise so unconcerned with results in a

---

* FTC, *op. cit.*, p. 1074. At this writing a federal grand jury is investigating GM for possible violation of the Sherman Act, but no indictment has been returned (December 1960).

† Of course, perfect competition is never fully attained in any industry because of immobile factors and imperfect market knowledge if nothing else. Perfect competition can still be used as a standard by which industries with varying degrees of imperfection can be judged, however.

‡ George Stigler, "The Extent and Bases of Monopoly," *American Economic Review,* Supplement on TNEC, June 1952, pp. 2–3.

particular market that their policies are not affected by ordinary commercial incentives arising out of that market.

4. Matters of commercial policy must be decided by each trader separately without agreement with his rivals.

5. New traders must have opportunity to enter the market without handicap other than that which is automatically created by the fact that others are already well established there.

6. Access by traders on one side of the market to those on the other side of the market must be unimpaired except by obstacles not deliberately introduced, such as distance or ignorance of the available alternatives.

7. There must be no substantial preferential status within the market for any important trader or group of traders on the basis of law, politics, or commercial alliances.*

He goes on to discuss the process of competition that these rules imply and then concludes:

Though such a process does not guarantee the best imaginable results, it affords a practical safeguard against intolerable ones and is consistent with progressive improvement of those actually achieved.†

Still others have decided that no generally applicable set of specifications can ever be written. They would examine particular industries asking: (1) In what respects do they differ from perfect competition? (2) Could antitrust action reduce these discrepancies? and (3) Would the gain be great enough to make up for any losses involved in the antitrust action? If they could devise no antitrust remedies that would do more good than harm, they would count an industry workably competitive.‡

Workable Competition in Automobiles

The auto industry gets a very different score depending on which of these approaches to workable competition is used. It comes off very badly in even a rough comparison with pure competition. If the five automakers count as a "reasonably large number," then practically every industry in the country would pass the test. A similar comment applies to entry into automobile production. There is no evidence of formal collusion, but price competition is very

* Corwin D. Edwards, *Maintaining Competition*, McGraw-Hill, 1949, pp. 9–10.

† *Ibid.*, pp. 10–11.

‡ Jesse W. Markham, "An Alternative Approach to the Concept of Workable Competition," *American Economic Review*, June 1950, pp. 349–361, reprinted in American Economic Association, *Readings in Industrial Organization and Public Policy*, 1958, pp. 83–95.

limited. The industry has succeeded in raising prices in the face of considerable overcapacity. Profits are high, and show precious little tendency to disappear.

By contrast, the auto industry appears in a fairly good light when the second concept of workable competition is used. The five firms do offer customers a variety of choices, perhaps somewhat less than before the disappearance of the independents but still more substantial than in many industries. All of the firms, even the two remaining independents, have proved capable of making important inroads on one another's markets, and though GM could undoubtedly intimidate the independents and Chrysler, Ford is so large and viable that GM is unlikely ever to engage it in all-out war. The present-day industry is certainly profit-conscious, and it avoids formal collusion. There is no evidence that the blockaded entry was intentionally sought by members of the industry. If automobiles get a D— when judged by the pure competition standard, they seem to deserve about a B using the less doctrinaire standard.

What Could Antitrust Do?

Taking the third approach, what could antitrust do in the automobile industry, and would it be worth the struggle? The economies of scale appear to make considerable concentration unavoidable. Firms in the half-million car class seem to be necessary for all the advantages of large scale. The industry might be able to support a big four or a big five instead of a big three, but not much more unless present competitive methods are changed.

Could antitrust do anything to increase price competition or to reduce the profit rate? If the government could get a conviction, the courts might give the industry a good scolding. If GM, in response, were to cut price and profit, it would very likely drive two or three of the remaining firms from the field. Alternatively, Ford and GM might become especially solicitous of the other firms in the industry, and reduce the selling pressure. It seems unlikely that such a result would be in the public interest either.

What if the courts went farther and ordered a dissolution? Since such action could only substitute a big four or big five for a big three, it would not increase the prospect of direct price competition and it would probably not do much to industry profits. It might be of some lasting value in providing a larger number of permanent healthy firms offering more alternatives to the buyer. Incidentally, the two quarter-billion-dollar mergers that formed American Motors and Studebaker-

Packard were pretty clearly in the public interest for just this reason. They offered some hope of preserving at least a few alternative cars on the market.

It is interesting to speculate on what form a dissolution might take. If the resulting units are to be viable, neither Ford nor Chrysler seems eligible. Their subdivisions, other than the Ford Division, would be too small. The same is not true of GM. Chevrolet would probably thrive by itself, or with appropriate segments of Fisher Body and a few of the parts divisions. In a good year it sells more than a quarter of the market. Individually, Buick, Pontiac, Oldsmobile, and Cadillac would just be well-heeled independents, but three or four of these together would sell a fifth to a quarter of the market and would certainly have the resources and reputation to introduce a low-priced car. In addition, some of the parts divisions could conceivably be made into separate firms serving the entire industry, so that neither of the automotive branches would have special advantages as to integration. It is difficult to imagine that much more could be accomplished in a dissolution move. The public might have another low-priced car, and perhaps some more in the middle- and high-priced ranges. On the other hand, in the competitive struggle that could follow, we could expect more advertising and styling expenditure, not less.

No one need conclude that the dissolution of GM is imminent. The courts have ordered very few such drastic remedies in 70 years of antitrust, and when they have it has usually been in cases where corporate misdeeds were blatant. A judge might have a difficult time convicting GM for successful internal growth. This is especially so because a dissolution would hurt a large number of "innocent" stockholders and employees who obviously had little or nothing to do with GM's size or behavior. Many of the people who did make a good thing out of GM have since sold their stock to you and me at prices that reflect the fine profit prospects. Antitrust cannot touch them, and we are making only a normal return on *our* investments.

Dissolution might still be called for, but it should not be undertaken to punish the corporation. The wrong people are apt to be punished. It should only be undertaken to improve the structure and performance of the industry.

SUMMARY

Product differentiation accounts for many of the features of the automobile industry. Its highly risky style game, its heavy advertising and tooling expenditures, its nation-wide dealer organizations, and its strong consumer loyalties go a long way toward explaining the disappearance of the independents and the virtual exclusion of new firms, though technical economies of scale are also very important. The enormous firms that remain have been able to avoid many of the administrative disadvantages of scale as a result of their decentralized organizations. They are in extremely powerful positions, able to require unusual concessions from their suppliers and their dealers and to earn some of the highest profits in all of industry. The prices of their competing cars often differ mildly but they ordinarily fall within a narrow range and show a price leadership pattern, with GM usually calling the tune. GM, in turn, seems to have long-run profit maximization built into its internal organization.

To maximize profits, the automakers must choose the most profitable combination of price, quality, and promotional activity. In the 1910's and early 1920's a policy of style stability and price cuts was very successful, but since then the most effective strategy has been one of product improvement and heavy promotional expenditures with stable or increasing prices. This shift seems to be explained by the saturation of the market in the early 1920's which probably reduced the elasticity of demand. It was shown that such a change would make selling efforts and product improvements more likely to be profitable. The willingness of the auto makers to engage in accelerating nonprice rivalry while avoiding price competition is due to the uncertain effect of nonprice moves, the time lag before retaliation can occur, and the need of the auto makers to compete with last year's cars as well as with each other.

Both competition in quality and in selling effort may be of value to the public, but both have been subject to criticism. Quality competition may result in consumers paying for improvements that many do not want. The problem might be avoided with wide choice, but the few automobile firms have often tended to duplicate each other's product. Advertising which introduces new products or firms, announces improvements or prices, or provides other useful information performs a valuable function for the general public as well as for the advertiser, but ads that simply manipulate demand are of questionable social value.

In spite of its extreme concentration and its high profits, the automobile industry has often been described as "workably competitive." At any rate, a frontal attack by the antitrust authorities could not possibly transform the industry into anything approaching perfect competition. A big four or a big five instead of a big three is conceivable. It might provide the consumer with a somewhat wider range of choice, but it probably would not alter industry performance greatly.

FURTHER READINGS

The automobile industry has been a continuous object of popular interest since the turn of the century. The two classics date from the 1920's: Lawrence Seltzer, *A Financial History of the American Automobile Industry*, Houghton Mifflin, 1928, and Ralph C. Epstein, *The Automobile Industry, Its Economic and Commercial Development*, A. W. Shaw, 1928. Probably the closest thing to a general scholarly study of the industry of more recent vintage is the FTC's *Report on the Motor Vehicle Industry*, 76th Congress, 1st Session, House Doc. 468 (Serial Set 10346), 1939. A very good recent study of the British automobile industry with many implications for the American industry is George Maxcy and Aubrey Silberston, *The Motor Industry*, Allen and Unwin, 1959. In addition, there are numerous popular histories of the industry. One of the best is E. D. Kennedy, *The Automobile Industry, The Coming of Age of Capitalism's Favorite Child*, Reynal and Hitchcock, 1941.

A number of economists have studied particular aspects of the industry. Hans Brems used the automobile industry as a continuing example in his book *Product Equilibrium Under Monopolistic Competition*, Harvard University Press, 1951. An interesting new approach to oligopoly appears in Martin Shubik, "A Game Theorist Looks at the Anti-Trust Laws and the Automobile Industry," *Stanford Law Review*, July 1956, p. 594, part of which was reproduced in his book, *Strategy and Market Structure*, Wiley, 1959, Chapter 12. He explains in easily understandable terms a relatively new form of analysis and does a good job of applying it to the auto industry. Much of the book would be very difficult for a beginner, but the article is written for the general reader.

The classic on nonprice competition is Edward Chamberlin, *The Theory of Monopolistic Competition*, Harvard University Press, 1933, Chapters V–VII. A good textbook discussion of nonprice competition appeared in M. J. Bowman and G. L. Bach, *Economic Analysis and Public Policy*, Prentice-Hall, 1949, Chapter 27.

The idea of "workable competition" first appeared in J. M. Clark, "Toward a Concept of Workable Competition," *American Economic Review*, June 1940, pp. 241–256. It is reproduced in American Economic Association, *Readings in the Social Control of Industry*, 1942. Corwin Edwards, *Maintaining Competition*, McGraw-Hill, 1949, particularly Chapter 1, and J. W. Markham, "An Alternative Approach to the Concept of Workable Competition," *American Economic Review*, June 1950, pp. 349–361, reproduced in *Readings in Industrial Organization and Public Policy*, Irwin, 1958, contain discussions of the subject from a different point of view.

9

MONOPOLISTIC COMPETITION—RETAILING

A large part of American industry does not fit very well into any of the pigeonholes used in this book so far. This is true of many service industries and much of distribution and light manufacturing—for the most part the sort of enterprise that congressmen and men in the street call "little business." Conditions in these fields are not very well represented by either the pure competition of agriculture or the oligopoly of automobiles. Like the auto makers and unlike the farmers, these businessmen often advertise and employ salesmen, and they ordinarily set their own prices. But landlords, shopkeepers, and apparel makers, like farmers, come in great numbers and more are usually available whenever profit prospects are good.

MONOPOLISTIC COMPETITION

The fields which combine some of the features of purely competitive and of monopolistic industries have been described as *monopolistic competition*. Table 9.1 shows where this category fits in. The distinction between monopolistic competition and oligopoly lies in the number of sellers. In oligopoly each seller is so large that he must expect his rivals to notice his policies and react to them. In de-

TABLE 9.1

TYPES OF INDUSTRIAL ORGANIZATION

	Many Sellers	Few Sellers	One Seller
Standardized product	Pure competition (agriculture)	Pure oligopoly (steel)	Pure monopoly (electric power)
Differentiated product	Monopolistic competition (retailing)	Oligopoly with differentiated product (automobiles)	

ciding on price or design or advertising, Ford had always to take the reaction of GM into account. In monopolistic competition, however, individuals are small enough so that any *one* of them can adopt a policy on its own merits without worrying about the direct reaction of others. If it looks profitable for any one of 100 storekeepers to improve his services, change his prices, or move his store to a new location, he can usually do so without the rest of the shops in town retaliating.

Product Differentiation Once More

The distinction between pure and monopolistic competition lies in the product rather than in numbers. The products of pure competition are standardized; the public is equally willing to buy the number 2 red winter wheat of Farmer Brown and of Farmer Smith and shows no loyalty to either. The products of monopolistic competition are differentiated. Each shop is somewhat unique in location, convenience, layout, or geniality of salesmen. Most have a circle of customers who trade with them regularly, as a matter of convenience, personal loyalty, or just plain habit. Each has a mild sort of monopoly on his own particular product—say, groceries sold on a self-service basis in the vicinity of Fifteenth and James Streets. His monopoly power is far less than the utility company's, of course, because there are many fine substitutes for his product, such as supermarkets in the vicinity of Tenth and James.

The distinction between monopolistic and pure competition shows up in the demand curves which individual sellers must consider. Farmer Brown has a demand for his number 2 red winter wheat like that in the left-hand diagram in Figure 9.1. The price will be the same regardless of what he sells. The James Street Super has a

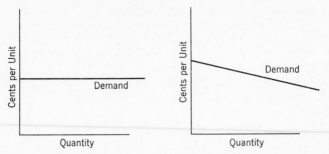

Figure 9.1. Demand curves of firms in pure (left) and monopolistic (right) competition.

demand like the right-hand curve in Figure 9.1. Its proprietor has some choice about the price he charges. He will still have some business if he raises prices, and at lower prices he can attract a large number of customers. The demand curve at James Street Super is apt to be quite elastic, however, because of the ready substitutes available.

THE STRUCTURE OF THE RETAILING INDUSTRY

Types of Retailing

Retailing is not just one field of enterprise but a whole collection of fields. Table 9.2 shows their relative importance according to the 1954 Census of Business.

Most retail outlets are fairly small, with sales on the order of $100,000 per year, but even our largest cities can support only a few department stores. Chains are all-important in some lines (variety stores) and unimportant in others (auto dealers). Some outlets (such as restaurants) have highly differentiated products, while others seem to be practically cases of tweedledum and tweedledee to the customer. Most retailing is highly competitive but there are legal limitations on price competition in a few lines and restrictions on entry set by law or the manufacturer in some.

To cover all these features as well as the many aspects of monopolistic competition, this chapter will discuss several different cases: (1) retailing in general—food and dry goods stores; (2) standardized products—gas stations; (3) restrictions on price competition—drugs; and (4) restrictions on entry—liquors.

The Revolution in Retailing

The trade of shopkeeper is an ancient one. At the end of the nineteenth century it was still the province of small proprietors for whom retailing, like farming, was a way of life. The shop was often part of the family home, and the family ordinarily supplied most of the labor. The typical shop was unrelated to other outlets except for the independent wholesale firms supplying them all. There are still large numbers of these stores but they account for a shrunken share of retail sales. Every decade since the turn of the century has seen some major new type of retailing grow at the expense of the family store.

The first great changes were the department stores and mail order houses, the former made possible by the concentration of transportation lines at the nodes of our large new cities, the latter by the

TABLE 9.2

NUMBERS AND TYPES OF RETAIL OUTLETS, 1954

Type of Business	Number of Stores	Total Sales (millions of dollars)	Sales per Store (dollars)	Chains of More than 10 Stores	
				As a Percentage of Total Number	As a Percentage of Total Sales
Food stores	384,616	39,762	103,381	5.6	35.1
Eating and drinking places	319,657	13,101	37,856	1.7	5.8
General merchandise	76,198	17,872	234,546	15.1	51.3
Department stores	2,761	10,558	3,823,977	61.2	54.6
Variety stores	20,917	3,067	146,627	32.8	77.5
Apparel, accessories stores	119,743	11,078	92,515	12.7	21.9
Furniture, home furnishings, & appliances	91,797	8,619	93,892	5.0	7.7
Automotive group	85,953	29,915	348,039	5.8	2.4
Gasoline service sta.	181,747	10,744	59,115	2.8	6.4
Lumber, building mats. Hardware and farm equipment dealer s	100,519	13,124	130,562	5.6	7.9
Drug, proprietary stores	56,009	5,252	93,770	4.6	15.8
Other retail stores	226,903	15,987	70,457	3.4	11.9
Liquor stores	31,240	3,181	101,824	7.1[a]	24.8[a]
Nonstore retailers	78,508	4,513	57,484	19.8	39.0
Mail order houses	2,019	1,605	794,900	2.2[b]	[b]
All major categories	1,721,650	169,967	98,723	4.8	19.9

[a] State liquor stores are treated as chains. There are very few chain stores in liquors other than these.

[b] The Census does not give sales of mail order houses because it would reveal data for particular firms if it did. Their annual reports show Sears Roebuck and Montgomery Ward together selling $3,981 millions in 1954, considerably more than the total mail order sales given here. Much of this was through their retail stores, of course.

development of reliable mail and express service.* The scale of such institutions permitted them to purchase in large quantities using specialist buyers and winning discounts from the prices paid by the small dry goods and hardware stores of the day.

The chain stores developed in the early part of this century. Some had their origin in the nineteenth century, but most of the growth occurred between 1914 and 1930. They brought large-scale buying, the advantage of Macy's and Sears to the variety, food, and drug fields, all of which sell in relatively small local outlets. Their spectacular growth in the 1920's and their advantages in price competition won them a place among the popular villains of the day.

The supermarket was the great innovation of the 1930's. By cutting out credit and delivery, letting the customer serve himself, and operating on a large scale, they were able to offer the buyer low prices at the bottom of the depression when he was extremely price conscious. The first supermarkets were converted garages and warehouses and seemed to be fly-by-nights or poor people's stores. Only after several years did it become clear that standard brands, modern packaging, and the family car had made the old grocery clerk and the delivery wagon obsolete. Since the 1930's the supermarket idea has spread to the hardware, drug, and variety fields and even to the corner grocery itself.

The 1940's and 1950's produced the shopping center and the discount house. The first is a sort of latter day, multifirm extension of the department store idea. With its acres of parking lot and, in the best of cases, its careful planning, it provides an improved version of "downtown" well adapted to suburbia. The discount house extended minimum service, low margin retailing to consumer durables. Like the supermarkets, they were greeted as barely legitimate at first, but when it became clear that a large part of the public preferred to provide its own service and not pay for large inventories and luxurious surroundings, the department stores and established appliance dealers began selling on the same basis.

Concentration in Retailing

Ever since the revolution in retailing began, there has been much viewing with alarm over the supposed destruction of competition that

---

* The United States did not really participate in an earlier "revolution in retailing," the rise of the cooperative, which did much to undermine the traditional retailers in England in the 1860's and 1870's. The very modest development of coops in the United States has been widely attributed to our relative lack of class consciousness and to the development of other innovations in retailing.

accompanied it. For decades a substantial portion of our people have pictured the A&P or Sears when they used the word "monopoly." Observers have regularly foreseen the extinction of the independent store and a retail trade dominated by a half-dozen giants.

Actually, retailing remains one of our most competitive lines of business. Until about 1930 the larger firms did seem to have a growing advantage, but they were probably increasing competition rather than destroying it. The mail order houses and chains, combined with improved means of transportation, undermined the quasi-monopolistic positions of the few local merchants in thousands of formerly isolated small towns. The new institutions certainly emphasized price competition to the embarrassment of the traditional firms. Many of the innovations since 1930 have helped to preserve the independents, rather than destroy them. By becoming super-markets, independent food stores could achieve enough scale to keep up with the chains, or even become small local chains themselves. The discount houses were independent stores almost by definition, to start with, though some have developed into chains or large department stores by now. Even in the variety store field, where the chains were dominant, it seems to have been the independents and small chains that introduced self-service.

It is true that many old-style family stores have lost out to the new retailers, but so have some revered old department stores such as McCreery's and Wanamaker's (New York). Figure 9.2 shows sales by the large retailers as percentages of total sales in the fields where they are important. In variety stores, where the chains had gone farthest by 1930, the chain store share of total sales has shown a continuous decline. The department stores have done equally poorly compared with the other outlets of the things they sell. Sears and Wards have expanded their share of the market slightly.* Only the food chains have actually expanded compared with their competitors, and a part of this growth has been accounted for by new, local chains that still have some claim to the "independent" status.

There are some enormous firms in retailing today, but they are seldom large enough to dominate their fields. Table 9.3 shows the 1954 sales of the four largest firms in the three fields where giant

---

* Both department store and mail order sales are compared with the total retail sales of the following census groups: general merchandise, apparel, furniture and appliances, hardware and farm equipment, drugs, "other" stores except for fuel and feed stores, and nonstore retailers. The chain store percentages in 1954 are different from those in Table 9.2 because chains of four or more stores are used here as against ten or more in Table 9.2.

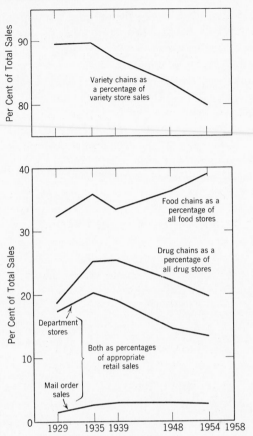

Figure 9.2. Sales of large firms as percentages of particular retail fields, 1929–54. Source: *Censuses of Business* and *Statistical Abstracts*.

firms are most prominent and compares them with total sales for the whole country. The billions of sales of the four largest food chains amount to only about 20% of total sales of all retail food stores. Total sales of the four largest general merchandise retailers amount to only 18% of the national total for general merchandise, apparel, and mail order sales.* In the variety field, the largest companies do account for half the sales, but their stores must compete with many drug and department stores as well. In most other types of

* If Sears, Wards, Penney's, and Allied Stores are compared with general merchandise, apparel, furniture and appliances, drug, "other" store and mail order sales, and most of them compete in all those fields, they account for only 12% of the total.

TABLE 9.3

TOTAL SALES OF THE FOUR LARGEST FIRMS IN THREE RETAIL FIELDS, 1954

in millions of dollars

Food Stores		General Merchandise Stores	
Great Atlantic and Pacific Tea Company	4,140	Sears Roebuck	2,966
		J. C. Penney	1,107
Safeway Stores	1,813	Montgomery Ward	888
Kroger Stores	1,109	Allied Stores	544
American Stores	625	Total, four largest	5,505
Total, four largest	7,687	Total, all general merchandise, apparel, and	
Total, all food stores	39,762	mail order sales	30,565
Percentage	19.8%	Percentage	18.0%

Variety Stores	
F. W. Woolworth	721
S. S. Kresge	338
W. T. Grant	317
J. J. Newberry	180
Total four largest	1,556
Total, all variety stores	3,067
Percentage	51.3%

Note: In a number of cases sales are for fiscal years rather than calendar year. In each such case, the fiscal year that covered the largest part of 1954 was used.
Source: Annual Reports and 1954 *Census of Business.*

retailing, *all* the chains put together do not come up to 20% of sales. Except for the dime stores, then, no branch of retailing was any more concentrated on a national scale in 1954 than the textile industry.

Of course, these are nation-wide percentages. Large retailers may be much more important within the localities in which they trade. The FTC recently surveyed food marketing in 15 metropolitan areas. It found that the four largest retailers or retail groups in 1958 accounted for from 39% to 90% of food sales in these areas with the average falling at 63%. It should be pointed out, however, that in most areas the four leaders included not just chains but also groups of independent stores with some sort of centralized purchasing arrangement. Two such groups were among the four leaders in eight of the areas studied, and one such group was among the four in four other cities. The three metropolitan areas in which all four leaders were chains had the three lowest concentration ratios reported in the study, ranging from 39 to 44.*

A merger movement among the medium-sized food chains got under way in the late 1950's. Some of the existing chains grew markedly as a result, and a few new large chains appeared as well. The FTC concluded, however, that most of these mergers took existing chains into new territories. If this is correct, the mergers have probably not reduced the numbers of competing retailers in particular local markets seriously.†

Even in those fields of retailing or localities where sales are fairly concentrated, the big retailers have several checks on their control over the markets in which they sell. The country is full of automobiles, so most customers have large numbers of alternatives. Moreover, many modern retailers are becoming less specialized. The supermarket that sells nylons and the drugstore where you cannot find the drug counter are famous. Any seller who tries to maintain high prices is apt to find the grocers or the gas stations or someone equally far removed trying to take over his profitable lines. At any rate, there seems to be a continuous supply of new shopkeepers, ready to appear whenever prospects are good, and often even when they are not.

Economies of Scale—Buying

The large retailers have several advantages over their smaller competitors. Probably the most famous is their ability to buy on preferential terms. Their large orders can sometimes reduce costs of production, handling, and selling for the manufacturer, and they are generally strong enough to insist upon participating in the gains that result. This advantage can be substantial. The tire companies have been able to show enough cost savings on tires sold to 62 large retailers to permit discounts of from 26 to 40% below the prices paid by their smallest distributors.‡

* FTC, *Economic Inquiry into Food Marketing*, Pt. I, *Concentration in Retailing*, Government Printing Office, 1960. The study was intentionally limited to medium-sized metropolitan areas ranging in size from Fort Smith, Arkansas, to Atlanta, Georgia. Concentration ratios would probably be lower for such metropolitan areas as New York, Chicago, or Los Angeles, but such cities cover too much area. Food stores in the Bronx hardly suffer from the competition of food stores in Jersey City.

† *Ibid.*, p. 17.

‡ Federal Trade Commission Docket 5677 (1954) in re B. F. Goodrich.

One of the main advantages of the large retailers when they first appeared was their ability to bypass the wholesaler. He had performed an essential function when retailers were small and scattered, acting as a representative for the manufacturers and buyer for the shopkeepers. He usually provided warehousing, delivery, and credit as well, and charged accordingly. In many localities wholesalers were few in number and quite able to reach and observe agreements among themselves about the prices and services they would insist upon.

The independent wholesaler was decidedly not essential to the large new retailers of the 1910's and 1920's. The buying, handling and credit functions had still to be performed, but the large retailers could often do it for themselves more cheaply. They were in effect entering the wholesaling business and undermining its oligopolistic structure. In spite of opposition from the wholesalers, the chains were able to gain direct access to the manufacturers.

Many old-style wholesalers have disappeared since the 1920's, and their successors have had to change their way of business to survive.* Many have switched to a cash and carry basis. Some have organized "voluntary" groups of retailers which make purchase commitments permitting the wholesalers to duplicate the chains' advantages. Some have been replaced by retailer-owned cooperatives. These "voluntary" groups and cooperatives often arrange joint advertising and sell products under their own labels. Some even do part of their own manufacturing. At least in the most favorable of circumstances today, a group of independent stores with their cooperative supplier are reportedly at little or no disadvantage in buying compared with the chains.† The shares of these groups in food store sales have grown as fast in the postwar years as the shares of the chains themselves.‡

Economies of Scale—Operating Efficiency

In addition to their buying advantages, the large retailers may be able to realize operational gains as a result of centralized planning,

* This is true mainly in fields like food and dry goods where new methods of retailing have put pressure on the old wholesalers and their clients. There are still plenty of old-style wholesalers in such lines as drugs.

† For a good account of the transformation of the wholesaler, see Ralph Cassady, *The Changing Competitive Structure of the Wholesale Grocery Trade,* University of California Press, 1949.

‡ FTC, *op. cit.,* pp. 6–7. The approximate share of cooperative wholesaling and voluntary groups in total food store sales rose from 22% to 33% between 1948 and 1958. Of course, a large part of this growth resulted from the formation of new groups or existing stores joining old ones.

promotion, and inventory policies and specialization in buying and management. Sales per worker in organizations of various sizes might be used as a rough indicator of the extent of such gains. Figure 9.3 shows sales per worker in 1954 in the five retail lines discussed in

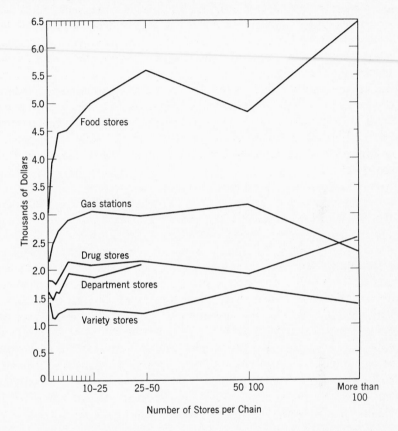

Figure 9.3. Sales per worker by number of stores per organization. ("Workers" includes both employees and proprietors.) Source: *Census of Business, 1954.*

this chapter. In each field except perhaps variety stores, the chains show fairly clear operating advantages over the independents.* In foods, the advantage is spectacular. The definite operating advantage of the food chains and the questionable one of the variety chains may

* The largest gas station chains show low sales per worker, but gas stations are a special case. A few of the major oil companies, particularly Standard of California and Standard of Ohio, operate their own stations. They dominate the "more than 100" group in Figure 9.3. Most of the other *chains* are independent of the major oil companies, but the bulk of the one- and two-station distributors are closely tied to the majors just as the more than 100 group is.

help to explain why the former should be still expanding at the expense of the independents, as shown in Figure 9.2, while the latter are yielding ground to them. With the chains' buying advantage reduced by various forms of cooperative purchasing, the possibility for further growth may depend on operating advantages.*

The operating advantages of chains over independents suggested in Figure 9.3 do not necessarily mean that we must look forward to a retail trade of a few dominant firms in the future. While the chains as a group have a clear advantage over the one- to three-store organization, the advantage of large chains over moderate-sized chains is much less impressive in most lines and does not exist at all in variety stores.† The 25- to 50-store food chains are far less vulnerable to the price competition of the A&P than are the corner grocers. A retail world of 25- to 100-store chains would still not be very concentrated.

COSTS, DEMAND, AND MARGINS

Retail Costs

Retailers' costs fall into two broad categories: the *cost of goods sold* and the *operating expenses*. The first of these consists mainly of the expense of merchandise purchased for resale and is obviously a variable cost. A retailer would ordinarily drop a line if its price did not even cover what he paid for it. The famous "loss leader" is an apparent exception. A store may sometimes offer merchandise at its wholesale price or even less to attract customers. Such a policy can only apply to part of what the store sells, of course, if it is to survive. The losses it takes on its "leaders" might best be treated as a sort of advertising expense designed to convince consumers that it is a store with exceptionally low prices.

---

* Department store chains, not shown in Figure 9.2, have been growing at the expense of independent department stores considerably faster than food chains. Their share of total department store sales has risen from 18% to 64% between 1929 and 1954. The drug chains have been losing ground, however, probably as a result of public policy. See pp. 384–385.

† The cost figures that are available support this. The Harvard School of Business makes surveys of costs in food and variety chains. The food chains show lower operating expense per dollar of sales the larger the chain, but the medium-sized variety chains have lower operating costs than either the small or large ones. In both cases the cost of goods sold are excluded. Harvard School of Business, Bureau of Business Research, Bulletins, *Operating Results of Food Chains,* and *Operating Results of Variety Chains*—various years.

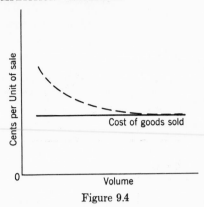

Figure 9.4

The cost of goods sold per unit of sale certainly does not increase as volume expands. In fact, so long as there are quantity discounts available, it will decrease somewhat as the broken line in Figure 9.4 does. However, to keep the analysis simple, it will be convenient to assume that the cost of goods sold remains constant over the usual range of volume. The solid line in Figure 9.4 will then represent the cost of goods sold.

Operating expenses are the costs of running the store and providing the retail services. Labor makes up more than half the total for practically all retailers.*

Operating expenses have traditionally been treated as fixed costs. Indeed, talk about "spreading overhead" seems to have originated in retailing. Labor is obviously a fixed cost for the old-fashioned family store. Shopkeepers cannot fire their wives any more easily than farmers can. A large part of the labor costs of more modern retailers should probably be classified as fixed also, although sales commissions and a part-time sales staff introduce some variable elements. Macy's and the A&P need the services of most of their basic staff just to have their stores open for business. In addition, most of the nonlabor operating expenses, such as real estate and tenancy costs, utilities, insurance, and taxes fall fairly clearly into the fixed cost category, though delivery and some inventory costs are possible exceptions here.

With their variable costs constant or declining and with most of their operating costs fixed, retailers should have a fairly continuously declining cost per unit of sale with expanding volume. Such a pat-

* Harvard School of Business, Bureau of Business Research, Bulletins No. 152, *Operating Results of Department and Specialty Stores—1957*, No. 153, *Operating Results of Variety Chains—1957*, and No. 154, *Operating Results of Food Chains—1957*.

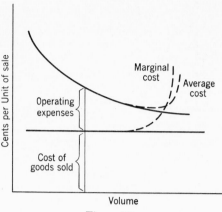

Figure 9.5

tern of costs is shown in Figure 9.5. Stores do have some limits on how much trade they can handle, as anyone who has been in a popular supermarket on Friday evening can attest. The store's capacity shows up in Figure 9.5 in the rising marginal and average cost curves after a point. Retailers can and do expand their capacity somewhat by employing part-time help, so the rise in costs per unit need not be completely abrupt. In general, except for occasional peaks, retailers can lower their unit costs by increasing volume.*

Demand at Retail

A retailer's demand curves depend on the types of goods sold. They fall into two broad categories, *convenience goods* and *shopping goods.* Convenience goods are the sort of things that consumers buy regularly, preferably at the nearest store, such as food, drugs, and gasoline. Shopping goods are the larger, occasional purchases, such as clothing, furniture, or automobiles, for which consumers will shop from store to store trying to find the best buy. Realistically, the

* A well-known economist made a statistical study of three departments' expenses at Lord and Taylor, a large New York department store, over a four-year period. Although he excluded general store overhead and the cost of goods sold, he got continuously declining costs per unit of sale over the *entire* range of sales observed. Even at peak periods costs per unit were still declining. In one department, operating costs per unit were only half as much at the peaks as in very slow periods. Joel Dean, "Department Store Cost Functions" in Lange et al. *Studies in Mathematical Economics and Econometrics,* University of Chicago Press, 1942, pp. 222–254. Some economists feel that this, and similar studies, exaggerate the declining cost character of retailing, however. They argue that in peak periods (during the Christmas rush, say) the customer gets far less service with each purchase than at other times. See comments of George Stigler, summarized in the *American Economic Association Proceedings, 1940,* p. 401.

distinction between the two is blurred, since shopping habits differ, but it is a useful distinction, nevertheless.

Location is very important in the case of convenience goods. If a buyer's time is worth anything at all, it will not pay to drive halfway across town to save a nickel. Retailers who sell convenience goods try to locate where the density of customers per store is high. As a result, food stores, drugstores, gas stations, and variety stores are usually scattered fairly uniformly across the city.

Stores selling shopping goods are more likely to be bunched together at the heart of the city, or, to an increasing extent, in *large* shopping centers in the suburbs. Since a woman buying a dress will try a half-dozen stores before she decides, clothing stores are more likely to make sales when conveniently surrounded by more clothing stores. Stores selling convenience goods are often bunched together in small shopping centers as well, but for a different reason. They share a parking lot and offer the housewife a drugstore, a hardware store, a gas station, and a supermarket, all at one stop.

The demand curves of sellers of convenience goods may not be very elastic on a day to day basis. Most consumers have only a dim notion of the going prices of the hundred small items they buy. On any given morning the demand for a particular grocer's steak may not be much more elastic than the demand for steak in general. Few of his customers will drive to another store if he charges too much. Most would not even know it. If he tries to take advantage of what his customers do not know, however, he will probably be in trouble soon. As times passes, they are bound to find out about other people's prices and shop elsewhere. A reputation for high prices, once won, is hard to live down. Any retailer planning to stay in business must disregard his attractive but misleading very short run demand curve (D_S in Figure 9.6) and set prices according to his more elastic, longer run curve (D_L in Figure 9.6).

The longer run demand curve is still not perfectly elastic, because each store is more convenient to some customers than any other. Housewives who live one block off or who like the grocer's friendly smile or friendly credit will go on buying there even if they know prices at other stores are lower. At somewhat lower prices, other customers will find this store attractive. If prices get low enough this store can draw customers from miles around.

The demand for shopping goods at any given outlet is likely to be more elastic than that for convenience goods. Most buyers shop around and have a fairly clear idea of the alternatives when buying a suit or a washing machine. And since the possible saving is substantial, many buyers are willing to go to considerable inconvenience

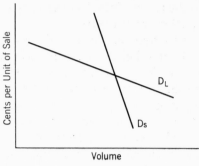

Figure 9.6

to get a good buy. There are differences in price among sellers of shopping goods, reflecting mainly differences in services offered. The buyer who wants a large selection, a courteous and expert salesman, a guarantee of service or right to return merchandise, and an air of respectability must pay more than another who wants the product without frills. No two stores are exactly alike in reputation and services offered so each is likely to have some regular customers. Most of us can be wooed away to another department store or appliance dealer if we find a bargain, though. Sellers of shopping goods seem to have downward sloping demand curves also, but they are ordinarily very elastic.

Margins

Retailers often speak of their selling prices as being made up of the cost of goods sold and their *gross margin*. If the gross margin covers a retailer's operating expenses, whatever is left may be referred to as *net margin*. Since cost of goods sold and gross margin are ordinarily expressed as percentages of selling price, they should add up to 100%. For instance, Figure 9.7 shows margins for six types of stores discussed in this book. Out of every dollar spent at food chains 80.6¢ goes to cover the wholesale cost of the goods purchased and 19.4¢ is margin. Of this, 17.8¢ goes to cover operating expenses and 1.6¢ appears as accounting profits.* Other retailers have

---

* These definitions will be used throughout the chapter. They are simplifications of a rather complex terminology made more complicated by differences from trade to trade. The words "markup" or "markon" are similar to gross margin, as defined here. They differ in that gross margin usually takes into account the effect of cash discounts, inventory shrinkage, and "markdowns." Many retailers use the term "net operating income" to mean what "net margin" means here. All of these concepts are usually calculated as percentages of selling price.

higher margins. For the most part this reflects more expensive services. In some instances, as we shall see, high margins may also
reflect monopolistic restrictions.

Margins are sometimes tricky. High margins do not necessarily
mean high profits. Sometimes a store can sell so much more at a
lower price that the increased volume more than makes up for the
lower profits per unit, leaving it with a higher total profit. In fact,
it is sometimes possible to *increase* net margins by *decreasing* price.
Figure 9.8 shows how this might happen. With rapidly decreasing
costs and a fairly elastic demand curve, the retailer can, by dropping
his price from 25¢ to 20¢, actually increase his *net* margin from 2¢
to 3¢. Of course, his total profits rise faster than his net margin.
Not only does he make more on each unit sold but he sells more units.

Something like this seems to have happened to the A&P in the late
1930's. In 1937 they intentionally experimented with their prices
and were able to increase their sales from $1104 per week per store

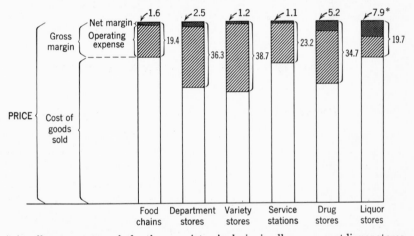

* An allowance was made for the proprietors' salaries in all cases except liquor stores.
For this reason net margins in liquors are somewhat exaggerated.

Figure 9.7. Source: Food chains: Wilbur B. England, Bureau of Business Research, Bulletin No. 154, *loc. cit.* (1957).

Department stores: Malcolm McNair, Bureau of Business Research, Bulletin
No. 152, *loc. cit.* (1957).

Variety chains: Anita C. Hersum, Bureau of Business Research, Bulletin No. 153,
loc. cit. (1957).

Service stations: *National Petroleum News Fact Book*, May 1958, p. 185.

Drug stores: Ely Lilly Company, *Lilly Digest*, 1958.

Liquor stores: National Cash Register Company, *Expenses in Retail Businesses*,
undated (approximately 1956).

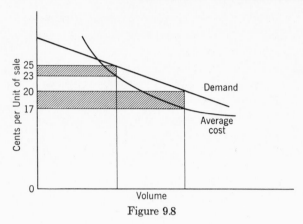

Figure 9.8

to $1226. They had to take a drop in their *gross* margins from 18.6% to 18.3% to do this, but the increased volume resulted in a drop in operating expenses from 18.4% to 17.2% at the same time. As a result, their *net* margins rose from 0.18% to 1.22%!*

MONOPOLISTIC COMPETITION IN THEORY AND PRACTICE

Prices and Output in Monopolistic Competition

The logical next question is just what price and margin will prove most profitable. The firm in Figure 9.8 obviously could not go on increasing profits by cutting price indefinitely. Where should it stop?

The customary analytical solution to this problem is shown in Figure 9.9. With the mild sort of monopoly shown there, a retailer trying to make maximum profits should set price P, taking a margin of PC, and as a result, sell a volume of Q. He would be equating marginal cost and marginal revenue just as the more impressively monopolistic Alcoa and USS did.

Realistically, it seems to be common for stores to take uniform margins on practically all the goods in particular departments. Such a price policy may seem very far removed from the strange-looking diagram in Figure 9.9; but the two are not necessarily inconsistent.

* Morris Adelman, "The A and P Case: A Study in Applied Economic Theory," *Quarterly Journal of Economics,* May 1949, p. 238. For the price cut to be of any significance, the A&P must have accomplished considerable economies in purchasing as well as taking a slight reduction in gross margin, something that seems quite plausible with a 10% increase in volume.

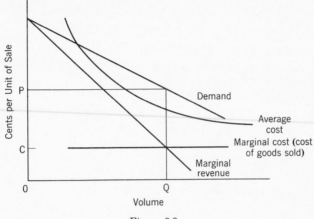

Figure 9.9

It just would not pay to try to work out the most profitable margin on each individual item among the hundreds handled by the typical retailer, especially when he can only guess about the demands for them. It is hardly surprising that he takes broad categories and adds 10% to wholesale in one group, 15% in a second, etc. It makes life easier.

Life would be easier yet if retailers took the same margin on everything, but they do not. Retailers take low margins on staples where interstore comparisons are easy, such as sugar and canned milk at the groceries. Low margins are also common where the retailer can hope to win large volume by making a special of an already low price, such as a chain's own brand of coffee or a special shipment at exceptional prices at department stores. Both grocers and department stores tend to take high margins on luxury foods or style goods,* where each store's offerings are somewhat unique and price comparisons are less easy. This is particularly true of some types of clothing, furniture, and sports equipment where the retailers have exclusive dealerships, and often in the case of imports where competing stores are unlikely to carry the same merchandise. What the food and department stores seem to be doing in each of these cases is taking low margins where elasticity of demand is great and high margins when it is not. They are engaging in price discrimination, like good, profit-seeking monopolists.

---

* To some extent high margins on style goods simply reflect high marginal costs. Because of the "perishability" of the merchandise, the wholesale price is not the whole marginal cost. The same is true of produce in a food store, of course.

Long-Run Adjustment—Overcapacity

The retailer represented in Figure 9.9 was making a profit in excess of a normal return on his investment. In most lines of retailing such a situation could not last for long. New stores would appear in the neighborhood to share in this firm's good fortune. As they did, each store would have fewer customers and could sell less at each price. Demand curves would shift downward as shown in Figure 9.10 until there were insufficient profits to attract new firms. Unusual profits completely disappear when the demand curve barely touches the cost curve, as D_2 does in Figure 9.10. When this equilibrium is reached, each store will be forced to take the fullest advantage of its mild monopoly simply to break even.

As things are set up here, the store would have considerable over-capacity. It could have more business and operate at lower costs, but only by cutting its price and margin so much that it would be taking a loss. The result of the entry of new stores is 20 super-markets, each doing half as much business as it could handle. If the same town had only 10, each fully used, there would be a substantial saving in grocers, buildings, parking lots, and neon signs.

Overcapacity in Perspective

It is easy to exaggerate the significance of the overcapacity in-volved in monopolistic competition. The long-run adjustment de-scribed here is not the only reason for half-empty stores. There is bound to be off-peak overcapacity. Department stores cannot help being pretty empty in January and groceries on Tuesday if they are to handle the Christmas or Friday rush. There can also be over-

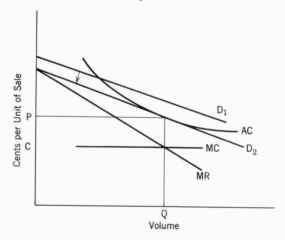

Figure 9.10

capacity because the men who build the stores guess wrong about population trends or public taste. Retailers can make mistakes just as well as farmers and steel producers—perhaps better in view of the ease with which untrained individuals can set up shop.

The overcapacity that is the result of monopolistical competition is not all waste either. A town with 20 half-empty supermarkets gets better service than it would with 10 busier ones. Customers need not drive as far to shop, and the saving in transportation costs makes up in part for the loss in unused grocer's services. Consumers differ in tastes as well as in the locations of their homes, and a town's stores can come closer to satisfying everybody's needs if they include stores that offer music while you shop, stores with congenial butchers, and stores with no frills but cheap goods. If everybody's tastes and location are to be provided for, there is bound to be product differentiation, and such overcapacity as may result may be thought of as the price we pay for it.*

The overcapacity involved in monopolistic competition would be less severe, the more elastic the demand for the products of individual firms. The elasticity of demand in retailing is normally very high. An economist employed at Macy's used statistical methods similar to those described in Chapter 2 to estimate the elasticity of demand for seven staple items and four broad categories of goods sold by the store. He found elasticities that ranged from 2.47 to 6.60 and the lower elasticities were explained as being little known brands (elasticity of 3.52) or off-season goods (elasticity of 2.47 in one year and 3.21 in the second).† The typical elasticity was about 5.0. This

---

* Of course, we can go too far in meeting every need of every buyer. We could keep increasing the variety of services until there was a store for every consumer, but obviously we would then be paying too much for product differentiation. There is evidence that retailing tends to carry product differentiation too far, but it is extremely difficult to say how much too far. See W. A. Lewis, "Competition in Retail Trade," *Economica,* Nov. 1945.

† Roswell H. Whitman, "Demand Functions for Merchandise at Retail," in Lange et al., *op. cit.,* pp. 208–222. In some respects even the high elasticities given here understate the actual elasticities. Prices of related goods at Macy's and prices of the same goods at rival stores were not taken into account in making the estimates. Moreover, the elasticities were all based on a few months' experience and should only show short-run adjustments. When elasticities were recalculated, taking the prices of competing goods at Macy's into account, the estimates were much higher than those given here.

In connection with the A&P price cuts of 1937 mentioned earlier, the discussions of A&P Regional Presidents at the time have been interpreted to imply an anticipated short-run elasticity of 1.91 to 2.33 and a long-run elasticity of 9.65 to 13.80. Morris Adelman, *A & P: A Study in Price-Cost Behavior and Public Policy,* Harvard University Press, 1959, pp. 472–473.

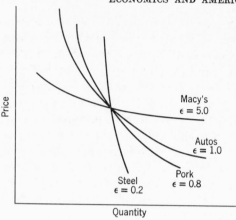

Figure 9.11

figure is extremely high compared with the results of other statistical demand analyses. Figure 9.11 compares demand curves with elasticities of 0.2 (steel), 0.8 (pork), 1.0 (automobiles), and 5.0 (staples at Macy's). If other retailers have elasticities as great as those indicated here, the overcapacity that results automatically from long-run adjustments in retailing would not be very severe.

The demand for goods at individual stores has certainly become more elastic over the last 50 years. At the turn of the century, when few families had their own means of transportation and consumers had little basis for judging the manufacturers, consumer loyalty to merchants who were nearby and "reputable" was likely to be strong. Since then nearly everyone has acquired a car and the manufacturers have conducted a 50-year advertising campaign. The consumer has shifted his loyalty (and the monopoly power that went with it) from the local merchant to the national manufacturer. He will now buy a washing machine or a box of soap from anybody, just so he gets the right brand. Retailers, though not manufacturers, have moved closer to pure competition as a result.

Some economists have argued that very high long-run elasticities are inevitable in cases of monopolistic competition. They contend that severe product differentiation is just not consistent with free entry. If other firms can enter into competition "freely," this automatically means that they can come close to duplicating the existing firms' services. If new firms are unable to produce closely competing products, entry into that segment of the market is not "free."

Nonprice Competition Once More

Since they are offering somewhat differentiated products, retailers like automobile manufacturers are apt to engage in nonprice competition. A retailer can raise his demand curve by having more clerks so that no one need wait, by carrying larger stocks so that customers have greater choice, by providing free parking, escalators, music while you shop, trading stamps, etc. All of these improvements add to cost as well as to demand, however. Figure 9.12 illustrates such a change. Say that a merchant introduces trading stamps. He succeeds in raising his demand curve from D_1 to D_2, but he increases his unit costs from AC_1 to AC_2 in the process. If the increase in gross revenue is greater than the increase in cost, as is the case here, the new service will be added. As a result the store can make more than a normal profit. It may not even have to raise its price to cover the cost of the stamps, because of the drop in average costs when volume increases.

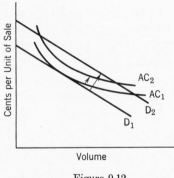

Figure 9.12

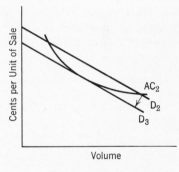

Figure 9.13

Other stores can play the same game, however. As other stores introduce competing improvements in product, the demand will shift back down toward D_3, as shown in Figure 9.13. In the long run profits should disappear again because of entry or imitation; but now costs at each store will be higher with each volume of sales because of the cost of the improved service. If prices are left unchanged, this means that every store must have more volume for its margins to be adequate. In other words, some of the stores have to be squeezed out for the remaining ones to be able to break even selling their new, more costly product at the same price. Alternatively, prices and margins may creep higher, to cover the increased costs, leaving most of the stores still in business.

Many people have criticized the high costs of distribution in the United States. They throw up their hands in horror at a country where every sixth person is a middleman. The high costs of distribution are often attributed to unwanted services forced upon the public by the process of nonprice competition described here.

The free entry that typifies most of retailing, however, puts a limit on the amounts of such services that can be forced upon us. Every decade since the turn of the century has seen some group of retailers who had gotten out on a high service, high margin limb dropping gracelessly to the ground as a result of new mail order houses, chain stores, supermarkets, or discount houses. Whenever a substantial number of customers pay for services they do not want, a new retailer seems ready to appear and give them fewer services at a lower price.

Advertising, a very controversial "service" in other industries, usually appears in a good light in retailing. It is almost entirely devoted to distributing information rather than simply building the prestige of already well known sellers. Far from destroying competition, as it may in other fields, the Sears catalogue and the grocery ads in the local paper provide consumers with better information about their alternatives and bring the retailers closer to pure competition. The ability to announce it to the world makes price cutting profitable where it might not be otherwise, because far more customers can be brought in for the sale.

PUBLIC POLICY IN RETAILING

Protecting Little Business

The new, low-cost retailers and the increasingly competitive pattern of modern retailing have meant trouble for the old-style retailers and wholesalers. These little businessmen have not accepted their fate with quiet stoicism. When faced with new competition that has threatened to destroy them, they have risen in righteous wrath and petitioned Congress or the city assembly for relief. As "pillars of their communities" and members of well-organized groups, the retailers and wholesalers have often been able to get quite a number of legislators to listen.

Most of the protective legislation dates from the 1930's.* Most states passed laws at that time putting limits of one sort or another on price competition at retail.† Twenty-eight states imposed special

---

* At the turn of the century, however, the hardware dealers tried to stop the introduction of parcel post because of their fear of the wicked "catalogue houses" and the old-fashioned dry goods dealers tried to get special taxes on the new department stores.

† The resale price maintenance ("fair trade") and the unfair practices acts— see pp. 418–426.

taxes on chain store outlets.*   Most of this legislation is still on the books, though in general it has not prevented the continuing changes in retailing.

The Robinson-Patman Act

The main federal action was the Robinson-Patman (or "Anti-Chain Store") Act passed in 1936.   The avowed purpose of the law was to make it illegal for "any person engaged in commerce to discriminate in price or terms of sale of commodities of like grade and quality . . . and to protect the independent merchant, the public whom he serves and the manufacturers from whom he buys, from exploitation by unfair competitors."†   Price differences can still be justified under the act if they do no more than reflect differences in the "cost of manufacture, sale, or delivery"‡ but it is up to the seller to prove that his cost savings are at least as great as any discounts he grants if the latter are challenged.   Since accounting is a complex art and costs can be allocated in a great variety of ways, such justifications are not easy to establish.

Moreover, the FTC can, under the act, put a limit on quantity discounts in a particular line of trade if it finds that the very large purchasers are so few as to render price differentials "unjustly discriminatory or promotive of monopoly."   In other words, the commission can prevent a manufacturer from selling to large purchasers at prices low enough to reflect all cost saving if it chooses to.   In view of the difficulty of a cost defense, manufacturers are under pressure by the act to charge large buyers more than their costs would call for.   In effect, they are encouraged to, and can be required to, discriminate *against* the large buyer, as the economists use the term.

The Robinson-Patman Act has received a mixed verdict from econo-

* Most of these taxes were progressive—the larger the number of stores, the higher the tax, so the chains were encouraged to close small, old-style stores and replace them with much fewer but larger supermarkets.   Fourteen of these taxes were still in effect in 1958; Institute of Distribution, *Retailers Manual of Taxes and Regulations*, 1958, pp. 73–78.

† Robinson-Patman Act, Preamble.

‡ Section 2(a) of the Clayton Act as amended by the Robinson-Patman Act. Exceptions were also allowed for sales to prevent deterioration of perishables or seasonal goods or for bona fide close-outs.   No express exception was made for functional discounts (to retailers, wholesalers, etc., because of their functions in the distributive system) but since a main purpose of the act was to preserve the existing distributive system, the FTC and the courts have not questioned these differentials in most cases.

mists. There is something to be said for eliminating advantages that
result from monopsonistic buying positions rather than from the
technical advantages of scale, but many feel that if strictly enforced,.
the law would impose high cost methods of production and distribution on the public. Moreover, in some cases the strong buying power
of large retailers might be beneficial in countering the strong selling
positions of manufacturers. For instance, it is widely assumed that
the powerful bargaining position of Sears and Wards serves to keep
tire prices lower than they would be if the tire companies had only
small, old-style retailers to deal with.* In actual practice the Robinson-Patman Act has probably not done much to limit the development of large retailers and reduce the competitive pressure on small
ones. The main reason for its mild effect is that enforcement has
been weak.†

Retailers and Antitrust—The A&P Case

Even without the Robinson-Patman Act, the antitrust laws would
probably apply to large retailers who follow predatory policies. The
Justice Department was able to win a notable suit against the A&P
for violation of the Sherman Act.‡ The chain never controlled more
than 21% of any area's food trade, over the country as a whole it
accounted for only about 10% of the total trade, and neither percentage had grown significantly since the early 1930's.§ Yet the A&P
was convicted of "monopolizing."

* The only application of the quantity limits proviso to date had to do with the
rubber industry. The FTC set a limit that reduced the tire manufacturers' discounts to 62 large customers. (Remember these limits were to be set where the
large purchasers were "few.") Since then a major tire manufacturer has been able
to justify its largest discounts on a cost basis [B. F. Goodrich FTC Docket 5677
(1954)]. The FTC's action was appealed and set aside on a technicality, FTC v.
B. F. Goodrich, 242 F. 2nd 31 (1957).

† For one thing, the FTC has limited enforcement resources, and the field
covered by the Robinson-Patman Act is vast. There are also some loopholes in
the act. One, known as the "good faith defense," is discussed on pp. 417–418.
Another possibility for evading the act is for a large retailer to buy the entire
output of some manufacturer. The low price that results is not discriminatory,
since there is no other price charged. Since the A&P can do this but a cooperative
wholesaler probably cannot, the Robinson-Patman Act might even work *against*
the more progressive independent retailers.

‡ US v. The New York Great Atlantic and Pacific Tea Company, 173 F. 2nd 79
(1949).

§ Adelman, "The A and P Case," *op. cit.,* p. 243. The 10% figure is based on the
A&P annual reports and the 1940 census. The 21% figure refers to "units" which
correspond roughly to metropolitan areas. A&P undoubtedly had a larger share
of the trade in individual towns in some cases.

The reader may recall that before the Alcoa case* the prohibition of "monopolizing" in the Sherman Act had applied to predatory or exclusive actions but apparently not to big firms just because they were big. A firm could be the only seller in the country and stay within the law if it behaved correctly. The Alcoa case altered this to some extent, in that market control by itself became a partial criterion of "monopoly"; but the old prohibitions remained in force or were strengthened under the "new Sherman Act." Firms with little control over their markets could be convicted of "monopolizing" if the court found them acting in a predatory way. This was presumably the case with the A&P.

The court decided that the chain had pursued a pattern of policies in the years just before World War II aimed at undermining its competition. It found that the A&P had consistently sought discounts that were preferential compared with its competitors; that it had set up its own brokerage firm and required suppliers to deal with it; that it had used its buying power to gain special treatment from produce growers; and that it had used profits in one line of business or one area to make up for losses elsewhere. While isolated acts of this sort might simply be good business, the general pattern reflected an illegal policy according to the court.

This decision has been the subject of much controversy.† Many economists felt that A&P was being convicted for engaging in competition rather than for destroying it. The case seems to have grown out of the complaints of grocers when the A&P experimented with reduced margins in the late 1930's. The government's brief quoted a statement by John Hartford, the key defendant in the case, that a spectacular increase in meat sales ". . . was accomplished by reducing the gross profit rate until the volume was built up to a point where the expense rate was low enough to permit the store to operate at a profit." The brief then commented, "We know of no more clear and concise words with which to express the government's charge."‡ Actually, the government's charge was nowhere nearly so

---

* See Chapter 5, pp. 204–205.

† Adelman, "The A and P Case," *op. cit.*; Rashi Fein, "Note on Price Discrimination and the A and P Case," and Morris Adelman, "Comment," *Quarterly Journal of Economics,* May 1951, pp. 271, 280; J. B. Dirlam and A. F. Kahn, "The Anti-Trust Law and the Big Buyer: Another Look at the A and P Case," *Journal of Political Economy,* Apr. 1952, p. 118; Adelman, "Dirlam and Kahn on the A and P Case," and Dirlam and Kahn "A Reply," *Journal of Political Economy,* Oct. 1953, pp. 436, 441. Adelman subsequently wrote a whole book on the subject: *A & P: A Study in Price-Cost Behavior and Public Policy, op. cit.*

‡ Quoted in Adelman, "The A and P Case," *op. cit.,* p. 241.

clear or concise. It covered a large number of other points, but to the extent that it attacked A&P's low margins it was going after what is usually considered a major competitive virtue in retailers.

The decision's critics also felt that A&P's ability to win price concessions from its suppliers might make for a more competitive economy, not less. Many have argued that large buyers like the A&P, especially when they have the alternative of manufacturing for themselves, do much to offset the monopoly power of producers and to undermine products which carry too heavy a load of advertising and selling expenses.* The government seemed to be attacking this bargaining power directly, and many deplored it.

Some have doubted that the government's charges were even plausible in view of the A&P's position in the market. Why would suppliers offer discriminatory discounts to a firm representing only a tenth of a very competitive market? If it cost them less to supply the A&P than smaller firms, they might offer discounts to win its attractive business, but only if the price concessions exceeded the cost saving would the discounts be discriminatory. Profit-seeking suppliers in competitive industries would not be likely to make such large concessions so long as they have a large number of alternative buyers, which they do in food processing. Again, why would a firm in an industry with such easy entry as food distribution pursue a predatory price policy? Local price cuts that eliminate competitors could not offer much prospect of long-run profits since high subsequent prices would simply mean new competition.†

Other economists have questioned whether the A&P case was unmitigated disaster. Many of the A&P's controversial discounts were won, not from large monopolistic sellers, but from inconsequential firms with large numbers of competitors. Of the 36 firms whose discounts were referred to during the case, 21 were not even listed in *Moody's Manual*, and many that were turned out to be in relatively competitive fields such as canning.‡ The most powerful producers, such as the sellers of canned milk and soap, were able to resist A&P's

---

* Adelman, "The A and P Case," *op. cit.*, p. 254; J. K. Galbraith, *American Capitalism, The Concept of Countervailing Power*, Houghton Mifflin, 1957; and R. B. Heflebower, "Mass Distribution: A Phase of Bilateral Oligopoly or of Competition," *American Economic Review*, May 1957, p. 275.

† Adelman, *A&P: A Study in Price-Cost Behavior and Public Policy, op. cit., passim.*, pp. 404–408. Aside from questioning the rationality of discriminatory discounts or predatory pricing in food distribution, Adelman presents a great deal of evidence seeming to show that neither occurred to any important extent.

‡ J. B. Dirlam and A. F. Kahn, "Anti-Trust Law and the Large Buyer—Another Look at the A and P Case," *Journal of Political Economy*, Apr. 1952, p. 129.

pressure for discounts. It could be argued that A&P was exploiting its weaker suppliers at least as much as it offset the monopolists' pricing power.

At any rate, the conviction did not destroy A&P or its usefulness to competition. A&P paid a fine of $170,000, which hardly broke its back. The government sued to dissolve it into seven regional chains, but in the final settlement the A&P had simply to dissolve the Atlantic Commission Company, its brokerage subsidiary. It could go right on buying directly. The A&P's policies were little altered by the decision. One conclusion was that:

> The great bulk of the good which grocery chains do—with their private labels, their large scale coordinated operations, their low markup and intense competition with established manufacturers and channels of distribution— they can continue to do.*

GAS STATIONS

Oligopoly in Retailing

Readers with some background in retailing often feel that oligopoly might give a better picture than monopolistic competition of the stores in their experience. Retailers are forever "shopping" their competitors. They often price to "meet the competition" and openly charge "customary markups." One might expect to find tacit agreements on price similar to those of auto and steel makers.

There may be some elements of oligopoly in retailing, but the result is likely to be very different from other cases of oligopoly in this book. Tacit price agreements are unlikely for several reasons:

1. There is no one uniform price to agree upon. Most stores sell thousands of different items and are always having a sale on something. The price of identical chickens on a particular morning can vary from 29¢ to 50¢ a pound at similar supermarkets. Those with high prices for chicken are likely to have low prices on something else. Only the average prices of a whole shopping cart of groceries need to be in line with each other, and even these differ from store to store according to the amounts of service offered.†

2. Retailers have strong incentives to cut price. Their main concern is to get us into their stores and keep us coming back, and a

---

* Dirlam and Kahn, "Anti-Trust Law and the Large Buyer," *op. cit.,* p. 132.

† A seller of shopping goods is under more pressure to meet his competition on each item, but he does not have to duplicate every sale price to stay in business, and it is impossible for him to meet the price of other sellers who offer more or less service.

reputation for low prices is usually an asset in accomplishing this. Most of the big successes in retailing have started off with aggressive price competition.

3. There are too many merchants in most large cities for a price agreement to work without some legal backing. One of the three big aluminum manufacturers can count on retaliation if he cuts price, but one of 40 grocers probably does not have much to worry about.

4. Even if all the established merchants in town were ready to observe an agreement on margins, it probably would not hold up because of the free entry and high turnover in retailing. New stores, including new branches of substantial chains, are always ready to appear whenever prospects are good, and the rate of business failure is much higher in retailing than in most lines of enterprise. Both those entering and those struggling not to leave are apt to cut prices in their efforts to win new customers or retain old ones. Established stores have to meet this price competition or join the train of stores on the way out. In general, there are too many stores, too complicated a product, and too easy entry for oligopoly pricing to offer mcre than a temporary explanation for price practices in *most* lines of retailing.

Oligopoly seems more plausible in the case of gas stations than for most retailers.* A single standardized product accounts for more than half of their sales, so prices are easily compared. At least the larger and better located sellers of major brands of gasoline must expect the rapid loss of customers if they charge substantially more than their rivals, and retaliation if they charge much less.

The Majors

Gas stations fall into two broad categories, those dealing in a well-advertised major brand of gasoline such as Texaco or Shell, and those dealing in relatively unadvertised local brands such as Site, Spur, or Hancock. We will refer to the first as major brand stations and to the second as independent brand stations. The major brand stations, in turn, can be classified as to ownership and control.

1. A few are actually operated by paid employees of the major oil companies.†

2. Some stations are owned by the operators or by third parties

* Franchised automobile dealers are an even better case. In many respects they reflect the automobile manufacturers' policies discussed in Chapter 8.

† In the 1920's more than a third of the stations were in this category, but practically all major refiners have found it profitable to change their stations to a lease basis.

and simply deal in a major refiner's product. The refiners typically provide equipment, paving, or at least paint jobs for such stations. In many cases the refiner leases the station from the owner and then leases it back on an advantageous basis. The leases can usually be canceled by either party on short notice.

3. Much the most important group of major stations are owned by the oil companies but leased to the operators, again with a short-term cancellation clause. The proprietors of such stations are technically independent businessmen. However, the major refiners assist them in promotion, financing, and operations and supervise them to assure minimum standards. As a result, these proprietors have much in common with the managers of chain store branches.

The major stations usually emphasize service. They attempt to attract motorists by having clean stations, lots of attendants, free road maps, and an air of respectability. They are often fairly small neighborhood enterprises, and do a large business in servicing and in tires, batteries, and accessories.

The Independents

Some of the independent stations are also operated by single station proprietors but a large proportion are really local chains, owned and operated by independent jobbers, or in some cases by small refiners. Such firms can buy full tanker or tank car lots. Their stations are commonly in locations with high traffic density. A survey of four large midwestern cities showed the modern independent stations selling from 58% to 130% more gasoline per station than the major stations.* Like the large retailers in other trades, these firms have been able to bypass the wholesaler or simplify his function and win substantial price concessions in the process.

The independent stations emphasize price in selling. Their antecedents of the 1930's were aften unattractive and unadvertised, and price was almost their only appeal. The modern independents continue to make that appeal, but many are as attractive as the major stations and sell products as well known within their local markets as some major brands. Most of the independents' business is in the sale of petroleum products. They do little in the way of servicing as a rule. The independent distributors buy some of their gasoline from independent refineries, but the largest part is the unbranded product of major oil companies.† The large refiners are willing to

* S. Morris Livingston and Theodore Levitt, "Competition and Retail Gasoline Prices," *Review of Economics and Statistics,* May 1959, p. 130.

† It has been estimated that 75% of the independent stations' gasoline comes from major refiners. *National Petroleum News,* Feb. 1958, p. 137.

do such business because it provides individuals among them with a means of increasing their sales without cutting prices generally. Sales to independents at bargain prices are especially likely when stocks of oil accumulate and must be moved, as in the period after the Suez crisis ended.

Retail Pricing of Gasoline

The proprietors of major brand gas stations make their own price decisions with more or less guidance from the major oil companies. The major refiners do control prices at stations they operate directly and at some leased stations where proprietors are on a commission basis, usually during a breaking-in period, but these are a small part of the total. Major refiners' pressure on the operators of leased stations could be quite effective, because of the contract cancellation clauses. In some case it appears to have been exerted in favor of stable and uniform prices. In other cases the dealers have been left on their own.*

The major gasolines are apparently identical in the eyes of many buyers, so that each station's individual demand curve is extremely elastic. At the same time, the elasticity of demand for gasoline in general is very low. Gasoline is only a small part of the cost of running a car. Having committed himself to the high depreciation, interest, insurance, and maintenance expenses involved in owning a car, a driver is unlikely to be swayed by a tenth of a cent more or less per mile when deciding whether to take the car or the bus.†

The position of a major station is represented in Figure 9.14. A price reduction met by other sellers would move him down his very inelastic D_2 curve and leave him poorer. Operators of badly

---

* R. Cassady and W. Jones, *The Nature of Competition in Gasoline Distribution at the Retail Level,* University of California Press, 1951, report numerous instances of majors in the Los Angeles area applying pressure on their retailers to stabilize price; see pp. 69–78, 92–95, 117–119. J. B. Dirlam and A. E. Kahn. "Leadership and Conflict in the Pricing of Gasoline," *Yale Law Journal,* June 1952, surveyed operators in upstate New York and found an equivocal policy. The major refiners ordinarily pressed for observation of suggested price, but some also urged defensive price cutting; see p. 838.

† One study by a major oil company indicated an elasticity of demand for gasoline of only 0.13, reported in Cassady and Jones, *op. cit.,* p. 21. The elasticity of demand in a particular market may be considerably greater because of the possibility of buying elsewhere. Lincoln Clark found an elasticity of 0.7 to 1.1 for gasoline in Tennessee when prices in neighboring states were held constant: "The Elasticity of Demand for Tennessee Gasoline," *Journal of Marketing,* Apr. 1951, p. 407.

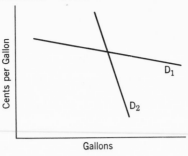

Figure 9.14

located or unattractive stations may look longingly at their D_1 curves, but they can only hope to pick up business if their price cuts are not met. Some do make small price reductions, but they usually refrain from advertising them for fear of retaliation. Many make "behind the pump" discounts to truckers or neighborhood businessmen. For the most part these price concessions are not large enough to encroach seriously on sales of other stations.* Operators of successful major stations usually emphasize service as a more successful way of winning customers.

Unlike the sellers of major brand gasoline, the independent stations depend on price to attract business. For the most part, their very existence depends on some differential from major brands, and they tend if anything to exaggerate the saving in their advertising. The majors cannot eliminate the differential short of eliminating the independents themselves. It is usually cheaper to live and let live, so long as the differential is not great enough to drain off excessive amounts of business. Just what differential is sufficient and what loss of trade is tolerable are obviously matters where judgments can vary. Most of the time a differential acceptable to both groups develops. Two cents a gallon for regular is common but small, unattractive, or poorly located independent stations may offer more. The independents have grown faster than the major stations in the years since World War II by offering increased service and convincing a growing share of the public that they sell good quality products. In the process the

* In a survey of all stations in six midwestern cities, from 1.5% to 31.0% of the major stations were found to have posted prices below the most common price for regular gasoline, but in most of these cities less than 1% were as much as 1¢ below the norm. More complete information on stations in four of the cities showed that the stations posting prices below the most common price were usually unable to sell as much gasoline per station as those selling at the higher price. In other words, discounts were used by less successful stations and were generally inadequate to make up for their disabilities. Livingston and Levitt, *op. cit.,* pp. 121, 128.

established differential from major gasolines has shrunk from prewar levels.

Price Wars

If the independents try to attract business by increasing the differential, or if the majors do by closing it, a price war is likely to result. Price reductions by one group lead to price reductions by the other until one of the sides gives in.

If the price war persists for any length of time, the oil companies must come to the assistance of their stations or lose some of them. The usual policy is to allow rebates from announced tankwagon (wholesale) prices. The unreal announced prices may be continued for long periods as public statements that the concessions are only temporary and that announced prices are considered "normal."

It is easier to describe the conditions that lead to price wars than to say who causes them. The immediate move that starts things off may be made by a reckless independent, the operator of a hard-pressed major station, or an overzealous salesman from a major refiner. The setting is more important. Gas wars are most likely to occur in areas where local refineries or easy water transportation offer the independents regular access to cheap gasoline, and in periods when surplus gasoline accumulates so that the independents' costs decline. They are especially common on heavily traveled through routes into the large cities such as Los Angeles, Chicago, and St. Louis, and in Connecticut and New Jersey between the large eastern cities. The demand for gasoline along such routes is much more elastic than the demand for gasoline generally, since low prices there can attract business from a distance. Price cuts by stations in Connecticut or New Jersey may seem to pay even if they are met by all the immediate neighbors.

The end of a gas war requires some sort of open or tacit agreement. Sometimes a chain of independents will announce a return to the pre-gas war price and the other stations happily follow. Sometimes the majors remove their rebates as a signal for operators to call off the war. It seems to be fairly common for local trade associations, local government officials, or even the major oil companies at times to arrange agreements ending severe gas wars.*

---

* Large oil companies are in a poor position to do this because of their vulnerability to antitrust prosecution. Ten of them as well as three large independents have been indicted by a federal grand jury for an alleged agreement to end a price war in the South Bend area. US v. Standard Oil et al., 165 F. Supp. 359. The indictment was dismissed on technical grounds but the case is being continued.

Gas wars are local rather than national, and, in most areas, are only temporary lapses from normal behavior. Most of the time the gas stations live and let live as far as price goes.

Overcapacity

Even if we conclude that they have an unstable form of oligopoly, the gas stations need not have exceptional profits. With free entry, profits can disappear here just as well as in other lines of retailing. For instance, in Figure 9.15 where the tankwagon price plus tax is 26¢, the station can make considerable profit at the accepted margin of 6¢ a gallon so long as it is selling 15,000 gallons. If there are opportunities for such profits, more stations are likely to appear, however. High profits can disappear, even if the 32¢ price is maintained, as the new stations draw off trade.

Entry into the gas station business is especially easy. Perhaps the most important form of rivalry among the major oil companies is their competition for outlets. The way to win a customer for Shell or Standard products is to have a station near his home and others easily available whenever he wants to stop. As a result the large refiners will go to great lengths to blanket the market with stations. They build and equip stations and finance them for the operator on an advantageous basis. Would-be proprietors need very little capital to enter the business, and, since the skills involved are widely known and hope springs eternal, there is practically no limit to the number of potential operators as well as stations.

If this picture of the gas stations is correct, cities with high mar-

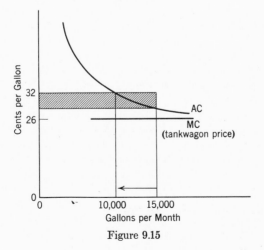

Figure 9.15

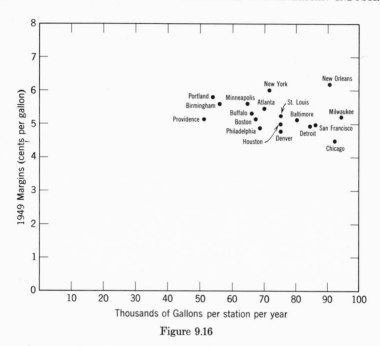

Figure 9.16

gins should have too many stations, with lower sales per station than the low margin cities. Figure 9.16 shows some slight tendency in this direction. It compares margins in 1949 with sales per station reported in the 1954 Census in 18 large metropolitan areas. Washington, D. C., and Youngstown, Ohio, were left out because 1954 was an unusual year for gas stations in both cities. Maryland and Virginia had just put in a 6¢ gasoline tax which the District of Columbia did not do until the following year. By contrast, Ohio had raised its tax by 1¢ in 1953 while Pennsylvania made no change. As a result, Washington stations picked up lots of business from their suburban competitors while Youngstown stations lost business to stations a couple of miles away in Pennsylvania. For the most part, cities with high margins in 1949 did have a mild tendency to have too many stations, each with very low volume by the time 1954 rolled around, but the relationship was not very close.*

* The margins are monthly averages for the year 1949 reported by Texaco and published in *National Petroleum News*, Jan. 1951. Sales per station are for stations operating all year in 1954 according to the 1954 *Census of Business*. Since we are trying to find the effect of margins on the number of stations, the appropriate margins must be for years earlier than the year in which output was measured. The years after 1950 were marked by a large number of gas wars and would probably not be considered "normal" by gas station operators. At any rate, figures

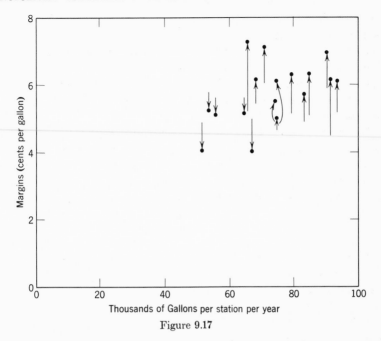

Figure 9.17

Figure 9.16 does not tell the whole story, however. Cities that develop great excess capacity may show a tendency toward price cutting. Operators of half-used stations are more likely to be tempted than busy ones. Figure 9.17 compares 1954 sales with 1957 margins this time.* Most cities show higher margins in 1957 than in 1949, but the low volume cities uniformly reduced theirs from eight years

available show only the nominal margins (the difference between official tank-wagon prices and retail prices) and do not include rebates given in time of price wars. The years from World War II through 1949 were marked by few price wars so the margins from that period are more reliable. The author attempted an analysis similar to that presented in Figure 9.15 using margins from other years and found the fit less good than even this one.

Only cities of more than 500,000 population were used because there is a clear relationship between city size and sales per station as well as the one noted here between price and sales. Margins were not available for stations in the following large cities for 1949: Cleveland, Columbus, Cincinnati, Pittsburgh, Indianapolis, Dallas, Seattle, Los Angeles, and Kansas City. Margins for the New York Metropolitan Area are the simple average of those reported for Newark and New York City.

* 1957 was used because it was a year fairly free of gas wars in the cities used so that margins were more meaningful than in years like 1956 and 1958. Other years show similar results except for a few unreal nominal margins associated with gas wars.

earlier. It would seem that, given a few years, capacity does affect average prices. In this respect gas stations resemble the competitive industries—where a high supply means low prices and vice versa— and are quite different from automobiles and steel where prices can go up in spite of considerable overcapacity. Oligopoly may give a reasonable picture of the gas stations on a particular day, but it seems less appropriate in accounting for long-term tendencies. This should not be surprising.* The tacit agreements of the gas stations' oligopoly are far more fragile than those of other oligopolies described in this book. Only in the most extreme of circumstances (1921 and 1931–32) did steel prices change as much as 30% in one year; such fluctuations are almost annual experiences in many local gasoline markets.

The Government and the Gas Stations

Public policy on gasoline retailing has certainly not been unequivocally on the side of more competition. Many communities have taken price cutting as an unquestioned evil when it comes to gasoline. Several states have laws prohibiting sales of gasoline at less than announced prices, in effect outlawing the "behind the pump" discount. Some cities prohibited self-serve stations when the independents introduced them in the early 1950's ostensibly for safety reasons, but the main groups advocating the laws were dealers' associations and appropriate trade unions. A number of cities have laws preventing gas stations from displaying price signs of more than a square foot in area, thus making price cutting to attract the passing motorist

---

* A number of studies of gasoline markets have reached a similar conclusion: that retail margins tend toward competitive levels in the long run. Edward P. Lerned, "The Pricing of Gasoline, A Case Study," *Harvard Business Review*, Nov. 1948, p. 749, felt that margins much in excess of operating "costs" led to price cutting by independents (pp. 742–743, 751) and suggested that the low margins in Ohio in the 1930's compared with other states accounted for the small increase in stations (p. 750). J. S. Bain, *The Pacific Coast Petroleum Industry*, University of California Press, 1945, Pt. II, pp. 227–233, noted a similar role for the independent and found that margins remained at levels that barely covered operating expenses over most of the period studied. Dirlam and Kahn, "Leadership and Conflict . . . ," *op. cit.*, pp. 838–842, summarize these views and concur. Livingston and Levitt, in their survey of six midwestern cities cited earlier, found that with one minor exception the higher the margins, the more stations there were pricing at less than the norm.

The reader must be warned that the conclusion reached here applies *only* to the retailing of gasoline. Most persons studying the refining segment of the industry conclude that oligopoly gives a better picture there. For discussions of the oil industry in general see Bain or Dirlam and Kahn listed above, or Melvin G. de Chazeau and A. E. Kahn, *Integration and Competition in the Petroleum Industry*, Yale University Press, 1959.

practically useless. Agreements among retailers seem to have been fostered in some localities, especially in small towns or where the unfair practices laws (discussed on p. 426) have been applicable to gas stations. There are instances where operators have met in public and voted on price.*

The Standard Oil Case

The federal agencies also have an equivocal record on competition in gasoline retailing. Their most important action in this field was a Robinson-Patman Act case in which the FTC found that Standard Oil of Indiana had discriminated illegally when it sold at low prices to four Detroit independent jobbers in the 1930's. As in other communities, these firms were the leaders in price competition. The FTC ordered Standard Oil to stop giving the discounts. Standard Oil appealed, and after years of litigation the Supreme Court ruled against the Commission.† It decided that a firm could justify price differentials under the Robinson-Patman Act if such "discrimination" were necessary to meet a competitor's price in good faith. The Detroit jobbers had alternative sources of supply at prices as low as Standard Oil's and the company would undoubtedly have lost their business if it had refused to meet these prices. The Court held that the law did not prohibit bona fide price competition of this sort.

The decision caused an uproar. Many felt that it largely vitiated the Robinson-Patman Act since few profit-seeking businessmen offer discounts except to meet competition. Bills to eliminate the "good faith" defense were introduced in the 84th, 85th, and 86th Congresses. During hearings on the amendment in 1957 hundreds of businessmen descended on Washington. Retailers' associations, especially those representing major brand gas stations, favored the new legislation. Independent distributors, manufacturers in many lines of business,

* For a more complete description of some of these practices see Ralph Cassady, *Price Making and Price Behavior in the Petroleum Industry,* Yale University Press, 1954, pp. 246–252.

Most states have active gasoline retailers' associations, many of which are continuously fighting for price controls of various sorts, including resale price maintenance, the enforcement of unfair practices laws, and even direct regulation of retail prices by special state commissions. The oil refiners usually oppose these measures. See Cassady and Jones, cited above, p. 279, or almost any issue of *The Gasoline Retailer.*

† Standard Oil v. Federal Trade Commission, 340 US 231 (1951). The FTC then issued a revised order and it too was appealed. It was finally set aside by a 5 to 4 decision of the Supreme Court, 355 US 396 (1958).

and both the Justice Department and the Chairman of the FTC opposed the amendment.*

Economists disagree about its advisability. Opponents argue that it would mean "soft competition." It would weaken or eliminate those retailers that have done most of the innovating and have proved most prone to price competition and would protect the small major stations from competition. It would eliminate one of the main elements of price competition at the refiner level. Advocates of the amendment argue that it is necessary to attain the objectives of the Robinson-Patman Act: the protection of small businessmen from unfair buying disadvantages. Some feel that manufacturers who are prohibited from discriminating may be forced to make price cuts across the board.†

Over-all, government at all levels has done little to improve the performance of gasoline retailing. If the trade is less efficient than it might be, it is because of overcapacity. The actions of federal, state, and local governments to check price competition intensify this problem, if anything. The independents have continued to grow, retail margins have continued to reflect supply conditions, and major refiners have continued to engage in some price competition by granting discounts and rebates, largely because the governmental actions have been unsuccessful.

CARTELS WITH FREE ENTRY—DRUGSTORES

Resale Price Maintenance Laws

Agreements among the firms in an industry to limit competition are referred to as *cartels*. Informal cartels have not been very successful in most lines of retailing. Discount houses thrive on such arrangements when observed by *other* stores. There must be some

* Hearings before the Senate Subcommittee on Anti-Trust and Monopoly, 85th Congress, 1st Session, on S11 and S1211, Mar. 12–Apr. 5, 1957, *passim.*

† The Attorney General's National Committee to Study the Anti-Trust Laws, a group of well-known economists, attorneys, and businessmen invited to review the existing law at a conference in 1954, came out in favor of the "good faith" defense established in the Standard Oil case, but two well-known economists, Walter Adams and A. E. Kahn, dissented for the reasons given above. *Report of the Attorney General's National Committee To Study the Anti-Trust Laws*, pp. 180–186.

sort of legal enforcement if agreements to restrict competition in retailing are to work.

The most important means of accomplishing this in the United States have been the resale price maintenance or "fair trade" laws of every state but Alaska, Missouri, Nebraska, Texas, Vermont, and District of Columbia.* They permit manufacturers to stipulate minimum prices in contracts with their retailers. Then if a contract is violated, the manufacturer can sue the price cutter. In fact, under the "nonsigner" clause included in most fair trade laws, the manufacturer may sue any retailer selling below list price even if he has not signed an agreement, provided only that some dealer in the state has. In effect, the manufacturer has the power to enforce a price agreement among the sellers of his product if he chooses.

Resale price maintenance is not used in every branch of retailing. It seldom applies to petroleum or food products or to most types of shopping goods.† It has been common in the sale of drugs, cosmetics, liquors, and small appliances.

Fair trade has a long history in the drug field and is more complete there than in most other branches of retailing today.

Fair Trade in Theory

The effect of fair trade laws or of any cartel with free entry is analyzed in Figure 9.18. The drugstore represented there might have a demand curve like D_1 in the short run, but since the manufacturer has specified that the price cannot fall below P, only the solid section of the demand curve counts. The profit that results will disappear in this case as in others because of the new stores it attracts into the trade. The new crop of pharmacists cannot drive down the price under the fair trade laws, but they can spread the volume of trade thinner and thinner until the demand at a prospective new store is down to D_2. After that the druggist's margin does not seem excessive. It barely "covers costs." The druggists may feel that it does not even do that. If they can convince the manufacturer to

---

* In a number of states, however, court decisions have undermined these laws. See p. 425.

† Fair trade does not seem to work when the typical sale is large because it is almost impossible to keep sellers from making secret concessions. It is clearly inappropriate when brand names are unimportant, as with many food and textile products. Some of the more powerful manufacturers, such as the oil refiners and cigarette manufacturers, have been able to resist pressure on them to fair-trade their products.

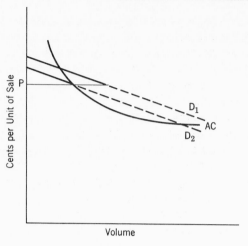

Figure 9.18

specify higher margins, they may be able to increase their earnings for a time. In the long run, of course, the greater the margins, the greater the overcapacity.

Unable to compete in price, druggists may try to expand volume by carrying a greater variety of brands, offering free delivery, or providing some other increased service. An individual store can certainly win customers this way, but drugstores in general will not gain much. The net effect in the long run is simply higher costs at each store (AC_2 in Figure 9.19) but no more profits than before.

Are Fair Trade Prices Too High?

Cartels with free entry would cause overcapacity only if the price

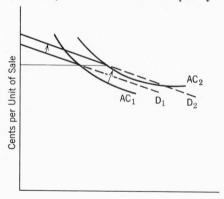

Figure 9.19

agreed upon were higher than that prevailing otherwise. In Figure 9.20, if the "fair trade" price were P_1, resale price maintenance would lead to no more excess capacity than we would have anyway, but if it were higher, say P_2, it would mean more drugstores with less business per store.

There has been much debate about whether fair trade actually raises prices or not. A number of surveys have been made by the sponsors of fair trade which seem to show that drug prices actually declined slightly with the coming of fair trade laws, that they rose less than nonfair trade prices during the inflation of the 1940's, and that retail drug prices are lower in fair trade than in nonfair trade states![*]

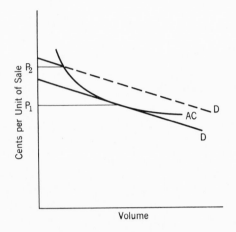

Figure 9.20

Other surveys have produced different results. The FTC found that after the introduction of fair trade laws in the 1930's prices charged by department stores and chains were definitely higher but that prices charged by small independents, especially in small towns,

* Some of these studies are suspect since they depend on the reports and often the memories of druggists who have a vested interest in fair trade. For instance, the most ambitious such survey, H. J. Ostlund and C. R. Vickland, *Fair Trade and the Retail Drug Store*, Druggists Research Bureau, 1940, depended on replies to a questionnaire sent to all druggists in fair trade states inquiring about prices before and after fair trade laws were passed. The same questionnaire appeared in a drugstore magazine with the caption "Cast your vote for fair trade." This and other such studies are criticized in Marvin Frankel, "The Effect of Fair Trade: Fact and Fiction in the Statistical Findings," *Journal of Business,* July 1955, pp. 182–194.

TABLE 9.4

SALES PER DRUGSTORE IN METROPOLITAN AREAS OF
MORE THAN 500,000 POPULATION

Metropolitan Area	Sale per Store (dollars)	Percentage of Stores with More than $500,000 Sales
Dallas	146,598	1.5
Houston	114,768	1.8
Kansas City	145,091	4.5
San Antonio	97,411	not available
St. Louis	103,942	2.0
Washington, D. C.	192,977	7.0
All six nonfair trade cities together	136,642	3.9
All other metropolitan areas of over 500,000 population	84,532	1.2

Source: *Census of Business,* 1954.

apparently were not.* An economist who had a commercial research firm sample posted retail prices of tooth paste in large cities
in both fair and free trade states found average prices significantly
higher in the fair trade areas.† Five years after having prohibited
resale price maintenance agreements, the Swedish government surveyed retail prices in four lines of goods and found them averaging
below the manufacturers' recommended prices in each case.‡

Most of this somewhat equivocal evidence seems to point toward
higher prices under fair trade at least in the large metropolitan
areas. Such a conclusion is easy to believe in view of the retailers'
vehement support of the fair trade laws.

Overcapacity in Drugstores

Sales per drugstore in fair trade and free trade states should provide some check on the possibility that resale price maintenance would

* FTC, *Resale Price Maintenance,* 1945, pp. xlvii–xlvix. The FTC survey also
depended on druggists' memories and probably suffered from some of the defi-
ciencies of those sponsored by advocates of fair trade.

† Ward Bowman, "The Prerequisites and Effects of Resale Price Maintenance,"
University of Chicago Law Review, vol. 22, Summer 1955, pp. 852–855.

‡ "Failure of Recommended Prices," *Cartel,* Apr. 1959. The article reports the
results of studies published by the Swedish Price and Cartel Office in 1958.

lead to overcapacity. Table 9.4 shows 1954 sales per drugstore in the six metropolitan areas of more than 500,000 population located in nonfair trade states. Every city shown has higher sales per store than the average of metropolitan areas over 500,000 in fair trade states. Drugstores in the six areas taken together do half again as much business per store as those in other large metropolitan areas. Of course, there are many reasons why some areas should have drugstores with higher volume than others. Table 9.4 does not prove that fair trade prices have attracted too many stores into the trade, but the high volume of drugstores in all six nonfair trade cities certainly supports that hypothesis.

The druggists themselves have commented on overcapacity in their trade at times. A detailed study of 12 representative drugstores sponsored by the Wholesale Druggists Association reached the conclusion that only about 35% of employee time was spent in selling; 25% was used up in simply waiting for customers to come in. With regard to the other 40% the study concluded:

> In many cases employees chose to arrange or clean stock rather than remain completely idle. The non-selling time (65% of all time) represents a reservoir of available selling time to a large degree.*

The slowness of large retailers to develop in drugs is also probably attributable to fair trade at least in part. Figure 9.2 shows that the chains' share of the retail drug trade rose from 1929 until the era of the fair trade laws and has declined since. This occurred in spite of the substantially higher sales per worker in chain than in independent stores, shown in Figure 9.3. Similarly, the nonfair trade cities in Table 9.4 show consistently larger percentages of their stores in the "more than $500,000 sales" class than do the large metropolitan areas in fair trade states. Fair trade laws prevent large retailers from passing savings on to the customer and hence eliminate their most effective means of expanding. A supermarket revolution in drugs does not seem likely so long as retailers are prevented from courting high volume with low margins.

Fair Trade and the Courts

Resale price maintenance was common in Europe, where it met few legal barriers, by the end of the nineteenth century. In the United States the National Wholesale Druggists Association won a resale

---

* D. E. Burley, A. B. Fisher, and R. F. Cox, *Drug Store Operating Costs and Profits,* McGraw-Hill, 1956, p. 5.

price maintenance agreement from the manufacturers in 1876, but it was only extended to the retail level in 1900.* These agreements were accepted by the courts at first,† but in a 1911 decision the Supreme Court concluded that they were "obvious" agreements in restraint of interstate commerce and therefore illegal under the Sherman Act.‡

Bills were introduced in every Congress from 1914 to 1936 to make such agreements legal once more, but no action was taken until the depression. The state of California passed the first modern fair trade law in 1931 and added the first nonsigner clause in 1933. Forty-one other states passed similar laws in the next three years. In 1937 Congress passed the Miller-Tydings Act exempting fair trade agreements from the antitrust laws wherever state law allowed them.§

The Decline and Fall of Fair Trade

The resale price maintenance agreements were clearly in the interest of many retailers, but what did they do for the manufacturers who had to enforce them? In the first decades of this century, companies with brand names newly established in expensive advertising campaigns seem to have felt that use of their products for "loss leaders" would destroy their prestige. Others, whose products were sold mainly through small outlets in trades with powerful retailers' associations, had to adopt fair trade to keep their dealers' favor.¶ A few manufacturers seem to have used high margins protected by fair trade to get dealers to push their products.‖

Many manufacturers have soured on fair trade in the last 25 years. If retailers were willing to push the product with low prices, why prevent them? This view was particularly to the point when large retailers had the alternative of selling competing products under their

* Bowman, *op. cit.*, pp. 826–827.

† Fowle v. Park, 131 US 81 (1889).

‡ Dr. Miles Medical Co. v. Park and Sons Co., 220 US 373 (1911).

§ It was passed as a rider to the District of Columbia appropriation of that year because of the possibility of a presidential veto.

¶ The Northern California Retail Druggists Association conducted a boycott of Pepsodent until the company agreed to fair-trade it in 1935. The Company made a public apology and contributed $25,000 to a fund of the National Retail Druggists Association to finance the fair trade law campaign in other states. FTC, *Resale Price Maintenance, op. cit.*, p. 143, and TNEC, *Final Report*, 77th Congress, 1st Session, Exhibit 2793, p. 233.

‖ TNEC Hearings, Pt. VI, p. 2564.

own labels, something they were prone to do when prevented from using their cost advantage in selling national brands.

Fair trade has declined in importance in the years since World War II. The discount houses thrived on the agreements which at once provided a "normal" price from which to offer discounts and kept the prices of "legitimate" stores above theirs. Many manufacturers who were lukewarm toward fair trade did little to enforce their agreements. Producers who did try to get enforcement met increasing difficulties. It was one thing to threaten the large chains and department stores of the 1930's and quite another to police a great number of small discounters. If an offender was brought into court the judgment was often slight.

Several judicial decisions have weakened the laws further. In 1951 the Supreme Court ruled that the Miller-Tydings Act had not exempted the state nonsigner clauses from the antitrust laws.* While the McGuire Act passed in the next session of Congress filled this gap, the discount houses got so much momentum during the interlude of poor enforcement that fair trade never really recovered. A lower court concluded that state fair trade laws did not prevent sellers in nonfair trade states from advertising and delivering through the mails in all parts of the country and the Supreme Court refused to review the case.† A number of state courts have gone further, 17 throwing out the nonsigner clause and 4 the whole fair trade statute under their state constitutions or subsequent legislation.‡

The increasing difficulty of enforcement has driven many erstwhile supporters to abandon fair trade. General Electric, one of the last big holdouts, finally gave up in 1958. By then a well-known business magazine could report that fair trade was practically dead outside of the drug field.§

A national fair trade act to restore fair trade throughout the

---

* Schwegmann Brothers v. Calvert Distillers Corporation, 341 US 384 (1951).

† General Electric v. Masters Mail Order Co. of Washington, D. C., 244 F. 2nd 681 certiorari denied 355 US 824 (1957).

‡ By June 1960, the fair trade statutes were unconstitutional in Ohio and Utah, unenforceable in Virginia, and repealed after first being declared unconstitutional in Nebraska. The nonsigner clauses had been declared unconstitutional in Arkansas, Colorado, Florida, Georgia, Indiana, Iowa, Kansas, Kentucky, Louisiana, Michigan, Minnesota, New Mexico, Oklahoma, Oregon, South Carolina, Washington, and West Virginia. Both the statutes and the nonsigner clauses have been upheld in recent decisions in other states, however.

§ "Is Fair Trade on the Way Out?" *Dun's Review,* 1958, p. 33.

country and eliminate the threat of mail order selling was introduced in the 85th Congress. Twenty-one representatives of 14 retail and wholesale organizations testified for the bill. Only 7 manufacturers did, and 3 of these were in the drug trade. Representatives of the FTC, the Departments of Justice, Agriculture, and Commerce, and the Bureau of the Budget all opposed the bill.* No change was made in the law.

Unfair Practices Acts

The "unfair practices" acts are close relatives of the fair trade laws. They are statutes passed in the 1930's by 31 states under which any dealer in a covered trade is prohibited from selling at prices which are less than his costs. The determination of "cost" is obviously crucial. As spelled out in the acts, it clearly includes operating expenses as well as the cost of goods sold. In 20 states the law specifies minimum markups—typically 6% at retail. In eight states, trade associations may make cost surveys which can then be used as prima-facie evidence against price cutters. That is to say, it is up to the defendant to prove that he is not breaking the law if his prices will not cover the costs shown in the surveys.

These surveys have sometimes been very unscientific.† Accounting costs are uncertain in the first place, and businessmen with a vested interest in high prices are not likely to be objective in making estimates. As a result, the surveys have tended to turn into price agreements among association members. Once a minimum margin is agreed upon, price cutters can be threatened with criminal prosecution. The mere threat of litigation may be enough to intimidate a small businessman, especially if the agreement seems to be in his interest anyway.

The unfair practices acts do not have a very impressive enforcement record. State law enforcement agencies seldom devote much time or money to them. Large chains and department stores are unlikely to be deterred by the prospect of lawyers' fees even though little businessmen may be. The acts have themselves been declared

---

* "Fair Trade" Hearings of a Subcommittee of the House Committee on Interstate and Foreign Commerce, 85th Congress, 2nd Session, Apr. 29–May 7, *passim*. Seven of the retail and wholesale representatives were from the drug trade.

† In one instance the president of the Colorado Food Distributors Association (wholesale grocers) is reported to have asked the membership at a meeting if there was anyone present whose costs were less than 12%. When no hands went up, they decided to raise their margin from 9%, which it had been for some time, to 12%. Reported in Vernon Mund, *Government and Business*, 2nd ed., Harper, 1955, pp. 494–495.

unconstitutional in five states. Their most important effect has been to grant permission to small businessmen to engage in open price agreements.

CARTELS WITH RESTRICTED ENTRY—LIQUOR STORES

If it is overcapacity that plagues cartels with free entry, why not restrict the number of firms? This has been done in some lines of retailing. Manufacturers do it when they limit the number of franchised dealers, as with automobiles. State and local governments do it through the licensing laws.*

Restrictions on Competition in Liquors

Probably the most regulated of retailers are the liquor dealers. Every state either licenses or prohibits private liquor stores. One is still dry. In 17 others liquor is sold through publicly owned liquor stores exclusively. Each of the remaining states licenses stores to control their number and location and to prevent violations of the liquor code.

Liquor is one field where resale price maintenance is still largely intact. In 22 states fair trade in liquors is of the usual sort and depends on the willingness of manufacturers to sign and enforce contracts. However, 10 states, including such populous ones as New York and California, have enacted laws making resale price maintenance mandatory in the case of liquor. Not only *must* distillers and wholesalers stipulate minimum prices,† but the liquor control authorities ordinarily do the enforcing. This makes the fair trade laws much more effective since the violators are threatened with almost

---

* There are very few state or local governments that have not performed this function for some little businessmen. In 1952 there were more than 1200 state laws licensing members of one occupation or another, including tree surgeons, egg graders, dry cleaners, real estate dealers, and pest controllers. "Occupational Licensing Legislation in the States," *State Government,* Dec. 1952, pp. 275–280.

In the same vein, 16 states "protect" the consumer by preventing sale of aspirin outside of drugstores. *Retailers Manual of Taxes and Regulations, op. cit.,* pp. 200–228.

† The regulations are often written so that they facilitate tacit agreement among distillers and jobbers. In California a price change must be published 45 days in advance though an exception is made for those meeting price cuts by rivals. For a good discussion of the distilling industry, see A. R. Oxenfeldt, *Industrial Pricing and Market Practices,* Prentice-Hall, 1951, Chapter 9.

certain license suspensions rather than more problematical lawsuits.

Even nonprice competition is prohibited to a considerable extent. The California Alcoholic Beverage Control Act prohibits any licensee from giving "any premium, gift, or free goods in connection with the sale of any alcoholic beverage."* Trading stamps and even free ice have been prohibited. The size and nature of shop window advertising is also regulated.† Liquor control has just about restricted competition to the clerk's disposition.

In California, at least, the liquor control laws have also been used to protect the old-style distribution system. Under ordinary circumstances manufacturers must go through independent wholesalers in distributing their products and neither the manufacturer nor the wholesaler may engage in retail operations.‡ The law also contains a number of rules similar to those of the Robinson-Patman Act, apparently aimed at preventing price advantages for large retailers.§

The one possibility of price competition in liquor retailing in mandatory fair trade states has been the private brand. Distributors in some of these states have been able to do very well buying unbranded liquor, often from the better known distillers, and selling it under their own labels. They can meet the fair trade requirement by filing a minimum price which includes only a nominal margin (6% is a common one, compared with about 20% on national brands). To fill this gap, two states have adopted measures specifying minimum margins of 20% and 33.3%!

Monopoly Price and Profits in Liquors

There can be little question but what the liquor dealers have exercised a safe sure monopoly as a result of these controls. In 1952 a study was made of retail prices of 13 nationally known brands of liquor in all states other than those with public liquor monopolies. The lowest prices were in nonfair trade states in each case (eight in

---

* California Alcoholic Beverage Control Act, Chapter 16, #25600. No two state regulations are exactly alike. This section on liquor stores is based mainly on California controls. For analysis of the somewhat similar experience of New York, see Charles H. Hession, "The Economics of Mandatory Fair Trade," *The Journal of Marketing*, Apr. 1950, pp. 707–720.

† California Alcoholic Beverage Control Act, Chapter 16, #25611.1, and California Business Regulations, Chapter I, Article 16, #106.

‡ California Alcoholic Beverage Control Act, Chapter 15, #25500, 25501, and 25502.

§ *Ibid.*, #25503.

Missouri, four in the District of Columbia, and one in Texas). The median fair trade state had prices 30% above these minimums on the average.*

The most impressive evidence of the exploitation of this state-bestowed monopoly is the value of liquor licenses. California has not allowed new liquor licenses since 1939,† so the only way of entering the business has been to buy a license from an existing proprietor. The value of liquor licenses has risen with prospective profits. Licenses that cost less than $1000 originally were running about $9000 apiece in Los Angeles County and as much as $23,000 in newly urbanized areas such as Santa Clara and San Bernardino Counties by July 1959.‡ The fact that retailers were willing to make such payments to get into the business is a clear indication that substantial profits were available over and above what would barely attract dealers. After paying $10,000 or $20,000 for a license, a new liquor dealer might just be able to break even, but those who were present when the restrictions were first imposed were beneficiaries of some substantial windfalls. The monopoly profits of these liquor dealers have been converted into rents.

The restrictions on numbers in liquor distribution is certainly not an exclusively economic question. At least ostensibly its purpose is the protection of public morals. That purpose does not require the supression of all price competition, however. If knockdown prices for liquor are to be prevented, surely high taxes rather than high margins are the sensible answer. The states with publicly owned liquor stores do limit the number of outlets, maintain high prices, and appropriate the profits for the states. States with tight control of private liquor stores accomplish these goals only very imperfectly, if at all.

---

* Charles F. Stewart, "Mandatory Resale Price Maintenance of Distilled Spirits in California," *Journal of Marketing,* Apr. 1954, p. 376.

† New licenses have been issued in one instance (Orange County) but this is the only exception.

‡ During the month of July 1959, there were 47 transfers of package liquor licenses in Los Angeles County at prices ranging from $5000 to $12,500. The average was $8890. There were four sales in Santa Clara County at from $20,000 to $25,000, averaging $23,000, and two sales in San Bernardino County at $23,000 and $23,250. Licenses may not be transferred between counties, so they are less valuable in counties where the population has not grown much in the last 20 years. In San Francisco County (which includes only the central city) they were averaging only $3,283 in July 1959. Information from correspondence with the California State Department of Alcoholic Beverage Control.

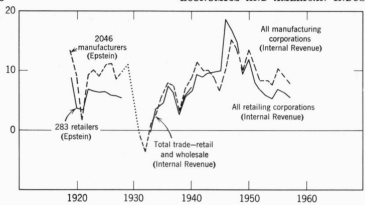

Figure 9.21.   Net income after tax as a percentage of owners' equity.
Source: 1919–28, R. C. Epstein, *Industrial Profits in the United States,* National Bureau of Economic Research, 1934. 1931–57, Internal Revenue Service, *Statistics of Income.*

PERFORMANCE

Retail Profits

Such information as we have on the number and profitability of retail firms provides fairly good support for the ideas suggested in this chapter. Figure 9.21 shows reported profits after tax as a percentage of owners' equity for incorporated retail firms and compares them with the rate of profits after tax for all manufacturing.* Separate profit figures for retailing go back only to 1938, but profits for all trade, wholesale and retail, extend back to 1934. It seems safe to take the total trade figure representing retailing in the earlier years, since retailing is much the largest part of the total and because the combined figures always move with retailing figures in the years since 1938.

Profits appear to have been consistently lower in retailing than in manufacturing except for the years 1944–48 at the end of World War II. This probably reflects the competitive character of retailing. It

* For consistency with other chapters, Figures 9.21 and 9.23 use profits after tax. This probably overstates retail profits because many retailers are small enough to benefit significantly from the low tax rates paid on the first $50,000 of profits and probably pay a smaller percentage of their incomes in taxes than manufacturing corporations as a group as a result. The profit rates shown in Figures 9.21 and 9.23 may also overstate retail profits because only the larger and more successful retailers are incorporated. On the other hand, profits of small corporations are not reported to the extent that they are paid to the owners of the firms as salaries or expense accounts rather than dividends.

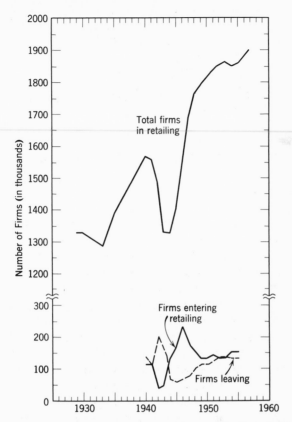

Figure 9.22.   Source: *Statistical Abstracts of the United States*.

cannot be due to any less risk.   Actually retailing is famous for its bankruptcy rate.   While about 41% of all business firms are in retailing, just about 50% of the failures occur there each year.*

The exceptional profits right after World War II were fairly clearly associated with inflation and the relative scarcity of retail outlets. Such retailers as there were did very well.   However, the profits disappeared very rapidly compared with those in manufacturing.   The reason is shown in Figure 9.22.   For several years new firms appeared at a great rate while relatively few disappeared.   Some of the influx can be interpreted as returning servicemen setting up shop, but the low rate of disappearance of old firms in those years pretty clearly reflects the high profits being earned.   By the time the number of firms had gotten up to roughly the level suggested by prewar rates of

* *Statistical Abstract of the United States,* 1959, pp. 487, 503.

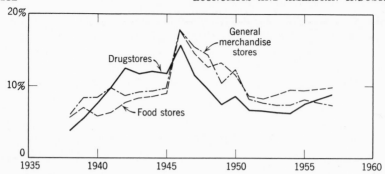

Figure 9.23. Net profit as a percentage of owners' equity. Source: Internal Revenue Service, *Statistics of Income.*

growth, profits had been competed away. Thereafter the number of firms entering was almost balanced by those leaving.

Profit figures are available for three of the lines of retailing discussed in this chapter: foods, drugs, and general merchandise (mainly department stores). They appear in Figure 9.23. Each follows roughly the pattern of retailing in general, though drugs show lower profits than the others except for the war years. Some have presented this as an argument for fair trade,* but it is really beside the point. So long as there is no restriction on entry, profits should disappear under the fair trade laws because of reduced volume per store. In fact, to the extent that fair trade reduces the risk in drugstore operations, it should result in lower profits than other lines of retailing. With less danger of failure, men might enter the drug field with prospective profits of maybe 6% while they would need perhaps 8% to go into the retailing of food or textile products. The discouragement of chains in drugs can also play a part in keeping reported profits low. It is the chains that are incorporated, and they, therefore, receive disproportionate weight in Figure 9.23.

Margins

Statistics on retail prices show more about the various commodity-producing industries involved than about retailing. Gross margins are more appropriate in evaluating the retailers themselves. Figure 9.24 shows the gross margins in all retailing and in five branches of retailing discussed in this chapter. Margins for all retailing and for incorporated food stores were derived from the reported net sales and

* "Proves Fair Trade Prevents Price Rises," *American Druggist,* Jan. 17, 1955, pp. 13–14.

costs of goods sold in income tax statistics. The other margin figures were reported in regular surveys of firms in the trade.

The gross margins for all retailing have declined consistently since World War II, and to some extent since the 1930's. This is a very rough figure, however, since the items sold vary so from year to year.

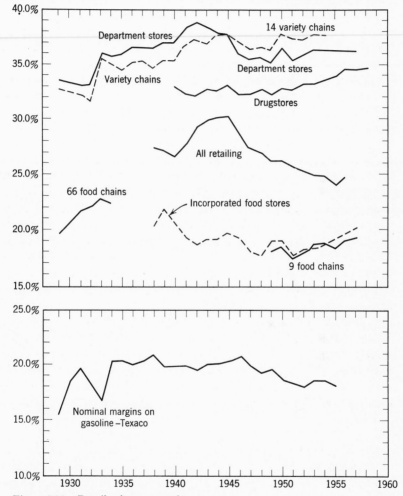

Figure 9.24.   Retailers' gross margins.

Source: Department stores, variety chains, and food chains, Harvard School of Business, Bureau of Business Research, Bulletins.

Drugstores, *Lilly Digest, loc. cit.*

All retailing and incorporated foodstores, *Statistics of Income.*

Gas stations, *Petroleum Facts and Figures.*

For instance, one reason why wartime margins are so high is that new automobiles and appliances and many of the lower priced items disappeared from the market. Most of these items customarily carry margins of considerably under 30%, the wartime average. When these goods reappeared after 1945 the average margin for all retail transactions dropped as a result.

Even compared with the prewar years of 1938–41, however, over-all retail margins were not particularly high in the early postwar years. The main reason for the high profits in the years right after the war was high volume, not high margins.

Margins in particular lines have followed divergent paths. Most of them reached high plateaus with the coming of NRA, fair trade, and similar price-fixing schemes in the mid-1930's. Food and gasoline margins are down considerably from those levels, department store margins slightly so, and margins at drugstores and variety chains not at all. The rise of the supermarkets accounts for much of the drop in food margins beginning in the late 1930's. Similarly, the spread of independent stations since World War II is an important reason for the lower gasoline margins. The rise of discount selling in the 1950's had little effect on the five lines of retailing shown in Figure 9.24, though it may help to account for the slight dip in department store margins. The decline in over-all retail margins in the 1950's, when most of the particular margins shown here did not fall, probably reflects the spread of discounting in the consumer durable field.

Stable or declining retail margins do not necessarily mean that retailers have lower dollar receipts. If retail prices are rising, retailers may be taking just as much or more margin in dollars while letting their percentage margins decline. On the other hand, the decline in over-all retail margins since the 1930's means that the price of retail services has not risen as much as commodity prices generally.

Productivity

The measures of productivity used in some of the previous chapters are hard to apply to retailing, since the "product" is extremely difficult to measure. One economist has made an attempt, however. His index of output per man-hour in distribution (retailing *plus* wholesaling) and a similar index for the commodity-producing industries (agriculture, manufacturing, and mining) appears in Figure 9.25.*

---

* Harold Barger, *Distribution's Place in the American Economy Since 1869*, Princeton University Press, 1955, p. 38.

Man-hour productivity has not increased in trade anywhere nearly so rapidly as in other fields. This would explain why an increasing proportion of our labor force should be employed in commerce. When we double our national productivity we do not improve all fields equally rapidly. The manufacturers and farmers may be able to produce twice as much output with no more employees, or even with fewer, but the retailers have not been able to distribute twice as many goods without more staff.

The slow growth in productivity in distribution is capable of more than one interpretation. It would seem to be consistent with the idea that the bigness and some degree of monopoly make for rapid innovation while competitive conditions like those in retailing discourage progress. On the other hand, it might simply reflect the character of the product. Retailers are selling services, and it sounds plausible that personal services are less capable of mechanization and mass production than are products.

Certainly retailing has been marked by numerous spectacular innovations in this century. Such developments as the mail order houses, department stores, chains, supermarkets, and discount houses all appear as momentous as such developments as continuous rolling of steel or assembly line production of automobiles, though of course

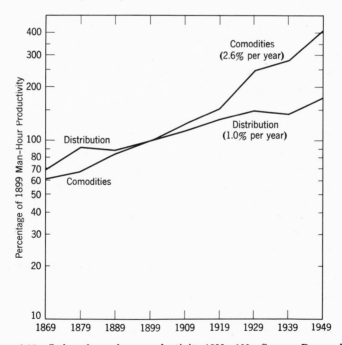

Figure 9.25. Index of man-hour productivity 1899=100. Source: Barger, *loc. cit.*

there is no way of comparing them exactly. At any rate, within retailing itself it has not been the fields which are protected from competition that have produced the great innovations. They have come in the wide-open fields where no holds are barred. The introduction of monopolistic restraints has unquestionably inhibited the innovation process in retailing rather than the reverse.

SUMMARY

In general, retailing is a highly competitive field of enterprise. Changing forms of retailing in the last half century have mostly worked toward more competition, especially more price competition. Economies of scale are significant in many lines of retailing and have resulted in some very large firms, but concentration ratios are still low.

Retailing has been analyzed in terms of monopolistic competition, where each seller has a somewhat differentiated product but is small enough to act independently of the others. The differentiated products result in a downward sloping demand curve for each firm and a mild form of monopolistic pricing. In the long run, the entry of new firms in such industries results in overcapacity and the disappearance of profits. The tendency toward overcapacity can be exaggerated, however, because of the high elasticity of demand for each firm's services and because the differences among firms that result in overcapacity are themselves of value to the consumer. Nonprice competition in retailing may result in a tendency for margins to creep up as services increase, but the free entry and price competition that mark retailing put a limit on this tendency.

Oligopoly may provide a more plausible model of retail price decisions, but the results are similar. Profits disappear because of free entry, and if prices are greater than the lowest average cost, overcapacity will result. Price competition is common in retailing, however, and at least in the case of gas stations, great overcapacity seems to lead to low margins while near-capacity operations are associated with high ones. The results resemble competitive industries such as agriculture and textiles more closely than they do oligopolistic industries with few firms and limited entry such as aluminum, steel, and automobiles.

Government policy has for the most part tended to restrict competition in retailing rather than encourage it. The Robinson-Patman Act has some economic justification in attacking the monopsonistic power of large buyers, but if enforced it would require discrimination *against* the large buyer, weakening the positions of just those retailers who have proved most likely to innovate and engage in price competition. Actually, the acceptance of the "good faith" defense by the courts has limited the effect of the act. The A&P case had motivations similar to those of the Robinson-Patman Act, though again it had limited effect.

Resale price maintenance would prevent price competition among retailers altogether. Far from solving the economic problems of monopolistic competition, however, it would probably result in more overcapacity. Restricting entry, as with liquor retailing, leads to an undeniably monopolistic position for retailers with questionable benefit to the community.

Retailing has continued to perform in a competitive way. Profits have disappeared, price competition has pushed margins down in many lines, and new low-cost methods of retailing have appeared. These changes have been possible in spite of the Robinson-Patman Act, resale price maintenance laws, and unfair practices acts, because for the most part the restrictive legislation has not been enforced.

FURTHER READINGS

The classic statement of monopolistic competition appeared in Edward Chamberlin, *The Theory of Monopolistic Competition*, Harvard University Press, 1933, especially Chapter V. A closely related concept was developed simultaneously by Joan Robinson in *The Economics of Imperfect Competition*, Macmillan, 1933, Chapter VII. Both went back to earlier discussions, particularly Piero Sraffa, "The Laws of Returns Under Competitive Conditions," *Economic Journal*, 1926, reprinted in American Economic Association, *Readings in Price Theory*, Irwin, 1952, p. 180. Few ideas in economics have been more extensively discussed. A famous interpretation and criticism of these ideas was Robert Triffin's *Monopolistic Competition and General Equilibrium Theory*, Harvard University Press, 1940. Many of the common criticisms of monopolistic competition are developed or discussed in Nicholas Kaldor, "Market Imperfection and Excess Capacity," *Economica*, 1935, pp. 33–50, also in *Readings in Price Theory, op. cit.*, p. 384. Later editions of Chamberlin contain an exhaustive bibliography of further comments.

There is no single definitive study of retailing. For a review of long-term trends in the industry, not exclusively statistical, see Harold Barger, *Distribution's Place in the American Economy Since 1869*, Princeton University Press, 1955. Two good articles attempting to work out an analytical model that will fit retailing are W. A. Lewis, "Competition in Retail Trade," *Economica*, Nov. 1945, pp. 202–234, and Jane Aubert-Krier, "Monopolistic and Imperfect Competition in Retail Trade," in International Economic Association, *Monopoly and Competition and their Regulation,* Macmillan, 1954. Both are by Europeans, but they make extensive reference to American data. A discussion of the same general topic by three American economists, Stanley C. Hollander, Morris Adelman, and Richard B. Heflebower, appeared under the general title "Price and Competitive Aspects of the Distributive Trades" in *American Economic Association Proceedings,* May 1957, pp. 252–292. The paper by Stanley Hollander in particular embodies a very good and extensive annotated bibliography of recent studies of retailing of all sorts. The FTC is conducting what promises to be a very complete study of food stores. Only one part of that study has been published at this writing: FTC, *Economic Inquiry into Food Marketing,* Pt. I, *Concentration and Integration in Retailing,* Government Printing Office, 1960.

There are several good sources on the gas stations, particularly Ralph Cassady and Wylie Jones, *The Nature of Competition in Gasoline Distribution at the Retail Level,* University of California Press, 1951, Ralph Cassady, *Price Making and Price Behavior in the Petroleum Industry,* Yale University Press, 1954, and S. Morris Livingston and Theodore Levitt, "Competition and Retail Gasoline Prices," *Review of Economics and Statistics,* May 1959, p. 119.

On the Robinson-Patman Act and related matters see Corwin Edwards, *The Price Discrimination Law,* The Brookings Institution, 1959. The A&P case was discussed at length in the journals, especially Morris Adelman, "The A and P Case: A Study in Applied Economic Theory," *Quarterly Journal of Economics,* May 1949, p. 238, and J. B. Dirlam and A. E. Kahn, "Anti-Trust Law and the Big Buyer: Another Look at the A and P Case," *Journal of Political Economy,* Apr. 1952, p. 118. A more complete discussion of the A&P case appears in Adelman, *A & P: A Study in Price-Cost Behavior and Public Policy,* Harvard University Press, 1959.

Vernon A. Mund, *Government and Business,* Harper, 1955, Chapters 21 and 22, is a good source on resale price maintenance and unfair practices acts. The classic on fair trade is Ewald Grether, *Price Control under Fair Trade Legislation,* Oxford University Press, 1939. For additional references on the same subject, of which there are hundreds, see Stanley C. Hollander, *Discount Selling, Retail Price Cutting, and Resale Price Controls,* American Marketing Association, Bibliography Series No. 3, 1954. On the special treatment of liquor stores, see Charles H. Hession, "The Economics of Mandatory Fair Trade," *Journal of Marketing,* Apr. 1950, p. 707, and Charles F. Stewart, "Mandatory Resale Price Maintenance of Distilled Spirits in California," *Journal of Marketing,* Apr. 1954.

10

FACTOR MARKETS— STEELWORKERS

$\mathbb{S}$ o far this book has dealt mainly with the markets for commodities such as milk, aluminum, or retail services. This chapter is devoted to an equally significant set of markets where the resources that go to produce these commodities are traded.

Traditionally economists have classified our productive resources into (1) *labor*—all productive human effort, (2) *land*—all natural resources, and (3) *capital*—all man-made productive resources. Each of these pigeonholes contains a great clutter of only distantly related items, however. "Labor" ranges all the way from little old ladies to professional football players and "land" embraces both Manhattan real estate and Texas oil pools. For many purposes it makes more sense to subdivide the broad traditional groupings into fairly uniform subcategories and speak of each of them as a separate factor of production. Much of the analysis that economists have developed to describe factor markets applies equally well to little old ladies or Manhattan real estate or to any other resource. Labor is much the most important factor of production if evaluated in terms of the share of the national income that it earns. For this reason, when distinctions are necessary, this chapter will discuss the market for labor, particularly that of steelworkers.

INCOME DISTRIBUTION

Factor Shares in the National Income

So long as we were discussing product markets our main concern was the efficient use of our scarce resources. Efficiency is also an important question in discussing factor markets, but the distribution of income, which has been largely ignored so far, is an inescapable issue now.

The distribution of income among various factors of production over the last 30 years is shown in Figure 10.1. Labor earns much the largest share of total income. Wages and salaries have regularly come to about two-thirds of the total national income. Moreover, this understates labor's share since it does not include the in-

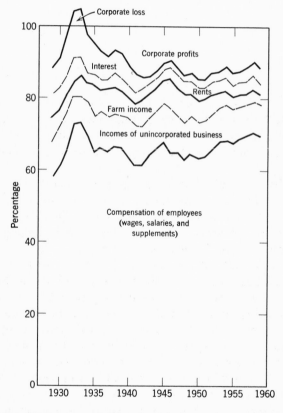

Figure 10.1. Percentages of the national income going to various factors of production 1929–58. Source: Derived from 1959 National Income Supplement to *Survey of Current Business.*

comes of the self-employed. Compensation for the effort of several million farmers, doctors, lawyers, and unincorporated tradesmen must make up a large part of the "income of unincorporated business." Altogether, labor takes about three-quarters of total income in this country. Its share has been about this as far back as the statistics go.*

The rest of the national income goes to various sorts of productive property. The interest and rents in Figure 10.1 are only those paid directly to individuals. In addition, a large part of the "profits" of corporations and the nonwage income of unincorporated businesses may be thought of as returns on the capital and land provided by the firms' owners.

Income Inequality

Figure 10.2 shows another aspect of distribution: the degree of inequality. The richest fifth of the nation's households consistently earns just under half of the nation's personal income. The lowest fifth earns only 5% of it. This understates the share of the wealthy because undistributed corporate profits, which are not included in income here, must be assigned mainly to the top 20% of the households. The income tax does not change things much. The left-hand chart in Figure 10.2 shows incomes before tax, and the right-hand chart incomes after tax. The differences between the two are slight.

Some of the inequality is more apparent than real, however. A third† of the lowest group of households are headed by persons over 65, most of them retired or semiretired. For others, incomes were temporarily low during a period of unemployment or bad business or while they were in school. Again, the high-income households are larger. In 1957 there were 3.82 persons per household at the top against 3.29 at the bottom.‡ If we could get the average *lifetime* income *per person* instead of income per family in particular years, we would probably find greater equality.

In spite of these quibbles, however, there is still more real poverty in our country than many people realize. One American household in five earned less than $2000 before tax in 1958. This included 33%

---

* There are short-run fluctuations in labor's share over the business cycle. Labor receives more of the total during depressions, largely because profits fall off so rapidly then.

† Selma F. Goldsmith, "Income Distribution by Size," *Survey of Current Business,* Apr. 1959, p. 11.

‡ Goldsmith, *loc. cit.*

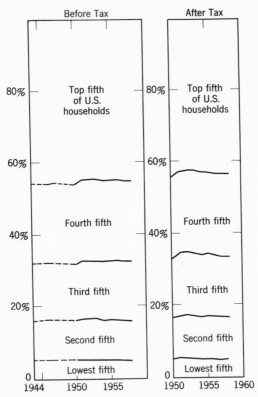

Figure 10.2. Percentage of personal and disposable income going to various income groups. Source: *Survey of Current Business,* Apr. 1958 and Apr. 1960.

of the farmers and the service and unskilled workers.* The greatest poverty was among small farmers, the racial groups with limited opportunities such as Mexicans and Negroes, and families faced with such tragedies as the death, long-term illness, insanity, or imprisonment of the breadwinner.

Income is probably more equally distributed today than it was before World War II. Figure 10.3 shows the share of the top 5% of Americans in total incomes since 1919. It ran 30% in the 1920's and 1930's but has been only about 20% since then. The decline would be less impressive, however, if undistributed corporate profits were included.†

* "1959 Survey—Financial Position of Consumers," *Federal Reserve Bulletin,* July 1959, p. 714.

† Selma Goldsmith, "Changes in the Size Distribution of Income," *American Economic Review,* May 1957, pp. 504–518. This article contains an excellent summary of the complicated literature on this subject.

There is a widespread feeling that greater equality is a virtue. Most Americans seem to be proud of the apparent increase in equality since the 1930's. Yet there is little basis for arguing with anyone who does not like it. If you and I can agree on our objectives—say increased output—then I can prove to you that some policy is good provided I can demonstrate that it has the desired result. But if you and I differ on the goals we think are desirable, there is no proving that one of our value judgments is better than the other. The statement that greater equality is a good thing is obviously a value judgment. The most that economists can say is that certain conditions result in more or less equality. It is up to the public to decide whether it likes the results or not.

WAGE THEORY

Factor Markets

Who is to be rich and who is to be poor and how much richer the rich are than the poor depends largely on what different people get for their effort and for the productive properties they own. This in turn depends on the working of the factor markets where these services are sold.

The business firms that were the suppliers on product markets are the buyers here. If we assume that these firms try to maximize profits, we can analyze their demand for machinists or downtown real estate or any other factor of production in much the same way that we analyzed their supply of milk or cotton cloth earlier. A profit-maximizing firm will only employ a factor if it pays its way, in other

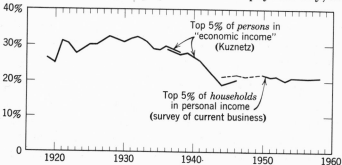

Figure 10.3. Share of the top 5% in total personal income 1919–57. Source: S. Kuznetz, *Shares of Upper Income Groups in Income and Saving,* National Bureau of Economic Research, 1953, Appendix Table 122, and Selma Goldsmith, "Size Distribution of Personal Income," *Survey of Current Business,* Apr. 1958 and Apr. 1960. "Economic income" is roughly noncorporate national income.

words, if it brings in at least as much revenue as it costs. The key to the demand for a factor of production, then, will lie in (1) what it can produce and (2) what the things it produces sell for.

The first of these questions may seem to be a stumper right way. There is no answer to the old question, "How much does labor produce?" If we eliminate *all* labor from a factory or farm we will usually eliminate all the output as well, but the same is true of other

TABLE 10.1

Machinists	Total Output (gimlets per day)	Product
0	0	
		5
1	5	
		7
2	12	
		8
3	20	
		7
4	27	
		5
5	32	
		3
6	35	
		2
7	37	

factors of production. Labor without tools is just about as unproductive as tools without labor. A combination is necessary to get anything done at all.

Marginal Product

Happily, it is not necessary to determine the total product attributable to a factor. All that the employer needs is the *marginal product*, the extra output that goes with a small addition of the factor in question, keeping other factors fixed. Table 10.1 works out the marginal product of machinists at various levels of employment in a hypothetical gimlet shop.* It is drawn up on the assumption that

---

* A gimlet is an old and famous product common to illustrations of this sort. The reader may take it as similar to a "whatchamacallit," though gimlets really do exist. Technically they are a form of hand drill.

the firm keeps equipment, materials, and other types of labor constant and varies only the number of machinists. The output of gimlets may increase at an increasing rate at first. Two machinists working together may be able to do more than twice as much as one working independently. Sooner or later, of course, the rate of increase is bound to slow down. The fourth machinist will not add as much as the third because there is less equipment per man after he is hired and because he does the less essential jobs that the first three did not have time to do.

The marginal product of labor in this case is shown in the third column of Table 10.1. It is just the difference between outputs with each added machinist. If three men produce 20 units and four men 27, the marginal product of the fourth man is 7. After a point the marginal product of machinists falls off. The reader should recognize this as the principle of diminishing returns. Whenever some factors are kept constant and one is varied, the marginal product of the variable factor must ultimately decline.

The numbers in Table 10.1 are plotted in Figure 10.4. Diminishing marginal product appears in the upper diagram as a flattening out of the total product curve. As more machinists are added, the curve continues to rise but at a slower and slower rate after a point. The marginal products of the first, second, third, etc., machinists are the steps labeled ΔQ_1, ΔQ_2, ΔQ_3, etc. They are plotted directly in the lower diagram.

We would have reached similar results if we had varied any other factor. Try keeping the number of machinists at four, say, and adding more and more machines. Sooner or later the marginal product of machines will have to decline. The same crew with more equipment will produce more gimlets, but there is a limit to what they can do no matter how much capital they have to work with.

Marginal Revenue Product

Now we can take up the second question that concerns the employer: what the products will sell for. To keep things simple, suppose that gimlets sell on a purely competitive market. Then it is easy to work out what an extra laborer adds to revenue for the firm. Table 10.2 does this. The marginal products are simply multiplied by the price of the product (say $2 per unit) to yield what might be called the *marginal revenue product,* the extra revenue attributable to one more unit of the variable factor. To make maximum profits the employer should hire machinists until the marginal revenue product just equals their wage. For instance, with a wage rate of $10 per day it would certainly pay to employ the first, second, third, and

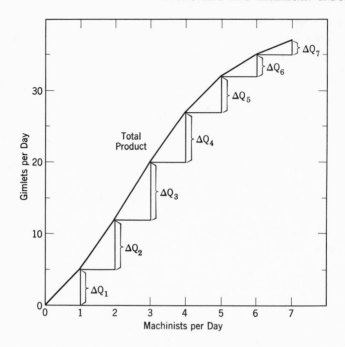

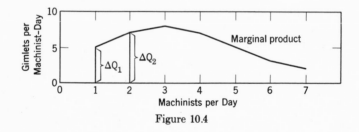

Figure 10.4

fourth man. Each of these adds more to receipts than to expenses and increases profit (or reduces losses) by the difference. The fifth man would bring in $10 in additional receipts, so the firm would neither gain nor lose by hiring him. The sixth man adding only $6 to receipts would reduce profits. It would only pay to employ him if the wage were as little as $6 a day.

Things would be a bit more complicated if the employer were something of a monopolist. Not only would the marginal product of labor in his shop decline as he took on more men, but he would have to cut his price or increase his selling costs to get rid of the extra output. The marginal revenue product would now fall off more sharply than in Table 10.2, but the employer would still maximize his profits by expanding until the marginal revenue product just equals the wage.

Our profit-seeking businessman should do the same with all of the factors he employs. He would not be earning maximum profits until:

1. The marginal revenue product of machinists equaled the wage of machinists.

2. The marginal revenue product of typists equaled the wage of typists.

3. The marginal revenue product of floor space equaled the rental of floor space.

4. The marginal revenue product of machines equaled the cost of employing machines, etc., all through the shop.

At first glance it may seem that we have imposed too many jobs on the businessman. Earlier in the book he was deciding how much to produce by equating marginal cost to marginal revenue. Now we also have him deciding how many of various factors to employ by

TABLE 10.2

Machinists	Marginal Product	Price of Product (dollars)	Marginal Revenue Product (dollars)
0			
	5	2	10
1			
	7	2	14
2			
	8	2	16
3			
	7	2	14
4			
	5	2	10
5			
	3	2	6
6			
	2	2	4
7			

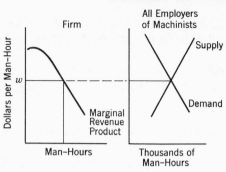

Figure 10.5

equating their marginal revenue products with the rates he must pay to get them.

Actually, these two jobs come to about the same thing. The profit-seeking businessman should expand so long as each addition to revenue exceeds the corresponding addition to costs. It makes no difference whether we visualize him as adding more and more to the output produced, or as adding more and more to the inputs he employs. In the first case he compares marginal cost with marginal revenue, and in the second he compares factor costs with marginal revenue product. Either way, his most profitable level of operation is where the last addition to cost just equals the last addition to revenue.

Demand and Supply—Particular Factor Markets

Marginal revenue product schedules have many of the features of demand curves. With other factors fixed they show how much of the variable factor (machinists here) will be employed. A marginal revenue product curve that might serve as a single gimlet firm's demand for machinists is shown on the left in Figure 10.5.

The over-all demand for machinists in the market as a whole would have a similar shape. Employers generally would find it worthwhile to employ more machinists at lower wage rates because (1) they could afford to use more men per machine in spite of the lower marginal product that results, and (2) they could sell their product for lower prices and would therefore increase production and employment. A demand curve for machinists is drawn in the right-hand diagram in Figure 10.5.

The supply of machinists would slope upward and to the right. High wages would attract young men into the trade, and low wages would tend to keep them out.

In a perfectly working competitive labor market, the supply and demand for machinists would yield the going wage which the gimlet manufacturer shown on the left in Figure 10.5 must pay if he wants to hire machinists. He may employ as many as he likes, however, and to make the most profit he should settle where their marginal revenue product just equals their wage.

Supply and Demand—Labor in General

The results are different when we talk about the supply and demand of *all* labor, not just machinists. For one thing, it is necessary to use real wages, i.e., wage rates measured in dollars of constant purchasing power. A general wage increase that is just offset by a general price increase is not likely to make much difference in how much people will work or how many will be employed.

The over-all supply of labor may have a very strange shape. High wages for machinists resulted in more machinists because workers were attracted from other employments, but a high general wage rate can only bring forth more labor if it makes the existing population do more work. It is not at all clear that this will happen. It is true that higher wages make it more expensive to stay home from work, but higher wage rates also mean more income. As we get richer we are apt to take part of our increased incomes in more leisure time. It is quite possible, then, that an *increase* in wages could result in a *decrease* in the amount of labor offered for employment! Try it out for yourself. How much would you work at $2 per hour? How about $5 or $25 or $50? Perhaps you will offer more labor for a while, but there are probably quite a number of people who would work *less* after a point. They can have increased take-home pay and still take Mondays off or arrange long vacations or retire young. Certainly this is what has happened to Americans as a group over the last century. In the 1890's the 60-hour week was common. Now we have a 40-hour week with paid vacations, six or eight paid holidays, and coffee breaks.

Going by past experience, then, the supply of labor may very well slope backwards after a point, as in Figure 10.6. At any rate, most authorities agree that social questions such as how many babies were born 30 years ago or how many immigrants are allowed or how many women work are much more significant than wage rates in determining how much labor is available in the national market.

The demand for labor in general would have a more orthodox shape. Just as with the business firm, you can think of the country's land and capital and technology as approximately fixed at any one time. After a point, the more persons there are working with these resources, the lower the marginal product of labor. High *real* wages mean that workers must have a high marginal product to be profitably employed. Lower real wages would mean that more workers could be used with each acre or machine.

Presumably the over-all supply of labor, which depends roughly on the population, and the over-all demand for labor, which depends roughly on the other resources of the country, will determine "the" wage rate.

Wage Differences

Of course, there is no such thing as "the" wage rate in the United States. Americans are paid wages all the way from a few dollars a

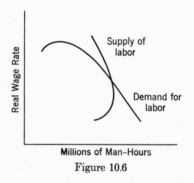

Figure 10.6

day for some farm labor to 500 for some movie star! The wage rate we just turned up must be taken as some sort of an average.

Some wage differences may be simply short-run affairs reflecting a temporary over-supply or under-supply of labor in particular trades or regions. A boom in electronics is apt to mean high salaries for electronic engineers, and a large supply of farm labor in comparison with the land and capital available in Mississippi would mean low wages there. However, this sort of wage difference would be only temporary in a perfectly operating competitive labor market. In the long run workers would be attracted into the high wage areas and industries and driven away by low wages until such differences disappeared.

Even in the long run there would be some differences, however. For one thing, not all jobs are equally attractive. Most of us would not be interested in a position as a structural steelworker 20 stories above the street even at twice our pay on the ground. Similarly, many are willing to work for less in a bank or department store than they could earn in a factory because of the white collar, tie, and supposed prestige. The final equilibrium situation where no one leaves the bank or enters structural steelwork would find money wages quite different on the different jobs.

Wage differences might also persist in the long run because of innate differences in individuals. So far we have talked as if all labor were the same. Of course it is not. Men may be more or less productive than women. Those with the higher marginal revenue product would have a higher wage. The same goes for workers who differ in age, intelligence, strength, dexterity, good looks, or just about anything else. If the special requirements of some job could all be acquired at a business college or a beauty salon, wage differences could not for long exceed the cost of breaking into the better paying trades, but where the special requirements are built-in features of the individual, wages might vary greatly without any tendency for the differences to disappear. Willie Mays and Brigette Bardot have special abilities that assure them higher incomes than the rest of us who are simply less well endowed. No one can compete away their advantages because no one can duplicate the special talents they have to offer.

Not all the barriers to movement between jobs are set by nature. In the real world there are all kinds of restrictions erected by unions, professional and trade associations, government licensing agencies, and social prejudice. At the high incomes available, we could probably have many more doctors than we do in spite of the long and expensive training requirements. At least there are large numbers of excellent students at the premed level who never gain admission to medical schools and probably more who would try if the obstacles to entry were not so great. Union rules that impose long apprenticeships and limit union membership do the same for the plumbers and electricians, while government-imposed entrance requirements and licensing rules keep down the numbers of real estate agents, morticians, beauticians, and what have you in one state or another. Of course, some licensing is essential. We cannot let just anyone call himself a doctor—but it is all too easy to use the power to limit competition.

At the other end of the income scale, Negroes, Mexicans, and other minorities, self-supporting women as a group, and persons entering new lines of work after the age of 45 earn low incomes on the average because they are limited to a few overcrowded and hence low-paying fields.

Summary of Wage Theory

Figure 10.7 tries to bring together the several dangling strands of wage theory that we have discovered so far. The right-hand diagram shows the over-all supply and demand of labor in the country. The middle two show the supply and demand for two particular types of labor, say textile workers and machinists. The left-hand diagram shows the adjustment of a particular machine shop to the wage rates with which it must contend.

The over-all supply and demand presumably determine the average wage rate. The wage for particular types of labor may be more or less than this. The high wage for machinists and the low wage for textile workers might lead workers to leave the latter field and enter the former, but this tendency will not go far enough to completely equalize wages if the supply of labor in the high-wage field is limited by disadvantages of the job, by the natural limits on the skills available, or by artificial restrictions of various sorts. Similarly, low wages may never be brought up to the average level if the supply of labor in some fields is especially high because of nonmonetary advantages or exceptionally large numbers of workers with limited alternatives. Each profit-maximizing firm would hire the types of labor it employs out to the point where the marginal revenue products just equal the appropriate wages.

Factor markets that worked this way would allocate our scarce resources very efficiently. For one thing, if every firm used machinists out to the point where the marginal revenue product equaled the wage, and if they were all in pure competition and all paid the same wage, all machinists would be employed in their most productive uses. If the marginal revenue product of machinists were different in different employments, we could increase output by shifting them from the less to the more productive uses, but profit-maximizing firms

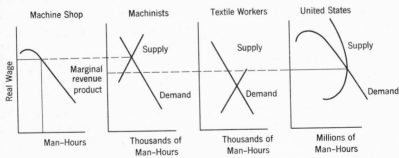

Figure 10.7

would do this automatically in a perfect market. Similarly, if workers moved whenever they could from low- to high-wage trades, the total labor force would automatically be used in its most productive employments. Finally, if the over-all wage rate were set by supply and demand, output would automatically be adjusted to the level where the marginal sacrifice of workers measured in dollars was just balanced by their marginal revenue products. We would not find ourselves working a 16-hour day when the extra goods were not worth as much to us as the free time given up.

This does *not* imply that perfect factor markets would necessarily result in an ideal income distribution. What income distribution is desirable is an ethical question. There are many who doubt that a GM executive or the owner of a West Texas oil field has a good *moral* claim to $500,000 a year, even if the factors they own have marginal revenue products on that order. At the other extreme, very few would argue that imbeciles ought to starve even if their marginal revenue product is nil. The case for the allocation of resources in perfect factor markets is one of efficiency, not fairness.

THEORY AND PRACTICE

Theory and Practice—Marginal Revenue Product

But do labor markets really work this way? Do businessmen really employ labor with an eye to the marginal revenue product? Do laborers really move from job to job to get higher wages? And are wage rates really determined by supply and demand? No other aspect of economic analysis has been subject to more questioning than wage theory.

Certainly very few businessmen consciously try to equate marginal revenue product with wage rates. Most of them do not even know what marginal revenue product means! This does not prove the theory wrong, however. If businessmen do maximize profits they will wind up where marginal revenue product equals the wage whether they can use the economists' jargon or not.

Maybe businessmen do not try to make maximum profits, though. They certainly do not take all they could in the immediate short run, and even over the long pull they might earn less than the maximum because of a concern for public welfare or just because they like the easy life. This is probably more true of their wage policies than other aspects of management. Public opinion usually approves of the manager who buys materials at the lowest possible price, and it certainly favors the manager who develops new, more efficient techniques, but it is apt to be critical of the man who cuts costs by paying labor the lowest wages he can get away with. Businessmen often seem to feel a moral obligation to let their help in on any success they enjoy. At any rate, a policy of paring wages to the bone is usually shortsighted. A firm that pays the bare minimum is not likely to get the cream of the labor supply and *is* likely to face a high turnover rate, a hostile work force, and difficult discipline problems among workers who have little to lose if fired.

On the other hand, competitive producers do not have much choice in the matter. They have to keep costs at a minimum or lose out to firms that do. Many of the competitive industries such as textiles, apparel, shoes, and retailing have been typified by exceptionally low wages. It is the monopolistic firm that is in a position to offer high wage rates. Aluminum, steel, and automobile workers earn half again what employees in the textile and shoe industries are paid.*

Even if the steel and auto companies do not try to maximize profits by depressing wages, however, they can still set marginal revenue product equal to the wage by adjusting their output and employment policies. To make the most profits, given their high wages, they can install labor-saving equipment, hire only the best labor, and stick to the most profitable products. Such policies are generally looked upon as wise and even public-spirited. The careful personnel officer who always gets the right man for the job, the efficient engineer who works out the lowest cost method of production, and the bright cost accountant who can identify the products that do not pay their way usually enjoy public approval, not censure.

Of course, the personnel officer, the engineer, and the cost accountant might prefer to spend their afternoons on the golf links. Few firms run at their very peak of efficiency. For instance, 36 of 43 southern industrialists, when asked how they would react to a lessening of the North-South wage differential, replied that among other things they would "improve efficiency through better production methods, organization, supervision, incentives, workloads, etc."† The implication is that they were not making all the effort they could to find and use low-cost methods at the time. Probably firms do have a tendency to move toward maximum profits (where marginal revenue products equal wage rates), but it is a matter of conjecture how strong a tendency it is.

* A more thorough discussion of this point will be taken up in Chapter 11, p. 506.

† Richard A. Lester, "Shortcomings of Marginal Analysis for Wage-Employment Problems," *American Economic Review,* Mar. 1946, p. 77.

Labor Mobility

If the picture of the profit-maximizing businessman hiring and firing labor to keep his costs down is imperfect, the idea of workers always on the lookout for higher pay and ready to move to better jobs is worse. A number of surveys have attempted to determine workers' knowledge of the labor market and their readiness to adjust.* Knowledge of conditions in other industries, in the same industry elsewhere in the country, and even in other plants in the same area has consistently proved to be very meager. Most workers have also shown a decided reluctance to quit one job for another. Seniority and pension rights, the security of familiar skills and surroundings, and the danger of unemployment make such attitudes understandable. It is the relatively young, unmarried worker with little seniority who makes such voluntary moves as do occur, mainly in boom years when there is some place to go. When they do have to look for a job, few workers make a systematic survey of the possibilities. They ask their friends and relatives, or they apply at random at convenient plants. A majority take the first job they find without shopping further.

In spite of all this, a tendency for competitive wage adjustments is still possible. A competitive labor market does not require every one to be on the move. It is only in the low-wage industries or regions that anyone has to quit his job, and even there only a minority have to move for some adjustment to occur. They do not have to pick their next jobs very intelligently, either. If more workers quit poor jobs than good ones, and if they choose their next jobs at random, there will be some net migration from the low- to high-wage industries and areas.

Some movements of labor toward better jobs are famous, such as the country boys who have been going to the city for centuries now. Table 10.3 shows that the interregional migration in this country has also followed the pattern that theory would suggest. In the South, where a surplus agricultural population and limited amounts of capital keep wages low, there has been a continuous outflow. In the West, which has no surplus agricultural population to supply its rapidly growing industry, high wages attract a substantial inflow. In the Northeast and North Central states, where wages are about average, in and out migration approximately balance.

* Several of them were brought together in *Labor Mobility and Economic Opportunity*, Wiley and Technology Press, 1954. A classic in the field is Lloyd G. Reynolds and Joseph Shister, *Job Horizons*, Harper, 1949.

TABLE 10.3

Region	Av. Straight Time Wage Rates (dollars) in Manufacturing (Apr. 1954)	Av. Annual In Migration (1953–57)	Av. Annual Out Migration (1953–57)	Av. Net In or Out Migration (− Means Out)
Northeast	1.67	396,000	425,000	− 29,000
North Central	1.80	726,000	730,000	− 4,000
South	1.36	849,000	1,024,000	−175,000
West	1.94	699,000	489,000	210,000
United States	1.68			

Source: Bureau of Labor Statistics Bulletin 1179, *Factory Workers' Earnings, April, 1954*, and Bureau of the Census, *Current Population Reports*, Series P-20, No. 82, 1958.

Wage Determination

For many people the idea of wage rates determined by supply and demand on a competitive market place is the most difficult of all to accept. It plainly does not work in short-term periods of general unemployment. In theory an oversupply of labor would cause real wages to fall. Nothing of the sort happens. In the real world of large-scale employers and unions it is no easy matter to get even money wages down in time of depression. Even when money wages drop, real wages may not if prices fall at the same time. Figure 10.8 shows that this is what did happen during the great depression. In the decline from 1929 to 1933 money wages fell, but the cost of living fell just as fast. As a result, *real* wages in manufacturing remained practically unchanged. Later, during the slow recovery from 1933 to 1939, real wages in manufacturing rose by a third although the lowest annual rate of unemployment during the period was 14% of the civilian labor force. The increase in real wages after 1933 may be partially attributable to government policy and to the rise of unionism, but neither was important in 1929–33. The real wage did not fall in that period in spite of the worst unemployment the country had ever known.

Wage theory makes more sense in explaining long-run tendencies. For instance, why do American workmen earn twice as much as their British counterparts? Certainly it is not a matter of union activity or social legislation. The British have carried these just as far as we have.

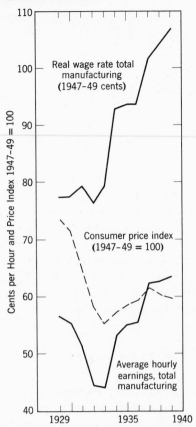

Figure 10.8. Source: *Economic Report of the President*, 1960.

The advantage of American workers is in higher productivity—not that they are intrinsically superior, but they do have more capital per worker, more and often superior natural resources per worker, and usually larger scale methods of production. As a result output per man-hour runs about twice as much in American manufacturing as in English. In some industries such as tin cans, pig iron, radios, and cigarettes it gets up to three and four and almost five times the British levels.*

This is just the answer that theory would have given for the high American wage rates. The left-hand diagram in Figure 10.9 might represent the British labor market and the right-hand one, the American. The high wage here is a matter of the high productivity of our

* Marvin Frankel, "Anglo-American Productivity Differences: Their Magnitude and Some Causes," *American Economic Review Proceedings*, 1955, p. 95. The productivities studied referred to 1947 and 1948 figures.

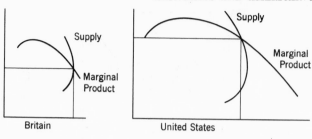

Figure 10.9

labor, which, in turn, is due to the relatively small size of our labor force compared with the land and capital it has to work with.

Altogether there is some tendency for labor markets to perform the way theory would have them do, but it is a long-run tendency and probably an incomplete one. Adjustments of production methods in response to wage changes, movements of labor to more attractive jobs, and changes in wage rates to reflect supply and demand conditions are often impeded in the short run and only have noticeable effects over a period of decades.

UNIONS—STEELWORKERS

The discussion so far has largely ignored the union and is therefore obviously incomplete. The rest of this chapter is devoted to trade unionism in general and to the unions of the iron and steel industry in particular.

Trade unions are almost as diverse in their organization and performance as the industries they organize. They are apt to yield widely different results if they: 1. organize practically all the plants in an industry (steel and automobiles) or only a segment of them (textiles); 2. have tight control over some skilled craft (the building trades) or organize masses of semiskilled workers (meat packing and automobiles); 3. deal with firms in highly concentrated industries (automobiles and steel) or with firms in industries made up of large numbers of small producers (coal mining and apparel), with regulated industries (the railroads), or with government agencies (postal workers); 4. operate primarily on a national basis with nearly uniform organization and conditions across the country (steel) or are primarily local organizations with loose national connections (teamsters and the building trades).

No single union can possibly represent all unionism simultaneously, any more than one industry can be taken to stand for all of private enterprise. Ideally, this book should cover a large number of different unions, but there is room for only one. The steel union has been selected for study because: (1) it now organizes two of the industries discussed in this book, aluminum and steel, and has many features in common with the automobile union as well; (2) it is one of the best known and most widely debated of American unions; and (3) a large number, though not all, of the major issues of unionism have arisen in connection with iron and steel unions at one time or another. Nevertheless, there will be a number of occasions in the next pages when it will be necessary to point out that what is true of the steelworkers is not true of either the teamsters or the carpenters or the textileworkers or some other segment of organized labor.

Craft Unionism in Steel

Most steelworkers, like the great majority of American laborers, went unorganized until the late 1930's. Yet there have been unions in or around steel since its very beginning. In fact, the union preceded the industry. The first union, known as the Sons of Vulcan, was founded in 1858 to organize the iron puddlers, who had a strenuous, glamorous, and highly skilled craft essential to the old wrought iron industry.* The union was small, but the strategic skills of its members made it powerful. It won the country's first nation-wide labor contract of any sort in 1865, and it was able to keep itself intact and to maintain wage scales in subsequent depressions—no mean trick for the unions of that day. In addition to the puddlers, some of the rolling mill workers were organized in the 1860's and 1870's. In 1876 these merged with the Sons of Vulcan to form the Amalgamated Association of Iron and Steel Workers. (It later became the Amalgamated Association of Iron, Steel and Tin Workers. We will just call it the AA.) The merged union ultimately expanded to include most of the skilled trades in the iron mills and was able to organize some of the great new steel mills being built in the 1880's. Between 1876 and 1892 its membership grew very rapidly. By 1892 it could be described by a famous scholar of trade union history writing in 1918 as the "strongest union in the entire history of the American labor movement."†

* This account of iron and steel unions in the nineteenth century is based mainly on John R. Commons and associates *History of Labor in the United States,* Vol. II, Macmillan, 1918, and John A. Fitch, *The Steel Workers,* Charities Publication Committee, 1911.

† Commons, *op. cit.,* pp. 495–496.

The AA was one of the charter members of the American Federation of Labor (AFL) formed in 1886. Like most of the early unions of that organization, the AA consisted mainly of skilled workmen. These were much more easily organized than the unskilled. Their skills made them hard to replace so strikes could not usually be defeated with outside strike-breakers. They were also relatively few in number so concessions were not too expensive to the employer. Since they were typically the better paid, more established workers with a large stake in their jobs, they were more easily convinced of the advantages of organizing and better able to survive long struggles with management. The unskilled, by contrast, came in great numbers and more were arriving from Europe or the farm every day. Except in periods of extreme labor shortage they were in a poor bargaining position because they could easily be replaced.

As one might expect, such craft unions pursued policies in the interests of their constituents. They avoided political activity of the general uplift variety though they would try to influence particular issues that affected them directly. For instance, the AA was a persistent and vigorous advocate of tariffs on iron and steel products. They bargained for wage scales and working conditions for their members rather than for the mass of unskilled workers in the mills. The skilled ironworkers felt they had an interest in long hours since they were paid by the ton. As a result the AA actually opposed a reduction from the 12- to 8-hour day.* The steel industry maintained a 12-hour day and a 7-day week until 1924.†

The old craft unions of the AFL such as the AA have often been criticized for their limited objectives. The goals of enriching the "aristocracy of labor" and of avoiding general social reform do not inspire many idealists. Yet these unions did succeed in establishing a permanent labor movement for the first time in the United States after almost a century of failure by other types of unions.

The Defeat of the Union

Until the 1890's the AA maintained cordial relations with the powerful new steel manufacturers such as Jones & Laughlin and Carnegie, though among Carnegie's major mills only Homestead near Pittsburgh had a continuing union organization. Then in 1892 Carnegie demanded cuts in the Homestead pay scales and threatened to

* Selig Perlman and Philip Taft, *History of Labor in the United States 1896–1932*, Macmillan, 1935, pp. 97–98.

† The workers affected had one day off in two weeks—not all steelworkers had such hours.

deal directly with the men if his requirements were not met. The result was a momentous strike that began with a pitched battle between strikers and Pinkerton men brought in by the company leaving half a dozen dead on either side. It ended five months later with the men returning to the job without a contract. The most powerful union of the day had been no match for the great corporation that was to typify the twentieth century.

Most of the other basic steel companies in the Pittsburgh area followed Carnegie in eliminating the union. It survived in the Chicago area and in some iron and finishing mills but its membership was halved.

When USS was formed in 1901 many of the remaining unionized mills were merged with the Carnegie empire.* With some mills organized and others not, the Corporation would be able to divert orders to nonunion mills in any dispute. Recognizing this threat, the union demanded that contracts be signed for all the unorganized as well as organized mills in three USS subsidiaries devoted to finishing. The company refused and a strike followed in which the union was again defeated. It had to accept a settlement that left fewer unionized mills than before and forbade any further organizing activity. Thereafter USS was free to eliminate the union completely whenever the time seemed ripe, something it did in 1909.

These events set the tone for much of large-scale industry. The great corporations that were developing in the first years of this century could apparently follow an openly antiunion policy with impunity. Such mass production industries as automobiles, tires, electrical equipment, petroleum, and chemicals were generally able to keep the union out until the late 1930's.

There was a major effort to re-establish the union in steel at the end of World War I. The war boom had seen a rapid growth in union activity throughout the country. In addition to expanded craft union membership, the semiskilled workers of the apparel industry and parts of the textile and meat-packing industries had been organized before the war ended. The successful leaders of these campaigns then turned to steel. Twenty-four unions claiming jurisdiction within the steel industry joined in a drive for members in 1918. Some of the unions gave only half-hearted support. The largest financial contributions came from the new Amalgamated Clothing Workers ($100,000) and the International Ladies Garment Workers Union ($60,000). There was much bickering about jurisdiction. In the

---

* Most of this section on the steelworkers in the first three decades of this century is based on Perlman and Taft, *op. cit.*

middle of the drive the leaders of the AA tried to make a separate agreement with USS. Yet in spite of all these difficulties the campaign was a big success. More than 100,000 steelworkers had joined by mid-1919.

The Corporation responded with mass firings which precipitated a nation-wide strike in September 1919, but the industry refused to budge. Strikebreakers were brought in and the mills were reopened. Violence was common—some 20 strikers were killed. The company was able to win public sympathy by capitalizing on the antiradical, antialien feeling rife in the country just after World War I. A large part of the press and the public was convinced that the strike was an attempt of Communists or anarchists or someone to take over our basic industry. Gradually the strike petered out. The organizing committee called a halt in January 1920.

This defeat marked an end to the expansion of unionism. Throughout the country union membership and union power declined during the 1920's. It reached a low in 1933, after four years of depression.

Steel Without Unions

The success of steel in excluding the union over a period of almost half a century rested on two important policies. (1) USS openly employed its great power to prevent organizing activity, and (2) it undertook to improve its employees' conditions without the union.

Along the first line, the Corporation, like many firms of the day, employed a formidable industrial espionage system with spies throughout the mills and the mill towns. Their main function was to discover union activity and to identify union sympathizers or those who led in disputes. The "troublemakers" faced discharge and blacklisting, which meant that other steel makers would not hire them. In the smaller communities the steel companies were often able to capture the local governments and the local press. Labor organizers were repeatedly arrested or beaten. Union meetings were virtually prohibited in some towns. The local police often fought the company battles. In some cases company guards were deputized or the companies supplied arms to the local police.*

* A report of the Interchurch World Movement, Report on The Steel Strike of 1919, Harcourt, Brace, 1920, brought many of these conditions to public attention in the years after the great strike of 1919. In the late 1930's a series of hearings by a Senate Education and Labor Subcommittee (The Lafollette Committee) publicized many similar cases. Hearings on The Violation of Free Speech and The Rights of Labor, 75th and 76th Congresses, 1938–40. They found, for instance, that four steel companies (not USS) had spent $178,139 on tear gas in connection with a single strike in 1937. Republic Steel at that time had ten times as much tear gas as the whole city police of Chicago! Report No. 6, Pt. 3, pp. 57, 65.

At the same time that it was erecting these obstacles to the union, big steel was introducing a wide range of employee benefits. As we shall see, steel wages were generally good. USS introduced overtime pay for work in excess of eight hours during the 1919 organizing drive, and under great public pressure it went from the two-shift, 12-hour day to the three-shift, 8-hour day in 1924. The corporation had introduced a profit-sharing scheme in 1901. It also provided some company-financed pensions, conducted an effective company-wide safety program, and built a number of well-publicized hospitals, housing projects, recreation facilities, and the like. These policies certainly improved the workers' lot, particularly that of older and better established men, just the ones most likely to lead in any organizing movement. It would be unfair to give the exclusion of the union as the only motive for these improvements. In the 1920's in particular, management was taking a new attitude toward employees. Yet one of the most common arguments for the new programs was that they protected the companies against the union.

Keeping the union out did not always mean avoiding labor trouble. From 1901, when it virtually defeated the union, until 1937, when it recognized a new one, USS had to fight three major strikes in 1904, 1909, and 1919. There were a half-dozen other such outbreaks in the remaining steel companies.* Even when strikes could be avoided there was a continuing hostility in the mills as witness the mens' readiness to join unions when the opportunity arose despite grave penalties.

By suppressing the union the companies had taken the power to make decisions unilaterally and without recourse. No matter how well this power was handled, there was bound to be complaint. In real life the arbitrary power was often mishandled, especially at the lower levels where favoritism in layoffs and even shakedowns of the workers by their foremen were to be found. The result was an accumulation of uncorrected grievances.

One approach to this problem was to establish some sort of employees' representation under company control. In steel these programs came to be known as Employee Representative Plans. Elsewhere they were called company unions. Bethlehem initiated such a program in 1918 and was copied by most of the major steel companies in 1933 and 1934. Employees elected representatives who could

* Some important ones were Pressed Steel Car Co., 1909, Bethlehem, 1910, Colorado Fuel and Iron, 1914, Republic, 1916, Weirton, (National), 1933, and Republic, 1935. Some of these involved terrible violence. In the first mentioned, state troopers at one point responded to the killing of one of their comrades by dragging strikers through the streets behind their horses. Perlman and Taft, *op. cit.*, pp. 263–265.

present grievances to management. These representatives had far less bargaining power than independent unions, but the mere possibility of communication was a real improvement.

The Coming of the Union—Legislation

The success of the large employers' antiunion policies finally ended in the 1930's. Big business, the hero of the booming 1920's, became the villain of the depressed 1930's. Great numbers of people who had accepted management's view of the unions previously became favorable to them now.

Government policy changed in response. As late as the 1920's the federal courts had been ready to issue injunctions enforceable by arrest and imprisonment against strikes, picketing, or just organizing activities. Now government policy was reversed. The Norris-LaGuardia Act passed in 1932 declared Congress' intention that a worker should have "full freedom of association, self organization, and designation of representatives of his own choosing to negotiate the terms and conditions of his employment. . . ." The main practical effect of the act was to eliminate the use of federal injunctions in labor disputes. The National Industrial Recovery Act of the next year required that the "codes of fair competition" adopted under it provide for freedom to organize and bargain collectively "without coercion from employers."

Later, when the NIRA was declared unconstitutional in 1935, Congress passed the Wagner Act with much the same labor provisions. Employees were to be free to organize without interference of any sort from the employer. A National Labor Relations Board (NLRB) was established to conduct shop elections to determine the will of the majority of workers as to bargaining representatives. It also had authority to issue orders against "unfair labor practices" by employers such as discrimination against union members in hiring, firing, and promotions, the establishment of company unions, or the refusal to bargain "in good faith" with the designated bargaining agent. This legislation was tested for years in the courts and only became really effective at the end of the 1930's, but it indicated the direction of public policy much earlier.

The Coming of the Union—Organization

The new setting made organization in steel seem practicable once more. The old and feeble AA experienced an upsurge of membership in 1933. The union accepted the new dues but did little more.*

---

* This section on the organization of the United Steel Workers is based mainly on R. R. R. Brooks, *As Steel Goes,* Yale University Press, 1940.

When the new members met separately to plan an active campaign the established leadership simply expelled them. Meanwhile the steel companies were adopting employee representation plans similar to Bethlehem's as token compliance with the NIRA requirements. Many workers who had found the AA useless switched to these company unions as safer and more likely to produce something.

Discontent with the older craft unions was widespread at the time outside the steel industry as well. The cry was for *industrial unions* that would organize all employees in whole plants of the mass production industries, not just specialized skills. The 1934 conventions of the AFL passed a resolution urging organizing drives in steel and similar industries. The next year when little or nothing had been done, the leaders of the existing industrial unions, particularly the United Mine Workers and the two apparel unions, formed a Committee for Industrial Organization (CIO) to take matters into their own hands. The craft union leadership of the AFL responded in August 1936 by expelling the CIO unions, and America had two rival labor movements. The AFL and the CIO were only united in 1955.

The CIO established a Steel Workers' Organizing Committee (SWOC) in June 1936, to which it (mainly the United Mine Workers) contributed $500,000 and a trained organizing staff. The AA was persuaded to affiliate with SWOC when faced with another internal uprising and with the certainty that SWOC would proceed with or without it.

Meanwhile the employee representation plans had shown an increasing degree of independence. Originally set up on a mill by mill basis to discuss local grievances, the representatives had by 1936 formed regional councils and were presenting demands involving wages, hours, and vacations. They were coming very close to collective bargaining. Many of the elected employee representatives were won to the support of SWOC after it came into existence. A SWOC sympathizer was even elected chairman of the USS employee representatives.

This put USS in an uncomfortable position. Repudiation of its employee representation program would be difficult, but dealing with it now was little short of dealing with the union. Moreover, SWOC's recruiting drive made a strike likely, and in the current political climate the Corporation would not have the public support it had in 1919. The permanence of the new climate was demonstrated by the landslide re-election of Roosevelt in 1936, and the likelihood of a successful strike by the victory of the United Auto Workers at GM in February 1937. Late 1936 and early 1937 was a period of rapid economic recovery and after a half decade of losses USS could ill afford a strike. Moreover, the Corporation had a new leadership in the 1930's that was trying to rebuild the ancient edifice. The adamant antiunion stand of Carnegie, Morgan and Gary was one of many old policies that could plausibly be reconsidered in the changed atmosphere of 1937. On March 2, 1937, USS signed a contract with the SWOC.

It was not the Wagner Act itself that wrought this revolution. The act was generally ignored by steelmen at the time. A circuit court had already declared it unconstitutional in a test case involving the discharge by Jones & Laughlin of ten men for union activity. A month after the USS settlement, however, the Supreme Court reversed the lower court and required Jones & Laughlin* to comply with the NLRB's order. After the USS settlement in March, this decision in April, and a brief strike in May, Jones & Laughlin also recognized the union. More than 100 other small steel firms jumped on the band wagon.

However, the union was not able to win immediate recognition from the rest of the major independents—Bethlehem, Republic, Youngstown, Inland, National, and Armco. Although the NLRB now had a right to exist, its powers were not clearly defined. Many of its orders in the steel disputes of 1937 were appealed and wandered through the courts for years. In the meanwhile, these "little steel" companies remained adamant. In May 1937, a strike was called against the most unionized of them—Republic, Inland, and Youngstown. One plant of Bethlehem Steel was also drawn in. The strike was reminiscent of 1919 with attempts to reopen struck mills, resulting violence, and intervention by local police. Eighteen strikers were killed. In the worst case, the famous "Memorial Day Massacre," a group of Chicago police charged an unarmed crowd at a meeting near the Republic Steel plant in South Chicago, killing 10 strikers and wounding 90. The little steel strikes failed at the end of the summer, partly because the country was going into another depression.

The organizing fight then shifted to the NLRB and the courts. By the start of World War II most of the NLRB orders had been upheld in court. The union won NLRB elections throughout the Bethlehem mills by 2 and 3 to 1 majorities in 1940 after which that company plus Republic, Inland, and Youngstown signed. During World War II, the union was even able to win shop elections and recognition in the South.

The war and the decade and a half of prosperity that followed it solidified the union's position in steel as in most of manufacturing

* Jones & Laughlin v. NLRB 301 US 1 (1937).

outside of the South. In the years just after World War II strong antiunion feeling appeared which found expression in the Taft-Hartley Law of 1947, but though the Law imposed important limits on the unions, it left the essential apparatus of the Wagner Act intact. It is conceivable that a major postwar depression might have brought an attempt to eliminate the union once more, but no such depression ever came. By the late 1950's it was plain that the union was permanent.

Steel has one of the bloodiest histories in American industrial relations, but in five major industry-wide strikes since World War II no steel company has attempted to operate a struck mill, and no significant instance of violence has been reported. Steel disputes are no longer wars of survival. Now they are just arguments about the terms of employment.

The United Steel Workers Today

SWOC changed its name to the United Steel Workers of America (USW) in 1942. It now has some 960,000 members, which makes it larger than any other union except the International Association of Machinists (992,689), the United Automobile, Aircraft, and Agricultural Implement Workers (1,027,000), and the International Brotherhood of Teamsters, Chauffeurs, Warehousemen and Helpers (1,418,246).* It represents almost the entire steel industry as well as aluminum, zinc, and many steel fabricators such as railroad cars and tin cans. Among major steel makers, all but one of National Steel's two mills and five of Armco's seven are organized by the USW.† The USW has never been able to win representation election in these mills, but it has still had an important effect upon them. To keep the national union out, National and Armco have consistently maintained wages as good or better than those paid in union mills and have provided grievance procedure as reliable as in organized mills. The workers have the advantages of belonging to the USW without having to strike for them.

The USW is made up of some 2800 local unions,‡ and it in turn is a member of the AFL-CIO. There is usually a separate local for each plant. The locals are governed by officers elected by the general

---

* "A Survey of Membership in American Unions," *Monthly Labor Review*, Jan. 1960, p. 6.

† In addition the steel facilities of some fabricators are organized by other unions, notably the Ford Motor Company, organized by the United Auto Workers.

‡ Bureau of Labor Statistics Bulletin 1222, *Directory of National and International Labor Unions in the United States*, 1957, p. 43.

membership. Their main function is the administration of contracts. The locals would be at an obvious disadvantage in dealing with the multiplant firms of the steel industry, so the lead in contract negotiations and in basic union policy is taken by the international head-quarters* ("international" because it has locals in Canada).

The international officers are elected in a general referendum among all members of the union every four years. There is also a biannual convention to which locals send delegates in proportion to their memberships. The convention must pass on major policy questions. The steelworkers' elections and conventions have yet to produce a shakeup in the leadership of the international. Philip Murray was installed as president by John L. Lewis† with the establishment of SWOC in 1936 and remained in office until his death in 1952. David McDonald, the original secretary-treasurer of SWOC, has been president ever since. Only once (in 1956) has there even been a serious opposition candidate.

Most of the rank and file take little interest in union politics. There is no continuing opposition party for the discontented to turn to. It takes widespread unrest for an opposition to build up, and when it does the incumbents have a definite advantage in their control of the union press.

In general, the USW leadership, like the national leadership of most unions, is in little danger of being removed by the rank and file,‡ just as most modern corporations are managed by men who can seldom be changed by the stockholders. Like most corporate managements, the USW seems to have represented its constituents' interests reasonably well in spite of this. At least its members have supported it in NLRB elections although they always have the alternative of choosing no union at all.

The lack of control over leadership has spawned corruption in some unions, though *not in the USW*. A minority of union leaders elsewhere have used union funds for their own purposes, have extorted money from workers in assigning jobs or from businessmen by threat-

---

* This is not true of all unions. In those dealing with industries that are local in nature, such as printing, construction, and trucking, it is the local or some regional division that does the negotiating. As a result a description of teamster or carpenter policy in one part of the country need not apply elsewhere. On the other hand, official steelworkers' policy is similar in Pennsylvania, Alabama, or California.

† John L. Lewis was president of the United Mine Works until 1959 and Philip Murray was one of his vice presidents until he went to SWOC in 1936.

‡ This is much less so at the local level, especially in smaller locals where the leadership is in close contact with the rank and file.

ening strikes, or have accepted bribes from businessmen in return for not enforcing contracts or for signing substandard ones. Spectacular Senate hearings in 1957 and 1958 produced a large number of cases of this sort in a number of unions, especially the Teamsters. USW appears to be largely free of such practices. Its centralized organization and its position in the public spotlight make the USW less susceptible to such tendencies than some other unions. Such unions as the Teamsters, which are locally organized and deal with many small employers, offer far more likely fields for the use of union power in the interest of union officials. A small trucker may be quite susceptible to extortion by the agent of the relatively inconspicuous local with which he deals, but it is almost inconceivable that a David McDonald would ask for personal favors from USS or that USS would give them.

The USW and SWOC before it were a part of the CIO from 1936 until the merger of CIO and AFL in 1955. The USW has been a member of the AFL-CIO ever since. The affiliation puts very few restrictions on the USW, however. The AFL-CIO is a loose confederation of quite independent unions. Its main functions are to lead in political action, to assist in the organization of nonunion segments of the economy, and to serve generally as a forum of the union movements. It can sometimes affect the policies of member unions by admonition or persuasion, but strong unions like the steelworkers may safely go their own ways if they wish. The worst that the AFL-CIO can do to rebels is expel them, but such unions as the United Mine Workers and the Teamsters have been able to do quite well outside the national federation.*

COLLECTIVE BARGAINING ISSUES

Steel Negotiations

There are hundreds of USW contracts, but the pattern for most of them is set in negotiations with the major steel makers. Each company has its own contract. However, since World War II, major contracts have been negotiated simultaneously and their main features have been almost identical.

* The AFL-CIO attempts to assign jurisdictions to its members, so expulsion might result in other unions being authorized to organize the expelled union's trade. This could be a significant threat for relatively weak unions, but it does not mean much to a strong one. The AFL-CIO expelled the Teamsters on charges of corruption in December 1957, but the union has gone right on expanding. Some have opined that the expulsion hurt AFL-CIO more than it did the Teamsters.

This virtual industry-wide bargaining is understandable. If the union could strike one company at a time it could very likely win more than in dealing with the industry as a whole. Both the union and the companies have an interest in standard contract provisions. The union needs uniformity to avoid internal unrest, while each company wants to be sure that its labor costs are no higher than those of its rivals.

Ordinarily the key contract in the steel industry is that between USW and USS. Table 10.4 presents a chronology of their settlements since World War II. Steel negotiations were regular annual events until 1956.* As a rule they resulted in wage increases, but the pay scale was only one of a great number of subjects discussed. The post-war steel negotiations have run the whole gamut of collective bargaining issues.

Job Classification

One notable accomplishment was the establishment of uniform job classifications in 1947. After two years of negotiations the union and the companies succeeded in working out systematic evaluation and ranking of the complicated assortment of skilled, semiskilled, and nonskilled jobs to be found in the mills. At USS, jobs were broken down into 31 categories separated at that time by equal steps of 3.5¢ per hour.† This classification made it possible for the industry to avoid negotiating each wage separately, something that had previously disrupted the union and collective bargaining regularly. Steel's job classification system has been widely copied.

Fringe Benefits

The great issue of the 1949 dispute was fringe benefits, particularly pensions. The union conducted a six-week strike and went without a wage increase to win pensions for all workers of more than 15 years' service and partially company-financed hospital and life insurance. Each contract negotiated since then has included some improvements in or additions to the fringe benefits available to steelworkers. By

---

* Steel contracts ran for two years in those days, but they always provided for one reopening on questions of wages and sometimes other issues such as pensions.

† The size of the steps has been increased from time to time since then to keep up with the rising basic wage rate. The differential was changed in 1948, 1950, 1952, 1955 and in the automatic increments from 1956 on. By 1960 the increments were 6.9¢ per hour. Whenever the differential changed, most workers wages rose by more than the base rate. The wage increases shown in Table 10.4 are averages which include the effect of these changes in the differential.

TABLE 10.4

USS CONTRACTS AND WAGE SETTLEMENTS
SINCE WORLD WAR II

Date	Strike	Av. Hourly Wage Increase (cents)	Other Major Contract Changes
Feb. 16, 1946	Jan. 14–Feb. 15	18.5	
Feb. 8, 1947		5.2	Job classification
Apr. 1, 1947		15	
July 16, 1948		13	
Nov. 11, 1949	Oct. 1–Nov. 11	....	"Fringe benefits": partially company-financed life and hospital insurance and wholly company-financed pensions to supplement social security
Dec. 1, 1950		16	
July 26, 1952	Apr. 4–Apr. 8, Apr. 29–May 3 and June 2–July 26	16	Modified union shop, six paid holidays
June 12, 1953		8.5	Eliminate North-South wage differential within a year
July 1, 1954		5	
July 1, 1955	July 1 (one day)	15.2	
Aug. 3, 1956	July 1–Aug. 3,	10.5	Three-year contract with: (a) automatic raises of about 8.3¢ each July; (b) cost of living escalator; (c) and supplemental unemployment benefits
Jan. 1, 1957	Automatic increases	3	
July, 1, 1957	and cost of living	12.3	
Jan. 1, 1958	increases under	5	
July 1, 1958	1956 contract	12.3	
Jan. 1, 1959		1	
Jan. 5, 1960	July 15–Nov. 7, 1959	....	Preserve work rules

Source: "Wage Chronologies: United States Steel," *Monthly Labor Reviews.*

1960 they included pensions, insurance, paid vacations, paid holidays, severance pay, jury duty pay, and shift differentials. Back in 1940 fringes came to only 7¢ an hour or 8% of straight time pay. During the second half of 1958 the comparable figures were 73¢ or 26%.*

Compulsory Union Memership

The central issue of the 1952 dispute was the USW demand for a *union shop,* an arrangement by which anyone hired under the contract must join the union within a specified period. The companies had stubbornly opposed the union shop for many years, but in 1952, after eight months of arguing, two months of strike, and much government pressure, they finally agreed to a limited form of it. Newly hired employees had to apply for union membership, but they had the right to cancel their applications within a specified period. Old employees who already belonged had to maintain their membership, but they could withdraw during the last 15 days of the contract. As it worked out, practically no one availed himself of his right to withdraw and these provisions were dropped from later contracts without any real argument.

Few aspects of collective bargaining have aroused such heated debate as compulsory union membership. Of course, much of management opposes it simply because it strengthens the union, but many people who have no direct vested interest still object that the union shop is an invasion of personal rights. They argue that individuals who oppose the union on principle should not be forced to contribute to it. Defenders of the union shop reply that it is no more of an invasion of personal rights than is the collection of taxes from everyone, even pacifists, to pay for defense.

The main case for the union shop is that it protects the union from "free-riders," nonunion employees who enjoy the benefits won by the union but make no contribution to it. By making the union's existence more secure, the union shop is supposed to encourage more statesmanlike union leadership. Without some sort of compulsory membership, it would be quite possible for the management to eliminate the unions by hiring nonunion men in some cases.

In recent years there has been widespread discussion of "right to work" laws which would prohibit all forms of compulsory union membership. Nineteen states had adopted such measures by the end of 1959, but practically all of them were southern or plains states where union members are few. The only major industrial state with a

* Department of Labor, "Background Statistics Bearing on the Steel Dispute," *Monthly Labor Review,* Oct. 1959, p. 1096.

"right to work law" is Indiana. Voters in a number of industrial states have rejected it by wide margins.

The *union shop* should be distinguished from the *closed shop*. Under a closed shop agreement a worker must be a union member *before* he can be hired, while a union shop simply requires that he join once he is on the job. This distinction is much more than mere hairsplitting. The closed shop gives the union the power to say who gets the job. Some unions such as the building and printing trades have combined it with strict admission and apprenticeship rules to severely restrict entry. This combination of closed shop plus closed union may be very convenient for those who are already electricians or typesetters, but it is hard on those of us on the outside. This criticism does not apply to the union shop where the employer may hire his nephews or blue-eyed blondes or anyone else so long as they join the union on time. The closed shop, but not the union shop, was outlawed in the Taft-Hartley Law, but so far the prohibition has had limited effect. Contracts no longer expressly provide for the closed shop, but in many of the old closed shop trades union apprenticeship rules and the practice of hiring through union hiring halls effectively exclude nonunion men. The steelworkers, like most industrial unions, have never sought the closed shop. It has been a feature of the older craft unions primarily.

The North-South Differential

A long-term goal of the USW was the elimination of regional wage differences. Even before 1937 the steel companies paid the same rates in the Pittsburgh, Youngstown, and Chicago areas,* but they paid less in other districts such as the East and especially the South. Under union pressure these differentials were gradually reduced until in 1954 even the southern mills were brought up to northern wage rates.

Some economists have raised doubts about the desirability of this policy of nation-wide wage uniformity. They point out that by raising southern wages the union eliminated any special incentive for the companies to locate new plants in the South. The higher southern wages would protect the jobs of northern steelworkers and would be very nice for the southerners already in the mills, but there might be fewer southerners hoeing corn on the hillside and higher wages in other southern industries if the wage differential had persisted.

* George Seltzer, "Pattern Bargaining and the United Steelworkers," *Journal of Political Economy*, Aug. 1951, p. 322–323.

Escalators and Improvement Factors

Until 1956 the union negotiated about wages every year, but by then many had come to doubt the usefulness of these annual crises. The auto industry had gotten along quite well under long-term contracts since 1948. In 1956 the companies were able to win a three-year contract from the union.

The contract provided for regular wage adjustments to make up for the raises the union had been able to negotiate each year previously. They were of two sorts. The workers were protected against inflation by an "escalator clause" under which wages were adjusted each January and July for any changes in the Cost of Living Index.* In addition there was an annual "improvement factor," an automatic raise that averaged 8.2¢ each July over the life of the contract. This amounted to an increase in real wages of about 3% a year, roughly what the steelworkers had been able to win by annual bargaining in the early 1950's but considerably more than many workers were getting.†

Supplemental Unemployment Benefits

The 1956 contract also introduced a provision for unemployment payments. For years the steelworkers had been demanding a "guaranteed annual wage" (GAW) to protect them against layoffs. The companies were understandably reluctant. In an industry where output could drop by half in a mild recession, an unalterable guarantee of any substantial part of the payroll could be disastrous. If the companies did have such an obligation they might find it worthwhile to substitute machinery and temporary help for the permanent workers to whom the guarantee applied.

What the USW actually got in 1956 was something called "supplemental unemployment benefits" (SUB), which falls far short of a full GAW. It is quite similar to a provision of the United Auto Workers' contracts of the previous year. The steel companies contribute 3¢ to 5¢ per man-hour to a fund which is used to supplement state unemployment insurance benefits during layoffs. Eligibility for SUB depends on the period of previous service. Maximum total benefit from the state and the company together would be 65% of

---

* A ceiling was put on each year's escalator increase in the contract signed in January 1960. More than a year of annual improvements were also passed in those negotiations and the strike that preceded them.

† The improvement factor in the auto workers' contracts came to about 2½% per year.

straight time pay after tax for 52 weeks, but many would be eligible for far less. If the fund runs low, as it did in the 1958 recession, benefits are scaled down. In other words, instead of a greater wage increase, the companies agreed to do some of the saving for their workers. One effect of SUB is to redistribute income within the mills. Men with low seniority who suffer most from layoffs benefit from SUB more than older employees.

Work Rules and "Featherbedding"

In the 1959 negotiations the main issue turned out to be the "work rules," the thousands of local customs governing size of crew, rest periods, pace and method of work, etc. The steel companies complained that they had inadequate control over these matters and were not able to manage their mills efficiently as a result. They charged the unions with "featherbedding," i.e., preserving unnecessary jobs and obstructing the introduction of labor-saving methods.

There are some famous instances of apparent featherbedding to be found in American industry, such as the railroad brotherhoods which have preserved the "firemen" in spite of the shift to diesel locomotives and the building trades which have fought hard to maintain many hand methods. The most obvious cases are usually to be found in craft unions whose members have specific skills to protect from mechanization. Industrial unions ordinarily have much less restrictive rules.

In the case of steel, contracts have provided that established local work rules should remain in force generally, but that the companies may revise them if their "basis" changes. If such revisions are disputed by the union, and if no settlement can be negotiated, the questions go to a neutral arbitrator whose decision is binding on both parties (see p. 477). Arbitrators have ordinarily ruled that the "basis" for a practice has changed if new techniques involving new equipment have been introduced. This means that there is practically no union obstacle to further mechanization ("automation") in steel, something that is far from true in many other industries.*

* This interpretation is based on "Labor," *Fortune,* Dec. 1959, p. 216, and the comments of George W. Taylor, chairman of the steel fact-finding board appointed by President Eisenhower in connection with the 1959 steel strike. Taylor's comments were reported in the *Monthly Labor Review,* Dec. 1959, p. 1330. At one point he told industry representatives: "If it is true, as the testimony before us has indicated, that under 2-B [the work rules section of steel contracts], the companies have had rather wide latitude in introducing technological change and adjusting manpower accordingly, this is a practice which, I assure you, many other industries would give a great deal to have." *Ibid.,* p. 1331.

On the other hand, the arbitrators have not allowed management to reduce crew size, say, simply because it could show that a job could be adequately handled by fewer men. Management could not correct its old mistakes. The adamant stand of the union seems to have been based on a fear that the wholesale change in work rules would put large numbers of its members out of work. When union representatives express this fear they tacitly admit that the steel mills are overstaffed in some instances.

This sort of stand by the union, and the far more restrictive policies of some other unions, makes some sense from the point of view of the workers involved, but it is harmful to the general public. Rising productivity is the main reason for our rising standards of living, and while general unemployment is possible, there are much better methods of dealing with it than keeping us all poor.

On the other hand, particular trades certainly can be hurt by labor-saving changes, especially if demand for the final product is inelastic and growing only slowly, as is true of steel. Attempts of workers in such circumstances to protect their jobs are understandable even if economically undesirable. A much better solution to their problem would be for the employer and the general public, who both stand to gain from the changes, to assist workers who must shift to new jobs. A settlement in the meat-packing industry simultaneously with the steel dispute did just this. Armour & Co. agreed to establish a jointly administered fund to be used to help retrain and transfer workers displaced by mechanization.*

In steel, the final settlement in 1960 left the work rules provision intact but established joint union-management committees to study work rules generally with the implication that some voluntary changes would be made.

Grievance Procedures

All this has had to do with the spectacular national negotiations that set the terms of steel contracts, but the union and management are dealing with each other continuously over local day to day issues that arise under the contract. Who gets disciplined or laid off or promoted and why? Before the union this sort of question was generally left to the foreman who could be completely arbitrary and even corrupt.

From the very first the USW has insisted on a reliable grievance

* Contracts of Armour & Co. with Amalgamated Meat Cutters and Butchers and with United Packinghouse Workers, Aug. 31, 1959, reported in *Monthly Labor Review,* Oct. 1959, p. 1108.

procedure to handle these questions. Today if a steelworker has a complaint he may take it up with his foreman and the shop steward, the union representative on the job. If either side is dissatisfied with the decision, the case may be appealed through several steps in the union and company heirarchy, and if the question is still not settled it is arbitrated. USS and the union maintain a permanent board of arbitration made up of union and company representatives with a chairman acceptable to both sides. Smaller companies may have a single umpire or may simply join the union in selecting arbitrators as cases arise. Both parties agree in advance to live by the decision.

This grievance procedure, which is typical of those found in most collective bargaining contracts today, has removed much of the old arbitrariness. The small and continuous disagreements which could be the basis for accumulated resentment or sporadic strikes are settled peaceably.

STRIKES

In winning its impressive list of gains since World War II, the USW has called its members out on five major industry-wide strikes. These have been much the most noticeable aspect of the union. They have usually aroused considerable criticism from the public at large.

They are an essential feature of the union as we know it, however. The whole point to workers bargaining collectively rather than as individuals is their ability to withhold all labor from a mill, i.e., to strike. Without the right to strike the union might be able to gain some of its ends by influence within the corporation or government, but this would convert it into primarily a political pressure group.

The man in the street often tries to assign the blame for strikes. This is an extremely difficult and usually fruitless project. In a certain sense both sides are always to blame since either could stop the strike immediately by giving in. To go any farther the observer would have to decide who was making the unreasonable demand, something that is very hard to determine in view of the complex issues and the habit of both unions and managements of asking for more than they really expect. Most experts do not even try.

The losses that arise from strikes are often exaggerated. To bargain effectively the union needs the threat of the strike, but it can often avoid actually calling one for years at a time. The left-hand portion of Figure 10.10 shows total man-days lost in all labor-management disputes during the years 1927–59 expressed as percentages of total

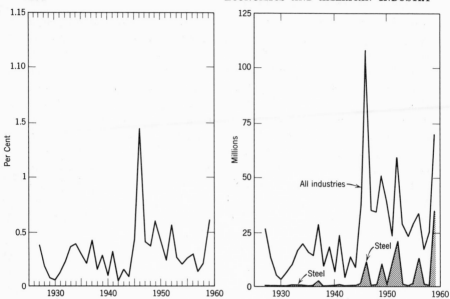

Figure 10.10. Left: Man-days lost in work stoppages as a percentage of total man-hours worked. Right: Total man-days lost in work stoppages (millions). Source: Bureau of Labor Statistics, Report No. 92, "Work Stoppages, Basic Steel Industry," *Historical Statistics of the United States,* and *Monthly Labor Reviews,* 1960. Figures estimated.

work time available in the economy. Only once, in 1946, did strikes take as much as 1% of the total work time. Usually they did not reach even 0.5%. This does not include losses of suppliers or customers of struck plants. On the other hand, it overstates the actual losses of the disputants since much of the time lost during the strike is made up in building inventories in advance and in supplying pent-up demand afterwards.

The strikes that do occur are uncomfortable, but in most of them the discomfort falls mainly upon the disputants. A strike that closes one of the meat packers but leaves the rest operating, or even one that closes every talcum powder plant in the country, is no more than a minor nuisance to the rest of us. We can leave the disputants to wait it out as long as they can stand it.

National Emergency Strikes

Steel strikes are something else again. They are just too big to be ignored. The shaded portions of the right-hand part of Figure 10.10 show the man-day losses directly attributable to steel disputes. They account by themselves for most of the peaks in strike losses since 1947. In addition to taking 500,000 men out on strike directly, steel disputes that last long enough can throw another 500,000 out of work in supply industries such as coal and in steel-using industries such as automobiles. By the end of the 1959 strike every GM assembly line had closed.

No government since the war, whether Democratic or Republican, has been willing to let a major steel strike run its course. The government has directly ordered the suspension of two strikes and its intervention has affected the outcome of all of them.

Seizure

To deal with the 1952 strike President Truman "seized" the steel mills. This had been the main weapon used by the government to deal with the few major strikes of World War II. The courts have repeatedly declared strikes against the government illegal, so seizure amounted to a prohibition of strikes. Seizure was just a formality. The management continued to manage, and profits continued to accrue to the owners. The most the government ever did was to change the terms of employment, and even this was uncommon. In the steel case the companies challenged the President's move, and the Supreme Court ruled that, barring an act of Congress, the President had no power to seize struck industries in peacetime.* The mills were "returned" to the industry and the strike continued.

Taft-Hartley Injunctions

This left the President with only one formal remedy in a national emergency strike, the temporary injunction provided for in the Taft-Hartley Act. It was used to end the 3½-month steel strike of 1959. Under the law the President appointed a "fact-finding board" which held hearings on the strike issues and brought pressure on the companies and the union to settle, but under the law it could make no recommendations. After the board reported no settlement, the Attorney General secured an injunction from a federal court prohibiting the strike for 80 days. The steelworkers appealed the order, but the Supreme Court upheld it, ruling that the procedure was constitutional and could properly be applied in this case.† Work resumed immediately. The last step in the Taft-Hartley procedure was to be a

---

* Youngstown Sheet and Tube v. Sawyer 343 US 582 (1952).

† United Steelworkers v. U. S. 4 L. Ed 2nd, 12 (1959).

polling of the membership on the managements' last offer by the NLRB. All indications were that the offer would be rejected by a wide margin and that the strike would resume. Shortly before the date of the vote the companies were persuaded by informal government pressure to give up their position on the work rules issue, and the dispute was settled.

This procedure has been the subject of much debate. The unions, harking back to the injunctions of the 1920's, see it as a "union-busting" procedure. In fact, it has been used quite sparingly. The steel injunction was only the seventeenth issued in 13 years under the act. No union has yet come close to being "busted" by one. On the other hand, it offers only a temporary solution to serious disputes. If the union and management have taken rigid and inconsistent positions, as in the 1959 work rules dispute, the procedure by itself can only postpone the evil day.

Informal Intervention

The ultimate solution to every major steel strike since the war has involved government intervention to affect the terms of settlement. In 1945–46, 1949, and 1952 the President or some government agency made public recommendations which the union then adopted as its final position. Although a strike followed in each case, the final settlements corresponded closely to the recommendations. Price controls were in effect in 1946 and again in 1952, and in both instances settlements were only reached when price control authorities agreed to change ceiling prices for steel. These changes contributed to the breakdown of controls both times. The 1949 dispute occurred during a recession so that the union was in a weak position. Many feel that it would not have won as much without the government's recommendation.

The Eisenhower administration professed a policy of preserving "real" collective bargaining free of government control. It avoided making public recommendations of settlement terms, but it was unable to avoid intervention in the steel strikes of 1956 and 1959. In 1956 the press reported that the end of the five-week election year strike was brought about by the intervention with the steel companies of George Humphrey, then Secretary of the Treasury and formerly president of National Steel. In 1959 it was Vice President Nixon and Secretary of Labor Mitchell who finally convinced the industry representatives to accept the union's position on work rules rather than let the strike begin again. 1960 was another election year and the steel settlement was obviously important to Republican prospects.

A number of economists in reviewing government intervention in steel disputes have concluded that, while it has not succeeded in avoiding strikes, it has typically resulted in more generous settlements than might have been expected with free collective bargaining.*

Compulsory Arbitration

This heterogeneous collection of incomplete *ad hoc* remedies regularly elicits demands for more dependable means of dealing with national emergency strikes. The most common proposal has been for some sort of compulsory arbitration. This is much more popular with the general public than with management, the unions, or industrial relations experts, however.

For one thing, it would almost certainly mean government determination of wages and working conditions in key industries since one or another of the disputants would be unwilling to compromise if he thought he could do better in arbitration than in bargaining. Steel unions and quite possibly the industry would receive a sort of public utility status with all the attendant problems of regulation.

Enforcement of the strike prohibition that would accompany compulsory arbitration would present another problem. During World War II the steel union, like most American labor, observed a no strike pledge, but this was a matter of wartime patriotism and would be hard to duplicate in peacetime. With our present attitudes an offending union could be fined and its leaders could perhaps be punished, but it is doubtful if the public would be willing to break unions or imprison workers to prevent strikes.

There are all sorts of other suggestions for dealing with national emergency strikes. Under one plan unsettled disputes would result not in strikes but in penalty taxes on both parties. Workers would receive take-home pay that barely exceeded unemployment benefits and management would pay such heavy taxes that the company would have net losses comparable to those in a real strike, but output would continue.

Most industrial relations experts do not take this and similar suggestions very seriously. Realistically, the country will probably continue to deal with periodic emergencies in steel and other essential industries as they arise with an assortment of stopgap remedies.

* Frederick H. Harbison and Robert C. Spencer, "The Politics of Collective Bargaining: The Post-War Record in Steel," *American Political Science Review,* Sept. 1954, p. 717, and Otto Eckstein and Gary Fromm, "Steel and the Post War Inflation," a paper prepared for the Joint Economic Committee, 86th Congress, 1st Session, 1959, p. 19.

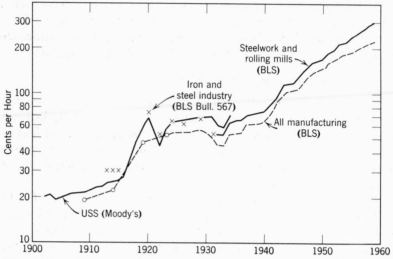

Figure 10.11.   Average hourly earnings, steel and all manufacturing.
Source: USS data from *Moody's Industrial Manuals.*
Bureau of Labor Statistics data from *Historical Statistics of the United States,*
Bulletin 567, *Wages and Hours of Labor in the Iron and Steel Industry,* 1931, and
Monthly Labor Reviews.

PERFORMANCE

Steel Wages

What have the steelworkers been able to accomplish with their
union? The answer is not as obvious as it may seem. Figure 10.11
compares average hourly earnings in steel and in all manufacturing
over the years. Steel wages are certainly higher than average, but
they always were. Again, steelworkers have been able to make spectacular gains since they were organized in 1937, but so has everybody
else.

Figures 10.12 shows steel earnings as a percentage of average hourly
earnings in all manufacturing. Steelworkers had generally earned
about 20% more than the average worker in manufacturing in the
1920's and the 1930's before the union. When SWOC was formed in
1936 the steelworkers' wage advantage increased sharply, first as the
companies tried to head off the union and then as the union made
demands to prove its worth. At the peak in 1939 the steelworkers
were able to push their average hourly earnings to about a third
more than the average of all manufacturing. The union seems to

have increased their wage rate advantage by roughly 10%. Other workers caught up during World War II, however, and it was only in the late 1950's that the steelworkers were able to regain the advantage they had held in 1939.

Of course, much of the rest of "all manufacturing" is also organized today. There have been a number of studies of the impact of unions in various industries comparing union and nonunion wages or noting the changes that have occurred with organization. One well-known economist reviewed these studies and made the following summary:

Let me attempt a rough guess, on the basis of our sketchy present knowledge, of the effects on wages of American unions during periods of relative prosperity and price stability. The United States membership of unions in 1956 was about 17.5 million, about one third of wage and salary employment excluding agriculture and domestic service. Of these members, perhaps one-fourth are in unions that have raised wages by 10–20 per cent. This group probably includes the skilled building trades and printing trades, the operating railroad brotherhoods, the coal-miners, the maritime unions, some of the teamsters, and various smaller craft unions. Perhaps half of the total number of union members are in unions that may have raised earnings by 5 to 10 per cent. Included here are the unions in durable goods manufacturing, some unions in non-durable manufacturing and communications, and the transportation workers and unskilled construction workers excluded from the first group. Finally, the remaining fourth are in unions with little or no influence, largely because they do not fully control their jurisdictions. Included in this group are the members of retail and white-collar unions, of the unions in the

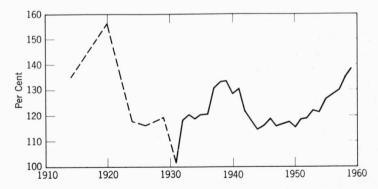

Figure 10.12. Average hourly earnings in steel as a percentage of all manufacturing.

Note: The figure for 1920 is approximate—based on 1920 figure for steel but 1919 figure for all manufacturing.

Source: *Historical Statistics of the United States, Statistical Abstracts,* and *Monthly Labor Reviews.*

shoe and textile industries, and of unions in the apparel industry. This group also includes members of government workers' unions, which do not really engage in collective bargaining over wages.*

If this is correct, the unions' effect on wages has been quite limited. Five, 10, and even 20% increases are not very large compared with the 100% increase in the average hourly earnings of manufacturing workers between 1936 and 1960. No union seems to account for more than a small part of wage increases of its members since the organizing drives of the late 1930's.

The over-all gain of labor in this period is no clearer. If the reader will refer back to Figure 10.1, he will find that the share of wages and salaries in the total national income has been remarkably stable over the years. Its slight increase over the period shown can be partly explained by the decline in the proportion of the labor force that is self-employed, particularly the decline in the number of farmers. If any of labor's gain was the result of the unions that appeared in the 1930's, it was pretty clearly not at the expense of profits. Their share was increasing too!

The relatively slight effect of organizing a third of the employees in the country is understandable. A small group could quite conceivably help itself to a larger proportion of the national income at the expense of the rest of us, but "labor," which already earned two-thirds of the total before the union came, can hardly hope to increase its share by much when it organizes. The way to get a bigger slice for the workers generally is to have a bigger pie.

Social and Political Gains

The noneconomic accomplishments of the USW and of unionism generally are much more impressive. One of USW's clearest gains is the grievance procedure. The worker undoubtedly improved his position when he won a means of appealing arbitrary decisions by the boss. The law of the steel mill is far less capricious than it was 30 years ago.

Many would count the political impact of the union as a gain also. There is little doubt but what the big political prizes usually go to the well-organized groups. Some economic groups, including business and the farmers, have had large and politically effective organizations for years, but until the appearance of the union the urban working class was largely unrepresented. Many argue that the development of the unions has brought our government closer to effective democracy by giving real representation to a large, inarticulate group.

* Albert Rees, "Do Unions Cause Inflation?" *The Journal of Law and Economics* Oct. 1959, p. 86.

This is primarily an accomplishment of the broad-based industrial unions such as the USW. They have been considerably more active than the older craft unions were in endorsing broad reform legislation that benefited the working class generally. Even today, however, American unions are politically less active and certainly less radical than their European counterparts. There is no American Labor Party like the labor or socialist parties of many European countries.

Steelworkers and Inflation

The steel union affects many other people beside the steelworkers. The main concern of critics is that it may contribute to inflation or to the extent of monopoly.

It has seemed obvious to many laymen that the USW's wage demands have led to rising prices. Economists have been much less certain about this. It is true that steel prices usually went up when steel wages did, but it has not always been clear that both would not have risen even without the union.

The worst inflation in recent years was associated with World War II. Table 10.5 shows the percentage increase in wages from the start of the war in 1939 to the peak of the inflation in 1948 in steel and in 12 industries where the union was weak. They all rose, but the increase in steel was relatively modest. A majority of the nonunion industries experienced greater wage increases than steel, and none showed increases that were much less than steel's. This helps to explain the decline in the steelworkers' wage advantage over other industries in the 1940's. By contract, from 1914 to 1920 steel wages had risen 10% *faster* than in manufacturing generally, although there was no steel union to speak of.* It is still possible that the steel union contributed to the post-World War II inflation, even though steel wages rose relatively moderately then. Perhaps the labor shortage was greater in the nonunion lines and in the World War I steel industry than in steel during the World War II period.† Maybe steel wages would have lagged even more without the union. However, it is very difficult to argue that the USW led the way up, as the man in the street seemed to think at the time. It is even possible that the union had a restraining influence! Some have argued that employers without unions might be willing to raise wages temporarily

---

* Rees, *ibid.*, p. 308. The organizing drive of 1919 had occurred during this period, but it had been defeated in late 1919. The steel wage increases went on until late in 1920.

† There is some evidence to support both points. See Lloyd Ulman, "The Union and Wages in Basic Steel: A Comment," *American Economic Review,* June 1958, p. 408.

during a labor shortage, but steel companies would be more reluctant because they know that any increases they grant are apt to be permanent.

The role of the union may be very different in the creeping type of inflation that occurred in 1953–58. Very few commodities were then in short supply. In fact, there was overcapacity and unemployment

TABLE 10.5

DEGREE OF UNIONIZATION AND PERCENTAGE CHANGE
IN HOURLY EARNINGS, STEEL AND 12 OTHER
INDUSTRIES, 1939–48

Industry	Percentage Unionized 1946	Percentage Increase in Average Hourly Earnings 1939–48
Basic steel	80 to 100	99
Crude petroleum	20 to 39	96
Nonmetallic mining	20 to 39	133
Cotton textiles	20 to 39	189
Silk and rayon textiles	20 to 39	181
Confectionery	30 to 39	121
Nonalcoholic beverages	20 to 39	193
Butter	20 to 39	123
Ice cream	20 to 39	87
Power laundries	20 to 39	99
Cleaning and dyeing	20 to 39	97
Wholesale trade	1 to 19	93
Retail trade	1 to 19	103

Note: The 12 industries other than steel were all of the industries of less than 40% unionization in 1946 for which information was available. Information on unionization for butter and ice cream referred to "dairy products" and that for wholesale trade and retail trade referred to "wholesale and retail trade."

Source: Albert Rees, "Wage Determination in the Steel Industry," *American Economic Review*, June 1951, p. 309.

in many industries. Yet the price level rose persistently if slowly, and it practically never declined.

During this period steel wages did lead the way. Table 10.6 shows how steel wage increases have compared with those industries from Table 10.5 for which information was available for 1953–58. Most of them were still nonunion. The greater gain of the USW in this period was *not* due to a shortage of steelworkers. The steel industry has not increased the number of production workers even in peak years over the 1952 levels,* nor have steel-producing centers been areas of labor shortage.†

Price increases could still have been avoided if output per man-hour had risen as fast as wages. Then labor cost per ton of steel would not have increased. There was some increase in productivity in steel, but not enough to offset the rising wages. As a result, labor cost per ton of steel has been creeping up almost continuously. The steel companies maintained their profits during the period, so the wage increases have been passed on as higher prices.‡

TABLE 10.6

Industry	Percentage Increase in Average Hourly Earnings 1953–58
Basic steel	33
Petroleum and natural gas	22
Nonmetallic mining and quarrying	22
Broad woven fabric mills	12
Confectionery and related products	23
Dairy products	17
Laundries	15
Cleaning	16
Wholesale trade	23
Retail trade	21
All manufacturing	20

Source: *Monthly Labor Review*, 1953 and 1958.

Altogether, there were many factors contributing to both the galloping inflation at the end of World War II and to the creeping inflation in the prosperous years that followed the Korean War. The steel

* James P. Mitchell, "Background Statistics Bearing on the Steel Dispute," *Monthly Labor Review*, Oct. 1959, p. 1093.

† Eckstein and Fromm, *op. cit.*, p. 18.

‡ See Chapter 7, p. 310. Steel prices have risen at about the same rate as steel wages since 1947–49, which means they have risen considerably faster than unit labor costs. However, going back to pre-World War II, steel prices and unit labor costs have risen at just about the same rates. The pattern of both steel prices and steel wages contrasts remarkably with the 1920's, a period of stable wages and falling prices.

union's role in the galloping inflation was a mild one or perhaps even a negative one, in spite of what the general public thought at the time. It seems more probable that the union played a role in the creeping inflation. This conclusion should be put into perspective, however. Everyone is agreed that galloping inflations can be ruinously disruptive. Creeping inflation is clearly far less of a problem.

The Union and Monopoly—Labor Markets

From time to time the newspapers and congressmen have been exercised about the "labor monopoly" of the USW and of other powerful unions. There is quite a bit of confusion about what this means, but in some respects it may be a legitimate concern.

The USW and other strong unions are certainly monopolistic combinations in labor markets. The workers of the steel industry price their services collectively in hopes of improving the terms on which they sell. If they were selling cheese or toothpicks on this basis, we would call their organization a cartel.

This need not cause great alarm, however. The market for steel labor without the union would hardly be purely competitive. Wages and working conditions were not determined by supply and demand before 1936, they were determined by USS. In 1937 the Corporation had 261,000 employees. In many communities it was the only signficant employer. When there were other mills in town they ordinarily hired on the same terms as USS. There was a wage pattern in the industry before the union, with USS leading on wages and working conditions as it did on price.*

Local markets for steel labor before the union might be called *monopsonistic* (one buyer) or *oligopsonistic* (a few buyers). Installing a monopolistic agreement (the union) on the opposite side of this market was a far cry from installing one in an otherwise competitive situation. The steelworkers were not in much danger of exploiting the big steel companies. In fact, if the steel companies had been using their powerful hiring position to depress wages, the union might bring the terms of employment closer to those that would prevail in a perfectly competitive labor market. The increase in wage rates under such circumstances might well be accomplished without any loss in employment if the employer had previously been restricting employment to keep wages down.

It is not clear that the steel companies were forcing wages down by exerting their monopsonistic power before the union came. Other

---

* USS led in 11 of 14 wage changes from 1913 to 1932. Seltzer, *op. cit.*, p. 322.

roads to profits were far more socially acceptable than taking them at the expense of the workers, and big steel was famous for its concern about public opinion. At any rate, as we have seen, steel wages were well above those in most manufacturing before the union was organized. If the steel companies can be accused of direct economic exploitation of their employees, it was in the continuation of the 12-hour day well into the twentieth century. The union did not actually bargain this away, but the organizing drive of 1919 was certainly an element in its elimination.

Clearer cases of exploitation are apt to occur where the product market on which the employers sell is competitive. Such employers must take every advantage they can, just to break even in the long run, and those located in isolated labor market may find that one of their "advantages" is the ability to hire and retain labor at substandard wages. This is more likely to be the preunion story of a coal mine in an isolated West Virginia valley than of a steel mill.

The Union and Monopoly—Product Markets

In addition to exercising monopoly power on labor markets, which is the whole point of the union, the USW may be able to exploit the steel companies' monopolistic position in product markets. This would be true if the steelworkers actually have been able to push prices up more than would have happened in their absence, something which may well have occurred during the late 1950's.

It is quite possible that the union might press steel prices up to levels that the steel companies by themselves would not have chosen if labor costs had not risen. For one thing, the union represents only workers who are already inside. If higher steel wages and prices limit employment opportunities for new men, the present members of the union are not likely to complain. USS is concerned to keep growing, but the USS locals of USW may not be. Again, USS must face the possibility of new producers if it sets prices too high, but the USW has far less to worry about on the entry score. If steel prices go up owing to union pressure, the threat of entry will probably not be increased. Any new steel company will almost certainly be organized by the same union and pay the same wages.

The possibility that the union may exploit the companies' monopoly power should again be taken in perspective. Remember that so far the steel union seems to have been able to increase its advantage over the average level of manufacturing wages by about 10% compared with nonunion days, and even this has occurred in only a few years.

The monopolistic effect of unions on product markets differs with the industry. In some fields, such as coal mining and contract construction, the union is in a position to raise wages and hence prices to levels that the producers could not attain by themselves because of their large numbers and free entry. The employers may well benefit from the union in such industries if it can eliminate any cost advantages of small producers in isolated labor markets or in low-wage sections of the country. Management in the larger firms in such industries has sometimes welcomed the union as a "stabilizing" influence. In slack periods the United Mine Workers have insisted on a short work week which not only passed around the unemployment but also served to restrict coal output and stabilize coal prices, something that the mines by themselves could not have done. Similarly, some of the building trades unions have insisted on materials produced by shops organized by the same unions, thus limiting competition at the supplier level.*

By contrast, the textile, apparel, and retail clerks' unions have little or no monopoly power because they organize only a segment of extremely competitive industries. Any gains that exceed those that would occur without the union are apt to drive the organized employers out of business in the long run.

Unions and Income Distribution

In the eyes of much of the public, the saving grace of unions is their effect on income distribution. It is widely supposed that unions result in greater equality, mainly because of increased wages.

Again economists are uncertain. If the union made its gains at the expense of profits, increased equality would be likely, because a large proportion of corporate profits do go to the top income groups. However, steel profits do not seem to have suffered much because of the union.† The gains of the USW seem to have been at the expense of other income earners in large part.

It can be argued that an important group of losers were nonunion laborers. Higher steel wages would tend to reduce employment opportunities in steel. The workers kept out would have to find jobs

---

* The courts have decided that such action by a union is illegal under the antitrust laws if it involves conspiracy with the employers [Allen Bradley Co. v. Local Union No. 3, International Brotherhood of Electrcal Workers, 325 US 797 (1945)] but not if it is taken by the union acting independently in its own interests [US v. Hutcheson, 312 US 219 (1941)].

† See Chapter 7, p. 313. Of course, steel profits might have been higher after 1937 if the union had never been organized, but at least steel profits are no worse because of the union.

in the nonunion lines of work. A large part of the real poverty in America is to be found in these nonunion fields. Table 10.7 shows the percentage of families that earned less than $2500 in 1957 within the broad industry classifications in our economy. More than half the farmers and a third of the service workers were this poor, but only a few of the families connected with the highly unionized mining, manufacturing, transportation, and construction industries were. If union members did gain by keeping nonunion workers out, they may actually have made the poor poorer!

TABLE 10.7

FREQUENCY OF LOW-INCOME FAMILIES BY INDUSTRY
OF FAMILY HEAD, 1957

Industry Classifications	Per Cent
Agriculture and farm labor	52
Personal and domestic service	34
Business and repair service	14
Retail trade	13
Construction	12
Professional	11
Wholesale trade	8
Finance	8
Transportation	7
Mining	5
Manufacturing	5
Government	4
All employed civilians	13

Source: Robert J. Lampman, "The Low Income Population and Economic Growth," a paper prepared for the Joint Economic Committee, 86th Congress, 1st Session, 1959, p. 23.

As we have seen, it is questionable how much unions have gained in higher wages. As a result, the adverse distribution effect of the union is probably not very great.

All this has referred to the direct effect of union wage demands. The union may have a greater political effect in the opposite direction. The apparently increasing equality of income in the United States in recent years has been widely attributed to the maintenance of full employment, to the improved incomes of farmers, to the improved opportunities of Negroes, to increased educational opportunities throughout the country, and to the progressive income tax. Most of these have been at least partly the result of government action, and the unions have been among the leading groups in society pressing for just these actions.

SUMMARY

In theory the general wage level is determined by the interaction of the demand for labor, which depends on its marginal product, and of the supply of labor, which depends on the size and makeup of the population. Wages in individual trades or regions might be above or below the average because of differences in the attractiveness of jobs, differences in individual abilities, or because of artificial barriers to movement between jobs. Profit-maximizing firms in competitive labor markets would employ each type of labor to the point where its marginal revenue product just equaled its wage.

In practice labor markets work far from perfectly. Wages respond to supply and demand only in the long run; labor is often very immobile; and business firms may fall considerably short of profit maximization. There are probable tendencies in the direction indicated by theory but they are certainly incomplete.

The union only became an important factor in mass production labor markets such as steel in the 1930's. Before that the unions had been largely limited to skilled craftsmen and had been no match for great corporations such as USS. The steel union was finally successful in 1937 after a major change in the political climate and a shift from craft to industrial unions.

Strikes, or at least the threat of strikes, are an essential feature of the union as we know it. Steel strikes are no longer the bloody battles they were so long as the union's existence was at stake. The issues today are the terms of the contract, not whether there should be one. The social cost of strikes in most industries is very slight, but in a few cases, including steel, strikes can become national emergencies. As a result, the government has intervened in all important postwar steel strikes. Usually this led to government proposals of terms considered generous to the union. They were ultimately accepted though often only after the strike which the government had sought to prevent.

Since they have been organized, the steelworkers have been able to win a fourfold increase in wages, as well as pensions and other fringe benefits, the union shop, supplemental unemployment benefits, and long-term contracts with automatic wage increases and a cost of living escalator. Many of these gains were highly controversial when introduced but are widely accepted now.

When compared with other industries, however, the gains of the steelworkers seem more modest. The greater part of their improvements are simply the steelworkers participating in the general rise in the national income. This comment is even more true of many other less powerful unions. The clearest accomplishments of the union have been in providing a grievance procedure and in giving the urban working class a political voice.

It may be just as well that the union's power to win economic gains is so doubtful.

If the union did have a drastic effect on its members' wages, it might contribute more to such problems as inflation, monopoly in product markets, and income inequality than it actually does.

FURTHER READINGS

The economics of labor is another major field within economics. Two excellent texts in the field are Melvin Reder, *Labor in a Growing Economy*, Wiley, 1957, and Lloyd Reynolds, *Labor Economics and Labor Relations*, Prentice-Hall, 1959.

An authoritative source on the distribution of income in the United States is Herman Miller, *Income of the American People*, Wiley, 1955. The apparent increased equality in income was noted in Simon Kuznetz's *Shares of Upper Income Groups in Income and Savings*, National Bureau of Economic Research, 1953. For extensive comments on this and other studies of income distribution, see discussions by Selma Goldsmith and Robert J. Lampman in the 1957 *Proceedings of the American Economic Association*, pp. 504–528.

The classic statement of wage theory appeared in J. R. Hicks, *Theory of Wages*, Peter Smith, 1932. There have been a host of studies trying to evaluate it in practice. An excellent summary and bibliography is to be found in Melvin Reder, "Wage Determination in Theory and Practice," Chapter III of Neil W. Chamberlain, Frank C. Pierson, and Theresa Wolfson, eds., *A Decade of Industrial Relations Research 1946–1956*, Harper, 1958. George H. Hildebrand, "The Economic Effects of Unionism," Chapter IV of the same volume, contains a survey of studies of the effect of unions on income distribution and price levels.

The classic source on the early history of trade unionism is the four-volume work by John R. Commons and associates, *History of Labor in the United States*, Macmillan, reprinted in 1951. A shorter sketch of the same material is Selig Perlman, *A History of Trade Unionism in the United States*, Macmillan, 1932, reprinted by Augustus Kelly, 1950. The organization of steel is described in R. R. R. Brooks, *As Steel Goes,* Yale University Press, 1940. The union's own history is Vincent D. Sweeney's *The United Steel Workers of America—Twenty Years Later, 1936–1956.*

There have been a number of studies of various aspects of the steel union's effect since World War II. Robert Tilove, *Collective Bargaining in the Steel Industry,* University of Pennsylvania Press, 1948, and George Seltzer, "Pattern Bargaining and the United Steelworkers," *Journal of Political Economy,* Aug. 1951, p. 319, cover industry-wide bargaining and its effect. Frederick H. Harbison and Robert C. Spencer, "The Politics of Collective Bargaining: The Post-War Record in Steel," *American Political Science Review,* Sept. 1954, p. 705, discusses the government's handling of steel strike emergencies. Albert Rees, "Post War Wage Determination in the Basic Steal Industry," *American Economic Review,* June 1951, p. 389, Lloyd Ulman, "The Union and Wages in Basic Steel: A Comment," and Albert Rees, "Reply," both in *American Economic Review,* June 1958, discuss the possible inflationary effect of the USW. Otto Eckstein and Gary Fromm, "Steel and the Post War Inflation," Joint Economic Committee, 86th Congress, 1st Session, 1959, cover the creeping inflation of the late 1950's. Jack Steiber, *The Steel Industry Wage Structure,* Harvard University Press, 1959, covers such subjects as job classification and grievance procedure in the industry.

11

CONCLUSIONS—
THE STRUCTURE AND
PERFORMANCE OF
AMERICAN INDUSTRY

This book has been able to cover seven industries; there are hundreds left to go. Much of the analysis and some of the conclusions which have been presented can be extended to other industries, but this should be done with great care. Every case will have its own unique features and yield its own answers. This book cannot begin to cover all of the important industries,* but it is possible to test the appropriateness of some of the conclusions of the last ten chapters in broad segments of our economy. Most of this chapter is devoted to such a project.†

---

* Those who wish to read up on some of the other industries which have been studied, and only a handful have been, will find Walter Adams, *Structure of American Industry*, Macmillan, 1961, to be a useful book. It contains descriptions of the coal, construction, chemicals, petroleum, cigarette, motion picture, tin can, airline, and newspaper industries as well as four that were covered in this book.

† The approach and conclusions of this chapter are quite similar in many respects to J. S. Bain's *Industrial Organization*, Wiley, 1959. It depends heavily upon that book.

CONCENTRATION

Concentration Ratios

The main question of this book has been what differences the various types of market structure have made in the ways that industries perform. There are many elements in market structure: how concentrated is production or sales; how easy is entry; what sort of product is involved; and who are the customers? All of these are important, but the main emphasis here will be on concentration largely because the statistics are widely available.

The most commonly used measure of concentration is the concentration ratio—the share of total shipments controlled by the four largest firms in the industry. Concentration ratios are available for all manufacturing though not for most other fields of enterprise. Concentration ratios are usually calculated for fairly carefully defined products such as "cotton broad woven fabrics" or "primary aluminum," while many of the measures of industry performance such as profits, wage rates, and advertising expenditure are regularly available only for broad industry groups such as "textile mill products" (which include cotton, synthetic, wool woven and knit goods) or "primary metals" (which include aluminum, steel, and various other metals). In order to make comparisons possible it has been necessary to use weighted averages of concentration ratios within the broad industry groups. These averages are shown in Table 11.1.

These average concentration ratios are, of course, only rough indicators of the structures of the industry groups involved.* Those with low averages such as textile mill products (average concentration ratio of 25) usually include at least a few products with high concentration such as hard surface floor coverings (concentration ratio of 84). Similarly, highly concentrated industry groups such as transportation equipment (average concentration ratio of 69) often contain unconcentrated segments such as boat building and repair (concentration ratio of 18).

* In one case, "products of petroleum and coal (except petroleum refining)," the average concentration ratio in Table 11.1 is positively misleading, though the fault lies in the underlying figures from which the average was derived. The leading product in this small subgroup is coke. Coke production is quite concentrated because all the major steel producers make their own. Most of this coke is not sold on the market place, however, and the profits, wages, and advertising expenditures of the steel companies appear under primary metals. The remaining coke producers are mostly connected with the bituminous coal industry where concentration is extremely low. Because this subgroup is so misleading it will be left out of subsequent analyses. At any rate, it is much smaller than the others shown in Table 11.1.

In a few cases the figures in Table 11.1 overstate the degree of concentration within industry groups. This is true where imports are significant because foreign supplies are not covered. The paper and nonferrous metals groups were the only ones where imports amounted to as much as 10% of total shipments in the year covered. Concentration ratios would also overstate the power of large firms if the different products definied by the Census are close substitutes. For instance, high concentration in beet sugar is less significant than it might appear because the average consumer cannot tell beet sugar and cane sugar apart. The clearest cases of close interproduct competition are within textile mill products and apparel products.

The opposite sin of lumping together noncompeting products is far more common. For instance, the product group "footwear, except rubber" includes men's and women's shoes, though competition between the two is hardly severe. Similarly, "periodicals" combines *The Ladies' Home Journal*, *The American Economic Review*, and comic books, while "pharmaceutical preparations" includes antibiotics, vitamins, laxatives, and veterinary medicines. Unless the leading laxative producers also dominate horse medicine production and by the same extent, the concentration ratio for pharmaceuticals will understate the degree of concentration.* Concentration ratios also understate the power of large firms when the products involved are sold on regional rather than national markets. In industry groups such as lumber, primary metals, stone clay and glass, petroleum refining, and some foods, it is the size of the four largest firms in the Middle Atlantic or the Midwest or the Pacific Coast states that really counts rather than in the country as a whole.

There is probably some understatement and some overstatement in most industry groups. Although the two tendencies will cancel each other out to some extent, the net effect is probably to understate concentration except in three or four of our least concentrated industries. With these reservations, we will have to make do with the existing figures for lack of anything better.

Concentration and Performance

What difference does it make that automobiles and tobacco products are produced in concentrated industries and textiles and apparel are not? A variety of answers have been suggested. High concentration. has been criticized because (1) it may lead to a misallocation of our

* The figures in Table 11.1 avoid this problem to some extent in the cases of refrigeration equipment, radios and related products, steel, motor vehicles, and a few other products by using more refined product definitions in finding averages.

TABLE 11.1

AVERAGE CONCENTRATION RATIOS IN 20 INDUSTRY GROUPS
AND 9 SUBGROUPS, 1954

Industry Group		Average Percentage of Shipments by Four Largest Firms in Each of Component Industries
Food and kindred products		34
Beverages	30	
Foods	34	
Tobacco manufactures		76
Textile mill products		25
Apparel and other fabricated textile products		14
Lumber and wood products		10
Furniture and fixtures		18
Paper and allied products		22
Printing and publishing industries		17
Printing and publishing (except newspapers)	16	
Chemicals and allied products		43
Petroleum and coal products		35
Petroleum refining	32	
Products of petroleum and coal (except petroleum refining)	47	
Rubber products		55
Leather and leather products		26
Stone, clay, and glass products		45
Primary metal industries		57
Primary iron and steel industries	55	
Primary nonferrous metal industries	62	
Fabricated metal products		27
Machinery (except electric)		33
Electric machinery		48
Transportation equipment		69
Transportation equipment (except motor vehicles)	48	
Motor vehicles	95	
Instruments and related products		43
Miscellaneous manufactures		21

Note: The figures given here are the weighted averages of the four largest firms' shares of total product shipments in the Census product class groups that make up the various industrial groupings. (Census product class groups correspond to four-digit industries and industrial groupings correspond to two-digit industries. See footnote on pp. 24-25 of Chapter 1.)

In nine cases where concentration ratios for the (four-digit) Census product class groups were not available, the weighted average of concentration ratios for country's resources and leave us poorer as a result; (2) it may intensify the inequality of income; (3) it may contribute to the problems of depression or inflation; and (4) it may even make political democracy less workable. On the other hand, concentration has often been defended on the grounds that (1) it may be necessary to attain the economies of large-scale production; and (2) it may accelerate economic progress. We consider each of these arguments in turn.

Concentration and Economic Efficiency

The country is supposed to use its resources inefficiently because firms in concentrated industries presumably set prices too high and therefore, produce too little. Imagine that a light bulb and a can of tuna fish both sell for 30¢. Consumers would buy enough of both products each year that the last light bulb would be worth just as much to them as the last can of tuna or the last 30¢ worth of anything else they consume. If the tuna fish industry can be taken as purely competitive, the last can would also take 30¢ worth of labor and capital to produce. Marginal costs would equal price there. At the same time, if firms in the concentrated light bulb industry were taking their maximum profits, the marginal cost of light bulbs would be well below their price. Perhaps it would take only another 15¢ worth of labor and capital to produce another bulb. Then we could gain by taking resources out of tuna and employing them in light bulbs. For every can of tuna we give up we would gain two light bulbs. That is, we would gain 60¢ worth of merchandise in the concentrated industry and lose only 30¢ worth in the competitive one. Of course, to do this we would have to sell more light bulbs, which would require lower prices for them. A price cut would be in the country's interest but it would make the light bulb companies less

---

the (five-digit) Census product classes were used. These cases were: full-fashioned hosiery, wool carpets and rugs, flat glass, steelworks and rolling mills, primary copper, primary lead, refrigeration machinery, radios and related products, and motor vehicles and parts. The resulting concentration ratios are probably somewhat higher than they might have been if the same method used in other industries were used in these. In most of these cases, however, the different product classes within the product class groups do not compete very closely if at all, so the overstatement is probably not severe. At any rate, only in primary metals, transportation equipment, and electric machinery are as many as a fifth of total shipments affected.

Source: Derived from *Concentration in American Industry*, Report of the Subcommittee on Anti-Trust and Monopoly, Senate Judiciary, 85th Congress, 1st Session, 1957, Table 38.

profitable. In other words, profit-seeking monopolists will tend to head down the wrong road from the whole country's point of view.

PROFITS

Concentration and Profits

It is impossible to compare marginal costs and prices directly in most industries, but throughout the book average rates of return on owners' equity have been used as rough indicators of economic performance. They will be used here as well. Assuming that new firms entering the industries involved would have no higher costs than existing producers, high profits would tend to indicate prices in excess of long-run marginal costs, with some economic inefficiency as a result.*

Figure 11.1 compares the average rate of return on owners' equity after tax for the years 1949–58 with average concentration ratios in 22 industry groups or subgroups. The more concentrated industries showed higher average profits fairly consistently.†

Concentration is only one of many factors in determining the profitability of an industry, however. Another obvious one is the rate at which it grows. Even a purely competitive industry can show high short-run profits if demand is rising or cost decreasing rapidly. Until the resulting profits have attracted new competitors, the firms lucky enough to be in the industry already can do very well. Similarly, even monopolists can show low profits if demand declines unexpectedly. However, there seems to have been no special tendency

---

* Low profits are also consistent with inefficiency if they result from overcapacity rather than low prices. Overcapacity may be found in any industry where demand has fallen off, or it may simply result from free entry in fields where prices are maintained well above minimum average costs. Government intervention has prevented price competition in some fields such as drug retailing, but publicly supported cartels are rare in manufacturing today. (The one important exception that comes to mind is petroleum refining, where state "prorationing" of crude oil output helps to support petroleum prices. This is not manufacturing, but the bulk of the refiners whose profits are shown in Figure 11.1 are producers of crude as well as refiners.) There may be a few cases where dominant firms stabilize prices at levels that attract too many new firms into the industry—something that seemed to be happening in certain types of aluminum fabricating in the 1950's (see p. 218). This cannot happen in industries of low concentration, however, because they do not contain dominant firms.

† The same result would appear for any period after 1948 except for the inflation from July 1950 to April 1951. An earlier study showed a similar relationship before World War II. See J. S. Bain, "Relation of Profit Rate to Industry Concentration: American Manufacturing, 1936–1940," *Quarterly Journal of Economics*, Aug. 1951.

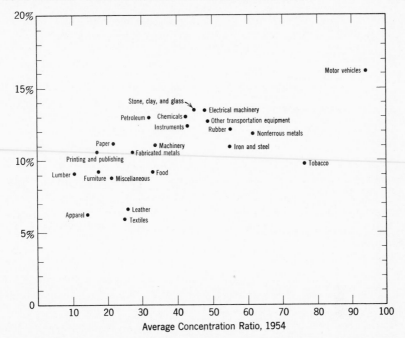

Figure 11.1.   Average rate of return on owners' equity 1949–58.

Note: Profits for petroleum refining based on profits of petroleum and coal products industries, 1949–51, and petroleum refining, 1952–58.

Source: Average returns derived from FTC-SEC, *Quarterly Financial Reports, United States Manufacturing Corporations.*

for either the more or the less concentrated industries to grow particularly rapidly in the 1950's.   Figure 11.2 shows the level of output in 1957 as a percentage of 1947–49 in the various industries covered.*
While some of the concentrated industries did expand very rapidly, so did some of the industries of low concentration, and both groups had their slowly growing industries as well.†

Some of the concentrated industries did show lower profits than others.   The tobacco industry is the clearest case.   At the beginning of the period its leaders had just been convicted of "monopolizing" under the Sherman Act and were on their good behavior.   Then came

* 1957 was used instead of 1958 to avoid the affect of the 1958 recession.

† A third possible reason for high profits might be rapidly increasing productivity.   Industries in which output per man-hour grows much faster than the average would experience declining costs provided that their wage rates increased no more than in other industries.   Rapidly growing industries do happen to be those with the greatest increases in productivity, by and large, so it is difficult to separate out the effect of rising demand and falling costs on profitability.   At any rate, there does not seem to have been any significant relationship between concentration and productivity increases in recent years.   See p. 517.

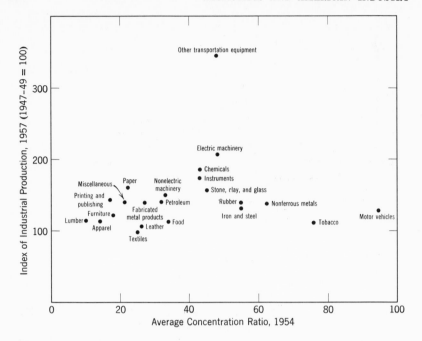

Figure 11.2. Level of output in 1957 as percentage of 1947–49. Source: *Federal Reserve Bulletin,* Dec. 1959.

the lung cancer scare, and the tobacco industry faced a stable or declining market in a period when most industries were expanding. In spite of all this, however, it succeeded in earning average profits that were greater than six of the nine industries with average concentration ratios below 30.

The most profitable industry among those with concentration ratios under 30 was paper and allied products. It had a long run of good luck in the 1950's with demand for its products growing much faster than the average of manufacturing. Capacity increased too, but not fast enough to compete away all the resulting profits. Still the average rate of return in paper making was lower than in all but 4 of the 13 industries with concentration ratios over 30.

Practically all competitive industries earned high profits in the shortage years just after Warld War II. Figure 11.3 compares concentration ratios and average rates of profit after tax on owners' equity in 1947 and 1948. In those years the less concentrated industries were the more profitable ones if anything. One possible explanation is that the monopolistic firms did not charge all that they could during the short-term sellers' market because of long-run

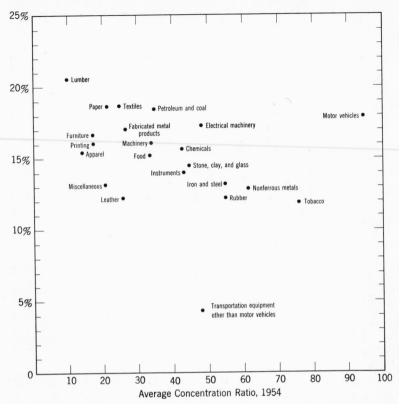

Figure 11.3. Industrial concentration and corporate profits, 1947–48.
Note: Profits were reported only for products of petroleum and coal together in those years.
Source: FTC-SEC, *loc. cit.*

considerations, but competitive prices were bid up by impersonal market forces. In other words, manufacturers' prices were allowed to ration scarce shirts and shoes but not scarce steel and automobiles.

When the shortages disappeared profits in most industries fell.* Figure 11.4 shows the decline in profits from 1947–48 to 1949–58. In less concentrated industries profits dropped drastically. The sellers could not control their prices in these industries. As demand became less intense or supply increased with entry, profits could not be maintained. In the more concentrated industries, profits were kept up much more successfully.

* The only exception was transportation equipment other than motor vehicles. This is primarily the aircraft industry, which was in the doldrums just after World War II because of the near suspension of the defense program.

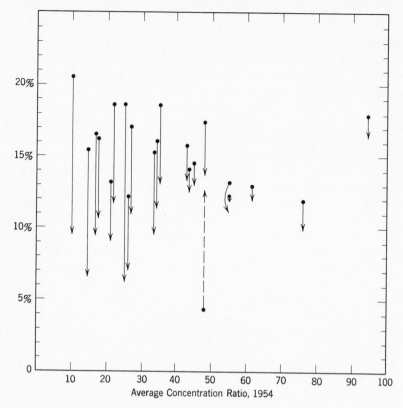

Figure 11.4. Concentration and change in profits from 1947–48 to 1949–58.
Note: Petroleum and coal products in 1947–48 were taken to represent petroleum refining alone.

Profits and the Public Good

Profits may exist for several reasons:

1. To some extent they are just interest on the stockholders' investment. If the firms involved had borrowed their capital from banks or by issuing bonds they would have had to pay 4 or 5% interest, which they would have counted as cost, not profit. Another way of looking at it is that firms will only enter an industry if their owners expect at least as good a return on their money as if they put it out at interest. As a result, when profits "disappear" in pure competition, there is still a return to the owners of the firm as good as they could earn elsewhere. In Figure 11.1 only the profits above perhaps the 5% line can be counted as true economic profits.

2. In addition to interest, profits often include some risk premiums. When "profits disappear" in competitive industries, there is still something more than mere interest left in the exceptional firm or the exceptional year to offset the inevitable failures. If oil well exploration as a whole is to break even, the owners of successful wells must earn substantial profits to make up for all the dry holes that are drilled. The profits in Figure 11.1 are averages for ten years and for all the corporations in broad industry groups. Losses and profits are averaged together, so a large part of the profits serving as risk premiums should cancel out.

3. Short-run profits are to be expected in competitive as well as monopolistic industries from time to time when someone hits upon a profitable innovation—a new product, a new low-cost method of production, a new location. It is only in the long run that such profits of innovation are competed away by imitators. These short-run profits must account for many of the earnings in excess of the 4 or 5% interest rate in the less concentrated industries in Figure 11.1.

Profits as imputed interest costs, as risk premiums, and as short-run returns to innovators all serve socially useful functions. They attract capital into industry and direct it to its most profitable use. These types of profit could hardly be avoided even in a purely competitive economy.

4. However, profits may also arise because sellers are sheltered from competition. Such profits may be very nice for the owners of the firms involved, but they do very little for the country as a whole. In fact, if the earlier story about the light bulbs and tuna fish is correct, monopoly profits mean that the country as a whole is poorer than it might be.

In Figure 11.1 the industry groups with concentration ratios under 30 averaged about 8.8% on the owners' equity over the 1950's. Much of this must have been interest, risk premium, and innovational profits though even these industry groups contained some concentrated segments which probably earned monopoly profits. The ten industry groups with concentration ratios of more than 40 averaged 12.7% on owners' equity over the same period—half again what the nonconcentrated industries did.

Hidden Profits—Rents and Wages

The higher profits of monopolistic industries may not seem very earth-shaking. An extra 4% on owners' equity for these firms cannot amount to more than a few billion dollars a year—only 1 or 2% of our 500 billion Gross National Product. Is is worth all the fuss?

Probably it is, because only a small part of monopoly profits appear in corporate accounts and therefore in Figure 11.1. When firms or their mines, plants, patents, or trade-marks have changed hands, the price has ordinarily reflected profit prospects. The purchasers often have to pay so much for a profitable property that after the transaction they receive only a normal return on their investments. After the purchase the new owners show no exceptional profits, but market performance has not changed. The profits have simply been transmuted into economic rents. By the same token, unprofitable properties are likely to sell at low prices, so that the new owners make a reasonable return even though the old ones lose their shirts. In other words, corporate accounts tend to overstate low profits and understate high ones.*

In addition, the employees of concentrated industries seem to receive some of the monopoly gain. Figure 11.5 compares straight time hourly wage rates in May 1958 with average concentration ratios. By and large, the more concentrated the industry, the higher the wage rate. Highly concentrated industries like primary metals and transportation equipment pay their help half again what very competitive industries such as textiles, leather, apparel, and lumber products do.

Of course, other things beside the monopolistic power of the employer go to determine wage rates. Skills, sex, location, and the relative power of the union are all important. For instance, the printing and publishing industry, which employs primarily highly skilled workmen who have a powerful union, has to pay a high wage in spite of its low concentration. The petroleum and coal products industries (primarily petroleum refining) pay very high wages, as might be expected in a field where labor is an exceptionally small part of total costs and the union is in a strong position as a result. Again, the tobacco industry, located almost entirely in the South and employing a high proportion of women, pays low wages in spite of its high concentration.

The high wages of concentrated industries and the low wages of unconcentrated ones are not due to regional differences, however. Figures 11.6 and 11.7 show the relationship between concentration and

* Profits in all industries, competitive and monopolistic, are exaggerated because plant and equipment is listed on the books at its original cost rather than its replacement cost. This overstatement is least in rapidly growing industries since most of their equipment has been installed during the expensive postwar years. There are a number of other difficulties with corporate profit figures. See Chapter 4, pp. 144–146.

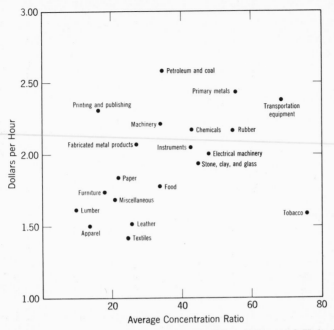

Figure 11.5. Straight time hourly wage rates, May 1958—total United States —and average concentration ratios. Source: Bureau of Labor Statistics, Bulletin No. 1252, *Factory Workers' Earnings, 1958,* June 1959.

wage rates in the South and in the North Central area. Southern wages are generally lower for comparable industries, but within both regions the more concentrated industries tend to pay their help more.

If wages as well as profits run half again as much in competitive industries as in monopolistic ones, the distortion that results from monopoly would appear to be quite significant. It was suggested early in the book that perhaps a quarter of the national income originates in unregulated industries of high concentration.* If those industries earn wages and profits of a third more than what is necessary to attract labor and capital from competitive industries, perhaps 8 or 9% of the national income would be "excess" profits and "excess" wages. That would be around $35–40 billion or almost as much as the defense budget!†

* See Chapter 1, p. 28.

† A third of a quarter is a twelfth or 8½%. The national income was running $480 billion at the end of 1959. The total defense budget was $46 billion in fiscal 1960.

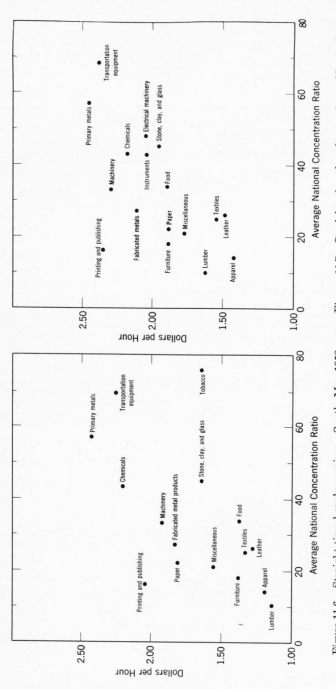

Figure 11.6.   Straight time hourly earnings—South, May 1958.
Note: Petroleum and coal, rubber, electric machinery, and
instruments are not available.

Figure 11.7.   Straight time hourly earnings—North Central
states, May 1958.
Note: Petroleum and coal, rubber, and tobacco not available.

Source: Bureau of Labor Statistics, Bulletin 1252, *op. cit.*

SELLING EXPENSE

Advertising

Another source of waste in market performance may be excessive selling expenses. Of course, not all selling effort is wasteful. To the extent that advertising or salesmen distribute useful information about prices, availability, or new products they perform socially useful functions. We would have to devote some of our resources to spreading information in our complex economy whether we called the process advertising or not.

A large proportion of the selling expenses of our country result in little or no useful information, however. Ads that simply repeat a familiar brand name or make vague claims for the questionable uniqueness or social prestige of some well-known product may do great things for the firm but they are not much help for the consuming public. They may actually do harm if they lead to irrational choices by consumers. About the same comment applies to salesmen when their main function is to give the consumer a feeling of personal obligation to buy, and to unnecessarily elaborate packaging designed to waylay the housewife on her way through the supermarket.

The only figures on selling expenses available are those on advertising. The cost of salesmen and packaging can only be surmised. No breakdown of "informative" and "manipulative" advertising is possible. Table 11.2 compares advertising expense per dollar of sale in 1956–57 with average concentration ratios. Industries that sell important parts of their output to consumers are shown in the left-hand column. Those that sell primarily to industrial users appear on the right.

Advertising expenses in the industrial materials and equipment groups never exceed 1% of total sales. By and large, the customers of these industries are well informed about the things they buy. Little informative advertising is necessary and manipulative advertising is of little avail.

When it comes to consumer goods, Table 11.2 shows a wide range of advertising practice. Most of the industries of low concentration seem to have low advertising budgets, the one exception being the relatively small beverage industry. Some of the more concentrated industries also show low advertising expenses, especially petroleum, motor vehicles, rubber products, and electric machinery. Most of the big advertisers are in the concentrated groups, however. Several of these show advertising rates two and three times as great as the firms with low concentration. Particular industries within these groups have even higher advertising expenses, and it is usually the concentrated segments that do the heavy promotion. For instance soap and liquor, both with concentration ratios of 63, were reported to spend 10% and 5–6% respectively of their sales on advertising

TABLE 11.2

CONCENTRATION AND ADVERTISING EXPENDITURES
IN MANUFACTURING, 1957

Industry Groups Where Consumer Goods Are Important			Industry Groups Producing Primarily Industrial Equipment or Materials		
Industry Group	Average Concentration Ratio (per cent)	Advertising Expenses as a Percentage of Gross Sales	Industry Group	Average Concentration Ratio (per cent)	Advertising Expenses as a Percentage of Gross Sales
Apparel	14	1.0	Lumber and products	10	0.5
Printing and publishing	17	0.7	Paper and products	22	0.8
Furniture	18	1.4	Textile mill products	26	0.7
Leather and products	26	1.1	Fabricated metal		
Beverages	30	4.9	products	27	1.0
Machinery (except			Stone, clay, and glass	45	0.8
elec.)[a]	33	1.1	Transportation equip-		
Food products	34	2.0	ment (other than		
Petroleum and coal			motor veh.)	48	0.2
products	35	0.5	Primary metals	57	0.4
Instruments and related					
products[b]	43	2.3			
Chemicals and related					
products[c]	43	3.6			
Electric machinery	48	1.8			
Rubber products	55	1.7			
Tobacco products	76	5.2			
Motor vehicles	96	0.9			

[a] Includes refrigerators and stoves.
[b] Includes clocks, watches, and photographic equipment.
[c] Includes drugs, cosmetics, soaps, and detergents.
Sources: Derived from Internal Revenue Service, *Statistics of Income*, 1957–58. preliminary.

in the years just after World War II.* Some other familiar advertisers are razor blades (concentration ratio of 97) dentifrices (78), breakfast foods (78), flour mixes (58), shortening and oil (55), hair preparations (51), candy bars (49), cough and cold products (46), coffee (45), flour (38), beer (27), "other cosmetics and toilet prepara-

* Bain, *Industrial Organization, op. cit.*, p. 390.

tions" (24), and bread (19).* The last four of these have fairly low concentration ratios but all of them are clearly understated. Flour, beer, and bread are sold on local or regional markets while "other cosmetics and toilet preparations" obviously includes a variety of noncompeting products.

Much of the very heavy advertising expenditure is of very doubtful information value. Actually, one would expect that it would be in markets with large numbers of sellers or with complex and ever-changing shopping goods such as automobiles and appliances that the public's need for information would be greatest. Where there are only a few well-known sellers with convenience goods like soap and cigarettes that go virtually unchanged for years, it should not take a great deal to tell the public what is available and at what price.

The discussion here has been limited to manufacturing. In retailing, the other segment of the economy where advertising is important, the problem of waste is probably less significant. The bulk of the advertising at that level seems to be pretty clearly informative.

Altogether, expensive advertising which is of little or no direct social value seems to be primarily a problem connected with certain concentrated industries, though by no means all of them. It is not completely clear whether it is concentration that makes these industries heavy advertisers, or advertising that makes them concentrated. Probably the direction of causation is different in various industries, though the two tendencies might have a mutually reenforcing effect.

POSSIBLE ADVANTAGES OF CONCENTRATION

Economies of Scale

The substantial amount of waste implied in the high profits, high wages, and in some instances high selling costs of concentrated industries may be inevitable if the economies of scale cannot be attained without very large firms. The most comprehensive information we have on the efficient scales of operations in various industries is based on a sample of 20 industries investigated in the early 1950's. The results of questionnaire material collected in that study are shown in Table 11.3. Column B shows estimates of the optimum size of plant

* *Concentration in American Industry, loc. cit.* Concentration ratios for dentifrices, hair preparations, candy bars, cough and cold products, and "other cosmetics and toilet preparations" are for more detailed product divisions than those used in deriving Table 12.1 (they are five-digit product groups instead of the four-digit classes used there) and would tend to be somewhat higher than those in Table 12.1.

expressed as a percentage of total national capacity. The survey often yielded a range of estimates of optimum scales so column B necessarily shows a range of percentages of the market in which the optimum plant would fall. Column C shows the minimum concentration ratios apparently required for efficiency in the various industries

TABLE 11.3

OPTIMUM PLANT SIZE AND MULTIPLANT ECONOMIES IN 20 INDUSTRIES

A Industry	B Percentage of Natl. Industrial Capacity Contained in One Plant of Min. Efficient Scale in about 1951	C Hypothetical Minimum Concentration Ratio for Single Plant Firms (per cent)	D Actual Concentration Ratios 1954 (per cent)	E Estimated Cost Advantage of Multiplant Firms
Typewriters	10–30	40–100	78	None
Tractors	10–15	40–60	67	No estimate
Copper	10	40	94	None
Fountain pens	5–10	20–40	55	None
Automobiles	5–10	20–40	98	No estimate
Cigarettes	5–6	20–24	82	Slight
Soap	4–6	16–24	63	½–1%
Rayon	4–6	16–24	79	No estimate
Gypsum products	2–3	8–12	89	Small
Rubber tires and tubes	1⅜–2¾	5½–11	78	No estimate
Meat—diversified	2–2½	8–10	39	None
Steel	1–2½	4–10	54	2–5%
Metal containers	⅓–2	1⅓–8	80	No estimate
Petroleum refining	1¾	7	32	None
Distilled liquor	1¼–1¾	5–7	63	No estimate
Farm machinery except tractors	1–1½	4–6	37	No estimate
Cement	⅘–1	3⅕–4	31	Small or 2–3%
Canned fruits and vegetables	¼–½	1–2	28	None
Shoes	1/7–½	4/7–2	43	Small or 2–4%
Flour milling	1/10–½	4/10–2	43	No estimate

Note: Concentration ratios listed for "copper smelter products", "pens and mechanical pencils; "soap and glycerin," and for an average of five-digit products that go to make up "steel mill products" and steel wire, sheet, and strip products.

Source: Columns B and E from J. S. Bain, *Barriers to New Competition*, Harvard University Press, 1956, pp. 72, 86. Column D, *Concentration in American Industry, loc. cit.*

covered. For instance, if copper production requires a plant with capacity equal to a tenth of the market to have all the economies of scale, the four largest firms must have at least 40% of the market. Column D shows the concentration ratios that actually applied in the indicated industries in 1954.

In each of the first five industries in Table 11.3 it seems likely that plants of efficient size would require enough concentration to result in substantial monopoly profits. It might be possible to have more and smaller firms in these industries, but only at some cost in technical efficiency. Costs were described as "substantially" higher at half of the optimum scale in typewriters, "moderately" higher in automobiles, and "slightly" higher in tractors.*

On the other hand, there are 15 cases in the sample, including some of the country's most concentrated industries, where we could apparently have minimum cost plants and still have concentration ratios of well under 30. In other words, none of the last 15 industries in Table 12.3 need be much more concentrated than textile mill products in order to attain technically efficient plants. It is notable that the actual concentration ratios in column 4 are greater than the hypothetical minimum concentration ratios possible in every industry except perhaps typewriters. In some cases industries are 10 and 20 times as concentrated on a national level as they need to be for low-cost plants. Of course, even these industries may have to be concentrated in relatively small local markets in some instances.

It might be that a firm could gain something in efficiency by operating more than one plant. Information on such economies of multiplant firms was available in only 12 of the 20 industries sampled. Column E shows the estimated reductions in costs available to a firm operating more than one plant in those industries. In 6 of these 12 the gains seem to have been nil. Only in steel did they really amount to much, and even then some respondents thought that one plant was as good as several. It seems probable that economies of multiplant operations also exist in some of the cases where no estimate was given.

Firms with much greater size than is needed for technical reasons may reap advantages over smaller firms in selling. The big cigarette or soap producers can blanket the entire economy with their ads or salesmen at a lower cost per dollar of sale than a firm just barely large enough to run an efficient plant. These selling advantages of large scale are difficult to evaluate. If the same amount of advertising would exist whether the industry were concentrated or not, the public as well as the firms could gain from the savings; but if the industry would do less advertising if less concentrated, the country as a whole might be better off with more and smaller firms.

In general, the gains from concentration may make up for the

* Bain, *Barriers to New Competition, op. cit.,* p. 78. No estimates were available for copper and fountain pens.

waste in some cases—perhaps automobiles among those discussed in this book—but in a larger number of cases we can apparently have the advantages of large scale and of competition simultaneously.

Concentration and Progress

A virtue commonly claimed for concentrated industries is their supposed superior progressiveness. There are various arguments. The high profits can serve as a source of capital for further investment, though many economists argue that a greater reliance on capital markets and a smaller use of plowed back profits might result in a better allocation of capital among industries. Again, the fact that the profits of innovation are not immediately competed away is supposed to make risky innovations more attractive to monopolistic firms. Finally, large firms, which need not mean monopoly if the market is big enough, can afford to finance research following 20 different paths at once instead of just one, and they therefore are less likely to find their entire research program wasted.

Against this it may be argued that leaders of the more monopolistic industries are in a position to slow the rate of change to protect their investment in plant or their peace of mind, and that they have less incentive than competitive firms to innovate since the wolf is usually pretty far from their door. They do not have the competitive pressure on them to keep them running. They can relax and enjoy their profits.

It is difficult to evaluate the progressiveness of different industries because there is no clear standard to employ. One would expect the young and rapidly growing industries to have an advantage in innovation whether they are competitive or monopolistic in structure.

Economic progress can take the form of new or better products or of more efficient methods of production. The product improvement aspect of progress seems to be practically unmeasurable, but improvements in efficiency would show up in increased productivity, i.e., increased amounts of output per unit of resources employed. Throughout the book we have used output per man-hour of labor to measure this because it is the only figure available in most of the industries covered. While man-hour productivity may be an adequate indicator of progress in many cases, it is an incomplete one. A man may accomplish more simply because he has more tools to work with, or he may do more with no more tools than before. The second case would be a much clearer instance of economic progress than the first.

What we need is a measure of productivity of labor *plus* other inputs. Something approaching this has recently become available

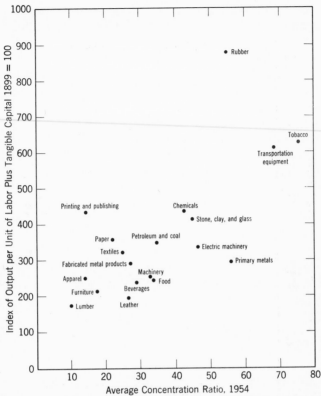

Figure 11.8. Total output per unit of labor plus tangible capital employed—1953 as a percentage of 1899. Source: Fabricant, *op. cit.*, pp. 46–47.

as a result of a study conducted by a well-known economic research organization.* Figure 11.8 compares their estimate of increase in output per unit of labor *plus* tangible capital employed from 1899 to 1953 with average concentration ratios in 1954. Concentration in earlier years would be more appropriate, but comparable figures are not available. In any case, there do not seem to have been any drastic changes in concentration in manufacturing since World War I.

The more concentrated industries do show a greater increase in productivity over the first half of the century. Part of their advantage lay in their youth, however. As Figure 11.9 shows, the

* Solomon Fabricant, *Basic Facts on Productivity Change, Occasional Paper No. 63*, National Bureau of Economic Research, 1959, quoting John Kendrick, *Productivity Trends in the United States,* a broader study by the same organization still in preparation (to be published 1961).

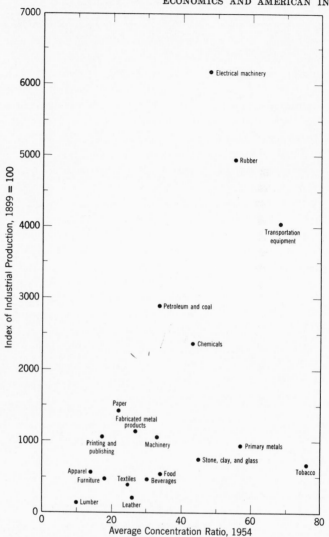

Figure 11.9. 1953 output as a percentage of 189 output. Source: Fabricant, *op. cit.*, pp. 46–47.

rapidly growing industries from 1899 to 1953 were mostly the more concentrated ones. No industry with a concentration under 30 in 1954 had increased its output by as much as 15 times (1500%) since 1899. Several of the more concentrated industries had shown increases of two and three times that much. Most, but not all, of the spectacular gains in productivity shown in Figure 11.8 correspond to spectacular gains in output shown in Figure 11.9. A more slowly growing concentrated industry such as primary metals or stone, clay, and glass usually did only moderately better than the less concentrated ones. It could be argued that high concentration encourages rapid growth in output. Perhaps the rate at which sales increase reflects the rate at which new products are introduced or new uses for old ones are developed. Unfortunately, there seems to be no way to evaluate such a proposition. The slow growth of the textile and shoe industries and the rapid growth of the electric machinery and transportation equipment industries are obviously a matter of the products involved in part. People have been wearing clothes for quite a while now, but they only started driving cars and running up electricity bills about the turn of the century. It seems impossible to say whether auto sales or shirt sales would have grown faster or slower if the industries had been more or less concentrated.

In more recent years the tendency for concentrated industries to grow more rapidly has weakened, and so has their advantage in

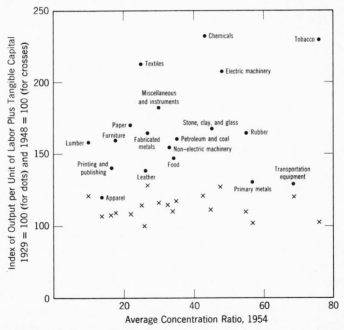

Figure 11.10. Total output per unit of labor plus capital employed—1953 as a percentage of 1929 (dots) and of 1948 (crosses). Source: J. W. Kendrick, *Productivity Trends in the United States,* Preliminary Mimeographed, National Bureau of Economic Research, 1958, Appendix Table D-IV, to be published by Princeton University Press in 1961.

productivity. Figure 11.10 shows output per unit of labor *plus* tangible capital in 1953 as a percentage of 1929 (the dots in the upper part of the diagram) and as a percentage of 1948 (the crosses at the bottom). No consistent relationship between concentration and increasès in productivity is visible in either period.* On the average the concentrated industries do not seem to do any better or worse than the competitive ones in the rate at which they improve efficiency. Any presumption that either competitive or concentrated industries have a special route to progress is open to question.

INEQUALITY, INSTABILITY, AND POLITICAL PROBLEMS

So far this chapter has been concerned almost entirely with the effect of concentration on economic efficiency: are we producing enough of the right goods and are we using efficient techniques and improving them as fast as we might. Economic concentration may affect other important questions as well. It probably plays a role in perpetuating the inequality of income within our country. It may have some significance in the nation's effort to avoid depression and inflation. It may even be important in the workability of political democracy. Each of these points is worth some comment.

Concentration and Inequality

The concentration of market power may well result in greater inequality than would otherwise be the case. Most of the very wealthy in our country can trace their fortunes either to an inside position in some concentrated industry or to the ownership of resources that are limited by nature such as oil reserves or urban real estate. Of 75 persons identified as having more than $75 million in 1957, 23 had derived their wealth from oil (including 7 Rockefellers whose wealth originated from the Standard Oil trust at the turn of the century), 9 from automobiles, 8 from chemicals, and 5 from aluminum (6 if Kaiser is included). Most of the rest came from other industries with high concentration. The only clear representative of the unconcentrated industry groups in the 75 was one whose wealth came from agriculture, and even here the ownership of scarce resources was important.†

* The same is true of any other subperiod after 1929 (1929–37, 1929–48, or 1937–48).

† These figures were derived from "America's Biggest Fortunes," *Fortune,* Nov. 1957, p. 177.

CONCLUSIONS—THE STRUCTURE OF AMERICAN INDUSTRY   519

Perhaps more important is the fact that the unconcentrated industries account for more than their share of the low incomes in our country. It is only in such industries as textiles or leather or retailing that actual wage rates are ever low enough to be affected by the minimum wage laws. Of course, agriculture has long had a special place in the United States as one of the country's greatest sinks of poverty.

The connection between concentration and inequality is quite plausible. If people could move freely from job to job, individuals with equal ability and willingness to work would wind up with about the same wage in the long run no matter what line of work they went into. If one job offered better compensation, all things considered, than another it would attract labor until the advantage disappeared. It takes some limitation on the movement of labor between employments to preserve marked waged differences for equally attractive jobs requiring equal skills.

Something similar can be said about the movement of capital from industry to industry. If there were no restrictions, a dollar would yield its owner about the same amount in the long run no matter where he invested it. With barriers to entry in some industries, however, some people's dollars are apt to prove better than others and to earn permanently better returns.

Concentration in industry must certainly be counted as one of the important barriers to the movement of factors of production from one employment to another. A major reason why man-hours and dollars of capital employed on farms and in textile mills earn so little is that prices of automobiles and steel are too high. If the steel and auto makers had lower prices and sold more as a result, they could employ more resources.

Monopolistic restraint by business firms is only one of many limitations on the movement of labor and capital between employments. Barriers to factor movements have been erected by the government through various licensing laws and by the unions through restrictions on the numbers in particular trades or simply through their establishment of high wages which reduce the number of jobs in certain lines of work. Social prejudice creates some of the most severe limitations on opportunity for some of our poorest groups. And even if all such restrictions on factor movements were eliminated, there would still be poverty due to illness, insanity, and old age. It seems likely that monopoly on product markets intensifies the problem of inequality, but it is only one of many contributing factors.

Even if monopoly had only a neutral effect on the degree of inequality in our country, however, it might still be objected to on the grounds of equity. A large proportion of our population clearly considers it unfair for one person to gain at the expense of another simply because he is in a strong position. This concern for fairness has probably been more important than any concern about economic efficiency in the development of our antitrust laws.

Market Structure and Price Stability

The effect of concentration in product and factor markets on economic stability is considerably less certain. During the 1930's there was much debate about whether prices in concentrated industries were more rigid than in competitive ones. Different economists reached different conclusions, depending on what measure of concentration they used. At any rate, it was not at all clear whether price rigidity during a depression was a vice or a virtue. There is not much doubt but what any one industry can increase its sales with lower prices, but it is very much open to question whether all producers taken together can do so. Certainly they cannot win customers away from someone else the way a particular industry can. The pros and cons of price stability in time of depression take far more space than we can give them in this chapter. Suffice it to say that a large number of economists are skeptical about price and wage reductions as a policy to deal with depression today. This question, and the general one of how to deal with depression, is best left to discussions of macroeconomics.

In recent years much more concern has been expressed about the role of concentrated industries or unions or both in inflation. Experience differs, depending on whether it is a galloping inflation associated with shortages such as 1946–48 and 1950–51, or a creeping one when few if any goods are in short supply such as the price increase that occurred in 1954–58.

The changes in average hourly earnings from 1946 to 1948 are shown in Figure 11.11 and the changes in prices in Figure 11.12. The really big wage increases were all in the *non*concentrated industries in those years. In a number of cases such as textiles and furniture, they occurred in industries where the unions were relatively weak. By and large the more concentrated industries with usually strong unions showed more moderate raises.

The connection between concentration and price changes was not nearly as close, but Figure 11.12 shows no tendency for the prices in concentrated industries to rise faster. The poor correlation between concentration and price increases is certainly not a matter of competitive firms absorbing the higher wages. The competitive industries were generally earning exceptional profits in those years. The trouble with prices was that they were apt to reflect the prices of materials as much as wages and profits within the industries involved. Fluctuations in the price of cotton textiles or of fabricated metal products say more about what is happening on the farms or at the steel mills than in the processing plant.

What happened in 1946–48 was that demand exceeded supply for most goods. In the competitive fields this naturally resulted in a bidding up of prices and wages. No one was to blame for the rise in the price of cotton cloth or the wage of textile workers. That was a matter of impersonal forces on a competitive market. The same could not be said of the concentrated industries. There was not much

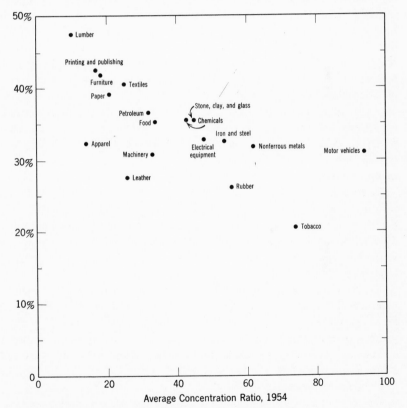

Figure 11.11. Change in average hourly earnings 1946–48.

Note: Comparable information was not available for instruments, miscellaneous, and other transportation equipment.

Source: *Handbooks of Labor Statistics*, Bureau of Labor Statistics, Bulletins 916 and 1016.

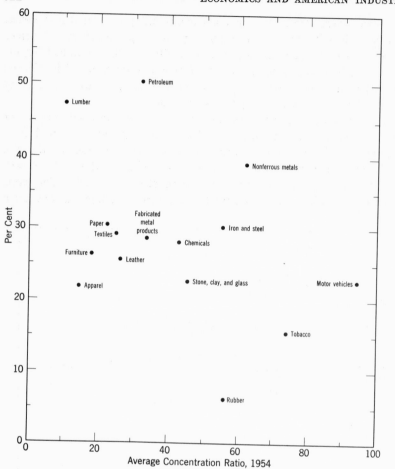

Figure 11.12. Percentage of increase in wholesale prices from 1946 to 1948. Source: Bureau of Labor Statistics, Bulletins 920 and 973, "Wholesale Prices in 1946" and "Wholesale Prices in 1948." Wherever index numbers had to be constructed, 1948 weights were used.

question of impersonal forces making the factory price of automobiles or steel go up. The automobile and steel producers certainly controlled those prices, and had to be circumspect in the use of their control. They seem to have been more careful in granting wage increases too—perhaps because with the powerful unions they faced, any wage increase would be impossible to reverse later on.

At any rate, it is very hard to place the main responsibility for the inflation of the 1940's on the monopolists or the unions. They restrained it, if anything!

The picture during the creeping inflation of the mid-1950's is quite different.   Figure 11.13 shows the percentage increases in average hourly earnings in those years and Figure 11.14 shows the price rises.   Here the more concentrated industries showed the greater wage increase.   The greatest price increases also occurred in concentrated industries, though again, as in the 1940's, the price change was not as closely related to concentration as the change in wage rate.

It is understandable that concentrated industries should lead the way up in a mild inflation like that of the late 1950's.   In the 1950's there were few shortages so unregulated supply and demand were not likely to push many prices up under such circumstances.   Individual products could still be scarce, but not all of them at the same time. In concentrated industries, on the other hand, firms and unions had sufficient market control to set their own prices over quite a wide range.   They could raise their prices to some extent even in the face of surplus capacity if they thought such moves were in their interest. It would be hard to identify either the union or the managements of powerful firms as the villains in the creeping inflation, but it seems likely that the concentrated character of their market contributed to the problem.

Bigness and Government

Some observers have seen in the concentration of market power a threat to democracy as well as to the efficient and equitable working of our economy.   American democratic institutions grew up in an

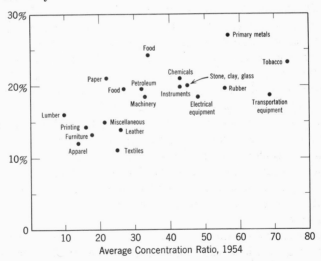

Figure 11.13.   Percentage increase in average hourly earnings from 1954 to 1958. Source: *Monthly Labor Reviews*.

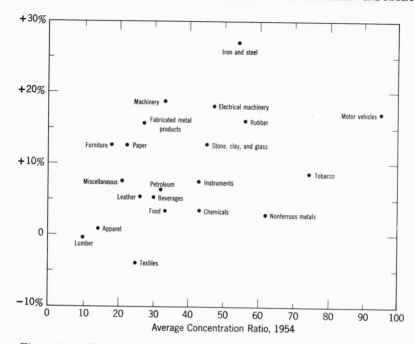

Figure 11.14.   Percentage increase in wholesale prices from 1954 to 1958. Source: Derived from Bureau of Labor Statistics, Bulletin 1257, "Wholesale Prices and Price Indexes, 1958."

atomistic environment where no individual outside of the government exercised significant control over the direction that society as a whole took.   Could democracy survive with great firms whose managers were much more than insignificant atoms in the markets where they traded and in the over-all life of the country?

A common prediction has been that our country would not allow powerful economic groups to go unregulated for long.   The existence of widespread monopoly power is supposed to lead naturally to the establishment of government regulation over large segments of our economy.   People who hold this view often go on to argue that personal freedoms were likely to disappear along with corporate freedoms so that the detailed intervention of government in important segments of economic life would result ultimately in the destruction of democracy.

Others have taken another tack.   The great power of concentrated business organizations leads naturally to the development of other economic blocks to offset them.   Some observers have predicted an increasingly bitter conflict between these great economic blocks that will end in the seizure of absolute power by the leaders of one group or another.

Neither fear is completely without foundation. Something approaching both of these tendencies has occurred in some European countries at times in the past. Yet the big corporation has been with us for more than half a century and the big union has held its powerful position for almost a generation now and democratic institutions still survive.

Even if we have not seen the demise of democracy, however, there are those who object that power has been so concentrated in the hands of small groups that only the forms of democracy are left. At the turn of the century there was real reason to believe that the government was the exclusive tool of a few industrial magnates, or at least was tending in that direction. In the 1930's and 1940's the powerful union that was supposed to really run the country became a familiar and widely held bogey. Even today there are many who fear the effective dominance over the nation's decisions by a small elite of military and big business leaders.

On a less horrendous level, many regret the great importance of organized pressure groups in modern government. Perhaps the groups are too diverse for any one to become dominant. Perhaps the different groups will often tend to offset each other's effect. Yet they unquestionably lead to a great outflow of special interest legislation, and they result in the partial disenfranchisement of the unorganized.

Finally, the employer and the union often exercise powers over employees or customers today that resemble those of government. These institutions are seldom answerable to the general public as are elected officials. Our recourse from arbitrary decisions may be inadequate. It can be argued that the concentration that gives them their exceptional power means that fewer decisions are subject to democratic processes than might be the case.

Most of these comments are a sort of speculation that cannot easily be verified. That is not to say that they are not important. Few concerns can be more significant.

SUMMARY

Some Conclusions

Monopoly in the sense of concentration sufficient for market control really does exist in an important group of American industries—and it makes a substantial difference in terms of high profits, high wages, and perhaps, in some cases, excessive selling costs. Altogether, its cost to the rest of us each year may well be on the same order of magnitude as the cold war or a good-sized recession. It is certainly worth worrying about.

Concentration may have other faults as well. It has probably intensified the problem of inequality. It seems to contribute to the creeping type of inflation that can occur even with adequate capacity in most industries, though not to the galloping inflations that arise from excessive demand. Some observers even see concentration of economic power as a threat to democracy itself.

In a few instances high concentration may be unavoidable if we are to enjoy the advantages of large-scale production, but industries for which information is available are much more concentrated than would be necessary for plants of optimum size. If concentration in such cases has a saving grace it lies in the possibility of more rapid technical progress, but even this is open to question.

For the most part the industries with low concentration show little more than normal profits, moderate or even depressed wages, and usually reasonable selling expenses. It is important to note that few of these industries could be described as purely competitive. Many of them would probably be characterized as oligopolistic, but weak oligopolies appear to perform very differently from strong ones.

The less concentrated industries are not without defects, however. Some of the industries discussed in previous chapters suffered from short-term instability traceable at least in part to their competitive nature. In such industries there is no one who can control short-run changes in price and output as is done in concentrated fields, while the large numbers may result in undesirable fluctuations in production and inventories owing to inadequate market knowledge.

In the long run some competitive industries faced with stagnant demand have experienced long periods of redundant capacity and depressed incomes because of the immobility of capital and labor. Of course, less competitive industries can have excess capacity too. In fact, they are especially likely to in cases where private cartels or government action maintain high prices that permit too many producers to enter or remain in the field.

The conclusions reached in this book have been based on an established body of theory, a handful of case studies, and some statistical tests applied to broad industry groups within manufacturing. Most of the industry studies and statistical tests rested on more complete studies made by other observers, and further studies covering other industries exist with somewhat similar conclusions to those reached here. Nevertheless, the industries not yet adequately studied and the questions still unanswered are vast. Most of the conclusions of this book are open to further questioning. They are definitely not proven by the broad gauge measures used in this chapter or by the limited group of industries described earlier. The empirical material presented in this book should be taken as illustrations of ideas widely accepted by present-day economists rather than as proofs that those ideas are correct.

What Can Be Done

Every economist has his own prescription for the state of affairs that apparently exists in the market place today. Some, especially those who put great emphasis on the economies of scale and the possibility of rapid progress in concentrated industries, would let well enough alone so long as overt collusion and clearly predatory attacks on competitors are prevented. Others, especially those who fear the political side effects, have taken strong stands for dissolution in all industries with more than tolerable degrees of concentration. Many others are ranged at various points between these views.

Neither extreme is very likely to be the route that public policy will follow in the near future. Judging by the events of the last 20 years, firms with powerful positions are not apt to be left free of government supervision. An all-out dissolution policy would appear even less likely. In 70 years of antitrust, the courts have only been willing to order the dismemberment of monopolistic firms in a handful of the most extreme cases.

Something can be done, however. Even if the present size of existing firms is left untouched, *effective* concentration can be reduced. One way would be to eliminate import restrictions so that large American sellers have to compete with their foreign counterparts. The United States has quite a good record on tariff reductions over the last 20 years, but sometimes the effect of these reductions has been offset by import quotas such as those imposed on oil and non-ferrous metals in 1958. Restrictions of this sort unquestionably make the country as a whole poorer as well as eliminating a major possibility for competition.

In addition, we may hope for some reduction in concentration if we can simply keep any future merger movements in check. In a growing economy, concentration will decrease unless firms expand as fast as the markets in which they sell. Most of them have not been able to accomplish this in the past without resorting to mergers. In fact, even with two substantial merger movements in the 1920's and the 1940's, concentration in manufacturing as a whole seems to have remained almost unchanged since World War I. Not every merger is harmful,* but a policy of close scrutiny for any horizontal or vertical combinations involving major firms in industries with concentration ratios of more than 30, say, would probably be in the public interest.

Further, more controversial steps would involve government intervention to reduce barriers to entry or concentration directly. Loans or loan guarantees might be used to overcome the severe limitations that capital rationing sets on entry. Such a policy is already in force on a small scale, but it could be expanded to offer credit facilities to even very large enterprises when needed for entry into industries requiring huge scale. The RFC loans to Reynolds and Kaiser which permitted them to enter the aluminum and steel industries probably yielded high social returns regardless of the interest paid. Again, the large-scale manipulative advertising which serves as a major barrier to entry in certain industries could be curbed, perhaps with a heavy progressive tax on expenditures in excess of a certain percentage of sales, leaving some exemption for new products. Vertical dissolution might be called for where the pre-emption of raw material sources or distributive outlets provides the basis for great monopoly power.

Direct action to deal with concentration would mean horizontal dissolution. This might be called for even in cases where no overt moves to maintain such power could be demonstrated, especially where high concentration and blockaded entry coincided with undesirable performance such as increasing prices and high profits in the face of excess capacity. Exceptions could be made where high concentration is clearly attributable to the economies of scale or to successful innovation. How far such a policy should go depends on how much weight is given to the argument that concentrated industries are more progressive. The writer is of the opinion that while an effort to establish anything approaching a purely competitive steel industry, say, might do more harm than good, an industry with leaders as large as Jones & Laughlin, National, Youngstown, and Armco would still be quite capable of developing and applying whatever new techniques are in the offing. A steel industry with those four firms as leaders would have a concentration ratio of only 20. Or again, it would be difficult to attack the petroleum industry, with a concentration ratio of 32, for lack of progress. In a number of our more concentrated industries

* See Chapter 4, p. 128. Instances of socially useful mergers have been cited in Chapters 4, 6, 7, 8, and 9 as well.

it would appear that some dissolution would be possible without killing the goose that lays the golden egg.

No one should swallow these suggestions whole. Some of them would meet violent opposition not only from the vested interests involved but from a significant number of informed scholars as well. The policies described in the last four paragraphs probably become more controversial as they progress. Few economists would favor trade restrictions in most concentrated industries. Many would oppose dissolution in the typical case.

When it comes to the competitive sectors of our economy, the problem is to improve the adjustment to competition by reducing instability and immobility. One essential function of the government in both respects is to maintain prosperous conditions throughout the country so that these problems are only local and so that new employments are available for those escaping from declining industries. Beyond this, it could do much to improve the market knowledge available within such industries by collecting and distributing earlier and more usable information about inventories, production plans, market prospects, and production techniques. Great strides in this direction have been made in recent years. Finally, government might intervene in the short run to stabilize the more volatile markets provided that it can limit itself to that objective and avoid shoring up declining industries by permanently supporting their markets.

There are many possible public policies to improve the flow of labor and capital out of permanently depressed industries. Some possibilities are government-sponsored retraining programs, regional redevelopment for depressed areas, special unemployment insurance, and public purchase of land and capital committed to dying industries. There are difficulties involved in most of these programs, but at least they point in the right direction. While assisting the depressed industries, they also benefit the general public by directing resources to more efficient uses.

On the other hand, the use of tariffs, price supports far above the market, resale price maintenance, licensing provisions, and similar restrictions on competition to bail out such industries are generally harmful. They may save some little businessmen from low incomes, but they do so by eliminating the price competition sought in other parts of the economy. They inhibit the movement of resources to their most effective uses. If they raise prices significantly, they lead to obviously wasteful overcapacity. Such policies are just palliatives

that suppress the symptoms—low incomes—but intensify the disease
—overcapacity.

All of the policies that have been discussed here assume the continuation of a largely unregulated private enterprise system. The wholesale extension of public utility status to concentrated industries would probably find few advocates among contemporary economists. Regulation may be unavoidable in some of the traditional public utilities, but it has certainly proved to be a far from perfect substitute for competition.

The alternative policy of nationalization for concentrated industries seems even more remote in present-day America. At any rate, the pro's and con's of such a policy involve great issues that are far beyond the scope of this book.

The writer is convinced, along with a great number of other observers, that while our present market system has major imperfections, it is quite capable of substantial improvement short of being completely scrapped and exchanged for another economic system. The problems of monopoly and competition call for reasonably small adjustments, not a revolution.

FURTHER READINGS

For an entire textbook devoted to the approach used in this chapter the reader could do no better than J. S. Bain, *Industrial Organization*, Wiley, 1959. It contains a more extensive discussion of almost every point that has been introduced here. We are indebted to the same author for our most thorough attempt to study the structure and performance of a large sample of industries in his *Barriers to New Competition*, Harvard University Press, 1956. This chapter uses both books extensively. Another broad gauge book appropriate to this chapter is the National Bureau of Economic Research, *Business Concentration and Price Policy*, Princeton University Press, 1955, which contains a number of important scholarly papers on such subjects as the measurement and meaning of concentration ratios, the merger movement, economies of scale, and price flexibility.

On the relationship of concentration to profits the classic source is J. S. Bain, "Relation of Profit Rate to Industry Concentration: American Manufacturing, 1936–1940," *Quarterly Journal of Economics*, Aug. 1951. On wages see Jacob Perlman, "Hourly Earnings of Employees in Large and Small Enterprises," TNEC Monograph No. 14, 1940, and Sumner Slichter, "Notes on the Structure of Wages," *Review of Economics and Statistics*, Feb. 1950. Perlman's conclusions emphasize the absolute size of the firm, and Slichter's its profitability, but both results are generally consistent with those in this chapter. An interesting attempt to evaluate the social losses from concentration appeared in Arnold Harberger, "Monopoly and Resource Allocation," *American Economic Review Proceedings*, 1954, pp. 77–87. He considers only the effect of excess profits, however. See George Stigler, "The Statistics of Monopoly and Merger," *Journal of Political Economy*, Feb. 1956, p. 33.

The classic statement on the advantages of concentrated industries in innovation appeared in Joseph Schumpeter, *Capitalism, Socialism and Democracy*, Harper, 1950, Chapter VIII. For a very readable textbook presentation of the case see Henry H. Villard, *Economic Development*, Rinehart, 1959, Chapters 4–7. G. Warren Nutter, "Monopoly, Bigness and Progress," *Journal of Political Economy*, Dec. 1956, pp. 520–527, presents a good statement of the opposite viewpoint. The best source of productivity estimates for various industries is John Kendrick, *Productivity Trends in the United States*, Princeton University Press, due to be published 1961.

The original study of price rigidity in time of depression was done by Gardner C. Means, "Industrial Prices and Their Relative Inflexibility," Senate Document 13, 74th Congress, 1st Session, 1935. It elicited a debate with great numbers of participants that lasted for a decade. A recent study which contains reviews of many of the earlier ones and presents a sophisticated approach to the old subject is Richard Ruggles, "The Nature of Price Flexibility and the Determinants of Relative Price Changes in the Economy," in *Business Concentration and Price Policy, loc. cit.* These studies referred mainly to the experience of the 1930's. The findings of several experts including both Means and Ruggles on price performance during the inflationary periods are presented in the hearings of the Senate Judiciary, *Administered Prices*, Pt. I, July 1957.

Some of the famous books emphasizing the possible effects of concentration on our political system and on the long-run development of our economic system are Henry Simons, *Economic Policy for a Free Society*, Chicago University Press, 1948, Robert A. Brady, *Business as a System of Power*, Columbia University Press, 1943, and C. Wright Mills, *The Power Elite*, Oxford University Press, 1956. For a more optimistic view see A. A. Berle, *The Twentieth Century Capitalist Revolution*, Harcourt, Brace, 1954.

Few books are written on public policy toward business without some discussion of possible changes. Two notable recent contributions are the *Report of the Attorney General's National Committee to Study the Anti-Trust Laws*, 1955, and Carl Kaysen and Donald F. Turner, *Antitrust Policy*, Harvard University Press, 1959. The first is the outcome of a conference of attorneys and economists to evaluate the current antitrust laws. The second is a carefully reasoned attempt to formulate a consistent set of public policies toward monopoly. Both are comprehensive.

INDEX